Peter Watson is a journalist, televi[sion] [...] [historian]
of ideas. He was a senior editor of t[he] [...]
correspondent of *The Times* and a co[...]
has written for many newspapers, in[...]
and the *Spectator*. His books, which have been translated into more
than 25 languages, include *Ideas: A History from Fire to Freud*; *The
German Genius* and *Convergence: The Idea at the Heart of Science*.

Also by Peter Watson

Peter Watson

The French Mind

400 Years of Romance,
Revolution and Renewal

SIMON &
SCHUSTER

London · New York · Sydney · Toronto · New Delhi

First published in Great Britain by Simon & Schuster UK Ltd, 2022
This edition published in Great Britain by Simon & Schuster UK Ltd, 2023

1 3 5 7 9 10 8 6 4 2

Simon & Schuster UK Ltd
1st Floor
222 Gray's Inn Road
London WC1X 8HB

www.simonandschuster.co.uk
www.simonandschuster.com.au
www.simonandschuster.co.in

Simon & Schuster Australia, Sydney
Simon & Schuster India, New Delhi

A CIP catalogue record for this book is available from the British Library

Paperback ISBN: 978-1-4711-2898-1
eBook ISBN: 978-1-4711-2899-8

Typeset in Sabon by M Rules
Printed and Bound in the UK using 100% Renewable
Electricity at CPI Group (UK) Ltd

For Kathrine

Anyone born on the blessed soil of France cannot bear life elsewhere.

−GERMAINE DE STAËL

France is the heart of Europe; as one gets further away, social life withers.

−FRANÇOIS-RENÉ DE CHATEAUBRIAND

We say strychnine, quinine, nicotine, aniline ... I say: Parisine.

−NESTOR ROQUEPLAN

Only France has the right to project herself as a model, because no people has merged its own interest and destiny with humanity more than she.

−JULES MICHELET

The French genius is certainly the most complete, the most balanced, and the most able to create a form of general intellectual culture.

−ERNEST RENAN

Anglo-Saxon intellectuals, who form a race apart, cut off from the rest of the nation, are always dazzled when they find in France men of letters and artists closely involved in the affairs of their country.

−JEAN-PAUL SARTRE

Of all languages, the French language is the only one that has an element of probity attached to its genius. Defined, social and reasonable, it is not only the language of the French, but the language of humanity.

−ANTOINE DE RIVAROL

It must be admitted that conversation in Paris has been perfected to a point where there is none other like it in the rest of the world.

−LOUIS SÉBASTIEN MERCIER

The most brilliant and most dangerous nation of Europe.

−ALEXIS DE TOCQUEVILLE

How does one recognise intelligence in a nation? By its ability to speak French.

–VICTOR HUGO

Vienna, Berlin, St Petersburg and London are only cities; Paris is a brain.

–VICTOR HUGO

Without France, the world would be alone.

–VICTOR HUGO

Elsewhere in Europe, you will encounter elegant manners, cordiality, warmth, learning, but only in Paris ... will you find in abundance the kind of genius that makes an irresistible whole of all these social accomplishments.

–HONORÉ DE BALZAC

Like other European peoples, and perhaps *par excellence* among them, the French were accustomed to define themselves in relation to an enemy.

–FRANÇOIS FURET

To exercise the kind of supremacy that belongs to it, France has been given a dominating language.

–JOSEPH DE MAISTRE

How maddening, says God, it will be when there are no more Frenchmen.

–CHARLES PÉGUY

France often comes across as a country that wants to pass off its failures and defeats as symbolic victories, concealing its points of weakness by displaying unrivalled strength in such areas as fashion, letters, luxury and the arts.

–CHRISTOPHE CHARLES

France is the light of the world, her genius is to light up the universe.

–CHARLES DE GAULLE

France cannot be France without grandeur.

—CHARLES DE GAULLE

The French have never recovered from being beaten at Waterloo and Sedan.

—CHARLES DE GAULLE

France must continue to behave as a great power precisely because she no longer is one.

—CHARLES DE GAULLE

Increasingly unable to control economic trends, the French state has moved to a re-defining of sovereignty from a political economic concept to a cultural one. If the Gaullist concepts of *prestige* and *grandeur* could not be achieved through economics, then they could be achieved through the affirmation of the strength of French culture.

—SOPHIE M. CLAVIER

The fact remains that the greatest English authors enjoyed truly universal recognition during the eighteenth and nineteenth centuries only through the translation of their writings into French.

—PASCALE CASANOVA

The Parisienne is the shining justification of the superiority of France over other nations.

—LÉON GOZLAN

In the history of Europe, I see only one country – France – that has always thought of the good of others.

—LOUIS GILLET

We French are, we must be, the world's conscience.

—ROMAIN ROLLAND

London may become Rome, but it will certainly never become Athens: that destiny is reserved for Paris.

—THÉOPHILE GAUTIER

France would not easily be content to count for no more in the world than a big Belgium.

–JULES FERRY

French cultural exceptionalism has never existed, thank goodness ... It might seem ridiculous when French political and cultural spokespeople trot out references to France's *rayonnement* [radiance] – as they habitually do. Taken literally, the word implies that we French consider France to be the sun of humanity, the stellar orb whose function it is to shine down on and warm the entire planet. But every orator who lapses into this cliché ... is fully aware of the image of national vanity he is presenting to foreign audiences.

–JEAN-FRANÇOIS REVEL

France! Great in all the arts, supreme in none.

–ANATOLE FRANCE

For half a century we have been obsessed by a doubt: are we still a great people?

–ÉDOUARD BALLADUR

In France, the equality that people dream about is: everybody gets to attain the same noble status.

–PHILIPPE D'IRIBARNE

Old France, weighed down with history, prostrated by wars and revolution, endlessly vacillating from greatness to decline, but revived, century after century, by the genius of renewal!

–CHARLES DE GAULLE

*

The English are, perhaps, greater philosophers; the Italians better painters and musicians; the Romans were greater orators; but the French are the only people, except the Greeks, who have been at once philosophers, poets, orators, historians, painters, architects, sculptors and musicians ... And in common life, they have, in great measure, perfected that art, the most useful and agreeable of any, *l'art de Vivre*, the art of society and conversation.

–DAVID HUME

A Frenchman who, with a fund of virtue, learning and good sense, has the manners and good breeding of his country, is the perfection of human nature.

–LORD CHESTERFIELD

A Frenchman must always be talking, whether he knows anything of the matter or not.

–SAMUEL JOHNSON

The French are the first People of the Universe; that in the Arts of living they do or ought to give Laws to the whole World, and that whosoever would either eat, drink, dress, dance, fight, sing or even sneeze, *avec Élégance*, must go to Paris to learn it.

–SAMUEL FOOTE

[It is] a pleasanter job to be a Parisian than a king.

–HM KING MILAN OF SERBIA

In ways that other literary cultures do not, French literary culture connects the narrow world of science or scholarship to the broader world beyond.

–PRISCILLA PARKHURST CLARK

There is no other culture than the French ... it is, by necessity, the right one.

–FRIEDRICH NIETZSCHE (TO AUGUST STRINDBERG)

CONTENTS

The Fascination with France, the French and the French Way of Life

In 2008, a Frenchman, Pierre-Louis Colin, a 34-year-old speech-writer at the Foreign Ministry, published a book entitled *Guide des jolies femmes de Paris*. Despite its jovial title, the book had a serious purpose in that Colin's 'high mission', as he explained it, was to help combat what he saw as a 'righteous' (he probably meant self-righteous) Anglo-Saxon-dominated world. His subject, he said, was especially French and very important. It was a guide to finding the prettiest women in Paris.

'The greatest marvels of Paris are not in the Louvre,' he confided. 'They are in the streets and the gardens, in the cafés and in the boutiques. The greatest marvels of Paris are the hundreds and thousands of women, whose smiles – whose cleavages, whose legs – bring incessant happiness to those who take promenades. You just have to know where to observe them.'

The book went on to classify the arrondissements of Paris according to their women. No less than the way France itself may be divided into its gastronomic regions, every neighbourhood in Paris, Colin insisted, had its 'feminine speciality'.

Ménilmontant, in the north-east, for example, was characterised by 'perfectly shameless cleavages – radiant breasts often uncluttered by a bra'. The area around the Madeleine Catholic church was the location to find 'sublime legs'. Even middle-aged Parisian women between the ages of forty and sixty, he observed, showed a unique 'saucy maturity', reflecting an 'ambitious sex life that refused to lay down its weapons'.

Colin was certainly doing his bit to combat the domination of the world by the Anglo-Saxons, many of whom would have decried his book as inherently sexist at the same time as shamelessly enjoying his approach, and acknowledging that he himself fulfilled the stereotype many foreigners have of the French, as being more obsessed with sex (and being better at it) than the rest of us.

I first came across the book when I read another one, *La Seduction: How the French Play the Game of Life*, by Elaine Sciolino, a former Paris bureau chief for the *New York Times*. In fact, I was more interested in Sciolino's book than I was in Colin's – not because I was a middle-aged, happily married man with no residual interest in radiant breasts or shameless cleavages, but because I recognised her book as one of a growing genre of titles that are written about France and the French but about nowhere and no one else.[1]

I call these 'cute' books because they are, for the most part, written with tongue firmly in the cheek but with an underlying serious point, that serious point being that the French are different from the rest of us. They are different from the rest of us in specific ways, and/or in more general ways that we nonetheless find difficult to fully pin down.

Among these titles we may include: *Sixty Million Frenchmen Can't Be Wrong (Why We Love France but Not the French)*; *French Women Don't Get Fat*; *French Women Don't Get Facelifts*; *French Children Don't Throw Food*; *French Parents Don't Give In*; *The Bonjour Effect: The Secret Code of French Conversation Revealed*; *Au Contraire: Figuring Out the French*; *How the French Invented Love*; *1000 Years of Annoying the French*.

This is not an exhaustive list, but it is enough to convey the flavour and reach of this genre. The themes that these books explore range across a colourful landscape of characteristics which, although for the most part hardly academic, do betray, among the non-French, who are the authors of these titles, an admiration for and, at the same time, a resentful irritation with and – yes – an envy of a people that can be so self-regarding and, at times, arrogant: 'Love of *grandeur* is one of the fundamental characteristics of French culture.' 'They have an innate disposition towards creative thinking.' 'Intellectual foreplay.' 'It is a centralised country with a penchant for authoritarianism and a disdain for compromise.' 'Since their World War II purgatory, the French have learned to live with the idea that they are neither the biggest, nor the strongest, power on earth. But they still believe they are the best.' 'They have a degree of self-assurance that few other countries have.' 'The gastronomic orgasm.' 'In France there is a residual belief in the intrinsic genius or superiority of the French language.' 'Not a week goes by in France without talk of *l'exception culturelle* (the cultural exception).'[2]

For the most part, these observations are not substantiated or followed through. They are meant half seriously but not properly investigated. In many cases, it would be difficult if not impossible to do so. How do you judge a disdain for compromise, or degrees of self-assurance?

Viv Groskop, a British broadcaster and comedian, has in all seriousness written a funny book on how French literature can teach us to be happy. Again, could/would anyone write a book about how German, Russian or Jewish literature could teach us happiness?

Sudhir Hazareesingh, born in Mauritius, a former French colony, and now an Oxford academic with a flat in Paris, makes a more substantial stab at things in his book, *How the French Think: An Affectionate Portrait of an Intellectual People*. Among his considered observations: the French evince an 'unrelenting dogmatism'; they have a 'magnificent rhetorical style' in conversation; 'the activities of the mind have occupied a special place in French public life'; 'the French devotion to culture is reflected in the weight given to the written word'; 'the philosophical spirit is more developed there than anywhere else'. France has 'a contempt for materialism'. There is a belief among the French 'that the possession of a high degree of culture provides (in and of itself) an entitlement to rule'. 'In France we have no oil but we have ideas.' France believes it is 'a beacon to the rest of the world' with an 'uncritical belief in the supremacy of the French *mission civilisatrice*'. 'The French café symbolises equal dignity.' There is 'a preference for abstract argument over concrete, evidence-based discussion'. 'All the great ideals of European civilisations have come through France.' 'French unhappiness might be caused by too much thinking.' There is an 'absence of interest in con-temporary French thought among progressives across the world'. Yet 'intellectuals continue to matter'. 'French elite thinking has drifted towards a strident form of ethnic nationalism.'[3]

It's a lot to take in, and some of these observations are paradoxical and/or contrary, others are dated, not all are flattering, but the cen-tral point is that it is France and the French that attract these kinds of bald, bold and provocative statements in the first place, when other nations do not do so. There are no books on why American women don't get facelifts, how the Irish think, why 80 million Germans can't be wrong or 1,000 years of irritating the British (though after Brexit that might change).

A clue to this phenomenon lies, I believe, in the fact that many of the authors of these books about France are American: this is not accidental. It is not accidental because, among the 196 nations of the world, only America and France harbour universal pretensions and suffer from a similar narcissism. We hear regularly about French exceptionalism and American exceptionalism but hardly at all about that of any other nation. Rooted in history and lodged in their peo-ple's collective psychology is the conviction that the French, like the Americans, have a special global mission. For the Americans it is the spread of democracy and free enterprise ('manifest destiny'); for the French it is the *mission civilisatrice*. As the American historian Richard Kuisel puts it, both nations – and only these two nations – are convinced that other people in the world *want to be like them*. Americans believe that they possess the secret to freedom and pros-perity and the French believe they are the champions of *civilisation*. This, in my view, accounts for why many non-French are drawn to – and at the same time irritated by – France and the French. Both nations have an inbuilt arrogance but that among Americans is more understandable since their country is so obviously richer and more open (though clearly by no means less corrupt) than anywhere else. But with the French it is much harder to pin down what it is that we admire/are jealous of/can't abide.

Most non-French people probably don't know that there is a thriv-ing French anti-American literature: *America the Menace: Scenes from the Life of the Future; Menace in the West: The Rise of French Anti-Americanism; L'Amérique est-elle trop riche?; Les Américains sont-ils adultes?; La France colonisée; L'Amérique dans les têtes: un siècle de fascinations et d'aversions; Le Défi américain; L'Obsession anti-américaine*. Unsurprisingly, not all these titles have been translated into English. The zenith (or nadir) of this 'literature' was Jean Baudrillard's *Amérique*, published in 1986, which claimed to find a 'chasm of modernity' between France and the United States, because America 'represents the end of European values and culture; it is a society without reflection or introspection, without reverence for cultural heritage, without depth or a sense of the tragic'. America was already in decline, he thought, 'at the facelift stage'.[4]

Charles de Gaulle agreed, *avant la lettre*. In one speech in the 1960s he listed America's faults: violence, racism, vulgarity, moral laxness, seductive materialism. De Gaulle disliked the American way of life, finding America to be 'a society without history and therefore without identity'. (In fact, as we shall see, it is France that has had a problem with its identity.) In particular, de Gaulle disliked the 'arrogance of power' that he felt the US showed. Yet his own policies were themselves grounded on his famous 'certain idea of France' where she 'is only really herself when she is at the forefront of nations'.

According to one distinguished French historian, François Furet, who died in 1997, French exceptionalism is now over. In 1988, Furet published with two colleagues a book entitled *La République du centre* and subtitled *La fin de l'exception française*. Furet looked at French exceptionalism in the long term and found that the areas in which the French *had* differed from their European counterparts (revolution, repeated ways in which governments have fallen by one form of violence or another, *dirigisme*, the absence of compromise or consensus, the need for glory) were finally on the wane and France was becoming more like other modern industrial nations. Furet's book attracted enormous attention in France, though it was never translated into English, and one reason for that may have been because he wasn't entirely right.[5] The American academic Richard Kuisel, already introduced, wrote two excellent books about French–American relations. In the first, published in 1993, he concluded that the American way had 'seduced' the French. In the second book, published in 2011, he concluded that the French had rejected American values, while maintaining their exceptionalism.[6]

The ambivalence which Americans feel about the French, and which the French feel about America, is reflected – to an extent – in the relationship between the British and the French. In their long book on *That Sweet Enemy*, a history of British–French relations, Robert (British) and Isabelle (French) Tombs subtitle their story 'a love–hate relationship'. Interestingly, their book has four entries in the index on 'Francophilia' and ten each on 'Francophobia' and 'Anglophilia', but no fewer than *forty-six* on 'Anglophobia'.[7]

So there *is* something special, something different, something fascinating about the French. Foreigners are at one and the same time envious of the French way of life and irritated by the French assumption that they are more civilised than the rest of us. There is of course a paradox here. If the French *weren't* more civilised than the rest of us, the rest of us wouldn't envy them their way of life.

But what *is* their way of life? What is their secret? How has that way of life come about? As already discussed, the raft of 'cute' books, though providing entertaining guides to this or that aspect of Frenchness, never really hit the nail on the head across the board. I believe there *is* an answer, a serious answer, and this book sets out to provide it.

A Culture of Defeat, a Genius for Renewal

The idea for the main theme of this book first arose when I read *The Children of the Revolution: The French 1799–1914*, published in 2008 by Robert Gildea, professor of modern history at the University of Oxford.[8] Gildea's argument in that book (which, despite its title, begins in 1760) was and is that, beginning with the French Revolution, and lasting until the First World War, there were five key generations that shaped the history of the country, and that these generations were marked by five convulsions that embraced France during those years: the Revolution itself, and the Terror that followed it, from 1789 to 1794; 1815, the Hundred Days, the Battle of Waterloo and the restoration of the monarchy; the revolution of 1848 and the coup d'état shortly after in 1851; the

Franco-Prussian War and the Paris Commune in 1870–1; and the Dreyfus Affair of 1897.

I was also taken by the work of French historian Pierre Nora and his interest in what is 'intangible' in cultures, in 'national mentalities', in his idea that France, even today, is still 'painfully seeking itself', his concern to run to earth how France's uniqueness as a nation was achieved, the 'obsessive cult of country' that he observed about him and, yes, what exactly a 'generation' is, how long it lasts, and what determines who belongs to a generation. Gildea and Nora were exploring the right questions, but so too were other French historians, who together provided a golden generation themselves: Maurice Agulhon on French sociability and the country's 'violent symbolic landscape'; Noëmi Hepp on what is and what isn't remembered; Fernand Braudel on 'collective destinies' and the country's 'distinctive cultural superstructure'; and Michel de Certeau's focus on the 'power of the well-spoken word' and the 'repeated wound'. Sudhir Hazareesingh also makes the point that 'loss, alienation and death' have 'deep roots' in French culture.[9]

All this, however, has to be put alongside the work and ideas of Wolfgang Schivelbusch, a German–American historian, in his 2001 title, *The Culture of Defeat*, and those of Jean-Marc Largeaud, the French historian who argues that there is in fact a culture of defeat that is 'unique to France'. Their theories all begin and end, in a way, with what Robert and Isabelle Tombs conclude in their book on the relations down the ages between Britain and France: 'The memory of defeat went [goes] deeper than the memory of victory.'[10]

Schivelbusch begins his original account in ancient times but it suits us to close in on his analysis of Hegel's nineteenth-century maxim 'that world history is the court of world justice [which] regards victory as a verdict – the end result of a previous struggle – that remains in force only until an opponent's challenge begins a new struggle ... In the classical liberal system, the winners at any one point in history must always be prepared to face challenges from rivals, who are often yesterday's losers, *whether the context occurs in industry or the marketplace, in the world of fashion or ideas, in sports competitions* or political elections.' (Emphasis added.)[11] The 'philosophy of defeat', he goes on, seeks to identify and appreciate the significance of defeat itself.

Reinhart Koselleck, a German historian who died in 2006, similarly drew a comparison between the historiography of victors and vanquished. 'While history may be temporarily made by the victors ... The historiography of the defeated is another matter entirely. Their defining experience is that everything turned out other than they hoped ... Therefore, they begin to search for middle- and long-term factors to account for and perhaps explain the accident of the unexpected outcome. There is something to the hypothesis that being forced to draw new and difficult lessons from history yields insights of longer validity and thus greater explanatory power. History may in the short term be made by the victors, but historical wisdom is in the long run enriched more by the vanquished ...'[12]

Putting Gildea, Nora, Certeau, Largeaud and Koselleck together with Schivelbusch produces the table below, a table that, I believe, acts as a clear starting point for understanding both the weaknesses and the strengths of the French and the contours of the French way of life. To address one of Nora's main points, I think it shows clearly that, as Gildea identifies, generational effects are crucial and are defined by *events*. Here, I argue, are the all-important ones:

1763	End of the Seven Years War
1789–94	French Revolution and the Terror
1815	Battle of Waterloo
1830	Revolution
1848–51	Revolution and coup d'état
1870–1	Franco-Prussian War and the Paris Commune
1896–7	Dreyfus Affair
1916	Verdun
1940	Vichy
1954–62	Dien Bien Phu and the Algerian War
1968	Events of May

The first thing to say about this list of dates is that, in fact, it is not exhaustive of the convulsions France has suffered. Barricades went up, and serious conflict followed, in 1832, 1834 and 1839, but the dates in the list are those that matter for reasons that will become clear.[13] More important, the second thing to say is that, on average, each pair of events is about a *generation* apart, never more than twenty-something years. The third is that each set of events in the list marks a real convulsion in French history: violence of one sort or another and, either for the nation as a whole (1763, 1815, 1870–1, 1940) or for large parts of it (the church, the army, the aristocracy, the *financiers*, the *pieds noirs*), a terrible experience of *defeat*. In other words, almost every generation of the French people, since it lost its place as the number-one nation in Europe (and therefore the world, at the time), at the end of the Seven Years War in 1763, has had close-up, first-hand experience of violence and/or defeat (the First World War is an especially complex and ambiguous case which we shall come back to). One could go further and say that many of these defeats (1763, 1815, 1870–1, 1940) were not just defeats but *humiliations*.

No other nation, certainly no other developed nation, has experienced so many and so regular defeats and humiliations. This 'repeated wound', in Certeau's words, it seems to me, helps explain to an extent the French way of life. As Koselleck phrased it: 'Being defeated appears to be an inexhaustible wellspring of intellectual progress.' Not only that, as Schivelbusch also says, yesterday's losers – as the table shows that the French have so often been – soon become challengers, not necessarily in the context of military affairs but 'in industry, the marketplace, in the world of fashion or ideas, in sports competitions'.

I am arguing here that the distinctive French way of life – the preponderance of high culture, high fashion, *haute cuisine*, intellectual activity – owes a great deal to the distinctive nature of French history, in particular its repeated wound of serial military and political defeats. These defeats have made France more reflective, more philosophical, more intellectual, more abstract, have helped divert its creative energies into its empires of art, culture, *haute cuisine* and *haute couture*. But the experience of repeated defeats has also ensured it is more dogmatic, defensively arrogant, envious of other peoples, and has helped stoke its contempt for materialism. Its repeated defeats have spawned its desperate need for a return to what is perceived as the grandeur of earlier times.

Though true enough, it is only half the picture. Ceri Crossley, in his book *French Historians and Romanticism*, makes the point that one of the long-term effects of the Revolution was to bring about an ingrained 'mood of renewal' in France. Whereas British history, for example, is reformist, French history is revolutionary, and we shall see that scenario in this book – a pattern of fairly swift returns to enthusiasm, a passion for work as often as not replacing the desire for power, so that in France the basic meaning of history lies in the *rede*velopment of man's productive capacities.[14] This is what de Gaulle meant when he referred to France's 'genius for renewal'.

But it is still not the whole story. Between the defeat of the nobility in the Fronde (the civil war which pitched the French king against the princes and the nobility and lasted from 1648 until 1653), which we might say created a more reflective, intellectual and stylish aristocracy in France than elsewhere, and France's next major defeat – in 1763, a century later, the end of the Seven Years War, when the country ceased to be the world's greatest power, ceding that title to Great Britain – French culture continued to evolve in a number of ways that made it the envy of the world. In the early eighteenth century, across a wide range of fields – from architecture and fashion to painting and chemistry, from food and philosophy to manners and theatre – the French led the way.

One of the effects of the Fronde was to inculcate in Louis XIV a dislike of Paris, which is one reason why he moved his court to Versailles, 12 miles and two to three hours away by horse-drawn coach. This decision would be to the long-term benefit of Paris and Parisians, which became evident as the eighteenth century progressed. Paris became the capital of the world.

After 1763, however, France changed. The change was not immediately apparent, because 1763 was only the first of the several defeats the nation was to suffer, and which together account for its cultural character.

According to Schivelbusch, the initial response to defeat, whether psychological, cultural or political, conforms to a pattern which cuts across nations. The first stage is 'dreamland'. This dreamland period, Schivelbusch says, normally lasts for weeks or months only, during which time memories of the actual reasons for defeat begin to fade, to be replaced by the losers' conviction that the nation laid down its arms more or less of its own free will, in a kind of 'gentleman's agreement' that placed trust 'in the chivalry of the enemy'. 'It is all the more surprising', he writes, 'how briefly the nation's depression tends to last before turning into a unique type of euphoria.'

And it is not far from dreamland, Schivelbusch says, to the most common – and often final – state, in which it is held that 'the actual losers were the moral winners', that the losers in battle were the winners in spirit. For example, the massacre of French knights in 1346 by English archers at Crécy is even today considered 'less a military defeat than chivalric martyrdom ... our enemies were anonymous, mechanical, soulless assembly-line workers, devoid of any imagination, who were only victorious because of their greater numbers'.[15] These sentiments, he says, recur throughout history and the underlying complaint is: 'Make it a fair fight and we'd have whipped you.'

The defeated party can always claim that the decisive factor in defeat was a violation of the rules. As Robert and Isabelle Tombs put it, the French account of their defeat at Waterloo is often put down, by Victor Hugo and other French historians, to the fact that the Prussians turned up late 'unsportingly to turn the tide'.[16] Much the same attitudes emerged in Paris during the First World War – see chapter 41.

And it is but a short step from here to the idea that victory achieved by unsoldierly means is illegitimate, a deceitful swindle, in some way false, whereas defeat is the experience of something 'pure and unsullied'. More even than that, victory tends to be seen as a mode of profit-making and therefore the victors inhabit 'the realm of tradesmen and merchants' rather than honourable military types. Against such adversaries, the losers make terrific sacrifices and, in so doing, 'the losing side attains a dignity in its own eyes that is as inaccessible to the victor in an age of profitable triumphs as the kingdom of heaven is to the rich man in the New Testament'. In a speech to the French soldiers returning home a few days after Sedan, Hugo assured them that 'you will always be the world best soldiers ... The glory belongs to France.' A statue erected to one of France's military leaders in 1874 bears the inscription '*Gloria victis*', 'Glory to the conquered' (there are in fact seven iterations of this scattered about France).[17]

And it further follows from this that, if the victor's triumph is seen as illegitimate in some way, and thus can stake no claim to glory or honour, an injustice has been inflicted that must be rectified. And this is where a new struggle begins, which is often an ethical or even juridical *levée en masse* in which the loser, 'casting himself as the personification of defiled purity, tries to score a "moral victory" against the winner'. In some ways this is the crucial step, for the onslaught cannot be cast in military terms. In fact – and again this is central to the argument – defeated countries can rely on one great consolation: their faith in their cultural and moral superiority above the people who have overpowered them. Linda Colley tells us that, following its defeat in the American War of Independence, Britain bounced back 'in one of the most formative and violent periods in the making of Britain and in the making of the modern world', where 'Lord North was made the scapegoat for national humiliation', and where one of the reasons for the enthusiasm for the abolition of slavery was because it helped the British feel superior to Americans.[18]

Schivelbusch describes a raft of intellectuals – French and German, mainly – who are sympathetic to the notion that 'victory threatens culture, whereas defeat might enhance it'. To quote only one example, Nietzsche was not alone in prophesying that, after the Franco-Prussian conflict of 1870–1 – in which Paris was besieged and France humiliated – France would only gain in culture while Germany, until then 'the land of poets and thinkers', would decline.[19]

The understanding of war as a 'purifying and renewing force' is, Schivelbusch says, the most important legacy granted to the defeated. And it is a short step from understanding defeat as an act of purification, humility and sacrifice – a crucifixion of sorts – to laying claim to spiritual and moral leadership in world affairs.[20]

As we shall see, time and again, this applied *a fortiori* in France. After Sedan, Hugo thundered: 'Like ancient Greece and Rome, France today is civilisation and a threat to France is a threat to all ... should the *unthinkable* transpire and France be defeated, it would be a sign of how far humanity has sunk ... Saving Paris means more than saving France: it means saving the world.'[21] Shortly after this, Parisians were reduced to eating rats and elephants from the zoo, and 30,000 of their number were butchered.

Undoubtedly, echoes of this sort can be found throughout history. For example, the French collapse of 1814–15, far from being acknowledged as a national disaster, was dismissed as the personal failure of Napoleon. The crimes of Vichy France in the Second World War were likewise dismissed later (by President Mitterrand among others) as not being the crimes of the real France – Vichy, he said, 'was not France'. The Napoleonic defeats had been carried out not by a single enemy but by a coalition, towards whose individual members the French nation could still feel superior. Following the First World War, Germany felt the same – that it had been defeated by a coalition (the 'stab in the back'), whereas it could have beaten any one individual of the opposition nations in a 'fair fight'.

Another pattern can be found in the 'parallel scourges' of English mercantilism and Prussian militarism, both departing from French *esprit* in their 'calculating coldness, heartlessness, methodicalness [and] lack of grace, fighting spirit and heroism'. In the aftermath of defeat in the Seven Years War, for instance, there was no doubt among the French public that the moral victor was not England – 'this restless people of accountants and egotists' – but France, thanks to the 'reliably loyal national integrity and strength of character'.[22]

Furthermore, every (new) defeat stirs up memories of earlier defeats and, as we shall see, and as Jean-Marc Largeaud has said, France has suffered more defeats – some humiliating – and those defeats closer together than any other comparable nation. In the Franco-Prussian War, the French army failed to win a single battle and its only actions were retreats.[23] It takes some doing to convert that sort of humiliation into a victory, but within a remarkably few short years, France was aglitter in the Belle Époque and Paris, not Berlin or London, was again the capital – and the envy – of the world.

If serial military and political defeats – 'the repeated wound' – help explain why France is a more reflective nation than others, why it defensively and aggressively promotes its successes in culture, the arts, the worlds of fashion, food and philosophy, as a sort of compensatory displacement activity, we still need to understand both why it recovered so quickly and so often from its defeats, and why the culture that it excelled in was, for much of the time, 'high culture'. France's image of itself as the premier home of high culture is part of its love of 'grandeur'.

This may be explained by one other aspect of the nation's history: an institution that is, if not totally unique, then pre-eminent in its history. This feature has been the subject of much recent scholarship about the French, and helps explain a great deal of what interests and intrigues us about them and, yes, sets them apart. That phenomenon is *sociability*.

Sociability is not a particularly user-friendly word in English. The word and the concept were first introduced into historiography in the 1960s to mark the study of the history of association (political and otherwise) and to describe intellectual networks. Conviviality, gregariousness, civility, liveliness, even 'clubbability' are given as synonyms in the dictionaries. But, in fact, they are all inadequate to some degree and sociability, for all its faults, is the most accurate and will have to serve. And in fact the French use it a lot themselves – they like it.

There were perhaps two reasons why the sociability of the French should take precedence. One is that the notion of sociability – in particular, its moral and political dimensions – was more thoroughly explored in eighteenth-century France than elsewhere, because theories of natural law were strongest there and ideas about association received more attention.[24] And there were those who felt, perhaps as a result of this, that the French were (are?) more sociable than other nations. Mirabeau, for instance, was one who felt that the '*vertus sociables*' were 'more natural to us than to any other nation'.[25] In Montesquieu's *Persian Letters*, Uzbec, his fictional Persian visitor in Paris, writes back to his homeland: 'It is said that man is a *sociable* being. On this score it seems to me that a Frenchman is more human than anyone else. He is man *par excellence* for he seems to be made uniquely for *société*.'[26] Daniel Gordon argues that 'it was common to affirm in the Enlightenment that France was the model of sociability to the rest of the world' and quotes Bernardin de Saint-Pierre, novelist and botanist, as saying that 'most of our writers brag about our nation's spirit of *société*',[27] while even Voltaire, in the dedication in his play *Zaïre*, wrote: 'Since the reign of Anne of Austria [mid-seventeenth century] they [the French] have been the most *sociable* and polite people on earth, and this politeness is not arbitrary ... It is a law of nature that they have fortunately cultivated more than any other peoples.'[28]

But a second, associated and arguably more important reason for the supremacy of French sociability was the emergence of the salon in French society.

TRADING THE SWORD FOR THE PEN – SUBLIMATED REVENGE

Depending on how you choose to understand modern French history, it began either with the Fronde in the seventeenth century, which helped lay the foundation for Louis XIV's removal of his court to Versailles and begin the *grand siècle*, but sparked the alienation of the nobility of Paris from the court, or it began in 1763, the end of the Seven Years War, when defeat by Britain marked the end of France's claim to be the greatest power in Europe, and left Britain to take over. This marked an enduring grievance of the French for their country's lost grandeur that it has never really overcome.

The Fronde pitched the aristocracy against the Crown, and the aristocracy lost. It was in fact a defining defeat for the aristocracy and is a good example, says Schivelbusch, of his theory, because, after their defeat, the Frondists, who opposed French absolutism, 'traded the sword for the pen', becoming typical losers of 'this reflective sort'. He cites as examples the memoirs and aphorisms of Saint-Simon and La Rochefoucauld, arguing that they 'were ultimately both a sublimated form of revenge and a social critique that led directly to the Enlightenment and the French Revolution'.[29]

More than that, the Fronde had a significant effect on the changing status of the aristocracy in France. As a result of the mayhem of religious wars, the commercial revolution sparked by the discoveries of the New World, and the scientific revolution, prices rose constantly between 1560 and 1640, roughly speaking, which had a disastrous knock-on effect in regard to the revenues of the nobility. This occurred in spite of the fact that *le monde* or high society in France was exempt from the *taille*, the tax that formed the basis of the French fiscal system. Nor was it helped by the *loi de dérogeance*, under which the nobility was forbidden from participating in business or commerce, welcomed by many among the nobility at the time as underlining their superiority and distinction.

The increased importance of the infantry in wartime also displaced the role of the cavalry as the elite corps. The nobility – traditionally linked with the cavalry – despised the infantry, one reason being that its advance took the stress off the military distinction associated with mounted warfare. This had the unintended consequence of severing the association between the aristocracy and valour and in so doing changed the very meaning of the nobility's claim to preference.

One all-important knock-on effect of this was that in the nobility's eyes the traditional superiority of arms was replaced by the superiority of breeding, 'the incontestable purity of lineage'. As Benedetta Craveri puts it: 'The outward signs of nobility – titles, positions, land, palaces, clothing and jewels – could no longer indicate membership by right of a certain class, since they had come to be used in the traffic between the Crown and the new men. The nobility therefore chose to define itself through the treacherous domains of style. Henceforth it would be by their way of living, of speaking, of acting, of amusing themselves, of enjoying each other's company that the nobles would persuade themselves of the unshakeable certainty of their own superiority. In place of arms, their touchstone would be provided by refined manners – *bienséances* – and by a body of unwritten law more powerful than any written one.'[30] They referred to themselves by the collective label of *le monde* to show that their worldliness was as separate from the divine realm of the church as much as from the court.

While these changes were taking place, Cardinal Richelieu appeared on the scene with his pronounced views about absolute monarchy and the forms of courtesy due to the king and his various offices. This was the beginning of the high point of absolutism in which one of the main aims of the monarch and his minister was to insist that the nobility conform to the strict, hierarchical etiquette of the court. 'A great monarchy must be reflected in the elegance of its language, the excellence of its artistic and cultural institutions, the prestige of its literature, and of course the splendor of its court.'[31]

This did not please everyone. As the American historian Daniel Gordon tartly remarks: 'How do people living in an authoritarian regime maintain their sense of dignity?' Almost the only practical possibility 'is to invest the seemingly insignificant areas of life that the authorities do not control with the maximum amount of meaning'. Citizens who lacked sovereignty, Gordon observes, had to 'take an inventory' of the social spaces that remained free and order them into a coherent whole.[32]

Given this context, coming on top of all the other changes of fortune that the nobility had suffered, it was only a matter of time before some of their number would seek an area of freedom separate from the increasingly oppressive nature of the court. And when it came it took the form of a protected space – secular, ethical and aesthetic – that was removed not just from the court but from the church too, a new collective ideal of life that lasted for centuries and set France apart from other nations. This was the salon, one of the main focuses of this book.

TEMPLES OF INSIGNIFICANT CHATTER OR SPACES FOR FRUITFUL DIALOGUE?

The first person to draw attention to this world was Comte Pierre Louis de Roederer, who in 1835 published his *Mémoire pour server à l'histoire de la société polie en France*. Since then there has been a raft of international scholarship exploring the 'complex web of influence between the salons and the savants', in particular their effects on the French language, on new forms of literature, on the role of philosophy in society, and in the realm of taste. One of the most up-to-date works on the subject is *The Age of Conversation*, by the Italian historian Benedetta Craveri. In admirable detail, she has identified the last half of the seventeenth century as the period when the French way of life as we know it first came into focus and the all-important part played by a dozen or so remarkable women.[33]

Many of these women were ridiculed in their own time, as we shall see. Despite this, it is the argument of this book that the salon appeared at a propitious time in European history, though it was no accident. Furthermore, it was both a symptom and a cause of several more or less simultaneous developments in social/intellectual life, which together determine what we so admire (and to an extent revile) about the French way of life. I will also argue that the mixing of sociability and intellect is an underappreciated lineament of history.

- The salon emerged as a social/intellectual and egalitarian alternative to the hierarchical absolutist courts of the French kings.

- The salons, hosted by female *salonnières* (for reasons we shall come to), helped to nourish a sympathetic and symbiotic relationship between men and women that set the relations between the sexes in France as different from – and much more agreeable and productive than – those elsewhere.
- The salons came on stream in France at the same time as (a) the maturation of high classical culture, formalised in the establishment of the great academies in French life, and (b) multiple innovations in the sophisticated realm of what we might call 'style' or 'taste', such as the introduction of *haute cuisine, haute couture* and *haute coiffure*; new forms of interior decoration (new colours and forms of furniture, such as mirrors); the invention of new wines, such as champagne; the science of cosmetics and dietetics; the greater sophistication of the toilette; and so on.
- This combination of stylish sociability and intellectual activity means that in France, more than elsewhere, intellectuality was more socially acceptable in *le monde*. This mix is what gave intellectual affairs – and intellectuals – a higher and more approved status in France than elsewhere.
- The simultaneous occurrence of these various activities comprised a unique event that gave France, and French culture, its unique flavour. Among other things – and this is all-important – it helped ensure that high culture in France was more a matter of fine art, poetry, theatre, novels, philosophy and later politics, rather than science. There *were* scientific salons, but they were nowhere near as numerous as other kinds. By and large, science is not as sociable an activity as the arts in any country. (But that is a topic for another book.) At the same time, the non-hierarchical nature of the French salons played an important role in the change of intellectual mood in France that helped to give rise to the eighteenth-century socio-political weather system that produced both Enlightenment and Revolution.

The word *salon* is – to an extent – an anachronism. Antoine Lilti, the foremost contemporary French authority on the culture of the salons, says it was first used in 1794 in Sébastien Chamfort's *Maximes et pensées*. Until then words such as *société, monde* or *cercle* were equally common. But *salon* has stuck and the literature on the subject is now both copious and contentious, starting in earnest in the 1970s in the wake of the new interest in sociability by historians.

The real question about salon sociability is whether salons were 'temples of snobbery and insignificant chatter', homes to precious trivialities, or convivial gatherings of proper intellectual debate, spaces for free and fruitful dialogue. Academics like the Canadian Jolanta T. Pekacz have argued that the salons had no real significance, that more than one man wrote about how he was relieved to be back among male company, in male-run salons or the cafés, which were mainly male affairs.[34] This does not sit well with the fact that many salons lasted for decades, or with the fact that many men of substance were members of multiple salons. Are we to conclude that such formidable individuals were content time and again with merely trivial goings-on in such surroundings? Common sense, as well as many quotations describing and extolling the virtues of long-lived salon life, suggest that their prominence was well earned. By and large, the French are not a frivolous people – droll, maybe, but that is quite different.[35]

Steven Kale, another of the several American academics who have taken an interest in French sociability and salons in particular, argues to the contrary that salons and *mondanité* (society life) existed 'in close proximity' to the worlds of politics, literature, art, fashion and business, all of which preoccupied French elites.[36] Salons encouraged socialising between the sexes, brought nobles and bourgeois together, and afforded opportunities for intellectual speculation.

In fact, the sheer *persistence* of salons during the nineteenth century, Kale says, underlined their remarkable ability to adapt to changing historical circumstances. In the wake of the worst excesses of the Revolution, salons largely disappeared, although to an extent they were reconstituted abroad by aristocratic émigrés.[37] In France itself, they were reconstituted shortly after the Terror ended, with Napoleon encouraging renewed salon activity as a way to enlist the support of the traditional aristocracy and boost the intellectual and social cachet of his reign in the eyes of monarchical Europe. This was an element in his politics of *fusion*. During the Bourbon Restoration (1815–30) and the July Monarchy (1830–48), salons extended their influence still more to become the principal focuses of elite political networking and intellectual exchange, albeit constrained by the norms of *mondain* sociability and still led by *salonnières*, 'whose traditional mediating function seemed all the more necessary in the face of growing political partisanship'.[38]

The 'feminine' characteristics of salons also came to be idealised by generations of male writers, artists, intellectuals and politicians, who treasured them 'as protected spaces for the reconciliation of differences'; their vital *neutrality* was understood to be guaranteed by the self-effacement and devotion to propriety of the *salonnière*.[39]

The salon was capable of an extraordinary flexibility, drawing its strength from not being one thing only. At times, the salon was like a royal court, at others a university, an academy, a republic or a monarchy, even a publishing house. 'Salons', says Kale, 'could be either marginal or mainstream, bourgeois or aristocratic, public or private, courtly or enlightened, hierarchical or democratic, mixed or exclusive, feminist or masculine, frivolous or serious, literary or political – or both.' They filled an institutional vacuum at the all-important intersection between public and private life that was so important to the emerging culture of the eighteenth century.[40]

There were those, such as Alphonse de Lamartine, who argued that salons 'determined the march of events' and manipulated political life from behind the scenes. Historian Marc Fumaroli says salons were an important basis for the evolution of French literature thanks to the development of polite conversation there.[41] Pierre Bourdieu sees in salons 'the birth of the writer ... in which the increasing autonomy of literary activity retains an independence of the power structure and the social elites'. The American historian Robert Darnton has a different take. He sees the literary world of the eighteenth century as divided – and divided bitterly – between elite writers with access to the salons, who were 'showered' with honours, and the 'low-lifes of literature' who survived by publishing pamphlets. The salons, he insists, were places where writers received 'consecration'.[42]

Underlying the resilience and longevity of the salons is an association between salon conversation, literature and the role of women in high society.

THE BEAUTIFUL HALF OF THE WORLD

Dena Goodman, professor of women's studies at the University of Michigan, argues that the eighteenth-century salons were in fact *the* central institution of the Republic of Letters, that they were almost invariably ruled by women and that they were central to the success of the Enlightenment. Her researches are part of a wider frame of reference which is investigating the role of women in French history, especially in the *ancien régime*, and emerging evidence (explored in several places below) that women were deliberately airbrushed out of that history.

Goodman and other (mainly American) colleagues therefore argue that the female-administered salons were part of the important emerging public sphere in the seventeenth and eighteenth centuries, part of the growth – along with journals and newspapers, letters circulating with the newly established postal services, academies and coffee houses – of public opinion, which was occupied as much by the bourgeois sections of society as the aristocracy. Indeed, the salons were arguably the most important point of overlap between these different social spheres. 'They were serious places, devoted to intellectual debate, in which the rules of politeness and a discreet governance by *salonnières* constituted the social grounding for the Enlightenment Republic of Letters, using an ideal of egalitarian sociability to bring together male philosophes' will to reform with female mediation.'[43]

After Goodman, perhaps the most sustained effort to reconfigure French history in this way is that by Faith Beasley in her book *Salons, History, and the Creation of 17th-Century France*. In this tour de force, she takes on in particular the habit of the French themselves to put down the influence that women have had on the intellectual life of the country during the past 400 years. She notes how conventional French histories continually (mis)reported the death of the salons (under Louis XIV), how the *salonnières* became 'mere' hostesses in the eighteenth century, rather than intellectual figures in their own right, how they disappeared after 1848 – how, in effect, they were always being sidelined by conventional (and of course male) French historians.[44]

In the seventeenth century itself, however, as Beasley points out, references to women's 'proficient ability' to discern the quality of literature were widespread. Women are even described as 'oracles'. Beasley quotes from Martin de Pinchesne, a would-be poet and royal official, who said in a preface to his uncle Vincent Voiture's Œuvres: 'This beautiful half of the world, with the ability to read, also is able to judge as well as we are, and today is the master of men's glory.' Beasley's argument is that, by the middle of the seventeenth century, the status of the salon milieu as arbiter of literary value 'was so established' as to incite intense opposition. More important in the long run, she says, and this is something we shall make much of, the salons' precise role was to offer 'worldly critique', as opposed to more academic assessment. And this, it is argued here, is an especially French characteristic. People in the salons, Beasley says, did not – at least in the seventeenth century – speak with erudition but they spoke, according to one of their number, 'with more good sense and less pedantry' than the exchanges which reigned in the universities. The salons countered the all-male academies and were deliberately designed to 'alter the entire literary field', and it is the case that 'many authors considered the opinion of the worldly public of the salons more crucial to their success'. There were, in the seventeenth century, 'over fifty active salonnières in Paris alone' and, according to Saint-Simon, they comprised 'a kind of academy of cultivated minds, of gallantry, virtue and knowledge ... it was a meeting place of the most distinguished in merit ...'[45]

Antoine Lilti only half agrees. The point of the salons, he says, was their 'worldliness', rather than 'a supposedly innate French talent for conversation'.[46] 'Le monde is an essential term for understanding Paris society of the eighteenth century ... Le monde occupied an important place in the aesthetic and intellectual debates of the century and many writers of the Enlightenment were fascinated by it, thus helping to give the customs and manners of the Paris elite a lasting literary aura ... Worldliness was the specific form taken in France by the fascination that the polite elites and the people of letters (gens des lettres) had for each other.'[47] Lilti has been roundly criticised, mainly by American female historians, for trying to trivialise and marginalise salons, as not part of Jürgen Habermas's newly identified 'public sphere', and we shall see that Lilti's critics have a point: there is no getting away from the fact that many of the Parisian *salonnières* were formidable intellectual, artistic and social forces.[48]

THE IMPORTANCE OF 'WORLDLINESS'

Moreover, 'worldly taste' was considered throughout the seventeenth century as a quality that women possessed innately and could pass on to men through social interaction. In this context, social education – not book learning – was held up to value, meaning that women had something to offer even when they were excluded from traditional forms of education. Education *in society* was held to be the equal of scholastic learning, and it is this, it will be argued here, that also marked the French way of life, what set French culture apart. It is, in effect, why (and where) the realms of taste and intellect came together.[49]

The fact that learning was a more 'worldly' matter in France than elsewhere implied and implies two further things. First, it means that this form of learning was more widely distributed in France than elsewhere – this is why the French overall are a more intellectual, abstract and cultured people than other nations. They do not have a greater proportion of 'blue-stockings' than the rest of us – professional academics in the universities, for example – but, for the above-mentioned reasons, the worldly bourgeois and upper classes *do* value learning and culture more than the social elites of other nations. Through the salons, and the agreeable forms of exchange within them, they were more familiar – and more intimate – with novelists, painters, musicians, philosophers and scientists. Through the French salon, those who were accomplished in one field met the accomplished in other fields rather more often than was the case in other countries. The longevity of the salons meant that these influences likewise solidified into accepted tradition.

But the salons served a separate, second function. As protected spaces, run mainly by women, they were relatively immune from the international politics – in particular the repeated defeats – that so shaped the masculine political life of the country. This was true even after the 'cabinet wars' of the pre-Napoleonic era gave way to

the world of 'levée en masse' conflicts from the immediate post-Revolution time onwards. And so the worldly learning and sociability
of the salons, which could not help but become more political in the
first half of the nineteenth century, helped sustain the intellectual
traditions that had emerged prior to the storming of the Bastille, and
in so doing played a major role in many of the post-defeat recoveries
that have so marked French history. The salons made it agreeable
and easy for people who shone in one field to meet others shining in
different fields, and the fellowship this created bolstered enthusiasm
and fellow-feeling so important in creating optimism going forward.
Though a wider world – of business, industry, travel, the media,
political and educational institutions – evolved around them, salons
continued as an elite form of engagement that embodied France's idea
of itself. While much of France wanted to forget its military/political
failures, the salon represented what France thought it was good at.

Salons and a Unique Female Literary Tradition

As we shall see in due course, Molière and contemporaries of his
were mainly responsible for the first great 'put-down' that women
suffered, together with Charles Perrault (1628–1703), who thought
that women 'took too much pride' in their minds and in so doing
damaged the self-image of the French nation.[50] Still others regarded
women as men's superiors in matters of the mind.[51] Such views were
there if you looked for them, says Beasley, but the French themselves
did their best to ignore them.[52]

In discussing the work of Dominique Bouhours, a seventeenth-century priest and grammarian, on the French language, Beasley finds
that he equates the finest French language with the way 'polite people
speak', as reflected in worldly society. In Bouhours's opinion, she
says, 'French bears the unique imprint of its monarch as well as
of its polite, worldly society', most often associated with the polite
society of the salons. Women who speak well are identified as 'one of
France's distinguishing characteristics'.[53]

Subtly, says Beasley, throughout the eighteenth century, and then
more openly in the nineteenth, literary critics, commentators and
historians 'sought to sever the strong relationship between the salons

and the classical literary field'; there was in fact 'a move to bury what was arguably in the seventeenth century the most influential and important product of the salons, namely its unique female literary tradition and female influence on the literary field in general'.[54]

Writers (female writers) such as Stéphanie Félicité de Genlis (1746–1830) sought – in, for example, her book *De l'influence des femmes sur la littérature française* – to revive the role that women played in intellectual life. Mme de Genlis's work was picked up on by the critic and editor of the *Revue des deux mondes*, Ferdinand Brunetière (1849–1906), in 1889, when he commended her for her work in drawing attention to female writers, adding that women in the seventeenth century inspired writers to try to please their contemporaries and not just follow the dictates of the ancients, and forced their compatriots to find new ways to express themselves. At the same time he felt that, as even Molière had said, they had gone too far in their influence, that they had made French literature too 'rarefied', forcing writers into a too-aristocratic style.[55]

In the nineteenth century, Victor Cousin (1792–1867), philosopher and administrator of public instruction, wrote repeatedly about women – Jacqueline Pascal (Blaise's sister), Mme de Longueville, Mme de Sablé, Mlle de Scudéry, Mme de Chevreuse – and, while praising them, nonetheless concluded that a 'woman is a domestic being, just as a man is a public figure'.[56] The same criticism applies to the other leading nineteenth-century critic of French literature, Charles-Augustin Sainte-Beuve (1804–69); he too found it difficult to accord women a proper place in history. For him they were confined to letters and memoirs, by implication 'inferior' forms of expression.[57]

Nowhere, insists Beasley, do we ever get the sense that Corneille, or someone like him, sought the approbation of the salons, that he treated them as a serious audience, whose opinion he valued and could learn from. Beasley says plainly that women have been systematically eliminated from the corpus of seventeenth-century writers 'considered to be the models of "Frenchness"'. Still others place women in the broader context of 'worldly culture', arguing that salons had no wider influence on more 'serious' literary tastes in France.[58]

Beasley's overall verdict is that there was a backlash against the achievements of women in seventeenth-century France, that backlash occurring mainly in the eighteenth and nineteenth centuries but not properly recognised either since then. Her own aim, she concludes, has been to show that the salons and the worldly public they created were 'major players' in the literary sphere, defining taste, creating new genres with important social messages.[59]

That there may be something to this was underlined in 1981, when Marguerite Yourcenar, the novelist, poet and translator, Belgian-born (and in fact a US citizen since 1947), became the first woman in 350 years to be elected to the Académie française. She said in her address to the academy that she felt it necessary to surround herself with the 'shadows' of the female contributors to French culture, adding: 'The women of the Old Regime, queens of the salons ... didn't dream of crossing your threshold and maybe they thought they would demean, if they did so, their feminine sovereignty. They inspired writers, ruled over them sometimes and frequently succeeded in getting one of their protégés into your company ... they cared little about being candidates themselves.'[60]

Yourcenar was a sign of change. She was more than hinting that the salon – and *salonnières*, and their form of sociability – had been essentially sidelined from France's memory of its literary past. And so – again according to Lilti, writing in 2005 – salons have now 'become an obligatory topic of study'.[61]

The Persistence of Salons

A final factor in the importance of salons, again especially so in France, is that they are a prime example of what Arno Mayer has called 'the persistence of the old regime'. Many historians, he says, have 'overdrawn' the decline of land, nobles and peasants, the contraction of traditional manufacture and trade and of organised religion, and the atrophy of high culture. Writing about Europe until 1914, Mayer says that in order to truly grasp the past 'it may be necessary to reconceive and perhaps even totally reverse this picture of a modern world commanding a recessive and crumbing old order'. Land remained the ruling and governing classes' principal form of wealth and revenue until 1914. No less significant, consumer manufacture continued to outweigh capital goods production in its share of national wealth, produce and employment and this was more true of France than anywhere else. The old governing class was both resilient and flexible.[62]

'The salon culture of Paris was far from being a lifeless fossil.' On the contrary, Mayer says, it retained a certain vitality but the salons of the modest (or 'counterfeit') nobility were without question more literary and artistic than those of the *ancienne noblesse*, which did not need intellectuality to consecrate its renown. Despite the fact that Edmond de Goncourt had announced the death of the salons and high society some years before, and however much Léon Daudet saw the cafés displace them, they remained very much alive well into the twentieth century. Mayer concludes that the salon culture of Paris 'was in the nature of a substitute court for a swarm of aristocrats without a king and without an aristocracy'.[63]

THE GREAT CHAIN OF SALONS

It is no exaggeration to say that there have been literally hundreds of salons in France since the middle of the seventeenth century.[64] We shall concentrate on a much smaller number that were the most influential. The nature of that influence was intimate at times, as the master list – the great chain – shows, below.

What distinguishes the list which follows is that these salons, all run by women, stretch *in an unbroken sequence* from the early seventeenth century until the day before yesterday. Their principal guests are included.

Catherine de Vivonne, Marquise de Rambouillet (c.1588–1665)
François de Malherbe, Jean-Louis Guez de Balzac, Claude Favre de Vaugelas, Pierre Corneille, Molière, Jean Chapelain

Élisabeth du Plessis-Guénégaud (d.1677)
Blaise Pascal, Nicolas Boileau, François de La Rochefoucauld, Jean Racine

Marguerite de La Sablière (1636–93)
Valentin Conrart, Charles Perrault, Bernard de Fontenelle, Jean de La Fontaine, Pascal, Pierre Gassendi

Marie-Madeleine de Lafayette (1634–93)
Molière, Racine, known for her own books

Madeleine de Sablé (1598–1678)
La Rochefoucauld, La Fontaine

Madeleine de Scudéry (1607–1701)
René Descartes, Paul Pellisson, Jean-François Sarrasin, Chevalier de
Méré

Anne ('Ninon') de Lenclos (1620–1705)
Bernard le Bouyer de Fontenelle, Louis, Duc de Saint-Simon,
Henriette de Coligny

Anne-Thérèse, Marquise de Lambert (1647–1733)
Fontenelle, Montesquieu, François Fénelon, Président Hénault

Alexandrine de Tencin (1682–1749)
Philippe d'Orléans, regent of France, Cardinal Dubois, John
Law, Marivaux, Comte de Mirabeau, Jean Astruc, Charles Pinot
Duclos

Marie-Thérèse Geoffrin (1699–1777)
Jean Le Rond d'Alembert, Denis Diderot, other *Encyclopédistes*,
Claude-Adrien Helvétius, Friedrich Melchior Grimm, André
Morellet, Jean-François Marmontel, François Boucher, Jean-Baptiste
Greuze, Carle van Loo

Marie du Deffand (1696–1780)
Voltaire, Hénault, Jean-Jacques Rousseau, d'Alembert

Julie de Lespinasse (1732–77)
D'Alembert, Jean-Frédéric de Maurepas, Jacques-Antoine de
Guibert, Anne Robert Jacques Turgot, Étienne de Condillac, Nicolas
de Condorcet

Suzanne Churchod Necker (1739–94)
Marmontel, François Jean Chastellux, Guibert, Paul Henri
d'Holbach, Morellet, André Grétry, Georges-Louis de Buffon, Louis
Carrogis de Carmontelle

Comtesse de Houdetot (1730–1813)
Rousseau, Morellet, Jean-Baptiste-Antoine Suard, Jean-Pierre de Florian

Madame de Genlis (1746–1830)
Grimm, Christoph Willibald Gluck, Holbach

Madame de Staël (1766–1817)
Louis-Marie de Narbonne-Lara, Charles-Maurice de Talleyrand, Benjamin Constant

Thérésa Tallien (1773–1835)
Daniel Auber, Rodolphe Kreutzer, Luigi Cherubini, Charles de Bériot, Maria Malibran

Juliette Récamier (1777–1849)
Jacques-Louis David, Luigi Galvani, André-Marie Ampère, Jean-Paul Murat, Anne de Montmorency, Gustave Moreau, Alexis de Tocqueville, Honoré de Balzac, Chateaubriand

Delphine de Girardin (1804–55)
Balzac, Victor Hugo, Alfred de Musset, Gioachino Rossini, Giacomo Meyerbeer, Théophile Gautier

Virginie Ancelot (1792–1875)
Chateaubriand, Stendhal, Ernest Renan, Sophie Gay, Alfred de Vigny, Prosper Mérimée, Alexandre Weill, Tocqueville, Charles Brifaut

Marie d'Agoult (1805–1876)
Franz Liszt, Heinrich Heine, George Sand, Mérimée, de Vigny, de Musset, Frédéric Chopin, Gustave Flaubert

Apollonie Sabatier (1822–90)
Charles Baudelaire, Ernest Meissonier, Auguste Clésinger, Eugène Delacroix, Hector Berlioz, Gérard de Nerval, Henry Murger, Maxime Du Camp, Gautier, Flaubert, Fernand Boissard, Louis de Cormentin, Auguste Préault, Edmond About, Charles Jalabert, Ernest Feydeau (father of Georges), Charles-Augustin Sainte-Beuve

Princesse Mathilde Bonaparte (1820–1904)
Claude Monet, Flaubert, the Goncourt brothers, Sainte-Beuve, Louis
Pasteur, Frédéric Durand, Hippolyte Taine, Alphonse Daudet, Jean-
Léon Gérôme, Guy de Maupassant

Lydie Aubernon (1825–99)
Leconte de Lisle, Ferdinand Brunetière, Paul Bourget, Leo Tolstoy,
Ivan Turgenev, Aléxandre Dumas *fils*, Anatole France, Hugo, Gabriele
d'Annunzio, Victorien Sardou, George Bernard Shaw, Maupassant,
Georges Lemaître. Foreigners were popular with Mme A.

Pauline Metternich (1836–1921)
Charles Gounod, Camille Saint-Saëns, Dumas, Richard Wagner,
Eugène Boudin, Edgar Degas

Marie-Anne de Loynes (1837–1908)
Flaubert, Émile de Girardin, François Coppée, Jules Verne, Pasteur,
Édouard Drumont, Taine, Renan, Georges Clemenceau, Jules
Renard, Sardou, Bourget, Emile Zola, Henry James, Sand, Gounod,
Georges Boulanger, Arsène Houssaye

Marguerite Charpentier (1848–1904)
Famously portrayed by Renoir. Zola, the Goncourt brothers, Sarah
Bernhardt, Gabrielle Réjane, Yvette Guilbert

Juliette Adam (1836–1936)
Lemaître, Pierre Loti, Daudet, Gounod, Paul Déroulède, Léon
Gambetta, Jules Ferry, Hugo

Geneviève Halévy Bizet, later Madame Straus (1849–1926)
Georges Bizet, Marcel Proust, Degas, Frédérick Mugnier,
Maupassant, Auguste Renoir, Daudet, Maurice Barrès

Anna de Noailles (1876–1933)
D'Annunzio, François de Croisset, Fernand Gregh, Augustine
Bulteau, Paul Hervieu, Proust, André Gide

Comtesse Greffulhe (1860–1952)
Proust, James Abbott McNeill Whistler, Serge Diaghilev, Moreau,
Gabriel Fauré

Marguerite Eymery 'Rachilde' (1860–1953)
Renard, Guillaume Apollinaire, Alfred Jarry, Remy de Gourmont,
Pierre Louÿs

Winnaretta de Polignac (1865–1943)
Gounod, Diaghilev, Igor Stravinsky, Erik Satie, John Singer Sargent,
Cole Porter, Nadia Boulanger, Sir Thomas Beecham, Fauré, Proust,
Darius Milhaud

Misia Sert (1872–1950)
Proust, Monet, Renoir, Odilon Redon, Paul Signac, Debussy,
Stéphane Mallarmé, Henri de Toulouse-Lautrec, Édouard Vuillard,
Pierre Bonnard, Maurice Ravel, Enrico Caruso, Paul Morand, Satie,
Coco Chanel, Diaghilev, Gide

Gertrude Stein (1874–1946)
Ernest Hemingway, Sinclair Lewis, Sherwood Anderson, Thornton
Wilder, Francis Picabia, Henri Matisse, Henri Rousseau, Joseph
Stella

Natalie Clifford Barney (1876–1972)
Ezra Pound, Paul Valéry, Djuna Barnes, Colette, Gide, Max Jacob,
Somerset Maugham, Rabindranath Tagore, T. S. Eliot, Rainer
Maria Rilke

Princesse Marie-Blanche de Polignac (1897–1958)
Elmer Fryer, Clemenceau, Luchino Visconti, Christian Bérard,
Francis Poulenc, Jeanne Lanvin

Marie-Laure de Noailles (1902–70)
Salvador Dalí, Jean Cocteau, Poulenc, Man Ray, Luis Buñuel, Balthus

Marie-Louise Bousquet (1885–1975)
Editor of *Harper's Bazaar.* Pablo Picasso, Aldous Huxley, Carmel
Snow

Paulette Nardal (1896–1985)
René Maran, Alain Locke, Claude McKay, Léopold Sédar Senghor,
Aimé Césaire, Léon-Gontran Damas, Langston Hughes, Suzanne
Lacascade, Suzanne Césaire, Louis Achille

Florence Gould (1895–1983)
Cocteau, Pierre Benoit, Henry de Montherlant, Jean Giraudoux,
Sacha Guitry, Marie Laurencin, Bérard, Ernst Jünger, Louis-
Ferdinand Céline

Edmée de La Rochefoucauld (1895–1991)
André Maurois, Jules Romains, Paul Morand, Anna de Noailles,
Léon-Paul Fargue, Valéry, Clair Goll, Mariel Jean-Brunhes
Delamarre, Suzanne Desternes

Almost all of the most important French literary, artistic and political figures are contained in these salons. True, there are not many
French scientific titans among them, but French scientists did have
their own form of sociability. Mme Lavoisier, wife of the celebrated
chemist, had a salon of scientists, as did palaeontologist Georges
Cuvier. A group of mainly physicists and chemists met at weekends at
the house of Claude-Louis Berthollet in Arcueil, a few miles outside
Paris, in the early years of the nineteenth century. Bonaparte took a
great interest in their findings. Saint-Simon also held weekly lunches
for scientists and social scientists in the early decades of the century.
Auguste Comte, one of the founders of social science, was much in
favour of salons as a way of spreading knowledge agreeably to people
who might not otherwise have access to it. Louis Pasteur frequented
more than one nineteenth-century salon. Sigmund Freud attended the
salon of Jean-Martin Charcot, the neurologist, but the other members were mainly writers and artists. Science does not lend itself so
easily to social conversation.

Of course, any one salon ended when its guiding light – the *salonnière* – died. But in many cases young soon-to-be *salonnières* acted as
apprentices in the salons of their elders, so that there was what you
might call an 'apostolic succession' down the generations. In some
cases, daughters actually inherited their mother's salons; in at least
one case, a daughter started her salon *in opposition* to her mother's
(chapter 22). But all along later salons were modelled on earlier ones,
in most cases inheriting their principal participants, the models gradually shifting over time (more political, less political, more musical,

more foreigners). In many other cases, participants were members of several salons all at once and this provides another link in the chain. (Charles de Rémusat attended three salons in one day at one point, Talleyrand was a member of five and Tocqueville eleven, though not all at the same time. Chateaubriand was a regular in the salons of the Duchesse de Duras, Mme Récamier, Mme d'Aguesseau and Mme de Montboissier.) The idea of one salon leading to another, making an unbroken line down the years, is a very appealing cultural theme.

There were differences as well as similarities. *Salonnières* had different characters, aims and ambitions, different organisational skills, different levels of political nous, intelligence and beauty. But they all had the gift of friendship. Some salons lasted for thirty and even forty years. They enable us to tell French social/intellectual and even political history in a fresh way.

Of course, we must be careful not to idealise salons as utopias, or overplay our hand. There were in France at all times different aristocratic cliques, with different aims and ambitions, and, as David Bell has pointed out, salons formed only a part of a far larger web of aristocratic sociability, 'much of it dominated by men, and relatively indifferent to the joys of literary conversation'.[65] Nonetheless, as Bell also concedes, 'there was no other early modern country in which women took on the effective leadership of a polite society so fully, and also helped shape the direction of literary life'. The enduring life of salons provided an informal institution in France, the combined intellectual-social nature of which, though difficult to calibrate exactly, played a role in helping France continually adjust to what history threw at it.[66]

The mixing of sociability and intellect is an underappreciated lineament of history, but it is this cocktail that makes the French the French in all their glory, glamour and would-be grandeur. And helps to render them both Gallic and galling.

The Intoxication of Simon Arnauld

On the evening of Wednesday 4 February 1665, Simon Arnauld, Marquis de Pomponne, arrived back in Paris after a year's exile 160 miles away in Verdun. He had been a close friend of Nicolas Fouquet, superintendent of finances under Louis XIV, the richest and most stylish man in the realm, who for years had outshone the Sun King in terms of the wealth, the properties and the art he amassed, and the cultural swagger he epitomised. But in 1661 Fouquet had been convicted by a jealous monarch of lèse-majesté and imprisoned for life, and Arnauld had been later sent away as part of the wholesale cleansing of the stables. After a year kicking his heels in the provinces, the marquis had finally been allowed back by the king, who was not blind to his diplomatic capabilities (he would soon become ambassador to Sweden, then a major European power).

That Wednesday evening, however, 'without even changing out of his travelling clothes', Arnauld went straight to the hôtel de Nevers, by the Pont-Neuf, which was the home of Mme Élisabeth du Plessis-Guénégaud, one of the more distinguished *salonnières* of seventeenth-century France. There, as he wrote to his father soon afterwards, with more than a touch of irony, 'I found only Madame and Mademoiselle de Sévigné, Madame de Fouquières and Madame de Lafayette, Monsieur de la Rochefoucauld, Messieurs de Sense, de Xantes, and de Léon; Messieurs d'Avaux, de Barrillon, de Châtillon, de Caumartin, and several others; there was also Boileau, whom you know and who had come to read some of his satires, which I found admirable; and Racine, who recited three and a half acts of a play about Porus, renowned for his rivalry with Alexander, which was assuredly of very great beauty. It would be hard to describe how I was received by all these people, for they were so agreeable and so full of friendship and pleasure at my return."[1]

Nicholas Boileau, the acerbic poet and critic, was a good friend of Jean Racine, then emerging as a pre-eminent playwright. Mesdames de Sévigné and de Lafayette were both innovative writers. François de La Rochefoucauld, a member of one of the most distinguished aristocratic houses in France, was a controversial soldier but also a much-envied lover and a noted author (*Memoirs* and *Maximes*), and a close friend of Mme de Lafayette. M de Sens was a prominent arch-bishop, de Châtillon was a cardinal, de Barrillon had been ambassador to England, and d'Avaux ambassador to both Venice and Sweden.

This was a not atypical salon *mélange* for the time, but what is perhaps the most striking aspect of Arnauld's account is the fact that, after a year's forced absence from the French capital, the marquis could not wait even to change out of his worn and dirty travelling clothes before hurrying across town to Mme du Plessis-Guénégaud's salon, which he knew met every Wednesday in season. For Arnauld, like many of his kind, the salons of seventeenth-century Paris were the high point of existence, the pinnacle of what was felt to be a new civilisation, the most exciting, pleasurable and intellectually satisfy-ing way of life that could be imagined. The offerings that Boileau and Racine read that night were new works, and the salon allowed Arnauld and the others to be part of a fashionable and privileged *avant-garde*. The salon experience was intoxicating.

Such intoxication was widespread, and of such moment that it is the argument of this book that the French *salon* – especially the Parisian salons, which lasted from roughly speaking 1650 to 1991 at least (much later than is generally realised) – comprised an infor-mal but nonetheless durable, crucial and exceptional institution in European social-intellectual life, and at the same time helps account for much that is distinctive and characteristic of the Gallic mind.

PART ONE

THE BIRTH OF THE SALON AND THE 'NEW CONSTELLATION' OF WOMEN

Catherine de Vivonne, the Blue Room and the Académie française

Imagine a palace in the very heart of Paris, near the Louvre and between the Palais-Royal and the River Seine. Now envisage leading away from the palace an avenue of sycamores towards a field – yes, a field – such that in late summer the owner could boast of 'being the only one in Paris to be able to see from her cabinet a field of hay being scythed'. It was a boast from an individual of some consequence, and that individual is now credited with making the first move towards what certain historians have called, with some exaggeration, a 'new civilisation'. She was Catherine de Vivonne, Marquise de Rambouillet, whose salon was probably installed in 1618, in her home in the rue Saint-Thomas-du-Louvre, which ran between what is now the Palais-Royal and the Louvre but then carried on down to the Seine.[1]

Catherine de Vivonne was not the only woman to open a salon at that time. The Vicomtesse d'Auchy opened a salon frequented mainly by poets, including François de Malherbe. However, he was interested in her for more than her intellectual hospitality, her husband found out and banished her to the provinces. Mme de Loges tried to emulate the vicomtesse, and her circle on the rue de Tournon included Malherbe (who seems to have gone everywhere), the essayist Jean-Louis Guez de Balzac, the translator Nicolas Faret and the grammarian Claude Favre de Vaugelas. But Mme de Loges was passionate about religion and politics and did nothing to hide her enthusiasm for Louis XIII's rebellious brother, the Duc d'Orléans. She too was sent into exile.[2]

No such unseemly fate befell the exquisite salon of Catherine de Vivonne. It had come about, according to her biographer, because she had grown ill at ease with the royal receptions at the Louvre. In her younger days, the beautiful marquise had played her part in some of the grand court occasions, including the famous ballet scenes but, over time, and despite the fact that 'Malherbe [again] had honoured the festivities with his verse', she had grown weary of 'the brutishness of the king's appetites' and had withdrawn.[3]

In 1618, Catherine was aged about thirty (the exact date of her birth is uncertain). She was the daughter of a French ambassador to Rome and had been born there to an Italian mother. In that year she began work reconfiguring her *hôtel*, in order to provide a setting suitable for the lifestyle she planned away from the court.

The innovations she introduced were to prove important in the history of taste and interior decoration. For example, she appears to have been the first hostess to move away from the ubiquitous red that everyone preferred and replaced it with blue, which is how her famous *Chambre bleue* (Blue Room) came about. This innovation was widely copied, as was her idea that her salon was conceived as a refuge from the world, 'with a feeling of intimacy and comfort, her cabinets filled with a thousand rarities, the air always scented by magnificent baskets of flowers'.[4]

As famous as the colour change was the reorganisation Mme de Rambouillet imposed on her house. The most significant alteration was that she had moved her actual bedroom into a closet and turned her bedroom into her official reception room, which enabled her to receive guests as she lay in an alcove on her daybed, a practice that seems unnatural to us but in fact became a social ritual. This alcove, or *ruelle* in French, was set to be imitated widely and become the 'revered space' where the seventeenth-century woman of the world received her guests.[5]

Gradually, then, and beginning in the rue Saint-Thomas-du-Louvre, the respect that was due to the king at court was, if not replaced, then at least paralleled by the respect given to the women who organised the salons, an important development the durable consequences of which we shall be following.

We know about life in the seventeenth-century French salons thanks to three unusual literary endeavours. In addition to the memoirs and letters of the time, which were little different in range from the memoirs and letters of other periods, our understanding of seventeenth-century salons can call on, first, the *Historiettes* of Gédéon Tallemant des Réaux; second, the prolix *romans-à-clef* of Mme Madeleine de Scudéry; and third, the *Divers portraits* organised by Anne-Marie-Louise d'Orléans.

Tallemant des Réaux (1619–92) was a Protestant who married Élisabeth de Rambouillet. His *Historiettes* were a mix of short biographies and anecdotes – scurrilous as often as not, occasionally cruel – that were circulated in private and not published until the nineteenth century. However, their accuracy is now generally accepted.

Madeleine de Scudéry, part of the Rambouillet salon before she opened her own (chapter 5), published several novels which, in the fashion of the times, were exceedingly long and extremely detailed. Two, *Artamène, ou Le Grand Cyrus* (ten volumes, 1648–53, set in ancient Assyria), and *Clélie, histoire romaine* (another ten volumes, 1654–61, set in ancient Rome), were also thinly veiled *romans-à-clef*, which depicted various members of the Rambouillet salon through pseudonyms: Mme de Rambouillet was 'Cléomire', Angelique Paulet – a red-headed singer and lute-player – was 'Élise', and Mme de Scudéry herself was 'Sappho'.

Cléomire had many gifts besides beauty – above all compassion and wisdom, traits generally associated at the time with a masculine temperament. She was by all accounts theatrical, and Tallemant, himself a member of her salon later on, describes her as 'commanding, demanding, exacting', and in precarious health, meaning she remained indoors a lot. Something of a prude, she was nonetheless not averse to risqué banter.

The third endeavour which tells us about those years in vivid detail was sparked by Anne-Marie-Louise d'Orléans, daughter of Louis XIII's rebellious brother, Gaston d'Orléans, and another fixture in the Blue Room. A prodigiously wilful girl and woman, officially known as Mademoiselle, and to history as La Grande Mademoiselle, she was proposed to by Charles II of England, Afonso VI of Portugal and Charles Emmanuel II of Savoy and turned them all down. Fabulously wealthy – she inherited five duchies when her mother died five days after Mademoiselle was born – she joined her father in the great adventure of the Fronde (see the next chapter), which rather spoiled her chances with the one monarch she did covet – her cousin, Louis XIV himself. Instead of marrying her, he sent her into exile where she wrote several (well-written, well-received) books under another name, penned her memoirs, and fell hopelessly in love with an impoverished nobleman, the Duc de Lauzun. The king approved the match, only to change his mind three days later and have Lauzun imprisoned. No reason was ever given for this spiteful act against an Orléans, the second family of France, and Lauzun languished in the Bastille for eleven years, until Mademoiselle sold two of her duchies, so she could afford to buy him out. Despite this extravagant gesture of affection and loyalty, they were never wed, and Mademoiselle died unmarried and without children.[6]

While she was exiled, she retreated to her estates at Saint-Fargeau, in deepest Burgundy, surrounded by great forests, and began to make a life for herself. She began by building a theatre (she loved dancing as much as she loved hunting), and among her instrumentalists was a young Italian composer, Gian Battista Lulli, who as Jean-Baptiste Lully would eventually become the king's composer.

Several notables (such as Mme de Sévigné) visited Mademoiselle in her Burgundy hideaway and news of Saint-Fargeau spread. She was eventually allowed back to Paris, where she invented a new form of sociability that both was and was not a salon. She and her friends developed the practice of writing and exchanging literary portraits of each other, intimate details in which an individual's 'prowess in conversation' was one of the main objects of description. The other main characteristic of the collection of *Divers portraits* – eventually published in book form – is that thirty-six of the fifty portraits are of women.

From these singular sources, we know that, to begin with, the chief aim of the marquise's salon was entertainment and diversion.

Practical jokes, for example, were extremely popular, one typical example being the trick played on the Comte de Guiche, who was invited for dinner and, to widespread amusement, given every dish it was known that he most disliked. Only after everyone had had their fun did Catherine make up for it and honour the comte with a splendid feast.

But the experience of the Blue Room was every bit as intoxicating as the Guénégaud salon. For Guez de Balzac, 'one day at the hôtel de Rambouillet is worth more than several centuries elsewhere'. Tallemant commented that Catherine's *hôtel* was 'the meeting place of those who were the most *galant* of the court and the most polished among the *beaux esprits* of the age'.

Literary debuts were common at the hôtel de Rambouillet. In 1638, Jean Desmarets de Saint-Sorlin offered a reading of his tragedy *Scipion l'Africain*, in the same year that Jean Chapelain presented the second part of his epic poem on Joan of Arc (not too well received), and in 1640 Pierre Corneille's *Polyeucte* was premiered (also not well received). On occasion works were performed, not merely read, because the theatre was also an intense passion in the Blue Room before Louis XIV claimed a royal monopoly on the practice later in the century.

Jean Mairet's *Sophonisbe*, considered the 'first truly genuinely classical French tragedy', was first staged in the Rambouillet salon in late summer 1636. Mairet's work, set in the Punic wars, featuring multiple murders of kings and their queens, is nonetheless a challenging work, and confirms that the members of Catherine's salon were not just 'pampered aristocrats enjoying frivolous pleasures and banal pastimes'.

But the single work most associated with the Rambouillet salon was what American historian Robert Schneider describes as a curiosity, the *Guirlande de Julie* ('Garland for Julie'), produced between 1633 and 1641 as a collective homage to Mme de Rambouillet's daughter, Princesse Julie, in the form of a number of poems each based on a flower 'representing her charms and virtues'. The driving spirit of this venture was Charles de Sainte-Maure, Marquis de Montausier, a distinguished soldier. A Protestant, well educated in Greek and Latin, both a warrior and a man of letters, 'at home on the battlefield and [in] the salon', he had been captured during the Thirty Years War and spent ten months as a prisoner of war – he was *experienced*.

In the aristocratic manner of the times, he never bothered to publish any of his works, publication being felt then as an indignity for a gentleman. But the *Guirlande* was the work by which he won Julie's hand in marriage, though it took time. There were sixteen contributors to the *Guirlande*, including Chapelain, Georges de Scudéry, Valentin Conrart, Gilles Ménage and Desmarets. In all, the collection included ninety-one poems, mostly madrigals, celebrating twenty-nine flowers, many alluding to Julie's 'mania' for the Protestant Swedish king, Gustavus Adolphus, who dominated the Thirty Years War. These Protestant sympathies gave the Rambouillet salon in Catholic France a subversive colouring.

The *Guirlande* enterprise is of especial interest for it is an early example of the developing close relationship between writers and aristocrats that was to be at the heart of literary culture in France in the seventeenth century.[7]

Tallemant also described the *Guirlande* as 'one of the most illustrious galanteries ever produced' and in fact the middle years of the seventeenth century saw 'galanteries' emerging as accounts of 'a distinct personality type'. They were works which 'combined virtue with the desire to please women and an ability to mix easily and playfully in their company'. The point was that such behaviour should never be pedantic or risk leading to unbridled passion.

For a warrior, indeed by any standard of the time, Montausier could be classed as an *érudit*; he was the author of a large collection of epigrams, apparently modelled on the Roman poet Martial, as a result of which, again apparently, Molière seized on Montausier as a model for the character of Alceste, the prig in *Le Misanthrope*.

Catherine's salon was in fact divided into two camps, who could be intellectual rivals at times. One was the warrior group, led by Montausier, the other a more literary set, led by Vincent Voiture. He was in fact the poet most idealised in the Blue Room, and was also known for serving as the secretary of Gaston d'Orléans (chapter 10), an opponent of the king: another reflection of the salon's subversive character. Voiture was a kind of master of ceremonies in the salon and his works revealed an openness with the aristocratic members, an approach which, again, would shape French intellectual life. And he was innovative. One of his works was entitled 'To a Lady Whose Skirts Were Raised While Falling from a Carriage in the Country'. Tallemant commented that Voiture 'is the first to have introduced libertinage to poetry'.

Just as Boileau and Racine were regulars at the du Plessis-Guénégaud salon, so Molière and Corneille were regulars in the Blue Room.

Corneille had been famous – notorious even – since publication of his play *Le Cid* in 1636, which had pitted him against Cardinal Richelieu. This turned into a very public quarrel, despite the fact that the cardinal had been drawn to Corneille's early work. So much so in fact that when the minister planned a journey to the playwright's native Rouen, Corneille was one of those chosen to write verses to commemorate the visit. Based on the success of that performance, Richelieu then selected Corneille to become one of '*les cinq auteurs*', or 'the society of the five authors'. This was a practice that could occur only in an absolute monarchy, the idea being that Richelieu himself would conceive ideas for plays and that the authors in the society would then dramatise the cardinal's notions, notions that were specifically designed to emphasise virtue, so as to elevate the moral climate of the realm.

But Corneille was not to be so easily suborned. His response was *Le Cid* and here too the controversy the play generated reflects the opportunities and problems of life in an absolutist monarchy.[8]

Le Cid, written in rhyming couplets with alternating masculine and feminine rhymes, is based on the life of the Spanish warrior Rodrigo Díaz de Vivar, a late eleventh-century figure who in real life appears to have been a 'sword for hire', fighting for both Christian and Muslim forces, though in Corneille's play he is shown only as a Christian soldier. In a typically complicated plot, Rodrigo is inveigled into killing the father of Chimène, the woman he loves. She vows to kill him in revenge, but before she can do so he leads the Christian forces to victory over the invading Moors (who are so soundly beaten that they call their victor's commanding officer 'lord' – '*sayyid*', 'Cid' being a French corruption).[9]

The play – regarded now as Corneille's finest work – was first performed at the théâtre du Marais in December 1636 and was a huge popular success, not least because in certain respects it diverged from the standard format of plays at that time. In the first place, it was described as a 'tragicomedy' and thereby contravened what was then regarded as a necessary and unbridgeable classical distinction between the two genres, tragedy and comedy. The play also had a happy ending, which was then regarded as another contravention, this time of Aristotle's theories in his *Poetics*. This was but one round in a seemingly endless fight in France over who were better, the ancients or the moderns.

Though the public responded enthusiastically to *Le Cid*, Richelieu was having none of it and this led to the so-called '*Querelle du Cid*' in which the cardinal, in what was then an unprecedented move, asked the newly formed Académie française to assess – in writing – the merits or shortcomings of the play. In reality, it was his intention that the academy condemn the work outright.[10]

Richelieu, fifty at the time, was the founder and the patron of the Académie française. Opened in 1635, just months before the premiere of *Le Cid*, one account has it that the academy began life in none other than the Comtesse de Rambouillet's salon. More likely, it started with the friendship between Valentin Conrart and Jean Chapelain.[11]

Initially, what was to become the Académie française met in Conrart's home. A Parisian and a Calvinist (and therefore a friend of fellow Protestant Tallemant des Réaux), he was employed by the Crown, but literature was his main love. The early discussions at his home ranged over current affairs but gradually literary topics assumed prominence. When Conrart and Chapelain took to meeting, and before Richelieu intervened, they adopted the hôtel de Rambouillet as their model.[12]

Since the meetings had not been sanctioned by the Crown, however, they were technically illegal, the law being that not more than six people could gather together at any one time. This forced the group to hold their gatherings in secret, hardly satisfactory. Eventually, the existence of the meetings leaked out but instead of being angry, or suspicious – qualities he had in abundance – the cardinal asked instead if the group would like to receive official status, which would mean it could meet legally and openly.

Richelieu – being Richelieu – had more than one motive in doing what he did. Chief among his aims was a need to promote the status of the French language, which reflected a fear at the time among the French cultural elite that it was inferior to that of Italy and that culture's widespread use of Latin. This comes out in the early history of the Académie française, by Paul Pellison (1743); an earlier account, by Nicolas Faret, called *Projet de l'Académie*, written to serve as a preface to the academy's statutes, was not published until 1983. These documents underline that there were no nobles in the early academy and that there was also a political side to the initiative.[13] Pierre-Paul Sevin's engraving of the early academy shows a raised seat set aside for Richelieu himself and the other members seated stiffly around a large rectangular table, each wearing a hat (to indicate privilege). The full complement of forty was not reached until 1639, the small number adding to the prestige of those elected.*

Not everyone was gratified by Richelieu's approach (later on the first members would look back on pre-Richelieu times as a 'golden age') but since they could hardly go back to meeting in secret, the few objectors had no choice but to cave in. While the negotiations had flowed back and forth Conrart had married and so the Académie transferred its premises to the home of Jean Desmarets. Several names were considered to begin with – 'Académie des beaux esprits', 'Académie de l'éloquence' and 'Académie éminente' – before they settled on 'Académie françoise', which later evolved into 'française'. Knowing Richelieu's interests, Chapelain used the opportunity to suggest that the academy should work towards the 'purity' of the French language, 'to render it capable of the highest eloquence'. In order to achieve this aim, he further proposed the creation of a dictionary and a precise grammar, together with a set of rules for writing in verse and prose 'to render [French] more capable of dealing with the arts and sciences, domains in which Latin had been pre-eminent as the universal language of learning'. The early Académie considered

---

* In 1855, Arsène Houssaye was to write an imagined history of the 'forty-first seat', in which he installed the many great French writers never elected, Molière being the first.

admitting women as members, but the proposal was voted down. It would later move into the Louvre.[14]

Before the academy could get going properly, however, Richelieu persuaded the new body to divert from its constitutional responsibilities, instead requiring it to investigate *Le Cid*. The newly elected members had no choice but to devote five months to preparing a report which damned the play 'for its violations of dramatic convention'.[15]

Richelieu's manipulation of the academy was part of a wider campaign of his to consolidate royal power. *Le Cid*, as Orest Ranum has argued, 'boldly set forth an ethic of conduct for the princes that placed them virtually above royal law as they pursued an heroic ideal'. The French princes were jealous of their independence and their rebelliousness was well known.

The newly elected members of the Académie were not at all keen to produce the report on *Le Cid*, though it was this which first brought their existence to the notice of a wider public. The assignment would never be repeated, the episode clearly illustrating the tension between politics and scholarship in an absolutist state. The report was in fact written by that stalwart of the Blue Room – and royal propagandist – Jean Chapelain, poet and literary critic, who was also the author of an epic poem on Joan of Arc. In his report, he argued that Chimène's character was implausible and immoral, in that she could not have loved Rodrigo after he killed her father. The play was a danger to the public.[16]

A second criticism of the play was written by Georges de Scudéry, brother of Madeleine de Scudéry and, like his sister, another habitué of the Blue Room. He was a poet and fervent dramatist (once described as 'not quite sane'), who argued that Corneille, in not sticking to tradition, was 'deifying' himself and, more to the point, did not respect the classical traditions of unity – the classical unities of time, place and action (a play must take place within twenty-four hours, a 'natural' day, rather than an 'artificial' day of twelve hours' daylight; there must be only one setting; and the action must be centred on a single conflict or problem). The academy did indeed conclude that the play broke too many of the unities.[17]

To begin with, Corneille responded robustly, even writing a poem in which he exalted his own talents at the expense of others, arguing further that drama did not need to be didactic only, that entertainment was just as praiseworthy. (He was supported by the members of the Rambouillet salon, which was often, a contemporary observer said, in a state of 'combustion' over literary disputes.) But eventually, wearied by the *querelle*, Corneille withdrew from Paris back to his native Rouen. There he licked his wounds for a time. After a break he would return to the theatre and enjoy more success; he would also reconcile himself with Richelieu, even to the point of dedicating a work to the cardinal, while also ensuring that his plays did adhere more closely to the classical unities.

ELOQUENCE ABOVE KNOWLEDGE

For its part, after issuing the report on *Le Cid*, the Académie turned back to its dictionary. Its work was painfully slow to begin with, so much so that in June 1639 the poet Boisrobert warned Richelieu that it would be best to give responsibility to just one man, and that man should be Claude Favre de Vaugelas, Baron de Pérouges, a grammarian, yet another habitué of the Blue Room. In fact, Vaugelas thought that the members of the Blue Room spoke the most perfect French possible and should be the model for the nation. (Vaugelas was mocked by the likes of Molière but French literary historian Roger Picard says he was a brave man, a man of taste and not a pedant.) Richelieu was persuaded by Boisrobert's arguments and provided Vaugelas with a 2,000-livre stipend to fulfil his responsibilities. Ultimately, he would become the main force in shaping what the dictionary would become, notably 'the association of correctness of language with polite society and the notion of superiority that accompanied it', making language an indicator of social standing.[18] The primacy of spoken over written language helped to usher in what has become known as 'the age of conversation'.

In typically French style, another of the aims of the academy was to mix sociably the literary and intellectual life of the country, and to reflect that 'eloquence is the noblest art', derived from conversation. Faret's document also links a revival of eloquence 'with the cultural renewal of France'. In fact, he looked for a dual renewal: the ancient vigour of the Gauls and the eloquence 'once thought buried in Greece

and Rome'. The reform of the language, Faret said, was a 'prelude
to the recovery of French greatness'. Conversation, he maintained,
engendered eloquence and eloquence was rarer (and therefore more
precious) than knowledge. For this reason, the early members of the
academy preferred to organise conferences than examine plays. Early
conferences tackled such subjects as 'The Defence of the Theatre',
'The Love of the Sciences' and 'Against the Sciences', and there was
even one 'On the *Je ne sais quoi*'.

Not that the Académie went uncriticised. Charles de Saint-Évremond,
soldier and literary critic, resented its 'pompous pretentiousness' and
Étienne Gantrel's engraving of the academy bears the ironic inscription
'To immortality'. A play, *La Comédie des académistes*, had been circulating in manuscript form for more than a decade before it was staged
in 1650 and mocked the academy as 'a den of pettifogging self-impor-
tant buffoons and drunkards', arguing over such 'important' linguistic
matters as whether closing a door means closing a door or closing the
room to which it gives access.

THE BIRTH OF FRENCHNESS

It is too much and too soon to say that the spirit of republicanism was
abroad in these salon gatherings: it was not. But the significance of
the Rambouillet salon is that it was an alternative to the court; that
was what counted in the early days. Society, the *gratin*, *le monde*,
whatever it called itself, was in the process of moving beyond the
king. 'The hôtel de Rambouillet', in the words of Tallemant des
Réaux, 'was, so to speak, the theatre of all their entertainments, and
was the rendezvous of all the most honourable gentlefolk at Court, as
well as for the most polished of the century's wits.' The Jesuit Pierre
Le Moyne referred to Catherine's salon as 'the court of the court'.
Most important of all, the salon was not hierarchical: 'affection,
agreement and wit took precedence over rank'. And, as a reflection of
le monde, salons – unlike the professions and the universities – were
not all-male affairs. In itself, this was a recognition that women were
then seen as embodying natural grace over the learned and artificial,
a level of sophistication that, it was felt, was not possessed in other
countries. And although diversion was an important ingredient it

was not the only one. There was a lineament of seriousness, too, such that it was said that there was 'a cultural revolution under way in the Blue Room'.[19] Not that the Rambouillet salon was academic in any way. (Both Guez de Balzac and Chapelain were on record as being scathing about 'learned' women.) On the contrary, Catherine – whose portraits show her as not always above showing too much flesh – went out of her way to disavow any such aim. Instead, she saw to it that her salon offered a mix of theatre, music, dancing, parlour games and conversation, the latter above all. Indeed, Mme de Rambouillet's salon can also be regarded as one of the stimuli to the 'Age of Conversation'.[20]

The developing relationship between men of letters and the nobility – what the salons brought together – was described by the notion of *honnêteté*, one of the most misunderstood concepts in the history of French culture. As Robert Schneider characterises it, *honnêteté* is a rhetoric of speech and behaviour that reflects 'the melding of literature and society', an ethical code and an ideal, a form of decorum designed to make men of letters 'appealing' to their 'less educated social betters'.[21] It overlapped with urbanity and worldliness, and implied an 'easy familiarity' with the social accomplishments from gambling to hunting to conversation. It was 'artful self-presentation in a nonchalant way'. It was, in a sense, the birth of Frenchness as we now understand it and as it likes to see itself.

As evidence that the academic world was not Catherine's model, the members of her group took as their main area of aesthetic and ethical inquiry the relatively new literary genre which at the time was despised and denigrated by the *savants* and the church, partly because it explored marriage, divorce and widowhood. This was the novel.

Benedetta Craveri, the Italian historian and biographer of Mme de Rambouillet, draws attention to the fact that, around the time that the salon of the hôtel de Rambouillet was being formed, Honoré d'Urfé's novel *L'Astrée* had just appeared. D'Urfé (1568–1625), Marquis de Valromey and Comte de Châteauneuf, was imprisoned twice in the wars of religion, giving him ample time to familiarise himself with the classics and conceive the plot of his novel.

This book, curious and even juvenile to modern tastes (although a film of it by Eric Rohmer was nominated for a Golden Lion at the 2007 Venice Film Festival), told a story that nevertheless resonated with the habitués of the Blue Room. A pastoral tale, it describes an ideal community of a few privileged people disguised as shepherds. In the forest of Forez (in the Loire region) an experiment is under way in which a small, free elite seek a utopian ideal on the basis of love, whose aim 'is to return women to the prestige once accorded them in chivalric society'.[22] It was not a million miles from the aims of the 'new civilisation' being born in the Blue Room.

A Woman's War: Élisabeth du Plessis-Guénégaud and Blaise Pascal

Two more sets of events will bring us back to that other early salon, that of Mme du Plessis-Guénégaud. In the first instance, it is by no means out of place to note that a prominent feature of French history just then was that, in less than a century, three queen-mothers had ruled as regents in France in the name of their young sons.[1] And that can be put alongside the Fronde, the catastrophe that overwhelmed France from 1648 to 1653, when the frustrated nobility rose up in armed rebellion against the monarch. The immediate reason for the rebellion was mounting taxes, but underneath the explosion was an expression of the aristocracy's resentment at the burgeoning strength of the Crown and more especially the third and most recent regency government, which had been installed five years before when Louis XIII's widow, Anne of Austria, had provocatively annulled her late husband's will and, in alliance with Cardinal Mazarin, who had succeeded Richelieu on the latter's death, expanded the reach of her regency for the nine-year-old Louis XIV.[2]

On top of everything else it stood for, the Fronde, 'more than any other conflict, seems to have been a woman's war'. Mme de Longueville, the Duchesse de Chevreuse, the Princesse de Palatine and La Grande Mademoiselle, together with others of their rank, 'devised plots, stoked rebellions, provoked discord and, not least, took up arms' – in time they became known as 'the great *frondeuses*'.[3] In particular, Mme de Longueville's exploits during the Fronde were such that the indefatigable Mlle de Scudéry dedicated yet another ten-volume novel, *Artamène, ou Le Grand Cyrus* – her 'fictional' rendering of the Fronde – to her, and lauded her as the story's predominant figure.

Anne-Geneviève de Bourbon-Condé, as she had been born, before being married to Henri d'Orléans, Duc de Longueville, the first gentleman of France after the princes of the blood, had all the arrogant qualities of the Condés, the cadet branch of the Bourbon royal house. They had regained political force after the deaths of Richelieu and Louis XIII had followed so quickly on one another, in December 1642 and May 1643 respectively, leaving the young king exposed and with no senior minister to guide and protect him. Mazarin had early sensed Anne-Geneviève's hidden threat to his schemes and the eruption of the Fronde reinforced his fears. At Mme de Longueville's goading, allied to the king's always-rebellious brother, Gaston d'Orléans, the Condés took against royal authority and declared open war on the cardinal, aiming for nothing less than to assume the country's leadership. Thus was France engulfed in a five-year civil war.[4]

Mme de Longueville's part in the fighting was contentious, but none of her opponents denied her extraordinary bravery. 'It is impossible not to be impressed by the iron determination with which she dominated her husband, stirred up her brothers, quarrelled with them, won them back over, allied herself with the Paris Parlement (a kind of court), threw herself with the help of her secretaries into civil rhetoric and political invective, rode a horse across France, incited Normandy to rebellion, took to the sea in a storm to find refuge in Holland, conducted negotiations with Mazarin from a small town of Stenay, the rebels' only remaining stronghold, and allied herself in Bordeaux with the popular [anti-monarchist] Ormée movement', a local revolt brought on by the fiscal activities of the Crown.[5]

After the Fronde's failure, she chose to remove herself to the Carmelite convent in the rue Saint-Jacques in Paris where she had been educated. She remained there until she died, twenty-six years later in 1679, 'as faithful in her mortification as she was in her pride'.[6]

And among her other contributions was the fact that it was she who introduced Mme de Sévigné to both the Blue Room and Comtesse

Élisabeth du Plessis-Guénégaud's salon. Like the Marquise de Rambouillet, the comtesse felt awkward at court, underappreciated in particular by the queen, and it was this that had prompted her to set up her own salon. Unlike the Blue Room, however, the du Plessis-Guénégaud gathering in the hôtel de Nevers was no retreat from the world. In the first place, Élisabeth was a convinced Jansenist, Jansenism being an austere heretical faith, much opposed by the Pope and the established church. Its main belief was in predestination for an 'elect' that was chosen by God and in which only God could confer grace. It followed that Mme du Plessis-Guénégaud's salon was a centre of political opposition. So much so that, at one point, Cardinal Mazarin was moved to send an envoy to the hôtel de Nevers to beg her 'to cease speaking ill of him so freely'. This shows the power of the salons in those days, which was further underlined when Blaise Pascal's *Lettres provinciales* appeared and the sixth and seventh letters were first read at the du Plessis-Guénégaud gathering prior to publication.[7]

On the evening when Simon Arnauld arrived back in Paris from Verdun, and hurried across to the hôtel de Nevers without changing his clothes, Nicolas Boileau was twenty-nine and Jean Racine three years younger. Though he would probably prefer to be remembered as a poet – and he did expand the capabilities of French verse, rendering it more flexible and supple – Boileau was also an exceptional critic, many of his satires (his preferred form) parodying and subverting what he saw as the overrated talents of his day, individuals such as Jean Chapelain and Georges de Scudéry.[8]

Born in 1636, the fifteenth child of a clerk to the Paris Parlement, Boileau was two when his mother died. Thereafter he was brought up by his grandmother and sent to study theology at the Sorbonne. In 1657, his father died leaving him comfortably off and he now decided on a literary career. Jean-Baptiste Santerre's portrait of him shows a slightly haughty man, looking out over a long, straight nose, and a smile that is definitely sardonic.

He had a great admiration for Molière as well as for Racine and, apart from meeting in the salons, they would all gather together at the café Mouton blanc on the rue d'Auteuil or the Pomme du pin cabaret on the place de la Contrescarpe in the area of the perfume-makers, together with Jean de La Chapelle, a dramatist, and Antoine Furetière, a fellow satirist.[9] This is an early sighting of the part played by the café in the intellectual life of France. Boileau's own satires attacked the writers whose style, he felt, was too flowery and more affected than those of his friends. He also translated classical works and in 1677 was appointed historiographer to the king, which gave him time to work on his wilder satires, *Sur les femmes*, *Sur l'amour de Dieu*, *Sur l'homme* and *Sur l'équiveque*, which latter attacked the Jesuits.

There was more than one parallel in the careers of Racine and Boileau, which probably aided their friendship. Both lost their mothers at an early age (Racine also lost his father), both were appointed historiographer to the king and both were elected to the Académie française. Racine is universally regarded as the great rival to Corneille, who was more than thirty years his senior. Born in 1639, in Picardy in northern France, Racine was taken up by his grandmother after his parents died. She removed him to the convent of Port-Royal in Paris, where she went to live. Port-Royal was run by fervent adherents of the Jansenist sect.

As Boileau had studied law for a time in Paris, so Racine was expected to do so. But, again like Boileau, he turned away from it towards letters. And in fact it was in his own role as a critic, rather than as a poet, that Boileau was one of the first to recognise Racine's talents. Apart from his style (Robert Lowell described it as 'hard, electric rage'), and his command of alexandrine lines, Racine's main concern was to update the ancient classics, to provide a contemporary fusion of the Greek idea of fate with the Jansenist belief in human helplessness, the age-old struggle of the will against the passions, which he regarded as doomed, especially in women.[10]

Whether it is in his masterpieces, *Andromaque* (1667) and *Phèdre* (1677), or elsewhere, Racine's dominant theme is the uncomfortable centrality of desire in life, the impossibility of controlling it, the fact that tragic characters are aware of their faults but know that they cannot overcome them, in a way do not *wish* to overcome them, that there is undeniable pleasure to be had from weakness, submission. Passion – in Racine as in the classical authors – is destructive of dignity, of duty, of hope. It is, in a way, a form of blindness.

Andromaque, the early drafts of which he read to Mme du Plessis-Guénégaud's salon on the night Arnauld got back from Verdun, established Racine as Corneille's equal, if not his superior, and sparked a rivalry that was only intensified when the younger man produced *Bérénice* (1670) at much the same time as a tragedy by another playwright on the very same subject. This was not as unusual then as it would be now. At the time Racine produced *Phèdre*, for instance, two other playwrights had written plays on a similar topic. In both cases Racine was clearly superior to his rivals. As things settled down, audiences seemed to relate more to Racine's characters as more human than Corneille's. When Boileau published his *Art poétique* in 1674 he concluded that Racine's understanding of tragedy was superior to Corneille's and this seems to have solidified into a permanent truth.

NOT A DAY WITHOUT PAIN

Just as there were parallels between Racine and Boileau, so too were there overlaps between the playwright and Blaise Pascal, who also read some of his works at Mme du Plessis-Guénégaud's salon. The portraits of Pascal – philosopher, mathematician, engineer, theologian – tend to show him as older than he was: he died at the age of thirty-nine. Those portraits give him bulbous eyes, a long, hooked nose, a fleshy mouth and a cleft chin. Perhaps the portraits do no more than reflect the fact that Pascal suffered chronic ill-health all his life, accounting for his early death.

There were three aspects to Pascal. There was the chronically ill Pascal, a man who, according to his sister – who wrote the first biography of her brilliant brother – never had a day without pain after his eighteenth birthday. This was put down to witchcraft by the neighbours but modern science ascribes his condition to nephritis or rheumatoid arthritis.[11]

Then there was the scientist and engineer, with a strong practical bent, who invented a calculating machine to aid his father Étienne, who was appointed chief tax administrator to Rouen at a time when there had been a crop failure, an outbreak of plague and a taxpayer revolt. Fascinated by the massive number of calculations his father needed to perform in order to carry out his new responsibilities, Blaise devised a machine to take the drudgery out of them. First called the *machine arithmétique* and later the Pascaline, the device was a set of interconnecting wheels in which the full turn of one ratcheted its neighbour one-tenth of a turn. He was awarded a royal patent on the device in 1649, when he was twenty-six.

Pascal corresponded with the Toulouse-based Pierre de Fermat, thirty years his senior, well known as a mathematician, as one of the creators of the calculus, and little known as a poet, which he also was, about the mathematics of probability. Using maths, Pascal also devised a shuttle timetable for the new horse-drawn omnibuses in Paris, making that city the first to operate a 'mass transit' system; and, in perhaps his most theoretically important coup, he devised an experiment – repeated on a number of hills of different altitude – to prove that a vacuum does exist in nature and is related to air pressure, then an important source of controversy. Some have seen this experiment as a historical turning point in the advance of modern science.[12]

At the same time, as a member of the nobility, Pascal was both in and out of the social swim. During the Fronde he and the rest of the family retired to Clermont (now Clermont-Ferrand) for safety's sake but afterwards he returned to Paris and for a while enjoyed the *vie mondaine* – at least up to a point. He was not a stranger to the salons but by all accounts not a regular. Undoubtedly for a time, however, 'he did show a weakness for silk and brocade and enjoyed the amenities of both a valet and a coach-and-six'.[13]

NIGHT OF FIRE

But we now remember Pascal as much for his philosophy as for his science: he, more than anyone else perhaps, successfully straddled these two worlds. This third Pascal is of interest because of the overlaps in his character that paralleled those of Isaac Newton, both men epitomising the transition to the modern view of the world, in that both were convinced experimentalists but equally fascinated by mysticism, ancient prophecy, miracles and bible hermeneutics. 'Modern readers are usually shocked to discover that the father of gambling odds and the mechanical computer wore a spiked girdle to chastise himself and keep him – as he thought – closer to God.'[14]

His religious conversion also came about via his father, who, one wintry day in January 1646, slipped on the ice on his way to stop a duel that was to take place in a field outside Rouen. Bone-setters were sent for and it so happened that the two bone-setting brothers, who moved into the Pascals' premises for three months to care for Étienne, were members of the Jansenist sect.

The conversion began in earnest, as Blaise tells us himself, on 23 November 1654, between the hours of 10.30 p.m. and 12.30 a.m., which he described as his 'night of fire'. He wrote his own record of what to him was a 'momentous experience of religious ecstasy', which he sewed into the lining of his jacket and which wasn't seen by anyone else until his death. It plainly underlined the absolute certainty that came over him that night that God exists and the feelings of 'peace and joy' that descended on him at that moment.

And it was while all this was happening that, in 1656–7, he produced his *Lettres provinciales*, some of which were first read in Mme du Plessis-Guénégaud's salon. The significance of the *Lettres* was that they were an entirely new phenomenon in theological debate. Pascal's style was new, an appealing breath of fresh air – witty, ironic, sarcastic, not excluding outright mockery and scorn.[15] The letters were composed in a conversational tone, which made them accessible to everyone. He was in particular vitriolic about the Jesuits.

The *Lettres provinciales* were accused of introducing a cynicism for the clergy into debate and the neologism 'Jesuitical' first appeared as a put-down. Equally important, the letters became known for the asperity of their style, which helped to shape French literary usage for many years. In substance, they are concerned with the distinction between natural and divine law, and tried to introduce a modicum of common sense into the dispute between the Pope and the Jansenists: that Christ did not die for everyone but only for the 'elect'. Pascal also argued that it is impossible for even the most virtuous to keep all the commandments (what then should we do?); that it is heresy to say we can accept or resist grace (how then should we live?); that we must free ourselves from all external compulsion (can it be done?). In the *Provinciales*, Pascal is eminently *human*.

In the second of his treatises, the *Pensées*, he again tried to add a modicum of common sense and straight talking to religion and argued that while belief in Christ is the only religion compatible with reason, he accepted that Christianity can never be *proved* by reason or authority alone. Instead, he insisted that it must be accepted in the heart: 'It is the heart which experiences God, not the reason.' And, famously, 'the heart has its reasons, which reason cannot know'.[16]

By now he was a long way from the salons and coach-and-six days. In his later *Pensées*, he condemned the pursuit of trivial matters, by which he meant the theatres, dancing, the salons, consumer goods and luxuries. These goods and activities, he says, are used by us as diversions.[17]

An extraordinary individual, he was proof surely that many different individuals can inhabit one body, and that consistency is not necessary to make your mark. His final notion was his famous concept that has become known as Pascal's wager, 'that we might as well believe in God because if, after we die, it turns out thère *is* another world, how much better will we be if we have given God the go-ahead in the past'. Voltaire called this wager 'indecent and childish'.

But it is also worth adding that recently Pascal's sisters and his niece have attracted historians' attention, research showing that all have been overlooked as philosophers themselves. While each of these women has traditionally been incorporated into Blaise's biography either as secretaries, correspondents or nurses of their brother or uncle, the American Jesuit academic John Conley has shown that Jacqueline Pascal, as headmistress of the Port-Royal convent school, made important contributions to the philosophy of education, that Gilberte Pascal Périer wrote the first philosophical biographies of Blaise and Jacqueline, and that Marguerite Périer 'defended freedom of conscience against coercion by political and religious superiors'. Each emphasised the right of women to develop a philosophical and theological culture.[18]

Marie de Sévigné, Molière and the Gradations of Love

Madame de Sévigné – the Marquise de Sévigné – who was also in the du Plessis-Guénégaud salon on the night Simon Arnauld arrived back from exile, must together with her daughter count as one of the most interesting women of the seventeenth century, with a range and depth unequalled even by many men. Although she had no official position (at court, for example), she carved out an independent role for herself that provides us with fascinating detail about life both at Versailles and in the Parisian salons, as well as the wider cultural and intellectual life in seventeenth-century France, ranging from maternal behaviour to the arts to philosophy.

Born Marie de Rabutin-Chantal, right in the middle of Paris, her family on her father's side were nobles from Burgundy, while her mother was Marie de Coulanges, a rich Parisian bourgeois. Like so many others at the time, Marie was left an orphan at the age of seven and was brought up by her uncle, the *abbé* of Livry. Things could have been worse because he saw to it that she had a good classical education and was taught Italian, Spanish and Latin.

She grew up to be famously blonde and famously beautiful, which for once comes across in Claude Lefèbvre's 1665 portrait of her, which shows an open, intelligent face, ready to smile, but not one to suffer fools gladly. She had – equally famously – 'flecked' eyes.

She was married in 1644, aged eighteen, to Henri, Marquis de

Sévigné, a nobleman from Brittany. To begin with they lived in Henri's manor house, Les Rochers, near Vitré, south of the Cherbourg peninsula, where she soon gave birth to a daughter, Françoise, in 1646, and a son, Charles, two years later. And then disaster – or opportunity – struck. In 1651, Henri was killed in a duel over his mistress.[1]

Marie never remarried. Despite being blonde and beautiful, she was, by some accounts, 'sexually cold' and thereafter strongly preferred the company of women. She never had her own salon but, with her husband being killed in the middle of the Fronde, once the hostilities were over she moved back to Paris and joined the Blue Room at the time of the fashion for *préciosité*.

Préciosité was a controversial phenomenon of the 1650s, an argument which lasted for almost a decade as to whether the women in the salons were affected, frivolous and superficial, whose intellectual aspirations were beyond them, a hubristic delusion, or whether in fact this was a deliberate put-down by misogynist men who couldn't – or wouldn't – cope with the changed standing of women after the Fronde. In the first half of the seventeenth century, it was considered 'unseemly' for women to even *think* of writing, but in the decade following the Fronde that all changed, and the idea of women writing became much more acceptable, except among one or two atavistic diehards.[2]

One view about the *Précieuses* was given in the *Divers portraits* put together in 1659 by La Grande Mademoiselle: 'They lean their heads on their shoulders, simper with their eyes ... and have a certain affectation in all their behavior, which is extremely offensive ... They have something like a private language ... they find fault with everything.'[3] Most famously, they were represented in Molière's two farces, *Le Misanthrope* (1666) and *Les Précieuses ridicules* (1659). In the former, Alceste rejects the *politesse* of aristocratic society and refuses to conform his behaviour to the standards required, arguing that such 'wall-to-wall niceness' is superficial, despite the fact that this makes him unpopular and despite the fact that he cannot help but love the 'flighty and vivacious' Célimène, whose wit and frivolity epitomise the courtly manners he so despises. She is as confirmed in her lifestyle as he is in his and refuses to change. Although Molière clearly puts down the flighty Célimène, it is not clear whether he regards Alceste as a hero, a villain or a fool – the play ends in a stand-off. As for *Les Précieuses ridicules*, it has stood the test of time better than a good many other 'classical' offerings. Two provincial ladies turn down the suitors their father has found for them because the men are 'insufficiently refined' (for which read 'insufficiently affected'). Instead, they take up with their suitors' valets, who have been disguised as nobles and coached in 'excessive manners'.[4]

But Molière wasn't the only one to make fun of the *Précieuses*. Nicolas Boileau and Antoine Furetière also wrote satires, as did the Abbé de Pure in his serial novel *La Prétieuse* (1656–8) and Antoine Baudeau de Somaize, yet another satirist, who published in 1660 the *Grand Dictionnaire des Prétieuses, ou La Clef de la langue des ruelles* and a play on the same subject, *Le Procez des Prétieuses en vers burlesques*, in the same year.[5]

So it does seem that, for a time at least, the *Précieuses* were fair game. On the other hand, recent scholarship shows that, again in the words of Benedetta Craveri, 'from the 1640s, a Pléiade of women held positions of prime importance in the social life of the capital. More than 130 – most of them nobles – have now been identified and each of them described in the singular by the adjective "precious", which had no pejorative connotations and was synonymous with delicacy, refinement and distinction.'[6] The *Précieuse* 'cultivated a high ideal of herself and of the respect due to her sex'.

In retrospect, then, the satirical controversy over the *Précieuses* concealed a real change that was taking place in France concerning the status and self-respect of women in the wake of the Fronde, which we should never forget was, more than most, a women's war.

This is supported by the fact that Mme de Sévigné, far from being the simpering affected type, lost in her own private language, had instead a robust intelligence and combative wit, and her writing style was anything but private – in fact it was a model of clarity and élan. However, instead of becoming a *salonnière* in her own right, she became a much sought-after member of other women's salons, noted for her conversational skills and the sheer liveliness of her presence. Moreover, during the course of her life, and even more so after it, she became noted for her extensive correspondence that reflected her brilliant conversational manner and is taught now in many French schools as a model of stylish clarity, wit and verve. Well over a thousand letters survive, in which three themes stand out.[7]

She began writing in earnest when her daughter, Françoise, whom she idolised, was married in 1669 to the Comte de Grignan, a nobleman from Provence who was appointed lieutenant governor of the region and so was required to live there. Mme de Sévigné was devastated at being separated from her daughter (who did not entirely reciprocate the feeling), and from then on wrote two or three letters a week to Françoise. These letters offer, first and foremost, a close reading of life in Paris, both court life and salon life, with a breezy affection in which Mme de Sévigné doesn't hide her feelings.[8] Given their extraordinarily limpid – even melodious – quality, we are taken into the conversational world in a transparent way that is second to none.

Mme de Sévigné was a confirmed neoclassicist, and sympathetic to Jansenism and its austere doctrines. She loved pulpit oratory – a literary form popular then but now of course dated. Much as she worshipped her daughter, she was not uncritical of Françoise's taste for the philosophy of Descartes (that life and the universe are essentially mechanical in character, which will eventually be shown to be reducible to mathematical constructs). Rather, Marie was an enthusiast for nature, with its incomparable beauty 'best pursued in disciplined solitude'.[9] Machines could never *love*, she tells her daughter, machines are not capable of *jealousy*, they cannot *fear*. It is these passions that make up a life. For her, introspection, religious contemplation and desire were the key elements of life and it is primarily through them that happiness was to be found.[10]

Her Jansenist sympathies crop up everywhere: in her conviction that the divine will is God's central attribute, so that even the smallest episodes of everyday life 'reflect the silent work of God's ordering of time'; and in her view that 'there is no moment of rest in this life'.[11] One of her greatest wishes was to be devout but she tells us she is only too well aware of how hard that is, that – in a way – following God is not entirely human. This is part of her charm, that she is too human, too weak, to live up to the exalted aims of the Jansenist faith, and this is why we like her, for her common sense and practicality. She condemns Ninon de Lenclos, a libertine we shall meet shortly, not only because she was a libertine (and had a liaison with Mme de Sévigné's own son) but for her dogmatism, an approach to life that Marie knows can lead only to dissatisfaction and disorder.

Throughout there is her concern with desire and love. In the salons, she shows, there was a widespread fascination with the gradations of love, the difference between love and friendship and how passion, desire, both determined and disfigured lives. In this regard, a second line of her correspondence was with her cousin Roger de Bussy-Rabutin, with whom she had a tempestuous relationship. One theme they explored together was the beginning, the end and the rekindling of love. 'I don't believe I have ever read anything as moving as the account you [Bussy-Rabutin] have given me of your farewell to your mistress.'[12] And this is key: Mme de Sévigné's achievement was to identify aspects of life – nuggets of experience, like a farewell to a mistress – that others had never noticed and in that way, as with true poetry, extend the reach of experience and enlarge it, enlarge life.

Marie-Madeleine de Lafayette, La Rochefoucauld and La Fontaine: Three Literary Revolutions

In his *Mémoires*, Charles-Maurice de Talleyrand described Mme de Sévigné, Mme de Lafayette and the Duc de La Rochefoucauld as a 'formidable trio' whose close friendship and 'robust conversations' comprised 'one of the high points of civilisation under the *ancien régime*'.[1] The second of the trio, Mme de Lafayette, was every bit as extraordinary as Mme de Sévigné, even if she is not as well known today.

She was born Marie-Madeleine Pioche de la Vergne in the Petit Luxembourg Palace in Paris in 1634, making her eight years junior to Mme de Sévigné. Her mother was lady-in-waiting to Cardinal Richelieu's niece – she was well connected. The entire family was required to vacate Paris in the Fronde, during which time her father died. She formed an early friendship with the poet Gilles Ménage, who encouraged her to study Greek, Latin and Italian so that, like Mme de Sévigné, she was well versed in the classics.

One can see why Mme de Lafayette would follow Ménage's advice. A lawyer who turned to the church, he wrote a history of women philosophers (published in 1690) and he too was a member of the Blue Room. Prominent among the female philosophers at the time was Mme Anne Le Fèvre Dacier, who Ménage described as 'the most erudite woman in the present or in the past'. Mme Dacier was an esteemed classicist, a translator of Greek philosophical works, including the *Iliad* and the *Odyssey*, who firmly believed that the ancients were superior to the moderns, and she had pronounced views on taste, which, she believed, was a guide to the health of civilisation. *Bon goût* would be an obsession in France throughout the seventeenth and eighteenth centuries. Dacier felt that there had been a decline in French literature owing partly to the sentimental novels so popular in the salons.

Though Mme de Lafayette resembled Mme de Sévigné in some ways, unlike her she suffered from several embarrassments that would help determine her character. The first occurred after her father's death, when her mother remarried Renaud-René de Sévigné, a cousin of her future close intimate. What was embarrassing was that *le tout Paris* had expected Sévigné to marry not the mother but the daughter. This had the unsurprising effect on the daughter that henceforth she was always somewhat wary of showing her emotions.[2]

A year or two later, in 1655, Marie-Madeleine married François Motier, Comte de Lafayette, eighteen years older than she, and in poor financial circumstances. The marriage was arranged in haste, leading some to speculate on another embarrassing possibility: that Marie-Madeleine was pregnant by another man and the comte agreed to a cover-up marriage provided it was accompanied by a generous dowry. They had two sons, but her husband preferred his country estates while she preferred Paris, and to a large extent they thereafter lived separate lives.

After these adventures, if they can be called that, she settled in the French capital and, unlike Mme de Sévigné in this regard, she inhabited both the world of the royal court and that of the salons. As a result of her friendship with Henriette Anne, daughter of Henrietta Maria and Charles I of England, and now wife of Philippe, Duc d'Orléans, brother of Louis XIV, Mme de Lafayette had free access to court society. This would help form the basis of two of the books she would become known for.

She was not a great beauty, we are told. Portraits show her as round-faced, on the chubby side, with a too-large nose, a too-small mouth and eyes that were too far apart. But her wit and ready intelligence counted for more and, not content with attending the salons of Mesdames de Rambouillet and du Plessis-Guénégaud – though she was very welcome there – she set up her own salon, on the rue de Vaugirard, where a raft of significant scholars, savants, poets and writers were drawn in. They included Molière; Racine; Pierre-Daniel Huet, renowned for his erudition; Jean Regnault de Segrais, poet, translator of Virgil and aide to La Grande Mademoiselle, who would help her write her novels when the time came; and La Rochefoucauld, who would become her closest male companion.[3]

THE FIRST (PSYCHOLOGICAL) NOVEL

Mme de Lafayette always had literary ambitions but not in the epistolary style of Mme de Sévigné. Her first novel, *La Princesse de Montpensier*, was published anonymously in 1662, Mme de Lafayette well aware that, at the time, it was 'not done' for court women to write books or appear in the public domain. Moreover, women were not thought of as intellectuals or artists. That did not deter her, however, and a second novel, *Zaïde*, appeared in 1670, and in which, apparently, both Huet and La Rochefoucauld had a hand, though it appeared under Segrais's name. It was reprinted more than once and translated into several languages.[4]

But all this paled alongside *La Princesse de Clèves*, published in 1678, again anonymously, and which, it is now accepted, revolutionised the novel, using a variety of innovations (Joan DeJean says plainly that this was the first modern novel, a timeless work concerned with the 'abyss of the heart'). Until that point, novels had usually been romances, action-oriented and recounting often-implausible narratives of heroes overcoming near-impossible odds to achieve a happy ending where, invariably, love triumphs. Marie-Madeleine changed all that. *La Princesse* is now regarded as the first psychological novel, making widespread use of interior monologues, where the study of character and motive are the main sources of interest, where analysis is as important as narrative, and where what we now take to be classical female interests – the inner workings of life – move centre stage.[5]

The plot tells the story of a sixteen-year-old heiress whose mother has brought her to the court of Henry II (i.e., a hundred years distant from Mme de Lafayette's own time) to make a match. Owing to court intrigues, the best prospects never materialise and the young woman accepts the only offer, that of a man of middling standing, the Prince of Clèves. Not long after the wedding, however, the newly minted princess meets the dashing Duc de Nemours and they fall wildly in love. Their passion is internal, though, and they meet only now and then in the princess's very own salon. Even so, the prince eventually realises that his new wife is in love with someone else and he confronts her. She confesses and it is this confession that accounted for the sensation caused by the book, and its wild success, as the world of both the court and the salons digested that her plot made explicit what so often took place in secret.

Following the confrontation, the prince falls ill. It is never spelled out whether from a natural illness or a broken heart, but on his deathbed he begs his wife not to marry the duc after his death. Following his demise, she is legally and psychologically free to pursue her passions. (Women in seventeenth-, eighteenth-, and nineteenth-century France often discovered their freedom on being divorced or widowed, as we shall repeatedly see.) Despite the continued attentions of the Duc de Nemours, however, she keeps herself to herself, reins in her feelings and removes herself to a convent for part of each year. The book also includes a very intense observation of life at court and – in a second scandalous theme – Mme de Lafayette implies that full satisfaction in life can only be achieved by removing oneself from the court, an argument that, of course, aligns her with Catherine de Rambouillet and Élisabeth du Plessis-Guénégaud.[6]

Mme de Lafayette was much affected by the death of the Duc de La Rochefoucauld in 1680 and although she lived on for more than a decade afterwards, she was never the same, though two other well-regarded books were published after her death: *Histoire de Madame Henriette d'Angleterre* and *Mémoires de la Cour de France pour les années 1688 et 1689*.

A Preference for Women

The third member of Talleyrand's 'formidable trio', François de La Rochefoucauld, the second Duc de La Rochefoucauld, was an extraordinary man whose career was divided sharply into two, though one of his biographers divided it into four, according to the four women in his life. He was born in 1615 into one of the most illustrious noble French families, whose military distinction dated back to the feudal eleventh century. Later '*seigneurs*', as they were known, fought in the religious wars, undergoing their share of casualties and honours and the second duc received the usual education of his class – military exercises, hunting, court manners, and a general socio-political grounding.[7]

He was sent into the army – incredible, this – at the age of nine, was married at fifteen to Andrée de Vivonne, a sixth cousin to Mme de Rambouillet, and at sixteen he took part in the Battle of Cassel, part of the Franco-Dutch War. By background and temperament, he was opposed to Richelieu and supported Gaston d'Orléans, the king's always-rebellious and always-plotting brother (chapter 10). These plots were invariably discovered and led to short stays in the Bastille for La Rochefoucauld, years of banishment and eventually to the Fronde, in which he was badly wounded twice, once in the head which left him temporarily blinded.[8] La Rochefoucauld recovered his sight but the battle marked the end of his active life.

There are those who argue that the violence, deceit and treachery that La Rochefoucauld experienced shaped the cynicism and the morality that he was to express so well in his celebrated *Maximes*. But this is to neglect the other aspect of his life, associated with four women: the Duchesse de Chevreuse, the Duchesse de Longueville, Mme de Sablé, and Mme de Lafayette, a glittering array of personages. He met the Duchesse de Chevreuse, one of the great beauties of the court and mistress to Louis XIII, while they were both in exile. The duchesse was in touch with the court of Spain, then enemies of the French king. La Rochefoucauld embraced the cause of his new lover, the plot was discovered, and this cut him off from all possibility of court favour.

It was the same in the Fronde. During those hostilities he met – and fell in love with – the Duchesse de Longueville, whose brave exploits have already been outlined. At the outbreak of hostilities, they fled together to Normandy. He left her at Dieppe and, while she was eventually forced to escape by boat to Holland, he moved to Bordeaux and, with the Duc de Bouillon, defended the town with the greatest bravery though in the end the parliament there compelled him to surrender as the only way to save the city from physical destruction. This made him distinguished but powerless.[9]

With the end of the Fronde, however, it can be said that in a sense La Rochefoucauld's real life began. He settled in Paris and, as someone coined the phrase, 'devoted himself to society', frequenting more than one salon.[10] In addition to those of Mme du Plessis-Guénégaud and Mme de Lafayette, he was also a regular at Mme de Sablé's. During this time he produced the two works for which he is chiefly remembered, the *Mémoires* of his own time (giving a faithful picture of the intrigues and scandals of the court during Louis XIV's minority) and his *Maximes* (everyone composed maxims at Mme de Sablé's, says Roger Picard).

One of the things he does in the *Mémoires* is describe himself. 'In the first place, to speak of my temper. I am melancholy, and I have hardly been seen for the last three or four years to laugh above three or four times ... I have ability. I have no hesitation in saying it, as for what purpose should I pretend otherwise? So great circumvention, and so great depreciation, in speaking of the gifts one has, seems to me to hide a little vanity under an apparent modesty ... The conversation of gentlemen is one of the pleasures that most amuses me. I like it to be serious and morality to form the substance of it ... if I do not make many witty speeches, it is not because I do not appreciate the value of trifles well said ... I do not dislike an argument and I often of my own free will engage in one; but I generally back my opinion with too much warmth and sometimes, when the wrong side is advocated against me, from the strength of my zeal for reason, I become a little unreasonable myself ... I have all the passions pretty mildly, and pretty well under control ... I keep the most punctilious civility to women ... When their intellect is cultivated, I prefer their society to that of men; one there finds a mildness one does not meet with among ourselves, and it seems to me beyond this that they express themselves with more neatness, and give a more agreeable turn to the things they talk about ... I have renounced all flirtation.'[11]

The *Maximes* were published first in 1665, containing 316 entries, later increased to 504, and there were five editions of the book in the seventeenth century alone. There have been eight English translations and, though they are not without their critics (Rousseau thought it a 'sad and melancholy' book), the *Maximes* have drawn praise from Pascal, La Bruyère, Chesterfield, Swift, Nietzsche and Montesquieu.[12] Voltaire thought that it was 'one of the works that most contributed to form the taste of the [French] nation', though he added that 'there is scarcely more than one truth running through the book – that "self-love is the motive of everything"'.[13]

The maxims are usually a few words, hardly ever running to more than two lines:

'There is something in the misfortunes of our best friends which does not wholly displease us.'

'If we had no faults, we would not take so much pleasure in noticing those of others.'

'The truest mark of having been born with great qualities is to have been born without envy.'

A CRUEL QUARTET

Though he was not part of Talleyrand's 'formidable trio', one of the other notable people in the salons of that time was the great French fabulist, Jean de La Fontaine, of whom La Rochefoucauld was a protector. The son of a *maître des eaux et forêts* at Château-Thierry, north-east of Paris, La Fontaine was educated in the law. A wife was found for him, a girl of fourteen but of course with a substantial dowry. The marriage was not a success, however. La Fontaine proved hopeless at business and after nine years of marriage – much of it lived apart – a financial separation of their affairs had to be arranged. From then on, the pair appeared to live amicably but separately, she in Château-Thierry, he in Paris. They had one son, who lived with his mother.

In Paris La Fontaine didn't follow the law but began his literary career with a translation of the *Eunuchus* of Terence. This brought him to the attention of Superintendent Nicolas Fouquet, who endowed him with a pension, in return for which La Fontaine was to compose verses each quarter when the pension became due. More notably, he wrote *Le Songe de Vaux*, Vaux being Fouquet's celebrated palace. When the superintendent was arrested and imprisoned by Louis XIV (see the Prologue), La Fontaine didn't entirely abandon his patron, composing *Pleurez, Nymphes de Vaux*. Following that, La Fontaine's reputation grew, and he crept up the social ladder. Always adept at making influential friends, at this time he made the acquaintance of one of Cardinal Mazarin's nieces, writing verse for her, and added the title of *Esquire* to his name. This was 'not done' and an informer caused him to be fined 2,000 livres.[14]

Perhaps the best example of his rise to prominence (in his early forties) was his membership of the quartet of literary figures who met regularly on the rue du Vieux Colombier, the other members being Racine, Boileau and Molière. With satirists like Boileau and Molière in the company, it is no surprise to find that this group had its sharp – even cruel – side. It is said that Jean Chapelain was a 'kind of outsider' in the group but this does not do justice to the situation. By all accounts, the group always left a copy of Chapelain's epic poem about Joan of Arc, *La Pucelle*, on the table, and any member who infringed its rituals was 'condemned' to read a few lines from the book as punishment.[15]

La Fontaine's next influential friend was the dowager Duchesse d'Orléans, who installed him in the Luxembourg. When she died, he was taken up by Mme de la Sablière, another great *salonnière*, who invited him to make his home in her house, and where he remained for twenty years. It suited him and he was able to concentrate on both his poetry and his interest in play-writing.

La Fontaine's oeuvre consisted of three elements – the *Fables*, the tales (*Contes*) and other works, of which the dramatic are the strongest. But it is the *Fables* for which he was best known in his day and which have most sustained his reputation ever since. There were twelve books published between 1668 and 1694. The stories are derived from many sources, mostly from Aesop and Horace initially, with more eastern sources in the later books, and he retells them in free verse. Some of them are ambiguously ironic and some of the *Contes* are licentious. He was after all a member of the same club as Molière and Racine.[16] By now in his late fifties, he was close to being the grand old man of letters and was elected to the Académie française in the same year as Boileau.

As well as being the author of many stories, La Fontaine was himself the subject of many anecdotes, often having to do with his absent-mindedness. Some of these were collected by Louis Racine, son of La Fontaine's lifelong playwright friend. In one, he met his son without realising it, and when it was pointed out he remarked: 'Ah, yes, I thought I had seen him somewhere.'[17]

Magdeleine de Sablé and the *Journal des savants*, Madeleine de Scudéry and the Tender Game of Love

Though the salons of Mesdames de Rambouillet and du Plessis-Guénégaud were the most distinguished gatherings to begin with, they were soon emulated by others no less so. Beginning roughly around 1654, with the return of peace and stability after the unpleasant rigours of the Fronde, Parisian society took on a new form. Since the king and Mazarin had won, and the nobles had now forfeited their claims to independence and autonomy, the aristocracy redoubled their concern with the social pleasures, withdrawing from the political scene into the realms of culture and taste. 'Salons multiplied, more and more of the nobility and the bourgeoisie became passionate for *sociabilité*, new forms of entertainment were introduced, and the *cercles* widened their interests.'[1]

Magdeleine de Sablé, for example, had been a habituée of the Blue Room since as early as 1620 and had enjoyed every moment. But the crisis of the Fronde was the beginning of the end for the Rambouillet salon. On the other hand, Mme de Sablé, who was a convinced Jansenist, fared better. Following her conversion, she moved into Port-Royal and had a house built specially for her in which 'her drawing room became one of the most creative meeting places in French cultural and society circles'.[2] As the Harvard historian of France William Wiley put it: 'The salons demonstrated too, that women

had won the centuries-old *Querelle de la Femme* and that she was
no longer man's chattel in society's marketplace. Courtier and savant
alike, therefore, visited the salons and knelt in ritualistic obeisance at
the feet of women.' Molière kept up the attack, however, ridiculing
them for preferring such expressions as 'I esteem the melon' over 'I
like the melon'.[3]

The *querelle* was an age-old battle over the equality (or otherwise)
between the sexes, dating back originally to the idea that women were
descendants of Eve, who had caused the expulsion from the Garden
of Eden, and so were in some existential sense inferior to men. The
issue was debated all over Europe but was especially sharp in France
as women increasingly rebelled against arranged or dynastic unions.
This is why in salon life there was endless discussion about love and
whether women were especially gifted in conversation, either born
to greater eloquence or failing at it. There was constant speculation
on how the women of the salons were best described, especially the
worldly ones – were they 'cultivated', 'precious', 'pedantic' (much the
same thing) or merely 'ignorant'? Molière and Boileau were just two
of the best-known critics of female abilities. Women were mocked for
both their learning and their ignorance. It is a notable fact of French
social/intellectual history that women who were widowed – which
happened a lot because of the practice of marrying off young girls
to much older men – did not remarry, preferring instead to branch
out, both socially and intellectually, now that they were (for the most
part) mature and economically secure. It is also true that widows
were a threat to two families if they were not financially independent,
an unwelcome drain on both their original family and their in-laws.
This too encouraged them to launch themselves into society.

Although Mme de Sablé's house in the convent was technically a
'retreat', she continued to be 'on excellent terms with society'.[4] Her
table was known as one of the best in Paris and for the mix of aristocrats, magistrates, scientists, doctors, diplomats, men of letters and
even Jesuits and Jansenists gathered together in her salon to discuss
not only theology, but to watch elementary experiments, and to
engage in arguments about metaphysics, morality and psychology.
Above all, there was still a fascination with love. *Questions d'amour*,
Benedetta Craveri tells us, 'were all the rage in the salons'. The

Marquis de Sourdis read out his thirty-two *Questions sur l'amour* and Roger de Bussy-Rabutin read from his *Maximes d'amour*. Among specific topics discussed were: 'Is it better to lose a loved one through death or infidelity?' and 'Is it possible to love something more than oneself?'[5]

La Rochefoucauld and La Fontaine were both regulars at Mme de Sablé's, and she helped with the production of the former's *Maximes*, even to the extent of producing several dozen maxims of her own. Magdeleine even went so far as to write her own review of the *Maximes* in the *Journal des savants*, which was published in March 1665. Going 'public' in this way, for a woman, was a definite step forward.[6]

'PLAYING' AT SCIENCE

Marguerite Hessein Rambouillet de La Sablière was married at the age of fourteen to Antoine Rambouillet de La Sablière, the younger son of another very rich banker, Nicolas Rambouillet du Plessis, the father of Élisabeth, married to Gédéon Tallemant des Réaux. Despite this concatenation of names, Marguerite was unrelated to the *maîtresses* of the Blue Room or the du Plessis-Guénégauds. Even so, her house became known as La Folie-Rambouillet because it was just as distinguished as the Blue Room.[7] On paper, Antoine was a good catch. In practice, however, the marriage was not a success and, although they had three children, by the time she was thirty Marguerite needed a separation. As happened with several other women in this book, that caesura was the making of her. She set up house in the rue Neuve-des-Petits-Champs, and opened her salon.

She had help beyond her apprenticeship in the Blue Room. Her brother was a friend of Boileau and Molière and her uncle knew Pascal and Racine. But it was Marguerite's own urbanity and accomplishments which made her salon such a success. Described by contemporaries as a 'convinced Cartesian', she had studied mathematics, geometry and astronomy with well-regarded instructors, including François Bernier (an early theorist on the world's races), who dedicated his work on the astronomer and philosopher Pierre Gassendi to her.[8]

By now, within Mme de Sablière's salon, the more frivolous aspects of salon life had been eschewed, in favour of literary, philosophical and scientific pursuits, though both Molière and Boileau poked fun at her. Nonetheless, she befriended La Fontaine and looked after him when he was in financial trouble; in return he dedicated more than one fable to her. And it was around her circle that the great quarrel, between the ancients and the moderns, broke out, a debate as to whether the recent invention of the printing press, modern fire-arms and the compass, which helped navigation to the New World, actually put modern scholarship above the age-old 'certainties' of the Greeks and Romans.[9]

Boileau led the charge for the ancients, who refused to recognise that contemporary society – and that included the women in it, who helped organise and maintain it – had any critical standing. Only men, and men of letters at that, could fulfil such a role. The importance of letters, and men of letters, would be a lineament of Frenchness for centuries.

Nicolas Boileau-Despréaux (1631–1711) was as formal in his appearance as in his literary style. A friend to all the main seven-teenth-century classicists, he was the first great French literary critic, the founder of a modern tradition of French writers who sought to emphasise that the ancients were great not because they were old but because they were good. Good literature, he said, and by that he meant poetry and the theatre, rather than the novel, was hard to pull off and modern writers could come closest to perfection by following the rules and example of the Greeks and Romans, their 'precision of regularity', soberly formal. He admitted his own inadequacy as a poet, saying he could not do justice in his language to the majesty of the great themes, which for him were tragedy and epic. (He thought Chapelain's *La Pucelle* was dreadful.) He counselled the king not to seek conquests but to look out for the welfare of his people, so that the literature of his time could be 'dignified and loyal'. He supported Racine's tragedy *Phèdre* against a cabal of critics. His *Art poétique*, based on Horace, was influential in England as well as France, and Mme de Sévigné tells us several times in her letters that the work was sometimes read aloud after dinner at salons she attended, describing it as a 'masterpiece'.[10]

Verse, said Boileau, should 'have the quiet dignity of a clear stream', not a muddy torrent, everything in its proper place with noble, elevated language, no 'dirty words'. He supported the unities, downplayed rhetoric; there should be nothing 'unbelievable', nothing sentimental. Verse should have a 'methodical order'. Boileau was a great admirer of Mme Dacier and her respect for classical rules (which he felt Corneille, Molière and Racine respected too) but believed that the alexandrine form was beginning to date. Critics of Boileau, however, felt that his 'minutiae of rules' had 'dampened the fire of poetry'.

The moderns, led by Charles Perrault, best known as the author of several classic fairy tales – *inter alia*, 'Little Red Riding Hood', 'Sleeping Beauty', 'Puss in Boots' and 'Cinderella' – disagreed, questioning the 'indisputable authority' that the ancient authors were endowed with, and instead encouraged freedom of expression and honest pragmatism in judging works of art. Perrault singled out La Fontaine as evidence that the moderns were better (he thought La Fontaine was better than Aesop and Phaedrus) but La Fontaine himself took the ancient side.

In his *Savante ridicule*, Boileau had accused Mme de Sablière of 'playing' at science, using astrolabes and microscopes as little more than toys and sitting on her roof all night 'watching Jupiter'. Perrault, in his *Apologie des femmes*, replied that in fact Marguerite had a good understanding of science, adding that Boileau had been corrected in one of her salons and that, perhaps, this accounted for his vitriol.[11]

After her death Mme de Sablière was described as the 'grande dame' who represented the ultimate 'in a half century of polite society'.

FEMALE GLORY

Recent scholarship allows us to conclude Part One on a high note so far as the 'new constellation' of women is concerned, and one that effectively puts Molière and Boileau, for all their gifts, in their place. For it shows that two of the women who were vilified by the chronic misogyny in seventeenth-century France (female writers being dismissed as 'insolent adventurers') were far more than the sum of their parts.

The first is Madeleine de Scudéry, who we have already met as the

author of several ten-volume novels yet 'long framed by her critics as
a pedantic *précieuse*' who has drawn scorn for the 'inordinate length
and unreadability' of her books.[12] This is not untrue so far as modern
tastes are concerned, but she was in fact widely read in her own time.
Her own salon, her *Samedis* as its meetings were called, has been dismissed as 'amateurish' – and there is no doubt that some sections of
society had it in for her. In fact, as time has gone by, another Scudéry
has emerged.

Born in Le Havre in 1607, into a minor Norman aristocratic
family, like so many others at that time she was orphaned early, in her
case at the age of six, and brought up by her uncle, an ecclesiastic who
ensured she had a full education, which included foreign languages
and a grounding in stoicism and Montaigne. She was introduced to
the salons of Paris by her brother Georges, also a writer (chapter 1),
and through him she became a frequent visitor to the Blue Room.

She produced the first of her books in the 1640s and in the Fronde
she and her brother sided with the Crown. In 1653, as the Fronde was
ending, she and Georges installed their own salon in a new building in
the rue de Beauce in the Marais area of Paris, on Saturdays. Among
the regular guests, apart from Mesdames de Sablé, de Lafayette and
Scarron (the future Mme de Maintenon, who would become the second
wife of Louis XIV), there were Catherine Descartes, niece of René;
Valentin Conrart, writer, secretary to the king and one of the founders
of the Académie française, as we have seen; and Paul Pellisson, a lawyer
by training, historian of the Académie française, historian to the king,
who had been imprisoned in the Bastille for his support of Nicolas
Fouquet. There was also the Chevalier de Méré, both a writer and a
mathematician interested – before Pascal – in probability theory.[13]

It is also worth saying that, even though Madeleine de Scudéry
was the object of widespread scorn – in Molière's *Précieuses ridicules* (1659), Furetière's *Le Roman bourgeois* (1666) and Boileau's
Satire X (1667) – the Académie française went so far as to award
her its first literary prize, for an essay 'On Glory' in 1671. And she
was elected to foreign academies who didn't discriminate against
women quite as much as the French ones did. She was translated into
English, Spanish, Italian, German and even Arabic. Roger Picard
tells us that no less a foreign figure than Leibniz sought 'the honour'

of corresponding with her. Her books appeared in instalments and, according to Picard, had much the appeal of Dickens in Britain in the nineteenth century. Joan DeJean says that the novel as extended conversation now began to disappear.[14]

Mme de Scudéry's philosophy is mainly contained in dialogues published towards the end of her life, based on the discussions held in her *Samedis* and which she called 'Conversations', with titles such as *Of Lying, Of Politeness, Of Glory, Of Hope, Of Anger.* Characters discuss various matters – the passions, the virtues, free will, God, the merit of this or that poet, how to phrase letters, natural history (butterflies, chameleons). She had an extensive exchange of letters with Catherine Descartes in which both rejected René's mechanistic explanation of animal life.

In fact, Mme de Scudéry was in general sceptical about philosophy: 'The result will always be an unstable mixture of half-truths and unanticipated difficulties. This problem arises because philosophers generally try to say something new rather than saying something true.'[15] She was in particular interested in the problems women faced in contemporary society, where she identified three moral virtues: magnanimity, politeness and discretion. And here perhaps there were some elements of preciousness. For example, in *Of Politeness* she conceives of it as primarily 'the capacity to engage in proper conversation with persons of elevated social rank'. In *Of Glory*: 'Ladies have glory when their mind exceeds their beauty.'[16] In *Of Hope*: 'The entire life of the court is nothing but hope; that is where one always dies in hoping for something.' She thought that repentance was the greatest manifestation of human reason, and that Descartes was right in that doubt was everywhere and its exercise the right use of our powers. She considered that self-knowledge can only emerge 'through scrutiny of one's social interaction'.[17]

Her novels, whatever their shortcomings (or 'longcomings'), addressed the 'tender game of love' but at the same time did not avoid such questions as forced marriage, domestic violence and abduction. She defended women's rights to participate in politics and public life, their rights to education and self-expression, arguing that a distorted view of modesty 'had reduced women to silence' and made self-expression in women 'a sin'. To refuse women the right to develop their intellectual gifts 'is to oppose Nature itself ... the Gods have made nothing useless in all Nature'.[18]

Several recent American female historians have drawn attention to the way women writers were excluded from the early literary canon-formation, which was first set in train in late seventeenth-century France, but the rehabilitation of Mme de Scudéry's reputation began as early as the middle of the nineteenth century when Victor Cousin – eminent philosopher, brilliant lecturer and educationist and president of the Sorbonne – wrote a history of society in France in the seventeenth century and highlighted de Scudéry's role. The latest assessment of her achievements was published as recently as the 1990s.[19] Precious or not, she continues to fascinate.

Corneille, Boileau, Racine, Molière, La Fontaine and La Rochefoucauld comprised a brilliant generation of French writers and dramatists (the artists, architects and scientists, no less brilliant, are considered in chapter 7). All of these figures were men. But we can no longer stop there, because it is not a complete picture. Around them, and in some senses above them, was a raft of women whose talents were equally deserving of attention. While they undoubtedly had their 'precious' moments, the very self-confidence that gave rise to the charges of 'preciosity' shows that in the last half of the seventeenth century (in particular, following the Fronde, the 'women's war'), women in France were beginning to assert themselves. Disappointed by the court, they had found in the salon a form of mixed-gender sociability that helped to advance both cultural affairs and the intellectual evolution of their sex. It was not a straight line by any means, but what the salons provided above all was a hitherto undiscovered form of intellectual excitement, as shown by Simon Arnauld's visit to Mme du Plessis-Guénégaud's salon that night in 1665. Roger Picard concludes that, throughout the seventeenth century, the salons had helped fix French as a modern language, replacing Latin as the 'perfect instrument of a universal culture'.[20]

We should not underplay the extent – and the novelty – of that excitement. It accounts for the sheer durability of the salon in French life with its unique mix of genders and the varied forms of intellectual activity. The importance of this sociable mix is too often overlooked.

PART TWO

THE LINEAMENTS OF FRENCHNESS I

The Philosophical Eroticism of Ninon de Lenclos

The same may be said about Ninon de Lenclos as of Madeleine de Scudéry, that she continues to fascinate, and perhaps even more so. Born in 1620 in Paris as Anne de Lenclos, she was nicknamed 'Ninon' by her father and labelled as 'sulphurous' by her many critics later in life, though some of them at least had the grace to concede that she was 'the most beautiful woman in France'. Her parents were very different from each other. Her mother was extremely religious – a bigot even – while her father was described as a 'debauched musician' who worked in the court of a rich *seigneur*.[1] Worse, he was accused of being involved in the assassination of a baron and therefore had to abandon his family, seeking the anonymous safety of Paris, where he died not long after.

So Ninon's life began in scandal and she was to amass a healthy collection of scandals before she was able to use her intelligence to turn events to her advantage. She grew up to be a notorious courtesan who shocked France by her numerous tumultuous affairs, not just with prominent politicians but even with ecclesiastics. (There was, at the time, it is worth saying, a strict hierarchy of prostitutes in Paris: in ascending order of status they were *filles publiques*, *courtisanes*, *filles entretenues* and *matrons*). Ninon justified her libertine behaviour as based on an epicurean philosophy and her insistence on the equal rights of women.

Though her mother was a devout Catholic, her father saw to it that, like many of the women considered here, Ninon had a good education, grew up with books, was taught Spanish and Italian and, like Mme de Scudéry, was given a grounding in the philosophy of Montaigne. She was in any case a child prodigy, with a singular intellectual cast of mind, who appeared in other women's salons at an early age displaying a precocious facility with the lute and clavichord.

THREE KINDS OF LOVER

She began her many affairs in her teens, becoming the mistress of almost countless prominent men, including the Grand Condé (the cadet branch of the House of Bourbon), the Abbé de Châteauneuf and the Duc de La Rochefoucauld; more than once she took two lovers at the same time.[2] She divided her lovers into three: those who paid her, her favourites and her 'martyrs', who genuinely adored her but were still required to spend what little they had on her. She set up shop first in the Marais, an area given over to prostitutes and courtesans, where she earned a reputation for her skill in bringing affairs to an end without rancour. So scandalised was one part of society that the queen, Anne of Austria (as we have seen, regent of France during Louis XIV's minority), had her placed under house arrest in a convent for 'lost women'.[3] Ninon was only released after another queen, Christina of Protestant Sweden – then in exile after converting to Catholicism and abdicating, and on her way to Rome – visited her in the more discreet convent cell in which Ninon had subsequently been hidden, and where they discussed the philosophy of Descartes, who had spent time in Stockholm, giving Christina instruction. Following this experience, Christina prevailed on the king to release her, saying that this 'exceptional courtesan' was the one thing that his monarchy lacked.[4]

As this shows, there was a whole other side to Ninon's life. In 1667, she opened her own salon, after which, as one biographer says, she alternated her 'intellectual and erotic encounters'. The salon was situated in the hôtel de Sagonne in Paris, a building designed by Jules Hardouin-Mansart, architect to the king and nephew of François Mansart, generally credited with creating the classicism of French architecture.

Lenclos's salon had a familiar roster of members – Boileau, the

Chevalier de Méré, La Fontaine, the Duc d'Orléans, the future regent, Molière (who read an early version of his anti-clerical *Tartuffe* there) and Fontenelle. This shows how this once-scandalous *femme fatale* (as she was also described, repeatedly) could hold her own with the most distinguished in the land.[5]

Nicholas de Largillière's portrait of Fontenelle gives him a strong, almost totally bald head, a somewhat florid skin, piercing black eyes, a long prominent nose and a mouth with lips that soften the rest of his features. Born in Rouen in 1657, the son of a lawyer, he was to be blessed with a long life – he died just a month shy of his 100th birthday. That long life took him all the way from the company of Corneille, Racine and Boileau to the next generation of Voltaire, Diderot, Buffon and d'Alembert. Although he was never regarded as a piercingly sharp thinker, the accessibility of his style and his enthusiasm for Descartes – and for science more generally – set him slightly apart from the more literary *philosophes*.

His early interests were in poetry – he tried his hand at Latin verse – but he also experimented as a man of the theatre. He was in fact a man of many parts, as well as being a nephew of Corneille. He enjoyed worldly society, was a noted gourmand (attributing his long life to eating strawberries), but he was also interested in theological matters and science, albeit science with a theological relevance. He is better known today as the author of two works of high originality, and high limpid style. In *Nouveaux dialogues des morts* ('New Dialogues of the Dead', 1683), he invented plausible arguments between mostly dead ancient and dead modern authors. Among the very enjoyable and intriguing imagined encounters are Montaigne and Socrates, Montezuma and Cortés, and Roxelane and Anne Boleyn.

His *Entretiens sur la pluralité des mondes* ('Conversations on the Plurality of Worlds') discussed gravity, infinity and turbulence, the latter an original innovation. And it did so in French, not Latin, again making his work more accessible, especially to women, part of his avowed aim. It was cast in the form of a series of conversations between a 'gallant philosopher' and a marquise, who walk in the woman's garden at night, the philosopher using the stars above as the starting point for his explanation of the heliocentric (Copernican) universe, and a discussion of the possibility of life beyond Earth.[6]

Fontenelle also took a prominent role in the quarrel between the ancients and the moderns, in which he sided with the moderns. He was against what he saw as the rigid formalism of classical times and in 1688 published his *Digression sur les anciens and les modernes* in which he pointedly asked if the trees of former times were taller than those of today. His answer was that they were not; therefore 'we can equal Homer, Plato and Demosthenes'. It was this which drew the ire of Racine and Boileau in particular, both seeing to it that he was rejected by the Académie française no fewer than four times before he was elected. The rejections didn't faze him. He continued to argue that the Cartesian method 'took the sheen off the butterfly's wing': that is, it undermined poetry. Despite this, he eventually became (in 1697) the perpetual secretary of the Academy of Sciences, a position he was to hold for forty-two years.

As well as being a follower of Copernicus, he also popularised the theories of Descartes and this underlines Fontenelle's significance, both then and now, as one of the first popularisers of science, someone who made natural philosophy, as it was then called, accessible in *le monde*, in the fashionable world of the salons.[7]

He had a gentle wit. When he was in his late nineties, he encountered Mme Helvétius, a noted beauty. 'Ah, Madame,' he said softly. 'If only I were eighty again.'[8]

THE INVENTION OF THE INTELLECTUAL

Louis de Rouvrey, Duc de Saint-Simon, was – if anything – even better connected than Fontenelle, though it is important to say that there were two prominent Saint-Simons in French history. The second was Claude Henri de Rouvrey, Comte de Saint-Simon (1760–1825), who was the grandson of the duc's cousin and a political-sociological figure during the post-Revolution era.

Louis's father had been a favourite hunting companion of Louis XIII, as a result of which he had been made 'Master of the Wolfhounds' and promoted to duc. By the time Louis inherited the title, their *duché* (dukedom) ranked thirteenth among France's eighteen ducs. At his christening he was sponsored by Louis XIV and he enjoyed an early career in the army, seeing action at the Siege of

Namur and the Battle of Neerwinden, both hostilities taking place in the 1690s, between France and the Spanish Netherlands, what would become Belgium.[9]

Well connected though he was, and though he undoubtedly added 'cachet' to Ninon's salon, Saint-Simon did not come to general prominence until much later, when he had been long dead. This is because he had from an early time begun to record all the gossip and goings-on at Louis XIV's court at Versailles. Saint-Simon was congenial company by all accounts, but also a disappointed man, whose career had not really fulfilled its early promise, and this mix – of congeniality and disappointment – combined to make him the perfect observer of the attractions and animosities of life at court.

On his death, at eighty, by which time he had exhausted his family's fortune, all his possessions were sequestered by the Crown. His memoirs – which were to become so celebrated and ran to thousands of pages – were at first circulated only among a favoured few, as excerpts in manuscript form. It was only in 1828 that the manuscript was returned to his family, and so it was only then that he achieved real fame.[10]

Saint-Simon's memoirs are entertaining because he is not averse to confessing his own foibles – he could be petty and vindictive, and was self-obsessed, acerbic and ill-tempered as well as truly witty. He uses slang, invents new coinages, such as 'intellectual' and 'publicity', while giving vivid descriptions of the intrigues at court, gossip about the strict but convoluted hierarchy at Versailles, the importance and consequences of the purity of the royal bloodline. The bishops are *'cuistres violets'*, 'purple pedants' on account of their ecclesiastical garb, and one politician is put down as having a *'mien de chat fâché'*, the appearance of a disgruntled cat. He had no time for the Jesuits, being more sympathetic to the Jansenists. He played a role in creating the public persona of such figures as Mme de Maintenon. The *Mémoires* influenced the work of authors as varied as Barbey d'Aurevilly, Flaubert and Proust.[11]

Saint-Simon shared Mlle de Lenclos's salon with Mme de Maintenon, though at the time she was still Françoise d'Aubigny. He described Ninon's salon as a place where there was a triumph of vice and irony conducted with *esprit* 'and redeemed by virtue', adding that everything that went on in her salon was done out of a respect for her wit and self-composure and that her conversation was invariably 'charming, disinterested and intimate'.[12] One of Ninon's lovers was Mme de Sévigné's son, at a time when he was twenty-three and she forty-eight, three years older than her young lover's mother.

As it flourished, Lenclos's salon – where irony, philosophy, worldliness and eroticism were mixed, as someone said, in a '*bon ménage*' – became identified with a sceptical attitude to Christianity, and an interest in epicurean philosophy, which notoriously espoused the pursuits of pleasure, romantic love, and sexual gratification as the only true way to happiness and fulfilment. By all accounts, Ninon led the discussions herself in her salon with wit and energy and with such success that she even offered a course of lectures (scandalous to the devout) on love, allowing female students in for free, while males had to pay. In her will she provided an allowance for a young Voltaire to buy books.[13]

She had another revealing exchange of letters, this one with Charles de Saint-Évremond, soldier, literary critic and self-confessed 'hedonist', who had been a disciple of Gassendi and, like Arnauld, had been involved in the fall of Fouquet in 1661. Like Fontenelle he was interested in the diversity of peoples across the globe and wrote a book about what he felt were worthwhile titles available only in Spanish and Italian. In other words, he was a committed internationalist. As with Fontenelle and Saint-Simon, his best work, *Conversation du maréchal d'Hocquincourt avec le père Canaye*, which has been compared with Pascal's *Lettres provinciales*, was published posthumously. He ended his life in exile in England, where he founded his own salon 'for love-making, gambling and spirited conversation', and he is buried in Poets' Corner in Westminster Abbey.[14]

Rather than the virtues, Ninon is saying in some of her letters to him, it is the passions that dominate the human will and moral life. But this must be seen against the fundamental equality of the sexes, confirmed in the reciprocity of behaviour. She thought that love was instinctual, not a matter of taste, and that while there are many kinds of friendship, love always 'maintains a close connection' with physical attraction. Love, she insisted, was a form of 'fanaticism', and cannot be 'restrained'.[15] 'The desire for love in a woman is a substantial part of her natural constitution; her virtue has only been patched on."[16] 'If I were you, I would not speculate on whether it is a good or a bad thing to fall in love. I would rather have you speculate on whether it is good or bad to be thirsty, or whether it should be forbidden to give someone a drink just because some people might end up inebriated.' The natural causation of human love, she argued, justified her own sexual libertinism. 'Personally, I have always believed that those lovers who try to keep themselves within reasonable bounds are not completely in love.'[17]

In the context of salon life, Mlle de Lenclos was not blind to the competitive nature of love, that individuals enjoyed the successes and failures of other people in the pursuit of affairs, but she thought that they should be more understanding of the pain that a failed love can bring. 'People truly in love can't help themselves and we would be priggish if we didn't from time to time enjoy the misfortune of others' (as La Rochefoucauld's maxim had it). But even so she sympathised with suffering women. And, in order to show the way, she chronicled the usual path of a love affair, from the earliest moments when 'for a period they are intoxicated with the belief that their love is of a superior nature ... But let us follow them as their affair unfolds ... Nature quickly recovers its rights and re-assumes its influence ... The day arrives when these lovers become dissatisfied with the pleasures of love.'[18]

Most important, perhaps, she insists on gender equality, that men and women do not differ in their psychological qualities, that both sexes are to be treated by the other with respect, that the purpose of charm and wit is to reinforce such respect in original and amusing ways, that this is the purpose of 'the gentle art' of flirtation which leads to full intellectual engagement.

Is it so surprising that a woman as experienced in love – in love-making – as Ninon de Lenclos should have such a mind? The last forty years, especially the last twenty, have seen a welcome re-evaluation. She had a well-thought-out life, one that would echo down the ages as the French – more than most – took flirting, love and love-making seriously.

The Formal French: Colbert and the Academies

'There has always been something Molièresque about the complicated and humiliating business of getting oneself elected to the [Académie française].' This is Cornelia Otis Skinner writing about late nineteenth-century France, by which time the election process had become more or less settled. 'First of all, the initial letter of application must be a gem of fine prose and brevity. Then come the weeks of personal soliciting for votes when the wretched candidate, bearing credentials like a servant with letters of reference, must pay a formal call on every accessible Academician.' By that time, too, a number of prominent *salonnières* – Mme de Lambert, Juliette Récamier, Princesse Mathilde, Juliette Adam – had become identified with successfully sponsoring candidates. (Anne Martin-Fugier described Mme Récamier as an indomitable 'Pygmalion', so successful was she at getting 'her' candidates into the academy.)[1]

No academy in the world has the prestige of the Académie française among its countrymen at large. Every writer of standing in France has been and still is at some stage stricken with what is called 'green fever' after the 'frog-footman' uniform the members wear – a palm-embroidered green jacket with gold trimmings, satin breeches with a sword bouncing against a silk-stockinged leg. In the late nineteenth century, they were also paid 83 francs a month, 'as often as not to sleep through the proceedings'.

All nations have their academies but few, if any, match the cachet of the six major academies in France where they are so well known to the public that in one of the cafés of the Belle Époque, the waiters wore mock green uniforms of the Académie française. The posts of permanent secretary to each of the other academies were keenly competed for, not just for the honour and power they conferred on the recipient, but also for the free lodgings that went with the job. These academies, which combine social and intellectual prestige, have been a major lineament of Frenchness down the centuries.

The academies came into being, reasonably enough, at the height of French classicism, when the nation's cultural achievements were second to none, when, in the words of Anthony Blunt, the eminent art historian (and Russian spy), 'there flourished one of the most brilliant groups of Frenchmen to have appeared at one time'.[2] What the French are pleased to call the *grand siècle* – what in fact without question was an incredible century – was the creation of five remarkable men above all others: two kings, Louis XIII and XIV; two cardinals, Richelieu and Mazarin; and Jean-Baptiste Colbert, perhaps the most talented – and most assiduous – of them all.

To Colbert (1619–83) must be attributed a major share in the creation of the *grand style* that was to mark the reign of Louis XIV, and has lived on as a central element in French taste. French classicism, which encompassed all the arts, marks the period in European cultural history when France takes over from Italy as the most buoyant and forthright expression of talent – even genius – across a wide range of expertise.

It is sometimes said that Napoleon was responsible for the great centralisation and *dirigisme* that is such a feature of French life, but Colbert predated him by more than a century. Born in Reims, the son of a merchant, Jean-Baptiste Colbert had a Jesuit education, then worked for a banker and, later, a lawyer whose son we have already met: Jean Chapelain, one of the founder members of the Académie française and the man Molière and his group loved to lampoon.

When Mazarin was forced to flee in the Fronde, Colbert was chosen to keep the cardinal informed of events. He came to prominent attention after a memoir for the reinstated cardinal that he drew up in 1659 and in which he showed that, of the taxes paid by the people, 'not one-half reached the King'.[3] This did him no harm at all and in 1661 the death of Mazarin enabled Colbert to become the first man in the king's administration.

Colbert eventually assumed several great offices. In 1665 he became comptroller-general (the minister in charge of finance) and four years later minister of marine. He was also appointed minister of commerce, the colonies and the king's palace but before all that, on 1 January 1664, he was appointed to the office of superintendent of buildings, giving him direct charge of most of the royal edifices, building projects, artistic enterprises, and in fact most of the artistic life of the nation insofar as the royal authority impinged upon it.

Aided by the author Claude Perrault, his brother, the architect Charles Perrault, the painter Charles Le Brun, the architects Louis Le Vau, Libéral Bruant and Jules Hardouin-Mansart, plus the designer of gardens André Le Nôtre, and a score of others, Colbert gave the artistic nation a stimulus that was to raise the French mind to great heights and to give the age one of its chief claims to the title of *le grand siècle*. As Blunt indicated, Colbert had a great generation to work with and on, for in addition to the dramatists, fabulists, poets and early novelists mentioned so far, this was the great age in painting of Nicolas Poussin, Claude Lorrain, the Le Nain brothers and Philippe de Champaigne.

Even more than that, the work of construction and reconstruction under Colbert is a roll call of many of the most famous buildings in the world and shaped much of the Paris that we know today. The Louvre and the Tuileries were continued, the Palais-Royal and the Château de Madrid were made over, the hôtel des Invalides was built, the Observatoire constructed and the *arcs de triomphe* of Porte Saint-Denis, Port Sainte-Martin and Porte Saint-Antoine all erected. But of all the work the most important was that on the royal *châteaux*. Some idea of its extent may be gained in monetary terms. A million livres were spent on Fontainebleau, 900,000 on Vincennes, 5.5 million on Saint-Germain, and nearly another million on Chambord.[4]

Above all there was Versailles. Colbert would have preferred to see the Louvre finished and he 'shuddered' at the sums that were poured out on Versailles's buildings, gardens, fountains and the canal: between 30 million and 50 million livres were expended. In all, under Colbert some 80 million livres ($40 billion today) were put into royal buildings of one sort or another. In some years, Charles Cole tells us, more than 4 per cent of the nation's budget went into the king's buildings.[5]

As Richelieu before him had taken a great interest in bringing on the Académie française, so Colbert took a great interest in the later academies. Academies had originally evolved in Italy, where the principle adopted was that the 'liberal arts' – painting, sculpture and architecture – should be organised into academies, leaving the guilds to administer the mechanical arts only.

The creation in Paris of the next academy after the Académie française, the Académie royale de peinture et de sculpture, in 1648, owed something to artistic rivalry, something to commercial competition and not a little to the envy of Rome, where there was already an academy for artists, the Accademia di San Luca. As Gill Perry tells the story, the Paris academy was also a response to a bid for greater powers by the Maîtrise, an artists' guild founded as long ago as 1391, whose members paid dues in return for protection by trade regulations. The Maîtrise had become increasingly resentful of the growing number of artists who escaped these regulations by obtaining royal commissions. These fortunate souls were known as *brevetaires* because the monarch offered them a *lettre de brevet*, which gave them legal exemption from the regulations of the Maîtrise. The *brevetaires* had other benefits too, such as free accommodation in royal buildings, including the Louvre.[6] The dispute was also caught up in the Fronde, for the Maîtrise was linked to the Parlement, which also took against the *brevetaires*.

The counter-attack was led by none other than Charles Le Brun. He sided with the *brevetaires*, and was familiar with – and impressed by – the teaching methods of the Accademia di San Luca, which he had seen during the four years he had spent studying with Poussin in Rome. As Mazarin and Anne of Austria consolidated their power, Le Brun's idea to establish in Paris an academy on the Roman model won royal support. The Crown forbade the Maîtrise from interfering.

Not all artists were as high-minded as Le Brun but the new academy did make its mission the redefinition of the status of visual art, the aim being to present it – as with the Rome academy – as a liberal art, the intellectual equivalent of epic poetry or ancient rhetoric. This involved a deliberate attempt to take painting and sculpture away from their origins as mere 'crafts', and in the process to turn artists into gentlemen-scholars.[7] To that end, members of the academy were not allowed to involve themselves directly in the commercial trading of their works, unlike guildsmen. Retailing and trade of any kind carried a social stigma, as seventeenth-century nobles knew only too well. And there were other restraints. Academy members could not keep shops, or even display their works in studio windows.

Instead, academicians were expected to follow the 'loftier' intellectual example of the Rome academy, where the more practical aspects of painting were augmented and polished by a knowledge of history, mythology and literature in order to produce history painting, then regarded as the highest possible calling.

Underlying this doctrine is the idea that painting appeals to reason or the mind, rather than to the eye.[8] This turns it into an intellectual and learned art, suited to educated people. Academicians acceded to the traditional definition that painting is an imitation of nature, but they insisted that this imitation must be carried out only according to the laws of reason. The artist selects from the haphazard richness of nature its most beautiful constituents but must go on to depict that nature according to the laws of reason – that is, the rules of proportion, perspective and composition. More than that, the true artist must concentrate on the *permanent* aspects of nature – form and outline – and devote rather less attention to those elements – colour, for example, and most notably – which are both ephemeral and appealing more to the eye than to the mind.

The academy used such thinking to arrive at a system of rules that was more complicated than any other on earth. 'The painter must only choose noble subjects. Like the dramatist he must observe the unities of time, place and action, though he may be allowed certain liberties in the matter of time to suggest what immediately precedes and succeeds the actual moment depicted.' The artist must observe the proprieties – everything must be suitable to the theme chosen.[9]

Not content with this, however, the academy set out its arguments in rigidly didactic form. Le Brun, in particular, produced a famous treatise on 'the expression of the passions' in which he went so far as to specify how to portray any particular emotion, complete with diagrams. Henri Testelin, the secretary of the academy, extended this method in his *Sentiments des plus habiles peintres*, published in 1680, which collated the agreed policies of the academy on such activities as drawing, expression, proportion, *chiaroscuro*, composition and colour.

And the didacticism didn't stop there. Instructions were added on the suitability of different artists as models and a strict hierarchy was specified here too. First, the ancients; second, Raphael and his Roman followers; third, Poussin. Incredible to our way of thinking, the student was specifically warned off the Venetians, 'since they took too great an interest in colour'.[10]

On arrival at the academy's school, the young student was made to copy the works of 'approved' old masters, first in drawing, followed by painting. Next, he must copy casts from antique sculpture. Finally, he was allowed to draw from life, because by then, 'his taste would have been sufficiently formed'.

The central aim of the Académie royale was to familiarise its students with a canon of great works produced by Italian Renaissance masters. In this way, the academy presented itself as the central transmitter of a great artistic tradition, and to underline this it established regular lectures which were open to everyone, professionals and laypeople equally. Using paintings in the French royal collection, these compulsory lectures for students – followed by discussion – helped to fashion a particular way of looking at pictorial art. In particular, they sought to strengthen the idea that art was a learned endeavour based on a critical familiarity with literature, the bible and history.

In line with this strict dogma, hierarchy surfaced everywhere in the academy. For example, there was a strict ranking of membership into pupils, probationary academicians, academicians, teachers (professors) and directors.[11] Full membership could be obtained only by submission of a suitable 'reception piece'. Hierarchy was further embodied in the award of prizes (for example, a scholarship to Rome), which went to those whose pictures best exemplified the academy's orthodox style and subject matter. André Félibien (1619–95), an architect and biographer, compiled a record of lectures which laid down the general principles of the academy's approach. This stipulated that representation of the human figure – particularly in historical, mythological or religious narratives or in allegorical compositions – 'was the highest form of artistic endeavour ... which distinguished art from manual craft'.[12] By the end of the seventeenth century this ranking had become set into yet another hierarchy:

1. History painting, including religious, mythological or literary narratives, sometimes of an allegorical nature, as well as studies of sacred figures, such as the Virgin Mary;
2. Portraiture (the higher the status of the sitter, the higher that of the portrait);
3. Genre (scenes from 'everyday life'; this was a term first used in the eighteenth century);
4. Landscape;
5. Still life.

Between them, Colbert and Le Brun succeeded in this way in imposing a uniformity of style all over France, if only because they needed commissions from this central authority. More and more, France overtook Italy in matters of taste and the other courts of Europe – even Holland and England, politically opposed to France – were not immune.

The Académie française, created by Richelieu, was still a semi-private group in 1661, under the patronage of Pierre Séguier, chancellor of France, who came from a distinguished legal and political family, and was related by marriage to Richelieu. The academy was working listlessly on its dictionary, and wielded but little influence. And so, when Séguier died, in 1671, Colbert took the academy in hand, gave it the king for a patron, moved it into the Louvre, 'provided it with pens, paper, ink, heat, light, and – it is said – a clock', and told it to finish its dictionary, 'that the language might be purified and made uniform'.[13]

After the death of Mazarin, Séguier had become the patron of the Académie royale also, but almost immediately afterwards Colbert had become assistant patron and channelled his energies in the academy's direction. He reinforced its monopoly of teaching, moved it into the Louvre as well, gave it Le Brun as director, and imposed on it severe regulations so that it might work in an orderly and proper manner and be ever ready to serve the king.

In 1663 the king and his administrators had the idea for a Prix de Rome, the award of which would provide for a French painter or sculptor to study for between three and five years in the Eternal City, at the government's expense, so as to study Renaissance and ancient art in close detail. The first award was not actually made until 1666, when Colbert gave the go-ahead. The Académie de France à Rome, as it was known, was housed first in the Palazzo Capranica, not far from the Piazza Colonna; the other directors were Le Brun and Gian Lorenzo Bernini, the eminent sculptor.

The academy was located in the Capranica until 1737, then moved to the Palazzo Mancini. Napoleon moved it to the better-known Villa Medici in 1793, by which time the prestige of the prize was substantial. Among the artists winning the award and acting as director of the academy were Charles-Joseph Natoire, Joseph-Marie Vien, Jean-Auguste-Dominique Ingres and, much later, Balthus.

The artists who won the prize were compelled to send back to Paris each year their '*envois de Rome*', works sparked by the inspiration of the Holy City. When they returned home, they generally became key figures in shaping taste and culture. As well as becoming instructors in the École des beaux-arts, they were invariably judges in the Paris Salon (with a capital 'S', an exhibition of paintings), which came into being in 1737. The prize was extended to architecture in 1720, to music in 1803 and to engraving two years later.[14]

So far as writers were concerned, the situation was slightly different. By all accounts Molière, Racine and La Fontaine were very popular at court, but they did not depend on it to the same extent as the painters and architects did. They kept their eye on the Paris public as much as on Versailles and this gave them a certain independence that visual artists could only envy. At one point, Boileau had tried to formulate some classical doctrines about composition but he did not hold the purse strings as Colbert and Le Brun did. It followed from this that literature was not much given over to royal adoration. Literature could be as varied as *Le Cid*, *Phèdre* and La Fontaine's fable *The Monkey and the Cat*.

Nevertheless, Colbert did support writers financially and provided pensions for artists and scientists of every stamp. In the field of drama, for instance, Corneille drew a pension of 2,000 livres,

Molière one of 1,000 livres and Racine one of 600. (To Colbert, Racine dedicated his play *Bérénice* in 1670.) Government largesse for the arts in France has a long pedigree.[15]

In the intellectual sphere Colbert showed himself as ready as in art to secure the service of foreigners, and thus it was that the chief scientific figures of the period in France were the Dutchman Christiaan Huygens, and the Italian Domenico Cassini. They helped make France the intellectual centre of Europe. One notable non-Frenchman convinced of this was Gottfried Leibniz, the German mathematician, who visited Paris in the early 1670s and was very impressed, giving us an independent viewpoint. The Académie royale des sciences, the fourth of the great academies, was created in 1666.

Ambitious for himself, the young Leibniz had corresponded from a distance (he was then in Nuremberg) with both the Royal Society in London and the Académie royale in Paris. Having made contact with both organisations, Leibniz was gratified to learn in July 1671 that the French academy 'desired nothing more than to benefit from Leibniz's learning'.[16] Soon after his arrival in Paris, he wrote home to Johann Philipp von Schönborn, his employer, that 'the fellows of the Academy are people extremely learned in various fields who could compose an Encyclopaedia of arts and sciences; they meet twice a week (on Wednesdays [when they discussed mathematics] and Saturdays [natural philosophy]) at the Royal Library where some of them also live. Their secretary is [l'Abbé Jean] Gallois, who also edits the so-called *Journal des sçavans* [the first academic journal in Europe, founded in 1665, later the *Journal des savants*]. The king, however, has also had an observatory constructed on the outskirts of the city, in Faubourg St Jacques, which commoners originally mistook for a citadel ... Near the Royal Library is the garden and laboratory of the Academy; for several years they have grown here almost all botanic specimens and analysed chemical elements.'[17]

At the time the academy was founded, in 1666, Paris was a city of nearly 500,000 inhabitants occupying between 24,000 and 30,000 houses.[18] One contemporary wrote of it as a confused mass of bridges (unlike London, which had only one bridge across the Thames) and filthy thoroughfares where its narrow streets, paved and unpaved, were lit at night by the reflecting candle lanterns installed in 1667. The houses were built mainly of stone, 'whited over with plaister'. Statues of the king and his forebears were 'everywhere'. One English visitor noted many monks and lawyers and that in the streets the coaches travelled at speeds that endangered pedestrians. The air was polluted but not as badly as in London. 'The city offered products ranging from glass eyes to carpenter's nails, and services from conservation of paintings to air disinfection.'[19]

Leibniz's French needed improvement at first and it was not his only failing. As he wrote home to another friend: 'Where one has to drink to impress, you can well imagine that I am not in my element.' Even after three years in the city, he could write: 'Paris is a place where one can achieve distinction only with difficulty. One finds there, in all branches of knowledge, the most knowledgeable men of the age, and one needs much work and a little determination to establish a reputation there.'[20] Access to the court, not just for Leibniz but for anyone, was not easy but in the autumn of 1672 he did meet Huygens, who was by then effectively the director of the Académie royale des sciences, having been entrusted by Colbert with its planning and organisation.[21]

Founded six years after the Royal Society, the Académie royale des sciences had similar aims but was in some ways very different, which affected the way its science was conducted. On the positive side, it was sponsored by the king and paid for out of the royal treasury. This meant that it had official premises from the very start and that its members received stipends – or pensions as they were called – to support their activities. Many of the more senior members also lived free in royal accommodation near the meeting places and laboratories. At the same time, the king's ministers administered the academy on the king's behalf. Known as 'protectors', they were in charge of funding, housing and recruitment and their function was to protect the work of the academy and the reputations of the scientists working there, but also to protect the reputation and image of the king. Louis XIV had no real interest in science as such, but he was very interested in the practical innovations it might introduce and which would benefit France and in particular his own reputation. From the start the Académie royale had a royal propagandistic role that the Royal Society in London never had.

As Leibniz also pointed out in his letters, the academy – which was usually referred to by its own members as '*la compagnie*' – had three principal locations: the King's Library, the King's Garden and the Observatory.[22] Like the academy of painting, the academy of sciences was organised hierarchically. Academicians were responsible for research and writing, but they also assessed new technology and advised the Crown on technical matters.[23]

This system, quite different from that of the Royal Society, had advantages and disadvantages. The academy was financially secure and had its own permanent premises. It had a direct line to the power structure of the state, and its members had status. But because of that power structure, and its role as a propaganda instrument, it was not as entirely free, as the Royal Society was free, to pursue its own interests. Because the king was always interested in activities that might usefully benefit his reign in practical ways, he was much less interested in basic theoretical matters.

Then there was the fact that, being effectively a state institution, the academy conducted its affairs – its meetings and its publications – in the vernacular French, rather than in Latin. This had the effect of making *la compagnie* somewhat nationalistic in outlook, more so than the Royal Society.

Instead of Newton and *Principia*, the Académie showed much more interest in botany and botanical research, and in cartography. There were several reasons for this. One was that the king was interested in the extent of his realm, and wanted as accurate a map as possible. Another was that French Jesuits were at the time leading missionary expeditions to the Far East, where lucrative spices could be found and exotic plants. There had been a traditional interest everywhere in plants for medicinal purposes.[24] In keeping with this, at the Académie royale des sciences botany was the field for which Colbert authorised the most significant funding after cartography.[25] The king took a keen interest in his gardens – he kept oranges in his greenhouses, and had 18 million tulips planted in one four-year period.[26]

Leibniz was able to stay in Paris for four years, and while there he was given access to some of the unpublished manuscripts of both

Descartes and Pascal. It was while reading the mathematical manuscripts of Pascal that he began to conceive what would eventually become his differential calculus.[27]

The Académie royale d'architecture was Colbert's own creation. Limited to ten members nominated by the king, it was founded in 1671. In architecture, as in painting and sculpture, the proper principles were those which had come down from Greece and Rome via the Italian Renaissance. For study, therefore, Rome was the proper place- and two architects were added to the six painters and four sculptors at the academy. In 1676 Colbert attached the academy in Rome to the Academy of Painting and Sculpture and so Le Brun became director of both.

The architecture academy's formal purpose was to advance official French culture and it became in time a leading think tank, disseminating a coherent aesthetic doctrine. It gave weekly lectures open to 'all men of taste', and helped to define the difference between architecture and civil engineering (a separate administration for roads and bridge-building was founded in 1669). In doing so, the academy helped elevate the status of architect from that of builder to liberal professional. It became a highly structured body of disinterested specialists which excluded commercial builders and property speculators on principle.

A project of the early academy was a study of the ability to recognise beauty, and members took a great deal of interest in the work of Vitruvius, Sebastiano Serlio, Vincenzo Scamozzi and Andrea Palladio, in particular the argument as to whether beauty was arbitrary – derived from custom rather than some unchanging 'transcendent set of divine, mathematical principles'. At the same time the academy was very practically minded, conducting a survey of quarries, to assess the systematic and formal qualities of various species of stone, and sending Antoine Desgodetz (1653–1728) to Italy to measure all of Rome's classical monuments, to assess what exactly *were* the mathematics of beauty. (Unfortunately, on the way there he was taken captive by pirates in the Mediterranean and held for months before a hostage deal could be worked out.) At other times the academy took a practical interest in maritime infrastructure (jetties, canals, bridges, lighthouses) and was involved in the choice of a new royal square (now the place de la Concorde), among other grand urban gestures to solidify Paris as the capital of Europe.

Jean-Baptiste Lully, a musician and composer of Italian origin, was the Le Brun of music. In 1659, the Abbé Perrin had produced the first French opera. Its success sounded the death knell of the older French musical forms like the ballet, and marked the triumph of the new Italian form. Two years later, Perrin dedicated one of his works to Colbert, and eight years after that, through Colbert, he was able to secure a monopoly of the right to present musical performances. Because of bad management the venture ended in failure and, while Perrin was in debtors' prison in 1672, Lully, with Colbert's aid, managed to buy the privilege. He was given the right to form the Académie royale de musique at Paris, and his permission was thereafter necessary for any musical presentation employing more than two instruments. Lully enforced his monopoly and fixed the Italian opera upon France as the dominant form of musical entertainment.[28]

In a somewhat similar fashion, a theatre monopoly was created. There had existed a number of theatrical troupes since at least 1402 (the Confraternity of the Passion, which presented religious plays), some of them enjoying aid from the state in the form of rent-free theatres and subventions. In 1673 a royal declaration united the troupes of the Marais and of the Palais-Royal, which was Molière's company. The king's brother, known as Monsieur, and his wife, had turned the Palais-Royal into an intellectual centre, a rare entity beyond the reach of Colbert. Under them the Palais-Royal became the home of the first Comédie-Française, where Molière lived for years. (It was also the location of the Académie royale de musique, where Lully and Rameau would make their homes.) Monsieur was especially influential in the career of Molière. It was he who 'discovered' the playwright, introduced by Gaston (now reconciled with the king, his nephew). Monsieur and Molière had several secret meetings before the playwright was brought into Paris, and it was Monsieur who was first to offer the actor-playwright a pension. Molière repaid the compliment by renaming his troupe 'Troupe de Monsieur, frère unique du roi'. Molière dedicated more than one play to Monsieur, though in the end Monsieur paid the price for introducing the troupe to the king, who took over as the main patron, when Colbert came into the picture. Over the united group Colbert exercised control, and to them he added in 1680 the troupe of the hôtel de Bourgogne. Once united thus in the Comédie-Française, they were given a monopoly of dramatic presentation in Paris.[29]

Like the academies, the Comédie had a hierarchy of levels. Actors were on trial/probation for their first year, after which, if successful, they became *pensionnaires*, with a fixed salary. The higher level was that of *sociétaire*, which was a full member, but it only became available when a more established member died, a bit like the Académie française.

Though Molière is by far the best-known member of the early Comédie, he was followed with great success by Florent Carton Dancourt, also an actor-playwright and a solid bourgeois individual from a 'good' family (when the stage was not quite a respectable stable). He was educated by Jesuits and had studied law. In 1680 he married Thérèse de La Thorillière and for more than thirty years they dominated the Paris stage. As with Molière, Dancourt specialised in ridicule, often basing his plays on current scandals and social pretence, lampooning middle-class types crassly trying to ape nobility.

ROYAL BOUNTY AND ITALY RANSACKED

By such means Colbert was able to impose upon the artistic life of France a degree of control, a uniformity of ideology, a unanimity of purpose that has seldom been equalled. That such regimentation did not stifle the arts is clear, for in almost every field it was a golden age of French culture.

Colbert did more than regulate. With royal funds he subsidised the art life of the realm. Pensions, salaries, lucrative appointments, orders for work were bestowed upon great artists, mediocre artists and minor artists. Nor was Colbert's bounty limited to Frenchmen, for he imported foreign talent and even subsidised foreigners who remained where they were. Abroad, as well as in France, art might glorify the *grand monarque*. French talent was supported in a variety of creative ways which are themselves a lineament of Frenchness and do the nation credit. Some were given fiscal, military or economic exemptions, or protected from their creditors. Others, like Bruant, Mansart, Le Brun and Le Nôtre, were ennobled. Others were made *valets de chambre* or artists of the king. Many received free lodging. Dozens and dozens were given pensions, varying from trifling amounts to handsome sums: 150 livres to 58,000 livres (the latter equating to $2.9 million today).

As foreign artists were summoned to France to the service of the king, so art objects of all sorts were imported to make France a treasure house of beauty. Colbert's motto was: 'We should seek to have in France everything beautiful that there is in Italy.' At his behest Italy was ransacked for its art works. Hundreds of originals were brought to France and hundreds of others were reproduced.[30]

One of Colbert's most notorious and least praiseworthy efforts was to steal the secret of mirror-making from the Venetians. For a culture so obsessed with itself, this was – perhaps – an obvious move.

Haute Cuisine, Haute Couture, Haute Coiffure: The French Taste for Grandeur

In the mid-1660s, Louis XIV bought no fewer than one hundred and forty-four mirrors all at once for his mistress of the moment, Louise de La Vallière. This extraordinary act of extravagance shows that there was in France at the time what we might justifiably call a 'mirror craze'.

Mirrors then, however, were not too much like mirrors now. For a start, they were relatively small accessories. For technical reasons, the largest that could be produced measured only about 28 inches high. More than that, they were extremely expensive and produced only in Venice.

Mirrors in the form of highly polished metal surfaces had been known since antiquity of course. But the most important breakthrough had been made by traditional Venetian glass-blowers when, in the late fifteenth century, they had discovered the secret of making clear, colourless glass (that is, without the 'bottle'-green hue common until then), and moreover in the form of plates, in which both upper and lower surfaces were flat and parallel, so that the images reflected in them were not deformed.[1] When this flat, clear glass was backed with a silvery, reflecting metal, the modern mirror was born.

The Venetians knew the value of what they had and did everything in their power to keep the technique of mirror-making a commercial secret. That value is underlined by the fact that, during the Renaissance, a fine Venetian mirror cost more than an old master painting. Louis XIV's mother, Anne of Austria, performed her toilette in front of a mirror that was so big it was considered worth going out of one's way to see it – yet the mirror measured just 18 by 15 inches.[2]

As with most things in the realm of taste, Louis XIV led the way. In 1665, 216 crates of mirrors were shipped from Venice to France with the king himself spending more than 20,000 livres – over a million dollars at today's prices – on 400 mirrors. This did not entirely please his new finance minister, Jean-Baptiste Colbert.

The Battle of the Mirrors

By now, Colbert was in full flood as the king's financial mastermind and, only too aware that France's deficit was his chief nightmare, he now conceived a plan intended to curtail the drain of monies out of France and into Venice. In the autumn of 1664, he gave a secret instruction to the French ambassador in Venice: to identify the principal Venetian mirror-makers and entice them to defect to Paris.

The government of *La Serenissima* had passed stringent laws to protect its monopoly. Those laws stipulated that if any workman went abroad, he would be ordered to return. If he refused, all his close relatives would be imprisoned. If even that failed to persuade him, spies would be sent abroad to seek him out – and assassinate him.

The French were not blind to the risks. Pierre de Bonzi, the ambassador in Venice, wrote to Colbert that he feared that the Venetians, once they found out about the French plan, would 'toss us into the sea'.[3] Nevertheless, by April of the following year, the ambassador had made progress and identified a few possible candidates. Colbert selected a character of his own, a roving diplomat named Sieur de Jouan, and sent him to Venice to bring back the people Bonzi had identified. De Jouan managed to smuggle past the customs officials three men, one of whom may have killed a priest and was therefore only too keen to escape.

The Venetians soon cottoned on to what had happened and began questioning the relatives of the men who had disappeared.

Interrogation pointed to the French, and the authorities asked their ambassador in Paris, Alvise Sagredo, to locate the missing men. What Sagredo didn't know was that Colbert had thought ahead and had secured a *second* batch of Venetian mirror-makers – four of them this time. They escaped by boat, heading south at first to Ferrara, then overland north to Paris. Not long after their arrival – by now it was December 1665 – the minister sanctioned the creation of the Manufacture royale des glaces de miroirs, in a handsome building in the rue de Reuilly in the Faubourg Saint-Antoine, the traditional centre of furniture-making.[4] The articles of the manufactory explicitly gave the company an exclusive monopoly on mirror production throughout France, with stiff penalties for anyone disregarding the agreement. The monopoly lasted for 125 years and the company in fact still exists, under the name Saint-Gobain, the oldest continuously operated company in Europe (it made the I. M. Pei-designed glass pyramids which mark the modern entrance to the Louvre).

There now ensued a series of tit-for-tat manoeuvres as Sagredo tried to entice or threaten his fellow Venetians, and the French did all they could to keep them in Paris. They were given bonuses and offered large dowries to take French wives, and the king paid them personal visits to underline how much their presence was appreciated. For their part, the Venetians forged letters from the men's wives, begging them to return home. Unfortunately for the Venetians, the letters were written in a style way beyond the literary competence of the wives and the husbands saw through the plot.[5]

Then things turned really nasty and there was a shoot-out at the Paris factory. One man was hit in the shoulder, two others lost fingers before a passing contingent of soldiers intervened. The Venetians now turned to poisoning, and one of the mirror-polishers died after a long agony. This seems to have done the trick for the Venetians. The mirror-makers in Paris realised that they would never be left alone, and so they collectively wrote to the Venetian authorities asking forgiveness and to be allowed home. Colbert was told by his French workmen at that point that they had learned all they could from the Venetians, so he let them go.

The glass-blowing Venetians had been a fashionable attraction for *le monde*, who had turned out in well-dressed droves to watch them practise their skills, but in fact it took a while for the Royal Manufactory to produce mirrors to rival the Venetians and it was not until 1682, when the king announced that he would now govern from Versailles, that the French could be said to have outstripped the Italians. On 1 December that year, the Galerie des glaces was opened to the public, when seventeen huge mirrors, each nearly 18 feet high and 6½ feet wide, gave people the first opportunity to see their *full-length* reflection. In fact, the large mirrors were made up of many smaller ones and the French had yet to properly overtake the Venetians.[6]

The real breakthrough was made by Barnard Perrot, ironically an Italian naturalised as a Frenchman who, in March 1687, after Colbert's death, was able to *pour* glass – not blow it – on to metal tables 'of any size he chooses'. The following month the Académie royale des sciences considered his invention – as it was their duty to do – and 'gave him a certificate'. This is when the French at last began to pull ahead. In 1696, Jean Haudicquer de Blancourt published *L'Art de la verrerie* ('The Art of Glassmaking'), including mirror-making, which he referred to as 'the most glorious of all works of art'. Now mirrors of a decent size began to enter private houses, which of course did wonders for the fashion business, as women (and men) could prepare themselves for presentation in everyday life in the privacy of their homes.

Price was still a factor. A large mirror – for example, say, one about 9 or 10 feet tall – could cost as much as 3,000 livres, more than $150,000 at today's prices. Yet in the last twenty years of the seventeenth century, half the households in Paris bought a mirror from the royal company.[7]

And there was one final advance to be made in keeping with the theme of this book. It came in 1699 when Robert de Cotte, one of the architects at work on Versailles, hung a large mirror over a fireplace. Cotte subsequently became a very fashionable interior decorator and everywhere he went he put mirrors over fireplaces. This 'fireplace look', known as '*cheminées à la royale*', or '*à la française*', was originally a way for everybody's home to have a 'touch' of Versailles but it turned out to be one of the very greatest interior decorating innovations of all time.

THE FOOD REVOLUTION

Just as the latter half of the seventeenth century was the time when salon life took off, and when the academies of French classical culture became established, so too was it the time when the crucial elements of what we might call French style fell into place.

To begin with, in 1651, the first year of the second half of the seventeenth century (and in the middle of the Fronde), François Pierre published *Le Cuisinier français* ('The French Chef'), and we may say that *haute cuisine* was thereby created. Born in Burgundy, Pierre became in time chef to the Marquis d'Uxelles, governor of Chalon-sur-Saône. He was always more than a chef, being the governor's kitchen clerk, a sort of below-stairs administrator. And it was while Pierre was in the employ of the Chalon governor that he began preparing his book. In fact, this book has come to be regarded as 'the first great cookbook, the first modern cookbook, and the harbinger of a culinary revolution as a result of which food became cuisine and cuisine became French'.[8]

One clever seventeenth-century marketing device was that Pierre wrote the book under the name La Varenne, chef to Henry IV, probably at that point France's most popular king who had by then been safely dead for more than forty years. As a result of La Varenne's book, which was reprinted twelve times in its first five years, and forty-six times by the end of the century, 'cooking and eating became more and more to be thought of no longer as a simple necessity but as a domain in which sophistication was possible and desirable'.[9] Terms were now applied to French cuisine that had never been heard before – 'refined', 'courteous', 'civilised' – a vocabulary very similar to that used about salon society, which of course adopted the new fashion with alacrity, a process that also ensured that Paris became accepted as gastronomy's international capital and a tourist attraction.

Le Cuisinier français included a eulogy on the superiority of the 'French way of life', the first of many. Until that point, as with Venetian mirrors, and the classical art available in Rome, Italian cuisine had been regarded as superior. But now food prepared *'alla francese'* or *'perfezionato a Parigi'* began to take over, and the French *cuisinier* (never a *cuisinière*) had a lock on *haute cuisine*. This was confirmed by the English translation of La Varenne's book, which appeared two years after its French publication.[10]

What, exactly, was this new cuisine? In the first place, La Varenne made explicit the techniques that have served ever since for the production of stocks, codifying recipes that produced the basic mixtures of herbs, such as the blend now called bouquet garni. He disliked the thin and sour sauces then common and instead much preferred butter as a basis; this was when thicker meat sauces began to proliferate. He helped popularise hollandaise sauce (eggs, butter, lemon, salt and pepper) and may have invented it.

Whereas beforehand cooking had been mainly about nutrition, La Varenne advocated that it should be about the pleasures of taste, and that richness of food was not to be dismissed. Importantly, he was one of the first to eschew spices from the Orient (nutmeg, cinnamon and ginger had been the staples of earlier recipes); he relied instead on plants nearer home – parsley, shallots, onions and leeks, and he identified bouillon as the basis for meat sauces.

Second, he explained – clearly and simply – a clutch of recipes, and these were numbered and alphabetised. Third, he presented his book not as literature exactly, but it was written in the first person, and was full of his ideas, views and personality, and he thereby invited readers to think about the philosophy of food and its place in a well-lived life. But perhaps above all what the book offered were his own new recipes and the clear exposition of those that would become classics: *bœuf à la mode, poissons au bleu, œufs à la neige*. He also separated salt and sugar, moving sweeter dishes to the end of the proceedings; this was the start of the concept of *le dessert*.

The concept of meat was also changed. Out went the big birds like peacock and in came veal, lamb, fowl and game birds.[11] Beef was used mainly for making stock – bouillon. Until this time, vegetables had been frowned upon, as indigestible and coarse, fit only for peasants, but La Varenne's book promoted vegetables as healthy.[12] As a result during the second half of the century, kitchen gardens and fruit orchards became increasingly popular.

When La Varenne's book appeared, according to Joan DeJean, no new cookery books had appeared in France for more than a hundred years, but the change in the air that was evident was underlined by the publication soon after of other cookbooks. In the same year as La Varenne published his book, Nicolas de Bonnefons released *Le Jardinier français*. Two years later La Varenne himself published *Le Pâtissier français* (the first book to be devoted entirely to pastry, then defined as 'making everything with a crust') and a year after that Bonnefons came out with *Les Délices de la campagne* and the culinary revolution in France was well under way.

Bringing up the rear in this new development was François Massialot's 1691 title, *Le Cuisinier royal et bourgeois*, almost as good a bestseller as La Varenne's books, which became well known for its author's invention, or popularisation, of the 'stew'. This was helped along by scientist Denis Papin's 1682 invention of the pressure cooker, which made it possible, as Papin himself said, 'to cook all types of meat in very little time'.[13]

Alongside all this, and not surprisingly perhaps, there arose a literature related to fine entertaining, which included the presentation of food (quite different from its preparation), the serving of food (in French service one helped oneself from the centre of the table), when to serve dipping sauces and with which foods, and how to fold napkins. This represented the growth of food sophistication.

By now, in late seventeenth-century Paris, food was served in a range of establishments but the nobles, when they weren't dining in the salons, ate out only '*chez le traiteur*'.[14] This was an early form of chic restaurant where as much attention was devoted to atmosphere and to the presentation of food as to the food itself. One guide to Paris in the 1690s listed thirty-four *traiteurs*: Aux bons enfants near the Palais-Royal, À la galerie on the rue de Seine, Aux bâtons royaux on the rue Saint-Honoré, and so on. By the end of the Sun King's reign a fully fledged *traiteur*/restaurant scene had emerged in Paris, chronicled by the Abbé Prévost, who set an episode in his novel *Mémoires et aventures d'un homme de qualité* in one of the best-known *traiteurs*, called Fracin.

The invention of *haute cuisine* also helped the invention of the dining room – and dining tables, dining plates and much else besides. Until the widespread circulation of porcelain (another stylistic innovation), in the 1690s, dining plates had invariably been metal – gold for the king, silver for the wealthy and pewter for everyone else. Antoine Courtine's 1671 book, *Nouveau traité de la civilité qui se pratique en France* ('A New Treatise on the Rules of Politeness in France'), stipulated that diners must not use their fingers to transfer food from the serving dishes to their plates, and use spoons instead.[15] (It is said that Louis XIV never touched a fork and that those who dined with him used only their knives and fingers.)

Inevitably the new culture of cuisine spawned names for those who now enjoyed food above all else. One word, which has survived, was *gourmet* but the first, not used now, was *côteaux*, in reference to the sloping hills where the finest wines were (and still are) grown.

PERFUMED GLOVES AND STATIONERY

In March 1656, Louis XIV, who is known not to have liked water, issued letters patent which conferred legitimacy on the first guild licensed to make perfume in his realm. The king, and later Colbert, were aware that France was paying out large sums, as with mirrors, for aromatics – in fact, the French were the largest consumers of such products, and the monies leaching out of the country were too much for them both to swallow. As a result, under the supervision of the French East India Company, aromatics were planted in large numbers on the French islands in the Indian Ocean – Île de France (now Mauritius) and Île Bourbon (Réunion). The move was a success: patchouli Bourbon and oil of vetiver Bourbon became perfume 'classics'.[16]

In 1673, Colbert built on this, giving glover-perfumers (perfumed gloves then being a very fashionable product) tax-free access to the aromatics from the Indian Ocean. And, at much the same time, he chose the town of Grasse, in the warm, fertile hills behind Cannes in the south of France, as the hub of the fragrance-producing business. Grasse rose to prominence on the strength of its involvement with scented gloves but in the seventeenth century it was producing oils from flowers such as jasmine, violet, orange and tuberose, introduced from Mexico only in 1670.[17]

In this way the fragrances of France – like its cuisine – were transformed. Until then, most perfumed goods – throughout Europe, not just in France – were made from animal products: civet was a musky fluid secreted by a cat-like mammal native to Africa and Asia; ambergris was formed in the intestines of sperm whales. Instead, Grasse began to specialise in more local vegetable products – orange blossom and lavender. Just as French chefs were breaking free of foreign ingredients, so too were French perfumers.

This provoked a change in commercial procedures, and shops began to open up in Paris selling the new substances, often marketed as powders or soaps. The perfumer Jobert, on the rue Croix-des-Petits-Champs, became famous for his potpourris (a variety of dried petals). The most celebrated perfumer was Simon Barbe, who, in addition to selling aromatic substances, published in 1693 a compendium, *Le Parfumeur français*. He followed it up with *Le Parfumeur royal*, 1699, which went into the intimate business of teaching readers how to make themselves smell good, beginning with soap.[18]

Barbe extended the concept of potpourri, advocating that people wear 'sweet bags' about their person to make them smell better, and also suggested that, in addition to scented gloves, handkerchiefs and even fans be powdered. For women he even proposed they wear potpourri sachets in their undergarments. This would, he tactfully suggested, 'correct imperfections'.

The one item above all that needed to be scented was the wig. And not only scented, for powders could also tint the hair or the wig. Hair colour at that time was changed – or enhanced – by pastes or ointments, known as pomades. However, by far the most popular colour for hair was silver, or silvery-white, what we would now call grey. This was a very difficult colour to achieve (for the young, that is). In fact it could only be found in the silvery powder known as argentine, and its rarity made it very expensive. Nor was its use much helped by the way it needed to be administered. To achieve a flawless grey-white look, Joan DeJean tells us, 'it was necessary to blanket the head with argentine. A perfumer-powderer threw an enormous quantity of powder up at the ceiling. Newly coiffed nobles then positioned themselves so that the falling cloud landed on their heads.'[19]

Alongside the growth of the perfume business, and with the widening use of mirrors, in about 1680 the phrase *la toilette* came into use, to describe the process by which the nobility prepared themselves every morning to face the world. The word *toilette* came from *toile*, meaning 'cloth', a *toilette* being the little cloth on which the accessories necessary for grooming were laid out. This process could take as much as three hours – and that applied equally to men as to women. This did not refer just to perfumes, of course, but to preparations regarding the health of the skin (adverts for which first appeared in the press in 1667), the coiffure (which we shall come to) and other aspects of grooming. The dressing table soon led to the dressing room. In fact, *la toilette* became a social ritual in itself. People visited each other while they were getting ready and the state of undress, even *déshabillé*, became in itself fashionable.

Incidentally, the one thing not considered essential to *la toilette* was water. People in Paris *washed* on a regular basis but rarely *bathed*.

'Big Hair'

Until the middle of the seventeenth century, in most places in Europe, and bizarre as it seems now, barbers doubled up as surgeons. But in 1659 a royal edict in France created the speciality of 'barber-wig-maker'.[20] To begin with they worked exclusively for men, and forsook all medical activity. Until that point women's hair was prepared by their maids and it was regarded as unseemly for men to touch a woman's head.

That all changed with the arrival of Monsieur Champagne. Champagne was the first hair stylist that we know about in history and the inventor of *haute coiffure*, the phrase itself being a new invention too. The usage came about because, during the Middle Ages and then the Renaissance, women across Europe wore *coiffes* – wimples, bonnets and other pieces of fabric which covered the head (it was a form of modesty). Beginning in Paris in the 1660s, however, the word began to refer to the hair itself, and the associated taffeta or lace was regarded henceforth merely as an accessory.

The word *coiffeur* was first used about Champagne in 1663, but by 1694, when the Académie française finally published its dictionary, it referred to '*coiffeurs and coiffeuses à la mode*'. By then, the speciality of hairdresser had emerged and matured, and was applied to women's hair as much as men's, with hairdressers inventing new styles for each new 'season'. As we have come to expect, their activities were widely satirised in the plays of the time, and it was in the script of *Champagne le coiffeur*, a satire about the number-one specialist, staged at the théâtre du Marais in 1663 shortly after his death, that the word *coiffeur* was first set down in print. Pierre Boucher, a seventeenth-century author specialising in travel subjects, identified a number of fashionable hair stylists in Paris, as did Gédéon Tallemant des Réaux, who recorded which elegant ladies visited which hair stylist every day, and which ones took Champagne or his later colleagues on foreign voyages so as to ensure they were always well presented wherever they were.

This development was helped by the creation of hairdressing shops ('salons', as we would say today). Until towards the end of the century, the hair stylist would visit the homes of their customers, but with the development of the shop, or salon, women visited the stylist, meeting other women there, of course, and seeing who liked what.[21] Fashions changed wildly, from very 'big' hair (literally: the styles could be 2 feet high; Saint-Simon quipped that women's heads were now 'in the middle of their bodies'), to very curly, to flat.

In March 1671, the Marquise de Sévigné, in one of her celebrated letters to her daughter in Provence, described women who had followed the new look for very short hair as 'completely naked', with 'little heads of cabbage', and she reported that the king had 'doubled over with laughter at the sight'. She went on to describe how, in order to achieve the new look, women were forced to sleep 'with a hundred rollers, which makes them endure mortal agony all night long'.[22]

Fashions changed so fast, and were so distinctive, that art historians say it is possible to date late seventeenth-century paintings from the hairstyles of the women depicted. The most celebrated of these styles was the '*fontanges*', so called because one of the mistresses of the king, Marie-Angélique de Scoraille, Duchesse de Fontanges, had tied her hair in a ribbon in a way that made her curls spill down over her forehead. The king liked it so much he asked her never to change it, and that meant of course that most of the women at court had to do the same.

The fashion for big hair vanished as quickly as it had arisen and by the end of Louis XIV's reign, according to Saint-Simon, '*l'extrémité du plat*' had been reached. Even so, as Montesquieu phrased it in his 1721 novel, *The Persian Letters*, 'whenever a lady has her hair done anywhere in Europe, she slavishly respects the edicts of French *coiffeuses*'.[23]

THE FASHION 'SEASON'

Hair and perfume were not the only elements of the fashionable world that took off in the late seventeenth century. In fact, it was in the 1670s that the fashion *industry* came into being.[24] What came together was an increasing number of people interested in clothes, increasingly sophisticated ways of supplying the demand, and for the first time new ways of spreading information about new trends, the beginnings of a publicity machine. Along with this went the growth of the speciality of fashion designers and shops selling clothes 'off the peg', rather than being specially designed for just one individual, though that existed too.

One interesting development occurred around 1650, when records show that women for the first time began to outspend men on their clothes. Another innovation occurred in 1672 when the fashion press began, and Jean Donneau de Visé launched his newspaper, *Le Mercure galant*. Its pages covered everything from general news to the social scene, arts and letters, trends in decorating and style, 'all things haute'. He aimed the bulk of his coverage at women and, in a remarkable innovation, he announced in January 1678 that he would publish a supplement at the beginning of every year, giving all the information that he could gather about 'la mode'. In that way the fashion 'season' was conceived, with the implied idea that fashions would change from year to year. Accessories began to be invented – or reinvented – on a seasonal basis.[25]

A couturiers' trade guild was formed in 1675 but they were allowed to sew only for women and children and were forbidden to design formal dresses for ladies of quality – that remained the privilege of tailors. Not to be outdone, the new guild members came up with the mantua or manteau, a sort of more or less fashionable housecoat women could wear about the house – and even in public – as a more relaxed look. Being loose-fitting, this garment allowed more of women's bodies – and their undergarments – to be glimpsed and this was a subtle form of female emancipation.[26]

The creation of *Le Mercure galant* and the invention of the fashion plate were both important elements in the growth of the *mode française* but so too was something less predictable. In that same decade, the 1670s, when Mme de Sévigné had worried that her words were failing her when describing to her daughter Françoise the lovely details of the latest fashions, she decided instead to send her – all the way to Provence in the warm south – a set of dolls. These too were an innovation of the times. They were decked out in miniature versions of the latest fashion concoctions and posted all over Europe as enticing ways to market the latest creations. Known as 'jointed babies' or as 'mannequins', they were usually about 2 feet high, made of wood, but with human hair.

Fashion mania spread everywhere and not least to shoes, including boots, high heels, which the king – being only 5 feet 5½ inches small – favoured, and, perhaps most influential of all, the mule or slipper. Once again, we find the Marquise de Sévigné in thrall to this fashion, writing to her daughter that a friend is on his way to see her, who has in his bag 'two pairs of shoes made by Georget', the 'in' designer of the moment. The mule – slight, elegant, casual, perfectly suited to the delicate female foot – was popular throughout the seventeenth and eighteenth centuries and may be seen in many of the paintings of Fragonard, Watteau and Boucher. Donneau de Visé, in his capacity as editor of *Le Mercure galant*, declared 1677 'the year of the shoe'.

THE CHAMPAGNE EXPLOSION

Far away from the world of fashion was Dom Pérignon, the man who invented the most fashionable drink of all, champagne, perhaps the *nonpareil* epitome of the French way of life.

It was an uncommonly rapid development. 'In 1669, champagne did not yet exist. By 1674, it not only existed but was being celebrated in the original guide to trendy food and wine as the "in" wine of the moment and one of the finest wines of France.' From then on, says

Joan DeJean, 'champagne's rise to prominence was unstoppable'. In his poem 'Le Mondain', Voltaire put it this way: 'The sparkling foam of this frosty wine / Is the brilliant image of our Frenchman.'[27]

The sparkling foam was the creation of just one man, Dom Pierre Pérignon, a Benedictine monk, and the seventh son of a clerk in the town of Sainte-Menehould, who attended the Jesuit school at Châlons-sur-Marne. The rule of the Benedictine order, which he joined, stipulated manual labour as one of the aspects of a fulfilling life and, since Pérignon's family owned several vineyards, when he joined the Abbaye Saint-Pierre d'Hautvillers, near Reims, he became *cellier* and remained in that post for the rest of his life.

Until that point champagne had been light red or pink still wine, made from pinot noir grapes. However, just then taste was moving towards white wine, or rather *vin gris*, 'grey wine', which was white wine made from red grapes. Change was in the air and Dom Pérignon made the most of it – he seems to have had an experimental nature. For example, he blended grapes from different vineyards, grapes of different quality and grapes at different stages of ripeness. It was this latter in particular that added sparkle to wine. He was alive to the ageing of wine and to the fact that wine aged better in bottles than in casks.

But his most important innovation, of course, was the double fermentation of champagne, which makes it bubbly. Because the Champagne region, being in the north, is the coldest wine-growing area in France, the low temperatures naturally halt the wine's fermentation before all the grape sugar has been processed. When warm weather returns, usually just after Easter, a second fermentation begins, a process that happens nowhere else. Dom Pérignon also understood that nature had to be helped along by adding a mixture of alcohol and sugar, what became known as the *liqueur de tirage* that facilitates the second fermentation. As a result, the added sugar in the *liqueur* is converted into alcohol and natural carbon dioxide gas.[28]

Other innovations were necessary – for example, extra-strong glass bottles to withstand the heavy pressure of the bubbles inside. But apart from the new method Dom Pérignon created, the most extraordinary thing about champagne is the way it took off. In 1674, barely five years after the invention, *The Art of Fine Entertaining*, one of the first books to mark the advent of French *haute cuisine*, also welcomed champagne as 'the hottest thing ... its taste is so charming and its aroma so sweet that it can revive a dead man'. In the 1712 edition of his *Cooking for Royalty and for the Bourgeoisie*, François Massialot was among the first to recommend that champagne was invariably better than other wines to be used in *haute cuisine*. Antoine Furetière, in the Académie française's dictionary – published at last in 1694 – said in his definition of champagne: 'If you want to *régaler* someone, you must serve champagne.'[29]

COFFEE/CAFÉ CULTURE

The final element in this set of virtually simultaneous extraordinary stylish achievements, made in France – and mainly in Paris – in the last half of the seventeenth century, was the café. And just as Dom Pérignon single-handedly created champagne, so – to begin with – one man created the café.

Coffee in fact arrived in France, to be consumed in private homes, as early as the 1640s. It came via the port of Marseilles, which would remain the hub of the coffee trade for some time. At that stage coffee was wildly expensive – a pound of beans could set you back 80 livres, the equivalent of more than $4,000 today, ten times what a bottle of champagne cost.[30] As often as not coffee was presented with Turkish or Armenian links and it was also said to have admirable medicinal qualities – it cured migraines and constipation, regulated menstruation and stimulated the appetite. It was to be drunk as hot as possible, preferably from a porcelain cup, and its bitter taste should be ameliorated with a lump of sugar (itself new and also very expensive). In a letter written in January 1690 the Marquise de Sévigné referred to the addition of milk, 'coffeed milk' or 'milked coffee'.[31]

Coffee was introduced to Parisians beyond the noble elite at the Saint-Germain Fair, an annual event held near the Abbey of Saint-Germain-des-Prés, where everything was sold, from wild animals to old master paintings. The coffee at the fair was sold from a booth operated by an Armenian called Harouthioun, also known as Pascal, and he went on to open a coffee house near the site of the fair. That foundered, however, and it was left to a Sicilian, Francesco Procopio dei Coltelli, who had worked for Pascal, to open the first establishment that really caught on.

Procopio – who soon Gallicised his name to Procope – spotted that the secret of coffee was that, because it was expensive, at least to begin with, and needed to attract the fashionable women of Paris, it needed to be made glamorous. His café, opened in 1675 or the year after in the rue de Tournon, had tables made of marble, and the coffee was served from silver pots, while chandeliers hung from the ceilings. On the walls were tapestries and old masters but also the new mirrors made in France, the ones that were much bigger than their Italian rivals. His waiters were decked out as Armenians – with colourful garb and fur hats. To begin with, going to a café was known in Paris as 'going to the Armenians'.

The café Procope was fashionable even at its opening, but its allure was added to when, in 1686, it moved a short distance to the rue des Fossés Saint-Germain (today's rue de l'Ancienne Comédie) where, three years later, the Comédie-Française set up premises more or less opposite. From then on, the Procope became *the* in place for actors and theatre-lovers, *la bonne compagnie*. Procope had the idea to serve interval drinks, where everyone came to see and be seen.[32]

Other cafés quickly followed – Laurent's for writers for instance – and the practice developed of going out for coffee after lunch, and to consume a small pastry. By 1715, according to one guidebook, there were between 300 and 350 cafés in Paris, where the secret was that women were a fixture, unlike in other countries, Britain, say, or Germany, where 'coffee houses' were more a male domain. Jean-Baptiste Rousseau's 1694 comedy, *Le Café*, suggests that there were even 'women's hours' in Parisian cafés, when the fashionable set were apt to meet.

Not only coffee was served. Tea and chocolate were also popular, and the cafés were also known as *limonadiers*, or places where 'soft drinks' were sold. The quotes are necessary because, in fact, many of them had alcoholic bases – they were what we would call cocktails. Some were very exotic. For instance, *rossoly* (*rosée du soleil*, or 'dew of the sun') contained fennel, anise, coriander, dill and caraway seeds. They were crushed together and macerated in the sun, and then a dose of brandy was added.[33]

By our standards the coffee offered in those days was weak. An ounce of ground coffee was added to a pint of water and brought to the boil ten times. It was then strained before being served. The first cup cost 2½ sous – roughly $6.

Newspapers were introduced at about this time, and cafés were natural places for the circulation of news. Newsboys would tour the cafés with their papers.[34]

Social life and public opinion were also aided by the introduction, in September 1667, of 2,736 glass lanterns positioned throughout the 912 streets of Paris. The city thus became the first to be lit at night, an amazing concept at the time and an equally amazing achievement. It was expensive (200,000 livres, $10 million annually for the candle wax alone) and had to be paid for by a new 'mud and lantern tax', with the Royal Academy of Sciences well placed to authorise the various reflector devices introduced. But the innovation more than paid for itself by creating a night life in Paris that had simply not existed before. The lighting changed the rhythm of the city in commercial terms (shopping did not have to end with the end of daylight), and the social life of the city could carry on until all hours, salon life included. In December 1673, the Marquise de Sévigné records how she and her friends were delighted that their dinner party did not break up until after midnight and that they were then able to help take one of their number home right across the city. 'We came home merrily, all because of the new lanterns.'[35]

Salons as 'Schools of Civilisation': Intellect in Fashion, Intellect *as* Fashion

I t is notable that in the history of salon life, and salon culture, what is stressed is the overlap between what we might call high culture – conversations about philosophy, literature, art criticism and collecting, natural history and science, interchanges between philosophers, writers, historians, politicians and *salonnières*. This is natural enough. But it is the argument of this book that the salons were also the crucible of French style and taste, and that style and taste included the bringing together of much else besides high culture, into a very cosmopolitan *mondain* mix of exactly those elements we have been considering in this section: *haute cuisine, haute couture, haute coiffure*, fine wines, all the fashionable ingredients of the *haute* or high life. It was this *amalgam* of classical high culture and style that first occurred to any extent in France in the late seventeenth century, and the fact that salon society of the high nobility enthusiastically espoused this approach, and led the way, that gave it a legitimacy that never existed anywhere else in quite this way. In effect, the intellect became fashionable, a phenomenon that has remained true in France, and is more true of French culture than of anywhere else.

WOMEN AS CIVILISERS

In most of the accounts of salon society, the stylish ingredients are ignored, overlooked entirely or downplayed, but the supporting evidence is there, once you look for it.[1] In his study of French salons, for example, Steven Kale says they encouraged socialising between the sexes, afforded opportunities for intellectual speculation, provided a setting for feminine literary expression and permitted the *philosophes* to display themselves to *le monde*, 'the fashionable world'.[2] 'Salons persisted because they were anchored to stable cultural norms defined by feminine attributes,' he writes, adding: 'Since the seventeenth century, those aspiring to elite status had "to go to the school of the ladies".'[3] Roger Picard in his study of literary salons phrased it this way: 'Salons became veritable schools of general culture for people of the world ... Civilised attention to the ladies required magnanimity between the sexes, ascribing to women the role of teaching men how to act toward "the fairer sex". Pleasing women therefore became not only the font of mondain civility but an ethical cornerstone that complemented the importance of patrimony and lineage in noble society. The counterpart of *galanterie* was the notion of women as civilisers. The salon eventually became the principal depository of this legacy of noble civility and sexual "commerce" ... and made France uniquely sociable.'[4]

We have already seen several times how the Marquise de Sévigné, in writing to her daughter, Françoise, took a keen interest in the craze for mirrors, in perfume, in the new 'cabbage-style' hair fashions, in the latest dresses on fashion dolls, and in the new taste for coffee.[5] We know she discussed these matters with her friend Mme de Scudéry and there is no reason to assume they were any different from the other people they mixed with.

In fact, if you dip into Mme de Sévigné's letters at random you can find references to the fads and fashions of the day wherever you look. Here she is in April 1671: 'Yesterday, I saw the Duchesse de Sully and the Comtesse de Guiche, whose head-dresses are charming. I am converted. This style is made for you, you will look an angel, and it takes no time to do.'[6] And here she is only a few weeks later, in June of that same year, in another letter to her daughter: 'I am glad you can turn your mind to dress. Do you recollect how tired we grew of that old black mantle you wore? No doubt it was meritorious but scarcely attractive to onlookers. I fear you will find it difficult to lengthen your short skirts. The fashion has reached us here;

the young ladies ... wear them just above the ankle.'[7] In October 1676, she again writes to Françoise: 'M de Langlée gave Mme de Montespan the gift of a gown of gold, lined and hemmed with gold and gold appliqué, and over all rolled gold, richly embroidered, superimposed over yet another kind of gold, the most divine material ever conceived, doubtless the handiwork of fairies unseen by mortal eye.'[8]

With such a description as this, one can see why Daniel Roche, in his 1994 book, *The Culture of Clothing*, originally published in French as *La Culture des apparences* (1989), not quite the same thing, reports that the majority of nobles, in pre-Revolutionary France, spent a hundred times more on clothes than did the working classes. Clothes, he says, were a way of demonstrating rank and acquiring prestige; the 'appeal of an attractive appearance' and care of the body were the 'imperatives of Parisian good form'.[9] He adds: 'The first readers of *Le Cabinet des modes*, *Le Journal des dames* and *Les Amusements de la toilette*, the aristocracy of court and town, played a role in proportion to their means and psychological resources ... Through these journals elegant citizens of both sexes breathed the air of Paris and found a subject for their worldly conversations.'[10]

CLOTHING AS A BRANCH OF PHILOSOPHY

The fashion merchant (*marchande des modes*) appeared at the end of the seventeenth century, at which time the toilette became 'a favourite theme of gallant painting' and accessories likewise became essential as aids to elegance.[11] At this same time under the aegis of the Académie royale des sciences, the Parisian master tailor de Garsault produced *L'Art du perruquier*, *L'Art du tailleur* and *L'Art de la lingère*, in which he explored the link between clothes, style, 'good form' and human psychology. *Les Règles de la bienséance et de la civilité*, published in 1703, which went into 175 editions, explored manners in polite society and was read by all classes. Even the *Encyclopédie*, which we shall come to, had 3,036 entries in it relating to style and fashion.[12] Many of these are about sociological, cultural, historical and moral issues having to do with style and fashion. The *Encyclopédie*, Roche says, 'asserted and exalted the conquest of manners ... The clothes trades were clearly ranked among the most important branch of philosophy', and included the activities of those 'occupied not in making us think we are happy but in actually making us so'.[13]

On the other hand, the philosophical critique of manners imposed a morality of dress.[14] There was a wide debate about the place of luxury in society. Montesquieu found that the social world 'seemed as natural as nature' but added that it survived only 'by magic and enchantment'. The Marquis de Saint-Lambert, who authored the article on luxury in the *Encyclopédie*, linked it directly to appearance and the comfort of life.[15] The very fact that the French insisted that they had invented *haute cuisine*, *haute couture* and *haute coiffure* shows that their longing for grandeur was a byproduct of the *grand siècle*.

Lucy Moore tells us that *salonnières* changed their clothes several times a day. Marc Fumaroli adds that salons were the *écoles supérieures* of fashionable society, where instruction was carried out 'by example and symbiosis, and not by explicit lessons'.[16] Roger Picard says that gastronomy, music, dance and satire were typical mixes of the salons. More than one notable admired the Abbé Morellet's 'skill in carving a pullet'.[17] Voltaire purged himself regularly before sitting down to table in order to eat his fill without any fear of indigestion.[18] 'The science of flavours gave the culture of the century an extraordinary verve and imparted enormous impetus to the scintillating ideas of philosophers and intellectual ladies ... French conversation, which earned for our books of quality their universal readership, attained its height of perfection at table.'[19]

THE ARTS OF LIBERATION

Clothing and its excesses were at times regarded as signs of moral disorder – 'Our clothes are fetters!' – and discussed as such in the press and salons.[20]

Yet Roche reports that fashion dolls were eagerly discussed at court. 'In France the Hôtel de Rambouillet and les Précieuses devoted exhibitions of these fragile mannequins made of wax, wood or porcelain, their clothes changing with the season.' He goes so far as to say that they were an aspect of the Enlightenment.[21]

Essentially, what developed, as Roche puts it, was an 'ideology of the wise use of fashion', as part of a 'pleasure ethic' associated with a new vision of life devoted to what were admitted to be 'minor arts' but which nonetheless were felt to be instruments of liberation. 'The educated and scholarly milieus, at least as they are revealed in the *Enyclopédie* or the socialised world of the academies, both observed and debated modes of dress; their fascination with manners did not prevent them from being taken as seriously as other branches of the tree of knowledge ... it was also the case that these men of letters and artists, amateurs and scholars, united "by the common good of the human race and a reciprocal sentiment of benevolence", could not but be influenced in their ordinary way of life and choice of clothes by the milieu with which they lived in symbiosis.'[22]

Victor Du Bled, a veteran observer of the French social scene, said this as late as 1900: 'The salons of the nineteenth century remained to some extent what they were in the past: schools of civilisation, where the art of conversation produced a charming *douceur de vivre*, thanks to women.' In our own day, French historians Mona Ozouf and Élisabeth Badinter find that the spirit of the salons lives on in French cultural life generally, where the country abhors 'the war of the sexes or their physical separation'.[23]

And so three elements came together in France, and in Paris above all, in the late seventeenth century: the salon; the establishment of the high-culture academies and equivalent institutions, such as the Comédie-Française; and the central ingredients of a stylish, sophisticated and pleasurable life. It is the *mix* which is important. It helps to show how high culture and intellectual matters became so prominent in the French way of life, and why what some people consider the 'minor' arts – fashion, food, interior decoration, entertaining – acquired a cachet in France long before they did elsewhere. It is what many French people, even today, believe sets them apart.

But there is another aspect to this mix, no less important. Montesquieu was to observe that the sociability of the salon was as natural as nature and that was no more than the truth. Salons, especially to some, were frivolous entities, run by *salonnières*, women whose intellects were not up to the serious business of thinking. But, as we shall see, salons were very stable affairs and that was because they fulfilled a real social/intellectual need.

In fact, the salons recognised, implicitly, that the social and the intellectual are not at all at odds with one another, or do not need to be. In many countries (Britain, for example, or Prussia) intellectual affairs were the business of the universities, or laboratories, and could be quite separate from the fashionable social life of those countries. In France, on the other hand, the salons arose naturally, as a reaction to the overwhelming centrality of the king's court, and so they evolved, over time, into relatively stable forms of activity, which were part seminar, part dinner party, part flirtation, part intellectual sharing and part intellectual competition. No doubt they had their frivolous moments – one certainly hopes so – but they were essentially stable, they endured. French thinkers maintained the inherent sociability of human beings, in contrast to a Hobbesian unsociable man.[24]

As a result the salons played a more important role in French history than they are usually given credit for. In the first place, as we shall now see, they were a formative element in the Enlightenment. Second, they played a contributing role in the intellectual transformations that brought about the Revolution of 1789. And third, in the nineteenth century, they played a vital role in keeping alive many of the pre-Revolutionary ideas that gave France an intellectual productivity – and stability – that she did not have in politics.

The Orléans Alternative

On 2 September 1715, the day after Louis XIV died, four days short of his seventy-seventh birthday, his nephew, Philippe d'Orléans, assumed the regency and instructed the Parlement of Paris to annul the late king's will. He installed the five-year-old Louis XV in the Tuileries and administered France from the Palais-Royal.

The whole world has heard of Versailles. Everybody knows about the Louvre. In this book a third building in France will feature prominently which is much less familiar but has had just as much impact on modern France as either of those better-known palaces. The building was once described as 'the most beautiful house in Europe'.

It is safe to say that without the Palais-Royal, in central Paris, the French Revolution would not have happened as it did – and arguably it might not have happened at all. This is a big, contentious thing to say, but the Palais-Royal was for nearly two hundred years the home of the Orléans family, the second family of France, the cadet branch of the Bourbons. Over those two hundred years – roughly speaking 1650 to 1850 – the Orléans family went from being rebels, leading the attempt to bring down their cousins, the senior branch of the royal family, to regents, running the kingdom on behalf of those cousins, to regicides, voting for their cousin's execution, to – in the final analysis – usurpers of those cousins, serving as kings of France themselves – though as very un-regal monarchs – until they were forced to abdicate in favour of a Napoleon. It is a story full of unrivalled drama, unimaginable wealth, heart-warming and heart-breaking love affairs, spectacular extravagance and sensational reversals of fortune; of incest, cuckoldry and other forms of sexual scandal; of poisonings, miscarriages of justice, murder and a major mystery. The Orléans' saga is the story of the longest-lived – and arguably most consequential – family quarrel in history.

More than that, the Palais-Royal served as the axis for what many historians regard as the most important and pivotal event in European history: the French Revolution. The biography of the Palais-Royal – in the very centre of Paris, unlike Versailles – is every bit as fascinating and contentious as the eight generations of the Orléans family itself.

For clarity's sake those eight generations are:

1. Gaston d'Orléans (1608–60), rebel brother of Louis XIII
2. Anne-Marie-Louise 'La Grande Mademoiselle' (1627–93), daughter of Gaston
3. Philippe I 'Monsieur' (1640–1701), cousin of Anne-Marie, brother of Louis XIV, cuckold
4. Philippe II (1674–1723), regent of France, roué and the nation's greatest collector
5. Louis (1703–52), who 'collected' (bought up) 20 *per cent* of the land in France
6. Louis Philippe 'Philip the Fat' (1725–85), under whom the Palais-Royal became 'the most beautiful house in Europe'
7. Louis Philippe Joseph 'Philippe Égalité' (1747–93), the most extraordinary Orléans of all; regicide; guillotined
8. Louis Philippe (1773–1850), against all the odds, king of the French

From Monsieur onwards, all the ducs d'Orléans lived in the Palais-Royal. The palace is situated at the eastern end of the rue Saint-Honoré and is located about 500 yards north of the glass pyramid that now marks the entrance to the Louvre. It is roughly the size of a New York City cross-town block and is shaped like a massive H but with two crossbars. In the bottom left-hand corner is the Théâtre-Français, otherwise the Comédie-Française. The famous cigar and rum shop À la civette is opposite.

The ironies in the Orléans saga are endless but the central one occurred in 1692, almost exactly a century before the outbreak of revolution, when Louis XIV, the Sun King, wished to marry off Mlle de Blois, his illegitimate daughter by his mistress Louise de La Vallière, Mme de Montespan. He settled on his brother's only son, the future regent. His brother, known as Monsieur, was not keen on the proposition, and so, as part of the deal the king agreed to make over to his brother the Palais-Royal. He couldn't know it but from that point on the Palais-Royal building gradually acquired a cachet for being a Parisian alternative to Versailles – artistically, intellectually and eventually politically.

The palace was not at first known as the Palais-Royal. It was originally built by Armand Jean du Plessis, Cardinal Richelieu, in 1629. Upon Richelieu's death, the Palais-Cardinal was ceded to Louis XIII, when it was renamed the Palais-Royal, because it now served as the childhood home of Louis XIV during the regency of Anne of Austria (1643–51). During her regency, she installed a 'throne room' in the Palais-Royal and ran the country from there, with the aid of Cardinal Mazarin. A close relationship developed between Anne and Mazarin, who were almost certainly lovers. Their major diplomatic achievement was organised from the Palais and comprised the remarkable feat of negotiating the Treaty of Westphalia, bringing a settlement to the Thirty Years War, and the end of chronic religious conflict across Europe.

Educated in the palace, the young Louis XIV was given his first mistress on palace premises ('the first ray of sun in the Sun King's life'), but it was also the place where, during the Fronde uprising, led in part as we have seen by his uncle Gaston d'Orléans, the young king and his mother were kept prisoner. Because of these experiences, Louis acquired a deep distaste for Paris, and this was one motivating factor in his desire to set up his court away from the capital, in Versailles. This decision, too, would have fateful consequences.

According to one historian, Gaston d'Orléans 'spent his entire adult life in and out of plots against Louis XIII's ministers and policies' and certainly the term 'colourful' does not even begin to do justice to his rebellious and rumbustious nature. Not only did he foment much of the turbulence of the Fronde, switching sides when it suited him, but he was forced into exile twice for his attempted assassination plots against Richelieu and Mazarin.[1]

In his private life he was equally headstrong. He fell in love at first sight with Marguerite de Lorraine at a time when France and Lorraine were enemies. On this account, the king refused him permission to marry but Gaston went ahead anyway and married Marguerite in secret. When the king found out, the marriage was annulled, but the Pope protested so vigorously that the couple were married a second time. The Parlement of Paris insisted on countermanding the Pope and annulled the marriage once more and it was only in 1643, on his deathbed, that Louis XIII authorised the union, so that the couple were then married for the third time.

Gaston's rebelliousness – the whole Orléans saga – stemmed from the fact that, from 1614 until 1638 – the birth of Louis XIV, when his mother was already thirty-six – he was heir presumptive in France, and again in 1647, when both Louis XIV and his brother, Philippe, were dangerously ill with smallpox. At a time when medicine was so primitive, and childbirth so fraught with danger, the Orléans were always on the edge of taking power. Although he was twice reconciled with his brother, and with the cardinals, Gaston was always a sort of 'king over the water'.

The Orléans 'alternative' was embellished early on by the character of Gaston's daughter, Anne-Marie-Louise d'Orléans, Duchesse de Montpensier. A wilful girl, officially known as Mademoiselle, and to history as La Grande Mademoiselle, her tumultuous career was outlined in chapter 1. La Grande Mademoiselle is one of the great romantic figures in history, with at least thirteen biographies dedicated to her, in French, English and German.[2]

Her immense fortune passed to her cousin and friend, the Sun King's brother, Philippe, Duc d'Orléans, known as Monsieur. In addition to Mademoiselle's huge legacy, Monsieur was doubly fortunate in that, in 1661, he was given the Palais-Royal to live in (where of course he too had lived as a boy, alongside his brother).

The relations between the king and Philippe were notoriously complex politically, psychologically and sexually. Monsieur was a flamboyant homosexual, who liked to dress in women's clothing and jewellery, even in public, and who seemed to enjoy being

humiliated by a young chevalier he had fallen in love with. When he
did eventually marry, to Henriette of England, daughter of Charles
I and Henrietta Maria, who had grieved in the Palais-Royal after
her husband's execution, he was cuckolded by none other than his
brother, the king. Not content with that, Henriette – before her early
death, aged twenty-six (possibly from poisoning) – just had time to
embarrass her husband with two affairs, one with his lover. So suspicious was her death that nineteen doctors were called to perform
the autopsy.[3]

There were reports that in fact Anne of Austria and Mazarin
deliberately pandered to Philippe's homosexuality, and inhibited his
education, so as to keep him from outshining his brother, so he could
never be a threat to the Crown. This possibly accounts for the antipathy Monsieur always had for Mazarin and, to an extent, and for
a while, his brother. They quarrelled badly several times, more than
once spitting at each other in public, with Monsieur even urinating
on the king's bed. These on–off relations culminated in 1658 when
both brothers were on the north coast, near Calais and Dunkirk, part
of the army that was fighting the English. The king became seriously
ill with typhoid fever and was not expected to live – a unit of the
army was despatched to take his body to Paris. At this time a cabal
formed around Philippe, because once again an Orléans was the heir
presumptive, as Gaston had been before him. The king survived but
Mazarin took care to disband the cabal.[4]

These were by no means the only scandals involving Monsieur,
and yet, at the same time, he and his two wives (he married Princess
Charlotte after Henriette died) created a fabulous court at the
Palais-Royal, whose splendour matched – and even at times eclipsed –
the king's.

The court at Monsieur's Palais-Royal didn't really take off, however, until the king gave it to him as his own property. At first, it was
a 'grace and favour' building – Monsieur was there thanks to the largesse of his brother, the king. When Richelieu had donated the palace
to the state, his will had specifically stipulated that it was to become
the residence either of future kings or of their direct descendants.
Monsieur, as head of a collateral line, was therefore legally barred
from ownership. But when, in 1692, the king wished to marry Mlle

de Blois to Monsieur's only son, the Duc de Chartres (the future regent), he had no small difficulty in obtaining his brother's consent. At the same time, it was a royal command and could not be gainsaid. The marriage was a sad affair by all accounts, attended by James II, the exiled king of England, but it did achieve its aim.[5] The deal by the king to make over the building to his brother must count as one of the most consequential ironies in history.

Monsieur – and in particular his first wife – had superlative taste. They began extensive redecorations and undertook the reconstruction of the halls where Richelieu had once housed his library and which had been the location of the royal academies from 1661 to 1691, in which Monsieur and his wives took a great interest. Despite Richelieu's aim to make the Palais-Cardinal the centre of a new and sophisticated area of Paris, its success did not outlast his death, and by the time Monsieur moved in it was far from being a fashionable centre.

The introduction of Monsieur changed everything. In 1663, *L'État général de la Maison de Monsieur* listed nearly 500 officers and servants, 20 ecclesiastical officers, over 100 maîtres d'hôtel, chefs, waiters and pages, over 100 gentlemen of the bedchamber, over two dozen doctors, surgeons and barbers, nearly 50 masters of the horse, a military guard of 150. In fact, Monsieur and Henriette turned the Palais-Royal into the intellectual centre of the realm. Richelieu had made it the home of the Académie française and the Académie des beaux-arts and under Monsieur and his wife it also became the home of the first Comédie-Française, where Molière lived for years. It was also the location of the Académie royale de musique, where Lully and Rameau would make their homes. Monsieur, as we have seen (chapter 7), was especially influential in the career of Molière. Henriette took against him by sponsoring Racine in opposition to Molière.[6] Two factions emerged at the Palais-Royal, the duke's and the duchess's, seething against each other. It was the talk of Paris.

Nevertheless, despite the in-house strife on all fronts, or because of it, it was under Monsieur that the Palais-Royal first acquired the reputation that would endure all the way down to the Revolution and beyond, as being an accessible centre of pleasure, intellectual stimulation, artistic brilliance, sexual licence and, by implication, an available *alternative* to the Sun King's self-conscious and excessively formal court, two to three hours away by coach, at Versailles. Unlike his brother, Philippe retained a fondness for the capital and took up residence there for long periods during the winter social season.[7]

Monsieur's son, Philippe II, Duke of Orléans (1674–1723), whose marriage of convenience to the king's bastard daughter had earned the Orléans their fabulous home, did manage to get his hands on the levers of power, becoming regent of France during the minority of Louis XV, from 1715 to 1723.

It had become clear early on that Philippe was far more intelligent and accomplished than his cousins. He had a lively interest in history, geography, chemistry and mathematics and spoke Latin, Spanish, Italian and German. He fought his first campaign at seventeen, and was a lieutenant-general at nineteen. He was interested in philosophy and was a superlative collector.[8]

During Philippe's regency, France was run for the third time from the Palais-Royal. Philippe showed himself as a competent ruler, his attitudes and policies epitomised by his taste in art, where he was responsible for the change from the heavy, formal, even gloomy world of Louis XIV's religious style, to the much lighter, more play-ful format of the rococo. He acted, he sang, he composed plays at the Palais-Royal which were actually staged. He was an omnivorous reader and he painted. He had studied in the Palais-Royal with Antoine Coypel, who in 1716 was made painter to the king.

Moreover, the regent turned into the greatest collector of fine art that France has ever had. He saw the Palais-Royal as a surrogate Versailles and modelled some of its decorations on the Salon des glaces and the Salon de guerre in the king's court, but in truth the collection he amassed outstripped anything the monarch had. He inherited from his father's first wife, who was the sister of Charles I of England, many of the pictures that had been in the English royal collection, including Van Dycks, Snyders and Titians. But his greatest coup was to secure, with the aid of Pierre Crozat, a wealthy banker but also his art agent, the collection of Queen Christina of Sweden, who had inherited from her father, Gustavus Adolphus, many of the masterpieces he had looted during the Thirty Years War (from

Prague, for example), when Sweden was a major power. The negotiations took ten years.[9]

But, Philippe being an Orléans, scandal was never far away. It fell into two categories. He stopped work every day at five and spent the evenings in what, in polite society, were called '*petits soupers*' and in everyday language were outright orgies – sexual encounters of the most flagrant kind, not excluding a competition one night for the 'best-looking sexual organs'. It was at these *soupers* that Philippe himself coined a slang word for his sensual male companions: *roué*. It meant 'rake', literally someone who has been broken on the wheel (*roue*). His wife, who thought a lot of herself because, though illegitimate, she was a king's daughter, naturally objected and from then on they had rival courts.[10]

Philippe was also several times suspected of incest with his eldest daughter and, at other times, of being a poisoner. He had a lavish laboratory on the top floor of the Palais-Royal, where alchemy was practised. When the Dauphin died in 1711, followed by the deaths of Louis XIV's eldest grandson, and then his great-grandson, all within the space of three weeks, the coincidence was too much for the rumour mill, though there was never any direct evidence.[11]

Because of this, it is no surprise to learn that the regent's style of rule was notorious. He was highly irregular sexually and rumours spread. More than that, the fact that Versailles was, for the moment at any rate, sidelined meant that social life in Paris revived. The great *hôtels*, now centred around the boulevard Saint-Germain on the left bank, rather than the Marais on the right, relit their lights and reopened their doors. 'Women abandoned the turreted coiffures of yesteryear, cut their hair and curled and powdered it; they rid themselves of the stiff court crinoline and wore the lightest of Indian silk just floating from the lightweight paniers of their skirts. Freed from its long servitude, French society yielded to all the excesses of a rediscovered freedom.'[12]

When Louis XV achieved his majority in 1723, at the age of just thirteen, the court was re-established at Versailles but, says Benedetta Craveri, the old monopoly 'of grandeur, of manners, of *esprit* and pleasure had been forever broken ... Paris had definitively regained the social and intellectual upper hand.'[13]

PART THREE

_____

Enlightenment:
'The Victory of Intelligence over Respectability'

'Esteem Is the Soul of Society'

By this time the first intellectual centre of the eighteenth century had emerged, according to the Marquis d'Argenson, a councillor of state under Louis XV and friend of Voltaire. This was the salon of Anne-Thérèse, Marquise de Lambert, on the rue Colbert and the rue de Richelieu in the second arrondissement.

Mme de Lambert is a good example of the recent research devoted to women in the French Enlightenment, being the subject of a 798-page study by Roger Marchal, for the Voltaire Foundation at Oxford.* This concentrates on the formation of her intellectual and moral life, her attendance at the *cercles* of Mme de La Sablière and Ninon de Lenclos, her neo-Platonism and her affection for Plutarch, Cicero and Pliny, her discipleship of Montaigne and La Bruyère, her friendship with Fontenelle, and a full appreciation of her own writings, which extended from 1688 until 1727. Marchal identifies an ethic known as 'Lambertinage' (an ironical play on 'libertinage', chapter 19), a disposition which encompasses military values, family values, the love of grandeur and the 'conquest of oneself'.[1]

He calls her salon 'La Cour de Minerve', and writes that its décor

---

* The Voltaire Foundation describes itself as 'the world leader for eighteenth-century scholarship'. Besides publishing *The Complete Works of Voltaire*, it also publishes the series Oxford University Studies in the Enlightenment (600 volumes to date), plus the correspondence of selected key Enlightenment thinkers (Rousseau, Bayle, Helvétius). It was founded in the 1970s by the Polish-British bibliographer Theodore Besterman (1904–76), who at one time lived in Voltaire's house.

was spiritually nourishing, that the 'sweet' arrangement of the
furniture encouraged her ambitions to create the perfect space for
stimulating conversation.[2] Marchal makes clear that Lambert's salon
was an amalgam of the Académie française and an aristocratic court,
preserving the manners and appearance of the latter, with gaming,
debauchery and libertinage strictly forbidden.[3] Her style, he says, was
one of refined elegance, reflecting both the baroque and the classical
worlds that were then the fashion.

By all accounts, Mme de Lambert had turned her back on the court,
just as Mme de Rambouillet had before her, and she also continued
the great chain by modelling her gatherings on those of Ninon de
Lenclos and Mme de la Sablière. She was a serious-minded woman,
with a taste for study, who was abandoned by her husband's family
after she was widowed in 1686. She suffered another misfortune
when her daughter died in her arms. The melancholy this caused
shaped her taste for literature rather than the exact sciences, and
she adopted a form of stoic Christianity. Every Tuesday she welcomed men of letters, scholars and philosophers, of whom the
most distinguished was the writer Bernard de Fontenelle, who we
met in the salon of Ninon de Lenclos. She tried to achieve a balance between the ancients and the moderns, and in so doing her
'famous Tuesdays' are now seen as inaugurating the reign of the
salons which came to characterise the eighteenth century. She was
the first to give writers and thinkers a pre-eminence alongside more
mondain types.

This was not her only innovation. In Mme de Lambert's salon,
greater knowledge was seen as a route to moral improvement, and as
part of this women were demonstrating their ability to get to grips
with Descartes. At one point, the salons explored whether Descartes
and Pascal's mathematics could be applied to love. We may smile at
this, but it was honestly enough meant and both men and women
were judged as capable of understanding such a link. More and more,
speech was seen as the pre-eminent domain of women, as was the
whole area of 'interiority', what we would call psychology, which was
seen as a new field and the chief area of exploration of the novel. Here
it is worth reminding ourselves of the earlier observation (chapters 4

and 5) that the novel was often conceived out of wedlock and its chief subject was adultery.

In earlier salons, a form of *écriture blanche* had evolved, in which each member of the salon contributed to the composition of any said work, but Mme de Lambert herself would make the most of that other literary form that proved so suited to women – pedagogical works about the education of children. Marriage was being seen more and more as a contract between like souls and less as a sacrament and there was a widespread reaction against too-frequent childbirth, promoted by the church. Women – though Mme de Lambert was an outlier here – still found it profitable to hide their learning behind a façade of worldliness, and plays continued to pit the learned academies against the 'less serious' and precious salons.

Another prominent member of Mme de Lambert's salon, no less distinguished than Fontenelle, and hardly less learned, was Charles-Louis de Secondat, Baron de Montesquieu. Born into a noble family with estates near Bordeaux, he lost his parents before he achieved his majority and was brought up by his uncle, the Baron de Montesquieu, who left Charles-Louis his estate and his title.

Montesquieu took part in the politics of Bordeaux, becoming both a councillor and president of the Bordeaux Parlement, but he later became known for three books of which at least one has had world-wide significance. This is partly due to the way politics was developing as he reached maturity. To the north, England had declared itself a constitutional monarchy following its 'Glorious Revolution' of 1688–9 and had joined with Scotland in the Union of 1707 to form the United Kingdom of Great Britain, underlining the power of parliament. In France, in contrast, Louis XIV had died in 1715, following a long reign, and was followed by Louis XV, aged five. Absolutism continued unchanged.

In 1721, while the regent was still alive, Montesquieu published – anonymously of course – *Lettres persanes* ('Persian Letters'), a satire on French society of the early eighteenth century.[4] The book was composed as if by two Persian visitors to France who are fascinated and puzzled by European society, by turns impressed, bewildered and half-frightened by the freer relations between men and women, compared with what they have left behind in Isfahan.

Montesquieu's second notable work, *Considérations sur les causes de la grandeur des Romains et de leur décadence*, displayed his theory that progress is less the work of great individuals and owes more to the moral climate of the times and the physical properties of a country, history being a reflection of cultural and social anthropology. This is what links him to Fontenelle, and also shows how his thinking would lead to *De l'esprit des lois* ('The Spirit of the Laws'), Montesquieu's most influential work, which we will return to later.

François Fénelon ranked third among Mme de Lambert's salon. He was a well-born priest who, after the Edict of Nantes was revoked, was one of several notable orators sent into Huguenot (Protestant) areas of France, to convince with his rhetorical skills the errors of Protestantism. He was also an instructor to the royal children. His best-known work was *Les Aventures de Télémaque* ('The Adventures of Telemachus'), ostensibly an adventure story about Ulysses' son, but in fact an outright attack on the concept of absolute monarchy, which is what made him appeal to the Marquise de Lambert. The book inspired many other works, including Jean Terrasson's *Séthos* (1731), which in turn inspired Mozart's *The Magic Flute*. Elected to the Académie française in 1693, Fénelon was also involved in the 'quietist' controversy, the heretical belief that 'stillness' and 'passivity' were preferable to active meditation and vocal prayer.[5]

But ultimately, Fénelon bowed to the Pope's authority and this is perhaps his true significance, that he was – in a sense – a stage on the way to the Enlightenment proper. He was a devout Christian, prepared to submit to the Pope's authority, but at the same time was aware that the king's authority needed reform. The king was – not surprisingly – angered by Fénelon's argument in *Télémaque*, which appeared to question the very foundation of royal authority, and as a result Louis required him to remain in the archdiocese of Cambrai, where he had been appointed archbishop. This prevented Fénelon from attending Mme de Lambert's salon.[6]

DOGMA IN THE MORNING, SONG IN THE EVENING

Mme de Lambert's salon was new in some ways. She had a mix of society people and scholars, but it seems that the scholars led the way.[7] She herself was well read in the classics and in Montaigne and she took her duties – as the wife of a great aristocrat, as a widow, as a mother – very seriously, and these were eventually reflected in her own writings, which explored her three-fold situation: *Avis d'une mère à sa fille, Traité de l'amitié, Traité de la vieillesse, Réflexions sur les femmes*. She applied the same approach with her salon. She was wary of being thought too intellectual, so that her Tuesdays were kept for men of letters and her Wednesdays for those in society.[8] Many, however, were welcome on both days.

The average gathering was for about twenty guests, who would arrive at about midday, for lunch, during which the subjects for conversation would be ironed out. People would be asked to give extracts from their works, and most were keen to do so. Montesquieu, for example, read parts of his *Lettres persanes*, which were warmly received.

The standing of Mme de Lambert's salon was most in evidence whenever new members were elected to the Académie française, because the hôtel de Nevers, as her salon was also known, invariably had its own candidate. 'You had to ask her to get into the Académie française,' said Président Hénault in his memoirs.[9] Not everyone was happy with this female influence on male culture.

On Wednesday evenings, erudition gave way to different forms of pleasure. As Hénault said elsewhere: 'I dogmatised in the morning and sang in the evening.'[10] In these evenings, the tone was light-hearted *galanterie*, but it was forbidden to play cards, get drunk or be ostentatious in one's clothing. Each guest brought a selection of novelties, anecdotes, witticisms, improvised verses and gallant compliments to share.[11]

Mme de Lambert believed that women had a right to an intellectual life, and that there was an inner dimension to the outward forms of living: that *politesse* in manners reflected a *politesse* of spirit, that good speech reflected good thought, that an *homme galant* was also a good man. And that the desire for esteem 'is also the soul of society; it unites us all'.

The subjects discussed were not so different from those of earlier salons – love, friendship, duty, taste, virtue, reputation. By now, however, the likes of Montesquieu, Marivaux, Fontenelle and Terrasson were more interested in the diversity of custom, the subjectivity of behaviour, the unpredictability of psychology and the emotions. They were also aware of the beginnings of secularisation and how that impacted Christian values. Underneath it all – and in the writing of Fontenelle and Montesquieu – was the problem of happiness on this earth, which was of course at variance with centuries of Christian teaching. In Montesquieu's *Mes pensées*, it seems that he first broached some of these ideas in Mme de Lambert's evenings.

And it was Marivaux, dramatist of the Comédie-Française, who made the most of this, who explored most thoroughly what became known as '*marivaudage*', the 'metaphysics of the heart', who developed a new kind of psychological introspection. Mme de Lambert helped this along by reviving the practice of literary portraits (her *petits écrits*) though in her case they concentrated more on psychology, originality and individuality than other aspects, such as appearance.

At the beginning of the eighteenth century, much of France showed a growing decadence. There was a gambling mania in the regency, as we have seen, and vulgar sexual licence was on the rise. But in Mme de Lambert's salon, the quiet pursuit of literary and philosophical eloquence, happiness and the well-being of others took centre stage.

Alexandrine de Tencin's Seven *Bêtes*

Alexandrine Claude Guérin de Tencin could not have been more different from Mme de Lambert. If, to begin with, she was known for one thing above all else, it was the night she drew the attention of Philippe d'Orléans, regent of France. The regent, as we have seen, was a brilliant man, an extremely cultivated man, but he was also known for his *petits soupers*. Every evening, he would retreat from affairs of state to enjoy the company of his friends, friends who were – to say the least – highly unconventional sexually. Mme de Tencin obtained an introduction to these *soupers* but Philippe's attentions were engrossed elsewhere at the time and he did not take as much notice of her as she would have wished.

That early in her career she had more faith in her body than in her conversational arts and so, a few evenings later, it suddenly appeared that one of the marble statues in the room stirred ever so slightly.

Everyone had been drinking so at first no notice was taken. But no ... eventually the regent – not to mention everyone else – could see that the figure above him, totally naked, was in fact a real woman. He approached the statue where the 'droll' voice of Mme de Tencin whispered: 'Monsieur, help me down.' Her influence over the regent did not last long, but still long enough to introduce him to the 'feast of the flagellants', copied from the days of Nero.[12]

She had had a difficult childhood. The fourth daughter in a family of the minor nobility, she was always destined for the church. But she knew her own mind early on and that mind told her she would hate convent life. Her parents were unmoved, even when she threatened suicide. But she was unmoved also and when, after she had been seven years in the convent, her father died and she became mistress of her own destiny, she managed – with the help of a lawyer – to have her vows annulled and even claimed the share of her family's fortune to which she was entitled. Her tenacity matched her beauty but she embraced for a time a career of scandal.[13]

When she had finally escaped the convent she hated so much, she had been introduced to the wider world via the house of her eldest sister, Angélique, who was married to Augustin-Antoine de Ferriol, the receiver-general (finance minister) of the Dauphiné, the area of eastern France around Vienne. Like Alexandrine, Angélique was described as 'beautiful, unscrupulous, ambitious, and quite culti-vated' and she too had her salon. The guests included Fontenelle and the young Voltaire.

Outside the convent Alexandrine threw herself into bolstering the career of her brother, who had also been sent into the church, but in his case more successfully because he had become an *abbé*. So close did they become that further scandal beckoned – when they were accused of incest. This was unlikely, but Alexandrine was certainly voracious sexually. She began a series of affairs, all with more or less distinguished men: Matthew Prior, the English ambassador; Lord Bolingbroke, English secretary of state and a political refugee; and Cardinal Dubois, the regent's tutor.[14]

Guillaume Dubois (1656–1723), the son of a doctor in Limousin, was the third of the four great cardinal ministers in France, along-side Richelieu, Mazarin and André de Fleury. He was an ambitious, scheming priest with remarkable diplomatic skills, and was rewarded by the king for the part he played in helping to bring about the marriage between the Duc de Chartres (the future regent) and Mlle de Blois (chapter 10). The Duc de Saint-Simon was unimpressed with this noted ecclesiastical libertine – he kept a portrait of the cardinal in his lavatory.[15]

On 17 November 1717, at what was then the fairly ripe age of thirty-five, Alexandrine gave birth to a son whom she immediately abandoned on the steps of the chapel of Saint-Jean-le-Rond, next to Notre-Dame.[16] She does not come out of the episode at all well, still less when we realise that the son grew up to be none other than Jean Le Rond (after the place where he was found) d'Alembert, the celebrated *philosophe* and one of the editors of the *Encyclopédie*.

Scandal was not yet behind her. One of her other affairs was with Charles de La Fresnaye, a well-known and well-regarded banker. Despite his reputation, he got into financial trouble and lodged with Alexandrine some bonds in exchange for a loan. When this loan did not help, and he returned to her for more money, she refused, and in addition refused to return the bonds she was holding. This threatened to exacerbate his disgrace and was too much for him. He returned to her house – this was in April 1726 – where she was entertaining friends, withdrew into a study next to her bedroom, and shot himself in the heart. He had left a will in which he accused Mme de Tencin of all manner of trickery, and incest at least twice over.

Alexandrine was incarcerated in the Grand Châtelet and later transferred to the Bastille.[17] Eventually, she was acquitted, after pressure from her family, but by then the damage had been done – her health was poor and, by some accounts, she was ready to give up the ghost.

An Intense Exchange of Ideas

In fact, she recovered in a matter of months and it is from this moment, 1728, that she formed her salon. Many of her habitués were regulars at Mme de Lambert's Tuesdays but when the marquise died (in 1733), most of them transferred to Mme de Tencin, also on Tuesdays, which were now free. It was in this salon, according to Craveri, that 'eighteenth-century *sociabilité* introduced a new criterion essentially based on intellectual prestige ... Madame de Tencin provided the first and most brilliant example of the victory of intelligence over respectability, a turnaround that did not depend on an abstract assessment of her intellectual ability (which no one doubted in any case) but rather on recognition of its value to society ... This authority would soon prove to be necessary in those intellectual salons where the *philosophes* came in strength and the dominant tone was no longer the easy, courteous spirit of leisure but an intense exchange of ideas.'[18]

There were in the rue Saint-Honoré what Mme de Tencin called her 'seven *bêtes*'. They included, besides Fontenelle and Marivaux, the physician Jean-Jacques Dortous de Mairan, Fontenelle's successor as director of the Académie royale des sciences; Claude Gros de Boze, numismatist and archaeologist and permanent secretary of the Académie des inscriptions; Jean-Baptiste de Mirabaud, translator of Tasso; Jean Astruc, author of an acclaimed treatise on venereal disease; and Charles Pinot Duclos, historian and novelist and permanent secretary of the Académie française from 1755.

Dortous de Mairan, or d'Ortous de Mairan (1678–1771), was a very distinguished scientist. He was educated in Ancient Greek and maths and at one time, like Dubois before him, was secretary to the Duc d'Orléans. He was interested in geophysics (in particular the shape of the Earth, whether it is flattened at the poles, as Newton had suggested and as we now know it is) and astronomy (exploring the exact measurement of the heat emitted by the sun), and, most originally, he was a chrono-biologist, one of the first to conceive the idea of biological circadian rhythms. He was drawn to the daily opening and closing of *Mimosa pudica*, and he explored this by – simply enough – exposing specimens to continuous darkness. From this he was able to conclude that the opening and closing continued even in the absence of sunlight. He did not draw the conclusion that they had 'internal clocks', rather that in some way they could 'sense' sunlight.[19]

He followed Fontenelle as secretary of the Académie royale des sciences but was also appointed editor of the *Journal des savants*. The *Journal* was first produced in January 1665, making it the first ever scientific journal, preceding the *Transactions of the Royal Society* by two months. It was launched by Denis de Sallo, a writer and lawyer, and was originally a twelve-page pamphlet, including obituaries of famous figures, church history and legal reports.

Jean Astruc was widely regarded as one of the most learned men of his day. Born in the Languedoc in 1684, he was precociously brilliant, earning his degree in medicine at the celebrated Montpellier school at the age of sixteen, and his doctorate at nineteen. He moved to Paris where he became professor of medicine at the Collège royal. His first major work was a discourse on venereal disease. He made some advances, recognising its contagious nature and its infectious aetiology, though he failed to distinguish between syphilis and gonorrhoea. He maintained that the disease had been introduced from the Americas (he thought Spanish soldiers had brought it back, the incidence of the disease being higher among them than others).[20] But his most controversial work in his later years had little to do with medicine.

In 1753 a small book appeared, ostensibly published in Brussels – to get around censorship – but in fact released in Paris, under the title *Conjectures sur les mémoires originaux*, generally known in English as *Conjectures on the Book of Genesis*. The 'conjectures' (a clever word in the spirit of the times) related to the fact that Moses' account of Jewish history could, on the face of it, have been vouchsafed to him either by revelation, or by oral history, but Astruc suspected instead that he obtained his information from *written* sources. The many repetitions in the scriptures, and especially the double accounts of some events, suggested to Astruc that Moses 'had more than one written document to hand'.[21] This was further underlined by the two words to describe God, Yahweh and Elohim. Astruc concluded there must be two documents, one which mentioned only Yahweh and another which mentioned only Elohim.

This conception of Mosaic authorship was as daring as it was new and Astruc published it tentatively and anonymously in case there was a backlash to publication.[22] The backlash took some time to occur and by then several other scholars had begun to focus on the inconsistencies in the biblical text.

THE SEPARATION OF POWERS

We can thus see that Mme de Tencin's salon was peopled by an extraordinary range of multiple talents, highly individualistic, where she would have been put to it to guarantee harmony and light, but where the gatherings would have been extremely exciting and rewarding. Her salon was firmly aligned with the moderns and among those who attended, her two closest friends, it appears, were Marivaux and Montesquieu.

In his unfinished novel, *La Vie de Marianne*, Marivaux has left us a description of Mme de Tencin's salon, where she is portrayed as Mme Dorsin: 'There was no question of rank or condition at her house; no one considered their own importance or lack of it; there were men talking to other men, between whom only the better reasoning prevailed over the weaker ... There were those for whom titles given them on earth by chance did not count, and who did not believe their fortuitous positions should either humiliate some or bring pride to others. This is how it was understood at Mme Dorsin's; this is how one behaved with her on account of the impression one received of the reasonable and philosophical way of thinking which I have told you was hers.'[23]

She showed her mettle in particular over the publication, in the autumn of 1748, of *De l'esprit des lois*, Montesquieu's masterpiece, which first appeared, anonymously, in Switzerland. Mme de Tencin, who had already listened as extracts were read out by the author in her own salon, received one of the first two copies, as a mark of esteem. She quickly spotted that the Swiss edition was riddled with mistakes and set about having them corrected: at her own expense, she had 500 copies printed of a list of errors and arranged for them to be distributed to bookshops and printed in the *Mercure* and the *Journal des savants*.[24]

De l'esprit des lois was twenty years in the making. Montesquieu was influenced by John Locke and in turn influenced Alexis de Tocqueville, Thomas Babington Macaulay and the founding fathers of America. There are three elements to the book, which was soon placed on the Catholic Church's index of prohibited works. The first aspect is a discussion of how to understand constitutional systems of government: Montesquieu offers the idea that *principle* should underpin any system, of which he identifies three kinds: republican, monarchical and despotic. For democratic republics, he says, the underlying principle is the search for virtue, a willingness to put the interests of the community ahead of private interests. In monarchies, he says, the love of honour – the desire to attain greater rank and prestige – is the motivating principle. And in despotisms, the fear of the ruler is the spring of the system.

In the second part of his argument, Montesquieu tackles the subject of political liberty and how to preserve it. He himself understood political liberty as personal security – citizens' rights as we would say today – and he warned that it was not to be confused with the idea that liberty and democracy are the same, or that liberty means being able to do everything that one wants. In order to combat the possible abuses stemming from these misunderstandings, he devised – most famously – his idea of the separation of powers, that the executive, legislative and judicial functions of governments should be administered separately. He also came up with an insistence on due process, the right to a fair trial and a presumption of innocence. He also opposed slavery.

A third and final element to the book is a more general discussion of how such things as climate and geography interact to help create the culture of a people and give them their 'spirit', which is to be reflected in their laws – laws should reflect the nature of a people. The book was swiftly translated into English and many other languages.[25]

Like many other *salonnières*, Mme de Tencin turned to novel-writing herself, publishing five in all and, like those by other *salonnière*-authors, they were at first published anonymously. For the most part, they were improbable tales of love and adventure, involving sieges, duels, abductions, shipwrecks and, as often as not, reconciliation. Her last, *Les Malheurs de l'amour* ('The Misfortunes of Love'), sums them all up. In truth, her fierce intelligence does not show in her novels.

Sceaux: 'The Best of All Possible Worlds'

Perhaps no detail about salons and salon life is as revealing as the fact that Mme de Lambert's and Mme du Deffand's salons both lasted for thirty years, and Mme Geoffrin's and Mme Ancelot's each for forty. That they were so stable, and so long-lived, in a period when the demand for change was building, shows that they must have been fulfilling an important function. In fact, as Roger Chartier puts it in *The Cultural Origins of the French Revolution*, a passion for novelty, innovation and change in the eighteenth century 'lived side-by-side with a jealous sense of attachment to tradition and past customs'. And this passion created new forms of sociability.[1]

The signs of that change, Chartier says, first appeared during the regency, 'when the royal court lost its exclusive prerogative to regulate aesthetic norms'. This lessened dependence on state authority – which had been growing since the debut of the Rambouillet salon – was 'marked by the emergence of an autonomous cultural sphere' with two all-important characteristics. One, it brought about a public whose critical judgements and literary practices were not governed by court decrees in the realm of taste or by the authority of the academies; and two, there was the emergence of a market in cultural goods, and that too did not always conform to the tastes and enthusiasms of the established authorities.

This emergence of the 'public sphere' was first identified by the German historian Jürgen Habermas in his renowned book *The Structural Transformation of the Public Sphere*, and in France that transformation was led by – and occurred in – the cafés, journals and salons.[2] But it was the salons, says Chartier, which were the primary form of conviviality, 'bringing together in an organised manner people from the worlds of fashion and literature who met to share pastimes such as gaming, conversation, reading and the pleasures of the table'. In particular, he notes that in the first three decades of the eighteenth century, the salon of the Marquise de Lambert at the hôtel de Nevers 'was contrasted to the "court" at Sceaux grouped around the duchesse de Maine, where the old etiquette was perpetuated'. In the run-up to the Revolution, he says, what was at stake in the Paris salons 'was control of an intellectual life that had been emancipated from the tutelage of the monarchy and the court'.[3]

In 1728, at the age of thirty-two, and already the Marquise du Deffand, Marie de Vichy-Champrond, as she had been born, composed – after the fashion of her time – a self-portrait. In it, she described herself as 'the enemy of all falseness and affectation', as neither beautiful nor ugly, as rational, with good taste though 'sometimes led astray by her high spirits'.[4]

In fact, the self-portrait appears to have been some sort of report-card, or taking of stock, in which the marquise, who already had a failed marriage behind her at this point, resolved on a make-over and a major change of direction in her life (there was more than one parallel between her life and that of Mme de Tencin). Born in 1696, in all likelihood at the family château in Champrond, at the centre of a vast estate in Burgundy, she grew up as a proud bearer of her rank.[5]

Educated in a convent, where she was known for her irreligion, she returned home at eighteen, soon afterwards moving to Paris as the bride of her distant cousin, Jean-Baptiste-Jacques du Deffand, Marquis de La Lande. Marriage was for Mme du Deffand, as with so many French women of the age, a source of many advantages. Sophie, Comtesse d'Houdetot, aptly quipped that 'I married in order to be able to enter society, to go to the ball, to take walks, to go to the opera and the theatre'.[6]

This meant, moreover, that Mme du Deffand entered society at the height of the regency, and she seems to have embraced the life of a libertine with enthusiasm. Her first lover was the regent himself.

It was a love affair, as she told her English friend Horace Walpole subsequently, between two people 'obsessed with ennui'. The success of her relationship with the regent was crowned by the award of a pension worth 6,000 livres and, less welcome, by the fact that her husband repudiated her. These scandalous activities came to an end with the death of the regent in 1723.[7]

It was now that she began to change. One way was that she began to value herself for her mind and her intelligence. This sounds glib and cannot have been easy to do, but she managed it by achieving success with a parody that she wrote in the manner of Antoine Houdar de La Motte's five-act tragedy *Inès de Castro*, a sentimental tale that had been making Parisian audiences cry for several weeks. It was also an act of friendship in aid of her friend Voltaire whose own tragedy, *Artémise*, had flopped. Marie also cultivated new friends, including Président Hénault.

Charles Hénault was substantial physically, portraits of the time showing him as being on the chubby side, with a round face and 'full' cheeks, but a mischievous grin. Educated at the famous Jesuit college the Lycée Louis-le-Grand, at the time he and Mme du Deffand met he was a young, rich magistrate, very accomplished and very successful with women. He was a good friend of Voltaire, credited with saving the manuscript of *La Henriade*, an epic poem of 1723, ostensibly written in honour of Henry IV but in fact an attack on religious fanaticism, when the author wanted to burn it. Vain, impetuous and anxious to please, in 1707 Hénault had been made a laureate of the Académie française and had won other prizes. He composed light verse in the style of Fontenelle, and two of his comedies had been produced by the Comédie-Française.

But there was also a political dimension to this many-sided man. In 1705, he became a councillor of the Parlement of Paris and in 1710 was made president of its chamber of inquiries. In 1723, the year Mme du Deffand wrote her own first work, Hénault was elected to the Académie française and in 1731 he gave up his position as *président au Parlement*. He gave up the position but kept the title, as American presidents keep the title until death – Hénault was known everywhere as *Président*.

He was also known as a historian. His *Nouvel abrégé*

chronologique de l'histoire de France, published (anonymously) in 1744, viewed French history through its institutions, and he spent much of the rest of his life updating and refining it. Hénault had an easy, graceful style so that the book was phenomenally successful, and was translated into several languages, including Chinese.[8]

A Stage Where the Curtain Never Falls

In the first years of their liaison, Mme du Deffand and the Président met at the famous court at Sceaux, a few miles outside Paris, on the south side. Originally built for Jean-Baptiste Colbert, it was designed by the Perrault brothers, decorated by Charles Le Brun, and had gardens laid out by André Le Nôtre, thus making it a perfect example of the architectural aesthetic of the *grand siècle*.

The chatelaine of Sceaux was the Duchesse du Maine, a greatniece of Mme de Longueville. Forced to marry the Duc du Maine, the legitimised son of Louis XIV and his mistress, Mme de Montespan, the duchesse proved herself 'incapable of forgiving her husband for his illegitimate birth' – the etiquette of the day stipulating that she was unable to take precedence at court. In response, the duchesse created her own private court at Sceaux. Because she was a royal of sorts, her gatherings there were always referred to as a court though they were, in effect, very grand salons.

Physically small, intelligent but overbearing, 'spoiled, unmanageable and insufferable', always sporting 'prodigious amounts of rouge', always craving a larger role and, like Germaine de Staël, longing to be talked about, the duchesse spent a not inconsiderable amount of time during the regency plotting with the Spanish ambassador to France, Antonio del Giudice, Prince of Cellamare, to stage a coup d'état to put the king of Spain on the throne of France. This was a sensational scandal when it was exposed, involving the queen of Spain and a raft of secret letters in invisible ink, though the regent himself was fairly phlegmatic, insisting only that the duchesse be exiled from Paris for a few years. This ensured that her court/salon always retained a somewhat racy reputation.[9]

Plays, we are told, were performed or rehearsed every day. Watteau was apparently thinking of Sceaux when he painted his second *Embarquement pour Cythère* (now in the Louvre), a picture which Rodin described as 'a psychological journey' through the three phases of love: persuasion, consent and full accord. The picture also described the situation at Sceaux – 'the urge to escape, to go on a journey, to remain on a journey rather than to arrive at anywhere specific, to be on a stage where the curtain never falls'.[10]

In a sense the court at Sceaux had moved on from where it had started out, as a meeting place for aristocrats who had turned their backs on Versailles, and instead it had become more literary. This was partly due to the fact that in Paris at that time, and before Mme du Deffand established her salon, which we shall come to, there was fierce competition between the salons of Mesdames de Lambert and de Tencin, which created its own fashion. The roster of writers at Sceaux included Voltaire, Fontenelle, Marmontel, Montesquieu, Diderot, Raynal, Prévost, Houdar de La Motte and d'Alembert. The 'flower' of the Académie française, we are told, divided their time between Mme Lambert's salon and Sceaux.[11]

Mme du Deffand was, by and large, a success at Sceaux, herself another victory of intelligence over respectability, much sought-after by Mme du Maine, and notable for her wit and dedication to the 'laborious theatricals'. As such, she was gradually able to put her libertine past behind her as Mme Tencin had done and, in effect, achieve a definitive metamorphosis, as a woman now concerned only with 'the seductions of the mind'.[12]

At this time the all-important change at Mme de Lambert's salon was taking place. This was the first where writers 'as such' met aristocrats in an alliance the nature of which was captured by d'Alembert: 'Some bring knowledge and understanding, others bring that elegance of manners and that urbanity which even a man of worth ... needs to acquire ... Society people came away more enlightened and men of letters more agreeable.'[13] This, then, was another phase in making the intellect fashionable in *mondain* France.

Both Morellet and Voltaire were at home at Sceaux and were agreed that good conversation can only occur when it is run by a woman, Voltaire typically adding that the great salon gatherings were always 'presided over by a woman who in her declining beauty shines by her awakening wit'.[14]

But the two most important people who were alongside Mme du Deffand at Sceaux, and who would have the most profound effect on the cultural life of France – of all Europe – were Voltaire and d'Alembert.

VOLTAIRE AND ÉMILIE

Nowadays, in the public mind, Voltaire is the satirical, even sarcastic, author of plays and poems culminating in *Candide*, his 1759 masterpiece about an improbably innocent young aristocrat brought up by his tutor, Dr Pangloss, to believe that he is living in the best of all possible worlds. Along the way, however, an indiscretion causes him to be cast outside this comfortable existence into a series of more or less hilarious catastrophes, following which he comes to question whether Dr Pangloss can be wholly right.

Voltaire was one of those individuals who show what can be achieved in a lifetime. As well as being a writer of poems, plays and novels, he was a social activist, getting involved in many of the socio-political issues of the day, he was a dilettante scientist who fought for the acceptance of (the Briton) Newton's ideas over (the Frenchman) Descartes's, he was an advocate of hedonism, scepticism and liberty, and, not least, he was a fantastic friend to many of those in his circle.[15]

Born François-Marie Arouet in 1694 into a well-bred family, he was educated at the prestigious Jesuit college, the Lycée Louis-le-Grand, in Paris.* As a young man he had a rather long, thin face,

---

* The number of impressive individuals who have attended this one school is itself impressive. Alphabetically, the names include: Alain Badiou, Henri Becquerel, Alfred Binet, Marc Bloch, Pierre Bonnard, Pierre Bourdieu, Paul Bourget, Robert Brasillach, Aimé Césaire, Jacques Chirac, André Citroën, René Clair, Paul Claudel, Léon Daudet, Régis Debray, Michel Debré, Edgar Degas, Eugène Delacroix, Jacques Derrida, Paul Deschanel, Camille Desmoulins, Denis Diderot, Georges Dumézil, Émile Durkheim, Laurent Fabius, Octave Feuillet, Augustin Fliche, Théophile Gautier, Théodore Géricault, Valéry Giscard d'Estaing, Louis Hachette, Victor Hugo, Jean Jaurès, Alain Juppé, Bernard-Henri Lévy, Émile Littré, Jean-François Lyotard, Émile Mâle, Louis Massignon, Pierre Mendès France, Maurice Merleau-Ponty, André Michelin, Molière, Charles Péguy, Henri Poincaré, Raymond Poincaré, Georges Pompidou, Romain Rolland, the Marquis de Sade, Jean-Paul Sartre, Léopold Sédar Senghor and Voltaire.

with large eyes and a prominent nose, but with an altogether pleasant aspect which, in portraits, gives no hint of the waspish qualities that would emerge. His father had literary tastes and was welcomed at Versailles and would have preferred his son to be a lawyer. But Voltaire adored the French classics – Molière, Racine and Corneille – and hoped to become a playwright himself. His young manhood coincided with the regency and, being a congenial soul, he enjoyed the libertine moment almost as much as anyone. Arguably more to the point, he did not suffer from the economic adventures proposed by the exiled Scottish economist John Law, which had led to the collapse of the Mississippi Company. Rather, he invested successfully, becoming financially independent in the process.

His first literary effort, released in 1718, was *Œdipe*, his reworking of the classical legend in the manner of Racine and Corneille. The play was first performed at Sceaux, when he was twenty-four, a sign of his rapid ascent on the social scene thanks to his family credentials. The title page of the play described it as by 'Voltaire', the name by which he was known ever after. There are several theories as to why he chose it. One is that it is an anagram of the Latinised version of Arouet = AROVET, plus LI, for 'le jeune'; another more likely version is that it is a reversal of the name of his hometown, Airvault, in the Poitou region.[16]

During the 1720s he produced a number of works that, truth to tell, were as much designed to promote his social standing as his intellectual one – these works illustrated the values of pleasure, *honnêteté* and good taste that were held to be of paramount importance in salon society. He was also drawn to the Englishman Lord Bolingbroke, a Jacobite in exile and a freethinker. This came in handy when Voltaire was accused by an aristocrat of defamation and – to avoid prosecution – went into exile in England from 1726 until 1729.

England profoundly affected Voltaire. Through Bolingbroke he met Jonathan Swift, Alexander Pope and John Gay, writers fusing their stories with biting social criticism. He was no less impressed by Isaac Newton. He didn't meet the great scientist himself, though he did meet the physicist's sister and a number of 'Newtonian scientists', and he was deeply affected by Newton's funeral, witnessing the accolade given to a scientist that was on a level with what would have been accorded a king in France. Newton's sister told Voltaire the story about the apple and her brother, and during his exile Voltaire became proficient in English, enough to write letters and even plays in the language. When he was allowed back into France, he was still denied entrance to Versailles, and this combination of admiration for England and Newtonian science and continued exile from the court produced in him the Voltaire the world knows.

But there was one final element in his make-up. This was his meeting in 1733 with Émilie du Châtelet. She was born Émilie Le Tonnelier de Breteuil, the daughter of one of Voltaire's early benefactors, who had a salon of sorts of his own, for men of letters. She had met and married the Marquis du Châtelet in 1722. In 1733 she was twenty-nine and had been given an excellent education by her father, being taught Greek, Latin and mathematics – her strong suit. She was an exceptional mathematician who produced a French translation of Newton's *Principia*. She and Voltaire formed a lasting relationship that, we are told, 'did not interfere' with her marriage. As well as the intellectual matters they shared, the relationship was also useful during later scandals in Voltaire's career – and before he moved to Switzerland – when he would seek safety at the du Châtelet estate at Cirey, where Émilie's aristocratic title meant it was a safe haven. The relationship lasted until 1749 when Émilie died during childbirth.[17]

Although Émilie du Châtelet is usually considered in relation to Voltaire, she was remarkably talented in her own right. Her intelligence was recognised early on and from the age of ten she received tuition in mathematics from the likes of Fontenelle, Johan Bernoulli, Pierre Louis Moreau de Maupertuis and Alexis Clairaut, several of whom are covered elsewhere in this book. And although her best-known work, the translation of Newton's *Principia* (still in use today), was published posthumously, she did release other works in her lifetime, showing her range. Her *Institutions de Physique* ('Foundations of Physics') was translated into several languages. When she lost a considerable sum to card sharks at the gaming tables at the court at Fontainebleau, she conceived a financing system to earn it back. She and Voltaire set up a laboratory at Cirey and each submitted a paper of their researches to a competition at the Academy of Sciences. Neither won, though both were commended.

On his arrival back in France after his English exile, Voltaire worked on the letters he had started in London, adding more with assessments of Francis Bacon and Locke and in particular Newton. This was fraught because, in effect, Newton had rendered Descartes and, to an extent, Leibniz, obsolete, and this raised all manner of nationalist grievances. In what became known as his *Lettres philosophiques*, Voltaire also described the English practice of inoculation against smallpox.

True to his fecund spirit, while all this was going on, Voltaire produced endless plays and poems (and copious letters), together with two works of history, on the reigns of Louis XIV and Charles II of Sweden. This triggered a rehabilitation in that he was now appointed royal historiographer of France, and this in turn gave rise to what was his most significant book in the eighteenth century, *Essais sur les mœurs et l'esprit des nations* (1751), the timing of which coincided with other titles by Montesquieu, Buffon and Rousseau and d'Alembert's preliminary discourse for the *Encyclopédie*. In effect, this consecrated Voltaire as one of the philosophic party, and aligned him with, among others, d'Alembert, also a prominent habitué at Sceaux.[18]

AGAINST REVELATION AND INTUITION

D'Alembert is known to history for a number of things, the first being his unusual birth. He was the illegitimate son of none other than Alexandrine de Tencin and the chevalier Louis-Camus Destouches-Canon, a cavalry officer. Destouches was abroad when the birth occurred and Mme de Tencin abandoned her son on the steps of the church of Saint-Jean-le-Rond de Paris. The new-born was placed in an orphanage and, as was the practice of the time, named after the protecting saint of the church where he had been found. His father found him and, although he didn't want his parenthood formally acknowledged, did do the decent thing and arranged for his son's adoption and secretly paid for his education. This education was substantial – he first attended a private school and then entered the Jansenist Collège des Quatre-Nations, also known as the Collège Mazarin. D'Alembert studied law, art and philosophy and graduated as an advocate, but his main loves were mathematics and, to a lesser extent, medicine.

Although in later life he would be at the very centre of the *philosophe* party as one of the main editors of the *Encyclopédie*, a member of the Académie royal des sciences (after several attempts), the Prussian Academy of Sciences and the Académie française, he was all his life a considerable mathematician, well aware that a scientific revolution had taken place in recent decades, and in touch and in competition with other first-rate mathematicians in Europe.[19] He was interested in – and made contributions to – astronomy (the movement of the moon), mechanics and fluid dynamics (fluids then had a wider resonance than now, in that they were felt to be responsible for electricity, magnetism and heat). But d'Alembert was also interested in one of the main issues of the Enlightenment, specifically the British Enlightenment – this was Locke's epistemology of sensation, the idea that all reliable knowledge reaches us via our senses, that there is no such thing as revelation or intuition.

Here he came across the work of – and formed a friendship in the Deffand salon with – Étienne Bonnot de Condillac, the Abbé de Condillac who, like Voltaire, had an aristocratic background (he was born in 1714 in Grenoble). Condillac was one of those savants who were early on interested in what would become known as psychology. In particular, he was interested in consciousness and how it was related to attention (why we notice some stimuli and not others), pre-linguistic abilities, the difference between animals and humans, and the role of language in thought (he argued that the languages of 'more primitive' peoples were more 'action'-oriented). He was interested in the nature of mind, memory, imagination, the evolution of morals, and how all this relates to our needs. One of the things that linked him to d'Alembert was his belief that mental life depended on sensations received by our organs, which impact the nervous system. He spent a lot of time considering the difference between animals and humans, believing that the higher cognitive functions depended on language and memory.[20]

By the same token, d'Alembert and his fellow Frenchman Alexis Clairaut (1713–65) were involved in the world of mathematics and mathematical physics that came after Newton's radical revision of Descartes's mechanical universe, to explore the range of ideas governing motion, mechanics (the motions of solid bodies), fluid dynamics (what laws governed the seas, the winds, the heavens), and the use of the newly imagined and devised calculus, brought into being jointly by Newton and Leibniz.

Clairaut was one of those who spent a considerable period of time examining Newton's conclusions, including leading an expedition to Lapland to confirm the great man's ideas about the flattening of the Earth at the poles and its implications for the way gravity varied across the planet. The Lapland expedition was carried out with Pierre Louis Moreau de Maupertuis (1698–1759), director of the Académie royale des sciences, and – like Condillac – a biologist whose work is now regarded as a significant precursor to evolutionary theory and genetics. Maupertuis thought that 'particles' from both father and mother made up an individual's constitution, that life forms – what came to be called species – may have changed over time, and that animals should be understood as populations rather than as individual selves.[21]

Sceaux was known for its musical entertainments and though d'Alembert was not himself a musician, he did have an academic interest in the subject. His particular concern was the mathematics of music and in 1747 he published an article on vibrating strings which contained the first manifestation of his 'wave equation' in print. This interest in vibration and in fluid dynamics led to what was perhaps his most important discovery, that as the speed of a fluid increases its pressure drops. This, in some ways, is the basic finding that allows flight to occur: the fluid passing over the top of the wing has further to travel and so its pressure drops relative to the fluid passing below the wing.[22]

MEMORY, REASON AND IMAGINATION

D'Alembert's mathematical contributions continued throughout his life. His *Opuscules mathématiques* – eight volumes between 1761 and 1780 – were a mixed bag of essays ranging from ideas about achromatic lenses to new thoughts about inertia, and included many creative and innovative ways of introducing differential equations to throw light on physical phenomena.

Despite these many significant contributions in mathematics, d'Alembert is chiefly known now as one of the editors, with Denis Diderot, of the *Encyclopédie*. Over the years of the *Encyclopédie*'s publication, d'Alembert would pen more than a thousand articles but his most valuable contribution was the *Discours préliminaire*, which he wrote when the work had just been conceived and he and his partner were seeking sponsors and subscribers. Published in 1751, it was immediately recognised as one of the seminal documents of the Enlightenment.

It is in two parts. The first part, ostensibly about why an encyclopaedia was needed, and what it could achieve, was in fact more of an exposition of the philosophy of sensationalism, in which d'Alembert's debt to both Locke and Condillac is clear. One theme is the link between scientific knowledge – to which he was wedded – and morality, in which science was pitched against the church. He was not as hard on the church as he would become, simply because, in order to get his document published, and the show on the road, he had to cope with the censors. The second part of the *Discours* was nothing less than a history of science and philosophy, in which his debt to Bacon and his idea of the tree of knowledge was also very clear, and in which the three functions of the mind were set out – memory, reason and imagination.[23]

At Sceaux d'Alembert had met Mme du Deffand, with Voltaire among several others. As their friendships blossomed, in the late 1740s the marquise began to consider holding a salon of her own.

She Who Made Voltaire Tremble

B y the mid-1740s, Anne-Thérèse de Lambert had been dead for a dozen or so years and the habitués who attended her Tuesdays at the hôtel de Nevers had migrated to Alexandrine de Tencin's. Mme du Deffand had attended Mme de Lambert's salon, but not Mme de Tencin's, a mutual hostility stemming from the fact that they had both been mistresses of the regent, the Duc d'Orléans. With the Duchesse du Maine now getting on in years, Marie du Deffand was ready to experiment on her own.

Since her premises in the rue de Beaune were so small, in 1746 Marie rented a pretty apartment in the convent of Saint-Joseph, situated in the rue Saint-Dominique in Saint-Germain-des-Prés. This practice of renting apartments in the convent was not uncommon and in the same building at the time other distinguished lodgers included the Princesse de Talmont, from the Polish nobility, 'ice cold but good company', who had married the Prince of Talmont but had become the mistress of 'Bonnie Prince Charlie', the pretender to the throne of Great Britain (who also lived in the building), and Félicité de Genlis, one-time mistress of Philippe Égalité.[1]

No less than Mme de Lambert's salon, Mme du Deffand's was sophisticated and cosmopolitan, combining aristocrats with guests from other social circles, in particular intellectuals and foreigners. The tone at Saint-Joseph, we are told, was ironic and light-hearted. 'Intelligence was the only quality required, provided it was accompanied by wit.' Understatement was especially admired. Her group was stable, and she treated everyone equally. She was impatient and egocentric; as one regular observed, 'it was impossible to be wittier than she'.[2] It is indisputable that she adopted the *philosophes* before they were well known.

As we have seen, Mme du Deffand had met d'Alembert at Sceaux. She had found him moody and uncouth to begin with but in time he would become the star of her entourage. Diderot was the one distinguished figure who was *not* welcome there. Probably, she sensed he was a far more disruptive radical than her protégé. Not that Diderot was the only – or even the main – disruptive element in her life. Her husband had died in 1751, adding to her chronic *ennui*, and, moreover, a serious eye disease was bringing about the gradual loss of her sight. In the early months of 1752, therefore, in an attempt to rescue herself from her predicament, she abandoned Paris and sought refuge in the family chateau of Champrond, where she had grown up. When she arrived there, to her surprise and delight she encountered Mademoiselle Julie de Lespinasse.

Born in November 1732, Julie was Mme du Deffand's niece, being the daughter of the Comtesse d'Albon and the Comte de Vichy, her eldest brother. Seven years after Julie's birth the comte married the comtesse's eldest daughter, making Julie both his daughter and his sister-in-law.[3] This did not make for a simple household, which was not improved when she was given the position as governess to her sister's children (who were of course her half-siblings). Mme du Deffand, when she arrived at Champrond, observed that Julie was accommodated only on sufferance. Captivated by the young woman's 'self-reliant character' and other clever and agreeable qualities, Mme du Deffand conceived the idea of attaching Julie to herself 'as a resource in [her] failing sight'.[4] She wrote Julie a letter of invitation which contained some words that would echo down the years: 'You must . . . resolve to live with me in the greatest frankness and sincerity, never to employ either insinuation or exaggeration; in a word, never to lose one of the greatest attractions of youth, which is candour. You have a good deal of intelligence, you have gaiety, you are capable of sentiment; with all these qualities you will be charming as long as you remain without pretension and without deceit.'[5]

When Mlle de Lespinasse reached Paris there was no denying that

Mme du Deffand, besides being a victim of insomnia, was close to being totally blind. And so, they were, for a time, totally dependent on one another. More than that, Julie was enthusiastically welcomed by the habitués of the Deffand salon, where Madame was back in her old familiar rooms with what had become her famous *tonneau*. (Literally speaking, *tonneau* is French for 'barrel' but in this sense it means a chair with a high back, curved to embrace and enclose the sitter and prevent draughts.) For ten years the arrangement between the two women worked perfectly.

The regulars at the salon soon became accustomed to the new arrangement, Mme du Deffand's acerbic wit and wide-ranging intelligence being perfectly set off against Julie's greater willingness to listen and to draw out the wit and wisdom of others. Julie's strength was explained specifically by Jean-François de La Harpe, a not-quite successful playwright, whom Voltaire had looked after for a time, and who was twice editor of the *Mercure de France*. Of her he wrote: 'I can say that I have never known a woman with so much natural intelligence and less desire to show it off.'[6]

Her circle of enchantment spread as the weeks and months passed. Particularly taken with Mlle de Lespinasse was Mme du Deffand's favourite, d'Alembert. Until that point – he was now well into his thirties – he had never shown much interest in women; in fact there were plentiful jokes referring to his impotence. He fell heavily in love with Julie but didn't reveal his feelings for years. This was especially poignant because Mme du Deffand now began to cherish a plan for d'Alembert to become secretary of the Académie royale des sciences.[7] She was unsuccessful in that endeavour but, at much the same time, two seats in the Académie française became available and she determined that she would do all she could to ensure that this bigger prize would be his.

Mme du Deffand had her work cut out. There was enormous hostility to d'Alembert as a *philosophe*, not only from court circles but from many academicians themselves. The academy just then, was – at it usually was – a conservative stronghold, faithful to the cult of Louis XIV, linked to the Jesuits, hostile to innovation and 'impervious' to the cultural renewal then taking place in France and which d'Alembert typified.

A New Class of Intellectual

There had been *some* change. As the years had passed, some new men had been appointed – Montesquieu in 1727, Voltaire in 1746, after three refusals, Charles Pinot Duclos a year later, Georges-Louis Leclerc, the Comte de Buffon, the celebrated naturalist, in 1753.[8] On each occasion, d'Alembert was defeated and Mme du Deffand was in despair.

Then, in August that year, the Bishop of Vence, Jean-Baptiste Surian, a well-known preacher, 'surrendered his soul'. There was by now a fairly widespread indignation that a man of d'Alembert's accomplishments should have been overlooked in preference to a raft of nonentities, and even Président Hénault – who had supported his rivals on earlier occasions – now rallied to him. D'Alembert was elected but it was Mme du Deffand who attracted most of the congratulations, 'as if on a personal triumph'.

This election, Benedetta Craveri argues, 'signified a turning point in the spread of the enlightenment'. In his book on the origins of the *Encyclopédie*, Franco Venturi says: 'First among the new generation of *philosophes* to be elected to the *Académie*, d'Alembert found there a territory in which to rally, just as he had wished, all men of letters to the new ideas, by turning them against the society of the great and the powerful. The *Académie* ... was to become the natural centre for the new class of intellectual.' Thus began a period of intense intellectualism in the 1750s, years in which the predominant ideas of the Enlightenment began to extend to a wider consciousness.

Mme du Deffand never relaxed her intelligence. Montesquieu was on record saying that he found 'inspiration' in her society, much as Voltaire had said, but she never swallowed her acerbic side. When Montesquieu was criticised in her presence for having made egotism the 'lever which moved society', she tartly quipped: 'Good, he has only revealed everyone's secret.'[9]

Her salon, Roger Picard tells us, was particularly open to British visitors – Walpole, Hume, Gibbon, Bolingbroke, Gray and the ideas of Isaac Newton – but her one weakness was that she could not bear solitude and wrote at least two letters a day, many to Voltaire. And what letters they were and are! Later in the nineteenth century,

Sainte-Beuve ranked her letters next to Voltaire's as 'the purest classics of the epoch'.[10]

Two Different Categories of Women

For ten years, then, from roughly 1753 to 1763, Mme du Deffand did not receive her guests alone. Most evenings at about six o'clock (when she got up) the doors of the buttercup yellow moiré drawing room were opened, and the habitués of her salon soon became accustomed to the unprecedented friendship between the far-from-well *femme d'esprit* and the slip of a girl from the country.

Julie might have been a slip of a girl, and she might not have been the most beautiful woman in Paris (portraits show her with a pumpkin-like round face and eyes too far apart), but she was what the French call *une jolie laide*, a plain woman who knows how to make the best of herself. Gradually, the psychology of the salon began to change. Visitors continued to admire Mme du Deffand's intelligence and to be enthralled by her sophistry. But Julie – not well educated, not especially beautiful – had a natural grasp of what we would now call interpersonal relations. She had the good sense to allow others to shine.[11]

This was especially true of d'Alembert. D'Alembert's love for Julie faced numerous obstacles other than his own nature. She was a very young woman recently arrived in Paris, and she was naturally looking for excitement – and romance. The salon was interesting intellectually, but Jean Le Rond was fifteen years her senior and somewhat academic, and she longed for passionate involvement. It was not long before she found it in a liaison with John Taafe, a visiting Irishman. So taken with him was she that she didn't spot that he was far from suitable. Mme du Deffand was appalled and told Julie she was risking her reputation. Julie responded by taking opium and in such a dose that many who knew her in Paris assumed that she had attempted suicide. She did not die but the opium habit would stay with her throughout her short life.

After the Taafe episode, Julie settled down for a while. She would join Mme du Deffand at about three every afternoon, and they would plan the evening's salon and write letters, and she would help with other administrative chores. D'Alembert, with his international reputation, was invited in 1763 to join the courts of both Catherine the Great and Frederick II of Prussia. He did go to the latter but spent only three months at the king's court. While there, he wrote to Julie every day, letters she did not share with Mme du Deffand.[12]

When d'Alembert returned to Paris, he fell into the habit of visiting Julie in her own mezzanine apartment where they could spend a few hours of gentle intimacy before Mme du Deffand got up and the salon proper could begin. Before long the practice spread, and a few of d'Alembert's closest friends joined him and Julie in her small apartment: Turgot, Marmontel, Chastellux, La Harpe, Grimm and Condorcet. Soon Mme du Deffand got wind of the early meetings – and she was furious. More than furious, incandescent with rage and disappointment. The wording of the letter she had written to Julie when she had welcomed her into her Paris home, all those years before – about being honest and frank at all times – came back to haunt her.

The break was immediate, abrupt, final. What was worse – for Mme du Deffand at any rate – was that she insisted d'Alembert take sides: he had to choose between her and Julie. D'Alembert chose Julie.[13]

A Supreme Masterpiece of French Literature

From the time of Julie de Lespinasse's defection, and even more of d'Alembert's, Mme du Deffand's salon gradually changed character, becoming more and more aristocratic. In her later years, now totally blind, she had three important friendships to keep her interested in the world around her. On a daily basis she was now looked after by her sister, but Marie's spirits were kept alive by the arrival in her life of Horace Walpole, by her correspondence with Voltaire and by the friendship of the Duc and Duchesse de Choiseul.

The friendship with Walpole was intense, amounting almost to love on her part but, in a book about France, he does not feature especially large. The fourth son of Sir Robert Walpole, Horace is known to history mainly as the master of Strawberry Hill, a neo-Gothic mansion once in the countryside but now in the south-western suburbs of London.[14]

The strength of the relationship between Mme du Deffand and Voltaire may be judged from their correspondence – it lasted for twenty years and comprised 100 letters from her to him, and 164 from him to her.[15] The exchanges were partly savoured by him as a way of keeping up with the news of aristocratic Paris while he was banished to Ferney (for being too outspoken in Paris, Germany and Geneva, where, in addition, theatre was forbidden), but the pleasure of writing was part of the point. They both knew they were good stylists and their letters would be read in the salons of the Faubourg Saint-Germain. Sainte-Beuve gave a famous assessment of Mme du Deffand as being 'with Voltaire, the purest writer of prose of the time'.[16]

Marc Fumaroli describes the alternating letters as 'one of the supreme masterpieces of our literature', and says that Voltaire had all he could do 'to keep up with her'.[17] The ironist feared by all Europe, Fumaroli concludes, had met his master. 'Before her, my shaken genius trembles.'[18]

At several points the letters refer to the Seven Years War and its legacy. Voltaire in particular was aware that a climate of general economic and political malaise brought about by the war was affecting attitudes towards the *Lumières*, the *philosophes* of the Enlightenment, and that attitudes were hardening.[19]

ALPHABETIC ABOMINATION: THEOLOGY V. PHILOSOPHY

In his later years, Voltaire's rupture with the French establishment was largely complete and enduring. He had established himself in Ferney, near Geneva, in 1759 and from then until his death in 1778 he adopted what would become his most recognisable outlook on life, announcing himself as a member of the 'party of humanity' and raging as eloquently as he could against the twin 'infamies' of fanaticism and superstition. In effect, Voltaire successfully entangled philosophy, science, social criticism and reformist political action into one all-embracing overview.

When the *Encyclopédie* appeared (chapter 14), and became embroiled in scandal, he joined in with gusto, on the side of the *Encyclopédistes*, contributing articles attacking the Jesuits as the chief form of infamy, bringers of darkness and superstition. He was especially close to d'Alembert and together they sought to use science and critical thinking to overcome the Jesuits, which they achieved in 1764, when the sect was expelled from France after refusing to reorganise under a French vicar rather than remain directly under the Pope's authority. But Voltaire was much more active even than this, writing fiction, satire, poems and pamphlets, and organising translations of foreign works sympathetic to the philosophers' arguments, such as Cesare Beccaria's treatise on humanitarian justice and penal reform, and his own assertive public defence of Jean Calas, a Protestant who was tried, tortured and executed for the murder of his son who had converted to Roman Catholicism, despite his protestation of innocence. Publicly exonerated in 1764, two years after his execution, Voltaire argued that Calas was the victim of a 'despotic' state and an irrational, brutal justice system.

Voltaire lived long enough to enjoy at least some victories of his campaigning. Enormously influenced by Newton, and growing up in the shadow of Descartes, Voltaire's greatest contribution was the *style* of life he lived, struggling heroically to understand the world, its natural laws and their implications for morality. His two books that sum him up most are the *Dictionnaire philosophique* and *Candide, ou L'Optimisme*.

First conceived in Berlin in 1752, while he was staying with Frederick of Prussia, Voltaire worked on the *Dictionnaire philosophique* intermittently until the first edition appeared in 1764. It is not what we normally mean by a dictionary. Yes, it is laid out alphabetically but, as Theodore Besterman, former director of the Institut et musée Voltaire, says: 'This epoch-making little book is in fact a series of essays on a wide variety of subjects, sometimes arranged under convenient headings arranged in alphabetic sequence, but sometimes placed under deliberately misleading or even provocative catchwords.' Thus for example, under 'Catéchisme chinois', the reader will find nothing about Chinese catechism, but instead an argument about the superiority of ethics over religion.[20]

Voltaire's overwhelming concern in the book is to pitch theology against philosophy. Even such entries as 'Friendship' and 'Beautiful' have ethical overtones. Friendship, for example, is a contract between virtuous persons. 'I say *virtuous* because the wicked have only accomplices, the voluptuous have companions in debauchery, self-seekers have associates, the politic assemble the factions, the typical idler has connections, princes have courtiers. Only the virtuous have friends.'

Above all, his treatment of religion is scientific. In his examination of Christianity in particular, he is most concerned to establish the truth: did an alleged event really occur? As Besterman puts it: 'When the *Dictionnaire* was first published men were still so naïve and so logical as to believe that sacred and inspired scriptures must be taken to mean what they say, and that it is blasphemous to select for belief what one chooses to believe.'[21] This underlay Voltaire's main concern – man's ignorance of himself, his world and his universe; how, without more knowledge, can we ever arrive at reasonable justice? So throughout his life, and throughout the *Dictionnaire*, he always sought out the facts, and then drew ethical conclusions from them, invariably laced with an elegant irony with which he lucidly exposed the 'infamy'.

He was, of course, obliged to 'disavow' the book, so as to avoid yet more time in the Bastille (he was incarcerated there twice), though everyone knew he had fathered it, not least for the scepticism he shows throughout. Here he is, for example, on Abraham: 'Abraham is one of the names famous in Asia Minor and in Arabia, like Toth among the Egyptians, the first Zoroaster in Persia, Hercules in Greece, Orpheus in Thrace, Odin among the northern nations, and so many others whose fame is greater than the authority of their history.'[22]

Voltaire triumphed in the end, returning to Paris from exile in 1778 as a frail octogenarian and welcomed by the city he had not seen for twenty-eight years as the hero of the Enlightenment that he now personified. A statue was commissioned in his honour, as we shall see, and his play *Irène* was performed also in his honour. The play is a tragedy, about the conflict between love and duty when a woman, Irène, is compelled to marry the emperor when she loves someone else. The opening night was performed in the presence of Marie Antoinette.

Voltaire was too ill to attend the opening but went to a later performance, when the actors crowned him with laurel leaves. 'Do you want to kill me with glory?' he cried. He died four months later.

A Longing for Revenge

By then, Mme du Deffand's situation had changed radically. After Julie de Lespinasse's involvement with John Taafe, and her suicide attempt (if such it was), the centre of gravity of Mme du Deffand's salon had shifted. D'Alembert may have been the first to warm to Julie but, one by one, a group formed in a corner of the Deffand salon around the younger woman, and the nature of the discussion moved away from literature to philosophy, political reform, constitutionalism, even republicanism.

After Julie had left, Mme du Deffand formed a firm friendship with the Duchesse de Choiseul, Louise-Honorine Crozat du Châtel, niece of Pierre Crozat. Born in 1735, she married the Duc de Choiseul, sixteen years her senior, who from 1758 until 1770, when he was exiled, was in effect the arbiter of French politics with all the authority of a prime minister. Louise-Honorine replaced Julie in Mme du Deffand's affections. She saw more and more of the Choiseuls at a time when the duc, 'a virulent and impenitent Anglophobe', was planning revenge for France's losses in the Seven Years War.

Choiseul was a 'pedigree-conscious' nobleman from the Duchy of Lorraine, still independent at the time. He could be vain, charming, a spendthrift, a ladies' man and a connoisseur (he had an excellent collection of paintings and – despite his Anglophobia – an English garden). But he was also a supremely effective administrator. Although France had lost the Seven Years War, Choiseul believed Britain had overreached itself, a view widely held both north and south of the Channel.[23] (Voltaire, too, writing to Mme du Deffand, remarked that 'England was ruining herself, thrashing us'.)

Choiseul wrote to the king that peace with England would 'take centuries' and that therefore 'we must employ the genius and all the power of the nation against the English'. He had in mind the biggest invasion of the British Isles ever. He read of riots in London with gloating pleasure but concluded that 'the English will never kill each other in sufficient numbers to satisfy us'. But to him it showed that, despite the recent defeats, France's political system and physical strength were inherently superior.

Britain's weakest point, Choiseul concluded, correctly enough, was America. He predicted that America would not allow itself to be taxed by far-away Britain. His idea was to await developments in America while building up French strength – primarily by building up the navy, which during the Seven Years War, he told the king, 'had been not only crushed, but disgraced'.[24]

During the Seven Years War, France had lost ninety-three ships (Britain had lost one) and, in view of this calamity, Choiseul took over the navy ministry and set to it. His aim was to replace the ninety-three and add a further forty-five frigates, an armada which he predicted would take four years to build up. Choiseul had the coasts of Sussex and Kent secretly surveyed, to find landing zones. Spies were recruited to assess the British naval strength in Portsmouth and Plymouth and others sent to the Black Country to discover techniques for casting cannon. Plans were made for a new harbour in Cherbourg, and Corsica was occupied in 1769 to deprive the British.[25]

All these impressively thorough plans came to nothing when Britain and Spain clashed in 1770 over the Falkland Islands. The king worried that Choiseul might now overreach himself and hurry to war, using Spain as a way of getting revenge over the old enemy. In the time-honoured way of the Bourbon kings, Choiseul was given twenty-four hours to quit Paris.[26]

He never saw high office again, Britain was never invaded, and the conduct of French foreign policy was taken over, in part, by the habitués of Julie de Lespinasse's salon, which is the subject of chapter 15. Meanwhile Mme du Deffand was invited to Chanteloup, where everyone gathered around her as they had done in Paris, because the duchesse had commissioned a *tonneau* identical to the one in Saint-Joseph. But the company was very different. The *tonneau* was the only thing that remained of her salon.

'All the Loose Knowledge of the World'

Now we enter the world of the Enlightenment salon at its most typical, most distinguished and most influential, with Mme Geoffrin. She was born Marie-Thérèse Rodet in 1699, 'a beautiful, devout orphan'. Her father was a *valet de chambre* for the Duchess of Burgundy and her mother was the daughter of a Parisian banker, who died a year later giving birth to a son. The children were subsequently taken to live with their grandmother, in the rue Saint-Honoré in Paris. The grandmother saw to it that Marie-Thérèse was engaged to be married at the age of only thirteen.[1]

The match found for her was François Geoffrin, a widower thirty-five years older than she, but 'an excellent settlement' was offered, M Geoffrin being the general cashier for the Manufacture royale des glaces of Saint-Gobain (chapter 8). They set up house further along the rue Saint-Honoré. Nearly two years after the wedding, which took place in July 1713, Marie-Thérèse gave birth to a daughter, also called Marie Thérèse, but without the hyphen. Thus, Mme Geoffrin was just fifteen years older than her own daughter. This closeness in age did not always make for a happy state of affairs.

In fact, Marie Thérèse, who was to become the Marquise de La Ferté-Imbault, said that the domestic peace of the household was ended with the appearance of a 'dangerous neighbour, the ambitious, intriguing, and amoral Mme de Tencin'. Just as Mme de Tencin had attended Mme de Lambert's salon, so Mme Geoffrin became a regular at Mme de Tencin's. In visiting the salon, again according to the

Marquise de La Ferté-Imbault, 'my mother's devoutness changed into a passion for people of *esprit* ... [and] the seed of her ambition began to spread rapidly'.[2]

One reason for this was that Mme de Tencin's salon had opened up for Mme Geoffrin a world she was unfamiliar with. She lacked a classical education – any kind of education at all in fact – and her introduction to the life of the intellect excited her beyond measure and even, according to her daughter, helped to relieve her of some of the boredom (*ennui*) she felt in having a husband thirty or more years older than she was. It was not long before she began to have thoughts about creating her own salon.

It was not easy. There were two problems. One was her husband, the other her daughter. M Geoffrin did all he could to stymie his wife's plans. He was a practical man, a businessman, and the life of the intellect did not interest him in the slightest. There were violent quarrels, François Geoffrin sometimes being humiliated in the process. Marie Thérèse hated these rumblings.

There is no doubt that the salon eventually created by Mme Geoffrin was even more impressive than Mme de Tencin's, though – like in a relay race – Mme G. took over many of Mme T.'s guests after her death in 1749. Mme Geoffrin's biographer credits her with three great qualities – her entrepreneurial talent, her psychological intuition, and her ability to understand the times she lived in.[3] The Enlightenment ideal had first emerged in Mme de Lambert's and Mme de Tencin's salons, to the extent that they had widened their circle beyond writers to include more and more individuals who would become known as *philosophes*, a term which came to mean not just philosophers but scientists, doctors, diplomats and natural historians who, most importantly, did not think that knowledge could only be assimilated, as Fontenelle did, by a 'small, select group', or constrained by the court or the academies, but should be available to anyone prepared to take it on.[4]

Mme Geoffrin's guests may be conveniently divided into three. At her Wednesday meetings there were those she inherited from Mme de Tencin and whom we have already met – the now aged Fontenelle, Dortous de Mairan, Marivaux, the Abbé de Saint-Pierre, Montesquieu at the height of his fame. To these we may now add the generation gathering around the *Encyclopédie* – the Abbé Raynal, Duclos, d'Alembert, Helvétius, d'Holbach, Grimm, Marmontel, Suard, Abbé Morellet, Chastellux. And third, perhaps her most original innovation, at her Monday salons she included one group of people never before part of salon society – the artists: painters such as Carl Van Loo, Claude Joseph Vernet, François Boucher, Jean-Baptiste Greuze and Hubert Robert, architects like Jacques-Germain Soufflot and engravers like Charles-Nicolas Cochin. This latter group, we are told, were included on the advice of Anne-Claude-Philippe, Comte de Caylus, himself an artist with an interest in archaeology, who acted as a sort of joint host on these Monday evenings, drawing out his fellow artists to talk about their work and their ideas in such a way as had never happened before.[5]

Mme Geoffrin herself was not in general a party to the discussions in her own salon. Without a proper education, she did not feel up to full participation. Rather she used her immense tact to ensure the continued harmony of the meetings, the more so as her guests were not chosen for their natural affinity.

By the middle of the eighteenth century the salons had become much more bourgeois affairs, places where a young author could bring his new play or poem, or his essay, to read before experts who 'in polished phrase or witty epigram, or with a silence more damning than faint praise' would make or mar the success of the enterprise.[6] Mme Geoffrin was not overly concerned about literary matters but she was very enthusiastic about art.[7] 'While Fontenelle and his *confrères* talked of the latest new play or book, and grew indignant at the restrictions of the Sorbonne ... artists would gather around the Comte de Caylus and discuss who were the likely people to obtain *appartements* in the Louvre, or when some lucky individual would be appointed to the long vacant office of First Painter to the King.'[8]

Mme Geoffrin's Monday evenings were famous all over Paris but not as fashionable as her Wednesdays. The manners of the artists were not always 'of the finest' and their speech was rougher than the writers'. (Boucher frankly preferred to meet actresses in the cafés, where he found his models.) Henri, Comte de Beauregard, has left an account of one of these Monday evenings. When he arrived (this was in 1768), 'each one had brought something; Vernet, a picture newly arrived from Italy, which they believed was a Correggio; M de la Rochefoucauld, a little picture painted in cameo upon marble, and encrusted by a process of which no one knows the secret; M Mariette [the man who virtually invented connoisseurship], a portfolio full of his most beautiful prints'.[9]

The presence of Abel-François de Marigny did not go unnoticed in Paris. Brother of the all-powerful Mme de Pompadour, the king's official mistress, he was one of the most influential men in the kingdom and at a young age had been sent to Rome with Cochin to make a study of the renowned classical works of art there. Mme Geoffrin attracted him to her salon where, she felt, with his privileges he was in a perfect position to help with *appartements* in the Louvre, and with commissions. Many of Mme Geoffrin's guests – not just artists but literary men too – had rooms in the Louvre at some point in their careers (d'Alembert, Mairan, Vien).[10]

ONE OF THE GREAT FORCES OF THE EIGHTEENTH CENTURY

But history remembers more about Mme Geoffrin's Wednesday suppers than her Mondays, for that was when the *philosophes* and the *Encylopédistes* met, that was the salon that earned it the title of 'fortress of free thought'.[11] Among the *philosophes*, we are told, Diderot was invariably unkempt and careless in his manners 'but fiercely aglow with wrath and enthusiasm'. With his hooked nose and high forehead ('like an ancient orator', as he himself put it), he was the early leader and founder of this *bande*. The son of a cutler in Langres (north of Dijon), Diderot had a mixed career to begin with. He tried being a tutor, he wrote two not very good books on free thought, for which he was briefly imprisoned, and his life had little to show for itself until he met a bookseller who had with him a French translation of an English encyclopaedia, published in 1727 by Ephraim Chambers of Westmorland. It was this modest work which gave Diderot the idea for his monumental undertaking, to gather together in one place 'all the loose knowledge of the world', to see where it might lead.[12]

Diderot had enlisted the aid of d'Alembert, already a famous mathematician, while still living with the glazier who had raised him. Between them they mapped out the reach of the book and set about recruiting contributors. Buffon wrote on natural history, Marmontel on literary subjects, Diderot himself on the Jesuits and on atheism. Given that the book was both a reference work and an instrument of propaganda for the Enlightenment, a surprising number of contributors were *abbés* or other men of the cloth, who would comprise the *philosophes*' main opposition. Many articles were unsigned but it is now known that several medical men joined in, while the cartographer Jacques-Nicolas Bellin wrote on naval matters, Louis Guillaume Le Monnier – best known as a botanist – wrote on magnetism and electricity, Louis de Cahusac, who wrote *libretti* for Rameau, provided articles on opera and ballet, and Jean-Jacques Rousseau wrote what became a famous article on political economy.[13]

Voltaire's contribution was modest – forty-three articles, mostly on literary subjects. Anne Robert Turgot and Dr François Quesnay – one of the founders of the 'physiocratic' movement – wrote on farming and grain, albeit under pseudonyms, and Jean François, Marquis de Saint-Lambert (1716–1803), contributed articles on fantasy, frivolity, honour and luxury. During his lifetime he was known for a successful poem, *Les Saisons*, and is now remembered as the lover of both Mme du Châtelet and Mme d'Houdetot, in which capacity he was connected to both Voltaire and Rousseau (chapter 20). Buffon actually produced little, just two articles: 'Nature (philos.)' and 'Nature, lois de la'. Diderot's bosom friend Friedrich Melchior Grimm (1723–1807) produced two signed articles, 'Motif (musique)' and 'Poème lyrique'. In fact, says John Lough, the mainstay of the articles in the *Encyclopédie* were produced by 'fairly obscure figures'. But that did not obscure its revolutionary nature.

A prospectus written by Diderot and d'Alembert's *Discours préliminaire* set out to examine '*la généalogie et la filiation de nos connaissances*'. Using Locke's then popular notion that all knowledge derived directly or indirectly from the senses, d'Alembert in particular traced the stages by which different branches of knowledge emerged. This led to the classification already highlighted by D'Alembert, according to whom three branches of knowledge – erudition (memory), literature and the arts (imagination) and sciences and philosophy (reason) – had developed since the Renaissance. The historical account is built up on a series of great names – Bacon, Descartes, Newton, Locke and Leibniz are all considered in some detail, followed by Fontenelle, Buffon, Voltaire and Montesquieu. Not everything was as it should be, according to d'Alembert. He regretted the loss of Latin as the international language of learning and was of the opinion that the literature of his own day was inferior to that produced during the reign of Louis XIV.

But beyond being a colossal work of reference (much greater than anything available in English), it was also clear that the *Encyclopédie* was a '*machine de guerre*', devoted to spreading the ideas of the Enlightenment, fomenting in the words of one critic 'the seeds of Anarchy and Atheism'. In this Diderot was always more outspoken than d'Alembert.

Opposition grew throughout the 1750s from the church, the Jesuits in particular, with the year 1760 standing out because of the performance in May of Charles Palissot's satirical comedy *Les Philosophes* at the Comédie-Française.[14] The Comédie was by then a state theatre, subject to rigid government control and censorship. By the end of the month there had been fourteen performances, and the play was published before the end of the run. Its text contained scurrilous attacks on Diderot (Dortidius) and Helvétius (Valère) while Rousseau (Crispin), still looked upon as a *philosophe* despite his breach with Diderot and the others (chapter 20), was lampooned by being dragged on stage on all fours, pulling a lettuce out of his pocket. Despite the fact that the attacks got under Diderot's skin, they are in fact few and far between as regards the *Encyclopédie* itself, and Palissot was sparing of Voltaire, who irritated his friends by exchanging letters with the play's author. In fact, Voltaire mounted a very clever – even eloquent – defence of the whole *Encyclopédic* enterprise.

Despite these trials and tribulations, and despite the fact that scattered throughout the pages of the volumes may be found cries of frustration at the obstacles which the state, church and Parlement put in the way of the free expression of their rationalist and secular approach to problems, the *Encyclopédie* faced head-on the three central intellectual realms at issue in the Enlightenment – philosophy, religion and politics.

A New Attitude to the World

In the realm of philosophy, both Diderot and d'Alembert took care to denounce scholasticism, which the latter described as a 'disease'.[15] They enthusiastically followed Locke in his rejection of innate ideas, were equally committed to opposing Thomas Hobbes's grim view of the human condition (this from Rousseau in particular), and throughout it all there was Diderot's committed materialism, in particular his scepticism about the soul and just where, in the body, it might be found. The books tackle the similarity between parents and children and early ideas about heredity as reflected in the thinking of Buffon, and the many articles on ethical and moral questions – treated rationally of course, as the editors saw it – were routinely attacked by the journal *La Religion vengée*, which never let up.[16]

In religion, what stands out most in the *Encyclopédie* is the call for toleration, though one article refused to extend toleration to atheists. Elsewhere, there were many moderate articles on the freedom of conscience, many of which were attacked mercilessly. (The prosecution of Huguenots was firmly condemned in the *Encyclopédie*.) By the 1760s the idea that an individual should be free to choose his or her religion, or no religion at all, was gaining ground but limited toleration was not granted to Huguenots until the eve of revolution in 1787. Diderot set out the principles of biblical criticism in an article entitled '*Canon, en théologie*', just one of many articles regarded as 'dangerous' by the church authorities.[17]

The politics of the *Encyclopédie* were less radical than its philosophy. It appeared before the 1770s and 1780s, when political discontent was becoming more vocal in France.[18] Lough says that one article has been subject to more minute analysis than any other and that is Rousseau's '*Économie (morale et politique)*', which appeared in 1755. Its views were more developed in his *Du contrat social*, published seven years later, but it was here that he first made the distinction between civil power and paternal power, removing the attempt by others to justify absolute power by tracing it back to the family.

The greatest storm was caused by Diderot's article '*Autorité politique*', in which he sets forth clearly the principle of government by consent, partially based on a quote from St Paul, and a 'contract of submission' between the ruler and ruled. Very different from what Rousseau would understand by his social contract, the *Encyclopédie* went on to consider the possibility of an elective monarchy, and a limited monarchy along British lines.

The *Encyclopédie* was not, as some were to claim, 'the first stage in the mighty conspiracy which brought the established order crashing down in the Revolution', but from the start people did take on board that it was a force to be reckoned with, and potentially threatening at least to some.[19] In private, Voltaire described the project as a '*Tour de Babel*' but there is no getting away from the fact that it stood for a new attitude to the world.

SOMETHING LOOSENS IN FRANCE

Mme Geoffrin was full of enthusiasm for this new undertaking and invited many of the contributors to her salon. After her death, her daughter, the Marquise de La Ferté-Imbault, discovered that her mother had given more than 100,000 crowns to the project, without which it is highly unlikely it could ever have been brought to fruition.[20]

All social levels in France at the time were vaguely feeling the oppression of the feudal privileges of the nobility, the iron grip of the Catholic Church and the gross unfairness of the taxation system, so that when, in the *Dictionnaire encyclopédie*, the grievances were set out in alphabetic form (and therefore easy to find), 'something loosened in France' and the desire for change was, to an extent, codified.

To an extent also, the fate of the *Encyclopédistes*, and the *philosophes*, was settled by the opposition they and the *Encyclopédie* aroused. A number of entries on theology in the book had been written by the Abbé de Prades, who argued for example that the soul is made of an 'unknown' substance and that justice in France was based on might, not the word of God. The Jesuits affected to find these articles heretical and the archbishops joined in, all over France. In this way, the *Encyclopédie* became famous (or notorious), and everyone wanted to read it.

In February 1752, shortly after publication of the second volume, a decree of the King's Council suppressed both volumes.[21] Ironically, the decree suppressed reprinting and selling of the book, but it contained no prohibition on the work itself. Diderot and d'Alembert therefore continued their exertions on the next volumes.

Rarely can a victory have been so pyrrhic, or so humiliating. The Jesuits, whose plan it was to take over the *Encyclopédie* and turn it to their own advantage, found that they simply did not have the resources – scholastic, administrative, imaginative – to take on their project and 'the Government was obliged ... to take measures to induce M. Diderot and M. d'Alembert to resume the work'.[22]

Mme Geoffrin's generosity was legendary. In addition to her liberal offering of commissions to her artist guests at her Monday salons, she settled generous pensions on Antoine Léonard Thomas, poet, the Abbé Morellet and d'Alembert. To Jean-François Marmontel (who Roger Picard calls 'a parasite'), she offered lodging in her house on the rue Saint-Honoré (he stayed for years). Marmontel was for a time editor of the *Mercure de France*, the leading newspaper of the day. He also wrote satires, mostly mild but enough on one occasion for the butt of his humour to ask for his incarceration in the Bastille.

Friedrich Melchior Grimm, an obscure German émigré to begin with, who managed to turn himself into a baron, had arrived in Paris in his twenties, as tutor to the children of the Count of Schönberg, and formed a friendship with none other than Jean-Jacques Rousseau, then as penniless and as unknown as Grimm. But when Rousseau featured him in his *Confessions*, both of them turned into overnight sensations. Grimm met Diderot in Mme Geoffrin's salon, and in this way he made the acquaintance of the Abbé Raynal, yet another guest. Raynal was editor of the *Correspondance littéraire*, a handwritten periodical which sent the literary news of Paris to certain northern princes. This was tailor-made for Grimm since a number of German princes also wished to be kept informed of what was happening in Paris. And so, after two years Raynal passed the editorship of his publication to Grimm, who never looked back. He too was welcomed by most *salonnières*, one of whom, Mme d'Épinay, who also had her own little theatre, became his mistress (chapter 22). His accounts of the Paris music scene were copious and included a description of the visit of the seven-year-old Mozart.[23]

Mme Geoffrin's fame and status were such that she, rather than any of the other *salonnières*, was invited to Vienna, St Petersburg and Berlin by their respective rulers. She made a more or less stately progression across Europe, faithfully reported in the press.[24]

When she died, in October 1777, after a long illness, during which her daughter forbade many of her long-standing *philosophe* friends from visiting her, she had already made arrangements for the pensions awarded to d'Alembert, Thomas and Morellet to be increased. More than anyone, d'Alembert was grief-stricken. He knew what she had done to help the Enlightenment cause. A cause that helped France think well of itself in the wake of the Seven Years War.

A HEN WHO HATCHED A DUCK'S EGG

Her daughter felt differently. According to the Baron de Gleichen, a German scholar of Greek who lived for a time in Paris, writing in his celebrated memoirs, 'Mme Geoffrin had a daughter who resembled her neither in face nor disposition, nor character ... She was even not very fond of her, and often said that she felt like a hen who had hatched a duck's egg.'[25] There is no doubt that Mme de La Ferté-Imbault was very different in character – and intellectual inclination – from her renowned mother.

Mme de La Ferté-Imbault cordially detested the *philosophes* she had grown up with, and who surrounded her mother, 'and she detested them to the end of her days'. Moreover, she never forgave her mother for forcing her into a marriage with an older man so that she might have a great name. When he died, leaving Marie Thérèse a widow at twenty-two, with one little girl, she might have married again but she resolved to keep her freedom. The outburst of happiness which she showed 'leads one to suppose that the marriage had not been a great success'. When her daughter died of consumption at the age of eleven, Mme de La Ferté-Imbault was inconsolable, and she became severely ill herself, which left her deaf for the rest of her life. She did not have an easy time of it.

On the other hand, her late husband's family, the d'Estampes, were one of the oldest clans in France and very close to the court. This was surely not unconnected with the fact that her tastes, quite unlike her mother's, turned aristocratic.[26] Her friends were the fashionable and frivolous souls of Versailles and she made no secret of her dislike of what she called 'the philosophic party'. This social divide reached its apogee in the middle of the eighteenth century, one symptom being the creation of several *sociétés badines*, orders of mock chivalry which were one of the ways that, in the last days of the *ancien régime*, the absolutism of French society tipped over the edge. One of these *sociétés* was the *Ordre de la mouche-à-miel* (Order of the Honey Bee), which had ridiculous rules about dancing and the punishments for not taking part.

Mme de La Ferté-Imbault had her own order, the Sublime Order of Lanturelus. Like her mother's salon, she also received on Mondays, in a separate section of the same house on the rue Saint-Honoré, but of course the guests were very different. Unlike her mother's salon, the daughter's was made up of older people who were, for the most part, very religious. One evening they passed the time in exchanging verses, in a parody of what they felt the *philosophes* and writers were doing and, in each case, that night, ended their verses with the words 'Lanturelu, lanturelu', which translates crudely as 'stuff and nonsense'.[27] An 'order' was quickly established, with mock solemnity, in which Mme de La Ferté-Imbault herself became 'Queen of the Incomparable Order of Lanturelus, and Protectress of Lampoons'.

Nonsense it might be, but the idea caught on, and all Paris was agog. 'When I devote myself to society and to my friends, I like only to laugh, to play, and to forget common sense,' she wrote in her *Plan de vie pour ma vieillesse*, which she wrote when she was sixty. She was now accepted at the highest social levels on the court side of society, but her eminence overall did not quite equal her mother's and to go with the passing of the years 'her youthful antipathy for the *philosophes* turned to violent aversion'. She judged Voltaire and d'Alembert to be 'the cleverest apothecaries of new poisons' and she devoted decades to manufacturing her own counter-arguments, which comprised a huge collection of thoughts taken from the greatest ancient and modern philosophers, all intended to underwrite the eternal verities of Christian morality. But when she suggested this might form the basis of an 'anti-*Encyclopédie*' she was quietly dissuaded.[28]

She did attempt a reconciliation with her mother, which also came about when she was sixty, when she sent Mme Geoffrin the plan for her old age, in which she vowed to let bygones be bygones. But it didn't really work. 'Everyone I frequent', she lamented, 'has a great regard for my mother and would like to meet her.' She was unable to overcome the raw fact that her mother 'preferred the company of d'Alembert and Julie de Lespinasse to that of her daughter'.

The Multiple Ménages of Julie de Lespinasse

After her spectacular falling out with Mme du Deffand, Julie de Lespinasse managed to rent two floors in a small house not far away. Moreover, Mme de Luxembourg provided her with furniture with which to set up house and, one by one, following d'Alembert, many of the habitués of the Deffand salon moved along to Julie's. It was of course the talk of Paris.

Not everything went well for Julie. She immediately came down with a bad case of smallpox. D'Alembert stayed with her, reassuring her that she would live. She did pull through but was badly afflicted with pockmarks that, as Marilyn Yalom says, wounded her vanity as much as her appearance. It didn't matter to the love-struck d'Alembert, who confided to David Hume that 'she was rather marked by small-pox. But, without being disfigured in the least.'[1]

Then d'Alembert fell sick with the same ailment. Now she had to nurse him. He too lingered near death, but Julie insisted he vacate the rooms he had always shared with his old nurse, and move into her building, where he could rent rooms above hers. He accepted, despite how it would look to everyone else – as though they were living as an unmarried married couple. It was never clear what the exact relationship between Julie and Jean was, though d'Alembert once told Voltaire that he had no intention of marrying Julie – he just didn't have the necessary wherewithal.[2] However, there is no question but that they enjoyed the same books, the same plays, the same music, and their peers treated them as a couple.

As far as Julie's own salon was concerned, it was every bit as successful as Mme du Deffand's had been. Of all those who followed d'Alembert to the rue Saint-Dominique, the most prominent were Turgot and Condorcet.

THE CONCEPT OF PROGRESS

Anne Robert Jacques Turgot was, arguably, the most original thinker of the French Enlightenment, whose efforts at reform would fail in the eighteenth century but succeed in the nineteenth, long after his death. Born in Paris in 1727, he was educated at the Sorbonne where, even as a student, he concerned himself with the 'big' questions of life, delivering two dissertations (in Latin, after the fashion of the time): *On the Benefits Which the Christian Religion Has Conferred on Mankind* and *On the Historical Progress of the Human Mind*. Indeed, Turgot was one of the first to envision the very concept of 'progress', which for him involved not just progress in manners and morals, but in the sciences, the arts, in law and, above all perhaps, in economics, which would come to dominate his thought.[3]

In the early 1750s, Turgot took office in the Parlement of Paris and became a member of the Chambre royale, a kind of supreme court when the Parlement was exiled for defying the king (this when he was still in his twenties). With his interest in economics and being so well connected, he was instructed to make a tour of inspection in the provinces, accompanying Vincent de Gournay, who, with François Quesnay, was one of the founders of the 'physiocrat' school, who believed that all wealth was founded in land. It was de Gournay who coined the phrase '*laisser faire, laisser passer*', which would become celebrated in modern classical economics and which would come to dominate Turgot's own views. During these travels, Turgot visited Voltaire and the two men became friendly and mutually supportive. Turgot also wrote several articles – on financial and economic matters – for the *Encyclopédie*, and began to attend the salons of not just Mme du Deffand, but Mme Geoffrin, Mme Helvétius and Mlle de Lespinasse.[4]

In 1761, such was his developing reputation in economics that he was appointed *intendant* (tax-collector) for the Limoges region. The appointment lasted for fully thirteen years, during which time he revised the tax structure of this very poor area and reformed the *corvée* system whereby the populace worked on the roads in lieu of tax.

While he was there, he wrote his best-known and most successful work, *Reflections on the Formation and Distribution of Wealth*, in which he expanded Quesnay's theories and developed his idea that only the *net* product of the land should be taxed. His ideas – and his achievements in Limoges – did not go unnoticed and in 1774 he was appointed minister to the navy and, a month later, was made comptroller-general of finances. This was at a time when France's public finances were in disarray and he set about enforcing the most rigid economies in all departments. He also ensured that a number of lavish state sinecures were dispensed with. This policy hardly made him popular, nor did his practice of imposing certain reductions on state contracts (for example, gunpowder and the royal mails) as they came up for renewal. (He replaced the slow and heavy mail coaches with more efficient *diligences*, which became known as '*turgotines*'.) His reforms did succeed in reducing government debt more than a little.[5] On economic grounds, he was opposed to France's involvement in the American Revolutionary War but was overruled.[6]

A Volcano Covered in Snow

The Marquis de Condorcet – Marie-Jean-Antoine-Nicolas de Caritat – was much in the mould of both d'Alembert and Turgot (whose biography he was to write), equally obsessed by the possibility of progress in society and the perfection of human nature, which were among the main objectives of the Enlightenment and the *philosophes*. He was born in 1743 in Picardy. His father – a cavalry captain – was killed only weeks after he was born and Marie-Jean was brought up in isolation by his deeply religious mother, who, a keen worshipper of the Virgin, chose to clothe him in white dresses until he was eight. He was then given a Jesuit instructor and was later enrolled for four years in a Jesuit school at Reims.

He did well at school but did not enjoy the regime, feeling that the competitive ethic of the *ancien régime* did not bring out the best in people. 'Human life', he was to write later, 'is not a struggle in which rivals contend for prizes. It is a voyage that brothers [*sic*] make together; where each employs his forces for the good of all and is rewarded by the sweetness of mutual benevolence ... By contrast, the crowns bestowed in our *collèges* – which induce the schoolboy to believe himself already a great man – arouse only childish vanity.'[7] The mix of dogma and corporal punishment that he encountered at Reims would colour his views all his life.

From 1758 to 1760 he continued his studies at the Collège de Navarre, a prestigious wing of the University of Paris, and this is where he began to show an aptitude for mathematics and science, which would form such a large part of his output. At the college, Jean-Antoine Nollet, an *abbé* but also a keen follower of Newton, had established France's first chair in experimental physics. Here Condorcet was able to shine in both mathematics and philosophy, overcoming family objections, and further exploring the world of integral calculus. Although his first written paper was rejected by the Académie royale des sciences, his talent was recognised and his second paper received the endorsement of d'Alembert and Jérôme de Lalande, an astronomer whose observations had helped in the discovery of Neptune, who went so far as to say that the then 21-year-old Condorcet ranked as 'one of the ten leading mathematicians in Europe'.

Through d'Alembert, Condorcet was given an introduction to Voltaire, who would become a great influence on the young man, and he began attending the salons of Mme du Deffand and Mlle de Lespinasse, where he met Turgot.[8] By all accounts, his manners at this time were not as graceful as they might have been – he was socially ill at ease, shy and introverted. Julie de Lespinasse called him 'a volcano covered in snow'.[9]

That so many mathematicians thought so highly of him so quickly was reflected in the fact that he was elected to the Académie royale in 1769, at the age of twenty-six, and this – together with the confidence that came from being in both Mme du Deffand's and Mlle de Lespinasse's salons – seems to have brought about a psychological transformation in him and he began to show himself as a passionate and accomplished polemicist. And so, when Turgot was appointed a royal official in Limoges, Condorcet offered his services as someone who could argue on his behalf. He agreed with Turgot on the matter of free trade in grain, the abolition of protectionist guilds and corporations and suppressing the *corvée*, which was, as he saw it, a taxation in kind, a system of forced labour in which people 'donated' part of their time to building roads and bridges. Condorcet was also in favour of Turgot's plans for representative government reaching up from the regions to the capital, via a hierarchy of assemblies. As the Revolution approached, he would come out from Turgot's shadow.[10]

PREDICTION OF A 'VAST GENIUS'

Thrilling as all these individuals were surrounding Julie, and though at about this time she told d'Alembert that she had never been so happy, in truth part of her still hankered after a passionate affair, the one element in her life that was lacking. This arrived almost on cue in the shape of the Marquis de Mora, son of the Spanish ambassador. He was a winning individual – handsome, personable and equally passionate. Again, it was d'Alembert who introduced the Spaniard to Julie.

By then Julie was thirty-six, Mora ten years younger. She spoke English, Italian and Spanish and was familiar with the literature of those countries, so there was that to share with him. Passion doesn't care about age difference, but Parisian society did. Baron Grimm remarked tartly about Julie that 'she had passed the season for love affairs'.[11] D'Alembert was the only one who didn't see it, blinded by his own feelings.

Even as she and Mora were exchanging passionate letters (twenty-two in ten days at one point), Julie met and was drawn to someone else. Jacques-Antoine-Hippolyte de Guibert was a military man and a writer, almost a *philosophe*. In fact, he was a friend of several of the *philosophes* and of Buffon. His 1772 treatise, *A General Essay on Tactics*, published originally in London and translated many times, even into Persian, took Paris by storm, even influencing the young Napoleon.[12]

Tactically, Guibert's main idea was to move armies away from passive infantry into autonomous divisions, permitting rapid movement, a rearrangement that would come into effect during the post-Revolutionary Napoleonic wars. Until that point, traditional military tactics had been based on long, slowly moving lines of men that required not just discipline but passivity. Guibert changed that type of approach and all Paris was fascinated – here was an intellectual soldier. Voltaire's well-known assertion 'I hate all heroes' comes from a poem he wrote in response to Guibert's *Tactics*.

More than that, as Robert Morrissey puts it, Guibert's thinking was at the 'crossroads' of a number of tendencies of that time – not just Enlightenment and absolutism, but ancient republicanism and military culture in the wake of the defeat in the Seven Years War. Guibert thought that the overall result of the changes introduced by Richelieu and Louis XIV had the effect of confusing 'glory for shine'.[13] He looked back on ancient Rome with affection – 'there was never a people with more grandeur' – and he called for a 'national discipline', an amalgam of politics, military endeavour and public education, out of which, he said, 'an enlightened mass' would emerge and out of *that*, he was convinced, one 'vast genius' would rise up.

This was, of course, a prescient view and one can see why Napoleon, then a young soldier, read Guibert's book with such interest. In fact, Guibert felt that France just then was 'degenerating' and quite unable to put such a system in place – he thought instead that Frederick the Great in Prussia had got it right, and he said he admired 'the grandeur of [his] resolution'.[14] Guibert felt that 'grandeur, audacity and genius' went together to produce a 'consistency of glory and renown', consistency being what France needed above all else. Guibert was not uncritical of the Enlightenment, feeling that critical reason was, to an extent, stifling the creative power of admiration and enthusiasm that was needed to forge ahead.

He also wrote tragedies that he would read in the salons with 'a captivating voice'. Because of this concatenation of talents, he was elected to the Académie française in 1785 where, in his inaugural speech, he returned to the theme of glory and grandeur, the cornerstone of which, he insisted, was a politico-military edifice under a brilliant man of genius. This – he remained convinced – was the best way for France to regain its former glory, following its defeat in the Seven Years War.

This was heady stuff and, with Mora's health now deteriorating fast, Julie turned to the military sensation. Unlike Mora, Guibert's star was in the ascendant (it was even said that he was 'the next Corneille'), and he made the most of his new-found fame. This is when, it appears, the couple first made love in Julie's box at the opera. (Boxes then were suites of rooms.)

Like Mora, Guibert was ten years younger than Julie and it seems that the general rule in such cases – that the older lover loves more – was true with Guibert. Nor was Julie's passion for Mora entirely dead. When she received news of his death in June 1774, once again she tried to kill herself, once again via an overdose of opium. Guibert was, meanwhile, still seeing *his* former mistress from time to time. And d'Alembert was still around, still in love with Julie, still running her errands. They were still a couple in the eyes of the world.[15]

Despite her suicide attempt, Julie still somehow managed to lead a full cultural life. She was present almost daily at the opera.[16] She dined with the upper crust of Parisian society at other times.

For her, the beginning of the end came in September 1775, when Guibert married someone else. Devastated, in her letters she compared her love for him as a 'great sickness', and asked for her own letters to be returned. Despite this, and despite sensing her failing health (she suffered from TB), she still found time – and the energy – to write him *forty-four* more letters. Her last letter contained the lines, 'Goodbye, my friend. If ever I return to life, I would like to spend it once more in loving you; but there is no longer any time.'

Julie de Lespinasse died on 23 May 1776, much too young at forty-three, and was buried the next day at the Church of Saint-Sulpice. D'Alembert and Condorcet led the mourners, who included 'a tearful Guibert'.[17]

THE GREAT GRIEF OF D'ALEMBERT

There was one more shock to come, for d'Alembert. Julie had asked him to burn her papers and to send back her letters from Guibert without reading them. This was normal practice for the time and d'Alembert did exactly as requested. However, she said nothing about the rest of her papers, and these he did read. The papers included her love letters from Mora and a memoir she had written about their affair. D'Alembert came across these entirely unexpectedly – and he was devastated. In his innocence and inexperience with affairs of the heart, he had never suspected that there had existed a ménage with three men.

He was inconsolable, so much so that he wrote two letters to Julie after her death, in which his distress is all too evident even at this distance. 'Oh you who can no longer hear me, you whom I loved so tenderly and so constantly, you who I thought loved me for a few moments, you whom I preferred to everything, you who would have taken the place of everyone for me, if you had wanted to; alas! If you can still feel some emotion in that dwelling place of death for which you have so deeply sighed, and which will soon be mine, look at my misfortune and my tears, the solitude of my soul, the horrible emptiness you have placed there.'[18]

The fact that Julie did not forbid him to read this part of her papers raises a question about her character. That she could love three men at the same time calls into question our ideas about the mutual exclusivity of love, but in France, Marilyn Yalom tells us, the French have accepted Julie as 'one of their own ... the woman who loves too much assumes a heroic dimension'.[19]

PART FOUR

Savoir Vivre:
The Lineaments of
Frenchness II

An Elevated Level of Living:
France as the New Greece

By 1749, when Montesquieu's *Spirit of the Laws* was published, and when the first volume of Buffon's *Natural History* appeared, carriages bound for Dunkirk and Calais left Paris every Monday and Friday from the Grand Cerf, a shopping arcade on the rue Saint-Denis, at eight o'clock in the morning. Carriages for the Low Countries left from the same location on Wednesdays and Saturdays at six o'clock in the morning in summer and an hour later in winter. Passenger coaches travelled usually only in daylight hours, but the mail couriers rode through the night. The post for La Rochelle left from the rue Contrescarpe every Monday, Wednesday and Friday at midnight, during peacetime, and messengers for Madrid left from the same place at the same time but only on Fridays, taking fifteen days to reach the Spanish capital.[1]

What this shows, among other things, is that by the middle of the eighteenth century, Paris, if not all of France, was temporally literate. Civic clocks were situated throughout the city and domestic clocks and watches were growing gradually more affordable as production techniques improved. In portraits of the time, for example, many people chose to be shown with their timepieces on display. They were a sign, not just of wealth, but of sophistication, for in many cases the clocks showed planetary movements as well as the time of day. The Enlightenment was as much about science as it was about philosophy and letters.

In fact, it was about quite a lot more than that, and clocks were but one sign of the new sensibility in France which was a marked advance on what had gone before. The new sensibility involved new thinking about all manner of things, from architecture and interior design to cooking and medicine, from hygiene and diet to aesthetics and sex, to new ideas about intimacy and individualism, and not least new ideas about the possibilities for happiness. In short, there was abroad in France a new art of living – and a new level of life. There were many new words to describe new activities and new ideas, and for the first time the words 'new' or 'modern' were themselves a mark of approval. Many of these developments were interlinked, and it is this interlinking which justifies the use of the words 'new sensibility'. The French believed it set them apart from – and ahead of – everyone else. They had made up for their defeats in the Seven Years War.

The French at this time were self-confident, even pleased with themselves. In 1776, Paul-Philippe Gudin de La Brenellerie, a dramatist friend of Beaumarchais, in his *Essay on Progress in the Arts and Human Reason During the Reign of Louis XV*, explained that during Louis's monarchy, 'human reason had reached a state of perfection' at the same time as, 'with an astonishing rapidity, comfort had replaced magnificence'.[2] The layout of homes – interior decoration, lighting, heating – had all been brought 'to such a point of perfection that it seems impossible that the degree of comfort that we enjoy today can ever be surpassed'. And he insisted that it took just as much 'genius' to invent a machine to pump water as to imagine a concept for a new tragedy.[3] This simultaneous progress in matters intellectual and in the art of modern comfort, says Joan DeJean, meant in turn that the French had created a 'veritable science of manners' in which 'their mastery is recognised all over Europe'. In that same year, Louis-Antoine, Marquis de Caraccioli – noted for his opposition to the *philosophes* – argued that as a result of having acquired 'comfortable and convenient' French beds and tables, 'Europe had become French'.[4]

In 1790, Arthur Young, an early English statistician and an agricultural expert, shared his first-hand experience of the Parisian way of life: 'In the art of living, the French have generally been esteemed by the rest of Europe, to have made the greatest proficiency.' 'The art of living' was a phrase that came into widespread use but throughout Europe generally it was applied to what were perceived as French strengths, and the French expression *l'art de vivre*. It referred mainly to interior decoration and the forms of furniture that came into use, plus two areas in which it was felt that the French had set the way since the time of Louis XIV: food and clothing.[5]

Voltaire agreed, arguing that 'every country had a national character' and that 'the essence of the French today' was to be 'the most civilised nation' in Europe, 'a model for all neighbouring countries'. More profoundly, a view began to form that furniture and décor had a subtle influence on the way people behaved, comfort rendering people more civilised and polite. On this account, 'France was the New Greece'.[6]

Not long after, the author of the first 'history of private life', Pierre Legrand d'Aussy, naturalist, antiquarian, and conservator of manuscripts at the Bibliothèque nationale, argued that 'the manner of thinking characteristic of the French' had been determined by such matters as architecture, furniture and dress. 'The French Way of Life', he insisted, was now 'universally recognised' to be superior to all others. 'Enlightened Europeans' were adopting all the 'interior arts' developed in France.[7]

The concept of civilisation itself went through three stages. To begin with it referred, narrowly, to the fact that comfort and ease were making people more civil to each other, that furniture did have an effect on behaviour as people found it easier to live well together in society. Next, the view formed that society was capable of achieving an ever higher and wider level of comfort, enabling more cultural development. Finally, there was recognition of what was called *'a* civilisation', that material well-being and intellectual progress went together in an integrated whole where, of course, France was the leader.

The change can be monitored in art. From the 1720s on, a new type of painting began to be seen in Paris. It was best exemplified by the canvases of Jean-François de Troy (1679–1752), who depicted settings that focus above all on the decoration of interior rooms. His 1728 painting *Reading in a Salon* shows seven individuals, two men and five women, all dressed in the most sumptuous velvets, silks and lace, in an equally splendid room, the walls lined with brocade, with an ornate gilt clock, an embroidered screen and an imposing fire-place – it is, above all, intimate. He first showed his pictures publicly in 1724 and 1725 at the Salon at the Louvre.[8] In fact, de Troy, who eventually became director of the Académie de France à Rome, made *tableaux de mode* famous. Instead of idyllic, theatrical depictions along the lines of his predecessors, de Troy showed the life of fashionable French society of the eighteenth century in an accurate, detailed, above all *non-judgemental* way – courting, card-playing, gossiping. These were small pictures, intimate, cosy and intended for use in the new, smaller rooms of individual houses.

Along with the proliferation of small rooms for dedicated functions (bathroom, dressing room, study), there were many innovations in the eighteenth century right across the board in the field of architecture, furniture design and interior decoration but in a book about French exceptionalism three stand out: the boudoir, the sofa and the secretaire. The boudoir spread steadily throughout Europe, perhaps showing, comments DeJean dryly, 'that the need for privacy and escape was as urgent as it is today'. But she also notes that in some cases the boudoir became 'the sexiest room in town', by which she means that it was a room where a woman could dwell on – and maybe try out – what to wear to attract the man of her choice. And she quotes from the 'boudoir book' of Marie-Anne Deschamps, a courtesan of note, in which she described one boudoir – that of a kept woman and chorus girl – which 'was anything but private', being more like a 'sexual paradise', equipped with erotic gadgets and mirrors galore. That this is not too far off the mark finds support in the 1832 edition of the *Dictionnaire de la conversation* (a twelve-volume tome with 'indispensable suggestions' for subjects people might talk about), which made it clear that 'everyone expects to find mirrors all over boudoirs'.[9]

LOVE ON THE SOFA

Notably – and this is what counted – a sofa accommodated two people, not one, and, no less important, it was upholstered. This, says Dena Goodman, 'was the real revolution' in furniture and behaviour, because the fact and sight of two people sitting together in close proximity 'was regarded as a rather racy innovation, part of the French "gallant" scene'. Stiff seating, such as that at Versailles, ensured that everyone was bolt upright at all times, which fitted well with the rigid hierarchy at court (this is what corsets were made for). More than that, the sofa brought into use – and took advantage of – *chantourné*, a new technical term meaning scrollwork or fretwork, which in turn was associated with the invention of a curved saw that vastly improved the possibility of producing woods swirled and curved in elaborate scallops and which facilitated the luscious swoops that so dominated the rococo. Finally, in this list of small developments that made a big difference to comfortable living, there was the *accotoir*, an armrest that was both curved and padded, which permitted yet more of the elegantly languid 'lolling' on the sofa that was such a feature of sophisticated love-making.[10]

The sofa set off a design and manners revolution so that by about 1760 all kinds of seating as we know it had been perfected. It also helped the upholsterers' craft to take off. In the first two decades of the eighteenth century more and more upholstery 'tricks' were concocted – for example frames within frames which gave more 'spring' to seating and backing, meaning that sofas became softer and more easeful than ever. By the end of the *ancien régime* there were more than 600 upholsterers in Paris.[11]

Also linked to the sofa revolution – and we shall come back to this – was a new expression which entered the French language in 1723: *tomber amoureux*, 'to fall in love'. It quickly won acceptance, says DeJean, for the phrase was included in a dictionary published in 1736, to be followed by the related phrase *coup de foudre*, or 'lightning bolt'.[12] Such intense pleasures had happened before, of course, but with the associated growth of letter-writing, the idea caught on as it had not done until then, and of course it was helped along by the development of the sofa, which made falling in love all the easier.

THE GOLDEN AGE OF THE LOVE LETTER

Letter-writing was helped by developments in the postal service. The postal service in France was hardly new, having been introduced at the very beginning of the seventeenth century, but the *petite poste*, which enabled three deliveries a day across Paris, did not begin until 1749.[13] And it was this which precipitated the high point of the Republic of Letters.

Letter-writing was a new and most pleasurable experience not entirely divorced from gallantry, and along with it went an explosion in the manufacture of desks.[14] Together with that went a concomitant rise in the use of locks. The secretaire was not just a place for writing but also a place for keeping secrets, suitably armed with locks and false bottoms. Jewels obviously needed to be protected but love letters were probably the documents that contained the most precious secrets. As a result, the locksmith was as important as any specialist. Locks could be elaborate and very beautiful, but they could also be diabolically cunning. All manner of trigger mechanisms were devised for preventing people opening locks. In some devices, the lock couldn't be closed once it had been opened; in others there was a mechanism showing how many times the lock had been opened since the love-letter-writer last locked it. Dena Goodman and Kathryn Norberg sum up in this way: 'French society had a particular capacity for creating secrets and engaging with technologies through which they were defined. In a number of ways, Parisian society especially appears to have been enormously at ease with the concepts of artifice, disguise and trickery.'[15]

Despite all these trickeries, DeJean argues that this was the golden age of the love letter. 'The new architecture facilitated the development of an area of private life that people everywhere still consider somehow particularly French: seduction ... Interior architecture provided visible proof of the desire to have a setting for flirtation, courtship, and a sexual life that was cleaner, more refined, more luxurious, and above all more private ... Eighteenth-century painting and literature – fiction and non-fiction alike – are massively devoted to the portrayal not just of sex, or courtship rituals ... but of an intricate process that involved learning how to be seductive, how to seduce, and even how to be seduced.'[16]

We may say, then, as a concluding generalisation, that private life was transformed between the 1730s and the 1760s. Pierre Legrand d'Aussy, in his *History of Private Life*, advocated that the coordinated history of architecture, furniture, dress and leisure activities helped to explain a nation's character, and that it separated the French from everyone else.[17] It was this growth of private life that, more than anything else, allowed our interior life, our psychology, to flourish.

The Fixation with Fashion

'The role of a pretty woman is much more serious than one might suppose: there is nothing more important than what happens each morning at her toilette, accompanied by her servant; a general of an army pays no less attention to placing his right flank or his reserves than she does to the placement of a patch, which can fail, but from which she hopes or anticipates success.' This wily piece of advice comes from no less an authority than Montesquieu in his *Lettres persanes*, written in 1721. During the early years of the eighteenth century, Kimberly Chrisman-Campbell tells us, the toilette evolved from an object (*petite toile*) to a set of objects (*service de toilette*) to a room to a ritual performance of taste and consumption 'synonymous with the morning'.[1] Although the toilette was in theory private, it was in fact more or less public, the ritual having been introduced at court by Louis XIV and his mother, Anne of Austria (chapter 8). What had begun as a formal court ritual evolved as the eighteenth century drew on 'into a vital exercise in taste and sociability ... Combining the ancient *vanitas* tradition with the ultramodern *tableau de mode*, the highly codified rituals of the toilette were reenacted over and over again in rococo art.'[2]

In fact, as the century lengthened, it became understood that women – some women at least – actually performed *two* toilettes, one truly private, when she performed the secret basics on her unadorned self, followed by a longer, more public toilette. According to that astute observer of Parisian ways Louis-Sébastien Mercier, 'the second toilette is nothing but a game invented by coquetry, with every move calculated to entice male ardour'.[3] Many observers commented on the application of pastes and other materials to women's faces but at the same time the sheer amount of time women spent at their toilette was of real concern to moralists and philosophers. People worried that this 'idle' time would breed further moral failings 'including narcissism, lust and gossip'. The Comtesse de Genlis (1746–1830) commented ruefully: 'In the country and in Paris, women received visits from men at their toilette, which took a long time for hairdressing, because of the long hair and the curls. They got dressed, even changing their chemises and lacing their corsets in front of men.'[4] She found this practice 'indecent' but she may have been overreacting, at least compared with her contemporaries. In general, the toilette was performed before a larger audience than just one male. Another observer countered: 'One went to women's toilettes as if to the theatre, and *petits-maîtres* [fops; see chapter 19], chambermaids, dogs and *abbés* made up the decoration.'[5]

After the toilette was over, a basin, water pitcher or ewer was used to wash one's hands. At the beginning of the century full bathing was considered a rare luxury. Clean water was a rarity but there was more to it than that: the doctors of the time believed that bathing – even washing one's face in water – was hazardous. Instead of washing, people relied on perfume and scented cosmetics on items of clothing to disguise body odours.[6]

Rouge put back the colour in faces painted white. 'Good taste dictated that rouge should be very thick, that it should touch the lower eyelids. That, they said, gave fire to the eyes.' Rouge 'imitated the enticing glow of a blush', which signified all at once modesty, robust health and sexual excitement. But rouge denoted another kind of blood – noble blood. In France, only the elite used heavy rouge. Although it could be bought in liquid or powder form, it was the creamy *rouge en pot* that caught on.[7]

Men's toilettes were less elaborate and less widespread than women's though many men went to the barber's or wigmaker's to have themselves shaved and powdered, but this practice declined in the years before the Revolution. That did not mean, however, that men were indifferent to women's toilettes – quite the contrary. Although there were fears in some quarters that the concern with fashion, cosmetics and hairdressing was making some men effeminate (even the *Encyclopédie* commented on this), throughout the eighteenth century, rouge, powder, paint and patches ('beauty spots') were worn by both sexes, together with lace, fur, jewels, embroidery and high heels. Napoleon, who was 5 feet 6 inches tall, famously banned high heels for both men and women, while Marie Antoinette wore 2-inch heels to her execution.

This concern with fashion undoubtedly had an effect on men but not always in the way that the moralists feared. Visiting Paris, the British author Tobias Smollett had this to say: 'A Frenchman in consequence of his mingling with the females from his infancy, not only becomes acquainted with all their customs and humours; but grows wonderfully alert in performing a thousand little offices, which are overlooked by other men, whos time hath been spent in making more valuable acquisitions. He enteres, without ceremony, a lady-bed-chamber, while she is in bed, reaches her whatever she wants, airs her shift, and helps to put it on. He attends at her toilette, regulates the distribution of her patches, and advises where to lay on the paint. If he visits her when she is dressed, and perceives the least impropriety in her *coiffure*, he insists upon adjusting it with his own hands; if he sees a curl, or even a single hair amiss, he produces his comb, his scissors, and pomatum [an old term for pomade], and sets it to rights with the dexterity of a professed *friseur*.'[8]

We should not be misled too much by this. A lengthy toilette did not necessarily imply a self-indulgent waste of the morning hours. Because the toilette took so long, women socialised and transacted business during those self-same stretches of time. They would write letters, read books, study music or foreign languages.[9]

In fact, the eighteenth century marked a major turning point in how men and women thought about the meaning of clothes.[10] More than other commodities, clothing became emblematic of modernity; in particular the emerging Parisian culture of fashion focused attention on the difficult relationship between femininity and modernity. Many foreign observers noted French women's pronounced interest in fashion.[11]

Between 1750 and 1850 there was a growing dimorphism of

middle- and upper-class male and female clothing. This transformation stood at the heart of what French historian Daniel Roche terms 'a new culture of appearances'.[12] There was now a new 'Enlightened society of taste' which many people considered frivolous.

It all stemmed ultimately from Louis XIV and the different roles of men and women in the theatre of absolutism. At Versailles there had been a culture of clothing based on power and rank, which helped 'encase the aristocracy in yards of silk, gold brocade and silver trimmings', all part of extending the royal grandeur. *La mode* was in fact defined as 'the manner of dressing that follows the received usage at court'.[13] Another view was that much of the fashion literature was produced by 'anti-courtiers'.[14] This gave fashion a political edge, which it would retain, to an extent, throughout the Napoleonic era.

Jennifer Jones has chronicled the changing fashions of *ancien régime* France and records the fashion for gold and silver brocade at the end of the eighteenth century and what she calls arguably the most important change in the history of French fashion since the fourteenth century – the three-piece suit. 'The adoption of the new style of male suit had as much to do with nationality as with gender and was sparked by international emulation and national rivalry between the French, British and Spanish.'[15]

Louis XIV's court got across its absolutist vision of French fashion via portraits, engravings and mannequins dressed in court clothing, but the most important medium was *Le Mercure galant*, established in 1672 by Jean Donneau de Visé, who had authored a number of popular farces and vaudevilles and was in fact the royal historian at the time. To begin with the journal appeared only fitfully but in 1678 it was renamed *Le Nouveau Mercure galant* and began to appear monthly. At that time, imports from India were especially popular. This was when fashion became more adventurously colourful but also helped set the taste for white, which was as important in interior decoration as with clothes.[16]

During the regency, the aristocracy had begun to form a new relationship with commercial culture. The main change came about because the court had temporarily been relocated to the Palais-Royal, and aristocratic sociability had increasingly centred upon Paris rather than Versailles. 'The culture of the Enlightenment flourished in social settings – academies and salons – in which nobility of the robe and nobility of the sword, aristocrats and bourgeois, rubbed shoulders.' New values of intimacy and domesticity took precedence, supported by the new architecture (smaller rooms, dedicated to specific functions).[17]

The most significant aspect of the new fashion culture was the way in which gender increasingly shaped patterns of clothing consumption. According to Jennifer Jones, 'women's buying habits began to diverge dramatically from men's in the eighteenth century. From mid-century going forward, the relative cost of women's wardrobes across all classes snowballed, up to five or ten times faster than their husband's.'[18] This difference cannot be exaggerated.

Everything was linked in France, says Roche, who argues that the new 'culture of clothing' played a crucial role in the development of modern individualism, and this was 'a prerequisite for liberal thought'.[19]

Eighteenth-century Paris increased its population from roughly 500,000 at the time of Louis XIV's death in 1715 to 750,000 on the eve of the Revolution. Out of that total population, there were 35,000 master artisans working in Paris in the early part of the century, of whom 15,000 worked in the clothing trade. By the late eighteenth century, roughly 3,000 men were master tailors, 3,000 women were mistresses in the seamstresses' guild, 2,000 women were in the linen drapers' guild, and 2,000 women dressed women's hair.[20]

The most significant item of clothing that seamstresses worked on was the new informal dress known as the mantua, which would set the fashion for what sometimes were known as *robes négligées*, worn by many noble and bourgeois women at the beginning of the century. It was a one-piece garment, cut a little like a kimono, and was very comfortable and less expensive to make than more tailored clothes. By the 1720s, however, it had been transformed into the flowing *robes volantes*, which Watteau made so much of. These were more fitted and, in turn, gave way later in the century to the *robe à la française*.[21] Another change that occurred during these times was the extended use of linen, both as underclothing and for accessories. Roche argues that a revolutionary '*invention du linge*' occurred at this time 'as linens acquired new meanings and gained new functions in social and bodily comportment as clean, white markers of propriety and civility'.[22]

Then there were the hairstyles. In early modern France this was a costly and time-consuming aspect of fashionable dress, which provoked much ribald comment and even concern, from the reign of Louis XIII, 'when religious authorities denounced the immorality of women's display of their luxurious locks', down to the era of Louis XVI, when it was the frivolity of women's elaborate, towering hairstyles that was the main cause for despair and denunciation. In 1700 more than 500 women were working as hairdressers in Paris, many of them named in the guidebooks of the time or mentioned in the *Mercure*. By 1777, six hundred male hairdressers had paid the required fee to join the corporation of the *barbiers-perruquiers*.[23]

THE MYSTERY AND IMPORTANCE OF TASTE

By the late eighteenth century, a group of mainly female merchants had emerged in France as the pre-eminent *marchandes de modes*, who insisted that they were the true creators of *la mode*. Technically, they sold and embellished goods, rather than manufactured them, though some did make outer garments and shawls. What was new was their self-conscious organisation: every year the *marchandes de modes* deliberately invented new hairstyles, new accessories in lace, wire mesh, feathers or ribbons, often in the most fantastic – not to say ludicrous – forms (one illustration, in Jennifer Jones's book, shows a woman with a four-masted, seven-sailed galleon on her head).[24]

The most celebrated of these was Rose Bertin, who numbered among her clients the more elegantly attired women in France, from Marie Antoinette to the actresses of the Comédie-Française. In Beaumarchais's *The Marriage of Figaro* (1784), Marceline delivers an impassioned speech arguing for women's 'natural right' to work in the clothing trade. Rousseau agreed, arguing that in the ancient world men were never tailors and that cutting, adjusting and sewing were 'women's work' and, moreover, such activities made men effeminate. This approach succeeded to the extent that in the late eighteenth century male *marchands de modes* and male hairdressers became common targets of ridicule. In the same vein, a link was 'discovered' between needlework and discipline and morality, in that the application needed for the 'delicate and dedicated task' of needlework was felt to be morally uplifting, especially for women.[25]

By the second half of the eighteenth century, French culture was enthralled by discussions of taste, genius and fashion. Philosophers from Montesquieu to Rousseau debated whether or not the taste for luxury and high fashion had sabotaged French culture and was making it too effeminate. Louis-Sébastien Mercier, for his part, said plainly that Parisians would not boast of having genius, 'because everyone knew what it was and who had it'. On the other hand, people often boasted of being an *'homme de goût'*, since it was difficult to contest but was increasingly important. And again, as Rousseau famously said, 'of all the natural gifts, taste is the one which is felt the most and which can be explained the least; it wouldn't be what it is if one could define it'. At the same time, however – and whatever Rousseau might say – the emerging science of aesthetics in the eighteenth century (and the development of connoisseurship) was predicated on the assumption 'that the influence of *le beau* on an observer could be precisely examined and measured'.[26]

THE 'AGREEABLE' ARTS

Now emerged, then, a difference between what were called 'the agreeable arts' (of fashion) and objects of 'high art'. 'Understanding the relationship of hats and fans to history paintings and sculptures ultimately required the construction of a new hierarchy of the arts and crafts – and of high culture and commercial culture – which assigned a different worth to the *beaux arts* and the *arts agréables.*'[27]

In the 1770s, critics began to poke fun at women's taste and the trend grew. Not long after the Revolution, Julien-Joseph Virey, pharmacist, medical doctor, early anthropologist and advocate of evolution, explored the 'pernicious' effect of women on the arts in his *De l'influence des femmes sur le goût dans la littérature et les beaux arts*. During the seventeenth century, under Louis XIV, said Virey, women had been 'firmly governed by men and the arts flourished'. During the reign of Louis XV, on the other hand, when his mistresses – Mesdames de Pompadour and du Barry – had influence, men let themselves be governed by women and it was a disaster for the arts and literature. (This was the age of Voltaire, Montesquieu, Rousseau, Boucher, Greuze.) The fine arts suffered, said Virey, due to 'the natural taste of women for tinsel and baubles'. Only with the Revolution did men reclaim the public realm and relegate women to the domestic sphere. Women and workers were clearly at the bottom of this new hierarchy.

Virey was not alone. Boudier de Villement, editor of the *Courrier de la mode ou journal du goût* and the author of no less a work than *L'Ami des femmes*, was equally disparaging: 'Women's imaginations continually nourish themselves on the details of jewels, clothing, etc: these so fill up their heads with colours that there does not remain any attention for objects which might merit it more.'

As ideas developed in the second half of the eighteenth century, a new distinction arose between those arts that were absorbed for sensual pleasure and those arts that were not to be 'consumed' in the same way because they could not and did not act on the 'base' level of the senses. There was, to underline the point, a radical distinction between the fine arts and the 'agreeable' arts, the mid-eighteenth-century neoclassical aesthetic theory thereby announcing an end to the unified, albeit hierarchical, understanding of the visual arts that had obtained prior to that time. 'No matter how strenuously fabric designers, wigmakers, or even portrait painters might proclaim their aesthetic talents and genius, according to the neoclassical vision, their products were essentially different from the pure arts of history painting and sculpture because they were meant to give pleasure through consumption by the senses rather than to elevate the soul.' As P. J. Mariette, the celebrated connoisseur, put it plainly: 'The history painter alone paints for the soul, other artists paint only for the eyes.'[28]

Cynthia Koepp says that this emerging distinction was painful for many who – whether tailors, dressmakers, silversmiths or furniture-painters – felt that their work was being devalued as the guilds became established.[29] 'As "artisans" they not only were denied the chance to attain the fame that painters enjoyed but were also denied participation in the high moral world of "Art" and relegated to the inferior world of the *arts utiles* and the *arts agréables*.'[30]

The *Encyclopédistes* helped exacerbate this distinction. They did indeed esteem such crafts as hatmaking, wigmaking and dress-making but in the process favoured these activities more for the mechanical skills of the human hand 'rather than any involvement of the heart or the mind'. In other words, they saw the agreeable arts as useful in a practical way, rather than offering something nourishing in a moral sense, which was the business of the high arts. Diderot himself rather neatly – perhaps too neatly – summed up the difference between arts and crafts when he said that the arts belonged to the realm of the heart and the crafts to the realm of the hand. Nor was it helped by the further distinction whereby the fine arts and the agree-able arts reflected the differences between *utile* and *frivole*.[31] These distinctions were felt all the more keenly in France in the run-up to Revolution because of fears that French superiority in the arts – and the luxury arts – was being eclipsed by an economic boom north of the Channel.

At the same time, and since the academies had traditionally been elite institutions, it seemed only natural for wigmakers or dressmak-ers who wished to elevate their crafts to have them accepted in the academies. In the beginning, many of the artisanal crafts had been based on secret knowledge (as we saw in the fight over Venetian mir-rors in chapter 8) but the academies were much more open, one of their goals being to disseminate knowledge widely, for the benefit of all, and France in particular, rather than for private or even corporate gain.[32] And so some in the agreeable arts suggested joining the estab-lished academies, others suggested starting their own (hairdressers in particular), still others used the academies to mock the ambitions of the artisans.

Another way the two forms of art were linked was when, say, the Académie royale des sciences examined and tested cosmetics. In February 1777 the *Journal de Paris* reported that the academy had examined a zinc-based rouge produced by a M Doucet of Normandy, to assess its health risk.

And there were, as always of course, short-cuts. Marie Antoinette's celebrated hairdresser, 'Le Grand Léonard', took as his title '*académicien de coiffures et de modes*'.[33]

THE USEFULNESS OF FRIVOLITY

Not that the traffic was all one way. The academies themselves came in for mockery as well, learned culture being lampooned as hardly useful, but trendy and banal and, even, politically subversive. And there were also those who challenged the idea that 'fashions and trinkets' occupied women's minds wholly; instead they praised women's taste and their abilities. Dom Philippe-Joseph Caffiaux, best known as a music historian, nonetheless wrote in his *Défense du beau sexe* (1753) that, insofar as the *beaux arts* were concerned, 'one sees everywhere that women are no less distinguished than men'. He identified a number of female artists, and even went so far as to argue that painting was invented by women. Nicolas Joubert de L'Hiberderie, a prominent figure in the Lyons silk industry, in a treatise on fabric design, also praised female abilities.[34]

Then there was Rousseau. In his novel *Émile*, he stressed that women excelled at fine observations; that women led the way when it came to assessing material objects or anything 'pertaining to the senses'; but in questions of morality or reason, men were better.

The upshot of all these events was that towards the end of the century a raft of female journalists were coming round to Rousseau's view about the dangers of commercial fashion culture, which meant – to their distress – that the artisans of Paris were even further removed from the fine arts than when the century had begun. 'By the eve of the Revolution attempts to elevate the clothing trades to the level of the fine arts and sciences were relegated to the realm of satire ... suggesting a growing recognition, even by craftspeople themselves, that the gulf between the world of craft and commerce and the world of art was too great to bridge.'[35]

But this did result in a useful trade-off. Whereas before the *arts utiles* and the *arts frivoles* had been looked upon as two distinct categories, by the run-up to the Revolution many French people had come to the view that the very frivolity of fashion made it beneficial to the French economy. Denied access to the serious realm of the fine arts, 'fashion found a warm welcome in the realm of commerce ... These new conclusions about fashion helped create a new vocabulary of social distinction: taste would become a powerful new code which separated working-class artisans from elite artists and connoisseurs.'[36]

This new way of thinking meant that a new understanding of women was forming by the eve of the Revolution. All women, it was now held, and whatever their age or condition, were incapable of resisting the blandishments of the *marchandes de modes*' boutiques. 'The excessive desire to consume was a particularly feminine trait, a weakness shared by all women from Marie Antoinette to the fish-mongers of *la halle*.' At the same time, says Craig Koslofsky, women's consumption of clothing added to, rather than subtracted from, their femininity and domesticity.[37]

NO LONGER A SIN

The most fashionable place to find luxury goods in Paris, certainly in the middle of the eighteenth century, was the Palais de Justice, which also was the site of the Parlement. It had a great hall and a number of arcades. J. C. Nemeitz, a German traveller, had this to say in his *Séjour de Paris*, released in 1727: 'Paris is full of boutiques in many locations where one can find anything one desires to buy; but the Palais is the centre and essence of all the beautiful clothing shops.'[38]

So far this leaves out one dimension of life entirely – the explosion of retail shops in Paris widened exponentially the opportunities for women *to be employed* as shop girls and as businesswomen. Over and above that, however, as Louis-Sébastien Mercier observed, many of these shops looked like harems, filled with women busily sewing, decorating hats and knotting ribbons. 'For many women the shops in which they worked must have seemed more like *serails* than *salons*.'[39] This being Paris, there was no doubt, Jennifer Jones says, that quite apart from the traditional forms of libertinism, the relationship between the shop girls (known as *grisettes* for the grey clothing many wore) and male customers was 'sexually charged'. Mercier agreed: 'Shopping is only a pretext.'[40]

By the late eighteenth century, the first daily newspapers in France, the *Journal de Paris* and the *Feuille sans titre*, included information on fashion alongside news of literature, music, theatre, *faits divers* and developments in the arts and sciences. The weekly *Feuille necessaire*,

1759, and its successor, the *Avant-Coureur*, 1760–73, also reported new clothing styles. Other publications were devised to report solely on fashion, and numerous collections of fashion engravings were also circulated from time to time. One typical title, says John Lough, was *La Publication mensuelle des modes, ou Bibliothèque pour la toilette des dames*.[41]

What had clearly occurred in the eighteenth century was a new definition of fashion. It was no longer, as it had been in the seventeenth century, about the display of luxury as a symbol of wealth and power. Rather, it was now about women's wish to be *jolie* and *belle*, so as to please the opposite sex. All over Paris there was a persistent desire by women 'to present their charms to men in a new and more advantageous light'.[42]

Moreover, the connection of fashion to current events became ever more obvious in the wake of the Revolution, when hats were designed to reflect the 'three estates' of the new realm, '*robes à l'Égalité*' were conceived, and buckles were made in the shape of the Bastille. The very concept of taste was now an attempt to sever the link between fashion and wealth and rank.[43]

In fact, across the years of the run-up to the Revolution, and beyond, a marked change came over the attitude to luxury in France. Whereas before, it had been condemned in many quarters as rooted in an unfortunate aspect of human nature – as grounded in vanity, debauchery or the passion for novelty – and had served as a proxy for criticising the *ancien régime*, by the end of the century a new concept of womanhood had arisen in which fashion and taste 'naturalised' women's interest in clothing. 'The frenzy for fashions was no longer considered a sinful state, harmful to the general health of society and the maintenance of social hierarchies, but rather a natural aspect of femininity.'[44]

So we may say that two things were happening in the late eighteenth century, which made it, as Sarah Maza points out, an important transition period, as French women saw the evolution of a new fashion culture linked with femininity but also frivolity, an extraordinary set of events when placed alongside Christine Le Bozec's devastating litany of the attempts to sideline and sabotage women's involvement in the Revolution.[45] In what was a mix of politics, economics and sexuality, clothing for men signified the role they played in wider society, the socio-political contract; for women, clothing meant something very different – it emphasised their sequestration in a more private sphere of maternity, domesticity and sexuality.[46]

To heighten difference was to excite desire, and on this Rousseau stressed that the proper wife performed neither for the monarch's gaze nor for the public's, but for her husband's eyes alone. More than that, this new theatre of bourgeois domesticity demanded costumes that expressed not aristocratic luxury, rather individuals' inner subjectivity as men and as women. With their enlightened identities firmly grounded in biology – in nature – women were now at least free to play with the range of roles that the fashions available in Paris offered. Female fashion, as Roche, Jones and Maza all agree, was ruled out of political power, but became instead a realm in which individuality might flourish.

The Philosophy of Food, the Cult of Coffee and the Rise of the Restaurant

'In the final decades of the *ancien régime*, French cooks achieved universal domination over the palate.' This is Sean Takats in *The Expert Cook in Enlightenment France*. 'By introducing something they called *la cuisine moderne* during the 1730s, cooks aimed at establishing themselves as expert engineers of taste ... Modern cooking's most important contribution was ... the emergence of a new type of cook, a "taste professional" who ... also saw himself as an intellectual of sorts.'[1] According to Antoine de Rivarol, a royalist and aggressively nationalist journalist of the time, 'by supplying theatre, clothing, taste, manners, language, and a new art of living to the nations around it, France had come to wield over its neighbours a sort of empire that no other people had ever exercised'.[2]

Despite their initial low social standing, cooks were ambitious for themselves and so drew on – and contributed to – the period's overarching project of 'systematising all human knowledge'. From these beginnings there emerged the century's greatest and most celebrated works on taste, making use in particular of the science and medicine of the Enlightenment. 'No less than the *philosophes*, cooks looked forward to a better society in which reason and science propelled human life to constant improvement,' and they conceived of themselves as fully part of the process. Though they didn't claim to be *philosophes* as such, their skills were written about in the *Encyclopédie* and they could therefore argue that they were, if not intellectuals exactly, practitioners of a serious speciality, on a par with medicine and science more generally, which contributed to food being regarded – in France more than elsewhere – 'a cut above mere pleasure'.[3]

A REVOLUTION IN THE ART AND STATUS OF COOKING

We also find that around the middle of the century, cooking began to be referred to in books of the time as an 'art', the basis of this judgement being that the practice both required knowledge of a set of 'rules' and also entailed 'method'. 'Cooking', says Takats, 'had gone from something one did to something one knew.' Another reason for the improving status of cooking, especially the *cuisine moderne* (which we shall come to), was its association with science, because it incorporated, to an extent, a knowledge of at least the language of chemistry, which was just then the most excitingly innovative branch of scientific knowledge. In keeping with this, many cooks made wild claims for their trade, promoting the view that they were able 'to refine the human spirit through the precise modification of diet'.[4]

Then there was the regent, in the Palais-Royal. His celebrated *petits soupers*, notorious as they were in some ways, were soon reputed to have set new standards in cooking and in the early 1730s there emerged a new raft of cookery books. The first of these, *The Modern Cook*, appearing in 1733, was actually released first in Britain but it appeared in French two years later, by which time the author had become chef to the Prince d'Orange, Orange originally being a small – and independent – principality in the south of France. This was a first sighting of a phenomenon that would recur in the kingdom – the concept of *nouvelle cuisine* or *cuisine moderne*, which took hold in the public mind of France more than anywhere else.

First among the individuals to make the most of this change in sensibility was the baldly named Menon, a writer about whom next to nothing is known but whose *Nouveau traité de la cuisine* was soon followed by his *Cuisine bourgeoise*, which became the most widely reprinted cookery book of the second half of the eighteenth century. What was new about *nouvelle cuisine* was the replacement of traditionally simple and crude roasts with prepared dishes, whether called *hors d'œuvres*, *entrées* or *entremets*, allied to an elimination of excess and above all the cultivation of delicacy. Leaner foods were now preferred to fatty foods.

The pace was stepped up from the 1730s through to the 1750s, as the *Encyclopédie* began its publication, with cookbooks now selling in much greater numbers than previously.[5] By mid-century, a marked revolution had come about in the status of the cook. They were now – at least in their own eyes – arbiters of taste, 'knowledge specialists' in connection with the ingredients they handled routinely.

This intellectual aspect of food, of cooking, was further helped by the way diet affected health. Chefs tried to dominate the understanding of taste and cooks even took upon themselves a new role as medical practitioners. This, as may be expected, was not without opposition. While physicians and surgeons could not avoid cooks' claims to improve health and even to prolong lives significantly (as the more extravagant did), they nonetheless mounted concerted campaigns to discredit cooks as specialist authorities.

There were many ways, it was believed, in which cooking affected health. Menon, for example, investigated the effects of 'overly strong flavours' on the 'papillae and fibres' of the tongue. Cooks, he maintained, had 'unique access' to one of the body's sensory organs, and as a result this gave them an inside track to understand metaphysical taste as well. 'Stimulating the anatomy of the tongue was tantamount to stimulating the spirit.'

Appetite and digestion were of wide interest in the eighteenth century and many experiments were undertaken to explore their mysteries. After all, for chefs, cuisine was regarded as a form of chemistry. This was underlined by the great Antoine Lavoisier, who carried out a series of experiments into bouillon. 'By comparing the specific gravity, fat and evaporated mass of various cuts of beef from a single animal, Lavoisier sought to maximise the efficiency of food production.'[6]

Lavoisier's name and other accomplishments were sufficiently distinguished to bolster the claims of cooks to scholastic status and it was not far from there to the notion of the *régime alimentaire*, which began to be a concern of medical circles in the middle of the century. Rousseau was just one who favoured moderation and pure foods, but there was no shortage of doctors recommending strict diets as a way to health. At one point, the diet of hospital patients was the subject of a dispute between doctors and nurses. The physicians at Nîmes took against the 'overplentifulness' of their patients' diets, which, they said, 'often impeded their recovery'.[7]

In 1765, Voltaire sniffed at the fashion for *nouvelle cuisine*, grumbling that such cooking 'messed up good plain food with nutmeg, pepper and mushrooms'.[8]

THE EFFECTS OF DIET ON REASON

The relevance of diet went even wider. One of the major maladies of the age was – or was thought to be – 'weakness of chest'.[9] The physically debilitated individual was understood to be, in some way, weakened morally and psychologically on top of everything else, to be lacking in 'personal sensitivity' and emotional responsiveness; moreover, it was a set of ailments that was believed to afflict in particular those of an artistic disposition. Emma Spary phrases it this way: 'the organs of ratiocination and digestion were commonly regarded as closely connected' and it was commonplace to suggest that digestive functions affected moral conduct. Mental function, in particular, it was held, could be enhanced through diet. In this way, between 1670 and 1760, cookery, political institutions such as food supply, and natural phenomena such as climate, were regarded as related.[10] Digestion came to be seen as crucial to the exercise of reason.

In fact, health was close to being an obsession of the time, generating an anxiety that opportunists could exploit. The city itself organised on occasion '*bals de santé*' (health balls) and, in like manner, restaurants 'made frailty into a quality to be exhibited and shared with others'. In an account of the restaurants of the Palais-Royal, written only a year before Revolution broke out, a visitor observed that 'even if he is not sick, a *petit maître* often orders consommé in the evening, because that gives him the aura of ill-health'. The 'delicate degeneration' caused by urban living was both a badge of illness and a sign of sophistication.[11] 'The sensitive soul – the philosophical young man or tender-hearted young woman who bursts into tears in front of a painting by Greuze, or while reading Rousseau's *La Nouvelle Héloïse* – was inherently delicate of body as well as of mind and heart.'[12]

Furthermore – and it comes as no real surprise – men of letters, it was widely believed, almost invariably suffered from, in addition to weakness of chest, either melancholia or else constipation – two ailments that responded to a particular dietary regime. It was likewise held that women were no less likely than literary men to be plagued by weak chests and unsettled stomachs. Female weakness, in the view of one Paris physician, was linked to their 'profound mental and physical laziness'. Having no real occupation (not being allowed to work by the mores of the time), well-off women were bound to give way to their 'passions and fancies', in terms of both food and sex. One particular danger was strongly flavoured items, which had a particular attraction for the female mind.[13]

The Gourmet as Scientist, the Gourmet as Artist, the Gourmet as 'Expert Eater'

In a section on 'the philosophical palate', Spary also argues that the concept of 'appetite' was an important area of discussion and disagreement in the middle decades of the eighteenth century, and in particular, 'were eaters in control of their appetites, or were they controlled by them?'[14] At times, the gourmet was held to be as grand and as accomplished as the scientist, 'knowing foods in the same way as the savant knew the truths of the natural or social world'. This was related to 'taste', which, then as now, was in fact held to be one of the defining qualities of 'polite' people.[15]

Stephen Mennell further argues that, during the eighteenth century, 'some of the leading figures in the land' did actually venture into the kitchen themselves and as a result may well have penned some of the *nouvelle cuisine* cookbooks, conferring on food preparation 'the title of a science as much as an art'.[16] Moreover, the personal involvement of the educated elite in cooking meant that cookery writing became a matter of acute interest in the Republic of Letters. Men of letters who were part of the 'polite' world saw the literature of *nouvelle cuisine* as a forum for discussions of the significance of taste, connoisseurship and consumption and for exploring the proper scope of learning.[17]

According to some contemporary theories, genius was a product of the arrangement and function of the organs. Materialist physicians like Julien Offray de La Mettrie (best known for *L'Homme machine*) or Antoine Le Camus (a doctor who did much to advance the cause of vaccination) had very definite views about mind–body relations. As Spary says: 'Culinary literature united philosophical accounts of mind and creativity with the chemistry and physiology of spirit in such a way as to legitimate the mental superiority of polite, literate city-dwellers.' This was sometimes explained, rather fancifully, by the 'fact' that various foods were made up of different shapes of corpuscles, which impacted special 'papillae or protrusions' on the tongue, palate or throat.[18]

'*Esprit* was both delicate and fragile, to be cultivated and preserved through lifestyle practices.' The self-conduct of *philosophes* thus operated simultaneously at an alimentary and at a literary level. Le Camus explicitly invoked the beneficial effects of wine upon creativity and polite table talk: 'Through the moderate use of this nectar, the blood circulates easily, the nerves obtain and preserve that irritability which is the first mobile of their entire play. Hence ... those agreeable comments one hears at tables served with prudence, which banish both stinginess and prodigality.'[19]

Particular foodstuffs were felt to 'refuel' the human mind, wine and coffee in particular, though Théodore Tronchin, Voltaire's Geneva-based doctor, well known throughout Europe for his advocacy of inoculation against smallpox, and despite his famous patient's fondness for coffee (and what he believed was its helpful effect on his imagination), nonetheless advised the sick to steer clear of all hot liquids, coffee most of all.[20]

Once more satire wasn't far away, with critics complaining that the French were merely making themselves ridiculous with claims that cuisine merited serious philosophical attention.[21]

The Mathematics of Pleasure and the Music of the Tongue

Balance, variety and moderation gradually came to the fore, rather than libertine excess or its opposite, extreme delicacy. 'Corporeal harmony', Spary tells us, was no mere metaphor. Would-be intellectuals speculated about a 'harmony of flavours', that just as there was a Newtonian theory of colours, so there might be a 'mathematical theory of pleasure', there might be a 'music of the tongue or the palate', just as there is one for the ears. And of course connoisseurship of food was equated with connoisseurship of the fine arts.[22]

As time passed, however, and more and more people were seen to succumb to excess, the medical profession began an attack on such practices, arguing that 'gustatory overindulgence' led to a loss of sensibility, in which *nouvelle cuisine* was particularly at fault, along with liqueurs.[23] The pursuit of 'unbridled pleasure' – seen as on a par with libertinism and the gambling mania, it was held – amounted to a flight from reason. The French were 'slaves to their mouths' and 'diseases were the inevitable consequence'. And there was always Rousseau in the background, with his influential ideas about how the development of civilisation and luxury was sapping the will and moral fibre in general.[24]

By mid-century a debate was raging as reformers began to question the claims of those who argued that reason 'could be extended' by the pursuit of sensory pleasure through cultivating the faculty of taste. Notably a number of Protestant thinkers took this line, advocating instead the advantages of abstinence.[25]

A 'LEARNED STYLE OF EATING': CHEMISTRY AND CREATIVITY

By the 1750s, then, there had emerged what we might call a 'learned style of eating', which juggled notions about chemistry and creativity. In one sense it was little more than an idea about healthy eating, but it was a major subject of discussion in the salons we have been considering. *Nouvelle cuisine*, according to some authorities, was 'necessary for mental labour', an idea that would prove very resilient. Antoine Le Camus put it this way: 'One should permit the moderate use of ragoûts and some succulent and spiced meats to men of letters, be it to stimulate their tardy digestions or to volatilise their nervous juices which gradually harden.'[26]

Against all that, there was the rise of what we might call the 'expert eater', who had been mentioned as early as the first (1694) edition of the Académie française's dictionary, which defined a *gourmet* as 'he who knows [*sçait*] how to know [*connaître*] and taste wine well'.[27]

At the same time, it was held that men of letters, the polite and the *philosophes* were most at risk from overindulgence *and* from too much delicacy, which, by the 1760s, was becoming a pathological condition, and one with both moral and even political consequences. Emma Spary again: 'Delicacy, sensibility, and imagination, formerly desirable attributes of the polite individual and hallmarks of French *génie*, were increasingly linked to effeminacy and pathologised.'[28]

Men of letters appear to have received special attention from the doctors, some doctors at least. Samuel Auguste Tissot, the Swiss neurologist and Vatican advisor who specialised in the 'diseases of the rich', as well as of men of letters, advised them to steer clear of 'fatty, pasty, viscous and windy foods', not to mention dried or hard meats (doughnuts, eel, pork and beans were all off the menu). Fish, cereals, root vegetables, bread, eggs, milk, chocolate and fruit were all approved, a vegetable diet most of all. The thinking man, Tissot advised, should 'avoid mixtures of different foods'.

His fellow Swiss colleague Théodore Tronchin had two favourite regimes, his 'white diet' and his 'dry diet'. The former consisted of 'milk ... which should merely be warmed, rice, pearl barley, gruel, millet, freshwater fish and white meat ... fresh eggs ...' The dry diet consisted of solid foods and was designed to rid the body of the excess humours 'caused by consuming hot liquids'.

Indigestion, Tissot said, ranked high among the medical conditions typical of men of letters.[29]

COFFEE, COFFEE SCHOLARS AND THE CAFÉ AS A CENTRE OF LEARNING

Alongside the new and more sophisticated interest in *haute cuisine* went a fascination with new substances – spices, liqueurs and, above all, coffee. 'Trituration', Emma Spary says, was now a way of life. What was meant by this was that, at various locations in the body (the stomach, the intestines, the 'lactation ducts' and so on), it was understood that solids were converted into liquids by chemical action, and these liquids were transported in the blood to the organs.

These movements, some alleged, were specifically sanctioned and set in motion by God, this religious dimension being kept alive by the observation of Lent, during which the abstinence that many people practised improved their health, or appeared to.

The most significant change to come over European eating habits in the seventeenth and eighteenth centuries was the consumption of new and exotic foodstuffs, notably coffee, tea, chocolate and sugar. Coffee, which Spary says is the drink most often associated with the French after wine, shows the clearest effect of diet on the mind, and this is, ultimately, where the foundation of the traditional French café as an intellectual institution is founded.

Coffee, Spary says, 'entered scholarship' between 1670 and 1730, and an important stage in the 'domestication' of coffee in France involved what were seen as its medicinal properties. Jean-Baptiste Colbert gave commissions to travellers to explore the world of coffee in the Middle and Far East so that a more thorough understanding of its preparation – and properties – would be available. In this way, coffee became an object of commercial gain *and* scholarly interest. People thought it should become an object of 'learned activity', and this was underlined by the fact that papers on coffee were presented to the Académie royale des sciences in 1713.[30]

Coffee scholars, as they became known, were invariably experts in other subjects, such as orientalism, horticulture or botany, and these areas of expertise were jealously guarded in the learned arguments over what, exactly, coffee was. Some cited coffee-drinking as the 'cause of ill effects', those ill effects ranging from weight loss and insomnia to dysentery. In the process, it came to be particularly associated with the exercise of reason. By the 1750s, some physicians were arguing that coffee was especially unsuitable for men of letters, but this was a minority view, given the advent of the coffee house, which came to be seen as the centre of *esprit* and a centre of learning. 'Coffee houses were a forum for the public presentation of knowledge and for displays of learned expertise.'[31] Though philosophy *was* discussed in cafés, their primary role was as a centre for the production of *belles-lettres*.[32]

Coffee houses were spaces of intellectual sociability in which many types of individual could lay claim to learned status, the café being a site of conversation and 'knowledge production', differing from the church or the universities. They were also associated with a rejection of erudition. In fact, cafés were given over more to a worldly, playful secular knowledge, and a culture of *esprit* 'to be understood as wit, mind and spirit' where the characteristic form was satire. Cafés were places where the public status of letters and science was contested, where the relationship between fame and insignificance was constructed, where intellectual authority was asserted – or not.[33]

MANUFACTORIES OF MIND

The café stood out from the cabaret, tavern or inn in three ways: the centrality of luxury ingredients to what it made available; the respectability of its polite urban elite clientele; and the inclusion of learning among the entertainments it offered (based on salon society).

To begin with, from 1700, the '*honnête*' ambitions of cafés attracted satirical attacks. Coffee-drinking was seen as merely a pretext for affected intellectual behaviour, a sort of public imitation of the salons. But cafés were successfully reformed in the early years of the 1700s and became seats of luxury, politeness and order. Along with this went the shift from wine as coffee began to be seen as a source of literary creativity. Papers along these lines were read to the Académie royale des inscriptions et belles-lettres.[34]

The café Laurent, founded in 1690 by François Laurent, was a prominent meeting place for lovers of *belles-lettres*, philosophers, musicians, painters and poets, and was frequented by Fontenelle, alongside other famous habitués.[35] However, this celebrity audience deserted the Laurent around 1714 for the café de Parnasse, and for Procope's café near the Comédie-Française.

Parisian cafés often specialised in particular areas of learning. Laurent's café was known as the café des Beaux-Esprits ('Wits' Café'), where 'all kinds of spiritual matters were discussed', while would-be men of letters would gather at the café Savant ('Learned Café'). The café, in the formulation of Augustin-Joseph de Mailly, an army general but also a *lumière*, whose ancestor had written a book on Paris cafés in 1702, had now become a localised space for dramatising and resolving disagreements over 'knowledge'.[36]

This being Paris, people were often critical of the standard of learning in cafés. Montesquieu commented dryly at one point on the gullibility of people who 'were four times as wise when they came out of the café as when they went in'. In the *Encyclopédie*, notably, cafés were described as 'manufactories of mind'.[37]

In a satire of 1740, Alain-René Le Sage identified a four-fold constituency for the café: *nouvellistes* (news specialists, people who went from café to café, picking up and relaying onward the latest news and gossip), chess-players, *philosophes* and poets. Entertainment, Le Sage said, took the form of listening in to the displays of verbal pyrotechnics so that cafés, in effect, became 'performative spaces', with elaborate word-juggling and erudition, where literary reputations could be made or broken.

Among the other intellectual entertainments, people met in cafés to hear the first public judgements on new plays. At the Procope playwrights sat out first nights and came to drown their sorrows after disasters. Voltaire himself once went to the Procope disguised as a priest to hear what was being said about *Sémiramis*, his powerful play about a queen in ancient Babylon who kills her husband and then falls in love, unknowingly at first, with her son.[38]

Cafés were the home of poetry, satire especially. Indeed, satire was the characteristic mode of eighteenth-century Paris, the epigram in particular generating a vast literature embracing every art of insult and parody. Cafés, notably, were outside the control of established authority so this was in effect the way writers negotiated with their social superiors. Every significant event was marked by poems, couplets and epigrams. Even ministers were known to commission satires in order to intervene in current affairs. The café was also the natural habitat for light poetry, the leading form of literary output between 1700 and 1750, which was universal in polite society.[39] For others, says Spary, the move to make poetry philosophical was a satirical inversion of its main purpose.[40]

The literary café was a very visible site of innovation in the sense that it generated not just new literature, but new exotic drinks. These were felt to go together to epitomise the newly fashionable and fashion-conscious lifestyles. The café was also socially innovative, leading to social mingling and levelling. It became known as a place of free expression for people of different social stations. As a result, violence was a not uncommon outcome of café conversations. Overall, though, coffee was credited with civilising people, with having a calming effect, and helping to distinguish truth from error, taste from caprice.

Cafés also became associated with celebrity. In the 1770s, when Rousseau was once in the café de la Régence, so many people came to see him that he was asked to move on. The café du Caveau, also known as the café du Sauvage, had someone they paid to be 'sauvage', leaping around wildly, gesticulating and making primitive noises. This sort of crush and behaviour meant that it was increasingly inappropriate for polite women to visit cafés.[41]

Between 1740 and 1789, the more so as women retreated, and as cafés specialised, and as merchants increasingly tried to expand and explore their wider interests in other matters there, such as science or literary affairs, and because they were automatically banned from the academies, it was only natural for cafés, as *the* public spaces, to start to become sites of political discussion.[42] The café Manury became known as a space where 'republicans can speak freely'. It was also clear to most that poetry and philosophy were a sublimated form of politics.

POLITE SCIENCE

Alongside the growth in knowledge, food shops – like shops in general – became increasingly elaborate, not to say luxurious places, with mirrored glass and giltwood and marble fittings, where the shopkeepers too could show off what they knew. Polite science, as it was called, was judged alongside artisanal skill and academic knowledge.[43] In the 1750s and 1760s, mustard, lemonade powder, rum, candy, cake and game pie all jostled with wigs, snuff boxes, natural history specimens, watches, fireworks, lamps, perfume and prints in these increasingly elaborate emporiums. Each of them, in effect, and in the spirit of the times, was a knowledge kingdom. The shops around the Pont-Neuf and the Palais-Royal were the most popular.

The point was that a complex system of knowledge production

went into the construction of a fashionable identity and its experts looked upon themselves as connoisseurs, persons of taste and high social rank. No less important, those who sold to them had to partake of the same system of knowledge, and this was as true of food and medicines as of dress and gesture. This is what polite science *was*, and it was gleefully satirised. One satire laughed disbelievingly at the 'fact' that there were in Paris 20 billion types of fan.[44]

In his banned materialist work, *De l'esprit*, in which he attacked all forms of morality based on religion, Claude-Adrien Helvétius (perhaps surprisingly) devoted several chapters to polite science, arguing that it should be systematised so that there would eventually evolve a homogeneous, public synthesis of such knowledge, which would benefit society and help with governance and stimulate the economy. The relation of the arts to the economy has been a lineament of Frenchness for a very long time, an alternative to its political instability.

There were even disputes about the philosophical significance of innovation. Antoine Hornot Dejean, a distiller, argued that France was especially favoured for the manufacture of liqueurs, and that they were a symbol of French inventiveness. 'It is necessary to invent ceaselessly,' he insisted. Indeed, invention was a *responsibility* of the French public. 'Every day savants make discoveries or useful attempts.' At the same time, the 'restless pursuit of novelty' was seen as a moral shortcoming peculiar to the French.[45]

THE INITIAL MEANING OF *RESTAURANT*

Into this increasingly sophisticated world was inserted the restaurant. Long before a restaurant was a *place* to eat, Rebecca Spang tells us, it was a *thing* to eat, no more and no less than a restorative broth.[46] In chapter 8, we saw that eating out in *traiteurs* had been a feature of late seventeenth-century society. But it was not widespread, and dictionaries of the time defined a *restaurant* as something not unlike a semi-medicinal preparation. Even the *Encyclopédie* described it as a 'medical term', and suggested brandy, chickpeas and chocolate as examples of 'restorative' substances.[47] Several French cookbooks of the eighteenth century provided detailed recipes for bouillon-based preparations, which they too called *restaurants*. Such preparations, they insisted, would restore health to incapacitated invalids.[48]

Some *restaurants* were concocted without the addition of any liquid at all, the final essence being little more than a juice of pure meat. Instructions called for whatever meats were being used to be 'sweated' for hours on end in a tightly sealed bain-marie. The prolonged sweating, so it was understood, began to break down and allow the juices of the ham or pheasant, say, to reach the eater already partially digested, making them easier to assimilate, entering an invalid's weakened digestive system without taxing it. *Restaurant*-bouillons were perfect for people suffering 'weakness of chest'.

And so, the restaurant, which we now understand as 'a space of urban sociability', evolved partly from the *traiteur* and partly from – for want of a better word – consommé. On this account, in the last twenty years of the *ancien régime*, one visited a 'restaurant' (or, as they were sometimes called, 'a restaurateur's room') to drink bouillon much as one went to a café to drink coffee. There was little in the way of solid food in these establishments, and it was common in their notices for them to say that they were particularly suited to those too frail to consume flesh. In this, restaurants were distinct from inns, taverns or cookshops, and were marked by their individual tables.[49]

In the first edition of the *Almanach dauphin*, compiled by one-time economist Mathurin Roze de Chantoiseau and published in 1769, in a section headed 'Caterers, Innkeepers and Hoteliers', there was a subsection for a 'Restaurateur', recommended for his 'delicate and healthful bouillons'.[50] In March 1767, *L'Avant-Coureur* ('The Forerunner'), a periodical specialising in innovation in the arts, sciences and 'any other field that makes life more agreeable', reviewed 'a new type of establishment' that had opened in Paris's rue des Poulies. The premises, the text said, specialised in 'excellent consommés or *restaurants* always carefully warmed in a hot water bath'. Furthermore, these *restaurants* were available 'at all hours, at reasonable prices, and were served in gold-rimmed, white faience dishes'. 'Those who suffer from weak and delicate chests, and those whose diets do not usually include an evening meal, will be delighted to find a public place where they can go to have a consommé without offending their sense of delicacy ... In order to leave nothing to be desired, it was also decided to make available the many new periodicals that appear every month in the capital, such that this new establishment offers both solace for the body and distraction for the soul.'[51]

THE GUILLOTINE AND THE GASTRONOME

Historians have long accepted that the French Revolution was a landmark in the history of French eating. More than that, the epoch of the great French restaurants is usually said to have had a romantic element in that it ironically began in the Revolution, to be followed by the rapid growth of elaborate, refined and luxurious food in the kitchens of the first cooks to become famous, in the Napoleonic and Restoration periods, when the chefs of the noble families who had either been guillotined or forced to emigrate, set up on their own account. Among them the most celebrated of all was Marie-Antoine Carême, generally conceded to have been the first 'celebrity chef'.[52]

This was the time when the gap in prestige between male and female cooks opened up (the Revolutionary and Napoleonic periods were anti-women in general). This era also saw the emergence of the bourgeois gastronome, someone who was not a cook himself, but instead an expert – a connoisseur – in 'the art of eating' and as such an accepted leader of public opinion in matters of taste.

Scholars in the new speciality of food history have pinned down the first manifestation of a new form of eating place, notable for being open to the public, and which now at last came to be known as the restaurant. Antoine Beauvilliers was the patron of Paris's first great restaurant, which opened in 1786 (though the date is sometimes disputed) as La Grande Taverne de Londres, near the Palais-Royal. Beauvilliers was famous for his triple chin, the fact that he always wore a sword, and his prodigious memory, which meant he never forgot a client. His 'signature dishes' included duck with turnips, and partridge with cabbage. Like the café Procope before him, La Grande Taverne featured chandeliers and superb linen tablecloths, plus waiters in uniforms, and an extensive wine list.

In the years immediately before the Revolution, the old system finally began to break down. The point about the Revolution is that it stimulated a demand for restaurants and made possible the means by which that demand could be satisfied. One reason for this was the arrival in Paris of a considerable number of revolutionary deputies from outside the capital, who put themselves up in boarding houses and acquired all too naturally the practice of taking their meals together, not least in the new establishments opening up in increasing numbers around the Palais-Royal and the rue Richelieu. The deputies also brought with them a fair number of recipes from their own local areas.[53]

It was in these circumstances that the gastronome emerged as a distinct and recognisable figure, and that gastronomic writing first appeared as a genre. The word itself, 'gastronomy', was deliberately (and grandiosely) derived from the Greek, and therefore seemed to have 'learned overtones'. It was coined in 1801 by Joseph Berchoux, who used it as the title of a would-be humorous poem.[54]

THE 'NOISY MIXTURE' OF OPINION

In place in Paris by 1820, restaurants were to remain a predominantly Parisian phenomenon until well into the middle of the nineteenth century. In 1844, John Durbin, the Methodist president of Dickinson College in Pennsylvania, wrote that 'restaurant dining [is] in many respects peculiar to Paris'.[55]

The first restaurants proper – and this is what differentiated them from the *traiteurs* – took care to demonstrate their concern for the well-being of their patrons like the cafés considered earlier. They were not averse to advertising that they made the most of the recent discoveries of medical science, which provided the basis for their new standard of cooking, always emphasising their bouillons' 'restorative powers' and that *nouvelle cuisine* also made the most of recent scientific advances. Entries in the *Almanach dauphin* might actually be formally endorsed by the Académie royale des sciences.[56] In the decades immediately preceding the Revolution, it was not uncommon for restaurants to style themselves *maisons de santé* ('houses of health'). Nicolas Restif de La Bretonne, the extraordinary author of some 200 books, noted that even in the 1780s restaurants were still offering 'health suppers' (*soupers de santé*).[57]

The review of the restaurant, above, which said that the restaurant stocked the latest periodicals, is crucial. This was a practice of the café as well, and Roger Chartier, in his book *The Cultural Origins of the French Revolution*, identifies a new political culture in France in the eighteenth century, which immediately preceded – if it did not exactly cause – the Revolution, in which salons, cafés, Masonic lodges, periodicals and restaurants all played a role in producing what d'Alembert called a 'noisy mixture' of opinionated individuals, who much enjoyed the sociability offered in these new institutions. Louis-Sébastien Mercier, for example, denounced restaurants for breaking up family life, enticing people away from their own dining rooms.

In eighteenth-century France, food, drink, fashion and interior decoration were all regarded as new forms of knowledge/learning, all contributing to the Enlightenment, earning their status as aspects of *savoir vivre* just as much as literature, science and philosophy.

The Serious Game of Love

What might be considered the most original form of the French imagination we might also call the most grotesque. It will be remembered from chapter 16 that the invention of the sofa brought about a revolution both in furniture design and in sociability, making it possible for the first time for more than one individual to sit intimately close to another. It is therefore perhaps not too much of a surprise that, in the eighteenth century, a number of novels were written in which the narrator *is* a sofa, giving that narrator an inspired 'ringside view' in eavesdropping on what the sofa occupants (i.e., lovers or would-be lovers) get up to. But for some writers this imaginative trick was not enough. In Denis Diderot's *The Indiscreet Jewels*, 1748, it is the female sexual organs which actually speak, betraying how female sexuality and seduction techniques differ from men's, or from what men *think* about female sexuality. Even in the twenty-first century, after decades of what we have been pleased to call a 'sexual revolution', the idea of speaking vaginas still takes some getting used to.

What this shows, however, is that libertinism, the fashion for predatory sexual seduction, which was popular in several parts of Europe in the late seventeenth and eighteenth centuries, but particularly prevalent in France, was rather more than what we mean when we say 'ladies' man', or 'philanderer', or 'womaniser'. In fact, before the eighteenth century the term had no sexual associations at all. It was used in a theological context, being not too distinct from 'atheist'. In the early seventeenth century, the term 'scholarly libertines' referred to an assortment of academics, poets and dilettantes who were 'freethinkers', opposed to dogma of any kind, seeking to demystify superstition and contesting both political and religious authority.[1] Later, libertines liked to consider themselves as emancipated from the court, a view that was strengthened following the crack-down by Richelieu and Louis XIV on aristocratic privileges. Marin Mersenne, a mathematician known for his theory of prime numbers and his musical-mathematical theories of harmony, calculated that there may have been as many as 50,000 'libertines', in the sense of atheists, in Paris during the reign of the Sun King.

Libertinism as we have come to understand it, however, began a little later, around the time of Ninon de Lenclos and Alexandrine de Tencin's many affairs and, of course, the regent's *petits soupers*. Its overall worldview was 'strategic retreat' in matters of pleasure, especially sexual pleasure. This was explained first in the *Dialogues de Luisa Sigea*, an erotic tale published anonymously by Nicolas Chorier, originally in Latin but translated many times into French in the early eighteenth century. Chorier was a magistrate 'in the eyes of the world' but a libertine at heart and what 'strategic retreat' means in this context is that 'when in public', as one of the characters advises the young heroine, 'live for other people; in secret and alone, live for yourself, covering yourself with a veil of decency ... Cover yourself with decency, the kind you can be easily rid of as needed ...'[2] In other words, public sociability and private sociability were very different – indeed opposed – worlds.

Following the regent and his roués – after 1715, say – libertinism pertained almost exclusively to erotic matters. It became firmly associated with the mores of the French aristocracy under the reigns of Louis XV and Louis XVI and it remained a major theme of French literature and art until the Revolution. Eighteenth-century art and fiction, says the Belgian philosopher Michel Feher, are practically synonymous with love-making. 'If we were to judge only by paintings, we would conclude that members of the upper classes had nothing to do than disport themselves as lovers.' Most importantly, this world is one where pleasure and vanity are understood as the only human motives. 'True love had apparently taken a back seat to serial sex,' Feher insists. 'One still said to a woman: "I love you", but this was a polite way of saying "I desire you".'[3]

What is too easily lost in any short summary of libertinism is the elegance of the encounters, the association of sex with refinement and delicacy, the favouring of nuance over plain and forceful assertion. Seduction involved the startling turn of phrase, the gentle affecting melody, the artfully designed garden, the easeful silks of a boudoir. In a consummate age of fashion and intimate architecture, attention was paid to 'the summarily sketched gesture', and in particular the partially glimpsed body. 'Libertinage occupied a space between reality and desire, the possible and the imaginary.'[4]

What was also new was that in the eighteenth century people acquired the practice more and more of committing their experiences to paper, in letters and journals kept in the secret places of their desks (chapter 16), matters that beforehand had been scarcely whispered in the confessional. 'They found in rhymed verse a way of making light of their pains and of playing within their desires.'[5] It was a sexual/behavioural revolution.

All that being said, libertinism was also in fact the very opposite of what Jean-Jacques Rousseau explored in *Julie, or the New Eloise*. This was easily the most popular French novel of the eighteenth century, describing an idealised romance between a young aristocratic woman and her love-struck tutor, who is unacceptable for love and marriage owing to his lack of both title and fortune. For Rousseau, true love was pure and ennobling as he sought to convince his contemporaries of the true value of the emotions.[6] Libertine literature, however, did not see anything pure or ennobling in love. On the contrary, for the libertine love was no different from lust and though libertine literature ranged from the light-hearted to the deadly serious, its view of 'romance' was regarded as important and revolutionary enough to engage the attention of naturalist and materialist philosophers such as Diderot, La Mettrie and Helvétius. Based in this view, which regarded men and women as equally motivated by lust, it followed that sexual pleasure was the only goal in life worth being pursued.

However, if that was point number one for the libertine, point number two was that there is an asymmetry built into the equation, an artificiality introduced by society. The aristocratic code of the time allowed men to give rein to their sensual desires, in which seduction was regarded as a meritorious achievement, whereas women were brought up to resist the appetites of *their* flesh and to derive satisfaction from modesty.[7] On this account, virtue is an artificial construct, amounting almost to an 'emotional disorder'. In such an artificial system, the only way out is the specifically human art of seduction.

There are, however, different types of seduction, based on the fact that there are – on this view – different types of men and women. One of the two male types is the *petit maître*, a decadent aristocrat who in English would be called a fop. He is motivated by the pleasure to be had from 'strategic retreat', to living on two levels without society guessing what he is up to. He enjoys his double life but sees no reason to publicise it – indeed, he derives satisfaction from *having* a double life. The second type is a more serious libertine – he is the 'grand libertine' or 'dangerous man', who is not content with the secret pleasures of the *petit maître* but wants to take revenge on the world he moves in, the artificial culture he inhabits, specifically to seduce a woman, in the process transforming her from someone who resists seduction into someone who welcomes it, and he then publicly humiliates her by announcing his conquest to the world at large. Through successive seductions, the grand libertine or dangerous man makes a name for himself. His vanity is piqued by the fact that others – less successful men – envy him.

The women who are the focus of seduction themselves fall into three types. These are, first, the prudes, women with a public reputation for austerity, 'who pretend to despise sexual pleasure'. Second are the coquettes, who take pleasure in their lovers' and would-be lovers' 'desperate passion'. And third are the so-called sensitive women, heiresses – as Michel Feher puts it – to the seventeenth century *précieuses*.[8] Disabusing these types is the greatest triumph a libertine can achieve.

A Total Loss of Innocence – Deliberate Cynicism

The campaign of seduction that forms the main thrust and theme of libertine literature has vengeance over a woman as its central element, but it is also a campaign against the mores of the time, with an underlying aim being to show that pleasure and vanity are the two main motives of the human comedy. It is a 'philosophy' – if we can call it that – born of the aristocracy's surfeit of leisure and the consequent prevalence of *ennui*, or boredom. In such an environment, many people of both sexes had suffered as a result of the 'erotic war games' that distinguished French – and especially Parisian – society in the eighteenth century, and in which 'tender love', the ideal for many women, was for men a 'fearsome threat' – another consequence of the asymmetry – carrying with it the possibility that the man who succumbed would end up being 'enslaved' to his mistress. And this is the point of seduction for the grand libertine. The campaign is intended to show to women that they are just as physically motivated as men, and that they are equally likely to become hostages of desire.[9] Its aim is to produce in the objects of the campaign a total loss of innocence. This is what being an adult means.

What can be glimpsed here is an attempt to create a serious philosophy, or make serious a game, to opt deliberately for cynicism, once more to create a level of grandeur in an area that may not entirely merit such treatment.

It is a point of contention that eighteenth-century painting is often conjoined with libertine literature as but another expression of the same phenomenon. In fact, eighteenth-century erotic art throws libertine literature into relief.

On close inspection, eighteenth-century French painting is an expression of *galanterie* – flirtation ending in consummation, but it is not evidence for the heavy-duty, self-regarding, seduction campaigns of libertinism. Eighteenth-century painting simply does not exist in such a multi-level world. The paintings of Boucher, Fragonard, Greuze and Lancret, for example, fall into the following categories (specific examples of paintings are given in the notes):

- There were regular depictions of nudes, often given a classical bent, as in statuary, to distance the art from the more obviously pornographic.
- There were a number of drawings and paintings showing female bodies (rarely if ever males) from behind, as often as not sprawled

across untidy bedsheets and silks. It is as if the artists could not risk too much full-frontal nudity but, at the same time, realised that an artfully – and languidly – posed nude rear or buttock can be extremely erotic.

- A number of figures – usually women – are shown sleeping, mostly in bed, or *on* the bed, and from the pose, and the thoroughness of the sleep, we are invited to assume that this is the sleep of sexual exhaustion.

- Many paintings confirm that it was the fashion of the time for women – even serving girls and maids – to wear bodices in which their breasts are forced upwards, so that the upper part of the bulging bosom and cleavage draws the eye.

- Lest we be minded to think that this is as far as artists could go, there is no shortage of paintings in which a stylishly dressed woman – and not always a young woman either – is depicted so that her décolleté shows not just her bulging upper bosom but both nipples as well.

- Women at their toilette, or in their boudoir, was another popular scene in which female figures are shown in various states of undress, mostly tame by our standards, but presumably eroticising at the time.

- By the same token, depictions of women showing their ankles, or lower legs, were also popular, not erotic to us but in the eighteenth century such exposure was seen as sexually enticing.

- There were innumerable scenes of couples on couches, sofas, daybeds and beds – in the music room, in the kitchen and sometimes out of doors – more or less closely disporting, touching, undressing, stroking, occasionally kissing.

All well and good, but libertine literature – libertine philosophy – goes considerably further than this and is much more thought-out. It is, first and foremost, a cynical analysis of what are seen as society's shortcomings.[10] On this account women are viewed as manipulators, revelling in the pain of their frustrated suitors. Just as men can glory in the conquests of their seductions, so women can take pride in their implacable modesty. The various authors bring different sensibilities to their stories – Sade brings irony, Crébillon *fils* bitterness, Diderot earnestness, Laclos ambiguity – but they all deal with the inconstancy of natural appetites and the hypocrisy this must entail.

The central idea is exactly that – natural appetites are natural, desire is a purely physical phenomenon, so that the impositions of society 'injure the human temperament'. Women who have been raised to be modest and constant are upholding 'unnatural virtues' and the libertine's aim is to free them from this unnatural state. Everyone who has ever been in love as a youth (and that includes almost everyone), and not had that love returned in equal measure, knows the lovesickness, misery, humiliation and loneliness that can occur – and endure. The aim of a successful seduction is to overcome such feelings, to hit back at a society which breeds such unpleasantness, and to inoculate the individuals (the seducers) from ever succumbing again. In losing their innocence, lovers become free.

Libertinism basically sees sexual relations as a form of commerce, not as in the modern evolutionary exchange where, to put it crudely, 'man offers love in exchange for sex; woman offers sex in exchange for love', but where 'female vanity' is the basic coinage in need of exposure. 'Love is a manipulation of a lover's desire by his vain mistress, rather than a pure impulse of tenderness.' The libertine refuses to recognise the existence of the heart. Although he retains a fond (and painful) memory of his lovesickness as a youth, he is now determined to ward off passionate love and never become its slave.

Nor does he seek exclusive ownership of a woman; this too may be seen as a form of slavery. As set out in both *Les Liaisons dangereuses* and *On the Education of Women*, Choderlos de Laclos sees love as a trap 'deliberately conceived' by women, a trap made all the more terrible in that its victims 'worship both their yoke and their tyrant'.

Claude de Crébillon *fils*, the author of *The Sofa*, was the son of a famous tragedian. His book and *The Indiscreet Jewels*, by Denis Diderot, were both 'inspired', if that is the right word, by *The Thousand and One Nights*, which had been translated into French at the beginning of the eighteenth century.[11] As with their Arabic prototype, both books revolve around a sultan who must be prevented from being bored. It is in order to fend off *ennui* that the sultan in *The Indiscreet Jewels* seeks the help of a genie, who offers him a magic ring. This ring if pointed towards a woman has the effect of making the woman's vagina – her 'jewel' – speak out loud.[12] In *The Sofa* another sultan, the grandson of Shah Riar and Scheherazade, is entertained by a young courtier named Amanzei. In the stories he tells, he remembers that his soul was locked up in a sofa; this was so because the god Brahma wished to punish him for his wicked lifestyle and his soul was therefore condemned to travel from sofa to sofa in search of true love. 'More precisely, Brahma told Amanzei that he would not be reincarnated into a human body until a man and a woman ... had consummated their passion on "his" sofa.'

In the course of Amanzei's travels, he witnesses close up the machinations of coquettes, the selfishness of cynical libertines, the hypocrisy of prudish ladies, and the manipulations of deceitful men. Over the course of the story, seven couples are eavesdropped on. In one, the hypocrite Fatima gives herself secretly to her slave; in another, Amina, a prostitute, allows herself to be humiliated by a steward, equally ineffectual; Almaida, already middle-aged, allows herself to be seduced by her spiritual guide; and so on. De Crébillon takes us through erotic play, relentless wickedness, while at the same time advancing the view that the greatest experience in life is love. He is showing how it can be manipulated, how we so often fail at it and that we reject modesty at our peril.

In *The Indiscreet Jewels*, the sultan's ring reveals the discrepancy – the duplicity – between the words emanating from the women's mouths and from their 'jewels'; there is only one woman – Mirzoza – whose mouth and jewel say the same thing. For the most part, the jewels produce what has been described as a 'syncopated' conversation in which the woman is quickly silenced, yielding to the 'chatter of the jewels'. In the book, the women panic and endeavour to silence 'the voices beneath her skirts', to the great amusement of the sultan. One jewel complains: 'I am visited, battered, neglected, perfumed, fatigued, ill-attended, bored ...' In another case, the jewel complains of being forced to witness 'nine proofs of love in four hours'.

Les Liaisons dangereuses is by far the most well-known libertine book.[13] Its central theme is: 'How can lovers surrender to the fires of passion while preserving their freedom?' – the classic libertine dilemma. For Laclos, amorous sentiment was a dangerous trap, and one in which the women in the story well realise that society places them at a disadvantage, confined to a limited set of roles, all of them circumscribed 'by the belief that female honour and pleasure are mutually exclusive'. One aim of the women in the story, therefore, is to shatter male domination.

The main difference between men and women is, as Laclos makes plain – and this is what sets the story apart from, and above the others – that whereas the male libertine can flaunt his victories, the female variety cannot: she must keep her triumphs secret. The man she defeats knows he is defeated, and suffers for it, but neither partner can broadcast this result, the man for fear of shame and dishonour, the woman because she must maintain her modesty at all costs in the eyes of the world and cannot come clean on what she has done. So even in seduction society puts women at a disadvantage.

This makes for a much more entertaining, and intertwined story, in which the difference between loving and pleasing is brought out clearly, and Laclos spends time explaining and exploring the asymmetry that, for him, is the principal danger of all liaisons. And this, to be frank, is how libertine literature, and behaviour, is to be understood, as a deadly serious game, but a game nonetheless, in which this asymmetry is played out, where the woman begins at a disadvantage and, even if she wins, can never broadcast her victory to the world. Never forgetting for a moment that all libertine stories are at one level pornographic, the libertine author makes – or tries to make – a serious point about love as a synecdoche for the human condition at large. While love may be the greatest experience to be had, its perils make one wonder if it is ever worth the price. The libertine has come to the conclusion that it isn't. 'Except that there is always, at the back of the mind, the worry that to miss out on real love is to miss out on something worth having ... There is always, deep down, a fear among libertines that they risk missing out.'[14]

Whatever conclusions are derived from these narratives, the significance of libertine literature is that it is an exploration of love – its carnal pleasures and its psychological/philosophical/hypocritical realities – that shows the French to have introduced a level of reality in place of the sugary sentimentality that is often the alternative. This is perhaps what the rest of us, without fully realising it, appreciate about the French.

PART FIVE

REVOLUTION, ROBESPIERRE, REGICIDE, RECOVERY, RESTORATION

The Discovery of the Bourgeois: Unpoetic, Unheroic, Unerotic

By all accounts, the salon of Louise Florence Pétronille d'Esclavelles, afterwards Mme d'Épinay, was somewhat more austere than Mme du Deffand's, or Mme Geoffrin's, less characterised by warm friendship and more given to the close discussion of politics, philosophy and morality.[1]

Born in 1726, into an ancient and noble Norman family, her father Baron d'Esclavelles was the governor of Valenciennes, in the far north of France, near the border of what would become Belgium. But he died when his daughter was only ten and she came under the protection of her mother's brother-in-law, Louis-Denis de Lalive de Bellegarde, one of the richest farmers-general in the kingdom, and grew up in the magnificent Château de La Chevrette, his country seat. Although she was dependent on family charity, so to speak, this did not prevent her cousin, Denis-Joseph Lalive, Bellegarde's second son (who had bought the title d'Épinay), from finding her attractive. He and Louise were married in December 1745. She was nineteen.

In the eighteenth century, farmers-general were given charge of all indirect taxes, which they fixed and collected, paying an agreed sum to the government/king. They were not always popular, but they were a necessary evil and as a result lived in luxury.

To begin with, the d'Épinays lived at La Chevrette but it gradually became clear that Lalive was not his father. Louise tried to conceal her husband's late hours – and his neglect of her – but her difficulties multiplied when, to escape her reproaches, he introduced her to a number of thoroughly unsuitable companions, of whom the most important was Louis-Claude Dupin de Francueil.[2] Francueil had good qualities – he was an artist and a musician – but he was also spoiled and dissipated and intent on seducing the entire family as much as Louise. (He certainly seduced her – she gave him a daughter and a son.) It was Francueil's arrival in Louise's life that would lead to her salon and its highly accomplished guests, not the least of whom was Jean-Jacques Rousseau, who took part in his own plays at La Chevrette.

At that stage, Rousseau was entirely unknown. In the first instance Francueil had given him some music to copy, during which encounter Rousseau had shown there was something to him, as a result of which Francueil made him his secretary. Rousseau in the meantime had written a three-act comedy in verse, *L'Engagement téméraire*, and this was produced, attracting the attention of Louise.[3] Thus was formed the first nucleus of what would come to be her salon.

THE WHITE TYRANT

Between, roughly speaking, 1750 and the Revolution, Paris was very cosmopolitan, with many German and – after 1763 and the ending of the Seven Years War – British visitors. Early on Louise was invited to the informal dinners held by Mlle Jeanne Quinault, a famous actress, where her co-host was the archaeologist the Comte de Caylus, and where a group of 'freethinkers overflowed with the ideas of the Enlightenment'. In addition to Rousseau, present at these dinners were Diderot, Crébillon *fils* (chapter 19), the dramatist Marivaux and Charles Pinot Duclos, author of both erotic novels and works of history (chapter 11). On occasion, Rousseau, Francueil and Mme d'Épinay 'sang for several hours after dinner', with a fourth figure, Friedrich Melchior Grimm, joining in.[4] Among the Germans newly arrived in Paris was the Count of Schönberg, who employed Grimm as tutor to his son. Grimm had been disappointed by his career prospects at the University of Leipzig and was licking his wounds in Paris, where he had formed a friendship with another German who would be a favourite in the salons, the Baron d'Holbach.

Through Mme d'Épinay, Rousseau met Grimm and was drawn to him via their joint interest in music. He also introduced the German to the *Encyclopédistes*, with whom he had not yet fallen out. Gauffecourt called Grimm 'Tyran Le Blanc', the white tyrant, partly on account of his personality ('He was always authoritative without being always correct') and partly because he always lathered his cheeks with white lead.[5] Different as they were in character, Grimm and Mme d'Épinay became intimate.

As Louise was absorbing the kind of society that was on offer in *ancien régime* France, Bellegarde, realising that his son would – sooner or later – bring ruin on the family, took care to settle an income on her. Louise and her husband were now, to all intents and purposes, separated but he continued to demand money from her, and infected her with venereal disease (which, amazingly enough, did not kill her). This produced a fetid atmosphere, and her health began to suffer, whereupon she relied more and more on what she called her 'five bears' – Grimm, Rousseau, Saint-Lambert, Desmoulins and Gauffecourt.[6]

A Meeting in the Mud

Not one of her five bears, but still a close friend, was the youngest of Bellegarde's children, Sophie, Comtesse d'Houdetot, Louise's sister-in-law. On paper Sophie was not an attractive proposition. Here is Rousseau's description in his *Confessions*: 'Her face was pitted with smallpox, her complexion was coarse, she was short-sighted, and her eyes were rather too round but, notwithstanding, she looked young [she was approaching thirty], and her features, at once lively and gentle, were attractive ... She overflowed with delightful sallies of wit ... which fell from her lips involuntarily.'[7]

In 1757 Rousseau, who set the fashion for simplicity in life, was living in a cottage on Mme d'Épinay's estate, composing what would turn out to be *Julie, ou La Nouvelle Héloïse*, his extremely successful novel. He and Sophie had already met by that point but to begin with there had been no electricity between them. However, in January of that year, Sophie was on the way somewhere else when her coachman took a wrong turning and then got trapped in the mud. Undeterred, Sophie got out and trudged on.

Before long, her path brought her to the cottage where Jean-Jacques was living. Despite her muddy attire, the chance meeting went well, and he invited her to stay for a light meal. Sophie had had a rapidly arranged marriage, after the fashion of the day, and was never in love with her husband. And so, not long afterwards, taking the initiative, Sophie returned to the cottage, this time on horseback and this time dressed as a man, which made riding easier. And, as Rousseau put it later, 'this time it was love … the first time and only time in my life'.[8]

A Wolf in Viper's Clothing

Has there ever been a more extraordinary figure than Rousseau? By turns brilliant, aggressive, childlike, quarrelsome, inconsistent and heartless, he may have only loved once but he regularly fell *out* of love with erstwhile friends in a series of explosive and embarrassing rages.

Born in Geneva in 1712, orphaned at the age of ten, he began adult life as an engraver's apprentice before he quit the city in 1728. From there he wandered Europe 'seeking an elusive happiness'. He converted to Catholicism in Turin, after which he had various escapades and forms of employment – as a footman, seminarist and music teacher or tutor, travelling around Switzerland and France. In 1732 he settled down for as much as eight years at the country house of Mme Françoise-Louise de Warens, a formidable woman who had divorced her husband when his business failed, and she introduced Jean-Jacques to the pleasures of intimacy. He remembered his time with Mme de Warens as an idyllic place in the *Confessions*.

In 1741 he arrived in Paris where he met Diderot, who later commissioned him to write about music for the *Encyclopédie*. Against that progress in his life may be set the fact that he sired five children by Thérèse Levasseur, a servant girl he met in Paris at a hotel where he took his meals, only to abandon them in a foundling home.

Never entirely stable, during the 1750s his quarrels spread to take in Voltaire and Diderot, and this was reflected in his writing, which was now characterised by a new note of defiant independence. In 1758 he turned on his former friends the *Encyclopédistes*, in the *Lettre à d'Alembert sur les spectacles*. This pilloried cultured society, especially the theatre, which he regarded as a corrupting influence, setting him against the *Encyclopédistes*, who thought drama helped educate the ignorant who couldn't read. They even advocated a playhouse for Geneva, Rousseau's home city, where theatre was banned. The previous year Rousseau had left Paris for Montmorency, now a suburb of the capital but then the site of a distinguished noble family, and the five years he spent there, he was to say later, were the most productive of his life. *La Nouvelle Héloïse* (1761) met with immediate and enormous success. In this and in *Émile*, published a year later, Rousseau argued eloquently 'for the inviolability of personal ideals against the powers of the state and the pressures of society'.[9] In 1762 he composed a withering attack on revealed religion, the *Profession de foi du vicaire Savoyard*, which brought about his arrest though he fled to England. This turned into a prolonged *cause célèbre*.

Religion, of course, was one of the ever-present vexed subjects of the day, with the Jesuits ever ready to pounce on any heresy, or what they maintained was heresy. In such circumstances, the fashion among the *philosophes* for deism was bound to figure prominently in the affairs of the salons, the more so as distinguished foreigners like David Hume passed through Paris. There was in fact a cult of Hume, who was entertained at a variety of salons, including that of Mme Helvétius, where he was warned about Rousseau but paid no heed.[10]

Hume was a man of pristine character, applauded in his own times for his 'uncommon virtue'. His friend, the economist and moral philosopher Adam Smith, saw him as a 'perfectly wise and virtuous man as perhaps the nature of human frailty will permit'. That frailty had its sternest test in 1766 when Hume offered to help with the exile of Rousseau.

At that time, Rousseau had cause to fear for his life. By then he had already been a refugee for more than three years, constantly having to move on. His radical tract *The Social Contract*, with its opening explosion 'Man is born free, but everywhere he is in chains', had been viciously condemned. Even more dangerous, in the eyes of the Catholic Church, was *Émile*, in which Rousseau campaigned for the clergy to be denied a role in the schooling of the young. A warrant for his arrest was issued and his books were publicly burned.

Forced to flee France, Rousseau first found sanctuary in a village in his native Switzerland, but a local priest managed to stir up cantonal feeling against him and he had no option but to move on yet again. But where?

This is where Hume came in. In Paris he had been rapturously received as secretary to the British ambassador, and the years he spent in the French capital were the happiest of his life, he said, and he earned the sobriquet *Le Bon David*. The *salonnières* who were most involved in bringing Hume and Rousseau together were Mme d'Épinay and Mme de Boufflers, in whose dazzling premises, with its four large mirrors, the young Mozart performed. Mme d'Épinay found Rousseau 'as poor as Job, but he has wit and vanity enough for four … Ugly as his face is, his eyes show that love plays a large role in his story.'

It has to be said that several of Hume's *philosophe* friends tried to warn him what he was taking on. Grimm, d'Alembert and Diderot had all gone through spectacular fallings-out with the combative Jean-Jacques. As d'Holbach famously warned Hume: 'You don't know your man. I will tell you plainly, you're warming a viper in your bosom.'[11]

At first all went well. Rousseau, by now a popular novelist as well as a philosopher, was lionised in London, where his weird Armenian garb, including a cap with tassels, in fact rather put Hume in the shade. But Rousseau was not drawn to London as a busy, noisy metropolis and moved, first to the village of Chiswick on the western outskirts, and then to Wootton, in Staffordshire, where he had been offered the use of a country house. And it was there that he conceived his idea of a plot against him, that his letters were being opened and that Hume was behind a plan to dishonour him. It was the sort of paranoid allegations he had made before against those he had previously fallen out with. Hume was worried – frightened even – because he knew that Rousseau was working on his *Confessions* and the books he had already published showed the power of his pen, in particular *La Nouvelle Héloïse*, which had been in such demand that Paris booksellers had rented it out by the hour.[12]

Hume began to denounce Rousseau to his erstwhile friends in Paris. He found that Rousseau had spoken of him to the great actor-manager David Garrick, calling him '*noir*, black, and a *coquin*, knave'. When Hume faced him with this, Rousseau slyly let it be known that he had overheard Hume speak ill of him in his sleep. This was a terrible development, vivid, original, and impossible to gainsay. Others joined in the imbroglio – Boswell, Walpole, Voltaire, even King George III.

A New Figure of Modernity

But of course Rousseau is known for far more than his quarrels, entertaining as they are. As more than one modern philosopher has said, Rousseau was a turning point in philosophy and, to an extent, politics. Rousseau was the first to identify the bourgeois – unpoetic, unheroic, unerotic, neither aristocrat nor of the people, a new figure of modernity and both a cause and a symptom of what ails modern culture. 'The bourgeois morality is mercenary. Within bourgeois society the arts and sciences tend to increase inequality, giving more power to the already powerful, and freedoms are lost. Class becomes decisive and there can be no common goal in bourgeois society without radical reform.'[13]

For us, today, this is all very modern, very pre-Marxian and very pre-Revolutionary. 'Rousseau was the presiding genius of the excesses of the French Revolution ... Civilisation had shattered man's unity.' Rousseau was insistent that equality could not be qualified.

He had made his feelings known to Sophie d'Houdetot in late spring 1757 and, for a few months, they were extremely close, enjoying the countryside, he expounding and exploring his views on freedom, the simple life, and living up to the ideals he had set himself. In time, Sophie became the model, or at least one of the models, for Julie, in the great romance which crowned Rousseau's career. Proof of this passion surely lies in the fact that, later, Rousseau copied out the two volumes of *La Nouvelle Héloïse* specially for Sophie, in his own hand.

The idyll didn't last. Jean-Jacques's servant girl, Thérèse, who he had treated so badly earlier on, informed Mme d'Épinay of the affair and she, it is said, passed on the news to one of her five bears, Saint-Lambert.

Jean François de Saint-Lambert is one of the lesser-known *philosophes* now, but he was colourful enough in his own day and his relationship with Sophie long outlasted her affair with Rousseau. Born in Nancy in December 1716, his interests combined poetry and philosophy, and he was also a soldier – he fought in both the War of the Austrian Succession and the Seven Years War. And he was an accomplished ladies' man, known for three affairs – with the Marquise de Boufflers; with Émilie du Châtelet, who was also Voltaire's mistress (chapter 12), with whom Saint-Lambert had a child (whose complicated delivery contributed to Émilie's death in September 1749); and with Sophie.

Saint-Lambert's best-known written work was a poem, *The Seasons*, which he read widely in a number of salons, not least Mme D'Épinay's, before publishing it in 1769. A masterpiece of descriptive verse, Voltaire thought it was the only work of eighteenth-century French literature that would last. Saint-Lambert published two philosophical works but not until after the Revolution and at the time he was one of Mme d'Épinay's five bears he was better known as a contributor to the *Encyclopédie*, where he published an essay on luxury. In 1770 he was elected to the Académie française.[14]

It was while Saint-Lambert was away fighting in the Seven Years War that Sophie met Rousseau. After Mme d'Épinay intervened, Sophie terminated her affair with Rousseau and returned to Jean François.

CULTURAL NEWS FROM THE WORLD'S CAPITAL

As for Mme d'Épinay and Rousseau, they had many interests in common, not least education. But Rousseau's disagreements with his former *philosophe* colleagues and friends became terminal after he published the *Lettre à d'Alembert sur les spectacles*, and Mme d'Épinay never saw him again.

By then she had begun to express her own interest in education. Like Mme de Lambert before her, this began as a series of hortatory letters to her son. In fact, her first letters had been couched at such a level as to be beyond the boy, and Rousseau had intervened, to make the language more accessible to a child. Later, she visited her son's school and, in conversation with the tutor, the shortcomings of the establishment were exposed. In her educational writing, Louise

Florence was at pains to explore the difference, as she saw it, between education and instruction, and what should be taught at home and what at school.[15]

She was becoming known and her social and intellectual profile was hardly harmed – not at all – by a visit she made to Geneva, beginning in November 1757. The ostensible purpose of the visit was to consult Théodore Tronchin, the world-famous Swiss doctor, described by Voltaire 'as wise as Asclepius and beautiful as Apollo', and known for his specialism in 'women's diseases', for recommending fresh air, exercise and looser corsets, and for carrying out groundbreaking research on inoculation against smallpox.

In Geneva, Voltaire honoured Mme d'Épinay with a few light verses and showered her with invitations. While there she studied botany and geology, which impressed Voltaire, who said: 'She is no scatterbrain: she is a *philosophe*, with a very clear, strong mind.'[16]

Grimm had not accompanied her. Despite her infirmity, he was hard at work with Diderot on the *Encyclopédie* and his *Correspondance littéraire, philosophique et critique*. During the near-forty years of its existence, until the Revolution, this monthly or fortnightly newsletter went out to its twenty or more royal and princely subscribers in handwritten copies produced by amanuenses in Zweibrücken, just over the border in the German Palatinate, thus avoiding French censorship. European courts welcomed this 'regular, candid, and cultural news' from 'the World's Capital'. As Mme d'Épinay joined the enterprise, with Grimm, 'her existence was transformed'. She began to express some of her own thoughts on education and started joining the Baron d'Holbach's coterie, where she first met Diderot (chapter 23).

On her return from Geneva, her salon re-formed and now included not only the *Encyclopédistes*, with whom she was fully identified, but several foreigners.[17] Her position was threatened, however, by the actions of her husband, who continued as a spendthrift and a gambler, so profligate that in 1762 they were forced to sell La Chevrette and move into a much smaller property, La Briche. Nor was that the end of her misfortune. Her son – it was equally clear – was taking after his dissolute father and acquiring a raft of debts entirely on his own account. This became so acute that Louise and her husband found it necessary to ask for a *lettre de cachet*, a singular device during the absolute monarchy which, under the seal of the sovereign, authorised the imprisonment of an individual without trial. Eventually, he was exiled from France.

None of these setbacks appear to have done Mme d'Épinay's reputation any harm with her *philosophe* friends, however, except Rousseau, who had returned from England after his high-profile falling out with David Hume. The readings of his *Confessions*, the earliest of which took place in Mme d'Épinay's La Briche salon, turned out to be so unpleasant and disagreeable – not just about her but also about Grimm, her long-term lover – that she succeeded in having the book stopped.[18]

A Treasure on Rainy Days

Still more unpleasantness occurred when, in the summer of 1769, the Duc de Choiseul demanded the recall of the Abbé Galiani, secretary to the Neapolitan embassy in Paris. Ferdinando Galiani was a cleric whose great wit, erudition and charm did not match his diminutive size – he was 4 feet 6 inches tall, so tiny that when he first arrived at court, he was subject to the most ribald laughter. He regained some lost ground when he brightly remarked to the king: 'What you see is but a sample of the secretary; the complete secretary will come later.'[19] He was in fact very learned, having made a number of excavations of archaeological sites near Naples at Pompeii and Herculaneum, where he discovered several papyrus volumes (this was when the Villa dei Papiri was being discovered), and he wrote a dissertation on Vesuvius. Diderot was no less fascinated by Galiani than Galiani was by Diderot. 'The abbé is endlessly clever and amusing, a treasure on rainy days.'

Galiani loved his time in Paris and was extremely distressed when he was recalled, but he had only himself to blame. He had committed an indiscretion when he let slip to a Danish diplomat that the pact that Choiseul was trying to form with Naples, as a bulwark against the alliance of Russia, England and Denmark, was in fact not going to happen, that the Neapolitans were stringing the French along. This news got back to Choiseul, who demanded his recall.

This development was felt keenly by both Galiani and Mme

d'Épinay, and by the rest of her salon. But it did spark a long and lively correspondence between the two, Galiani entrusting to Louise and Diderot the manuscript of his great work, *Dialogues sur les blés*.[20] They saw it through the press, the work being both a 'narrative and a sermon', consisting of dialogues in Socratic form, in which Galiani argued that there is a need for an 'infinity' of exceptions to free trade. (See chapter 22 for a fuller discussion.) The work received praise from all corners – Holbach, Mme du Deffand, Helvétius, Catherine (the Great) of Russia, Frederick the Great, all of whom were cheered as much by his jovial writing style as the substance of his argument.

In 1762 Grimm had been recalled to Germany and so, for a while, Mme d'Épinay oversaw production of the *Correspondance littéraire*. One way and another, as noted, these handwritten communications were circulated for thirty-seven years to many of the courts of Europe, confirming Paris as the cultural capital of the continent, and Mme d'Épinay as someone of substance in that milieu.

It was now that Louise began to spread her wings on the literary front. She tried her hand first at portraits of her friends, such as Mme d'Houdetot, personal sketches and a few verses, letters and essays, dedicated to her mother (in *Mes moments heureux*), and fictional letters and diaries (a popular form). But *Les Conversations d'Émilie* was a different matter.

Today this work seems unexceptional. It has an educational theme but is no more than the common sense that any reasonable mother would impart to her child. In those days, however, it was a revelation and a revolution.[21] Émilie was her granddaughter and Louise gave a sympathetic account of Rousseau's argument that, until the age of ten, children cannot grasp a long series of ideas and arguments, cannot take in arid abstract notions, and should be allowed to explore the world in their own way. Their questions should always be answered truthfully but as simply as possible, in this way gradually leading up to the time when the young woman is introduced to *le monde*.

The book was published in 1775, received widespread attention and went into many editions. Catherine II (Catherine the Great), to whom the second edition was dedicated, adopted Louise's recommendations for the education of her own grandson. Catherine also gave Louise a pension, which was sorely needed.

Louise's ups and downs continued. When, in 1778, Voltaire returned to Paris to great acclaim, he took rooms near her, which cheered her greatly. But then, not long after, the great man died and was refused a grave in the city that had once worshipped him. Her anguish was acute.

She continued to write on many themes. She ridiculed the new fashion for towering coiffures (chapter 8).[22] She continued to attend what she called Baron d'Holbach's 'synagogue', and she started taking opium, which enabled her to write, commenting dryly that half the human race existed on opium.

But then, in 1783, *Les Conversations d'Émilie* was crowned by the Académie française when she was the first recipient of a new award, the 'Prize of Utility', founded by the Baron de Monthyon, a French lawyer who donated 10,000 francs for a prize to be awarded to a French person who had produced the book 'most beneficial to morals'.[23] Four months later Louise d'Épinay was dead, at fifty-seven.

'Literification'

In the eighteenth century, says Marc Fumaroli in his book *When the World Spoke French*, 'the French were at home wherever they went'. Paris was every foreigner's second homeland, and the Enlightenment was a 'disposition to happiness', making this French century 'one of the most optimistic in the history of the world'. The world (that is, Europe) spoke French in the eighteenth century not merely due to power alone, he says, but because the public 'had above all endorsed the talent, wit and clarity of expression in French of the realm's writers and thinkers'. The Enlightenment spread out from France, he maintained (and despite what a raft of recent British and American scholarship has shown), because the aristocracies of the rest of Europe were 'fed on philosophical reading obtained from Paris'.

According to Fumaroli, the academies and salons of eighteenth-century Paris, in effect its urban aristocracy, had achieved a fine art of living unparalleled anywhere else. 'The academies created or reformed under Louis XIV', he goes on, 'shifted the centre of the Republic of Letters [from Italy] to Paris, and Parisian high society, living in symbiosis with the royal academies, has become the audience and arbiter of the European reputation of books, as it has become, with the institution of the salon, the audience and arbiter of taste in painting and sculpture; its favour becomes the criterion of an artist's European reputation.' The efforts of the urban aristocracy 'had raised the leisure of private life to the rank of a fine art of living, served by artists from the first master of the hunt to the last kennel keeper, from the chef to the gardener, from the dressmaker to the jeweller, from the wigmaker to the perfumer, from the painter to the architect, from the poet of light verse to the philosopher – director of conscience and leader of thought', all 'united to offer the art of conversation and gallantry a euphoric milieu ... On all these levels France was now mother and uncontested mistress'.[1]

Eighteenth-century France and in particular its language, he says, going slightly over the top, were quite simply contagious and irresistible 'because their image was that of the small amount of happiness and intelligence of which men are capable during their brief passage through this earthly vale of tears'.[2] Or, as Dena Goodman has put it, with less rodomontade, the salons were transformed in the eighteenth century from a characteristic of the life of the leisured classes to a central institution of the Enlightenment.[3]

Mathieu Marraud, in his comprehensive inquiry into this Parisian urban nobility in the eighteenth century, is more discerning than Fumaroli. He has identified what he calls a 'second order' nobility, ranking below the very highest nobles, on which the social and intellectual life of the capital was centred, and among whom military men, financiers, rentiers and farmers-general were most prominent.

And it was this second order which spread itself among the great salons of Paris, being attracted by the lure of 'new knowledge, belles-lettres and erudition', so much so, Marraud concluded, that one could even talk of a 'mode of thought that was typically noble'.[4]

This owed not a little to the demographic make-up of the upper realms of society where, in 1788, although men made up the majority of nobles (57 per cent), there were no fewer than 1,556 women who were either separated from their husbands or widowed, and a further 405 who were not (yet) married. It was from this sizeable base that the *salonnières* were drawn. We saw earlier (chapter 5) that widows were a threat to two families and so becoming a *salonnière* was a 'safe' solution both from an economic and a social point of view.

At the same time, the number of writers in France more than doubled between 1750 and 1789, going from roughly 1,200 to around 3,000. During that time the number of noble authors dropped from

25 per cent of this total to 14 per cent by the time of the Revolution (which still means that their actual number rose from 300 or so to around 420). The lure of literature was ever-present.

Writing, Marraud says, was an attractive new or second form of activity for the nobility. For example, many men who had had a military career began to write – he quotes Mirabeau, Saint-Lambert, the Marquis de Lezay-Marnésia, the Marquis de Saint-Marc and Billardon de Sauvigny. The Duc de Chaulnes had a 'veritable second vocation' in science, having given up his military career and passing well beyond the stage of an amateur. The Comte de Guibert, military tactician and lover of Julie de Lespinasse (chapter 15), also published a tragedy in 1786, *Le Connable de Bourbon*.

The number of books mentioned in the inventories of the day was highest for military men, clergy and lawyers though no more than 22.5 per cent of nobles had a library. In these libraries, theology and science were notable by their relative absence, the proportion of religious books dropping from 20 per cent to 10 per cent in the last half of the century, whereas *belles-lettres* accounted for more than two-thirds of books between them. History remained strong throughout though the nobility naturally took an active interest in the current affairs of the day.

A literary career should not be thought of as the 'last resort' (*pis-aller*) of a déclassé group, Marraud says. On the contrary, many of these individuals were well able to 'play the game' thanks to a privileged education that enabled them to enjoy the *mondain* benefits of the salons. Many had received personal and private tuition not just in letters and languages and history but in every form of activity including dance, design, music and equitation. This contrasted, he said, with the education of women: many of the *salonnières*, as we have also seen, were autodidacts.

Belles-lettres were the central intellectual activity of the salons, though in the run-up to Revolution, interests widened and there were many books written about the status of the Third Estate, about the trade in luxury items and the status of the rich in society, and about the morality of this situation, and there was a spate of books defending the privileged way of life, the legitimacy of the nobility and arguments supporting the omnipotence of the king.[5] It was also true that in all cases forbidden titles formed a sizeable proportion of works – fully three-quarters of inventories mention such books.[6]

Overall, Marraud says that in noble libraries between the 1750s and the end of the 1780s works on law more than halved, dropping from 13 to 6 per cent, while the sciences and the arts grew from 9 to 14 per cent, and history from 34 to 44 per cent. The second order was concerned with its professional advancement but also with wider cultural pursuits, and the nobility did its best to foist its cultural tastes on everyone else. And in essence this was an alternative to absolutism. (The salon at Sceaux was an early example of being seen as *contre*-Versailles.) The changing status of women was an important ingredient in this. Eighty-four per cent of the women in the salons were legally noble.[7]

Marraud notes, as have others, that the salons were not always as 'open' as they might have been, and that social barriers between members could be a bar to spontaneous conversation. Many aristocrats were more interested in the ideas of the *philosophes* than in the *philosophes* themselves, and were content to read their books without inviting them to dinner. The Duchesse de Choiseul was not untypical when she said she was quite happy to know what they looked like from their portraits, though this did change as the Revolution approached.[8]

It is also true that in the first place, the *philosophes* were read more for their works of fiction, or poetry, or dramas than for their philosophical ideas. D'Alembert was regarded as an interesting mathematician before he was read as a philosopher. The anti-*philosophe* mood flourished not just in the theatre but in literature too.[9]

The salons took little part in the first popular anti-royal movements, which were about the abuses of absolute power, not philosophy. But then, as the American historian Robert Darnton noted, and as Napoleon was to make so much of, literature became politicised. This was the 'literification' of the public domain. 'More and more the act of writing became a means of contestation.'[10]

Simultaneously, attitudes to the salons were evolving on the eve of the Revolution. Many of them were regarded as embodying values that acted against the traditional interest and habits of the nobles of the *épée*, and so were seen as subversive, while many other people believed that the salons were the epitome of what France did best. Salons represented a zone of communication emancipated from both the censure of the monarch and the '*étiquette curiale*', the influence of the church.[11]

Marraud concluded that there was abroad in France in the run-up to the Revolution a world of ideas and a world of power and that these two worlds could coexist in the same person – this is what literification was all about. One group of nobles existed in a world dominated by *antériorité, lignage, endogamie, fidélité, clientélisme, patrimoine seigneurial* and *ségrégation professionelle ou idéologique*. But parallel to this, little by little, there was the development of a more mixed society. By means of the *mondain* and intellectual worlds, this '*mésalliance*' inaugurated a France which consolidated the place of *belles-lettres* in the national psyche and helped to propel the French way of life on its exceptional course. The fact that these differences could exist in the same person, Marraud says, is one reason why the nobles came back so quickly after the Revolution.[12]

Debt, Madame Deficit and an Undimmed Versailles

In December 1797, at a dinner party given by Talleyrand, General Napoleon Bonaparte was placed next to Germaine de Staël, wife of the Swedish ambassador in Paris and daughter of the famous Swiss financier and former minister in Louis XVI's government, Jacques Necker. 'Who is the greatest woman, alive or dead?' demanded Mme de Staël, at her most importunate. Smiling, Bonaparte smoothly replied: 'The one that has made the most children.' This somewhat flummoxed Mme de Staël, who was more used to doing the flummoxing. She got her own back a short while later, however – or at least she tried to – when she turned up unannounced at the general's house in the rue Chantereine. The butler explained that the citizen-general was in the bath and naked. 'No matter,' countered Germaine, 'genius has no sex!' Napoleon, who could be positively Victorian when he wanted to be, was flummoxed in return.

These well-known exchanges introduce us to four women who, while still playing the role of *salonnière*, were far more formidable (*redoutable*), pursuing actively wider roles as the French Revolution approached, arrived, exploded and passed, and, indeed, as Napoleon himself approached, arrived, exploded and passed. These individuals are: Suzanne Necker, Félicité de Genlis, Germaine de Staël and Juliette Récamier. Their lives take us forward across those remarkable years in some style. Despite the limits that society placed on them, they each managed to shine.

*

Our first stop is with Germaine's mother, Suzanne Necker, *née* Churchod. This was another case in which the mother's salon was handed down, for not only would Germaine inherit her mother's list of guests, but her own daughter, Albertine – Suzanne's granddaughter – took over *her* salon in due course, with much the same list of participants.

Suzanne was the wife of Jacques Necker, a Swiss banker who came from a long line of Calvinist pastors, though his father was a solid bourgeois professor of law. At an early age Jacques was transferred to the Paris branch of his bank and by 1764 he had won a respectable position in the banking world but was hardly known outside it. He lived modestly, kept no mistress, wrote no books at this stage of his life, was never seen in any prominent salon and was not universally popular. One associate described him as 'the most humourless fellow in the whole world', arrogant and ignorant in equal measure, his 'outstanding defect', in spite of these shortcomings, nonetheless being inordinate vanity. He did not have a great deal to be vain about and was hardly congenial company.[1]

This unprepossessing character did attempt a love affair in 1764 with the widow of a Swiss officer but she too found him dull and frequently left him alone with her young son and his governess. The governess was a Swiss girl of twenty-seven, Suzanne Churchod. In no time she and Necker were married, breaking the news to the widow only after the ceremony had been completed. The widow remarked tartly that 'they will bore each other to death'.[2]

ÉDOUARD DE GUIBON

In fact, they had some things in common. Like Necker, Suzanne came from a family of pastors, though there were French Huguenots in the background as well and some minor nobility. She grew up poor but – thanks to her father – was surprisingly well educated, in Latin, Greek, mathematics and the sciences. She played the harpsichord and violin and was an adept painter. She was also ambitious, very ambitious. Many of the young local pastors who came to practise their sermons before her father also had eyes for her but found her condescending. One, who wrote poems dedicated to her, commending her eyes, her breasts and her complexion, nonetheless concluded:

> But your ceaseless moralising
> Which forever is my bane
> Spoils all the joys I am devising.

Her ambition led her to make frequent trips to nearby Lausanne, where she joined the Academy of the Waters, a society where young people would meet for dancing, flirting and 'the discussion of interesting topics'.[3] And it was at the academy that she met the man who would fulfil her early ambition. In Lausanne he was known as Édouard de Guibon, but he was in fact English and is better known as the author of the *Decline and Fall of the Roman Empire*.

Having inclined to the papacy at Oxford, Gibbon had been consigned to a staunch Protestant ideologue in Lausanne to reconvert him. It was, apparently, love at first sight, not with the ideologue but with Suzanne, on both their parts, though we should not overlook the fact that Gibbon was 'a gentleman of birth and means' and at twenty he had not yet grown triple-chinned or achieved his 'legendary corpulence' which, on one later occasion, had ensured that when he fell to one knee to woo a lady, he was unable to rise up again unaided. The young Gibbon's gentle manners and dazzling conversation appealed to Suzanne and overcame the fact that, even at twenty, his 'pudgy cheeks, tiny mouth and the bags under his eyes were not made to inspire passion'.[4]

In the event, the passion came to nothing. Gibbon's father was resolutely against a match to a 'foreigner' and, after much anguish, as Gibbon himself put it in a letter to Suzanne, 'I sighed as a lover, I obeyed as a son'. They agreed to remain friends.

To begin with, Suzanne did not have it easy. She had moved to Geneva with her mother after her father died in 1760, where she began giving private lessons to children. She may still have burned a torch for Gibbon but when her mother died, in 1763, leaving her penniless, her teaching paid off. She was taken in by one Pastor Moultou, whose children she was teaching. Through him she met Voltaire.

Children Are Not 'Miniature Adults'

As luck would have it, Anne Louise Germaine Necker was born two years into the marriage and just four years after the publication of Rousseau's *Émile*, and Suzanne determined to bring up her daughter according to the *philosophe*'s arguments. Rousseau's views on education, which are contained in *Émile*, were surprisingly modern if not quite as original as he made out. His main argument was that children are not 'miniature adults' but develop through various cognitive stages, as we would say, and that they should not be taught in any fixed curriculum laid down by an authoritative teacher, but be encouraged to develop their own skills in a spirit of equality and friendship, and be led to draw their own conclusions from experience.

At the beginning, the child's relationship with its mother is most important, Rousseau said, and he stressed the need for women to breast-feed their own children and to beware 'swaddling' them too tightly – the difference between love and constraint is especially important. This view is to be got across early on, during infancy, when the child should learn that it can't get its own way by crying but, at the same time, parents should not be authoritative or domineering. The child should be protected from physical harm but, other than that, left to go its own way. From the age of twelve or so, the child is now capable of acquiring abstract concepts and the skills appropriate to such concepts, again not by using books but by practical experience. Adolescence is the time when the child becomes more interested in others and must learn to live with them in mutual and reciprocal regard. Rousseau thought that compassion was central to life, and this is where *Émile* overlapped with his other great work of that year, *The Social Contract*. The child must come to understand the difference between manipulation and freedom.

To begin with, Suzanne tried breast-feeding, which practice, following *Émile*, had become very fashionable among *le monde*. 'Madame Necker heroically offered her celebrated bosom to her daughter' but after withstanding the pain and discomfort for four months, she was informed that Germaine 'was starving'.[5]

Jacques Necker by this time was the Paris manager of the Banque Girardot and proved very adept, trading on the stock exchange, becoming a partner in another bank, Thellusson & Vernet, and – having learned English and Dutch to improve his contacts – speculating during the Seven Years War in British bonds. His next step up was to be appointed, first, as minister of the Republic of Geneva to the Court of Versailles, a modest enough promotion but added to, a couple of years later, in 1769, when he was made a syndic (director) of the French East India Company. His star was at last on the rise and he was accepted at court.

MOTHER V. DAUGHTER

Necker's new status was soon underwritten further by the salon that his wife had been busy creating. She had laboured for four years – beginning in 1766 – to create something special, and she succeeded. The salons of Paris at the time were busy and so arranged that *philosophes* rarely had to dine at home: Mme Geoffrin entertained on Mondays and Wednesdays, as we have seen, Mme Helvétius on Tuesdays and Thursdays, Baron d'Holbach on Sundays, and Mme Necker, therefore, chose Fridays.

Suzanne chose well, so well that her daughter, Germaine, never had a playmate her own age until she was twelve, though by then she was 'on familiar terms' with Diderot, d'Alembert, Gibbon and Buffon. Every Friday, she would perch on a small wooden stool and listen. Being Protestant in a Catholic country, Suzanne was averse to religious discussions, and they were avoided. Her husband maintained his judicial silence and was admired for it.[6]

The Necker narrative existed on three levels. At the top there was Jacques's involvement in the economic theories – and therefore the politics – of a failing France. Second came Suzanne's salon, where the economic theories – and therefore the politics – of the realm were aired. And third came the family level, where, as we shall see, Suzanne and Germaine, mother and daughter, became rivals for the affection of their husband/father.

Suzanne's salon would – within four short years – come to overshadow Mme Geoffrin's, at least for a time. In fact, the house in the Marais soon became too small and the Neckers – who had taken to Paris life with alacrity – moved into the 'sumptuous' hôtel Leblanc in the rue du Cléry. Her earliest recruits, her biographer tells us, were 'in the second rank of fame but well chosen': Suard, Marmontel, the abbés Raynal, Galiani and Morellet, 'all zealous missionaries of the philosophic creed', and Melchior Grimm. Diderot joined in 1769, noting modestly to his mistress Sophie Volland that Mme Necker 'raved' about him.

High-flown Pomposity

Since Mme Necker's salons were held on Fridays, this meant fish for those who preferred to keep to Catholic dietary laws. Later, she added a Tuesday afternoon salon for more intimate guests. As one anonymous observer put it later: 'Madame N. has two days: one for the wits, another for the simpletons; I belong to the latter.'[7] According to Grimm, who was a regular in several salons down the years, the food 'left something to be desired'. Though Suzanne did her best to be welcoming, the Neckers had an austere side and her husband was known to be reserved on occasion, even distant, 'absorbed in his thoughts'. Because she was not the most robust of souls, Necker bought Suzanne a chateau at Saint-Ouen, on the banks of the Seine between the capital and Saint-Denis, where she could escape the heat of central Paris. Her salon followed her – it was close enough for guests to drive there for dinner.

Jean-François Marmontel was his usual sardonic self in his portrait of Mme Necker as being 'without taste in her dress, without care in her manner, without charm in her politeness, her mind and also her face is too artificial to have in them an air of grace'. He was in particular critical of her language, which, he maintained, 'was so highflown that its pomposity would have been laughable if one did not know that she was perfectly artless'. Everything about her, he says, was 'premeditated, nothing came as though from chance'.[8]

The Abbé Morellet added to this picture. He accepted that the literary talk in her salon was agreeable, 'where Mme Necker could hold her own', but that she was very unforgiving when it came to religion. D'Alembert was never as close to Mme Necker as he was to Mme du Deffand or Mlle de Lespinasse, but when Mme Necker heard of the death of the Marquis de Mora, Julie's Spanish suitor, she wrote to her, expressing her sorrow, and it was d'Alembert who replied.[9]

The family were what we would today call priggish, even cold. When Suzanne did put pen to paper, the title of one of her efforts was *Maxims Necessary for My Happiness*; another was *Journal of My Failings and My Faults, with the Best Means Not to Do the Same Things Again*. And she always maintained that there were seven claims on her, in this order: her husband, her child, her friends, the poor, household duties, society and her dress, and she took care to expatiate on the number of hours she was to spend each day on these various activities.[10] And, at a time when love between spouses was not held in very high regard, 'she was prodigal of the signs of her great affection for her husband'. She was therefore doubly devastated as she realised, later, as her health began to trouble her, that her daughter counted for more in M Necker's heart.

'Love' was part of the sensibility of the age, to be discussed in the salons, but Mme Necker had a Calvinist background and although she brought up Germaine along the lines laid down by Rousseau in *Émile*, or thought that she did, in fact her daughter was starved of real affection, feigning coughing fits to persuade her mother to pay her more attention. Despite this, Suzanne preferred the family habit of writing letters to each other, even when they were in adjoining rooms. Everything was directed to the development of Germaine's mind. By the age of eleven the young woman was a regular theatre-goer.[11]

Germaine's love for her father was unconditional. She grew up worshipping him and, before long, the bond between father and daughter would grow stronger than that between husband and wife. In return he never criticised her, allowed her talk to range wherever it would, and applauded her wit and her performances in the plays she took part in, in front of Raynal, Marmontel and Buffon (who always spoke of Necker as 'our great man'). In fact, as her biographer confirms, a grim struggle was taking place within the family between wife and daughter for the heart of Jacques Necker.[12]

For his part, Necker was meanwhile making a name for himself as a financier and economist.

EARRINGS THE SIZE OF CHANDELIERS

Everyone – everyone who thought about serious matters – knew that France was in trouble, that the state was running up an increasingly massive debt and that there was little chance the country could avoid bankruptcy.

Beginning in the early 1770s matters began to come to a head. In May 1774, Louis XV died of smallpox and was succeeded by his nineteen-year-old grandson, Louis XVI, and his 'beautiful and frivolous' queen, Marie Antoinette, also nineteen. Some measure of France's plight may be had from the fact that the country had the biggest government of any nation other than Russia, had incurred massive debt during the Seven Years War (1756–63), and suffered a three-year-long famine between 1769 and 1772. But it still seemed unwilling to change its ways, with the splendour of Versailles undimmed.

Among the palace's massive staff were eight architects, forty-seven musicians, fifty-six hunters, 295 cooks, 886 nobles of the court with their wives, children, secretaries, doctors and priests, together with some 10,000 soldiers. 'Almost every week, there were two banquets, two balls, and three plays held at Versailles.' Marie Antoinette made a bad situation worse by her profligacy, spending thousands of livres on her dresses and on diamond earrings famously 'the size of chandeliers', and squandering large sums at the card tables.[13] In order to pay for this, there were 1,600 customs houses throughout France; on the Loire, for example, between Orléans and Nantes – a distance of about 200 miles – there were twenty-eight. These took taxes equal to 20–30 per cent of all goods transported. Something had to change, but what?

The first of the quartet of names culminating in Necker was Joseph Marie Terray (1715–78), who first came to attention in 1736 when he was selected to specialise in financial affairs. He was good at his job, so much so that René-Nicolas de Maupeou, Louis XV's chancellor, made him comptroller-general, from where, in 1764, he helped bring down the Duc de Choiseul by showing that the government could not afford to go to war with Great Britain. To an extent, Terray was able to stabilise the economy, partly by repudiating segments of the national debt, suspending interest payments on government bonds and introducing new, compulsory loans. He reformed the collection of the *vingtième*, the 5 per cent tax on income, and the *capitation*, the head tax of Paris. While this brought about a sizeable increase in government revenue, he faced opposition over the free trade in grain, which was the main issue of the time. People suspected that Terray's system maintained artificially high grain prices so as to benefit the king. When Louis XV died in 1774, Terray was dismissed.

Anne Robert Turgot, who was eventually to take over from Terray, was the real financial revolutionary before 1789. His early accomplishments were described in chapter 15, not least his pleas for religious tolerance and the abolition of slavery. But it was his relationship with Jacques Claude Marie Vincent, Marquis de Gournay (1712–59), that turned him into an adventurous economist. The marquis was inspector of factories and he invited Turgot to accompany him on his rounds. On their journeys around France they saw how privilege had invaded all aspects of the economy and concluded that this could only be mitigated, or overcome, by free trade. Turgot wrote up his findings in Diderot's and d'Alembert's *Encyclopédie*, where he also took on the arguments of the physiocrats.

Where Turgot differed from the physiocrats was in his realisation that the basic ingredient in prosperity was not land but industry and commerce – exchange. He also worked hard to transform the traditional idea that interest was immoral. Arguably his most important written work was *Lettres sur le commerce des grains*, seven letters addressed to Abbé Terray while he was still in office as comptroller-general. This was Turgot's most passionate defence of laissez-faire, in which he argued that 'government is incapable of guaranteeing economic security ... it is not the master of seasons'. Terray was unmoved and, as we have just seen, in December 1770 ruled that grain could be sold only in government-controlled marketplaces. This helped to keep power in the hands of grain monopolists.

In August 1774, after the change in kings, Turgot was appointed comptroller-general, shortly afterward sending the new king a famous memo in which he said there would be no bankruptcy in the nation provided there was no increase in taxes and no new loans.[14] But his most controversial move was to establish the freedom of the grain trade. When bread riots broke out, first in Dijon, then elsewhere, he abolished duties imposed in various towns. He said publicly that people should prepare for self-government, which hardly made him many more friends at court. He also opposed an extravagant coronation for the new king. He lost that battle, and the coronation was as extravagant as ever.[15]

This subject of the free trade in grain had been one of the issues to divide the salons of the time, where an alternative view to Turgot's was put by the Abbé Galiani, whose eloquence and ambassador status gave him a large following. In 1769, with the help of Diderot, who was the most prominent regular of the Neckers' Friday evenings, and Mme d'Épinay, the *abbé* published his *Dialogues sur le commerce des blés* ('Dialogues on the Trade in Wheat').[16] In the modern world, economics is sometimes referred to as the 'dismal' science but that never applied to Galiani. His work managed to be both stylishly written and full of caustic wit. 'No one', commented Voltaire dryly, 'has ever written more amusingly on famine.'[17]

In the *Dialogues*, Galiani also argued that the best system of commerce is to have no system, and that it was wrong, as some economists of the time believed, that one country could not gain in commerce without another losing. Galiani also noted, as Turgot had noted, that the physiocrats were wrong, but he argued that there were diminishing returns in agriculture and that the wealth of a nation depended more and more on manufacturing and trade. He also thought that the business of bread was so basic that its organisation needed to be a matter for government control.[18]

Turgot tried to consolidate his position by producing what became known as his *Six Edicts*, designed to further strengthen – and regulate equitably – the economy. The most important edicts were one suppressing the *corvées* and another which sought to suppress the *jurandes* and the *maîtrises*, through which the craft guilds retained their privileges. Each of these measures conformed to Turgot's ideas about the benefits of free trade and the abolition – essentially – of privilege, that every man should be free to work without restriction. This was underlined by his further plan to subject all three estates of the realm to taxation. These attempts at many kinds of reform all at once – against the nobles, the *parlements* (which he thought should confine their activities to the administration of justice, with no economic or employment role), against the royal household, his views on free trade all round – were just too much.

Turgot tried to rescue his situation with a *Mémoire* that he submitted to the king, in which he proposed that landed property owners were to form the electorate, but in which no distinction was to be made between the three orders or estates, and that members of different municipalities would elect provincial bodies, which would together elect a grand overall body which should administer taxation, combined with education, relief for the poor and other socially progressive ideas. Once again this was altogether too much for the king, but it was a vivid example of the way informed, educated and non-partisan people could see the state beginning to unravel.

A further twist in the downward spiral came with the budget of 1775, which illustrates the French predicament perfectly. At the beginning of that year, the government had revenue on paper of 337 million livres but in practice only 213 million was left after interest was paid on the debt – in other words, no less than 37 per cent of the budget was used to pay down the debts already incurred. The costs of government that year were 235 million.

Turgot responded by cutting many sinecures for idle aristocrats and again attempted to abolish the guilds and the *corvée* – all measures that he had successfully put in place on a smaller scale in Limoges. These moves made him yet more enemies, in particular Marie Antoinette.

By now Turgot was also out of kilter with the prevailing view of the American Revolution in France. He was not against its aims – indeed, he was sure it would succeed. But with the economy in mind, he did not share the more popular view that the American war would provide France with a chance to avenge its defeat in the Seven Years War.

His fall came in spring 1776 after a series of intrigues. 'In the wake of his dismissal, government spending zoomed out of control, guilds regained their previous monopolies, restrictions again throttled trade, the regime brought back forced labour.'[19] Turgot spent the rest of his life involved in scientific and literary ventures and, a year later, was made vice-president of the Académie royale des inscriptions et belles-lettres.

The situation continued to deteriorate. By 1788, *half* the budget was now needed to service the debt, military spending consumed half of what was left, and Marie Antoinette became known as 'Madame Deficit'.

Salon Tactics

This, then, is the complex (but in a way straightforward) background to both the advent of Jacques Necker and his economic theories, and at the same time highlights why there was something inevitable about the French Revolution.

It seems that Galiani's treatise was the document that spurred Necker himself to put pen to paper and a couple of years later he published his *Éloge de Colbert*. This was a clever piece of work, being in effect a defence of state corporatism, an analysis flattering to the French. In corporatism, it is argued that society is not so much a collection of individuals as a collection of organised groups each with a common interest – farmers, labourers, lawyers and so on – and state corporatism means therefore that the ruling class *is* the state. This, it will be remembered, was a major achievement of Colbert's and helped to make France strong under an absolute monarchy.

By this time, so successful had Mme Necker's salon become that it was regarded in some quarters as a shadow Académie française, much as Mme de Lambert's salon had been earlier in the century. This was underlined by the fact that, when the *Éloge* appeared, the academy crowned Necker with its first prize.

This made Necker better known but, just then, when the Abbé Terray's economic policies were seen to have benefitted Louis XV too much at the expense of the people, and he was dismissed, it was Turgot and not Necker who was chosen to replace him. Turgot, as we have just seen, attempted to restore free trade inside France, but his efforts coincided with an exceptionally bad harvest and the resulting famine was blamed on him. Necker cleverly chose this time to produce *On Legislation and the Commerce of Grain*.[20] In his book, Necker attacked the physiocrats and their view that the only real form of wealth derived from the land, but he also questioned Turgot's advocacy of laissez-faire – he thought it was too easily open to abuse. This caught the attention of many people, including the king, and happened to be followed by a poor harvest which, in turn, was followed by a rise in the price of bread, followed further by the disturbances in Dijon, themselves giving rise to an outbreak of bread riots which became known as the *guerre des farines*, and which some people now regard as a precursor of the Revolution.

This timely manoeuvre of Necker's paid off when, in 1776, Turgot was forced out of office. Louis XVI appointed Necker assistant comptroller-general in that same year and, a year on, made him head of France's financial administration. This was unusual, because foreigners could not sit in the council of ministers. In addition, in order to be naturalised, Necker would have to give up his Protestant faith – which he refused to do. He was therefore given the title 'director-general of finance', with direct access to the king but without being part of the cabinet. This meant he had the king's ear, whereas other ministers could only work with the monarch via cabinet.

This mattered because, by the time Necker took office, it was widely assumed that only major financial and administrative reform could save France from ruin. The king's expenditure, on himself, his relations and his buildings, was still lavish (this is when he spent more on his brothers than on public health) and the almost constant wars – including French support of the Americans against the British in the War of Independence – were ruinously expensive too, so much so that national bankruptcy seemed imminent.

The ambitious Neckers, mindful of their advancing social position, moved into the official residence of the comptroller-general. This advance was not without its critics and is an aspect of the Neckers that has received specific attention from historians. Both Mme de La Ferté-Imbault and Marmontel revealed that Suzanne Necker's principal concern when she began to receive men of letters in her salon was not literature as such, but the advancement of her husband's career. Research has shown that this aspect of the Necker salon was obvious to contemporaries. 'The salon was broadly seen as that of both the Neckers, even at times of Necker alone.'[21] The central purpose of Suzanne's salon was that it permitted a Geneva Protestant banker to participate in the Parisian *monde* at a stage in his career when he was in fact doubly foreign to it. Part of what he was doing was finessing the codes of the *gratin* ('upper crust') by passing himself off as a cultivated man of letters. Necker deliberately let his wife shine in her (their) salon – as camouflage in effect – while he was happy to stand in her shadow as an indulgent and discreet husband.[22]

This tactic enabled him to muster a following not only among distinguished men of letters, but also with the fashionable aristocracy of Paris, who were pleased to attend his wife's salon and who in turn invited them back. Mme du Deffand was just one who organised a weekly supper around Necker, while his wife was able to ally her interests with the more established leaders of high society, so that Jacques and she frequented the salons not just of Mme du Deffand, but of Mlle de Lespinasse and Mme Geoffrin as well.[23]

The Necker salon therefore had both a political and a social aim, so that Jacques was seen to attract the support of men of letters, giving him an aura as a cultivated man, not just a banker or politician. In 1773, in his *Éloge de Colbert*, delivered before the Académie, he was able to present himself less as a Calvinist banker and to pose instead as an enlightened reformer.[24]

Another example of the Neckers' salon tactics was the famous episode of the Voltaire statue. This was paid for by subscription, and it is true that the idea was conceived originally in the Necker salon. But it was in effect a prominent episode in Necker's promotion of himself as a protector of men of letters. Anyone could subscribe, not just poets and dramatists, but aristocrats too. Grimm, who was so close to Mme d'Épinay and her salon, nonetheless found the Necker gatherings better than he expected and it was his account of the seventeen literary figures at Mme Necker's table that told so many about the decision to raise a statue to Voltaire. Although she had been taken to see him at Ferney all those years before, and attended his performances, Voltaire always eluded her Friday evenings. Only when the idea of the statue was mooted was her final victory secured. Grimm reported the event in his *Correspondance littéraire*: 'On the seventeenth of the month past [April 1770] there has been held at Madame Necker's an assembly of seventeen venerable philosophers; in the course of which, after having made the prescribed invocations to the Holy Ghost and eaten a copious dinner, and talked nonsense on a number of subjects, it was resolved by unanimous vote to erect a statue in the honour of Monsieur de Voltaire.'[25]

These salon tactics matter because our interest in Necker, in addition to his role in France's all-important debt crisis, lies in the fact that he was one of the first to grasp the growing role of public opinion and popularity in advancing his aims. He used the salon – ostensibly his wife's but in reality just as much his – to introduce his ideas to celebrated men of letters who relayed his ideas to a wider public, a role filled by Grimm and Diderot in particular.

SALONS AND REVOLUTION

Necker was one of the first to realise that the people who attended the salons were a wider public than the coteries around the king, who were always likely to attack and criticise outside views.[26]

Keith Baker, the British-American historian of France, has shown that Necker had an idea of public opinion 'as a rational and stable tribunal to which those who governed owed an account'.[27] For Necker, public opinion did not come about by, for example, the diffusion of printing, which was available to everyone. It equalled only the opinion of *le monde*. In the 1780s, *esprit de société* and *opinion publique* were two different entities but Necker conjoined them and in so doing he saw this kind of public opinion as specifically French. For him, it took its colour from the French monarchy. 'Public opinion corresponded to the specific nature of French society, ruled by honour, politeness and gallantry, where opinions converged thanks to the spirit of society.' In other words, public opinion began in the salons, went wider than court opinion and was where ideas and concepts were accepted and developed, before being carried to a still wider public. But the wider public didn't count, not to Necker. It is in this sense that salons, as a sort of half-way house in helping form opinion, played a role in the genesis of the French Revolution.

Necker's campaigns did not go uncriticised.[28] His 'suppers' for *beaux esprits* were part of his strength, but people were aware of 'the fanaticism that he has inspired within *la bonne compagnie*', and the habitués were sometimes dismissed as '*grandes dames*, beautiful women, pretty ones, witty ones, and above all intriguers'.

As Baker pithily puts it, Necker's public opinion was not public opinion as we would recognise it, 'but rather a simulacrum of it destined for the court'.[29]

Too Much Candour

So much for Necker's style. As far as content was concerned, he rec-ognised – as the king was loath to do – that tax reform was needed, and needed urgently, and moreover that reform needed to be fairer to the less well-off segments of society and that free trade – the new orthodoxy promulgated by Turgot – was all very well in theory but needed some state control so as to avoid abuses, which were all too common. In his *Essai sur la législation et le commerce des grains* he had shown that he understood perfectly the mess the country was in, the places where reforms were urgently needed and where the weak parts of the king's administration were located. Although he attacked the laissez-faire ideas of Turgot and the Abbé Galiani, at the same time Necker did abolish 500 sinecures (thus making that number of enemies, as Turgot had before him) and other posts he deemed superfluous. He tried to get taxes received on time, and to establish provincial authorities throughout France to aid in this task. Along with Suzanne, he visited hospitals and prisons and took action to improve conditions therein. He refused a salary. All of which made him wildly popular, at least for a time.

As with Terray and Turgot before him, there were hopes that Necker would be able to stem the debt crisis. But in 1781 Necker overreached himself. In order to convince the public that he was doing a good job, he daringly persuaded the king to let him publish *Compte rendu au roi*. On the face of it, this was a candid report on the financial state of France, and a first public airing of details that were traditionally kept confidential. But the revelations created a sensation. In reality, his treatise was a defence of Necker's own administration, and even contained a flattering reference to his wife Suzanne.[30] He glossed over the national debt and many of his figures were optimistic and self-serving and were challenged. Furthermore, when he used the alleged success of his figures to demand full mem-bership of the king's council of ministers – despite the fact that he was a foreigner – opposition boiled over. Other ministers threatened the king with their resignation – and Louis gave way. Necker would serve the next seven years in opposition, but it is important to note that throughout that time he was lionised much as before.[31]

While he was in exile, he occupied himself with writing about law and economics, publishing another widely reviewed work, *Traité de l'administration des finances de la France* in 1784. This was so controversial that Charles de Calonne, comptroller-general since 1783, who favoured infrastructure projects as a way out of the impasse, tried to prevent publication. He failed and the *Traité*, despite its high seriousness, sold 80,000 copies. Its subject – of course – was France's national debt, which everyone by now knew was the critical aspect of absolute monarchy, and which had reached 4 billion livres, with an annual deficit north of 100 million livres. One effect of this, as Necker pertinently pointed out, was that while Britain could borrow money at 3.5 per cent, France's indebtedness meant she was forced to pay 6 per cent. Unless there was reform, Necker insisted, the country could not afford to go to war.

FIREWORKS

It was this humiliating threat of national bankruptcy that would force Calonne to convene the Assembly of Notables, which had not met since 1626. On becoming comptroller-general in November 1783, he had discovered that France had deficits of 110 million livres, partly brought about by its obsession with supporting the Americans in the War of Independence against the British. Convening the Assembly of Notables underlined the seriousness of the situation, for much of which Calonne chose to blame Necker, because he had not raised taxes. However, a series of financial scandals implicated Calonne himself, he was dismissed and in April 1787 he fled to London. Necker was eventually called back to office for a second time in August 1788, possibly on account of the discreet support of Marie Antoinette. His return was celebrated by fireworks.

Now, as chief minister of France, he introduced paper money for some financing, and forbade the export of grain – grain was still a critical issue. In the vicious winter of 1788–9, when famine threatened, he intervened personally with the Hope Bank in Amsterdam to help finance the supply of grain and lent 2 million of his own fortune to aid the venture.

When the Assembly of Notables finally met, Necker, ambitious as ever, took care to compose a three-hour address regarding the financial health of the kingdom. Suffering from a bad cold that day, after fifteen minutes he got someone else to take over and read the rest. He also tried to get the king to accept a constitution not unlike that in Britain, in effect a constitutional monarchy, as others had attempted before him. But the king would not go along with this, a decision that was swiftly followed by the new National Assembly – in what was now Revolutionary France – declaring all taxes illegal. Necker knew that this would spell disaster and said so, but that did not prevent the king from dismissing him a second time and, because he was a foreigner, requiring him to leave the country immediately. Neither Jacques nor Suzanne so much as changed their clothes before going and when news of this dismissal became public, it famously provoked the assault on the Bastille, the first violence of the Revolution.

In fact, Necker was recalled and reappointed for a third time, but he could do little to prevent the financial chaos that reigned, as various desperate measures (such as confiscating ecclesiastical possessions) were tried and failed. Other ideas of his, such as turning a private bank into a national bank, like the Bank of England, were also jettisoned. The more his ideas were rejected, and the more they were attacked, from the likes of Danton and Mirabeau, and the more his popularity waned, the more depressed Necker became, until, in the autumn of 1790, he resigned, and, after being briefly arrested, retired to his estate at Coppet near Geneva.

Today, Necker would be nowhere near so controversial. He well appreciated that France was rich, that only the government was poor, and that credit is the heart of prosperity, credit needing trust to operate in a stable and unexcitable fashion. And he was not blind to social justice. Absolute laissez-faire, which Turgot promulgated, meant in Necker's eyes that everyone was out for themselves. But government regulation, he argued, was necessary to protect against exploitation.

Germaine saw in her father the embodiment of kindness. More generally, Necker is remembered with respect rather than enthusiasm.

Respect rather than enthusiasm also applied to Suzanne Necker. This was reflected in her relationship with the Académie française. With her canny social antennae, she had taken care to see that nearly all the men of letters who frequented her Friday salon were themselves already members of the Académie and they used her salon to consult with one another with regard to the prizes in their gift (M Necker himself won two prizes from the Académie). This was also true of the election of new members. No sooner had one of the *fauteuils* become vacant than Mme Necker had an inside track on who should succeed. Just like Mme Lambert before her, Mme Necker was assumed to have power in directing the academy's decisions.

Despite her 'starched intolerance', Mme Necker never lost her forcefulness, and despite the competition between mother and daughter, she retained great ambitions for Germaine. In 1783, when Germaine was seventeen, Suzanne had plans that she would marry William Pitt the Younger, who in that year had just resigned as chancellor of the Exchequer and would soon become Britain's youngest prime minister at the age of twenty-four. Her daughter had other ideas.

Mme Necker died in 1794. Starched to the end, she had made elaborate plans for a mausoleum for herself and her husband to be erected at Coppet (she insisted on being embalmed). The tomb was reopened twice, once on the death of her husband and again on that of her daughter. Then it was sealed permanently.

Coppet would become home to Germaine's salon in the turbulent years ahead.

The Maître d'Hôtel de la Philosophie

aron Paul Henri Thiry d'Holbach, together with his second wife, Charlotte Suzanne, were both occasional members of Mme d'Épinay's salon and elsewhere. We have already noted that the word 'salon' is to an extent an anachronism when applied to the eighteenth century. This is seen clearly in the case of d'Holbach's own gatherings on the rue Royale, for his meetings were known as either a 'coterie', 'the synagogue', 'the bakery' or merely 'the club'.

They were, however, according to Alan Kors in his detailed account of the coterie, the most intellectual, the most scientific, and one of the most lavish in terms of the food served and the wines consumed. The term 'coterie holbachique' was first used by Rousseau and he did not intend it to be flattering. In his *Confessions*, Rousseau argued that Grimm, Diderot and d'Holbach were part of a 'jealous conspiracy' against his person and reputation which he believed they had inspired and coordinated. But the dinners and conversations at which d'Holbach was the host were by no means closed affairs. As Kors puts it: 'From a gathering of friends in 1749 through 1751, the salon of Baron d'Holbach developed into one of the most intellectually stimulating and widely known private groups in Europe.'[1]

The core of the coterie consisted of many of the names we have repeatedly encountered – Diderot, d'Alembert, Turgot, Galiani and so on – plus some that are new, such as La Condamine, Helvétius, Morellet, Naigeon and Buffon, though the great naturalist didn't stay long, together with a raft of prominent British intellectuals, among them Adam Smith, David Hume, John Wilkes, Horace Walpole, Edward Gibbon, David Garrick and Laurence Sterne, the Italian Cesare Beccaria and the American Benjamin Franklin.

Earlier accounts of d'Holbach's dinners portrayed them as excessively earnest affairs, describing the gatherings variously as 'uniquely fanatical', 'rabid in [their] antireligiosity', 'a huddled little company of rationalistic enragés' or 'a little band of monomaniacal materialists'.² None of this was true, says Kors, but the coterie *was* very serious-minded, and its intellectual accomplishments were allegedly more substantial and more coherent than most of the other, female-led, salons. During the roughly thirty-five years that d'Holbach held his Thursday and Sunday gatherings he became, as Galiani called him, the '*maître d'hôtel de la Philosophie*'.

NATURE DOES NOT CARE FOR MAN

Baron d'Holbach was the heir to a large fortune, acquired variously through tax collection, the wine business and speculation on the stock exchange, and this enabled him to entertain his friends lavishly. Born in Edesheim in the Rhenish Palatinate in 1723, he studied at the University of Leyden from the mid- to the late 1740s, Leyden at that time being known for its sociable intellectuality – coffee parties, club suppers and 'constant group conversations'.

In its early days, his salon attracted more scientists than the other gatherings, including Paul Joseph Barthez, an anatomist and vitalist, and Gabriel François Venel, a chemist interested in France's mineral waters, though they both left Paris and moved on to the University of Montpellier. In 1759 d'Holbach bought a house on the rue Royale, Butte Saint-Roch (*butte* means 'mound' or 'rise'), where his dinners first became famous.³ In summer, he also held weekend parties at his family estate at Grandval, several miles from the capital.

Kors says that d'Holbach's salon had a glitter beyond its intellectual pleasures because, owing to his great wealth and taste, he employed an excellent chef, serving 'abundant and memorable' foods. His home had a cabinet of natural history, a library of 3,000 volumes and large numbers of paintings by France's leading artists. D'Holbach was equally lavish in his generosity, supporting several writers, artists and musicians, including Rousseau for a while. The baron published perhaps 400 articles himself and as many as fifty books, though all – in the manner of the time – were released anonymously. His most famous work was the *Système de la nature*, which was published in 1770 and which, says Kors, 'because of its aggressive atheism' raised a storm in France second only to Montesquieu's *De l'esprit*.[4]

D'Holbach's books were actually united by three themes which were intended to widen his audience: one, 'that the only coherent deduction from a sensationalist epistemology was a rigorous materialism'; two, that the only cohesive understanding of matter was as an 'uncreated substance containing motion as an essential property'; and three, that the only 'humane and beneficial' morality was one based on imperatives for the 'happiness and survival' of humankind, such imperatives to be brought about by the interaction of an amoral material universe, in which the human animal was neither favoured nor especially protected.[5] D'Holbach took care in his book to eschew the readiness to personify nature, to embrace the idea that nature 'cared' for man in some special sense and to call 'natural' those aspects of the world that man 'deemed good' and 'unnatural' those aspects that man 'deemed evil'. He was convinced that this had been the cardinal error of the deists and their idea of a 'God of Nature'. To him this showed evidence of an inability to face the 'amoral necessity' of the world realistically. A study of the universe, he said, does not lead us to God or a symbolic nature, but only to a 'vast chain of causes and effects' upon which manifold occurrences our relative happiness and unhappiness are based.[6] *Système de la nature* promulgated these arguments in detail.

THE PURPOSELESSNESS OF LIFE

Of the members of his coterie who we have not already met, Charles-George Le Roy (1723–89) is, according to Kors, one of the forgotten men of the eighteenth century. He too published all his works anonymously, in his case under the rubric 'the Physician of Nuremberg'. But he was, says Kors, an original thinker and a close friend of Helvétius. His interests were agriculture, forestry and animal behaviour. Diderot recruited him to write on these subjects for the *Encyclopédie*.

Le Roy was famous among his circle for his confession that he was an atheist, something that would contribute to the notoriety of the coterie as a hotbed of such views. He was first and foremost a natural historian of animal life.[7] His 'Letters on Man' were appended to his animal studies and they reflected his basic scientific approach, in particular his view that physiology determines the fundamental aspects of behaviour. He held it absurd to suggest, as Rousseau did, that society began with any form of social contract. 'Social organisation arose from the sexual bond created by the absence of a limited Particular Season for social relations among humans; from the need for nurture in the long period of infant dependency; from the physical inability for men in certain circumstances to raise food without cooperation, and the physical vulnerability of man to the elements creating "first necessities" which could only be satisfied by certain arts requiring social organisation.'[8]

Following on from this, Le Roy insisted, the organisation of humankind into societies fostered patterns of behaviour 'quite unlike' any other animals. 'All animals have certain basic needs, giving rise to a demand for satisfaction and each creature uses its reason to obtain satisfaction, followed by satiations.' And perhaps his most controversial/profound conclusion: 'Meaningful life is a simple pattern of repetition.'[9]

This important conclusion, he says, gives rise to a conception of history 'as a series of socially, politically, intellectually and artistically purposeless cycles'. We are condemned to a 'blind desire' for well-being.[10] He makes partial cause with the libertines in saying that vanity and compassion are humankind's guiding principles. 'Vanity gives rise to power, status and recognition, the public life. Compassion gives rise to reciprocity, justice, social morality, the bonds of society.' Le Roy remained close enough to the evidence to see how, for example, hunting tribes were alike, and yet different from fishing tribes, and how that led to the development of different moral codes.[11] An original thinker, as this shows, Le Roy was one of the first to argue that only the positive sciences (can) advance.

RED BLOOD AND FROST

It is also the case that Le Roy – like some of the others in d'Holbach's circle – was not as dry as some made him out to be and was for a time at the centre of a complicated romantic intrigue which revolved around d'Holbach's wife, the baronne, Charlotte Suzanne. Clearly exceptionally beautiful, she became involved – perhaps unknowingly – in two 'betrayals' virtually simultaneously.

In the first place, Jean-Baptiste-Antoine Suard declared his love to Charlotte, while Charles Pinot Duclos, Grimm's rival for the affection of Mme d'Épinay, informed the latter – falsely – that Grimm had in fact seduced the baronne. Mme d'Épinay was furious to learn this and immediately relayed the news (of both these episodes) to d'Holbach. He, needless to say, was hardly best pleased.

This awkward situation (no doubt amusing to outsiders) only began to be resolved when Suard was persuaded to apologise and agreed to look for a wife not already attached to someone else, thus absolving Grimm of any wrongdoing. Duclos was expelled from the coterie – for lying, for one thing – relations between d'Holbach and Mme d'Épinay were frosty for a time, and the baronne was so upset by the imbroglio that she fell into a depression and was only rescued by being put on a milk diet and a regime of riding in the fresh air. This was the further twist because Le Roy, who was royal lieutenant of the hunt, was an accomplished equestrian and had access to the most beautiful woods at Vincennes, and so was chosen to be her companion on these rides. In no time at all, he too had fallen for the baronne. She rejected his advances, told her husband, and once again the coterie was upended. Now Le Roy had to apologise but, like Suard before him, he was eventually forgiven. Given the high-sounding affairs we are in the middle of, this near-farce puts into context that these men, who sought to be so different in some ways, were like men – even boys – everywhere.

THE BEGINNING OF WISDOM

Jacques-André Naigeon (1738–1810), also little known now, was hardly popular even in his own time. He had a reputation of being annoyingly combative and volatile, described by one contemporary as 'a great book-collector and a little atheist ... he had an insupportable vanity'.[12]

For Naigeon, as for d'Holbach, there was nothing 'inherently' beautiful or horrible in the world. More than that, Naigeon was far from convinced by the claims of the scientists who stressed their belief that progress in their disciplines was inevitable.[13] This view was shared by Grimm, who, in his *Correspondance littéraire*, reviewed almost every title released at that time, and claimed to find the great majority severely wanting. For example, he condemned even Voltaire's poem on the Lisbon earthquake as sloppily doctrinaire and, moreover, containing as much illusion as the viewpoint it lampooned. He further condemned Rousseau's *Émile*, which, he said, embraced a major misconception, in fact 'a fictive model of man'.

What d'Holbach, Naigeon and Grimm were sniping at was what they felt was a naïve belief that progress was occurring and that it was possible to approach perfection. They thought that the use of such terms as 'natural' or 'providential order' was intellectually dishonest. It was plain to them that 'nature' was as destructive as it was innovative. 'The real truth was that nature was indifferent, and ideas about the "natural" and the "good" were illusions.' Realising this, Naigeon said, was the beginning of wisdom.

Naigeon was not without hope, Kors says. But we should look around us, observe the world as it is without preconceptions, and decide what it is that brings about 'the simple pleasure of existing', and not stray too far from that.

EVERYONE IS EQUAL

Claude-Adrien Helvétius (1715–71), originally a tax-farmer, is best known to history as the author of what Kors describes as '*the* dramatic *cause-célèbre*' of the 1750s, the philosophical treatise *De l'esprit* ('On Mind') of 1758. According to some accounts, until publication of this work Helvétius had frequented the salon of Mme Geoffrin, though others dispute this.[14]

Helvétius, with large, heavy, lugubrious features, spent only part of the year in Paris. According to Grimm, who wrote his obituary, he spent just four months a year in the capital. The rest of his time he was at his estate at Voré (south-west of Paris, near Le Mans), where he invited many other fellow members of the coterie to visit. He was from a family of doctors, originally called Schweitzer ('Swiss' in German), which was Latinised to Helvétius. Interested in poetry to begin with, as so many were, he turned to more scientific matters later on. His wife had her own salon for more than five decades, with much the same cast of characters as d'Holbach and Mme Geoffrin.

De l'esprit was partly intended as a response to Montesquieu's *Spirit of the Laws* and its main claims were three-fold: first, that all man's intellectual activities can be put down to physical sensation – including those that d'Alembert had singled out in his preparation for the *Encyclopédie* – memory, judgement, comparison. The only difference between man and the animals – taking a line from Le Roy – he said, was organisation. Second, as Turgot had hinted before him, and Suard, and the libertines, self-interest 'founded on the love of pleasure and the fear of pain' is the sole spring of action. Third, there is no such thing as absolute good and evil just as there are no absolute rights ... all the things we value are the product of society.

In summary, it doesn't sound so very different from what others were saying at much the same time, but its comprehensive clarity, plus his arguments that everyone was equal, and could/would benefit greatly from education, that nothing came from 'above', set Helvétius as firmly against the church as the throne. At one point he argued that if life in London was better than in Paris, it wasn't because Londoners were more gifted than Parisians but that they enjoyed greater freedom to think, to educate themselves, create and act. This is where he set himself against Montesquieu, who had argued that climate had a fundamental effect on character.

The book was quickly condemned, in the Parlement and in the Sorbonne, deemed 'heretical' and publicly burned. Helvétius was upset by this and issued more than one retraction. Like Turgot, he had the interests of his fellow men at heart and when he retired from tax-farming (having earned enough money, as he said himself), he used his fortune for the benefit of agriculture and poor relief.

Finally, we should mention Nicolas-Antoine Boulanger (1722–59), an engineer, scientist, linguist and eventually *philosophe*. Kors tells us that this man was 'one of the most creative and influential thinkers of the eighteenth century'. Among his better-known books were *Recherches sur l'origine du despotisme oriental* (1761) and *L'Antiquité dévoilée par ses usages* (1766). In both books he argued – again a very modern view – that the origins of religion and despotism could be found in the response of early civilisations to the catastrophes of nature.[15]

DIFFERENT FORMS OF SALON

D'Holbach's coterie was not to everyone's taste. In one of his letters from Paris, written in 1765, Walpole had this to say: 'I forgot to tell you that I sometimes go to the Baron d'Holbach's, but I have left off his dinners, as there was no bearing the authors, the philosophers, and savants, of which he has a pigeon-house full. They soon turned my head with a new system of antediluvian deluges ... The Baron is persuaded that Pall Mall is paved with lava or deluge stones. In short, nonsense for nonsense.'[16]

In exploring the d'Holbach bakery, Kors also set out to describe the various forms of salon in Enlightenment Paris. He says the great salons run by women – Mme Geoffrin, Mme du Deffand, Mlle de Lespinasse and Mme Necker – were great centres of sociability but with rules in which there was a strict limit to the 'earnestness and honesty' of their talk. (Not at all true at other times.) 'These hostesses insisted upon the rules of polite conversation, and the philosophes adapted as best they could. The women repaid them by intriguing for them to obtain places in the Académies, taking their sides in various feuds.'[17] The *philosophes*, Kors says, abided by these rules and were happy to do so. They 'delighted in these assemblies, delighted in the good company, the good food, the dazzling conversation'.[18]

But for Morellet, the atmosphere at d'Holbach's made it the most valuable of Paris salons. 'Now it was there that one could not fail to hear the freest, the most animated and most instructive conversation that ever was; when I say free I mean in terms of philosophy, of religion, or government ... there was no bold thought in politics and religion that was not brought forward there.'[19]

One such evening was described by Diderot in a letter to a friend.

He wrote that they began with d'Holbach defending Boullainvillier's *Traité de l'astrologie judiciaire*, a work that concerned an early theory of materialism, ambitiously linking the movement of every piece of matter in the universe with the movement of every other particle, and using this set of movements to explain everything that happens. Diderot's contribution, he says, was to dispute this and to argue that, for example, 'Saturn has about as much effect on us as the effect of an atom of dust has on the face of a great clock'. With the help of champagne, Diderot went on, the conversation moved on to a consideration of pre-existent germs, and what effect that had for this system of events, and then, 'as one insanity leads to another, the thought came to me that just as there are bad years for apples, pears, peaches and grapes, perhaps there are also bad vintages for men'. He says the company took up the idea and immediately began compiling a list of experiments that might or might not confirm it.[20]

This does at least convey something of the charm of such evenings, and the intellectual excitement. But Kors identifies three particular areas in which the members of d'Holbach's coterie went further in their deliberations, to form part of the backbone of the ideas of the Enlightenment. These were the 'cause of tolerance', the 'implications of history' and the 'fruits of wisdom'.[21]

The man who led the way here was Jean-François Marmontel, who in 1762 produced *Manuel des inquisiteurs*, a satire and abridgement of a text by a fourteenth-century inquisitor, which set out in a deadpan style the typical deceits, ruses, false promises, tortures and punishments to be employed to secure the regime's ways. He followed this with a very successful novel, *Bélisaire*, published in 1767, which, as one critic maintained, 'has no other goal but to establish Deism and to cause Christianity to be regarded as an odious or at least most indifferent religion'.[22] The chief business of religion, Marmontel maintained, was to console man and, in order to do this, God had to be presented to humanity as kind, merciful and 'exemplary'. For atheists, on the other hand, any 'divine intelligence' would immediately 'become accountable for the sufferings and unrequited tragedy of man's history and present state'. The universe, Marmontel concluded, was uncaring and amoral, and within it man must make his way as best he can.[23]

And he went on to say that God would not punish men for their theological errors, since if there was a God he would be well aware of man's limited understanding 'which necessitated his indulgence of error'.[24] It followed from this that no one could assert the necessity of any one form of faith (such as Catholicism, or even Christianity itself) as the means to salvation. Moreover the monarch, as God's representative on earth, must accept that moral precepts 'are freely available to all men *in nature* and can be enacted in secular law' (italics added).[25] Knowing this, kings must assume that the sword of power 'can just as easily be placed in the hands of error as in those of truth'.

The Sorbonne, the Archbishop of Paris and other critics were scandalised by *Bélisaire* and sought changes, while other *philosophes*, such as Voltaire and Turgot, orchestrated a campaign of support. It took a year for *Bélisaire* to be formally censured but by that time it had been defended by a raft of grand personages who included Catherine the Great, the king of Poland, Frederick the Great and the prince of Sweden. Marmontel, personally, suffered no penalties. As Kors sums up: 'D'Holbach and Naigeon never would win enlightened Paris to their cause of atheistic materialism. Marmontel, by stressing political over theological points of contention, succeeded in making the issue of tolerance a safe and popular cause for the philosophic community as a whole.'[26]

PUBLIC HAPPINESS

A particular interest of the coterie was history. At that time, two areas were felt to be important. There was a fascination with the natural movements and events of the past but there was also a keen interest in discovering the *purpose* of history, why it changed in the way that it did. It was, in a sense, an early form of *'longue durée'* history, aided by the new approach to the collection and use of statistics. Prominent here was François Jean de Chastellux.

'For Chastellux', as summed up by Caroline Warman, 'the subject of the historian was – and must be – man in organised society.' And at the very least it was conceded that if perfection was not possible, the historian must at least investigate how man's condition on earth could be improved. This is how Chastellux came to approach what he called 'public happiness'.

Private happiness was too varied and too personal to be sensibly measured, he felt, but he became convinced that the public happiness of a society/civilisation 'was capable of rational enquiry'. As he put it, happiness in this general sense 'could be understood as what remained of *a* after subtracting *b* and *c*, *a* being the amount of work a man is required to do without becoming miserable, *b* being the amount of work a man is required to do in order to secure the necessities and basic amenities of his life, and *c* being the amount of work demanded of a man by his sovereign authorities. Public happiness was the sum of private happinesses calculated in this way.'

This was original, to say the least, if a bit crude and oversimple. But the greatest risks to happiness, both private and public, Chastellux said, were 'superstition and warfare', the greatest 'scourges' for humankind throughout time. He began by looking at ancient Egypt and Sparta where, he said, priests and military commanders 'expropriated' the happiness of the many for their own ends. This also applied to ancient Rome, he insisted, where 'Christianity emerged as a desperate inchoate attempt by the people to overthrow the ancient superstition but had itself degenerated into a new superstition that the emperors adopted for their own ends. The two most pernicious superstitions were supernatural religion and the myth of martial glory.'

Looked at in this way, the history of Europe for Chastellux boiled down to a perpetual struggle among three groups of 'expropriators' competing for available rewards. These three were kings, nobles and clergy, who taught the people to anticipate rewards 'in a world to come' with, as a result, most people accepting their misery. In this the eighteenth century was worse than ever. 'Lulled by the bullion of the New World, the European monarchs embarked on ever-more costly wars, to the point where these wars – because of new technology – could not be afforded.' For Chastellux, the result was plain: kings were borrowing more and more (in the form of taxes), from people who were less and less inclined to believe, so that the arguments of the *philosophes* were being used more and more to fuel Christian fanaticism, producing ever-more staggering debts imposed on the people, 'a direct attack on public happiness'.[27] On this analysis, Chastellux thought that the British had had the right idea: it was time 'to despoil the monasteries'.

D'Holbach's friends were known in their time, and since, as the first high-profile grouping of atheists. But as Alan Kors's investigation shows, they were much more than this. They were figures emblematic of their time but also adventurous thinkers, willing to follow the scientific evidence wherever it led. There are many claims on the origins of modernity, but this small group was one of them.

Félicité de Genlis and *Égalité* in the Palais-Royal

S andwiched between Mme Necker and her daughter came Stéphanie Félicité de Genlis. In due course, Mme de Genlis and Germaine de Staël would become rivals, political and literary, the one exiled by Napoleon, the other his eyes and ears in that part of Paris opposed to his administration. But whereas Mme de Staël played a prominent role in Napoleonic France, Mme de Genlis played a crucial supporting role in the pre-Revolutionary and Revolutionary period.

She had been born in January 1746 into a noble but impoverished Burgundian family, but was so weak that she was baptised at home on the day of her birth. At the age of six she was received as a canoness into the noble chapter of Alix, near Lyons. This was a normal procedure of the time for women of her class, in preparation for the possibility that she would not find a husband. Not that she was not pretty. Contemporary accounts described her as having a beautiful, oval face, with a dimple in the middle of her chin. Her eyes were the colour of chestnuts, sparkling with mischief against curly hair 'black as shoes'.[1] Her bust, it was felt necessary to remark, was 'well curved'.

Her parents were neglectful of her education – her father was more interested in the pastimes of a country gentleman (hunting, fishing and his own private laboratory), and her mother was frankly dismissed as a 'social butterfly'. The inevitable result was that Félicité remained largely untaught, brought up by rough peasants. But then a young Breton girl was appointed to look after her and, through her,

Félicité discovered the books of Mme de Scudéry and the theatre, which became a passion. She also discovered a talent for music – learning to play the harpsichord, the oboe and, above all, the harp.[2]

Later in life she was to write her memoirs – in no fewer than ten volumes – and in these she tells us that, after the Breton Girl, her education was taken over by a certain M de Mondorge, who introduced her to La Fontaine's *Fables* and the poems of Jean-Baptiste Rousseau, whose turbulent, argumentative verses caused him to be barred from the café Laurent. Mondorge also encouraged her to write for herself.[3]

Then two strokes of good fortune came her way. Her aunt – her mother's sister, Mme de Montesson – had contracted a secret marriage with the Duc d'Orléans, a prince of the blood and a cousin of the king. In time this would lead to Félicité's presence in the Palais-Royal in its most turbulent and important days. The second stroke of good fortune occurred when, ironically, her father, Pierre-César du Crest, was returning to France from Santo Domingo, where he had unsuccessfully sought to make his fortune (the slaves in Santo Domingo were exceptionally restless). This was during the Seven Years War with Britain and du Crest was taken prisoner and sent to Launceston in Cornwall. There, he happened to share quarters with another French prisoner of war, a captain in the navy, Charles-Alexis Brûlart, Comte de Genlis, aged twenty-six. The two men formed a friendship during the course of which the naval officer noticed in du Crest's hands a miniature painting on the lid of a snuff box, from which he was inseparable. It was a portrait of Félicité playing her harp and, it is said, Genlis fell for her there and then. When they met in person (the comte having been exchanged for a British prisoner of war) it was a love match on both sides.[4]

Félicité was on the whole now comfortably off and settled down at the comte's country estate. She quickly gave birth to a son and a daughter, but she now also realised how inadequate her education had been and began to read – and write – in earnest. She familiarised herself in particular with the letters of Mme de Sévigné and the dramas of Corneille. She kept a diary in which she summed up what she was reading, and wrote her first book, *Les Réflections d'une mère de vingt ans*.[5]

In Paris, whither the family moved in 1758, her harp-playing was an instant success and she was invited to several salons to display her gifts. And this is where Mme de Montesson came in. Through her, Mme de Genlis was presented at court (she came from a noble family) and slept at Versailles. Mme de Montesson introduced her to several lesser salons – those of the Comtesse d'Harville, Mesdames de Balincourt and de Custine, and the Duchesse de Liancourt. But in the first instance, the next move in Félicité's career was the invitation – again via Mme de Montesson – to the chateau of Villers-Cotterêts. This immense chateau, about 50 miles north-east of Paris, was distinguished historically as the site where, in 1539, François I had signed an ordinance making French the official language of France. Years before it had been given by Louis XIV to his brother, the Duc d'Orléans. By the time Mme de Genlis arrived, that duc's grandson was the prince in residence. He took a deep interest in the theatre and literature and Félicité's prowess at acting and music appealed to him. It was at Villers-Cotterêts that Félicité met the duc's son, the Duc de Chartres, a relationship that was to have far-reaching consequences for both of them.

Roger Picard, in his history of salons under the *ancien régime*, dismissed Mme de Genlis as a pedant in all matters, but this can't be quite true as she began to count for something in society when she returned to Paris in the winter of 1767 (she was now twenty-one), still under the wing of Mme de Montesson. An early success was an opera ball which featured a ballet at its heart (as was normal for the times), when Maximilien Gardel, a well-known dancer and choreographer of the day, used her music as the base.

At the same time, preliminary negotiations were under way for Mme de Genlis's appointment to a position in the Palais-Royal. This came about because of the Duc d'Orléans's affection for – and impending marriage to – Félicité's aunt, the aforementioned Mme de Montesson. The king, however, would only accede to the marriage if it was a morganatic union, something which, in the years ahead, would prove critical.

Thanks to Mme de Montesson, Félicité was appointed to the suite of the Duchesse de Chartres, wife of Orléans's elder son and heir. Though she was the richest heiress in France, and pretty, graceful and modest, the duchesse – Louise Marie Adélaïde de Bourbon-Penthièvre – was not overly sociable and held very few receptions. In fact, the circumstances were ripe for the introduction to the Palais of Mme de Genlis. She had no sooner arrived than there was seen to be 'an immense change in its ordinary life ... As if by enchantment, conversation there took a higher and more lively tone.' Intellectually, Félicité was a cut above the other women of the duchesse's circle, and her facility with the harp – now very accomplished – inaugurated an era of musical evenings which brought the Palais to life.[6]

It did not take her long to extend her influence by organising an intellectual salon on Tuesdays for 'men of letters and men of the world', and musical evenings on Saturdays. Through her Tuesday salons, she formed a close association with the natural historian the Comte de Buffon and through him she met Jean Sylvain Bailly, astronomer and mathematician, who would go on to preside over the Tennis Court Oath, and Marie-Jean Héraut de Séchelles, lawyer and magistrate, who took a leading role in the storming of the Bastille, joined the Jacobin Club and became a member of the notorious Committee for Public Safety. And then there was Bernard Germain de Lacépède, a close collaborator of Buffon and an early thinker about evolution.

Despite the advantages that had come her way, Félicité's ambition was undimmed, and when the duchesse – who was anaemic, and distressed at the fact that she was childless – was taken to Forges-les-Eaux, in Normandy, where therapeutic thermal waters had been discovered, Félicité accompanied her. In her memoirs, she always glossed over this episode but in 1904 Gaston Maugras, a French historian, discovered in the archives of the Ministry of Foreign Affairs documentation proving that, at this time, Félicité and the Duc de Chartres were having an affair, and from then on, says her biographer, 'let there be no mistake: the Prince was for a long time under the empire of Mme. de Genlis ... Immensely his superior, she arrived at the point of ruling him even in the smallest details of his life, exerting her power even to tear himself away from his despicable pleasures ... Soon Mme. de Genlis controlled the secrets of his policy as well as those of his household.'[7]

In August 1777 the Duchesse de Chartres finally gave birth to twin girls and it was agreed – to everyone's surprise – that Mme de Genlis would be their governess. More than that, Félicité determined that they would not be brought up in the Palais-Royal itself – busy, brilliant and decadent as it was (and it would become more so as time went by) – but she would retire to the convent of Bellechasse. This too would come to matter.

She also gave up rouge. The duc laughed at her and bet her she wouldn't be able to keep to it. This was not the only bet he lost. 'Old women who always wore rouge were talked about and criticised,' she said, when she was thirty.

Every Saturday Félicité hosted her salon.[8] Her main guests were men of letters and artists, the most notable of whom was Buffon, but others included Gabriel-Henri Gaillard, painter and historian, who wrote a history of the rivalry between France and England and a biography of his friend Malesherbes. The Abbé des Vauxelles, famous as a bibliographer, was also a member, alongside the Chevalier de Chastellux, who we met in the previous chapter. Marmontel was there too, and the notoriously bad-tempered Jean-François de La Harpe, a good friend of Voltaire, whose best play was *Warwick*. Félicité's salon was sometimes graced with the presence of Mme du Deffand and d'Alembert, who would send his latest essay, newly printed, on ahead, for discussion.

And so Félicité had enlivened Bellechasse as she had previously enlightened the Palais-Royal. But more was to come on her part, and on the part of the Duc de Chartres. In 1782 one of Adélaïde's twins died, after contracting smallpox, then a scourge in France and elsewhere. It was just before then that Chartres had taken the unusual and fairly scandalous step of appointing Mme de Genlis to be governess of his sons, the Duc de Valois and the Duc de Montpensier. This too would prove very controversial in the long run but by then both Chartres himself and the Palais-Royal would lie at the centre of what some people call the most important event in European history – the French Revolution. We now need to take a step back to 1780, when it all started.

THE CAPITAL OF PARIS

On Saturday 30 December 1780, Louis-Philippe Joseph d'Orléans, Duc de Chartres, inherited from his father the Palais-Royal, which, as we know, was one of the most opulent and striking buildings in Paris, boasting magnificent gardens and housing the theatre of the Comédie-Française. Although Louis-Philippe was unimaginably rich, and married to the wealthiest woman in France, his extravagant lifestyle and his prodigious gambling meant that all his properties were mortgaged for four years ahead and he was in massive debt. He had, however, conceived an audacious plan to transform his finances by completely renovating and expanding the palace in what was described as 'one of the most comprehensive urban developments that Paris had ever seen'.

How far he succeeded may be judged from the remarks of Dr Edward Rigby, a Whig physician who, in early July 1789, left London for Paris on the first leg of his grand tour. A well-educated Englishman, he was nonetheless unprepared for the degree of tension he encountered on his arrival in the French capital. Soldiers of the king's army were visible on every street corner.

Amid this air of foreboding, Dr Rigby stumbled across the very nerve centre of political activity. In a letter home he said: 'We had not been long in Paris when we found that the Palais-Royal, a large square lately built by the Duke of Orléans, was the place where all political intelligence was to be obtained; for it was here that all persons assembled who took part in the great political drama – here that political questions were first discussed – and popular resolutions formed and arrangements made.' At other times, he heard it described as the 'capital of Paris'.[9]

No sooner had Chartres acquired the palace than he announced an ambitious plan to redevelop the site. The owners of the adjoining properties were incensed. This gilded public regarded access to the (vast) gardens as their right by ancient usage. There was an immediate outbreak of scurrilous and libellous underground tracts, an early sighting of the illicit pre-Revolutionary and Revolutionary literature that Robert Darnton has written about so entertainingly.

Because the public was so incensed, however, Chartres gave way and announced that the gardens of the renovated building would be open to the public – the general public, not just the aristocratic neighbours of the Palais. To an extent, this placated the opposition. As one observer put it, the gardens of the renovated Palais-Royal, when they opened in May 1784, were 'of all the promenades of Paris the most celebrated and the most frequented ... The public, which had so vociferously expressed its opposition to the new Palais, now ratified with its feet what it had failed to do by word of mouth.'[10]

But in developing the Palais-Royal over the heads of his neighbours and the wider Paris public, and in making the gardens accessible as they had never been accessible before, Chartres made what turned out to be a fatal mistake. No one knew it in 1784 but it was a decision that would lead, only a few short years later, to the Storming of the Bastille, which actually began from the Palais-Royal, and to Chartres's own death on the guillotine, after he had voted for the death of his cousin, the king.

Chartres would become Duc d'Orléans in his own right in 1785, on the death of his father, Philippe the Fat, a flamboyant character, sometimes decried as a despot 'on a par with the great Turk of Constantinople'. He was married in June 1769 to Louise Marie Adélaïde de Bourbon, daughter of the immensely wealthy Duc de Penthièvre, grand admiral of France and bastard son of Louis XIV and Mme de Montespan. Louise was by far the richest heiress in France but this made little difference to Chartres's lifestyle or his fortune. He remained heavily in debt and, having been given his first mistress at the age of fifteen (his parents were worried he might have inherited the family's proclivities for homosexuality), he had soon turned into a dedicated libertine that not even marriage could alter.

On top of this there was Chartres's relationship with the king and, in particular, Marie Antoinette. For Louis-Philippe Joseph d'Orléans was probably Marie Antoinette's most implacable and bitter opponent. Later in the 1780s they waged a 'pamphlet war' against each other, commissioning writers to pen the most scurrilous accusations. France looked on, half in glee and half in horror.

Louis-Philippe was a noted Anglophile in all manner of ways. (Marie Antoinette was an Anglophobe.) He dressed in English-style frock coats, he became a close friend of the Prince of Wales, he adored horse-racing and introduced it to France. He admired the English constitution and political system, especially the constitutional monarchy, and he almost certainly squirrelled away part of his fortune in London banks. He was brave and one of the first intrepid souls to try out the craze for the initially dangerous enterprise of ballooning. He joined the navy and distinguished himself at the Battle of Ushant, though that was not without controversy either. He had a succession of mistresses – Mlle de Cambis, Mme de Genlis, Princesse de Lamballe, Mme de Buffon, daughter of the great naturalist, and Grace Dalrymple Elliott, who was also the mistress of the Prince of Wales (by whom she had a daughter). Louis-Philippe was also grand master of all the Masonic lodges of France.[11] Many of these aspects – Orléans's heritage, his links to England, his secretive Masonic involvement, his hatred of Marie Antoinette – would be brought together by his critics later on to query his loyalty and his role in the pre-Revolution.

When his father died in 1785, Louis-Philippe inherited four dukedoms, two other great houses in Paris and one in Fontainebleau, and eight domains, amounting in all to 2½ million hectares. But it was the Palais-Royal that mattered most.

'ANTI-VERSAILLES'

Since the Palais-Royal had been given to the Orléans family by Louis XIV (chapter 10), many changes had been made – to the gardens, the battlements, the picture galleries and the opera. But what Louis-Philippe planned was of a quite different order, because his reforms were unprecedented. He was an aristocrat, a prince of the blood, but he had succumbed to commerce, an unheard-of initiative in the upper classes, who were actually forbidden by the *loi de dérogeance* from taking part in any such activity. 'We don't see our cousin at court much these days,' quipped another royal prince, 'now that he has become a shopkeeper.'

The contentious genius of the Palais-Royal lay in the fact that it succeeded as a commercial enterprise and – if inadvertently and to begin with – as a non-political experiment in social amalgamation. The aim of the Duc de Chartres, as he still was, was 'to attract the curious more and more to his palace by all sorts of games and recreations and public transactions'. Its reputation as 'anti-Versailles' was consolidated.

We know about this new palace and its attractions in detail. There were several theatres, including a children's theatre, a ventriloquist's theatre and one offering 'magic, illusion and science'. There were fireworks every night. There was a small circus and many individual entertainers – conjurors, singers, acrobats. A defrocked *abbé* sang bawdy songs, and rafts of prostitutes 'shouted out lewd possibilities'. The Palais-Royal was home to forty jewellers, eighteen tailors, fourteen silk merchants, nine engraving shops, nine drapers, seven clock merchants, five florists, four dressmakers, three fan shops, three tobacconists, a horse and carriage equipment store, and a store selling arquebuses.[12]

For those whose taste was for more exalted pleasures, there were a number of museums, where one could listen to lectures, sit through readings or see exhibitions. There were numerous pseudo-scientific booths that 'performed experiments' and displayed recent inventions. There were eight bookshops. A number of private clubs were organised (mostly on the second and third floors). The Club du salon des arts provided a forum where men of letters and artists could exchange ideas, read books and listen to music. Louis-Philippe himself started the Club des planteurs, whose membership was confined to people who owned land in America. And we haven't mentioned the baths, the restaurants and the cafés. One individual who studied the palace in the eighteenth century concluded: 'The ownership of the Palais-Royal by a prince of the blood ... and its location in the heart of royalist and aristocratic Paris made it the logical playground of the highborn.'[13]

Yet alongside this narrowly defined public of old there commingled a new expanded public and, in historical perspective, this is the all-important change. The duc instructed his Swiss guard to refuse entry 'only to drunkards, women in excessively indecent dress and those in tatters', thus opening his gates to the people of Paris. The result was the immediate juxtaposition of the various estates and their respective subdivisions. This was new. 'Pushing ever greater numbers of French men and women to think of this space as in some way their own, and bringing together an array of social groups only rarely present at such close quarters, Chartres' innovations had an important impact on the political landscape of pre-Revolutionary France.'[14]

ORLÉANS'S POLITICAL MACHINE

More than that, given the palace's official status as the private home of a prince of the blood, royal police were barred from the premises. And although the king's spies canvassed the grounds, the freedom for political expression, contestation and exchange was much greater in the Palais-Royal than elsewhere. As one important consequence, underground (unsupervised, uncensored) printing activity could flourish in the palace as nowhere else, generating a steady flow of illicit, subversive literature.

Libels were only part of the picture. The duc himself gathered around his person an extensive 'brains trust' or political machine, a network of political pamphleteers and a cabinet of individuals who, in the words of one historian, 'invented something novel in the history of French politics: the assertive use of wealth, research and propaganda for the purposes of forming public opinion and swaying public policy'.[15] This political 'Machine', as it has been called, was gathered together in the Palais-Royal after 1785, by which time the new garden project was up and running and bringing in enormous funds. The Machine included three individuals who would play significant roles in the Revolution.

Pierre Choderlos de Laclos, a soldier, Freemason, ballistics expert and early friend of Napoleon Bonaparte, was better known as the author of the notorious *Les Liaisons dangereuses*, published in 1782, which was itself an account of the decadence of the *ancien régime* in the run-up to revolution (chapter 19). However, there was more – much more – than this to Laclos, who had an interesting mind and varied achievements. He had studied at the École royale d'artillerie de La Fère, which in time would become the École polytechnique, and as a young officer served in the La Rochelle garrison during the Seven Years War. Becoming bored with military duties, he tried his hand at poetry (as almost everyone did in those days), composed an opera libretto (not a success), and established a new artillery school at Valence, where Napoleon was a student in the mid-1780s.

Choderlos was a great admirer of Rousseau but his own major work, in which he deliberately set out to write something 'which departed from the ordinary, which made a noise, and which would remain on earth after his death', would scarcely have found favour with Jean-Jacques. It is an exploration of libertinism and it was a scandalous success, 'pernicious and damnable', though in the twentieth century André Malraux argued that the book marked a new departure in French literature, in that the conspirators' actions were determined by an ideology.

After publishing the book, in four volumes, in March 1782, Laclos was ordered to return to his regiment (he had been granted a long vacation to complete it), and in 1788 he left the service to join the staff of Louis-Philippe d'Orléans, who he met through the Freemasons, where Orléans was the leader. After his time at the Palais-Royal, he survived the Revolution, met up again with Napoleon, became a brigadier-general in the Army of the Rhine and invented the modern artillery shell.[16]

Like Laclos, Jacques-Pierre Brissot, although chiefly known for his actions in the Revolution, was also a much more accomplished and multi-dimensional figure. Born in Chartres, the son of an innkeeper, he received a training in law but, at an early age, moved to London to pursue a career in journalism, founding French-language periodicals, marrying a Frenchwoman and fathering three children with her.

In London he became influenced by the abolitionists, and returned to Paris in 1788 to found the 'Society of the Friends of the Blacks', and started yet another newspaper which advocated republicanism, *Le Républicain*. He also travelled to the United States to make himself familiar, in the first instance, with the abolitionists there. He was elected to the American Academy of Arts and Sciences.

Employed by the Duc d'Orléans, to begin with he was one of the duc's secretaries at the Palais-Royal: 'My work consisted of examining all the projects that the prince could carry through with his immense fortune. We wanted to attach the intellectuals to us, to patronise the arts and the learned societies. Thus, we gave pensions to farmers and provided aid for new research.'

He went on to propose an Orléanist political party, and in time his ideas and activities (funded by the duc) would give rise to the Brissotin faction in the Revolution, better known later as the Girondins. He was one of the most enthusiastic supporters of the Revolution, famous for his speeches at the Jacobin Club, and later became a member of the National Convention. But he fell out with Robespierre; he was less extreme and, following the arrest of the king, favoured a national referendum to decide on his fate. This tactic wasn't followed up, and the king's execution was ordered immediately. Matters were turning against the Brissotins/Girondins and when they were blamed for the military defeats on the battle-field, and the food shortages which followed, and in particular when Brissot himself advocated a constitutional monarchy as a way to stem the increasing violence, he was – inevitably – one of the Girondins arrested, caught travelling with false papers. He was charged with being a counter-revolutionary and as a spy in the pay of Britain, where it was known he had good contacts.[17]

Emmanuel-Joseph Sieyès (the Abbé Sieyès), a third member of the Machine, was also bankrolled by Orléans and he would become famous as the author of *What Is the Third Estate?*, one of the sem-inal essays of the pre-Revolution. François Furet described Sieyès as the French Revolution's most profound political thinker. 'He gave it an initial impetus, in the winter of 1788–89, with three successive pamphlets: *Essai sur les privilèges* (Essay on Privilege), *Vues sur les moyens d'exécution dont les représentants de la France pourront déposer en 1789* (Views on the means of action available to represent-atives of France in 1789) and lastly, *Qu'est-ce que le Tiers État?* (What is the Third Estate?). Published between November 1788 and January 1789, the third essay made Sieyès's name resound across the nation.'

Sieyès was a priest from Fréjus on the Mediterranean coast of France. Intellectually gifted, he was educated by the Jesuits at the seminary of Saint-Sulpice, where he was looked upon as being 'sly' but with an 'insatiable' appetite for books. Ordained in 1772, Furet says he had read everything about the philosophy of the Enlightenment, both French and English, 'which would have also meant Scottish'. He eventually became canon of Chartres, in 1783, and then vicar-general, in effect assistant to the bishop. 'He was not at the centre of power in the church but no longer a nobody.'

Sieyès's first pamphlet, the *Essai sur les privilèges*, which appeared in November 1788, set the tone for the momentous events that were to follow: hatred of the aristocracy. For Sieyès it was plain that dem-ocratic universalism was the 'natural law of society'.

Two months after the first essay came the third, in January 1789, *Qu'est-ce que le Tiers État?* Not unlike Karl Marx's *Das Kapital* this is above all a battle-cry, a voice and tone that in itself, in its consistency, sets the scene for revolution. The economic activity of society's members is central and on this basis there is no place in such a society for the nobility. It is an absurdity, Sieyès says, to have at the head of state those who are *defined* by that which separates them from the wider public. Without nobility, he says, a society shaped by reason and science can prevail and thrive, to the benefit of all.

All people whose labour and activity produces wealth, he says, or contributes to public service, together comprise the political community, which, Sieyès submits, amounts to a 'nation', and this goes directly against the kind of society mapped out by Richelieu, Colbert and the Bourbon kings, who argue the opposite – state corporatism. 'For Sieyès, the nation means the community formed by the association of individuals who decide to live freely under a common law, forged by their representatives.' The nobility have no part in this because they have their own 'private assemblies'. This analysis led to the idea of the next Estates-General, which, in his famous phrase, 'was nothing, yet it was everything'. In fact, Sieyès emphasised that the Third Estate was the *sole* guardian of the national will. The triumph of this pamphlet, says Furet, lies in the simplicity of its argument: 'Public opinion is burying years of contempt under a rediscovered equality.'[18]

The *abbé* was a resentful man, observes Furet, intent on settling old scores with the old society, but his essays identified the French Revolution's 'biggest secret': hatred of the nobility. Written when Sieyès was part of the Orléans entourage, the thrust of the pamphlet was, to say the least, audacious. But could it really be said that hatred of the nobility was a secret?

Laclos and his lieutenants in the Palais-Royal drew up plans for government and reform, devised philanthropic works, issued libels, and prepared the campaign for the Estates-General. If we add together the many accounts of the period, we learn that not only Laclos, Brissot and Sieyès, but Mirabeau (who, like the duc, admired the English constitution), Desmoulins, Danton, Dumouriez and Marat all 'passed through the Orléans receiving line'. The duc himself led

the defection of the aristocrats to the Third Estate in the National
Assembly. The Palais-Royal was thus the busy epicentre of much
pre-Revolutionary activity.

ANARCHY OF THE APPETITES

Félicité de Genlis was well aware of how she was regarded by the
general public and she was, if not at ease being talked about, still
ready for the notoriety, and met it head on. In the very month in
which she was appointed governess of Chartres's sons, she published
Adèle et Théodore, ou Lettres sur l'éducation, in effect an adaptation
to practical life of the educational principles of Rousseau (originally
set out by Locke) but which was so clear and commonsensical that
readers – and the book was very successful – thought they could find
in its pages the spirit of both Plato and Fénelon.[19]

The book was also an attack against the *philosophes* and
their *Encyclopédie* in the name of religion and morality. Diderot
had learned of the book's imminent publication and persuaded
d'Alembert to try to intervene. He approached Mme de Genlis
and went so far as to propose that if she withdrew her book, the
Académie française – of which he was then the permanent secretary – would be made open to women and she would be the first
recipient of a chair. This was quite a daring move on d'Alembert's
part but it was quite the wrong tactic, and the book was the start
of a 25-year war between Mme de Genlis and the *philosophes*. She
was even forceful enough to propose her book for one of the prestigious prizes awarded by the academy, but this was too much. It so
happened that Mme d'Épinay had just published the second volume
of her *Conversations d'Émilie*, dealing mainly with early infancy,
and – as we have seen – the academy awarded her the prize instead.

Mme de Genlis's salon was full of literary and artistic people
until 1789, and only then did they become political.[20] Although she
detested the irreligiosity of the *philosophes*, she could not help but
be 'impregnated' with their democratic ideas, making her impatient
with the society then in place. She was also set against the court
because of the duc. She thought the throne was tottering and the duc
the man to hold it firm.

It was in 1789 that her Sunday salons began, described by the Goncourts as her '*salon bleu*', an ambitious back reference to the Rambouillet *Chambre bleue*. Among the guests now were some very familiar names to anyone interested in the events of the French Revolution: Bertrand Barère, who was to be a leading member of the Committee for Public Safety, Brissot, Talleyrand, and Alexandre de Lameth, a hero of the American War of Independence, a friend of Jefferson, who was accused of treason and fled, only to be captured by the Austrians and imprisoned in a dungeon for seven years. Others included Antoine Barnave, a noted orator who tried to set up a constitutional monarchy with Marie Antoinette, and the painter Jacques-Louis David. On occasions, the salon even included Danton, Lechapelier and Robespierre.

This tumultuous mix of personalities in Félicité's salon shows, if nothing else, that in every respect the Palais-Royal was the antithesis of Versailles, indeed, as Simon Schama says, its nemesis. 'At the core of Versailles was a pavilion block where the king's control over business was formalised by apartments enfilading off one another so that access at each stage could be barred or yielded as ritual and decorum required. Immense half-mile wings extended north and south, dependencies in every sense, housing the governmental and palatial services of the theoretically omnipotent monarch. The Palais-Royal, in contrast, was a Parisian equivalent of republican spaces like the Piazza San Marco in Venice. Its architecture "invited sauntering, watching, browsing, reading, buying, talking, flirting, pilfering, eating". While Versailles was the most carefully patrolled place in France, the Palais-Royal prohibited the presence of any police whatsoever. If Versailles set great store by the hierarchy of rank, the frantic business of the Palais-Royal subversively jumbled it up. Versailles proclaimed corporate discipline; the Palais-Royal celebrated the public anarchy of the appetites.'[21]

But ... but, as the 1780s lengthened, the skies at the Palais-Royal darkened. In early 1789, Nicolas Restif de La Bretonne produced his three-volume work *Le Palais-Royal*. La Bretonne was an extraordinary French writer, 'inordinately vain, and of extremely relaxed morals', who produced 200 books. *Le Palais-Royal*, among other things, chronicled the often-tragic lives of thirty-two courtesans of the Palais, the elite of the trade. These darker aspects of the Palais-Royal were very real, rendering it by the end of the century synonymous with all manner of depravity.[22]

'KING ORLÉANS'

These deteriorating circumstances began to come to a head with the convening of the Estates-General. This is, of course, a well-known event in the French Revolution. The Estates-General had not met since the beginning of the seventeenth century, but Louis XVI was so strapped for cash, as we know all too well, that he needed major taxation reforms. The Estates-General, however, would not agree. The king himself intervened and on 19 November 1787 insisted that the people submit to his demands. This was a fine but fundamental legal point because the form of words he used confirmed that the meeting of the Estates-General was in fact not that but a *lit de justice*, a very different legal entity, a sort of Privy Council that could endorse the king's wishes but not debate them. It was now that Orléans rose to his feet and, his voice quivering with anger – genuine or counterfeit – he asked the king what the status of the meeting was. The king was forced to acknowledge that it was a *lit de justice*. So the meeting that had begun as one thing was now something else entirely because the king couldn't get his own way, another naked display of arbitrary attempted absolutist authority. Still standing, Orléans replied that therefore what the king was proposing was illegal.

This stunned the Estates-General, stunned all of France: for a prince of the blood to address the king, his cousin, in such a manner was unprecedented, unthinkable, and brought back disturbing memories of the excesses of another Orléans, Gaston. But it made the prince wildly popular. The king was minded not to make too much of this, but Marie Antoinette was having none of it, and within hours Orléans was exiled to his estates.

Various attempts were made to get the duc back to the Palais-Royal; they all failed at first. But when the king brought in – and then quickly dismissed – Jacques Necker, who had recommended sweeping fiscal reforms to benefit both the national debt and the poor at the same time, opposition to him increased. This was the period when the clubs of Paris were seething with talk of sedition and now Orléans broke his exile and attended a meeting of the Club des enragés at the restaurant Masse in the arcades of the Palais-Royal. There he spoke enthusiastically in support of Emmanuel-Joseph Sieyès's calls for reform.

The 1788–9 winter was harsh, and the Seine froze over. Orléans ordered that bread be distributed throughout his estates and the old and infirm given warm refuge. His popularity soared.

The price of bread was still fluctuating menacingly. Violence broke out early in 1789 when a mob attacked the Réveillon paper factory in Paris following a rumour that wages were about to be cut in the harshest winter of all, pushing even bread beyond the reach of many. At one point the mob shouted 'Long live King Orléans' and it is now known that the rebels were paid by Choderlos de Laclos, using Palais-Royal money.[23]

Although Orléans had played little part in the everyday debates of the Estates-General, he did stand up on 30 June and lead forty-seven nobles across the floor to join the Third Estate. Three days later the rest of his colleagues joined them. When this news reached the Palais-Royal, rioting began, and that evening 3,000–4,000 people attacked the Abbaye prison to release fourteen members of the Gardes françaises who had been imprisoned for refusing to fire on the crowds during the Réveillon disturbances.[24] On the back of this the duc was elected president of the new National Assembly and at this point many regarded him as being the next king.

But matters were overheating and rumours rife. The Venetian ambassador reported back that Orléans's 'intentions are suspect and all that passes in the Palais-Royal must be condemned by anyone of sense'. The Parma envoy claimed that the duc was paying the troublemakers 20–30 sous a day. At the same time, there is little doubt that the king, apprehensive of what might happen, was planning to take on his opponents and was amassing both foreign and loyalist French troops. It was at this point, on 11 July, that he finally lost patience with Necker and ordered him to leave the kingdom.[25]

The following day, a Sunday, news of Necker's sudden departure reached the Palais-Royal and was interpreted as a prelude to more draconian action by the Crown. A young lawyer, Camille Desmoulins, pistol in hand, leaped on to a table outside the café Foy, known for the ices it served and the shade of its chestnut trees. There he delivered 'the most famous call to arms in modern history'. Snatching a cluster of leaves from one of the chestnut trees, he urged his listeners to take 'this green cockade' as the symbol of their imminent liberty.[26]

This was not the only revolutionary event to begin or take place at the Palais-Royal. Fighting in the gardens there continued on and off until 1795. At one stage there was a self-proclaimed fighting unit, the 'Patriotic Assembly of the Palais-Royal', whose resistance was eventually overcome by forces led by a young commander, one Napoleon Bonaparte.

The Great Mystery

Following the king's flight to Varennes, on 20–21 June 1791, and his capture, the scene was set for Orléans to take over, either as regent or even as king. This is what Laclos and Brissot expected – and hoped – would happen, as did others like Danton and Mirabeau, who patrolled the streets of Paris near the Palais-Royal extolling Orléans's qualities.

At this point there occurred one of the great mysteries of French Revolutionary history. It seems that Mme de Genlis had the duc's ear most just then and advised against him taking over. And this was the course he took. Was it a failure of nerve, of imagination, of character? It is one of the great unsettled questions, but amid the turmoil Orléans accepted an invitation from the king to go to England on a diplomatic mission. In retrospect this was a manoeuvre by Lafayette, the hero of the American War of Independence, to get the duc out of the way, and it was a major miscalculation on Orléans's part. In a sense, the Revolution now went on without him.[27]

His time in London was not a great success and when he returned to Paris his first problem was a domestic crisis at the Palais-Royal. His wife had become morbidly jealous of her children's close relation with their governess, Mme de Genlis. As part of this, the young Duc de Chartres had become a Jacobin and was in favour of a decree that had abolished all titles of the nobility. The son was so out of kilter with the mother that he announced he would dine with her no more than once a week. It was now said that Mme de Genlis was the lover of both the father and the son.[28]

Relations between the duchesse and Mme de Genlis continued to deteriorate, Genlis eventually being expelled from the Palais and decamping to Tournai. This prompted the psychological collapse of Orléans's daughter and, seeing this, the duchesse decided that she had had enough – and herself left the Palais-Royal.

THE NAMELESS CITIZEN AND THE FATAL VOTE

The year 1792 was the most chaotic – and the most violent – yet. Austria declared war on France, intent on counter-revolution; the monarchy was abolished; the king and queen were imprisoned; Orléans's sons joined up and fought against the Austrians; Orléans himself wanted to fight but was denied the opportunity. Brissot, Laclos and Danton, all of whom he had helped financially, seemed happy to abandon him. James Christie, the London auctioneer, was ensconced in the Palais-Royal, trying to agree values for the old masters in the collection, which Orléans needed to sell.[29]

Then there was the problem with Orléans's name. Since the abolition of titles, what did he call himself? His own commune (the new word for the area he lived in) referred to him as 'the nameless citizen', a belittling reference if ever there was one. The president of the commune suggested that 'Égalité' would be a good choice. Henceforth, he became Philippe Égalité; his sons also took that epithet, the Duc de Chartres as Général Égalité, his brother as Montpensier Antoine Égalité. The Palais-Royal, which had already been renamed the Jardin de la Révolution and then the Palais Égalité, finally became Maison Égalité. The fall of 'the most beautiful house in Europe' was complete.

As the violence spiralled out of control (the 'September massacres' that year were the worst bloodshed of the entire Revolution, when up to 1,600 were murdered), there were calls – by Robespierre, for example – to send all former aristocrats into exile. But Brissot spoke up for Égalité, acknowledging that he had bankrolled so much of their pre-Revolutionary activity (a vital admission, historically). Marat agreed with Brissot, so Égalité – fatally, as it turned out – stayed in Paris, where, as a member of the assembly, he was expected to take part in the upcoming trial of the king – and Marie Antoinette – and vote on the death penalty. That duly took place in December, when

Orléans did indeed vote for the execution of his cousin, the king – and Marie Antoinette.

By this time, although there were still many colourful activities in the Palais-Royal gardens, aristocrats were not welcome and some of the clubs on the second and third floors had closed. Still, more than once, stylish rendezvous were held there, one organised by Jacques-Louis David, who made a speciality of designing Revolutionary celebrations, this one in order to induce young men to enlist in the army, at a time when many thought that invasion by Austrian or British forces was imminent.

Then a plot was discovered for a section of the army to mount a counter-revolution. The leading figures escaped to the safety of the Austrians, and these included Général Égalité. He wrote a letter to his father explaining what the plan had been, how it had been conceived at the exile home of Mme de Genlis in Tournai, and this letter was intercepted. So it finally appeared clear to many that the Orléans clan *had* planned to take over the kingdom, after all.

Égalité's fate was sealed. Not long after, over a dinner of sole and lemon at the Palais-Royal, he was informed that he was to be arrested the next day. After several months in several prisons, and after a further dinner that we know consisted of oysters and lamb cutlets, he was guillotined on 6 November 1793.[30]

On the day that Philippe Égalité was guillotined, the state took over the Palais-Royal. The gardens remained open and as lively as ever, once the fighting had died down, though many of the clubs had closed, as we have seen. But of course by then many of the more elegant aristocrats who hadn't been guillotined had fled into exile, so that the entertainments lost a lot of their style. Gradually, the joy went out of life in the gardens, not helped by Napoleon's later policy of housing the poor and the destitute in the apartments.

In the wake of Égalité's death, there was a massive outpouring of books arguing that he was the evil spirit behind the Revolution. Memoirs of the Revolution, and of the last days of the *ancien régime*, poured from the presses throughout the nineteenth century, offering arguments both pro and con Égalité. The matter is still not settled.

The Most Eloquent Love–Hate Affair in History

Having known her since she was a girl, Mme de Genlis found Germaine de Staël 'ill-bred and a most embarrassing person'. Living down her own scandalous life as she aged, or at least trying to, Félicité wrote two novels, *Mélanie, or The Female Philosopher* (1803) and *The Chateau of Coppet* (1807), each of which is a direct attack on Mme de Staël. She professed to be disappointed by de Staël's form of romanticism, though in practice she was influenced by it as much as any of her contemporaries. By this stage of her life most of Mme de Genlis's time was spent 'promoting religion and describing sin in an unfavourable light'. Edward Gibbon summed up Germaine more generally and more accurately: 'Wild, vain, but good-natured and with a much larger provision of wit than beauty.'[1] More wit than tact, too. As someone else said, she was so spoiled by admiration for her wit that it was hard to make her realise her shortcomings.

Given the family she was from, and because she grew up seated at the feet of Diderot, d'Alembert, Buffon, Grimm and the other *philosophes*, Germaine's ambition – or her ease with accomplished figures – should surprise no one. But that did not guarantee her talent and the fact is that, as she was to show many times over, she equalled and even surpassed many of those around her in that department. Mme de Genlis published some 150 books but her writings are not read as Germaine de Staël's still are.

Germaine Necker became de Staël by marrying the Swedish ambassador in Paris. The Neckers drove a hard bargain – the ambassadorship must be guaranteed for life, a healthy pension was to be guaranteed, de Staël was to be raised to the rank of comte and Germaine was never to be forced to live in Sweden. They didn't get their way entirely (Baron de Staël was never made a comte) but her residence in the Swedish embassy would have its advantages.

To outsiders, the de Staëls seemed a united couple but there was little in the relationship in the way of tenderness and he never gained from her more than an affectionate cordiality. Aged twenty-three at the time of the Revolution, her main interests in life were love, politics and literature. She was to love three men in her life – Charles Maurice de Talleyrand-Périgord, Louis-Marie de Narbonne-Lara and Mathieu de Montmorency-Laval – though her most important companion from a psychological, intellectual and political point of view was Benjamin Constant.

Often flashily dressed, it was unkindly – but perhaps not unjustly – said that she used her bosom to distract attention from other aspects of her form. This agreed with her general approach to life, in which she needed noise, activity, movement. 'What I love about noise', she liked to say, 'is that it camouflages life.' 'With the sublime self-righteousness of a true Necker,' says one of her biographers, 'Germaine was able to walk through life, leaving in her wake a host of exasperated lovers, of ruined causes, of disastrous intrigues, and a crowd of onlookers who gaped or laughed at her.'[2]

No sooner had she been married and become an ambassadress than she took over her mother's salon. She installed it in the Swedish embassy in the rue du Bac. And there, next to love, conversation was the principal *raison d'être* of her gatherings. Several people have testified that the art of conversation reached its perfection in France in the years preceding the Revolution and Germaine was, as Christine Le Bozec tells us, the most brilliant talker of her time. And she was not averse to displaying her physical advantages – what were described as voluptuous arms, a 'generous' bosom, which was left uncovered even when travelling, and legs designed to show that she was 'more than just an intellect'.[3]

She gave birth to her first child, a daughter, in the summer of 1787 but lost her in April 1789, on the very eve of revolution. When the decision was made to call the Estates-General, her father was again recalled to ministerial office and, as we have seen, he played a role in treating the famine that attended the crop failure of the harsh winter of 1788–9. In August 1790, when Necker was forced out of office a final time, and exiled to Coppet, his estate near Geneva, Germaine did not accompany him. On the 3rd of that month she gave birth to her eldest son. At this time, she also had a lover.[4]

The first of Germaine's lovers was Talleyrand. Described as 'undoubtedly one of the more intelligent men of his age', he is often remembered for his statement that 'only those that had lived before 1789 could know the sweetness of living'.[5] He had damaged and deformed his legs in a childhood accident, as a result of which he was unfit for a military career and, on these grounds, forfeited his right of primogeniture and went into the church. His 'refined libertinism' scandalised even a society which took a lenient view of 'sinful clerics'. (When he was named Bishop of Autun in 1788, it was over the protests of his own mother.) He was not, it would appear, physically prepossessing. The Duke of Argyll likened him to 'a corpse considerably advanced in corruption', but note that the duke then went on: 'His feet are distorted in every possible direction. His having learned to walk steadily with such wretched materials is proof that he is a man of considerable abilities.' When Germaine met him, she was seduced by his feminine sensibility, combined with 'virile intelligence and strength'.[6] He managed to hold high office across a wide range of political regimes and, despite his feet, enjoyed the favours of a wide range of mistresses. He may even have been the father of the painter Delacroix.

It was probably Talleyrand who introduced Germaine to her second love and the father of her son: Louis, the Vicomte de Narbonne-Lara, handsome, intelligent, sensitive, a noted lover. He was born in Italy in a castle belonging to the Duke of Parma, but no one could be certain who his parents were. When Germaine and he met all he had to show for himself, at thirty-three years of age, was a succession of mistresses and massive debts. Germaine's husband was not at all pleased with her affair with Narbonne-Lara and she tried hard to pretend that there was nothing there – hardly easy when she was pregnant by him.[7]

But for her, loyalty in friendship was placed above sexual fidelity.[8] This was shown in the way that she took her next lover. When Narbonne-Lara had abandoned his former mistress, the Comtesse de Laval, for Germaine, Germaine repaid the compliment by falling in love with the comtesse's son, Mathieu de Montmorency-Laval. Like Narbonne-Lara he was a soldier, but Mathieu – a tall, blond, vigorous man – had served in the American campaign with Lafayette, and was one of those who brought back to France American ideas of liberty, and so greeted the Revolution initially with enthusiasm. He would survive the Revolution and the Terror, and accept high office in later administrations.

By now Germaine's salon in the rue du Bac had become a political meeting place for the liberal aristocracy which was soon to carry out the first phase of the Revolution. Gouverneur Morris, the American representative in France, who we know was a frequent guest, confessed to his diary that he felt 'very stupid' among her group. The year 1791 was when Germaine came closest to playing a part in the Revolution. That was the year when a constitution was drawn up. It was a constitution which in truth satisfied no one, but it was drawn up by Sieyès and Lafayette, and Sieyès was a steady fixture in her salon.[9] Her own preference at this time was to arrest the course of the Revolution and consolidate its gains; she preferred a constitutional monarchy along British lines, with a strong leader who would overcome the demands of fanatics, which she could already see beginning to form. For her, that meant Narbonne-Lara.

Operating on the assumption that intelligent men could always find the basis for agreement, she made her salon the forum for all manner of moderate opinion and brought together the likes of Brissot and Condorcet, on the left, with Antoine Barnave, a fine orator, who believed the king could be made to see sense, and Narbonne-Lara, who she felt was the monarchy's last hope of salvation. Also present were the brothers Charles and Alexandre de Lameth, two more constitutional monarchists, who helped draft the Declaration of the Rights of Man and of the Citizen.

There was more than one play about Germaine and her role at

this time, and a number of pamphlets. In the *Acts of the Apostles*, by the royalist author Antoine de Rivarol, she was described as the 'Bacchante of the Revolution' and 'the only person in Europe capable of deceiving the public on her sex', a gratuitously offensive reflection on her physical appearance. A comedy, circulated as a pamphlet, called *The Intrigues of Madame de Staël*, also appeared in 1791, and described her as a nymphomaniac 'who stirred up riots to keep her lovers'. The amount of abuse she was able to take was impressive, but it was not all against her. The same Rivarol, in his *A Little Dictionary of the Great Men of the Revolution*, released in 1790, dedicated the book to her with the words: 'We take the liberty to place your name in front of our collection, for to publish a dictionary of the great men of the day is merely to submit to you the list of your adorers.'[10]

With war in the air, Germaine moved nearer to the centre of events in one respect at least: in December 1791, Narbonne-Lara was appointed to the War Department. On top of that, Talleyrand was despatched to London to secure a promise of British neutrality in the event of war. Heady days.

Yet she and her husband were in a difficult position, not helped by the fact that Gustavus, the Swedish king, tried to mastermind the escape of Louis XVI and Marie Antoinette and, when he learned of their capture at Varennes, and their forced return to Paris, he began 'to pose openly as Europe's god-appointed champion against Jacobin tyranny'.[11] He was shot to death at a masked ball.

As the mood shifted against the Constitutionalists, Germaine devised an escape plan for the king. It came to nothing, the queen refusing to accept help from that direction. Germaine herself was forced to leave Paris, accompanied to the town gate. By 7 September 1793, 'when the ambassadress stepped out of her carriage at Coppet to fly into her father's arms', 1,368 prisoners, including 43 children, had been butchered in Paris alone.[12]

THE GYPSY LIFE

She made no pretence of liking Coppet. 'I hold all Switzerland in a magnificent horror,' she wrote to her husband and even, for a while, thought of returning to Paris in the middle of the Terror. But then her mother died. Germaine made no pretence of mourning either.[13] But soon after two events occurred which were to have long-lasting effects.

One was the Thermidorian Coup or Reaction, a liberal–conservative counter-revolution that followed the toppling of Robespierre in July 1794. Within hours of Robespierre's head 'hitting the wicker basket', as someone couldn't wait to put it, the Thermidorian Reactionaries set to work to create a conservative republic, 'free of centralised power, rigid economic controls, contrived religion and state terror', though they did embark on a 'White Terror', designed to purge government of any remaining Jacobins. A new constitution was passed that dissolved the National Convention and replaced it with the Directory, a five-member council, and a bicameral executive, which came into force in November 1795.

Seen by some as a rather desultory wasteland between Robespierre and Napoleon, the Directory did attempt to achieve stability without a return either to Jacobinism or the monarchy. It saw the early return of émigrés, ended the cult of Robespierre's Supreme Being, and voted to allow freedom of religion and worship, though it had to be carried out in private, the state no longer paying clergymen.

If not perfect, this was more to Germaine's liking, but it was to an extent overshadowed by the second event, the arrival in her life of Benjamin Constant, a relationship that would become, as one observer described it, 'the most eloquent love affair in history'.[14]

The existing portraits of Benjamin Constant – some of them at least – are misleading. They show a chubby-faced cherub, with languid fair hair and a general air of innocence. Nothing could be further from the truth. Benjamin was a cosmopolitan, sensual, highly intelligent individual, the son of a high-ranking officer in the Dutch army, from a Huguenot family with links to Paris, London, Brussels, The Hague and even China.

He freely confessed to preferring young girls to the classics. Though he attended Oxford University for only two months (no one knows why), he confessed that 'I sometimes see an English girl of my age whom I prefer to Cicero, Seneca, etc. She teaches me Ovid, whom she has never read or heard of but whom I discover in her eyes.'[15]

He then spent two years at Edinburgh University (when the Scottish Enlightenment was at its peak), which he later described as the happiest of his life, the basis of his lifelong Anglophilia.

He was also a gambler, and addicted to prostitutes, whom he visited often, admitting it publicly; he contracted syphilis.[16] He kept a diary, one of the main features of which was a number code with which he recorded recurring feelings, and which shows his priorities:

1. Physical [i.e. sexual] pleasure.
2. Desire to break my eternal chain [with Mme de Staël].
3. Reconciliation with this bond, because of memories or a monetary charm.
4. Work.
5. Disputes with my father.
6. Tenderness for my father.
7. Travel projects.
8. Marriage projects.
13. Indecision about everything.
16. Projects for a voyage overseas [i.e. America].
17. Desire to make up with certain enemies [i.e. Napoleon].

His diary shows that, in the summer of 1811, when he was in Germany, in one 46-day period he spent thirty nights gambling. It marks 'small winnings' on three nights and 'mad' losses on sixteen occasions. His diary also records that Germaine was 'the easiest person to live with in all small matters provided she has her way in the big ones'. From time to time, he bemoans 'the lack of "1"'.[17]

Though they were undoubtedly soul mates, Germaine described her life after Thermidor as a 'myserable gypsy life' and the same could be said for Benjamin. Though she never tired of his intellect, she said she was repelled by his physique – he was no match for the handsome aristocrats who 'occupied her heart'. But he became her political collaborator, and together they still hoped to unite the moderates in the country and mediate a peace between Revolutionary France and the European coalition. Together they drew up her next pamphlet, *Reflections on Peace, Addressed to Mr Pitt and to the French*, printed secretly, in which she argued for the acceptance of the Revolutionary status quo and showed that, however split the nation might be, it was ready to fight to repel foreign counter-revolutionaries.[18]

AN IMMENSE JUNK SHOP

On Germaine's return from Coppet to Paris in summer 1795 a strange sight greeted her. The fashionable areas, the Faubourg Saint-Germain for instance, were deserted, the smart hotels stripped of their furniture, and the churches denuded of their marble statues. Pavements were lined with objects for sale: 'The capital of the world', remarked one observer, 'looks like an immense junk shop.' Police records show a sharp rise in suicides and begging. At the same time (and obviously elsewhere) there were 644 public ballrooms operating in Paris (someone had the leisure to count them), and restaurants, jeweller's shops and bordellos had never done so well. Cemeteries were used for dances.[19]

This was a time when the tension between the republicans and the royalists was growing. It also meant that Mme de Staël's salon was needed more than ever and was resurrected, the roster of figures now including, besides Suard and Sieyès, Paul Barras, executive director of the Directory regime, Jean-Lambert Tallien, who had helped engineer the fall of Robespierre, and Marie-Joseph Chénier, brother of the martyred poet André Chénier, and himself a poet and dramatist. She was back with a vengeance.[20]

The new constitution, as envisaged, accorded well with Germaine's ideas – a five-man directorate, a cabinet, a bicameral legislature, and suffrage limited to property-owners, that is, the rich. The only feature that was a worry was the requirement to hold elections, at a time when the monarchists might revive. It was in trying to think their way out of this that Benjamin began his career as a political thinker.

Germaine meanwhile had now formed a new relationship with the Chevalier de Pange, a young cavalry officer and a classmate of André Chénier.[21] He was a thoughtful soul who, when the Revolution turned violent, condemned the violence but not the Revolution. He admired Germaine but did not reciprocate her passion, nor could he stop the groundswell of emotion that turned against her towards the end of 1795, when many thought that she was the intriguer-in-chief, or conspirator-in-chief, and that her salon was a hotbed of suspect ideas – this despite the impeccable roster of its members. At the end of the year, she was ordered out of France again and returned to Coppet with Benjamin. 'The universe is in France,' she wrote to de Pange after a few weeks, 'outside it, there is nothing.'[22]

During the winter that followed, everyone at Coppet was writing – Germaine was working on the *Passions* and Benjamin on *The Strength of the Present Government in France and the Necessity of Supporting It*, and Jacques Necker was writing on religious morality.

Feeling in France was turning more and more against Germaine. In April 1796 the French minister of police signed a warrant for her arrest if she set foot on French soil. She was not one to take this lying down. She despatched Benjamin to Paris with a consignment of copies of her new book, *On the Influence of the Passions*. It was in this work that she distinguished two types of happiness – happiness as it is desired, and happiness such as can be achieved. Her most original point is that to reach happiness one's passions must pass through a 'sublimated' stage in which, for example, love becomes friendship 'or conjugal tenderness', and love of glory must be transmuted into religion. Otherwise, happiness is too great a burden.

This was not a great intellectual success; nonetheless, she expected great things of it, and she was not disappointed. All her friends in Paris did indeed rally round – Suard, Chénier and the economist Pierre-Louis Roederer – so that the government relented, allowing her to reside in France provided she remained at least 8 leagues (about 20 miles) from Paris.

At this time, she was never not surrounded by a bevy of bright young men. One visitor who called on her said that at no time did she have fewer than fifteen persons in her room.[23] Noise again.

THE EMPEROR OF MATTER AND THE EMPRESS OF MIND

If Germaine had died in 1799, she would be remembered, if at all, as 'a curious period piece'. Her writings, before 1800, despite flashes of brilliance, would be worth barely a footnote. But in December

1797 she met Napoleon for the first time. As one of her biographers (there have been at least forty-four) says: 'Napoleon happened to Germaine.' He had just returned from the campaign in Italy where he had negotiated a victorious peace which had changed the face of Europe, and Talleyrand had arranged a grand reception at the foreign ministry. As Talleyrand later recalled, Napoleon didn't pay much attention to Germaine but she paid a lot of attention to him and, as another biographer tells us, 'there can be no question that, at least until 1800, Germaine wooed Bonaparte and praised him hyperbolically ... Doubtless, she felt that the greatest living man and the greatest living woman owed it as a duty to humanity to conjoin in spirit and, if at all possible, also in the flesh.'[24]

Napoleon thought the idea repulsive. He had once been impressed by her father but even that would change as time passed. Germaine sought glory, he told others, but had achieved only notoriety.

His hostility collided with her intransigent resistance, producing a fourteen-year duel between – as Sainte-Beuve was to say – the Emperor of Matter and the Empress of Mind, where the emperor ended up with no matter and, which is what counts, the empress's mind was broadened and sharpened. 'Her struggle with Napoleon made her the Conscience of Europe; her equally relentless fight to dominate the men she loved made her its spectacle.'[25] It was in these years that she wrote her three 'epoch-making' works – On Literature, Corinne and On Germany.

THE SIGNIFICANCE OF LITERATURE

In these works, she founded – or helped to found – a new sensibility, romanticism, often seen as a reaction against the Enlightenment. But this is somewhat to mischaracterise her. She was herself – and wanted others to be – a product of intellectualism and rationalism, combining politics, morality and a philosophy of history which would lead to liberal idealism.[26]

Above all, Germaine was no narrow French nationalist, much as she loved Paris. She readily bought into the idea – derived from Voltaire and Montesquieu – that France could learn from other nations, England and Germany in particular. She was as assiduous as anyone in advocating the idea of progress, much more practically minded than her father and, in truth, far more of a child of the Enlightenment than her reputation for romanticism makes her appear.

In the French manner, she regarded literature as the most significant record of the evolution of the human spirit, though she felt that progress was most visible in the sciences.[27] She grasped that civilisations passed through stages, from epic poetry and mythology to ethics and philosophy, and then to science. Christianity, she conceded, had introduced the idea of equal dignity of all human beings. Christianity stressed sympathy rather than strength. She was among the first to reject the idea that the Middle Ages were dark. She distinguished between the serene, brilliant, light-hearted south, and the cloudy, gloomy, meditative, striving, melancholy north. Absolutism encourages the fine arts, poetry, music and architecture but discourages philosophy, ethics and history. The court stifled originality and enthusiasm.

Whatever one's attitude to Germaine's views, her way of thinking was original and modern. 'It is the task of writers to serve the development of all generous ideas.' Scientific progress makes moral progress a necessity for if man's power is increased, the checks that restrain him from abusing that power must be strengthened too.[28] She did not deny that the Enlightenment inspired the Revolution. At the same time, some of her specific literary judgements were unfortunate.[29] She never fully appreciated Condorcet.

In 1799, she returned to Paris without authorisation. It was the very day that Napoleon overthrew the government by having his troops charge the Council of Five Hundred with bayonets. The Council of Five Hundred was the lower house of the Directory, and it was after this that Napoleon mounted his coup d'état and appointed himself ruler of France as first consul. Within a few weeks, Germaine's salon was again up and running in all its former glory, and Benjamin was in the government, appointed by Napoleon to the Tribunate, a sort of senate of oligarchs, which debated the government's proposals and made recommendations. All went well for two years, at which point Napoleon vowed he would 'crush' Germaine. Within another twelve months she was back in exile.

Her 'Elusive and Dangerous' Salon

Her salon was not, as she understood it at least, a rallying point of opposition to Napoleon's regime but merely a sounding board of public opinion. It was open to all convictions, and therefore could not be seen as a threat. If her salon (in the rue de Grenelle) had been the meeting place of an opposition party, the first consul need not have feared her (and Napoleon famously thought fear the most important emotion in politics). However, it was something much more 'elusive and dangerous'. The most prominent of Mme de Staël's regular guests were taken not from Napoleon's political enemies but from among his own ministers, officials, generals, even his own family. For Napoleon, it was unnerving.[30]

This was shown by the fact that, on 5 January 1800, Benjamin was due to make his maiden speech, on a government-sponsored initiative that would require the Tribunate to discuss each proposed law on a fixed day. This was too much, too rigid, for both him and Germaine, and together they drafted his speech, 'a sharp blast' against the government. On 4 January, the eve of his speech, there was a brilliant gathering in her unnerving salon which included half the government and several members of Bonaparte's own family. At one point, Benjamin took Germaine aside and whispered: 'Tonight your drawing room is filled with people whom you like. If I make my speech, it will be deserted tomorrow.'

Germaine responded: 'One must follow one's convictions.'

Next day, Benjamin accused the government of 'presenting its propositions to us on a wing, in the hope that we shall be unable to catch them', winding up with the sentiment that without an independent Tribunate, 'there would be nothing left but servitude and silence – a silence that all Europe would hear'.

That night Germaine had planned a sumptuous dinner in Benjamin's honour. By five o'clock she had received ten notes telling her that her guests had found something better to do. Napoleon, we are told, that night gave one of his first exhibitions 'of calculated rage'. 'There are, in the Tribunate,' he railed, 'twelve or fifteen metaphysicians fit to be drowned. They are vermin I carry on my clothes, but I shall shake them off.' He was backed up by opportunists everywhere, many of whom saw Germaine as equally culpable as Benjamin. An editorial in the pro-Jacobin *Journal des hommes libres* said of her: 'It is not your fault that you are ugly, but it is your fault that you are an intriguer ... You know the road to Switzerland ... Take your Benjamin with you.'[31]

A Great Bad Novel

Exiled once more in Switzerland, she was reunited with her children, one of whose teachers was a German pastor. Bored by being away from Paris, she used the pastor's presence to start learning German, and began her novel *Delphine*, three volumes, and then, three years later, *Corinne*. The themes of these books revolve around extraordinary women in society, how women are less able to impose themselves *on* society, how men are less capable of love than women, always remaining under the influence *of* society, which in the end kills the relationship.

Her switchback life continued, for while this was going on Napoleon had passed through Geneva and met her father, who persuaded the first consul to let her back to Paris. Still she didn't learn. Everything that was said in her salon – revived for a second time – reached Napoleon's ears. This is when Mme de Genlis acted as Napoleon's 'special agent' or, as some people have conjectured, his 'spy'. Having lost her husband and fortune in the Revolution, Mme de Genlis continued to write but, unlike Germaine and Benjamin, never criticised Napoleon, instead turning to him for support. In return, he provided her with an apartment in the Arsenal Library and a pension of 6,000 francs a year, and required her to write him regular letters.[32]

Delphine was an instant success. This did not endear Germaine to Napoleon, who took the extraordinary step of having a digest made of the book and then penning an anonymous review of it in the *Journal des débats* in which he damned it for its 'dangerous principles' and 'total lack of a moral aim'.[33]

Set in the early years of the Revolution, the story of *Delphine* focuses on the virtues of a woman, pitted against the weakness of a man. Delphine is a dazzling conversationalist, but her superiority is not that of the intellect but of the heart, *à la* Rousseau. All the mistakes she makes, the ruin she brings on herself, are occasioned by her (too) generous nature, her (too) passionate convictions, her (too) naïve trust. She loves Léonce de Mondoville, who has one characteristic flaw – he is too easily swayed by public opinion, too confined in an artificial code of honour. 'Instead of relying solely on his own reason and heart, as Rousseau taught, he looks on himself with the eyes of others.'[34]

Through a series of adventures, Delphine is persuaded to enter a convent and take holy vows. Léonce searches her out but then drops her, too influenced by what others think, and enlists in the army, where he is captured even before joining his unit and sentenced to death for a crime he did not commit. Delphine catches up with him, to no avail, and commits suicide on the execution ground.

The book is a savage attack on the culture of the *ancien régime* but also on marriage unsanctified by love, and it is an argument for the rights of women. Despite its Revolutionary setting, it was an obvious criticism of the reforms that Napoleon was trying to bring about, in particular his attempt to make women 'stick to their knitting'. One critic summed up *Delphine* in this way: 'There are great bad novels, and there are worthless good novels; Germaine's belong to the former category.'[35]

There is in *Delphine* a long portrait of Benjamin (as Henri de Lebensei), showing him as having a 'kind of savage and proud timidity [which] often makes him taciturn in company'. His main qualities, she said, which she admired, were truthfulness and kindness. By then their relationship had been platonic for years. In his own diary, Benjamin confessed he had felt no love for Germaine 'for a long time now ... I need a being whom I can protect, who will follow me, whom I can hold in my arms, whom I can make happy without effort.'[36]

The tenseness of her situation was getting to Germaine and it was now that she began taking opium, on which she subsequently became increasingly dependent. Moreover, Benjamin felt she had developed the knack of persuading others that 'anyone else's unhappiness was negligible beside hers'.[37]

IN GERMANY

Constantly irritated by her situation in France, in 1801 Germaine decided on a visit to Germany. Her literary fame was such that, in 1797, Goethe had sent her a magnificently bound copy of *Wilhelm Meister's Apprenticeship*. Though touched, she openly admitted that all she could intelligently admire was the spine. After taking up German with her pastor, since 1800 she had been familiarising herself with many German travellers in Paris, when even Wilhelm von Humboldt had helped her. By 1801, according to him, she could read – but not converse – in German.

In Frankfurt, Goethe's mother reported to her son that 'she oppressed me like a millstone'.[38] Weimar was different, however, Germaine being moved 'by the indefinable poetic atmosphere ... that interior life, that poetry of the soul, which characterises the German people', though she thought there was a strange contradiction 'between the elevation of the Germans' thoughts and the vulgarity of their forms'.

She finally did meet up with Goethe, and with Schiller and Wieland, who she got on with best. But the difference between the French and German approaches was nicely summed up by Goethe, who wrote: 'To philosophise in a social setting [a salon] means to indulge in lively conversation on insoluble problems ... Quite naturally, she usually carried speech and repartee to matters of thought and feeling which by right should never be discussed except between an individual and his God ... Because of all this the evil genius in me was provoked, and whatever subject came up, I addressed myself to it in a spirit of contradiction ... My obstinate contrariness often drove her to despair. But it was then that she was at her most amiable and that she displayed her mental and verbal agility most brilliantly.' Schiller said that she had no sense for poetry as he and Goethe understood it.[39]

From Weimar she travelled to Leipzig and then Berlin. She met Fichte and the Schlegel brothers, one of whom, August Wilhelm, fell in love with her and would become part of her entourage (he was famous as a brilliant translator of Shakespeare, but he was poor). She was called back from Germany because her father was dangerously ill. He died before she could reach him. When told, she collapsed and it took her nine days before she was well enough to carry on.

GREAT DAYS AT COPPET

The years 1804 to 1810 were 'the great days at Coppet'. 'Her house at Coppet', said Napoleon when he was on St Helena, 'became a veritable arsenal against me. One went there to win one's spurs.' In fact, it was not all about Napoleon, much as he might like to think it was. It has been described as a permanent seminar and debating club, a laboratory of ideas, where 'talking seemed to be everyone's chief business'.[40] Despite the fact that opium, which Germaine took like we might take sleeping pills, left her 'stupefied for days', she wrote plays to be performed, and in many she gave a leading role to Juliette Récamier, on account of her great beauty (chapter 26).

During these great days, Germaine was still collecting lovers and Benjamin was still frequenting brothels. She seems not to have been bothered by these regular visits, assiduously recorded in his diary where the sign ± indicated sexual intercourse. Her umpteenth lover was Dom Pedro de Sousa e Holstein, future Duke of Palmela and prime minister of Portugal. He combined nobility and sensitivity and was a considerable poet, while conforming to Germaine's requirement in a lover: 'It is a statistical fact that Germaine only fell in love with aristocrats.'[41] Germaine swept Dom Pedro away to Naples, where they were both excited by their age difference – he was twenty-four, she thirty-nine. For three weeks they savoured the heavy scent of the flowers in the soft, warm evenings, and explored Vesuvius, Pompeii and Herculaneum, much of it on horseback.[42]

Moving on to Rome, they did their best to maintain what they had. Germaine gave him short verses, in the manner of the time, but she knew they were not contemporaries and that that would come to count, more for him than for her. So, after she gave him a ring, they parted.

Corinne, her next book, based on her time in Italy, came out shortly after. It is, in the words of one critic, 'the worst great novel ever written – ineptly plotted, hysterical, and romantic in a ludicrous sense. Yet it is the product of an extraordinary mind, relentlessly intense.' Corinne is an idealised Germaine, an improviser in life and a would-be poetess. Oswald is a melancholy traveller from the north, by no means enamoured to begin with of the warm, sensuous Roman scene. But she shows him the *campagna*, explains its history and its beauty to him, and his reserve melts under her eloquence and the fact that she is at the centre of a brilliant society. She proposes a romantic trip to Cape Miseno, beyond Naples, where their secrets begin to leak out and melodramatic coincidences begin to afflict the story.[43] Oswald was intended to be married to an English girl, Lucile Edgermond, who happens to be Corinne's half-sister. Marriage plans for her collapsed when her father died and she escaped to Italy, spreading a rumour that she too is dead, and with her independent fortune she starts a new life as a poetess.

As in real life, Corinne (Germaine) loves Oswald (all the men in her life) more than he loves her. Oswald returns to England and to Lucile. Corinne follows, incognito, and watches their love in secret. Oswald is genuinely torn between the two – between duty and desire – which is one of the main themes of the book. But Corinne – implausibly to many critics – maintains her silence, does not approach Oswald, and dies in despair. This bald summary leaves out many wild and sentimental scenes, which accounted for the great success of the book, and the many criticisms.

The press denounced *Corinne* as anti-French, but the public were taken by its sentimental and romantic aspects. Napoleon declared it 'junk'. On St Helena, he tried to read it again, but said he was unable to finish it, though he added later: 'I want to see how it ends, for I still think that it is an interesting work.'[44]

While Germaine was finishing *Corinne*, Benjamin had begun a novel of his own, *Adolphe*. As the writing progressed, the heroine, Ellénore, began more and more to resemble Germaine. He did not publish the book for some years, but he did read it to Germaine. Her reaction, we are told, was 'fulminating', and went on for hours and days. At one point, according to his diary, he coughed blood.

The 'Silence' of France

At the end of December 1807, Germaine asked her son Auguste, then seventeen, to approach Napoleon as he passed through Chambéry in Savoy, not so very far from Geneva. The boy was shown into Bonaparte's presence as he was just finishing breakfast. Auguste had come to make two applications: that his mother be allowed back into Paris to live, and that she be repaid the 2 million livres her father, Jacques Necker, had loaned the state on the eve of the Revolution. On both counts Napoleon was implacable. He accused Necker of being responsible for the overthrow of the monarchy. In regard to his mother, Auguste pleaded that all she wanted from Paris was her friends and literature. Taking him by the earlobe, according to some accounts, the first consul remarked: 'Literature, is it? I won't be taken in by this. You can make politics by talking literature, morality, arts, anything ... Women should stick to knitting.'[45]

Of course, far from knitting, Germaine was still writing. Of all her writings, *On Germany* created the greatest contemporary interest. Like Voltaire's *Letters Concerning the English Nation*, the book is a protest against the suppression of intellectual freedom in France and a largely successful attempt to revitalise French life by the injection of fresh ideas from abroad. Like Tocqueville's *On Democracy in America*, its aim is to interpret an entire culture and to highlight for a complacent public the very different direction taken by a new nation – because in some ways that was what Mme de Staël's Germany was. It also had a polemical intent as she tried to embarrass Napoleon and her fellow countrymen over 'the silence' that had overcome France and which Benjamin had been the first to lament.[46]

German critics of the book have complained that her treatment of their philosophy was lightweight, and that she didn't fully grasp the main aim of German literature or idealism. In many places she went easy on Germany for her own, anti-Napoleonic purposes. Even so, the book was and is an extraordinary achievement. It was divided into four parts, over three volumes. Part One has been described as a thinly veiled satire on France, as she explores the institutions of Germany and the country's mores, espousing the view that the precious French language is actually less suited to poetry than German. She defends *Naturphilosophie* and even mysticism at the expense of English (and to an extent French) utilitarian philosophy, and the application of the empirical method to social/moral problems. It is in this book that she enthusiastically espouses romanticism, perhaps her most enduring legacy. Part Two explores the arts and literature, Part Three philosophy and ethics, and Part Four religion and 'enthusiasm', an old preoccupation of hers.

Not everything German was to her taste. She deplored the lack of conversation, of good critical standards and what she thought was the absence of social cohesion. She thought that the German taste for abstraction was a possible threat to liberty, and she was surprised by the 'warlike atmosphere of Germany, where one sees soldiers everywhere'.[47]

In her final chapter, she concluded that what the Germans had above all, and what the French had lost, 'was the faculty of enthusiasm', by which she meant 'the vivifying force of the generous emotions', the force that had created Goethe, Beethoven, Herder, Frederick the Great and *his* enthusiasms. In the past, she concluded, Germany had learned from France. Now, France could learn from Germany.

Napoleon had installed an office of censorship in 1810. Germaine's publisher submitted the first volumes of the book to the censorship office, which approved them with only minor changes, which Germaine accepted. Volume 3 was to prove more troublesome. Parts were read out in the salons of the Faubourg Saint-Germain and the news soon reached Bonaparte. By now Joseph Fouché, minister of police, had been dismissed, to be replaced by René Savary, a different animal entirely. Germaine's publisher had gone ahead and printed 5,000 copies of each of the first two volumes, obviously enough at considerable expense. While she was herself travelling, the authorities caught up with her, via her son Auguste, who informed her that Savary was insisting she must leave, 'within forty-eight hours', for one of the Atlantic ports and there await passage to the United States. She was also ordered to surrender all proofs and manuscripts of her book.

She did, in the event, surrender one copy of the manuscript, which she said was the only one. She wrote to the censor and to Napoleon, asking them to read the book, to prove that there was nothing that they need fear. There was a great deal of toing and froing, horseback travel through the night, letters criss-crossing, deletions to the text. Napoleon did read the book and wanted many passages – especially those 'exalting England' – suppressed. The text was described as 'un-French'.

And then, in October 1810, a detachment of gendarmes surrounded the plant in Lyons where the book was being printed, destroyed the type that had been set up, seized all the copies already printed and carried them away.[48]

Germaine did not go to America but hurried back to Coppet. On the way she passed through Dijon, which was filled with Spanish prisoners of war in torn uniforms. As Germaine herself summed up in her memoirs: 'Nothing can convey to the few free nations that remain on this earth the complete absence of security which was the normal condition of all human creatures under Napoleon's Empire.'[49]

Since Napoleon, the world has known much worse than him but, for its time, 1810 was a nightmare. War seemed permanent; it had gone on for eighteen years, stretching from Spain to Poland, Amsterdam to Corfu; French soldiers were garrisoned seemingly everywhere, demanding tribute and 'imposing the will of one man'. Bonaparte created state prisons, where people were held without trial, drastic new censorship laws were introduced, the church was deprived of its independence and even the Pope was arrested.[50]

Germaine and Napoleon were never reconciled. She remained in exile in Coppet, telling Juliette Récamier that 'exile is a tomb where you can get post'.[51] But her book did appear in England in 1813. She had lied about there being only one manuscript – of course she had – and another was smuggled first to Berne.

THE FIRST WOMAN OF EUROPE

At the time, however, Germaine had a new interest. John Rocca, half her age, was quite unlike Benjamin Constant. Extremely handsome, and very virile and sporty, he climbed, he swam, he hunted and he sought danger. In the romantic idiom of the time, he had run away from his Geneva family and enlisted in the army. He had fought in several wars, been riddled with bullets in Spain and had his horse shot from under him. By the time he met Germaine, he could not walk without crutches. He fell passionately in love with her and though she found his mind uncultured (she once remarked to a friend to whom he had offered an inanity, 'Ah! Words are not his language'), she did succumb, however dull he might be, and in August 1812, found herself pregnant, at the age of forty-six. By now she was haggard, and her skin sallow. She was regularly prescribed digitalis (commonly foxglove, used for heart conditions). Later, in April of the next year, she gave birth to a son who – it was soon clear – was mentally disabled and was sent away.

During her pregnancy she had been jeered at in public in Geneva. She embarked on extensive travels, taking in Russia and England, where she was feted and described in the press as 'the First Woman of Europe'.[52] About six weeks after her arrival, however, came the news that her son Albert had been killed in a duel. She received the news after an evening at Covent Garden. 'Although her son's death undoubtedly stunned and shocked her, she showed no such signs of convulsive despair as at her father's death.'[53]

PARIS OCCUPIED

In the tumult of events leading up to Napoleon's fall and the Restoration, both Germaine and Benjamin played minor but significant roles. Benjamin was close to Marshal Jean-Baptiste Bernadotte, one of Napoleon's most effective generals, who was surprisingly offered the throne of Sweden in 1810 and might have been made king of France also. Benjamin now wrote what many consider his most brilliant book, *On the Spirit of Conquest and on Usurpation*, which was vehement in its attacks on Napoleon, the empire and the military culture that the Napoleonic wars had fostered in France.

After Napoleon arrived in Paris, Benjamin first took refuge in the American embassy, and then fled Paris altogether. To everyone's surprise, however, and no doubt to his own and Napoleon's as well, he returned to Paris within three weeks and even agreed to work in Napoleon's new administration. He had a personal meeting with Bonaparte and confessed that the general was, as he put it, 'an astonishing man' and later set to work on drafting a new constitution.

The best-known elements of Constant's liberal principles are his defence of individual liberties, the assurance of free expression, and the protection of all means of providing individuals with access to political representation. In addition to Montesquieu's separation of powers, and diametrically opposed to Hobbes, Constant added the idea that there must be a *balance* of power between the different arms of government.

He observed that there were two stages to revolutions. The first was when the old order was overthrown, and the second occurred 'when by means of an artificial prolongation of a movement no longer nationwide, there is an attempt to destroy everything contrary to the viewpoint of a few'. He noted that the English and American revolutions had stopped at the moderate first stage and were the better for it.[54]

Events overtook him, as they overtook Germaine. Napoleon, in his long retreat after his failed invasion of Russia, in 1812, was faced with what became known as the Sixth Coalition – Russia, Austria, Prussia, Great Britain, Sweden and Spain. Even though the French had won the early skirmishes, they and the Pro-French German Confederation of the Rhine had collapsed after the Battle of Leipzig, in the autumn of 1813, and the tsar had driven on. His forces had been sceptical at first but then found, once inside north-east France, that the population was war-weary, and it suddenly became clear to the tsar that his main objective should be to enter Paris rather than chase Napoleon.

Napoleon had left his brother Joseph in defence of the city but his forces of between 20,000 and 30,000 were no match for the coalition's 150,000 and more. The fighting lasted barely a day, Joseph Bonaparte fled, and Talleyrand gave the keys of the city to the tsar. Six days later, Napoleon abdicated and went into exile. More than that, Talleyrand, Germaine's first lover, persuaded the tsar and the Senate to proclaim the restoration of Louis XVIII. Germaine, who was now free at last to return to Paris, wrote to her son: 'All London is drunk with joy.'

A Salon of Sixty

Germaine de Staël had not been in Paris properly, so to speak, since 1802, but her old life resumed. In her salon in her apartment at Clichy, the names were bigger than ever: the tsar himself, Wellington,

Bernadotte, Canning, Talleyrand, Fouché, Lafayette. One visitor said he found sixty people in the house at one time.

Benjamin found her changed. 'She is absent-minded, almost arid, thinking only of herself, listening little to what others say, caring for nothing, not even for her daughter, except from a sense of duty – and for me, not at all.'[55]

The news of Napoleon's escape – conveyed by the recently invented telegraph – shocked all Paris. The newly installed king fled to Belgium, and Germaine returned quickly again to Coppet. Benjamin – most astonishing of all – wrote a 'fervently pro-Bourbon' article for the *Journal des débats*, offering to risk his life 'to repulse the tyrant'. He fled, first to the American embassy, which gave him a passport, then to Angers, where he changed his mind, returned to Paris and visited Joseph Bonaparte, who made emollient noises. Two days later Benjamin gave Joseph an article he had written *supporting* Napoleon, which was published anonymously in the *Journal de Paris*. Several meetings with the emperor followed, after which Benjamin was appointed to the Conseil d'État, charged again with drafting a new constitution.

That evening he read his novel *Adolphe* at the salon of Juliette Récamier. Victor de Broglie, Germaine's son-in-law, was there. 'We were about a dozen or fifteen of us, listening,' he later wrote. 'The reading had lasted almost three hours ... As he approached the end, his emotion increased and his fatigue increased his emotion. At the end he could not contain himself; he broke into sobs. The entire audience, itself very moved, was caught by contagion. The room was filled with sobs and groans. Then, suddenly ... the convulsive sobs turned into peals of hysterical, irrepressible laughter.'

When *Adolphe* was published in London, 'all Europe immediately identified its heroine with Madame de Staël'.[56] She didn't mind, although his picture was hardly flattering. In the novel, Adolphe falls in love with a much older woman and their love isolates them from their friends and their social world. The story is driven not by real-life events but by the intensity of the couple's internal life.

'If Napoleon wins,' Germaine said, on learning that he had landed in the south of France, at the beginning of the Hundred Days, 'liberty is done for; if he loses, national independence is done for.' But

Napoleon by this time knew that he needed the support of liberal opinion – hence his overture to Benjamin. And both Fouché and Joseph Bonaparte hinted that Germaine might now get back the 2 million her father had loaned the state all those years before.

Germaine still had enthusiasm enough to form a new salon in the rue Royale, where she rented a new apartment, and completed *Considerations on the French Revolution*. Her salon was still rated as the most brilliant in all Paris.[57]

Benjamin thought otherwise. He had fallen in love – as had so many others – with Juliette Récamier. For twelve or thirteen years he had known her, without the least 'flutterings' of love. But a belated thunderbolt had struck him on the evening of 31 August 1814 and 'was to deprive him of his wits for fourteen months', when he recovered from his infatuation as abruptly as he had succumbed to it. During the interim he had lost all hold on himself, gambling at times through the night, enduring crying fits, visiting prostitutes.

On 21 February 1817, Germaine attended a reception given by Élie, Duc Decazes, Louis XVIII's chief minister. Walking up the stairs, she swayed and fell. De Broglie caught her before she could hit the ground and she was taken home. Her eyes were open, but she could not speak or move – she had suffered a stroke. For ninety days she lay flat on her back and her speech was recovered after a fashion. People came to visit her, including Chateaubriand and the Duc d'Orléans, and, to an extent, when she was transferred to a wheelchair, her salon continued. But then gangrene infected her body. The day after she died, in July 1817, she had been expecting the Duke of Wellington. She was fifty-one.

Benjamin would live on for more than another decade, much of it spent in the salon of Juliette Récamier.

Napoleon Spurned

Juliette Récamier, who shared a good friendship with Germaine de Staël, became a fellow exile and spent considerable amounts of time at Coppet, was very different from her in certain ways. For a start, she was extremely attractive – seductive even – qualities that come across directly in her portraits by David and Gérard. Scores of men fell in love with her, even Napoleon, and though she charmed most men into giving up hope of ever capturing her heart, the first consul never forgave her and, on that account, refused to help out her husband when he went bankrupt in 1806.

She had been born, as Juliette Bernard, in Lyons in December 1777, eleven years after Germaine. Her father was a notary and her mother, described as flirtatious and '*singulièrement jolie*', had an ambitious head for business.[1] Juliette was brought up by her mother 'to play some great part in the world' and was present at all her parties. She was given a convent education (which she loved) and was taught the piano, the harp and singing.[2] The family moved to Paris when her father was given the job of *receveur des finances* by Charles Alexandre de Calonne, comptroller-general to Louis XVI and, as we have seen, a rival of Jacques Necker. This favour came about because Calonne was probably one of Juliette's mother's lovers.

Her parents enjoyed Paris to the full, taking a box at the theatre and giving opulent parties. Juliette, then aged eleven, was an enthusiastic reader, in English and Italian as well as French. And, Lucy Moore says, 'she submitted to her mother's assiduous attention to her toilette', and was always dressed in 'elegant, expensive clothes', with her hair carefully curled. On a visit to Versailles, even the queen remarked on her beauty.

One person who had long remarked on her beauty was Jacques-Rose Récamier, a regular visitor to the Bernard household. He was a tall, blond man with great classical learning, a number of Revolutionary friends and a taste for the *demi-monde*, all in all a 'butterfly man about town'.[3] Despite this, the execution of the king shook him. He forced himself to watch as the blade of the guillotine 'kissed' the royal neck so as to prepare himself, as he thought, for a similar fate in the not-too-distant future. Despite this, in the wake of the king's death, and before the Parisian women began rioting over rising bread prices, and just as the Jacobin repression was being born, he showered Juliette with presents, sweets and 'the most beautiful dolls', before making an offer.[4] He was accepted in serial order. First, Juliette's mother gave her consent, then her father – and finally, Juliette herself. He was forty-two, she was fifteen.

The age disparity may not have been the most awkward part of the relationship. Récamier had been a close friend of the family before Juliette was born and admitted to 'tender feelings' towards Mme Bernard, who was, after all, *'singulièrement jolie'*.[5] It is not known whether the daughter was aware of all this, but it would certainly explain, in an ironical way, the comment, widely recounted, that she was so chaste 'she would not even sleep with her husband'. On the other hand, she later asked her husband for a divorce in order to marry someone else, so that suggests there was nothing wrong with her physically.

A VIOLET IN THE GRASS

As the Reign of Terror began, and women started giving their children Revolutionary names such as 'Civilisation', 'Cérès' or 'Phytogneâtrope' ('mother of warriors'), Récamier began buying up abandoned or confiscated aristocratic property. In the chaos of revolution, there were still fortunes to be made. This is an often-overlooked aspect of those times. The bank that he started was just then the strongest in the capital.[6]

Benjamin Constant, Germaine's great friend, was one of the first to remark on Juliette's arrival on the Paris social scene. Also a good friend of Thérésia Tallien – another famous beauty, with her own salon notable for its music, and who had a brief flirtation with Napoleon – he commented in 1796 that the exquisite Thérésia had 'reigned in peace until Juliette had appeared'. Not that there was overt rivalry to begin with – quite the contrary. For a time, Juliette and Thérésia moved in the same circles as Joséphine de Beauharnais. Juliette even took part in a tableau alongside Joséphine and Thérésia at a reception at the Luxembourg celebrating Napoleon's victories over Italy.[7] They attended the same balls, watched the same plays, and 'were dressed by the same couturiers and admired by the same men'. Their subsequent rift may have been caused by Thérésia's resentment at Juliette's undoubted success.[8]

By late 1797, says Moore, the 'careless gaiety' that had marked the first years since Robespierre's fall had faded. A new idol, freed from any taint of Revolutionary violence, was needed. The virginal Juliette, with her carefully nurtured image of modest chastity, seemed to fit the bill. An early portrait of her, by Joseph Ducreux, an aristocrat-turned-painter, had been widely admired in the Salon of 1796. Her modest dress at balls compared well with the *déshabillé* of Mme Hamelin, another beautiful seductress.[9] This is where Juliette evolved her famous '*danse du schall*' ('shawl dance'), which Germaine was to immortalise in *Corinne*.

Her quiet piety, the charitable works she lavished attention on, also met the mood of the day, as did her growing flair as a hostess. Always 'radiantly pale', her face bare of make-up, invariably in white dresses, with only pearls as jewellery – to enhance her chestnut curls – she was described by one admirer as 'like a violet in the grass'. In truth, says Cynthia Gladwyn, she was an outrageous coquette, 'completely lacking the flame of passion'. Very conscious of her powers of seduction, Juliette never pretended to be intellectual, and both 'enjoyed and despised' her celebrity. This tension showed when she stood up to get a better view of Napoleon as he finished a speech at a reception given in his honour at the Luxembourg in December 1797. Every head in the room turned to look at Juliette and 'a rumble of appreciation' swelled through the audience. 'For a moment it was she and not Napoléon on whom all eyes rested.' He 'threw her a look of intolerable harshness'.[10]

She met Germaine when her husband took her to a house he was intending to buy and then left the two women alone without introducing them, saying only that Germaine was there to talk about the sale of the property. When conversation began, Germaine said how delighted she was to meet Juliette at last and then went on to mention her father, Jacques Necker. Juliette was flabbergasted. Germaine, she knew, was supposed to be in exile but here she was in Saint-Ouen. She stammered out her compliments, and Germaine responded warmly with fond praise about Juliette's beauty. It was the start of a friendship that was typical of the intense female emotional relationships which characterised that age and were a way for women to enjoy intensity when it was riskier with a man, at a time when contraception was crude and imperfect.

The house which Jacques Récamier bought from Necker was at 7 rue de Mont-Blanc and under Juliette it would become one of the most celebrated salonnières in Paris. The interior, we are told, was a masterpiece of Directory style (that is, mainly neoclassical), designed by Louis Bertaut and assembled by the Jacob brothers (sons of Georges, Marie Antoinette's furniture-maker), who had fitted out the newly wed Bonapartes' house the previous year. Within it, Juliette entertained lavishly. In these, her 'frivolous' years, she danced all night, went to masked balls and slept all day. Callers were curtly informed: 'It isn't yet daylight with Madame.'

Although the playwright Jean-François de La Harpe was one of the first to be received by her, many – in the early days – were bankers interested in forming firmer friendships with her husband. Camille Jordan was an early member of Juliette's salon, as were Talleyrand and Pierre-Louis Roederer, the professor of political economy introduced earlier. And of course, she was invited out herself to many of the other salons – of Mme Hamelin, Mme Roger and Mme Marmont.

After Bonaparte returned from Egypt, Juliette enlarged her list of visitors, among them Admiral Joachim Murat and Marshal Bernadotte, 'who generally interested himself in Mme Récamier', which gave her salon 'a slightly antagonistic air'.[11] And she became good friends with Mathieu de Montmorency. He, of course, had been good friends with Germaine de Staël and was a distinguished politician and soldier, as well as something of a *philosophe*. He had been a *maréchal de camp* and accompanied Louis XVIII in his hurried flight to Belgium during the Hundred Days.[12]

On the nights her salon was convened, the house was lit by thousands of the most expensive candles, and decorated with masses of shrubs and plants and Turkish carpets. As with the masked balls, so with her salon – inevitably she was in white, 'emblematic of her purity' as she alternated 'between diffidence and an almost roguish coquetry'.[13] She sometimes allowed herself to be persuaded to perform 'the shawl dance'. People would stand on chairs to get a better look. 'She had more need of being amused than of being loved.'[14]

Female guests were invited into her gold and violet bedroom, 'reckoned to be the most beautiful in Paris', the walls and bathroom panelled in mirrors, the bed made of mahogany and ormolu with large, gilded bronze swans at either end.[15] On one notable occasion Juliette retired to bed during a party and, like Louis XIV decades before her, she – 'completely undress'd and in bed' – was admired by a roomful of men.[16]

Next to her bedroom there was a daybed very similar to the one painted by David in 1800. Juliette didn't warm to David's portrait, perhaps because he successfully caught the 'uneasy balance' she maintained between passivity and provocation.[17]

In the summer of 1799, Lucien Bonaparte wrote to his brother urging him to return to France. Political change was needed. Moreover, he began gathering potential allies at Juliette's house. Later, he would claim that he orchestrated the coup of Brumaire with her in mind.[18] The situation was further complicated by the fact that, in May 1800, Lucien lost his wife. There followed a period in which he wrote thirty-three letters – more than a hundred pages – to Juliette, which turned up for sale at the hôtel Drouot, the Parisian auction house, in 1895. The letters were full of 'burning declarations' on Lucien's part, and complaints: 'I noticed tranquil indifference seated between us.'[19]

Juliette held him at bay for a year and her careful way of keeping her independence (she enjoyed pointing out to her friends the grammatical faults in Lucien's letters) make her actual involvement in the plot unlikely. But, since she was so close to Germaine, it is highly likely that Juliette was at least aware of the plot to overturn the Directory. Napoleon abandoned his post in Cairo, after several French victories, and reached Fréjus in early October. He hurried to Paris through adoring crowds.

The coup was completed on 19 Brumaire (10 November). Germaine had returned to Paris the previous day and received messengers in her salon with news every hour.[20]

The relations between Juliette and Lucien had turned. Sainte-Beuve nicely observed that Juliette had 'a wish to make everything stop in April'. At a dinner given by someone else, attended by Mme Tallien and Lucien, one guest, drunk on champagne, proposed to toast all the pretty women present. 'The suggestion was quickly carried out.' Then Lucien stood up and proposed to drink to 'the most beautiful of women'. Both Mme Tallien and Mme Récamier cast down their eyes and prepared to be toasted. 'Well, gentlemen!' said Lucien gently. 'Her name is Peace, the peace we desire so much.'[21]

Juliette's discomfiture didn't last, her situation being helped by Napoleon's particular views about manners. Now that he was in power, he was insistent that clothes be less revealing, that manners be gentler. Arms and bosoms were to be covered up, and starch and stiff silks returned to fashion. Juliette took up painting, receiving tuition from Hubert Robert, who had been imprisoned during the Revolution.

But for a time she did become more involved in politics. Benjamin Constant asked her to bring together Bernadotte and Jean-Victor Moreau, the French general, to see if they would unite against Bonaparte, and it would appear that a plot was mounted in 1802. It failed, Moreau decamped for America, and Joseph Fouché, minister of police, paid her a visit.[22] This was not the only time he visited her with much the same message of caution, and Juliette was eventually forced to make a hasty, unplanned visit to London. It was not entirely clear, however, whether she fled because the plot had been hatched in her salon or whether she was unnerved by the attentions Napoleon was beginning to show her. Either way, London took to her as enthusiastically as Paris had done – she went everywhere and met everyone, the hat she wore with a white veil that reached the ground attracting particular admiration in the newspapers.

BONAPARTE'S OTHER CAMPAIGN

With Napoleon's greater control of the government, following the Battle of Marengo, he felt more secure and in March 1804 his Civil Code became law. In some ways it seemed aimed at Germaine and Juliette. Women were given the status of legal minors throughout their existence on earth, passing from the custody of their father to that of their husband. In the new marriage vows, women were to 'obey' their husband, in cases of adultery women were always seen as the guilty party and in child custody tussles the law favoured the man. Secondary education was provided only for boys.

And it was now Napoleon began his pursuit of Juliette in earnest. He sent Fouché to confront her and promise her a position at court. She turned him down. Bonaparte countered by sending his sister to invite Juliette to visit her, whereupon she offered Juliette the position as her lady-in-waiting. She turned that down too. The sister also offered Juliette a box at the Théâtre-Français. She accepted that a couple of times but on each occasion she found Napoleon seated across from her, his opera glass trained not on the actors on stage but on her. Finally, Fouché was sent to her once more, this time offering her the position of lady-in-waiting to Napoleon himself. To refuse such a plum was unheard of but refuse she did.[23] And so, when Jacques Récamier went bankrupt, and sought help from the Bank of France, Napoleon refused to authorise a loan.[24]

In some ways, however, Juliette had the last laugh. She bore her reversal of fortune stoically, sold all her jewels (but was allowed to keep her horses) and continued with her charity work. When this leaked out, and partly out of contempt for Napoleon, *le tout* Paris made a point of calling on her to show support.

And she still had Coppet, where she was always welcome and where her friends included Constant, Mathieu and Adrien de Montmorency-Laval, Prosper de Barante, August Wilhelm Schlegel, the Swiss writer Charles-Victor de Bonstetten and, above all,

Chateaubriand. She continued to capture hearts but refused to give hers, save where Chateaubriand was concerned.

The Next Finest Intellect after Voltaire

The relationship between Juliette and François-René de Chateaubriand was as fascinating as that between Germaine and Benjamin Constant. At the height of their relationship, Chateaubriand arrived punctually at 3.00 p.m., when he had Juliette to himself for an hour. When the others arrived, they would find the chairs arranged in a circle, sometimes more than one circle, but the armchair on the left of the fireplace, directly opposite Juliette, was always reserved for René. It was Juliette who started the fashion for meeting at that early hour – in most other salons friends usually called in the evening. A few of the chosen would remain for dinner. Sometimes there was music or recitations by François-Joseph Talma, the renowned actor. When Mathieu de Montmorency-Laval was made a member of the Académie française, Juliette's salon became known as 'the antechamber to the Académie'.[25]

Chateaubriand said that Constant had the next finest intellect after Voltaire but in his dealings with Mme Récamier he scarcely showed it. The first time he met her he was talking to Germaine when Juliette came into the room. He was immediately smitten, even though he wouldn't see her again for some years, but he was, in any case, says one biographer, a grumbling lover – like her he had a melancholy nature – who could never stop disputing with the woman he was at the time in love with. And Mme Récamier, there is no doubt, was able to use her beauty to her advantage.

Benjamin had known Juliette for ten years without being attracted in a romantic or sexual way (much the same in his case, as we have also seen), but in his *Journal intime*, in 1814 (three years before Mme de Staël died), we find this: 'Madame has put it into her head to make me fall in love with her. I am forty-seven years old ... My life is topsy-turvy ... I am the most unhappy of men.' Later, his anguish grows: 'I find it impossible to discover whether I have made the slightest progress in her heart.'[26]

In many cases Mme Récamier did not reply to these ardent entreaties. As more than one observer noted, she was the perfect coquette, cold and calculating. Sometime later – much later – Benjamin even fought a duel over her. At the time he was so ill that he had to sit in a chair as he held his pistol.[27] There is something both magnificent and ridiculous about the whole matter of his love for her, and through it we begin to see a far from attractive side of Juliette, as several biographers (there have been at least twenty-one) have noted.

The one exception to this pattern was Chateaubriand. (Sainte-Beuve, that clever old critic, once said women should never fall in love with Voltaire, Rousseau, Goethe or Chateaubriand.) Portraits show a rather dashing figure, with wild, even Byron-esque dark hair flying in all directions, large piercing eyes, a prominent nose and sensuous lips.

After her reversal of fortunes, when Napoleon had refused to help out, Juliette retreated to the Abbaye-aux-Bois convent, where Chateaubriand described her apartment: 'A gloomy corridor separated two little rooms ... The bedroom contained a bookcase, a harp, a piano, a portrait of Madame de Staël and a view of Coppet at midnight. On the windowsills were pots of flowers. When, panting after having climbed three flights of stairs, I entered the cell at twilight, I was delighted. The windows looked upon the gardens of the Abbaye. Amidst the green verdure nuns walked and schoolgirls ran to and fro ...'[28]

In these rooms, readings were held, and verses recited. 'Everything, however, was subordinated to the disposition of Chateaubriand.'[29] He was, certainly, a most accomplished man in a wide range of activities, one of those figures who – far more than Benjamin Constant, for example – achieved a great deal in several walks of life, becoming the model for others in France (Claudel, Hugo, Lamartine, Malraux) who achieved a mixed career of literature and politics. In his history of the Enlightenment, the American historian Peter Gay says that Chateaubriand 'saw himself as the greatest lover, the greatest writer, and the greatest philosopher of his age'. Certainly, another biographer argues that 'for the first time Juliette had met a man who, instead of being interested in her, insisted on she being interested in him'.[30]

He was born in the northern port of Saint-Malo, the tenth of ten children, and was raised in the family's chateau at Combourg in Brittany. His father, a gloomy soul, had been a sea captain but had become a shop-owner and a trader in slaves. As a boy, René couldn't

decide whether to join the navy or become a priest and the sheer gloom
and solitude of his circumstances seem to have got to him. Although
he formed a firm friendship with his sister, Lucile, he attempted suicide with a hunting rifle, which thankfully failed to go off.

Educated in Rennes and Dinan, he did eventually join the navy,
being rapidly promoted to the rank of captain. In 1788, on the eve
of the Revolution, he visited Paris, where he met La Harpe, André
Chenier, poet and journalist, and Louis-Marcellin de Fontanes, poet
and translator of Pope, who was commissioned to write an *éloge* on
Washington by Napoleon. Like them, Chateaubriand was originally
sympathetic to the aims of the Revolution but, like them, as events
turned violent, he opted to leave France and chose to visit America.
This was to have fateful consequences, because René's colourful
accounts of the wildlife and geography that he encountered in the
United States, and the vivid style in which he reported his adventures,
were to help spark the romantic movement in France.

He did not publish *Voyage en Amérique* until 1826, but in that
book he says he arrived in Philadelphia in July 1791. From there he
visited New York, Boston and Lexington before taking a boat up the
Hudson River to Albany. He then followed the 'Mohawk Trail' up to
Niagara Falls, 'an enterprise for which I was equipped with nothing
but my imagination and courage'. He dined on 'a collation of fruit
and milk', bought a pair of horses, hired a Dutch guide who spoke
several Indian languages and 'set astonished eyes on the first savages I
had ever seen'. They were painted 'like sorcerers', with bodies half-na-
ked, 'ears slit, crows' feathers on their heads, and rings through their
noses'. He fell over the edge of a gorge and broke his arm and spent
weeks in recovery in the company of a Native American tribe. He
depicted their customs, and made a number of zoological and botanical descriptions.[31]

Although later on the accuracy of his colourful account was called
into question, the three novels he based on his experiences, *Atala*
(1801), *René* (1802) and *Les Natchez* (written in the 1790s but not
published until 1826), his 'captivating' description of the wilderness
he found in America, especially the Deep South, where he encountered forests untouched by man, were composed in a style unknown
before and it was this that helped spark the romantic movement.

But that was only the beginning of his career. After returning to France he joined the army of royalist émigrés in Koblenz, who were led by Louis Joseph de Bourbon, the Prince of Condé. He also got married, pressured by his family to wed a woman he did not love and to whom he had no intention of being faithful. Before much else could happen, however, he was seriously wounded at the Siege of Thionville, a major clash between royalist troops and the French Revolutionary Army, the one raised by the *levée en masse*, referred to earlier. Badly injured, he was taken first to Jersey then to England in exile.

His time in London was just as gloomy as his childhood had been. He had no money and was forced to give French lessons and perform translations.[32] Exile proved important in some ways, though, as he recovered from his injuries. Being at a distance from France, a France in which events had cost the lives of many of his friends and family, brought about a set of reflections which comprised *Essai sur les révolutions*, published in 1797. This did not do very well, though the reflective nature of the work brought about another, more consequential set of reflections, which would lead to his conversion back to the Catholic faith, around 1798.

In 1800, with the new century being born, Chateaubriand was allowed back into France under the amnesty offered to émigrés by Napoleon's Consulate, whereupon he became for a short time editor of the *Mercure de France* (then the arbiter of taste in French arts and letters, until Napoleon closed it down in 1811). Chateaubriand won more fame, however, for his book *Génie du christianisme* ('The Genius of Christianity'). Conceived and at least partly written while he was in exile, and at a distance from France, the book is a defence of Christianity, which had come under such an attack from both the *philosophes* and the anti-clerical Revolutionaries in the successive stages of the turmoil of the 1790s (he absolved Rousseau of this but condemned Voltaire). Divided into four parts, the book examines in a sympathetic way the evidence for the existence of God (proved *inter alia* by the marvels of nature) and the immortality of the soul (proved is the existence of conscience), but perhaps what really catches the eye was the sheer enthusiasm, the rich, sweeping style which he brought to his vivid accounts of Christian writings, music, architecture and

art – poetry, the bible, the psalms, the fabulous paintings and buildings of the Middle Ages, the passions of the church, its orders and
notions of chivalry, the feelings which the faith aroused in so many
people and in so many ways. One critic observed that the book's main
strength was its 'grandeur', which kindled in a whole new generation
a renewed interest in the distant past of the church's epic narrative. It
too was one of the foundations of the romantic movement. Napoleon,
who had just signed his concordat with the Pope, originally used the
book to enlist the support of French Catholics but before long the
two men fell out and Chateaubriand was, like Germaine de Staël and
Juliette Récamier, sent into internal exile.

During the rest of his life, after Napoleon fell and the Restoration
had come about, Chateaubriand was in and out of favour in the
corridors of power, and in and out of diplomatic postings. He was
ambassador to Prussia in 1821, to the United Kingdom a year later,
and minister of foreign affairs from 1822 to 1824.

A fervent, very public – albeit liberal – supporter of the 'legitimate' Restoration (Louis XVIII and Charles X), Chateaubriand
refused after the 1830 revolution – which brought in the July
Monarchy – to swear allegiance to the new House of Orléans, King
Louis-Philippe, and this marked the end of his political life. He
retired to write the other book for which he is best remembered,
his *Mémoires d'outre-tombe* ('Memoirs from Beyond the Grave').
These, which were indeed not published until after his death in July
1848, were very different in mood from *Génie* – pessimistic about
the future, melancholic, even regretful. Excerpts were read in the
salons during Chateaubriand's life, including Juliette's. The fact is,
Chateaubriand needed money and so, every day at 2.00 p.m., distinguished gatherings 'of only fifteen' assembled in the Abbaye, and
René brought his manuscript, wrapped in a silk handkerchief, and
the company listened as excerpts were read out. The daily papers
clamoured for extracts.[33]

DEMOCRACY = MEDIOCRE MINDS

Two other formidable figures who graced Juliette's salon were
Charles Augustin Sainte-Beuve, arguably the greatest literary critic

of the century, and Alexis de Tocqueville, historian and politician, who were almost exact contemporaries. Sainte-Beuve formed a much more active participant of Princesse Mathilde's salon.

Alexis de Tocqueville, a distant relative of Chateaubriand, was born in Paris on 11 Thermidor in year XIII of the French Revolutionary calendar, 29 July 1805, the son of a Normandy count.* He became a magistrate, with an abiding interest in prison reform, and looked forward to a career in politics. However, because of his father's allegiance to the deposed Bourbon monarchy, Alexis found it expedient to travel to America with his friend and colleague Gustave de Beaumont. The ostensible reason for their visit was to study prison regimes in the New World but they travelled widely.

They remained in the United States for about nine months, criss-crossing the country more extensively than Chateaubriand had done, and took in New York, Boston, Buffalo and Philadelphia, also crossing into Canada. They travelled the frontier, down the Mississippi to New Orleans, and back up through the South to Washington. In Boston they stayed at the Tremont Hotel, the first large luxury hotel in the United States, where each guest was provided with a pair of slippers while his boots were polished. 'Here luxury and refinement prevail,' wrote Tocqueville. 'Almost all the women here speak French well, and all the men we have seen so far have been to Europe.' It made a change, he said, from the 'stinking' arrogance of the Americans in New York, where people would spit during conversation.[34]

To begin with, and until they reached the frontier, they were disappointed by the 'lack of trees' in America, and by the Indians, whom they found small, with thin arms and legs, 'brutalised by our wines and liquors'. They visited Sing Sing, a prison on the banks of the Hudson, met John Quincy Adams and Sam Houston (the founder of Texas, who brought his stallion aboard ship on the Mississippi), and were entertained by the American Philosophical Society. As their journey progressed, Tocqueville's admiration for America grew and on his return to France, he resolved to write a book about the most important feature which he felt distinguished America: democracy.

---

* The French Revolutionary calendar lasted from 1793 to 1805.

His book, simply titled *Democracy in America*, appeared in two volumes, the first in 1835, which concentrated on politics, and the second in 1840, which added his thoughts and observations on what we would call the sociological effects of democracy. That word in France, at the time, was equivalent to revolution and Tocqueville addressed what he felt was the main problem with democracy – the danger that it would make men's minds mediocre and in that way damage their ultimate freedom.[35]

But in almost all other ways he was full of admiration for the democratic spirit and structure of America. Americans formed a society, he found, in which classes were much less distinct than in Europe and where even the ordinary sales clerk did not have the 'bad form' of the lower classes in France. 'This is a *commercial* people,' his colleague Beaumont wrote at one point. 'The entire society seems to have melted into a middle class.'

Both men were impressed by the advanced position of women, the hard work, the general good morals, and the absence of military force. They were further impressed by the sturdy individualism (a word Tocqueville claimed to have coined) of the small landowners, who they saw as the most typical Americans. 'The Americans are no more virtuous than other people,' Tocqueville wrote, 'but are infinitely more enlightened (I'm speaking of the great mass) than any other people I know ...' In *Democracy in America*, Tocqueville made much of the stability of the American system (though he drew attention to the danger of rising expectations), which he contrasted with France and, to an extent, Britain (which he had also visited, as well as Ireland). He put this down to ordinary Americans being more involved than their European counterparts in (a) political society, (b) civil society and (c) religious society, and to the fact that America operated in ways which were almost the direct opposite of those in Europe: 'The local community was organised before the county, the county before the state, and the state before the union.'

Tocqueville greatly admired the role of the courts in America, where they took precedence over the politicians, and the fact that the press, though no less 'violent' than the French press, was left alone: no one even thought of censoring what was said. He had a section on juries, which he thought were very important, not just for meting out appropriate justice, but because the experience of being *on* a jury helped make people more familiar with the law and helped spread the thinking of the judges.[36]

He was not blind to the problems of America. He considered the issue of race to be insoluble. He thought both the blacks and the Indian population were undemocratic and 'without the qualities, intellectual and otherwise needed to live in a democracy'.[37]

In the realm of pure ideas, he felt that democracies would make more progress in practical than in theoretical sciences. He expected poetry to blossom in America because 'there was much nature'. He found families more intimate and more independent-minded than in Europe, and was heartily in favour of the trend whereby marriage was based more on love and affection than on economic or dynastic considerations.[38] Though he was in favour of individualism, he thought there were dangers in that the 'omnipotence of the majority' could lead to a stifling of intellect.[39]

Tocqueville's other notable works included *The Ancien Régime and the Revolution*. His argument here was that the Revolution had failed, and it had done so because of the inexperience of the deputies, who had been too wedded to abstract Enlightenment ideas and ideals, meaning that 'bureaucratic tyranny' – Bonapartism – was bound to come about. In another on Algeria, he thought that the treatment of the Arabs was 'barbaric' but he made a distinction between 'dominance' and 'colonisation'. He defended the occupation of the country in broad geo-political terms (controlling access to the Strait of Gibraltar, for example), and because such actions added to France's prestige, but he advocated a form of apartheid, in which the Arabs would govern their part of the country, as second-class citizens, while the French whites had their own administration.

He was what he was, a liberal, right-of-centre aristocrat with a private income, much travelled by the standards of the day, well educated and informed, an elitist but not a snob, who was convinced that literary types had too much influence in the *ancien régime*, thought that democracy was acceptable and safe, provided it was modified by education (available then, of course, in Europe, only to the better off) and admired the British House of Lords as, in fact, the most enlightened political establishment (he was also married to an Englishwoman – he described Britain as his second home intellectually). He saw liberty as a continual *process*, not just voting now and then but requiring continual active participation in the political infrastructure at all levels.[40]

He campaigned against Louis-Napoleon Bonaparte in the presidential election of 1848 and was among those who tried to resist Bonaparte's coup and have Napoleon III, as he became, tried for high treason. Detained briefly, he quit politics, and started on his book about the *ancien régime*.[41] He died of tuberculosis in April 1859.

AN ANGEL IN EVERY WOMAN

When Mme de Chateaubriand died in 1847, René asked Juliette to marry him. She answered that, had she been younger, she would not have refused but 'she was wise enough to know that he was happier anticipating his visits than if he were seeing her all day'. She was going blind, he was less and less able to move.

A woman of great beauty – and all are agreed that Juliette Récamier was unequalled on that score – who 'at forty-three looked as if she was thirty', who also had the gift of friendship, which can only succeed if it appears genuine, even if it is in fact calculated, is never going to be too popular with other, less well-endowed women. For a time in her life, as Joseph Turquan – the biographer of several of the Bonapartes and other figures of Napoleonic times – noted, it was 'good form to fall in love with Mme Récamier', and even Wellington, we are told, succumbed, though she received him coldly. Despite the playwright Mme Ancelot's criticisms of Mme Récamier's flirtatiousness, she herself invited Juliette back to her own salon in the company of Pierre-Simon Ballanche. And it was Ballanche, the counter-revolutionary philosopher, who wrote to Mme Lenormant, another *salonnière*, in 1829, giving a list of those attending Juliette's: Pierre-Chéri Lafont, actor of the Comédie-Française; Chateaubriand; Mesdames Appony, de Fontanes and Sophie Gay; Messieurs Cousin, Villemain, Le Brun, Lamartine, La Touche, Dubois, Saint Marc Girardin, Valéry, Mérimée and Gérard; the Ducs de Doudeauville and de Broglie; Messieurs de Sainte-Aulaire, de Barante and David; Mme de Boigne; Mme de Gramont; the Baron Pasquier; and so on.[42]

Among this list of names, we glimpse the way the story of the great chain of salons moves forward. Victor Cousin was, among other things, the teacher – one of the teachers – of Honoré de Balzac, who read *Le Peau de chagrin* at the Récamier salon (without too much success), but he was to have a more permanent presence at the salon of Sophie Gay, whom we shall meet soon, alongside Victor Hugo, Alfred de Musset and others.

To dismiss Mme Récamier as no more than a coquette is to misrepresent the art (or maybe it's a science) of friendship, which skill she had in as close to perfection as is possible. In her later years her friends did not desert her, as they might have done if her friendships were less than they were made out to be, even though her old age was spoiled by her failing sight, despite two cataract operations, which did not succeed. The Vicomtesse d'Agoult visited her, researching a book on de Staël: 'She rose to meet me, advancing with the hesitation of a person whose sight is dim ... The name of Lamartine entered our conversation. She assured me that she cared greatly for him, that she defended him constantly, for friends were very severe in regard to him ... She left me with an agreeable memory.' Alphonse de Lamartine, arguably France's first romantic poet, who famously 'saw an angel in every woman', was more of a presence in Mme de Girardin's salon than Juliette's, where we shall meet him again.[43]

In the end she was carried away by cholera, on 11 May 1849. One biographer concluded that she had never been a real woman because she had never been a mother. Needless to say that biographer – who shall remain nameless – was a man.

'The Return of Conversation'

The most famous battle in modern history took place on Sunday 18 June 1815 across sloping, rain-sodden fields straddling the main road south from Brussels. But Waterloo did more than rid the world of Napoleon. It marked the end of what some historians have called 'The Second Hundred Years War'. Since 1689, France had been at war more years than it hadn't, mostly against Great Britain but not only. The sheer cost of so much fighting had been one of the prime factors in creating the circumstances that led to the 1789 Revolution, but the Revolutionary Wars had been no less bloody. It is estimated that, over the course of the Second Hundred Years War, some 6 million people were killed, 'equal to the total population of England in the 1750s'. Between 1792 and 1815, 1.4 million French and 200,000 British lost their lives.[1]

The battle was fought in characteristic style. Napoleon had the larger army, but he knew that he had to smash through Wellington's lines before Blücher's Prussians arrived. It was, say Robert and Isabelle Tombs, the tactics of the Revolution against those of the old regime, 'unleashed enthusiasm against disciplined stoicism, *la furie française* against *le flegme britannique*', summing up each nation's idea of itself.[2] The confined space of the battlefield created an intensity of violence, where the French failed to break through before Prussian reinforcements arrived; Napoleon returned to Paris and, after trying to rally resistance, abdicated for the second time on 22

June. Europe would not know a war of that scale again for almost exactly one hundred years.

In Britain Waterloo was a permanent source of pride but, as the Tombses also point out, it was quietly commemorated in street names, railway stations and pubs, rather than anything deeply stirring. It was not recalled like the Armada, Trafalgar, Dunkirk or the Battle of Britain.[3]

The French response was very different. There, the memory of defeat went deeper, enriching what the French historian Jean-Marc Largeaud has called 'a culture of defeat unique to France'.[4] As we have had cause to note before, they dwelled on what they chose to consider as a 'glorious defeat', which offered a lesson in sacrifice; France had survived and would rise again. The French did not minimise the disaster but instead heightened the tragic aspects and emphasised the 'defiant heroism' of their forces.[5] Moreover, because the Prussians had turned the tide, despite turning up late, the French could always deny that any one nation had beaten them. General de Gaulle went so far as to make his first broadcast from London in the Second World War on the anniversary of Waterloo. Essentially – as had happened before and was to happen again – France celebrated a 'moral victory' in a conflict which, by any other criterion, it had lost. In his history of France, de Gaulle left out Waterloo entirely.

But again – as before, and as would happen again – the French recovery was remarkable and remarkably swift.

By the time the treaty of the Quadruple Alliance (between the United Kingdom, Austria, Prussia and Russia) was signed on 20 November 1815, the salons of the Faubourg Saint-Germain were already at work assisting in the creation of a climate of opinion that would persuade the alliance leaders to sanction a Bourbon restoration.[6] Mme de Staël was just one who counselled that Restoration governments would have to come to terms with the salons, now much more politically active and influential.

Aristocratic high society, Steven Kale says, was at its pinnacle during the Restoration. Virginie Ancelot, herself a prominent *salonnière*, observed that men of letters and politicians had both become more urbane than before, much more involved in affairs.[7] The most agreeable house in Paris at this time, according to Mme de Boigne, who could be construed as a rival, was the *hôtel* of the Duchesse de Duras (the French writer who inspired John Fowles's *The French Lieutenant's Woman*), who entertained in spacious premises at 21 rue de Varenne. She received her visitors late, between 9.00 p.m. and midnight, in rooms of exquisite taste, full of books, flowers, paintings and prints, globes of the world and antique vases. She would sit at her desk, rolling pieces of paper between her fingers, an enemy of what she dismissed as 'stupidity, gossip, frivolity', inviting only those she considered the most distinguished men in Paris. These included Alexander von Humboldt, who regarded her as 'a luminous point in my life', and Baron Cuvier, the man who had conceived palaeontology and was now professor of anatomy at the Jardin des Plantes and president of the Commission for Public Instruction. Cuvier was accompanied by Talleyrand, Charles André Pozzo, the Russian ambassador, the painter Baron Gérard and the American writer Washington Irving. George Ticknor, the American traveller and linguist, remarked that he was 'positively bewitched' by her salon, which was 'as interesting a society as could well be collected'.

More than one observer noted that, despite the books she wrote, Mme de Duras's salon was her 'career' and that she was a force to be reckoned with when she tried to wean Gérard and Cuvier away from their admiration for the emperor. One of her hang-ups, as we would say, was her looks – she was not pretty, and her husband was often unfaithful. Her predicament was reflected in some of her epigrams: 'If you have never been pretty, you have never been young.' 'How many times one dies before the real moment of death.'[8]

Chateaubriand was one of the stars of her salon, as well as of Mme Récamier's. When he fell for Juliette and started attending the Récamier *cellule* in the Abbaye-aux-Bois , he was so punctual in his times of arrival that neighbours set their watches by him. He stopped for a time going to Mme de Duras's, and she wrote him a note: 'I have had all the clocks stopped in order no longer to hear the hours striking when you will no longer come.'[9] The irony was that although her salon has been described as a 'European institution', she herself always felt a bit of an outsider. This showed in her work. Her novels pleased a range of people, from Goethe to the Parisian public, and they are undoubtedly original. But they are invariably about *isolés*, individuals cut off from happiness by race, class or sex. In *Ourika* (1822) there is the hopeless passion of a black girl for a French noble, she always 'alone, never loved'.[10]

When Napoleon had deliberately revived *la vie mondaine*, in an effort to enlist support for his initiatives, salons that had proliferated under the *ancien régime* reopened their doors only cautiously as returning émigrés nervously tested the waters. In 1814 and 1815, however, the reaction was very different. People were only too ready for a return to the old life and in no time, says Kale, 'each class, each party, and each political nuance, it seemed, had its salon'. Compared to a lacklustre royal court, Alphonse de Lamartine observed that 'conversation had returned with the Restoration'.[11]

Public opinion now established the intellectual underpinning of perpetual debate, and politics enthralled *le monde*, as it had done in the immediate wake of the Revolution.[12] More than that, the ethic of polite society helped to make the salon an antidote to the inevitable divisiveness of politics. François Guizot, leader of the conservative constitutional monarchists, who relished the altercations in the chamber as much as anyone, nonetheless insisted that partisanship 'hardly ever penetrated the house of Madame Rumford (the former Mme Lavoisier)'. Germaine de Staël applauded Mme Récamier as 'an angel of peace', who repeatedly calmed the partisan rancour that otherwise divided Germaine's friends.[13]

It is not surprising that, after years of such turbulence, the Restoration should have been especially well suited to the maintenance of stable political sociability.[14] In fact, the more the salons became politicised, the more the *salonnières* sought pacification.[15] Women continued to have a prominent role via the salons but a number of women in the nineteenth century were to achieve prominence in other ways, and ideas about their capabilities could not help but change. An added factor was the perceived tediousness of the court, so that even normally dedicated courtiers left Versailles as soon as possible to return to the salons. After 1830 the legitimist aristocracy (who wanted the Bourbons back on the throne) went even further, making it plain that the Faubourg Saint-Germain was an alternative centre of 'political sociability'.

Napoleon had invented *salons de fusion* where he hoped the traditional aristocracy would mix with his new aristocracy of merit. Though the aristocrats were well aware that merit was needed, this did not make for as easy a fusion as the first consul wanted and, gradually, as time passed, in the first half of the nineteenth century, salons became more and more politically conscious, and politically divided, with *salonnières* now being judged according to their ability to keep political opponents together.[16]

In the political salons, the *salonnière* usually had strong political views of her own but such was the variety that every political hue could find a home somewhere. Mme Schwetchine was home to liberal Catholics, Mme d'Abrantès to Bonapartists, for example. The salons of the 'Ultras' sought to adhere to the narrow (pre-Revolutionary) tradition of the aristocrats, who kept up their resistance to the Enlightenment. There were still 'old-fashioned' salons open to men of letters and artists but there was no doubt that society now was more doctrinaire.[17]

Nonetheless, outside politics salon life was as busy and as enjoyable as ever, because it was so varied and because most of the salons in the Faubourg were so close that people could easily walk from one less formal location to another. A salon was again, in the words of Mme d'Agoult, whom we shall meet more fully in chapter 29, 'the supreme ambition of the Parisienne, the consolation of her maturity, the glory of her old age'.[18]

Social life in early nineteenth-century France, says Philip Mansel, was considered a duty, as one factor in maintaining social order. Salon social life could also be regarded as offering part of a good education, with a raft of books underlining the point: *Manuel de l'homme de bon ton, ou Cérémonial de la bonne société* (1823), *L'Art de briller en société, ou Le Coryphée des salons* (1824), *Nouveau manuel complet de la bonne compagnie, ou Guide de la politesse et de la bienséance destiné à tous les âges et à toutes les conditions* (1845).[19]

The intrusion of politics did mean, however, that salons by and large ceased to be part of the cultural avant-garde.[20] One notable exception was the salon of Baron François Gérard, by now the most fashionable painter in Europe. For more than thirty years he received a variety of guests in his four-roomed apartment on the rue des Beaux-Arts (now the rue Bonaparte). A firm royalist and music-lover, his regular guests included Rossini, Meyerbeer, Ingres, Delacroix, Stendhal and Humboldt. 'One of Balzac's definitions of happiness was to have a salon as "astonishing" as that of Gérard.'[21] Other guests included Mme Récamier from time to time, and the Duchesses de Broglie and de Dino. The latter was the subject of a particularly sharp remark. Dorothée de Dino was the daughter of Talleyrand and was, like him, close to being a libertine. When she married the Duc de Dino, Parisians cuttingly remarked on how unsuitable her new title was: 'She was not accustomed to say no.'[22]

The other effect of politics was that the salons became listening posts. During the revolution of 1830 fresh news was relayed to Mme de Boigne's salon 'every quarter of an hour'.[23] Another effect of the intrusion of politics was that in many cases speeches destined for parliament were aired first in the political salons.[24]

The revolution of 1830, however, 'cleaved "society" in two', which had two longer-term knock-on effects. First, *salonnières* began to build their evenings around one '*grand homme*', to whom everyone else paid deference. And second, musical salons became more popular, obviously enough because risky conversation was reduced to a minimum. With these changes a hierarchy of salons emerged, based on the eminence of the *grand homme* that the *salonnière* could attract.[25] At the same time, more and more *salonnières* would begin to shine outside and beyond their salons.

Delphine de Girardin and her 'Collection of Superiorities'

In 1910, Léon Séché, who liked to be thought of as a French poet, though he was better known as a literary biographer, published a book about his fellow French poet Delphine de Girardin (née Gay), who was herself in fact better known as a literary muse. His book was cleanly and helpfully organised. After an opening chapter on her youth, the other chapters were headed: 'Delphine and Lamartine', 'Delphine and Victor Hugo', 'Delphine and Balzac', 'Delphine and Rachel', 'Delphine and Eugène Sue' and 'Delphine, Jules Sandeau, A. Dumas and George Sand'.[1] As neat a collection of illustrious names as you could find.

Her father was receiver-general and her mother, Sophie, was the daughter of a financier ruined in the Revolution but who provided her with an excellent education. She married well, at least the second time round, to the wealthy Jean Gay. Besides being an excellent pianist, Sophie Gay published several successful novels in the early years of the nineteenth century and under the Restoration. She was a *salonnière* herself, in Aix (en Provence) in the summer and Paris in the winter. She was '*une femme du monde*', spirited and spiritual, and known for her repartee.

And she wrote her own book about salons in which, to begin with, she set out various 'laws of the salon', the first being that the *salonnière*, 'without being old, must have passed that age in which one is only celebrated for one's lovely person or exquisite dress, and reached that period of life when talents and genius command homage'. The second law was that the master of the house must be polite 'but not in the way; he must be a nullity, or absent ... and in no way take precedence over her who is the presiding genius'. 'She should have a decided taste for superiority of all sorts, and soar above those narrow feelings of envy or jealousy ... She must place her enemies at their ease.'[2]

She covered the salons of Mme de Staël, Mlle Contat, Comtesse Merlin (where there was much singing and piano- and harpsichord-playing), Mme Lebrun and the Empress Josephine (who had several dandies in her group), which she called a half-formed court, and where letters from the emperor were occasionally read aloud. She spent most time on the salon of Baron Gérard, who was 'the first artist at whose house the nobility of all nations, men and women illustrious in science, learning, or art, desired to be admitted'.[3] There Champollion would describe the wonders of Egypt, and a raft of singers and musicians gathered around Rossini.[4]

Delphine showed a talent for composing verse and made her entry into society in 1822, at the age of eighteen, when she began reciting her verses in her mother's salon.[5] But Sophie was very ambitious for her daughter and ensured that she accompanied her to other salons both aristocratic and literary. She also stage-managed a much-publicised – and widely lampooned – meeting between her daughter and Lamartine. The encounter took place in the spring of 1825, at the Velino waterfall in Italy. This was a well-known beauty spot which had impressed and inspired poets since Horace. The encounter was arch because Lamartine was perfectly aware that Mme Gay and her daughter were nearby and desirous of making his acquaintance. And indeed, on cue, the poet 'stumbled' across 'the plump young Muse sitting by the river, where her mother had arranged her in an artful pose, one shapely arm on the parapet, the other nonchalantly holding a bouquet of wildflowers while the wind caressed her light brown hair'.[6] Ever the *galant*, Lamartine dutifully recorded the encounter in his *Souvenirs et portraits* (1872).

Among the aristocratic salons mother and daughter attended were those of the Duchesses de Duras (chapter 27) and Narbonne and the Marquise de Custine; the latter's (homosexual) husband was a good friend of Chateaubriand and Germaine de Staël, and was known for his travel-writing about Russia. Among other literary gatherings, Delphine also attended those of Charles Nodier and Victor Hugo. Nodier was a novelist and librarian at the Arsenal, but also with a lively interest in insects. And he had other varied preoccupations – he was briefly imprisoned for writing a short play satirical of Napoleon, he called for the restoration of the monasteries (to escape the rigours of the world), and his own Sunday salon, known as *Le Cénacle*, was designed to encourage the romantic generation of authors (Lamartine, Hugo, de Nerval, Vigny). He adapted John Polidori's short story 'The Vampyre' to the stage, as well as Mary Shelley's *Frankenstein*.

Little by little, Delphine – whose many portraits confirm that her head was indeed covered in those tubular ringlets, surrounding a fairly pious expression – became a sort of official poet. She started to commemorate events – the unveiling of a great painting, the death of a well-known general, the opening of a new department store – to the point where she asked for an audience with the king so as to compose a work 'worthy of him'. Her petition was successful, and she was granted a small annual pension.[7] Her declamations of her writings were dramatic. On one occasion, at Mme Récamier's, she read out a hundred verses of her poem *La Vision*, where she was compared with the great actor Talma (who spoke at Récamier's the following night). Her performance ended with her raising her arms and clutching a handkerchief to her face.

Her first love was not Lamartine but Alfred de Vigny, another romantic, but both sets of parents were against the match – there was not enough money to go around. Observers accused Sophie of 'pimping' her daughter ('*se conduit comme une maquerelle*'). Delphine might have slipped down the social rankings, given her mother's 'pimping', had it not paid off in the form of Émile de Girardin. They were married on 1 June 1831, when she was twenty-seven and he two years younger. According to one observer, it was not a marriage based on affection.[8]

Émile was the illegitimate son of Count Alexandre de Girardin, whose name he publicly adopted, when it was not at all the done thing, confirming his resolute character. Émile was passionately convinced that there had to be education for the greatest number possible, and to that end he believed the press had an important role.

By the time of his marriage, he had already founded two newspapers, *Le Voleur* ('The Thief') in 1828, a kind of press review (articles were 'stolen' from other publications), and *La Mode* in 1829, a weekly in which he published young talents – Dumas, Eugène Sue, Balzac, George Sand. For the illustrations he had identified the witty illustrator Paul Gavarni, then twenty-five, whose work would mostly decorate the pages of *Le Charivari*, a political review which specialised in cartoons and caricatures, not one of Girardin's publications but a title which would last more than a century from its inception in 1832.

In October 1831, Émile launched the *Journal des connaissances utiles*, the 'Journal of Useful Knowledge', medical, legal, geographical and other information that was presumed to be needed from one day to another. By December of the following year, it was selling 132,000 copies. Other titles followed, equally successfully. Émile had invented the cheap press in France and by 1834 he and Delphine were rich.[9]

THIS, THAT AND THE OTHER

More than that, though, Émile was keen to make use of his wife's talents, and so he gave her a weekly column, which she wrote under the pen name of Vicomte de Launay. The vicomte was presented as a witty man of the world, where he attended all the fashionable goings-on of Paris high society – the erection of a new statue, the opening of a railway station, the races at Longchamp, eating ices at Tortoni's, which was famous for them, details about the inner workings of the Académie française, gossip – as she herself put it – about this, that and the other. Here, for instance, she is on the theatre: 'The success which Madame Ancelot's dramas have obtained for her at every representation has confirmed us in a remark we made a long time since, that the French public is, of all things, the one that demands the most flattery.' Or again, here she is referring to Prince T***, 'who sent to his mistress, at this time last year, a simple basket of oranges; but each orange was wrapt round with a bill of a thousand francs'. At the same time, Émile appointed Balzac to write a weekly 'Letter from Paris', modelled on the articles in the British *Spectator*.[10]

Her salon, attended also by her mother, was at first held in a small apartment in the rue Louis-le-Grand, then moved twice until it ended up in the grand hôtel Marbeuf on the Champs-Élysées.[11] She received her intimates every night but her grand receptions, filled with poetry readings and music, were held on Wednesdays.

These evenings were filled with a glittering array of the greatest writers of the day – Gautier, Lamartine, Hugo, Balzac, Lautour-Mézeray, Sue, Dumas, Musset, Vigny, Mérimée, Sand, Jules Michelet, Félicité de La Mennais, Eugène Scribe and Alphonse Karr. Among the artists were Delacroix, Horace Vernet, Paul Delaroche and Théodore Chassériau, notable for his orientalist paintings, and amid the politicians were Guizot, Étienne Denis, the Duc de Pasquieur, the chancellor, Gabriel Delessert, the prefect of police, and Ferdinand de Lesseps, engineer and diplomat. Jules Adolphe Cabarrus, the fashionable homeopath, also attended. The composers were represented by Meyerbeer and Rossini.

Delphine and Émile, for a time – a long time – were *the* fashionable power couple in Paris. There were no mediocrities in their salon, which was also known in particular for the fact that such society was far more stylish than that of the court.[12] As Lamartine's wife put it, Delphine and Émile had assembled a 'collection of superiorities'.[13] This kind of society was under increasing threat during the July Monarchy, as privilege was more and more expected to be earned, but the aristocracy hung on, constantly revivified by its alignment with the aristocracy of talent.[14]

The Arrogance – and the Wreckage – of the Poet

As the roster of names above suggests, Delphine de Girardin's salon was a home to romanticism, and therein lay its contribution to French civilisation. Romanticism developed later in France than it did in Britain or Germany. It was in large part a reaction against the Enlightenment and its celebration of reason, which, in many people's eyes, had led to revolution, regarded by some as a victory and by others as a disaster.

The origins of romanticism may be found in several places, but one was in Chateaubriand's novel *Atala*, which described in luscious detail the pristiñe forests of North America – fulsome descriptions of nature would be a central element in romantic novels and poetry for years to come. The other was the sheer musicality of the wording in Lamartine's verse, the idea that what mattered in life was not intellect so much as emotion, passion, the air of doom overlying sublime beauty, all surrounding a view that, in some ways, the early nineteenth century was a 'sick' time, that individuals were isolated, and that the human condition was basically tragic, melancholic and disillusioned (a view obviously at odds with life in Delphine's salon).

Despite his reputation as a romantic, Lamartine's themes were scarcely original: laments for a lost love, regret for childhood simplicity and innocence, and an almost mystical religious meditation in such works as 'La Prière', 'La Foi', 'La Providence à l'homme' and 'Le Chrétien murant'.[15] But the sales figures spoke for themselves. *Méditations*, published in March 1820 in an edition of 500, was reprinted at the end of the month in an edition of three times the size, which had all gone by the end of April. In the words of critic/historian Frederick Hemmings: 'The astonishing success of the *Méditations* was due in part to what still charms its readers two centuries later: its muted musicality, its hypnotic fluidity ...' In other words, sound – music – more than sense, which is perhaps one reason why Stendhal was puzzled by Lamartine and thought him trite, 'as effaced as the effigy on an antique coin'.[16] What also mattered with Lamartine was that his verse 'seemed to come from the heart'. Such 'outpourings of the soul' had been absent from French verse since the sixteenth century, and so 'confessional verse' had at least the aura of freshness.[17]

The other aspect central to romanticism was highlighted by the works of Alfred de Vigny (1797–1863). In two of his main prose works, his novel *Stello* and his play *Chatterton*, he set out the idea of the Poet's (with a capital 'P') superiority to the crowd and others, artists who look upon themselves as the lords of this earth. At the first night of *Chatterton* (12 February 1835) the theatre was, according to Théophile Gautier, 'full of pale-faced, long-haired adolescents, firmly believing that there was no other occupation worthy of pursuit on this globe than to write poetry or to paint pictures – to practise art, as the phrase was; they looked on the *bourgeois* with a contempt . . . The *bourgeois*! That meant pretty well everybody . . . whoever did not belong to the mysterious *cénacles* and earned his living prosaically.'[18]

The character of the poet as both pariah and martyr was a myth deliberately manufactured by Vigny but it did have a basis in fact. *Stello*, which he published in 1832, was based on the life-stories of three eighteenth-century poets of whom Thomas Chatterton was one, the others being Nicolas Gilbert and André Chénier. All three died young though at this distance we can recognise that only Chénier would be regarded today as a genius.[19] Vigny's underlying argument was that whatever political system is in office, there is, in the words of the narrator in *Stello*, 'a natural antipathy between the man of genius and the common crowd'. The crowd is egalitarian, 'and cannot help but resent what it sees as the arrogance of the Poet, because he sets himself above it'.[20]

But the second aspect of *Chatterton* that attracted attention was Vigny's argument that there are circumstances in which suicide is morally justified, and the plot raises the question as to where the guilt for this lies.[21]

The subject was not entirely new. Flaubert admitted that some of his schoolmates in Rouen in the 1830s were attracted to the idea, that one had blown his brains out while a second had strangled himself with his tie. More than that, there were several high-profile suicides reported in the newspapers at that time, not least that of the neoclassical painter Antoine-Jean Gros, who drowned himself close to the time that *Chatterton* premiered.[22] As Hemmings tartly observes: 'The extraordinary glamour attaching to the profession of man of letters during the romantic period accounts for the misguided efforts of too many men of modest talent to win celebrity through their writing. As Flaubert put it with pardonable exaggeration: "Every notary carried within him the wreckage of a poet."'[23]

George Sand was another of Delphine's habitués. She was born Amantine Lucile Aurore Dupin in 1804. She had a remarkable succession of celebrated lovers – who included Alfred de Musset, Prosper Mérimée and Frédéric Chopin. Brought up in the village of Nohant, in the very centre of France, she first married someone who lived nearby. That didn't last and she began the first of her many affairs, leading her eventually to Paris, where early on she formed a firm friendship with the editor of *Le Figaro*, who suggested she try writing. To begin with she wrote both newspaper pieces and an early novel in collaboration with the man who was her lover at the time, Jules Sandeau, and they used the pen name Jules Sand. That affair went the way of all the others and at that point she adopted the pen name George Sand. This was when she tried her first novel all by herself, called *Indiana*. This told the story of a woman trying hard to break the restrictions that, under French law, bound a wife to her husband against her will.[24]

But, more than that, what many people responded to were her so-called 'rustic' novels. Set in *la France profonde,* they became popular throughout Europe as she sought – and succeeded – in attracting sympathy for the female condition in the nineteenth century. In *Consuelo*, regarded by many as her masterpiece, she narrated the misfortunes of a Spanish gypsy singer as she performed through Italy and Germany but who baulked at the importunities that came her way.[25] Sand was just as famous for her love affairs as for her books, and though her behaviour scandalised the more strait-laced of Paris, her work (more than sixty full-length books) did address serious issues of women's rights and their (lack of) independence. At the same time, she was criticised for not carrying through with her 'sentimental socialism' and mixing with the lower orders.[26]

ART FOR ART'S SAKE

But of course the most distinguished figure of all in Delphine and Émile's salon was Victor Hugo. By 1830 he had become established as the leading man of the romantic movement, the title conferred on him – if it hadn't been already – by the staging of his play *Hernani*.

The plot of *Hernani* is – like a lot of plots – complicated. Essentially it is about three men in love with the same woman – one is a king, Charles of Spain, another is her uncle and fiancé, and the third is a bandit – Hernani. The king is foiled at every turn, despite having more power than anyone else, which he repeatedly uses to try to stop the bandit having his way. The fiancé/uncle behaves well towards the bandit, protecting him from the king at times, until he finds out that the bandit is his rival for his fiancée. The king is elected emperor, the uncle commits suicide and the woman and Hernani take poison.

The play is remembered more now, however, for its stormy reception. Hugo knew what he was doing in writing the play, which was a direct romantic attack on the values of the classicists who were mainly in charge of French theatre. Along with Gautier and Berlioz in their work (such as the latter's *Symphonie fantastique*), he was deliberately staking his colours to the mast. The play was written very quickly, in less than a month, and got past the censor, despite his dismissive remarks. 'This work is stuffed with every kind of impropriety. The king talks frequently like a bandit ... the daughter of a Spanish grandee emerges as a shameless hussy ...' But he went on, somewhat surprisingly: 'It is desirable that the public should see into what aberrations the mind of man may lapse when all the rules are cast overboard.'

Among the audience on the first night were Chateaubriand, Mme Récamier and Benjamin Constant. It was the tradition then for the author of a play *not* to attend the first night, as it was considered bad luck. As it turned out, nothing much happened on that first night, but on the fourth the classicists began to use the weapon of loud laughter at inappropriate points in the text, or else left their boxes in the middle of the play, shouting loudly 'I can't stand this' and slamming the doors, generating in the words of one critic 'pandemonium'. But Hugo had the last laugh. The commotion ensured that the play was a great commercial success, even after the pandemonium got so bad that the play had to be suspended.[27]

Hugo was always hard to pigeon-hole. His next three collections of poetry were each different. *Les Orientales* was colourful and strongly rhythmic but offered no help in pointing the way forward. *Les Feuilles d'automne* explored nostalgic memories of childhood, described the pleasures of family life, waxed lyrical about the joys of nature in its gentler manifestations, and offered a few love poems and affectionate encomiums to artist friends such as Louis Boulanger and David d'Angers. And Hugo was insistent about the value of poetry. 'Whatever the tumult in public places, it is proper that art should persist, that art should stubbornly endure, remaining faithful to its own nature ... revolutions transform everything except the human art.'[28] *Les Rayons*

Heroine of the Fronde: Anne-Geneviève de Bourbon Condé, Duchesse de Longueville (1619-1679), by Jean Frosne, 1642.

Marie de Rabutin-Chantal, Madame de Sévigné (1626-1696), by Claude Lefebvre. Her writings are now taught as models of clarity.

Madeleine de Souvré, Marquise de Sablé (1599-1678). Everyone composed maxims in her salon.

Marie-Madeleine de Pioche de La Vergne, Comtesse de Lafayette (1634-1693). Her books revolutionized the novel.

Anne-Marie-Louise d'Orléans, La Grande Mademoiselle (1627-1693), by Charles Beaubrun. She inherited five duchies five days after she was born.

Anne 'Ninon' de Lenclos (1620-1705), attributed to Louis Elle Le Vieux. Sexually 'sulphurous' but 'the most beautiful woman in France'.

Marquise Anne-Thérèse de Lambert (1647-1733), by Nicolas Largillière, c. 1710. Her salon was known as 'La Cour de Minerve'.

A reading of Voltaire's tragedy, *L'Orpheline de la Chine*, in the salon of Madame Geoffrin (1699-1777), by Anicet Charles Gabriel Lemonnier. Not all of these crowded eighteenth-century luminaries, presided over by a bust of the great writer himself, were members of her salon.

LA BOUILLOTTE, D'APRÈS BOSIO.

A 'typically louche' salon of the Directory period (1795-1799). Engraving after Jean-François Bosio.

Claudine Alexandrine Guerin de Tencin (1682-1749), French school. The mother of D'Alembert, she introduced the regent to 'the feast of the flagellants'.

Marie-Thérèse Rodet Geoffrin in 1738. By Jean-Marc Natter. Her salon lasted for forty years.

M.me DE L'ESPINASSE.

Stéphanie-Félicité du Crest, Madame de Genlis (1746-1830) by Adélaïde Labille-Guiard, 1790. Rumoured to be Napoleon's spy in fashionable Paris, she was an arch-rival of Germaine de Staël.

Julie de Lespinasse (1732-1776), engraving by Louis Carrogis Carmontelle, 1760. Her many affairs devastated the naïve d'Alembert.

Germaine de Staël (1766-1817) as Corinne, the heroine of one of her many books. Copy of her portrait by Élisabeth Vigée-Lebrun. At first Napoleon thought *Corinne* was 'junk' but on St Helena he read it again and found it 'an interesting work'.

Juliette Récamier (1777-1849), by François Gérard, 1805. Scores of men fell in love with her, even Napoleon.

Delphine de Girardin (1804-1855), by Louis Hersent, 1824. Her salon was home to many romantics.

Marie d'Agoult (1805-1876), by Henri Lehmann, 1843. The mistress of Franz Liszt. Details of the affair were leaked by her 'friend' George Sand to Honoré de Balzac, who used them as a basis for a novel.

Mathilde Bonaparte, Princess Mathilde (1820-1904), otherwise known as 'Notre Dame des Arts'. By Edouard Louis Dubufe, 1861.

Juliette Adam, née Juliette Lambert (1836-1936). Her family ate twelve dozen oysters every Friday. An early friendship with Marie d'Agoult soured. She grew to be an ardent feminist.

Apollonie Sabatier, née Aglae Josephine Apolline Savatier (1822-1889), La Presidente. Drawing by Vincent Vidal.

Geneviève Halévy, Madame Émile Straus (1849-1926), by Nadar, 1887. Bizet's widow, she also had an affair with Maupassant.

Laure de Sade, Comtesse Adhéaume de Chevigné (1859-1936), by Federico de Madrazo y de Ochoa. Men were so entranced that a weekly salon was not enough – they insisted on visiting her every day.

Anna de Noailles (1876-1933), by Philip de Lazslo, 1913. Even Jean Cocteau envied her facility with words.

Winaretta Singer, Princess Edmond de Polignac (1865-1943). 'Diaghilev's Muse.'

The Duchesse Edmée de la Rochefoucauld (1895-1991) at the end of the 1980s. The last salonnière?

Paulette Nardal (1896-1985), hostess to the Négritude salon. She and her sister were the first black students to enrol in the Sorbonne.

et les ombres (1840) came with a subtitle, 'Fonction du poète'. And here Hugo changed his tune. 'The function of the poet is not to write hymns to nature but to prophesy, illuminate and point the way to the promised land.' Here too the artist was the leader of society.

This was the last book of verse Hugo was to publish for more than a decade. He was now well into his vast saga about the desperate world of the poor, *Les Misérables*, though publication was years away – 1862. In the run-up to the 1848 revolution Hugo seems to have replaced his interest in literature by his political ambitions. His *cénacle* had stopped meeting at his house though his young followers stayed together, forming their own group, the *petit cénacle*. The most notable of these were Gérard de Nerval and Théophile Gautier.

It was at this time and place that the word 'art' came into use with a wider meaning than hitherto, to mark all aesthetic activities that served no 'useful' purpose. Until that point the common usage was in the plural, as in *les beaux-arts*. By emphasising the word in its singular manifestation, the 'Jeunes-France' (as members of the *petit cénacle* referred to themselves) underlined the singleness of their vocation as an exclusive cult. 'For these gentlemen,' wrote one sarcastic critic in the *Revue de Paris* in 1833, '*art* is everything; painting; poetry, etc; these gentlemen are in love with *art*; these gentlemen despise anyone who does not work for *art's* sake, and they spend their lives talking *art*, discussing *art*.'[29]

There is some dispute as to whether this phrase, 'art for art's sake', was invented by Hugo, as he claimed, or by Gautier, who was very much at the forefront of this attitude. The men who saw themselves as part of this cult were united in hostility to the entire safe, self-satisfied – and as they saw it philistine – '*juste milieu*' establishment, led by the unexciting family at the top.[30]

UN ENSEMBLE DE PHÉNOMÈNES

Delphine, aka the Vicomte de Launay, at least to begin with, wrote fairly critically of the receptions given by the royal family at the Tuileries Palace, where she judged the guests – especially the foreign guests – to lack renown; they were not 'superiorities' at all. As she once put it: '*Le banquet royal a toujours l'air d'une table d'hôte.'* More and more her columns overlooked royalty and instead described the world of the fashionable salons, such as her own, in which she portrayed Paris as not so much a town as *'un ensemble de phénomènes'*, from the elegance of the fashions and the high quality of its manners to its exceptional conversational abilities.[31]

In her own salon, beyond the raft of romantic poets and novelists, there was Hugo's rival in the theatre, Alexandre Dumas. By and large the romantic dramas that were so popular in the 1830s have not stood the test of time and it seems that they achieved the success that they did due to the exceptional talents of a few outstandingly gifted players, among whom Marie Dorval and Frédérick Lemaître were the best known. But the plays did break new ground.

Dumas's *Antony* was based partly on his own life. Its narrative followed the development and consummation of an adulterous love affair.[32] The plot was straightforward, but the ending packed a punch. The husband is about to discover his wife and Antony *in flagrante* and so, in order to save her honour, Antony stabs the wife, his mistress, and pretends that he did so 'because she repulsed him'. As with Julien Sorel, in *The Red and the Black* – Stendhal's novel published in 1830 – Antony conceived of himself as a social pariah; as with Julien he seduced a married woman and ended by assaulting her. But the public's reaction was very different. Sorel's action evoked only outrage, but Antony's actions were admired by the young romantics of the time 'and pitied by all the young women'. Not irrelevant here were the 'Byronic railings against society' which Dumas put into Antony's mouth: 'The individual is rarely in the wrong, the social order always is.'[33]

Eugène Delacroix was the best known of the painters who were regulars in Delphine's salon. It is now recognised that the Salon (the regular exhibition) of 1827 launched the romantic school in painting. The older generation was represented that year by Gros (a portrait of Charles X on horseback) and Gérard (a ceremonial view of the coronation), while Ingres's *Apotheosis of Homer* was as classical as ever. But this was the year when, for the first time, the young romantics were present in numbers. Delacroix's contribution was *The Death of Sardanapalus.*

The sensation was on a par for that with *Hernani*. 'M. Delacroix's *Sardanapalus* has found favour in no one's eyes,' declaimed Étienne-Jean Delécluze, a pupil of David and a critic for the *Journal des débats*, 'neither among artists nor among members of the public ... The *Sardanapalus* is an artistic aberration.'[34] It was certainly new in image terms – there were contorted bodies writhing all over the large canvas. *Le Moniteur* noted the division among the salon-goers. A few thought it a masterpiece; most considered it absurd.

One of those who thought it a masterpiece was Hugo, who spoke out about it repeatedly. In fact, he actually thought the painting should be even more contorted. As he remarked to a journalist: 'The one thing I regret is that he did not set fire to this holocaust, the splendid scene would have been more splendid still if there had been a basket of flames licking around its base.' This shows Hugo's robust sense of romanticism compared with Delacroix's more tormented version. Hugo wanted 'orgiastic passion' whereas Delacroix painted his *fear* of it. This is reflected too in his reaction to the scandal: he took the picture away from the Salon and hid it. Well known as it is now, it was hardly seen at all until 1892 when it was bequeathed to the Louvre.[35]

Delacroix's other great picture was *Liberty Leading the People*. Produced in response to the events of July 1830, this shows a bare-breasted and bare-footed woman clambering over the barricades – and a number of dead bodies – brandishing the tricolour flag of the Revolution in one hand and a bayonetted musket in the other. She looks over her shoulder as the others follow and this leads us to the outline of Notre-Dame in the background, where the tricolour is also flying. The symbolism is fairly obvious, but it is the lush style – part-Rubens, part-Michelangelo – that sets it apart, its vivid detail bringing home the drama and chaos of revolution. It was bought by the government, who intended it to play a part in the Tuileries of the Citizen King, but that never came about and, after a while, the painting was returned to its author.

IDENTIFYING THE RENAISSANCE

Adolphe Thiers (1797–1877) was yet another of the 'superiorities' in Delphine's salon. He had made his name as a historian, publishing a celebrated (though much criticised, especially abroad) history of the French Revolution, in ten volumes, released between 1823 and 1827. Despite the number of volumes, more than 10,000 sets were sold and made him a rich man. A key figure in the July revolution of 1830 (which his books had helped bring about), and in the revolution of 1848, in a long career he served as prime minister in 1836 and 1840, and was responsible for the dedication of the Arc de Triomphe and the return of Napoleon's remains to France. He would go on to be prime minister for the third time in 1848 and served as president of France from 1871 to 1873. His history was fundamentally sympathetic to the aims of the Revolution and, broadly speaking, the conduct of the revolutionaries (but not the Terror). He criticised the monarchy, aristocracy and clergy for their obduracy.

The other historian in Delphine's salon was even more successful – as a historian – than Thiers: this was Jules Michelet (1798–1874). Like Thiers, Michelet wrote a history of the French Revolution, which his twentieth-century colleague François Furet described as 'the cornerstone of all revolutionary historiography and ... also a literary monument'. Like Thiers, Michelet's masterpiece was a multi-volume work, in his case a nineteen-volume *Histoire de France*, which he completed in 1867.

Michelet's father was a master printer and he might have followed that career in the imperial printing office except that he attended the famous Lycée Charlemagne, where he did so well that, on graduating from university in 1821, he was offered a professorship at the Collège Rollin. Michelet also produced a large number of lesser – but still interesting – volumes on a breathtaking, imaginative and eclectic range of subjects: vice, Luther, women in the Revolution, insects, birds, priests, love, mountains, sorcery.[36]

In his history of France, he brought the Middle Ages in particular to vivid life, though his most original innovation was to conceive and coin the word 'Renaissance' as an epoch in European history that represented a drastic break from mediaeval times.

In 1838 he was appointed to the chair of history at the Collège de France. Just then the Jesuits were making a comeback and Michelet, with the support of his friend Edgar Quinet, began a violent polemic against their influence. He was a left-wing republican, very opposed to the influence of the church. As 1848 approached, his views were expressed ever more forcefully and, despite their eloquence (acknowledged on all sides), he was suspended by the authorities. Being a republican, he refused to take the oath to the empire after Napoleon III's coup d'état and was dismissed from his position. When the Siege of Paris occurred, and then the Commune, he determined to write a grand history of the nineteenth century. He had not got beyond Waterloo when he died in 1874, aged seventy-five.

'For twenty years,' said Delphine in one of her later letters, 'we have heard salons abused for their tediousness, puerility &c. The railers seem blind to the fact that all our statesmen, all our men of genius, are men of the salons. Because Jean-Jacques [Rousseau] had been a lackey, it has been said that, to be eloquent, a person must be born in a low condition, or, if well born, must live with the vulgar; forgetting all the beautiful creations of genius that the elegant world has teemed with; and now, notwithstanding this experience, we hear unceasingly of the intellectual poverty of our salons, of the incapacity of the men of the world, of the futility of their ideas, and littleness of their views; and we hear these phrases everywhere, even in a salon, seated between Lamartine and Victor Hugo, or between Berryer and Odilon Barrot, who are, in our opinion, as delightful in conversation in French salons, as they are in poetry and oratory for the nation at large.'[37]

Anne Martin-Fugier picks up on this, and in *La Vie élégante* (her history of '*le tout* Paris', 1815–48) makes the point that during the July Monarchy politeness was menaced with extinction, but that Delphine de Girardin in particular worked hard to invest *le monde* with a moral and social dignity, and she did this by running her salon with a synthesis of two types of comportment – the serious and the frivolous. This, she says, was basically a traditional aristocratic mélange inherited from the court of the *ancien régime*, constantly revivified by the new developments of fashion and the ideas of the members of her salon.[38]

'A Life Based on More than Motherhood'

In 1830, when the revolution broke out that brought in the July Monarchy, Delacroix was 32, Balzac 31, Hugo and Dumas 28, Berlioz 27, Sand 26, and Gautier still in his teens. Balzac, in particular, had already written thirteen of the works that would eventually go to make up his extraordinary conception of the Comédie humaine, no fewer than ninety-one finished – and forty-six unfinished – stories, novels or essays about the France of the Restoration and what would become the July Monarchy, under the Citizen King, Louis-Philippe d'Orléans.

The Comédie was a quite unique exercise, consisting of 'Scenes from Private Life', 'Scenes from Provincial Life', 'Scenes from Military Life' and 'Studies of Manners in the Nineteenth Century'. There were fantasies, among them *Un peau de chagrin*, translated as 'The Wild Ass's Skin' – in which the magical epidermis of the title confers unlimited powers on its owner but shrinks each time it is used; philosophical works (*The Quest of the Absolute, The Elixir of Life, Christ in Flanders*); and straightforward essays (*The Physiology of Marriage*). In the Comédie, Balzac explores the use of money and power in the July Monarchy, ideas of heredity (bloodlines, parental secrets), the collective guilt of France hanging over from the Revolution and the Terror, the role of women and sex in society (the masculine and domineering title character in *Cousin Bette*), history and crime (*The Ball at Sceaux*, and *Old Goriot*, one of the most important titles, about an impoverished pasta-maker anxious to marry his daughters well and the near-criminal machinations by others to better themselves in society), religion (*The Atheist's Mass*) and so much else. It was and is a breathtaking accomplishment but in among the many fascinating (and occasionally tedious) stories there was one where Balzac let himself down.

Balzac was a friend of George Sand, who was in turn a friend of Marie d'Agoult. Marie d'Agoult is by no means as well known as Sand, but in many ways was far more consequential. She was one of the most romantic figures of all time, who gave up an enviable social position in Paris to elope with the Hungarian composer and virtuoso pianist Franz Liszt. Despite the scandal this caused, despite the (temporary) happiness Marie d'Agoult achieved by her drastic course of action, Sand – her supposed friend – shared details of the affair with Balzac, with the predictable result that he lightly disguised them in his 1839 novel, *Béatrix*. In this story, a handsome young lover falls for an older woman, Félicité des Touches (Sand), a celebrated writer who uses the pen name of Camille Maupin. (Sand was of course a pen name; her real name was Amantine Dupin.) To begin with, Félicité does not return the lover's affections and he moves on to 'a blonde marchioness', Béatrix de Rochefide (d'Agoult). Béatrix is represented as a beautiful but selfish woman, unequalled 'for cold-blooded cruelty and vulgarity'.[1] Balzac was pitiless in his depiction of d'Agoult and the story ends by Félicité/Sand entering a convent and Béatrix/d'Agoult finding love elsewhere.

The background to this story may lie in the fact that, while Marie d'Agoult was having her affair with Liszt, George Sand was having an affair with Chopin. However, at one point, Chopin dedicated one of his compositions to Marie, sparking a fit of jealousy in Sand, and provoking her to share what she knew with Balzac.

MIDNIGHT CHILD

Born Marie de Flavigny late in the day on 31 December 1805, in Frankfurt, Mme d'Agoult always described herself as a 'midnight child', there being an old saying in Germany that a child born at midnight 'is influenced by dark forces which show themselves in dreams and premonitions'.[2] Her father, Comte Alexandre-Victor de Flavigny, was known as a 'footloose', intransigent French royalist émigré. Her mother was Marie-Elisabeth Bethmann, daughter of a very wealthy German banker. The parents' relationship was both romantic and had its dark elements also: Flavigny had been incarcerated for a time in prison; Marie-Elisabeth visited him in his cell and stayed so long that scandal threatened unless they married.

Marie d'Agoult spent her early years in Germany where she met Chateaubriand, but after the Bourbon Restoration the family moved to Paris and she was sent to the Sacré-Cœur convent for her education. While there she showed a talent for the piano to such an extent that she was given additional lessons by Johann Hummel, who had himself been taught by Mozart. Later, at sixteen, by which time she was 'a striking, tall blonde with large blue eyes', when she was introduced to Parisian social life, she still found much the same attitude as in her convent. 'She attended balls with her mother but was not allowed to dance the waltz as the French considered that there was too much bodily contact which might arouse desire.'[3]

The high life of Paris, as Richard Bolster tells us, consisted at this time of three groups which would provide part of the backbone of Balzac's great work: the old aristocracy, which had survived since before the Revolution; the new nobility, deliberately created by Napoleon in his quest for social 'fusion'; and the ever-more important class of high finance, reflecting the Citizen King's ambition for people to 'enrichissez-vous'.[4]

After the comte died in 1819, Mme de Flavigny, with only herself to answer to, decided to open her own salon. Her timing was just right because she soon attracted a number of royalist members of parliament, not the least of whom was Joseph de Villèle, an ultra-royalist, who would become prime minister (for the first time of several times) in 1822. He was the first of five prime ministers Marie would come to know.

Marie met Delphine Gay at the latter's salon in 1826, by which time she was earning a reputation as a pianist. That did not obviate the need for a husband. Richard Bolster says that aristocratic manners had not changed much across the years of revolution and Napoleonic wars. In fact, it was hardly different even from the seventeenth century 'when the young Saint-Simon went to see the duc de Beauvilliers and expressed a wish to marry one of his daughters, leaving the choice to him'.

Charles d'Agoult, the choice of Marie's parents, was a soldier, who had fought in Spain during the Napoleonic wars, a man 'more thoughtful and regretful than eloquent'. The union was a marriage of convenience which would prove fatal in the long run. Marie never spoke about her own marriage but in addition to everything else, her husband was in an unfortunate position politically and militarily. Following the Restoration, Charles X had opted for policies that were popular among the Ultras – the fervent Bourbon monarchists – to the extent that he had dismissed many generals who had served with Napoleon, as d'Agoult had, and replaced them by members of the *ancien régime*, who were markedly inferior to those they replaced. For many, this was seen as deliberately provocative, as were the new draconian laws introduced to satisfy the demands of the church. In one example, those who stole valuables from ecclesiastical properties were condemned to wear black, walk shoeless to the guillotine and, once there, have their hands cut off before decapitation. The growing power of the priesthood under Charles was just one side of change.

This change was surprising to those who had known Charles before the Restoration. Well known for his libertinism in the *ancien régime*, during the Napoleonic wars he had betrayed a fulsome cowardice when he was given command by the British of an expeditionary force of French royalists charged with attacking the Quiberon peninsula in southern Brittany. During hostilities he had remained cowering aboard ship when his men were slaughtered by the opposing forces.

This was all background for Marie. A serious woman, as well as a passionate one, her sociological/political interests centred for a time on Saint-Simon and his programme for the eradication of poverty and the use of science and industry to ameliorate hardship.

LES TROIS GLORIEUSES

Despite her serious interests, Marie's moment had not yet come. She only became swept up in events when she was sitting in the opera one night and heard a rumour that Jules de Polignac, an ultra-royalist who had been exiled in London after the Revolution, and was now

ambassador to the Court of St James, had been recalled and was
about to be appointed prime minister. The rumour turned out to be
true but it was not quite the good news it might have been. Polignac
and the king introduced a number of new measures that, they
thought, would bring order to the realm but were instead repressive
and unpopular.[5] It was the height of summer, and protests began. In
an effort to maintain order, troops fired on the protestors and the
first barricades – made of cobblestones taken from the streets – were
erected. During the night a rash of posters went up across the city all
in favour of the Duc d'Orléans. In only three days – what became
known as 'les trois glorieuses' – the Bourbons fell and Louis-Philippe
d'Orléans became the Citizen King, not of France, but of the French.

The three days might have been glorious but the new king, from
the Orléans alternative line we have heard so much about, though
intelligent and moderate, was hardly exciting. In exile he had experienced poverty and carried out menial jobs, so in theory he should have
been in tune with many levels of French society. Instead, his reign was
dominated by those opposed to him, who fell into two very different
camps. On the one hand were the 'Legitimists', ultra-royalists who
wanted a return to the direct Bourbon line from Charles X; on the
other were the republicans, many of whom wanted Polignac executed.
When he escaped the guillotine, the republicans attacked the aristocracy for looking after their own. This meant that although aristocratic
life was still thriving, plots for change appeared to be everywhere.

In the middle of all this, however, and despite being beautiful,
rich and talented, Marie was growing increasingly anxious. How,
she continually asked herself, could she have contracted a marriage
to someone – however upright in so many ways – she did not love?
Gradually, she came to realise, motherhood was not enough for
her. She had experimented with religion, but that did not satisfy
her either, and she looked about her, noting that several women she
knew – Mme de Rauzan, Mme de La Bourdonnaye, Mme de La
Grange – held their own salons. At this time, too, a magnificent chateau became available at Croissy, near the River Marne, and she and
her husband snapped it up.[6]

Her first guests included Alexandre Guiraud, a poet from Limoux
in the south of France, now not so well known but who, in 1826, had

beaten Lamartine for a seat in the Académie française. Alexandre Soumet was another guest, also from the south, whose story *Norma, ou L'Infanticide* was adapted by Bellini for his well-known opera *Norma*; and there was Émile Deschamps, a romantic poet, a disciple of Hugo, who worked on the libretti for Berlioz's choral work *Romeo et Juliette*, and with Meyerbeer and Eugène Scribe on two operas, *Les Huguenots* and *Le Prophète*. Scribe was a prolific playwright who also produced a raft of libretti for some of the best-loved operas and operettas of all time, working with Rossini, Meyerbeer, Halévy, Donizetti, Bellini, Auber and, not least, Verdi.[7]

As this suggests, dramatics and music were just as much a backbone of Marie's salon as literature. She arranged concerts of the latest music by Berlioz, Chopin and Schubert (she was after all almost as much German as she was French), not surprisingly since she was so adept on the piano. In fact, 'adept' doesn't do justice to her level of talent. One evening she played the overture to Rossini's opera *Semiramis* when he himself was in the room, and the composer declared it 'the best performance since its writing'.[8]

In these circumstances, it is no surprise to learn that one of the guests in her salon was Franz Liszt. Marie herself described their first meeting in a memoir intended for publication after her death. It took place in December 1832, shortly after she had been to Geneva to help recover from a depression (and she was therefore at her most vulnerable). Liszt was five years younger than she (twenty-one to her twenty-six), but had taken the concert halls and the salons by storm when he was thirteen, everyone speaking of him as 'the new Mozart'. To her he seemed to float on air and she thought 'he had the anxious and distracted air of a ghost waiting for the chime of the clock to recall it into darkness'.[9]

Eventually, she invited him to Croissy, where she did her best to put him at his ease because he was always aware that he was not a member of the aristocracy.[10] For his part, he was keen to show her the parts of Paris life that he enjoyed, inviting her to a performance of *Antony* and one of the *Symphonie fantastique* by his friend Berlioz. Well connected and talented as she was on the piano, her friendship with Liszt took her to another level in the musical world.

A New Species of Melody

By the time Marie met Liszt, the grand opera of Meyerbeer and his contemporaries had succeeded the *bel canto* style of Rossini and Bellini. French music might not be as daring as, say, Wagner's harmonies, but it was in many ways more enjoyable, with melodic singing, and the Opéra in Paris had developed spectacle to the highest reaches. There was nowhere comparable at the time.

During the 1830s, led by Meyerbeer, opera became big business. Louis Véron, the first of the great directors of the Opéra, was overweight, a dandy in his dress, and liked a lot of jewellery but he sorted out the Opéra's finances and made it the most important house in Europe, where Eugène Scribe was the main librettist, François Habeneck the chief conductor, Marie Taglioni and Fanny Elssler the chief dancers, and Gilbert-Louis Duprez the great dramatic tenor. Heading the *corps de claque* was a man known to everyone only as Auguste, though his full name was Auguste Levasseur. The Opéra had its claque just as other theatres did. In the words of the *Musical World* in London: 'It would be folly for a new singer to appear without engaging the *chef de claque.*'

Meyerbeer was born in Berlin in 1791, a child prodigy. His first French opera, *Robert le Diable*, played in 1,843 European theatres in the 1830s. Meyerbeer had a simple set of beliefs: audiences did not go to the opera to be bored. As a result, in his operas no aria lasts too long and *bel canto* is eschewed, being replaced by lush orchestration, large, sweeping choruses, athletic ballet, melodies that everyone could whistle.[11]

Meyerbeer's style was overtaken by that of Liszt's great friend, Hector Berlioz. The most extraordinary aspect of Berlioz, perhaps, is that he was *not* a prodigy. He could 'pick out' notes on the guitar and the flute 'but that was it'. Paradoxically, not having a formal training may have been partly responsible for him becoming the first French romantic composer. For Berlioz not only created a new type of music, he also created the modern orchestra. He was the first person to express himself autobiographically in music, 'resulting in a new species of melody'.[12]

From the first he had the appearance of a romantic. Here is one description, by a music critic: 'He believed in neither God nor Bach. The high forehead precipitously over-hanging the deep-set eyes; the great, curving hawk nose ... the enormous shock of light-brown hair, against the fantastic wealth of which the barber could do nothing.'[13]

Size was part of Berlioz's appetite. Until that point, orchestras had rarely contained more than sixty instrumentalists. Berlioz's plans envisaged an orchestra of 150 but in his dreams he wanted three times that number, with a chorus of matching size, with thirty harps, thirty pianos and sixteen French horns. His concept of the symphony was aggressively new too. It was the first piece of 'programme music', meaning it told a story, painting pictures or scenes that led from one to the other, not at all easy to do in music.[14]

The *Fantastique* had been premiered in 1830, and people heard for the first time another Berlioz innovation, a theme that keeps running through the entire piece. He now produced a steady stream of great scores – *Harold en Italie* (1834), *Roméo et Juliette* (1839), *La Damnation de Faust* (1846), the oratorio *L'Enfance du Christ* (1854), *Les Troyens* (1859) and many other great works, 'in which in each case there is something that stirs the skin, something that doesn't seem quite right, something that veers vertiginously from the wild to the intimate that marks Berlioz at his coruscating best'. Théophile Gautier, in his *History of Romanticism* (1854), placed Berlioz with Hugo and Delacroix as the three great French romantics.[15] Marie was swept away by Berlioz almost as much as she was by Liszt.

BETRAYAL

Marie and Liszt became lovers in December 1833, though their relationship was as much intellectual as it was sensual. Liszt had many celebrated friends, not the least of whom were the critic Sainte-Beuve and Victor Hugo but also Balzac, Sand, Musset, Chateaubriand, Nodier and Heine, in exile in Paris.[16]

In May 1834 Marie discovered she was pregnant. At the time adultery counted as a criminal offence and in theory she could have been sent to jail for as much as two years, though in truth this punishment was rarely imposed. One way out might have been to resume sexual relations with her husband but she chose not to go that route. Having the child would provoke a scandal but it could, to a point, be weathered. Delacroix was thought by some to be the bastard son of either Émile de Girardin or Talleyrand and he was invited everywhere.

In this way began an itinerant period in Marie's life, starting in Geneva where, in addition to preparing for her next child, she began writing – in the first place in conjunction with Liszt – articles in musical journals. While she was in Geneva a friendship blossomed with George Sand, who knew Liszt well, originally through Chopin, who was one of her own celebrated lovers. Marie was an admirer of Sand's novel *Indiana* but, it turned out, Sand was only too ready to begin a friendship. She eventually dedicated her novel *Simon* to Marie.

Back in Paris, after a protracted stay in Geneva, so the world could get used to their arrangement, Marie and Liszt resumed their former lifestyle, consorting with Custine, Sainte-Beuve, Sue, Berlioz, Chopin and other musicians and a number of exiled writers who included Heinrich Heine and Adam Mickiewicz, poet, dramatist and translator, now regarded as the national poet of Poland. Marie invited Sand to be part of their 'set'.[17]

But then Marie's relationship with Sand began to falter and in fact a great act of betrayal was about to come off. Balzac had visited Sand at her home in Nohant, where she had given him an intimate account of the relationship between Marie and Franz. Sand sanctimoniously added that she herself could not write such a story 'out of loyalty', 'though it was perfect for a novel'. This led, in time, to Balzac's work *Béatrix*, about the disintegrating relationship between an aristocratic woman and a musician. It bore the subtitle 'Prisoners of Love', a phrase Marie had actually used in one of her letters to Sand.[18]

There was also no gainsaying the fact that Marie's relationship with Liszt was deteriorating too. In May 1839 she gave birth to Daniel, her fifth child and only son. Because Liszt was away on another of his long international tours, she decided to reopen her salon and take up more writing.

What Is a Classic?

Her friends at this time included Sainte-Beuve, Vigny and Jean-Jacques Ampère, the son of André-Marie, the creator of thermodynamics. She shared with Vigny a dislike of the bourgeois society then coming to prominence under the July Monarchy and she shared with Sainte-Beuve an admiration for Victor Hugo. Charles-Augustin Sainte-Beuve had in fact trained as a doctor – and practised as one for a time. But he had an abiding interest in literature and began writing for the newspapers as a critic. Marie was taken with his autobiographical novel, *Volupté*, published in 1834, but he would become better known for his exhaustive (five-volume) history of the Jansenist abbey of Port-Royal, a major piece of religious/philosophical history. He wrote a series of 'Causeries du lundi', light pieces that were published every Monday in *Le Constitutionnel*, and a celebrated essay, 'What Is a Classic?' The battle between the ancients and the moderns was an old tussle in France but Sainte-Beuve breathed new life into it, by reconciling the fact that there were ancient classics and there were modern classics and that a productive intellectual life should seek to discover these, become familiar with them, and then relax, knowing one had 'gone as far as one could'.[19]

Very familiar with English, German and Eastern literature, as well as with French, Sainte-Beuve made the point that it took time for a classic to be acknowledged, that, for example, Pope had in his time been elevated above Shakespeare, but that views had later changed. He conceded that Dante, Milton and Shakespeare were pre-modern classics, that France had little to show before the seventeenth century, that La Fontaine had not been favoured in his lifetime but had worn well, that Montaigne was a kind of 'proto-classic', that for him, Sainte-Beuve, Molière was superior to Racine and that the eighteenth century had produced four classics – Montesquieu, Buffon, Voltaire and Rousseau. He thought classical culture was healthy, romantic culture sickly. His point was this: the classic disturbs and runs counter to fixed ideas of what is beautiful and appropriate, and that there is a 'second order' of classics (Pope, Goldsmith) who add to the charm of life 'but do not disturb'.[20] Once we are familiar with the classics, he said, we can 'rest and cease from wandering'.

Marie would have liked to use Sainte-Beuve to recruit Hugo to her salon. She had met the latter at one of Delphine de Girardin's glittering evenings, together with Lamartine, Gautier and Balzac, on a night when Hugo had read lines from *Feuilles d'automne*. In the event, Hugo did not respond to Marie's overtures and she turned instead to Lamartine, also there that night, and he did become a good friend and a regular habitué of her salon. He was not the only one to respond to her. That same night she also – not surprisingly – met Delphine's husband, Émile, and it seems he was very taken with her too. Impressed by her intelligence, he made his publications available to her. Marie chose to write under the male name of Daniel Stern.[21]

The offer by Émile was not, apparently, totally professional and he began courting her assiduously, something she relayed to Liszt with a mixture of concern and amusement. Liszt was slightly thrown when Émile took Marie to the Champs-Élysées to watch the return of Napoleon's remains from St Helena. But she continued true to Franz, even when Émile gave her a whole page to review Sand's latest novel. She used the opportunity to criticise it as a feeble work, an example of a writer 'in decline'. It was welcome revenge for what Sand had done with *Béatrix*.[22]

Despite her feelings for Liszt, the relationship was increasingly rocky. His many European tours, rapturously received, had led him into any number of liaisons and she, being aware of this, had found solace of a kind in Georg Herwegh, a German poet who she had got to know through Liszt, who had set a number of Herwegh's verses to music.

In fact, Herwegh was rather more than a poet. He was in Paris in exile from Germany, after a 'career' of one political protest after another. He had taken part in a failed uprising in the German revolution of 1848, and even before all that he was in close contact with both Karl Marx and Arnold Ruge, co-editors of the journal the *German–French Yearbook*. Ruge went so far as to suggest that he and Marie and the others live together in a commune.[23]

MAL DE SIÈCLE

With her relationship with Liszt over, she began to pay more attention to her writing. Her new novel was called *Nélida*, an anagram of her pen name, Daniel (Stern). Nélida is a young woman who wishes to become a nun but is dissuaded by the mother superior, who is herself having doubts about convent life.[24] This was followed by *Valentia*, another story of an orphan brought up in a convent and sexually ignorant. This was seen as yet another attempt by Marie to confront George Sand on her own territory, which became even more apparent when, in 1847, she started to publish her 'Thoughts on Women' in a progressive publication, *La Revue indépendante*. Here she took the gloves off, writing that 'owing to the ponderous mediocrity of the recent works by George Sand' she had decided to insert herself into the debate about the social situation of women, going on to urge them to stop thinking of themselves as victims. This was quickly followed, in the same year (and on the eve of the events of 1848), by her *Essays on Liberty*, a step up in the level of her ambition. These essays embraced a very modern set of concerns – the protection of the environment, an attack on the death penalty, free healthcare for the poor.[25] It doesn't sound like it but this was in fact still part of the romantic sensibility, an aspect of what Musset had called the *mal de siècle*, the idea that the nineteenth century was leaving behind the world of the *ancien régime* but had not yet found a new direction, that the new world of science and industry had not yet provided the answer.

Change was under way within her. At the outbreak of the 1848 revolution, she was forty-two, still attractive, still dressing stylishly, and one of perhaps four women – with Delphine de Girardin, George Sand and Princesse Mathilde (chapter 30) – who defined the age, and all of whom, to some extent, were rivals. Unlike the others, however, Marie was turning away from the aristocracy, sensing that its political influence was now all but played out.

OVERTAKING GEORGE SAND

She followed the events of 1848 closely. Even in this she had Sand in mind. Being so close to the events of the revolution, Marie quickly determined to make a proper account of what was happening and, while Sand published mainly sentimental articles supporting the proletariat, Marie went around the city taking notes and carrying out interviews. Her approach, just as with the themes of her novels, was very modern. Even Lamartine, briefly foreign minister, agreed to see his old friend, and asked her who might serve 'the Second Republic' as foreign diplomats.[26]

The uprisings of 1848 were, we are told, the first 'class war' in history. Hatred by the French for the French was again an issue, as it had been in the 1789 Revolution, and would be again in the Commune and the Second World War. The articles that Marie now composed, the 'Republican Letters', written before her great, sweeping history, were a step up for her from anything that had gone before. She responded to the moment – tackling the big questions such as the meaning of freedom, the understanding of democracy, the very idea of social justice. Her pen portraits of the leading politicians were factually precise, psychologically insightful. Finally, she had overtaken George Sand.

Impressive as this was, it paled alongside the *History of the Revolution of 1848*, without question her finest work. In this book, she combined two unrivalled qualities. In the first place, there was her direct contact with the participants which gave her book an immediacy lacking in other, later accounts. In one incident, when Lamartine faced a rebellious mob, mayhem could have broken out at any time: 'Twenty times during these critical hours, Lamartine's life depended on every word and gesture he made. At one moment someone swung an axe near his head, while the crowd anxiously drew breath. Whether he did not see it, or whether he coolly reflected that this incident would help him, he summoned up all his strength and continued to speak with consummate eloquence.' The insurgents dispersed back to the dark slums of the city, singing on their way. And this was the second quality of the book and makes it still worth reading – the narrative drive. The thrust of her history so impressed Flaubert that he used it for his great work, *L'Éducation sentimentale*.[27]

An Impressive Extended Family

Marie may have overtaken George Sand, and written a masterpiece, but not everything was going smoothly in her life. For one thing, the Republic of 1848 had not lasted long – Louis-Napoleon Bonaparte's coup d'état of December 1852 had brought in, among other things, the Haussmannisation of Paris and her own house was one of those marked for demolition. Another problem was the increasing distance between herself and her children with Liszt, two of whom had married considerable personages. Blandine had married Émile Ollivier, who would become prime minister of France, while Cosima first married Hans von Bülow and then Richard Wagner.[28]

But in the last phases of her life – now that she was accepted as a writer of the first rank – her salon assumed a higher profile. Her opinion of the emperor was as low as to be expected and her reunions became one of the centres of opposition. The country seemed politically stable, and the economy was booming, but Marie maintained her taste for trouble and kept up a lively correspondence with, among others, Louis Blanc, Lajos Kossuth and Giuseppe Mazzini. Blanc was in exile in London for his role in the 1848 revolution, Kossuth was a fellow journalist but also governor-president of Hungary during the events of 1848, and Mazzini was Kossuth's opposite number in Italy and an ardent advocate of unifying that country. Her letters to these individuals, a mix of the personal and the political, were often read aloud in her salon.

In the 1860s, in the run-up to the Franco-Prussian War, Marie's salon continued as a centre of opposition to Napoleon III, if anything gaining in importance as the regime began to lose its earlier popularity. Another reason for the importance of Marie's salon was the decision by the emperor – dissatisfied with the increasingly reactionary advice of his notoriously interfering Spanish grandee wife, Eugénie de Montijo – to turn to the more liberal Émile Ollivier, Marie's son-in-law (though Blandine had died some years before). Ollivier had started out as far more liberal than the emperor but they had gradually both modified their views and, although they were still some way apart, Ollivier could not resist the lure – and allure – of power.

Ollivier took office in January 1870, just months before the outbreak of the Franco-Prussian War (chapter 36). Marie spent the early part of the year in the country, returning to Paris after an absence of seventeen months. It was not possible just yet to re-form her salon and she stayed with her daughter Claire, who suffered from clinical depression. Following the disasters of the Franco-Prussian War, in the summer Ollivier had moved to Italy, living under an assumed name, but Marie wrote to him, describing in detail what life in a ruined Paris was like. Ironically, paradoxically, in the Commune she was able to resume her salon (though the fall in the stock market had hit her earnings) and she reported that there was more life now than during the siege. Among her regulars was Jules Grévy, who would serve as president of France after her death.

Amid all the change and mayhem, one pleasant accolade was to come her way. In 1872 the Académie française honoured her with a literary prize. However, this was not for her history of the 1848 revolution but for a history of the Low Countries in the seventeenth century – a non-controversial subject. All the same she was very pleased; George Sand was never so honoured.[29]

The award prompted Marie to write her memoirs, which were published after her death in March 1876, three months before Sand's. *Mes Souvenirs 1806–1833* has been described as a 'softened form of feminism'. She was hard on the aristocracy, which, she felt, had progressively withdrawn from politics as the decades had passed, and she advocated proper education for women, so they could play a proper role in society, though she did not go so far as to argue for them to be given the vote.

The memoir did not cover her relationship with Liszt (who died ten years later), which she had intended to cover in a subsequent work. A version was eventually published by Blandine's son in which Marie forgave Liszt a lot of the heartache he had caused her. She felt he had played a pivotal role in her destiny, lifting her to celebrity and drama, and that the course of their love was 'timeless'. Above all, 'she had based her life on more than motherhood'.[30]

'Notre-Dame des Arts'

One evening in the early 1840s, Princesse Lætitia-Mathilde-Frédérique-Aloïssia-Élisabeth Bonaparte attended a costume ball in Florence in which she was dressed as Diana the Huntress. So impressive and beautiful did she appear that applause broke out among the fellow guests. Warmed by this reception – and emboldened – Mathilde, as she was known, took the opportunity to insult a fellow female guest who she happened to know was her husband's mistress. Whereupon her husband approached her – and slapped her across the face for all to see.

Mathilde's husband, Anatoly Nikolaevich Demidov, was in some respects her third choice. Born in Trieste in May 1820, when the Bonapartes were banned from France, when Napoleon himself was still on St Helena and had just less than a year to live, Mathilde was Napoleon's niece, daughter of his youngest brother, Jérôme, once king of Westphalia but now known by the 'derisory' title of Prince de Montfort. Very well educated, both academically and socially (she had been forced to stand in a box, so she knew how to curtsey properly), Mathilde could – on her mother's side – boast quite a lineage. Her mother's stepmother was a daughter of George III and also related to the tsar. Her English ancestry, however, was by no means central to who she was – as a Bonaparte, England for her would always be the country of Nelson and Wellington.[1]

But, of course, in France being a Bonaparte was not nothing. A change seems to have come over her in 1835 when her mother died, when she was fifteen. After the period of mourning, her thoughts – and of those around her – turned to marriage. The first candidate suggested was her cousin, son of Louis-Napoleon, who had been king of Holland, and was also called Louis. According to what she said later, he 'courted me assiduously'. There is no doubt that he gave her a splendid ring set with turquoise forget-me-nots but whether that amounted to an engagement band is somewhat doubtful. A marriage of Napoleons might have been a formidable alliance, but we shall never know for his political aims interfered. Louis was to stage three coups d'état, in 1836, 1840 and 1852, the first two of which failed, meaning that he was variously exiled to America, then imprisoned for six years before he escaped to England.

The second candidate was similarly attractive politically. In the summer of 1837, Adolphe Thiers arrived in Italy with an audacious plan. Thiers was a lawyer and journalist, one of two (the other was François Guizot) who through their writings, as we have also seen, had changed the understanding of the French Revolution. In January 1830 he had founded his own newspaper which had campaigned for a British-style constitutional monarchy and when Charles X had mounted *his* coup d'état in July 1830, reducing the size of the electorate, removing press freedom, and provoking revolt, as we have seen, Thiers had led a delegation to the residence of Louis-Philippe, Duc d'Orléans, offering him the post of lieutenant-general of the kingdom. The duc accepted, becoming Citizen King, on the side of modest reform.[2]

Thiers was prime minister several times throughout the July Monarchy (1830–48) and so was well placed to approach Mathilde in 1837 with the idea of an alliance between her and none other than Louis-Philippe himself. In its way it was an imaginative and bold idea: a union between the House of Bonaparte and the House of Orléans 'would give glamour to an unattractive bourgeois monarchy, and it would lessen the danger of a Bonaparte restoration'.[3] Mathilde, being banned from France, had never met Orléans but no matter – she was sympathetic to the proposal and she was to say later that, had the arrangement gone through, Louis-Philippe's disastrous excursions would never have come about.

The arrangement did not go through, but more because of what was happening on her side in Italy, than anything that was happening in Paris. For just then a suitable suitor had appeared. This was the 25-year-old Demidov. His background was far from straightforward. He was descended from blacksmiths who the tsar had warmed to – quite by chance – and awarded a plot of land, which was, unknown to anyone at the time, rich in iron ore. This had been successfully converted into enormous wealth, and social position, but marriage to Mathilde would seal the Demidovs' ascent.

Mathilde's father was not drawn to Demidov, however. Anatoly was widely known as a philanderer. Even when Demidov made it clear he would curb his behaviour, matters dragged on, the financial side of things taking time to sort out. While she was waiting, Mathilde was pleased to welcome the arrival that summer in Florence of none other than Franz Liszt. In a letter to Claudius Popelin, a history painter and enameller, she reported that Liszt had a beautiful woman with him. 'She's left her husband and 5 children, she's the Comtesse d'Agoult. I met her at Bartolini's where she is having her bust done like I am and I found her very pleasant. She is tall and thin, she looks like the figure of Hunger ... she has done very wrong, there's no doubt of that, but at least she has been carried away by genius, not by self-interest.'[4]

The marriage with Demidov eventually took place in the Greek chapel in Florence in November 1840. By some accounts, when Louis-Napoleon – who was then in exile in London after his second attempted coup d'état – heard about the marriage he dissolved in tears. Caroline Murat, Napoleon I's sister, said in her memoirs that had Mathilde married Louis, and become empress, the Franco-Prussian War would never have been 'allowed' to occur.

Meanwhile, Mathilde had a war nearer home, for the marriage was far from being a success. Anatoly, suffering from a series of ailments, was irascible and reverting to his old habits, going so far as to suggest that they should both take lovers and avoid having children, which was not at all to Mathilde's taste. This was when she met the man with whom she was to first find an emotional attachment. Émilien, Comte de Nieuwerkerke, was by profession a sculptor who would, with Mathilde's help, become a very influential fine arts civil servant in Second Empire France. Mathilde and he met in 1845 and before the following year was out they fled to Paris together.[5]

In Paris, besides stimulating Mathilde's emotions, Nieuwerkerke knew everyone in the art world, the social world, the intellectual world – *mondains* of every stripe – and he helped her to establish her first salon in the rue de Courcelles. She was swiftly at home, for Louis-Philippe continued to show her every affection. (He had finished his exile not long before in 1846.)

Events moved swiftly around her. The revolution of 1848 resulted in the Second Republic and in the ensuing elections Louis-Napoleon was voted in with a large majority. People asked themselves if the old plan – for the houses of Orléans and Bonaparte to be united – was again in the offing. But Louis was busy, now had an English mistress, and his mind seems to have been elsewhere. He did appoint Jérôme, Mathilde's father, as president of the Senate, to which was attached an enormous income and residence in the hôtel des Invalides. This did nothing to quell Mathilde's ambition, which now lay more in the direction of the creative and intellectual worlds, and would lead in time to her soubriquet of 'Notre-Dame des Arts'.[6] Her proximity to the powers that be, in the form of her father and Louis-Philippe d'Orléans, meant that she was always trying to bring her influence to bear on appointments in the arts – elections to the academy, for instance, or directorships of museums. She was in particular very hopeful that her position would help Nieuwerkerke become superintendent of France's major museums.

Her salon was now in full swing. Some of her habitués were names we have become familiar with – Mérimée, Jules Sandeau, who had collaborated with George Sand, Émile and Delphine de Girardin, and even Liszt and Marie d'Agoult.[7] In 1850 she took the opportunity to rent from the Marquise de Custine – a travel-writer, a friend of both Mme de Staël and Chateaubriand, whose father and grandfather had been guillotined in the Revolution – a chateau she had admired for some time. This was Saint-Gratien, near Enghien (now a northern suburb of Paris), which she used to extend her salon. One of her first visitors was Louis-Philippe himself, in July 1851, who made an odd remark. He admired Saint-Gratien, he said, but added that, come 1852, her house in Paris would be too small for her.[8]

On the night of 1 December 1851, Louis-Napoleon held his usual Monday-evening reception at the Élysée. The last guests left at around half past ten, after which he and a handful of close confidants removed themselves to his study. There, he handed each the text of three separate proclamations. In one it said that the Assembly was trying to seize the power that Louis-Napoleon held directly from the people, as a result of the vote in the most recent election. The second said it was his *duty* to protect and preserve the republic. In the third it said that he had re-established universal male suffrage, which the Assembly had reduced, and so he now intended to hold a plebiscite two weeks hence so the people could decide for themselves which government they wanted.

The next morning 300 deputies arrived at the Palais Bourbon to find it locked. Before they could adjourn, the police arrived to arrest them. Later that morning Louis rode out of the Élysée on a black stallion alongside Jérôme Bonaparte, the former king of Westphalia, the former emperor's brother and Mathilde's father, a symbol of what was to come. What was to come immediately was an attempt to erect barricades across the city, but no one's heart was really in it, and when troops marched into the city three days later, they found it easy enough to smash what had been erected, killing many bystanders and wrecking several well-known cafés. If anyone put up a fight, they were shot on the spot. Overall, some 27,000 protestors were arrested and tried, 9,000 deported to Algeria. By French revolutionary standards, not much blood had been shed, but tens of thousands of lives were disrupted.

When the plebiscite came off, 7 million voted for Louis-Napoleon and fewer than 600,000 opposed him, a resounding victory. Technically, France was still in the Second Republic but that vision of Jérôme accompanying Louis on horseback did not lie. On 2 December he had announced that he would be president for ten years. On 4 January 1852, it was announced that the currency would bear his effigy.[9] Later that year the imperial flags were restored to the army, surrounded by their gilt eagles, and Louis announced an imperial building programme in which the Louvre would finally be completed and joined to the Tuileries. This also presaged ideas he had about rebuilding Paris.

Mindful of her position more than ever now, and recalling Louis's strange comments of the year before, Mathilde now moved into nobler premises and reopened her salon in the rue de Berri. Louis had himself made it available and he came to her first gathering in the new location.

In short order, the social side of the Second Empire began to glitter. Mathilde herself went everywhere, but she was most interested in the theatre and in music. In addition to the familiar roster of writers – Dumas, Mérimée, Viel-Castel – this was a good time for French theatre, Mathilde in particular following the plays of François Ponsard, Émile Augier and Gustave Nadaud.

Many of Ponsard's plays feature women in the title roles, this being partly a result of his liking for Rachel, a well-known actress of the day. His *L'Honneur et l'argent* cleverly incorporated the values of the empire, while *Le Lion amoureux* dealt with the revolutionary period, not without some wit and sympathy for women. *Galilée*, a play about the life of Galileo being forced to recant his work by the Inquisition, drew criticism from the church. The plays of Augier were also anti-clerical and anti-romantic, in particular *Le Mariage d'Olympe*, where the courtesan is presented more realistically than in Dumas's *La Dame aux camélias*, while in another play, the husband is treated more sympathetically than the romantic lover, an original twist. Augier also wrote light comedies. The phrase '*nostalgie de la boue*' – meaning an attraction to low life and degradation – is taken from *Mariage d'Olympe*. Gustave Nadaud was a *chansonnier*, a songwriter whose songs were often banned under the Second Empire, thus underlining the eclectic nature of Mathilde's tastes.[10]

Like a lot of people drawn to the arts, in particular the performing arts, Mathilde was no earnest or academic egghead, but she did recognise talent when she came across it. This was true in music, for example, where she formed a firm friendship with Camille Saint-Saëns, 'a small, dandified, peppery man', who became a regular in the rue de Berri. He has been described as the most awesome child prodigy in the history of music, more so even than Mozart. Blessed with absolute pitch, he was able to master the piano at two-and-a-half, and could read and write music at three, at which age he composed his first piece. At five he gave his first public performance on the piano and at seven he was reading Latin and collecting biological specimens, for he also had an interest in science, becoming later a member of the Astronomical Society of France.[11]

He made his official public debut at the age of ten when, for an encore (and showing off not a little) he offered to play 'any of' Beethoven's thirty-two piano sonatas from memory.[12] Extremely forceful, 'dangerous to cross' as an adult, he had restless, piercing eyes and was a quick-fire talker. He was also blessed with total recall, which helped him become one of the finest pianists – and organists – of his day. He was organist at the Madeleine for many years.

Saint-Saëns was an early advocate of Wagner and in 1861 was appointed a teacher at the École Niedermeyer, a school for the study and performance of church music. Here his most gifted pupil was Gabriel Fauré. Like the writers in Mathilde's salon, and despite his enthusiasm for Wagner, he was opposed to romanticism, in favour of classicism, clarity and refinement. The irony is that, despite his enormous gifts, Saint-Saëns never really lived up to his potential. Only one of his thirteen operas ever looked like being popular – this was *Samson et Dalila* and that was premiered in Weimar, not in Paris. Also still popular is 'The Swan', sometimes known as 'The Dying Swan', a piece for solo cello and the penultimate movement from *Carnival of the Animals*, a symphonic poem of fourteen movements. Saint-Saëns dedicated his *Sérénade* for piano, organ and violin to Mathilde. It was performed in her salon in January 1856.

She was also taken with Gounod and saw to it that his comic opera *Le Médecin malgré lui*, based on Molière's play of that name, went ahead at the Théâtre-Lyrique when the management of the Comédie-Française objected that they had the exclusive performance rights.

THE STRUGGLE AGAINST ANONYMITY

This gives an idea of the forcefulness of the princess, something that was noted by the Goncourt brothers, who had had their doubts about her to begin with but gradually warmed to her, as they realised that she was an agreeable mixture of shyness and kindness but didn't make a show of it. The brothers, especially in the famous photograph of them by Nadar, were brooding and terribly serious-minded. They were flattered by Mathilde's evident interest in them, though they might not have been, for their first novel – they had begun writing together after a sketching holiday – was published on 2 December

1851, the very day of Louis-Napoleon's coup d'état, so that their eagerly awaited debut was quite overwhelmed by larger events. They were to write more novels, very detailed psychological studies but with minute descriptions of material things, in which they affected to show that the passing of life has no order, and that that is the way to enjoy it.

But they have become best known for their journal, which they kept from 1851 until 1896, full of caustic, searing *bons mots*, replete with snobbery, 'soaring accounts of pettiness' and superciliousness (they felt they were arbiters of intelligence), and a 'repository of all the woes and disappointed hopes suffered in their hard and horrible struggle against anonymity'.[13] The details of their everyday Parisian existence come to life in this way. 'Baudelaire was at the table next to ours. He was without a cravat, his shirt open at the neck and his head shaved, just as if he were going to be guillotined.' 'Everything is unique, nothing happens more than once in a lifetime.'[14] On another occasion they recorded an outburst by Mathilde against what she called 'empty' women, whose only concern was a preoccupation with their children. 'All this occupation', she said with a shiver, 'with creatures who give you no return.'[15]

Despite their sometimes coarse behaviour, Gautier and Flaubert were prominent regulars in Mathilde's salon. Flaubert also shared with Mathilde, and with the Goncourts, a notorious alienation from the common herd.[16] 'Between us and the crowd there exists no link, unluckily for the crowd, unluckily for us above all. But since there is a reason for everything, and since the whim of an individual appears to me as legitimate as the appetites of a million men and can take up as much room in the world, it is necessary, leaving material considerations out of account and neglecting humanity which rejects us, that we should live for our vocation, climb up into our ivory tower, and there, like an Indian dancing girl surrounded by perfumes, live alone with our dreams.'[17] Flaubert's distaste for his own age was legendary – he compared it at one point to excrement in his mouth. Flaubert and the Goncourts occupied a privileged position – they did not need to rely on the proceeds of their works for their livelihood, they had inherited wealth. This emboldened them in their views, but it also distanced them. This was especially true of the Goncourts' novels, which have not stood the test of time. 'Anyone who opens them today is aware of a kind of sepulchral chill wafted from the printed pages.'[18]

In addition, Flaubert thought that art was converging with science. 'Literature will more and more take on the aspect of science; it will be above all else *expository*, which is not the same thing as saying it will be didactic.' It was something the Goncourts agreed with; they felt they had identified 'nerves' as an important ingredient of the era's sensibility.[19] Mathilde, too, was – up to a point – interested in science. Later on, she would play a not insignificant role in the public career of Louis Pasteur, though she never warmed to the impressionists, who were also interested in new scientific theories about light.

James Wood summed up Flaubert in this way. 'Novelists should thank Flaubert the way poets thank spring; it all begins again with him. There really is a time before Flaubert and a time after him. Flaubert decisively established what most readers and writers think of as modern realist narration.'[20]

Mathilde had a benign attitude to Flaubert and looked on generously as he fulminated against the horrors of the bourgeois society that the emperor was intent on creating. She even went so far as to recommend to Victor Duruy, the minister of public instruction, that he should in turn recommend to the emperor that Flaubert be given the Légion d'honneur. It gives us some idea of her standing that Duruy replied: 'I am glad to be able to comply with the wishes of Your Imperial Highness.'[21]

Being so close to power – socially if not intellectually – was not without its problems for Mathilde, and one of them was Émile de Girardin. As we have seen, he and his wife, Delphine, were a sociable couple, even a 'power couple' as we would say. To begin with, their relationship with Mathilde had blossomed. Émile had asked Mathilde to be godmother to his daughter. But, as time went by, in his newspapers Girardin started more and more to attack the emperor and his government. At the same time, his papers also published some snide comments about Nieuwerkerke, hinting that he was no longer quite so faithful to Mathilde. The end of the friendship was sudden.

Another setback occurred when there was a break with Nieuwerkerke. Since their flight from Florence, and under Mathilde's influence, he had made his mark as a sculptor, securing several high-profile commissions, and – again with her help – he had parlayed that into a plum job, first as *intendant* of fine arts in the emperor's household and then as *surintendant* of all the imperial museums. This made him responsible for four great institutions – the Louvre, the Luxembourg Palace, Versailles and the chateau of Saint-Germain-en-Laye. This was no small domain and Nieuwerkerke became in fact a sort of minister of cultural affairs, looking after the paintings and other objects, and being responsible for new commissions and for the organisation of the Paris Salon. He got around and he knew everyone – and he became a senator.

Nieuwerkerke was not universally popular – his tastes, as mentioned earlier, were for the ancient and classical and he was violently anti-romantic. In 1869 Mérimée, down in Cannes, read about the break between Mathilde and Nieuwerkerke in the press and wrote to Eugène Viollet-le-Duc, a fellow member of Mathilde's salon and the architect who had restored many of the fine buildings in France disfigured during the Revolution: 'The *Surintendant* is said to be in love and very cruel to our friend.'[22]

But she wasn't down for long. We gain a glimpse of the affection in which her guests held her in a letter from Gautier, sent from Egypt. It was November 1869, and he had been invited there for the opening of the Suez Canal. Following his successful books *Voyage en Espagne* and *Voyage en Italie*, he had become known as a travel-writer though by that time he had lost a lot of his taste for travel. In one letter to Mathilde, he wrote: 'Princess, I'm grieved to think that the honour of being watched from the top of the pyramids by forty centuries and a half will cost me my Wednesday with Your Imperial Highness.'[23]

In January of the following momentous year – 1870 – Mathilde opened her first salon of the season with a duet from Rossini's *Barber of Seville*. Present that night were Nieuwerkerke, Flaubert, Baron Haussmann and someone from her earlier life in Italy, Claudius Popelin. His attendance attracts attention for we are invited to think that it was about now that he became her lover. Fuel is added to the fire here because, in that very month, Nieuwerkerke was removed from his high office, and of course Mathilde was now hardly minded to intervene to save him. Moreover, his demise was overshadowed by a much greater one only three days later, when the world learned that Baron Haussmann, also present at the Rossini duet, and the great redesigner and rebuilder of modern Paris, had been forced to resign his office as prefect of the Seine *département*, a post he had held since 1853. Long criticised for his 'fantasy' accounting, it was now revealed that the prefect had landed the city of Paris with a deficit – brought about by his virtually uncontrolled extensive building programme – of no less than £30 million sterling.[24]

When the Franco-Prussian War broke across France, Mathilde made for Mons in Belgium. She took with her sixty-two pieces of luggage. She kept in touch with the emperor and urged him to speak to the people of France. He realised, too late, that he had been tricked into war by Bismarck (chapter 36) and, following Louis-Napoleon's capture, on 4 September, Mathilde's old friend Adolphe Thiers, who had originally suggested an alliance between the houses of Orléans and Bonaparte, became head of the administration. At the age of seventy-three.

The capture of the emperor was disastrous news for Mathilde, but things got worse. On 26 February 1871, Thiers had no choice but to sign what was clearly a shameful peace with Bismarck. Three days later, even more shameful, the Prussians marched into Paris. The day after that, Dumas *fils*, who was only too aware that the princess might storm back, wrote to her, begging her not to return.[25] It did the trick.

But circumstances still did not improve. On 24 May, three days before Mathilde's fifty-first birthday, the Communards set fire to Paris. It was the ultimate disaster of French against French but, after four days of fighting, the Commune was overthrown and Paris was liberated (again, see chapter 36). Gautier dashed off to Brussels to bring her back, but she hadn't waited – she had taken a train by herself and, we are told, 'arrived at the Gare du Nord incognito'.

It did not take her long to revive her salon after the war was ended, where her later 'lions' included Hippolyte Taine and Alphonse Daudet. Taine was an Anglophile, who taught at Oxford, wrote a well-received history of English literature and was influential with his idea that a work of art is best understood as the product of three influences, race, milieu and 'moment', what we would understand these days as zeitgeist. Daudet wrote several plays but was noted for two books, one a vivid account of his last years of syphilis, which attacked his spine. *In the Land of Pain* was to become a classic of its kind though it was not published until well into the twentieth century. His other book was *L'Immortel*, a bitter attack on the Académie française, which he was never to enter, and in which he portrayed Princesse Mathilde (as Maria-Antonia, Duchess Padovani) as without respect or compassion, 'the fullness of her life belying the emptiness of her heart'.

La Grande Française

Verberie is a small town in Picardy. It was famous in medi-aeval times, being the residence of the Frankish kings, and it was there that, in the ninth century, Ethelbald, King of Wessex, came to wed his thirteen-year-old bride, Charles the Bald's daughter, Judith. By the time that Robert Louis Stevenson found his way to Verberie, in the late nineteenth century, it was chiefly known – if it was known at all – for its Sauternes and its oysters. And it was oysters that featured large in the young life of Juliette Lambert, Juliette Adam as she would later become better known. Juliette well remembered the Fridays of her childhood when, at ten o'clock in the morning, the oyster cart from Boulogne would arrive, 'bringing twelve dozen oysters for the family'. Yes, twelve dozen: her father and grandfather ate four dozen each, her mother and her grandmother two dozen each.

It was typical of *la France profonde*. Her grandmother lived her life in thrall to the 'Human Comedy' of Honoré de Balzac. 'Turning over the pages of his ninety-seven novels, or sitting over her embroi-dery frame, she lived the lives of his five thousand characters.'[1] Although she owed a great deal to her grandmother, as we shall see, Juliette Lambert never needed to live through fictional characters for she experienced a raft of momentous events, some of which she helped to shape.

She lived through the revolution of 1848, the coup d'état of 1851, the Siege of Paris, the civil war of the Commune, and two invasions of her homeland. She became the hostess of a leading political salon, and the founder and editor for two decades of an influential fortnightly periodical, *La Nouvelle Revue*; she was for many years the intimate friend and colleague of Léon Gambetta, Alphonse Thiers and Émile de Girardin, together with George Sand, Gustave Flaubert, Victor Hugo, Pierre Loti, Paul Bourget and Maurice Barrès. By the beginning of the First World War, she was known everywhere as '*La Grande Française*'.

She grew up as the daughter, granddaughter and – for a while – the wife of doctors. Her childhood, until her marriage at the age of sixteen, was marked – but, given subsequent developments, not marred – by a series of what we might, with justification, call kidnappings. These were brought about by the fact that her father, a lovable but chaotic man, a revolutionary in many ways, squandered money on his scientific experiments, leaving Juliette and her mother in privation, so that her maternal grandparents – much better off, and better organised with more common sense – carried her away from her parents more than once.

Throughout her childhood and youth her grandmother's and her father's influence alternated (he wasn't all bad, being a gentle feminist) but Juliette always said, as an adult: 'My love for my grandmother and for my daughter have been the two great passions of my life.'[2] They were also at odds politically and religiously. Her father was an aggressive agnostic, bitterly anti-clerical, and had refused to baptise her, whereas her grandparents were staunch conservative Catholics and managed her baptism later in secret. The constant family quarrels exerted a profound effect on her character.

Thanks to her grandparents she received a good – intellectually rigorous – education and thanks to her parents and their brothers and sisters – her uncles and aunts – she was given experience of living in a more relaxed way in the countryside, and learned about nature, and how to enjoy it.

In this, her father was much influenced by Rousseau, but he was also a firm believer in the right of all men to work, and in Pierre-Joseph Proudhon's syndicalism – a form of proto-Marxism. Though in years to come some of her father's notions were to appear to her quixotic, and as time went on his lack of common sense was to make her 'tremble' for his safety, she never – not even when they had drifted apart – ceased to respect his breadth of knowledge, the range of his charity and his unfailing good nature.[3]

Dr Lambert was in fact among those earnest souls who would help bring about the revolution of 1848 and his daughter would never quite forget or abandon those 'men of forty-eight'. She herself lived through four revolutions, the first being that of 1848, when she was eleven. But, despite her raw age, she could not help but be interested in politics because her family was so divided. Her aunts favoured a constitutional monarchy, and held her father's heroes – Louis Blanc, historian and advocate of cooperatives, Alexandre Ledru-Rollin, minister in the post-revolution provisional government, then an exile in London for many years, and Proudhon – in the greatest horror. As for Proudhon's notorious maxim, 'Property is theft', the aunts looked upon it as nothing less than 'the end of the world'.[4]

For his part, Dr Lambert cherished a dream that Juliette would one day forge a working-class marriage. A thoroughgoing revolutionary, he was delighted by the February revolution, and went so far as to break open an extra bottle of wine at dinner.[5]

Juliette met the man who was to become her first husband in early 1851, when she was in her mid-teens. To begin with she was merely told by her father that he was a republican and a Comtist.[6] At that point, Juliette had never heard the name of Comte, which would feature so large in her life later. The guest was a barrister by profession, his name was Lamessine, and his main strength was as a brilliant conversationalist. At fifteen, however, she found his worldly, cynical views upsetting. After the initial encounter, more meetings took place and were awkward, mainly because he was twice her age. Despite this, she was eventually told that he had asked to marry her and that the financial side of things had been already sorted out to everyone's satisfaction. She was furious and appealed to her father's better nature, and for months there was a drawn-out war of words between Dr Lambert and Juliette's grandmother.

The marriage went ahead and was a disaster. In the course of it, however, there was one bright spot – a visit to Paris from Soissons, where the couple were living. After staying there a fortnight in a hotel, she found herself, as she put it, 'uninitiated into the hundredth part of what she wanted to know'.[7]

Back home in Soissons, her world turned a little when, after the birth of a daughter she read an article in the weekly periodical *Siècle* by the multi-talented Alphonse Karr, sometime editor of *Le Figaro*, a novelist and a man of many parts. At the time, he had a column entitled 'Buzzings' ('*Bourdonnements*') and on that occasion he wrote about the crinoline, then very much in fashion despite, as Karr saw things, its absurdity. He went on to conclude that, despite the garment's obvious 'obtuseness', there was not one woman in all France 'with sufficient independence of mind not to wear it'. Juliette was having none of this and concocted a letter to Karr saying as much and, as far as she was able, penning it in a parody of Karr's own writing style. Karr played his part to perfection and the letter was duly published, and in its entirety. She was thrilled.

But her husband's friends bored her, and he was forever extolling the virtues of Auguste Comte, whose positivism seemed to Juliette to vitiate all her idealism. Comte held to the very French view that positivists were specialists in generalisations.[8]

Born in Montpellier in 1798, Comte was notable physically for his unusually short legs. He entered the École polytechnique in Paris, then well known for its courses in science and engineering, where Comte concentrated on the study of the French and Industrial Revolutions. It was at the École that Comte discovered his lifetime aim, to 'apply the methods of the physical sciences to society'. He also became the secretary to Henri de Saint-Simon, and both men may be regarded as early sociologists, an intellectual discipline where France was at the forefront.[9]

These ideas of Saint-Simon and Comte – and later Émile Littré – fascinated Juliette's husband and her father but left her cold. In fact, it was worse than that, for her predicament brought on an attack of neuralgia. Seeing this, her father – practical for once – recommended her to a medical friend of his who quickly realised that what she needed was the 'stimulant of congenial society'. He introduced her to two circles, one poetical, the other philosophical, where she speedily improved.

She became first a member of the Union des poètes and it was at a meeting of this union that she was taken to meet her first true celebrity. This was the aged Pierre-Jean de Béranger, a very popular poet and *chansonnier* in his day, the composer of a prodigious number of anti-establishment popular songs, many bitingly political, which had landed him in jail in the 1820s and where, undeterred, he continued to compose. His many friends included Chateaubriand, Félicité de Lamennais and Victor Hugo.

Béranger read some of Juliette's poems and delivered a prescient verdict, though it didn't seem so at the time. 'My child,' he said, 'you will never be a poet, but you may one day be a writer.' She was crushed, never wrote poetry again and withdrew from the union.

As for the philosophical circle to which her father's doctor friend had introduced her as part of her treatment, this was the salon of some new friends, M and Mme Fauvety.[10] Charles Fauvety was editor of, among other journals, the *Revue philosophique*, one of the contributors to which was Charles Renouvier, a post-Kantian philosopher, and through him Juliette was introduced to the work and ideas of Hippolyte Taine (chapter 30), who would prove to be a major influence on Zola, Maupassant and Paul Bourget. Another member of the circle was a certain Jenny d'Héricourt, who ran an underground network of early feminists and had written a polemical book attacking Proudhon. Juliette was never overly fond of Jenny in personal terms, but their interests overlapped.[11]

It was Mme Fauvety who introduced Juliette to the theatre, helping her enjoy more sophisticated pleasures. Juliette was also taken to her first fancy-dress ball, where she met Giacomo Meyerbeer, the musical idol of the early empire and arguably the most successful opera composer of the century, and who, it happens, was very taken with her. 'Why! She will make me forget my Selika,' he is said to have remarked, Selika being the heroine of his opera *Vasco da Gama*, the composition he was then embarked upon. He was also heard to add: 'I am too old to fall in love with a new face,' and left the ball abruptly.[12]

In April 1858, the great work by Proudhon finally appeared. Released in three volumes, it bore the title *De la justice dans la Révolution et dans l'Église*. Originally scheduled for 1854, the book had been eagerly awaited, so much so that Juliette's father, Dr Lambert, sent his daughter a letter begging her to buy the book and imploring her that, as she finished each volume, she must send it on to him. Juliette followed her father's recommendations to the letter, and it was as well that she did so, for within a matter of days the book was suppressed. Proudhon, condemned to three years' imprisonment and a fine of 4,000 francs, fled to Belgium.

Reading the book, Juliette could not help but be impressed by the sheer cleverness of the author's arguments. But for her, that couldn't hide the fact that his attitude to women, and his idea of what a 'just' world was, in relation to the sexes, could in no way be defended. On top of which, she was irritated by the fact that he had singled out for particular criticism two women among her contemporaries who she had most time for: George Sand and Daniel Stern. She was still boiling with indignation when, a few days later, she found herself in Mme Fauvety's salon where she made a point of buttonholing Jenny d'Héricourt: 'You ought to defend the women who are thus insulted ...'[13]

Jenny d'Héricourt didn't see it that way at all. 'George Sand and Daniel Stern', she was adamant, 'have only what they deserve. I insist upon virtue and practise it. Proudhon has not dared to attack me, I am certain of it, though I have not yet read his book.'

Astounded at this response, and disliking d'Héricourt even more than hitherto, Juliette hissed: 'Very well, I am a nobody, it is true, although I am as virtuous as you ... I will reply to Proudhon. Women must be defended by women.'[14]

She threw herself into the task with gusto and for two months it took up almost all her attention. Mostly the writing was done at night, closeted in her own room, where her daughter Alice was sleeping. When it was done, she gave it the title *Idées anti-Proudhoniennes*. She showed it first to M Fauvety, who liked it well enough but had doubts as to whether she would find a publisher.

Those doubts were well founded. Showing an admirable bravura, she began at the top, sending the text to Michel Lévy, publisher of Hugo, Sainte-Beuve and Dumas, and whose big success just then was Ernest Renan's *Life of Jesus* (released in 1863). No one was surprised when he turned her down, nor the next eight publishers – including Proudhon's own.[15]

Juliette refused to give up, her desperation provoking her to try something different. She approached a book- and map-seller, Taride by name, who had his shop on the ground floor of where she was living in the rue de Rivoli, and where she was a regular customer. She asked him if he would publish her book provided she underwrote all costs. 'Why not, Madame? We neither of us run any risk, for we are both unknown, and if we fail, no one will hear of it.'

She advanced him 800 francs and the book was duly printed and released on 15 August 'when there was not a cat in Paris'. Still, she sat in Taride's shop and inscribed fifty copies with carefully crafted dedications and sent them to a raft of celebrities, among them George Sand, Daniel Stern, Émile Littré, Émile de Girardin, Prosper Mérimée, Edmond About, Octave Feuillet and others. She herself delivered copies of the book to various newspaper offices, and then, of course, sent one to her father.

Her visits to the newspapers paid off and the book was covered widely. As Winifred Stephens observes, in that year, 1858, 'three years before John Stuart Mill began to write his *Subjection of Women*, three years before Britain's first female doctor, Elizabeth Garrett Anderson, Juliette Lamessine began her campaign'.[16]

She insisted that all liberal professions should be open to women, that women should be admitted to a share, if not in the legislation, at least in the administration of their country. She thought that the role of mayoress was particularly suitable for women. Other specific suggestions included the admission of women to the *conseils de prud'hommes*, organisations which in France regulate the disputes between employers and employees.[17] 'Work alone has emancipated man. Work alone can emancipate women ... I, like Proudhon, believe that a woman's first duty is to be a wife and a mother. But I maintain that family life need not absorb all women's activities, physical, moral and intellectual. The part of a broody hen is honourable without a doubt, but it is not suited to everyone, neither is it so absorbing as it is represented.'[18] And she echoed the statement of Mme de Rambouillet, in the very first salon, that women can debrutalise society.

D'Héricourt was wrong. Juliette's book brought her influential friendships and distinguished acquaintances, elevating her almost overnight into the cream of Parisian literary and political society. The two women writers she had especially defended both wrote to thank her, though Marie d'Agoult wondered if she was a man writing under a woman's name, the reverse of what she and George Sand had done. After Juliette corrected her, she was invited to one of the comtesse's salon evenings.[19]

No Stomach for Determinism

In the d'Agoult salon the divide between *abstentionnistes* and *sermentistes* was still going strong. Though the members of Mme d'Agoult's salon were all convinced republicans, they could not agree on the best form of opposition.[20] In 1858, when Juliette first appeared in the d'Agoult salon, two distinct groupings were beginning to form. On one side were the more extreme republicans who, like Juliette and her father, were determined to remain completely aloof from the emperor and so refused point-blank to swear allegiance to Napoleon III – these were the *abstentionnistes*. On the other hand, and just coming to prominence, was a more moderate republican party led by none other than Mme d'Agoult's son-in-law, Émile Ollivier, who, it will be recalled, had married Blandine, her daughter with Liszt. In their view, opposition to the empire could best be managed by entering the Corps législatif and playing as active a role in the administration as possible. In order to do that, however, it was necessary to take the oath of allegiance.[21] This party, known as the *sermentistes*, was to grow in strength until, in the elections of 1863, a Liberal Union was formed, which ended the absolute monarchy forever. Juliette would have no part in the *sermentistes* but from the first Mme d'Agoult formed a highly favourable impression of her.

And for her part, Juliette – at least to begin with – formed a similarly high impression of Mme d'Agoult and her salon. Given the people who populated her gatherings, it is not hard to see why. One of the more important guests was Émile Littré, a firm believer in a hierarchy of nations (Anglo-Saxon, Scandinavian), an eloquent follower of Comte and whose famous *Etymological Dictionary of the French Language* was just going through the press.[22] 'Littré', wrote Juliette, 'inspired me with a sentiment which was almost worship.'

Littré was very famous in his day. Born in Paris, he was educated at the famous Lycée Louis-le-Grand, where fellow pupils included Louis Hachette, the future publisher, and Eugène Burnouf, orientalist and Sanskrit scholar, whose ideas had an early influence on Littré. Elected to the Académie des inscriptions et belles-lettres, and then to the Académie française, Littré later became interested in politics and this is where his interest in Saint-Simon and Comte came in. He was not an original thinker, but he was a better stylist than Comte and he pushed further their ideas about what the 'laws of society' might be, and the long-term consequences of where industrialisation and scientific discoveries might lead. Try as she might, though, Juliette could not stomach determinism – it seemed to her the very negation of imagination. Nor did she like its association with John Stuart Mill and England – she would be anti-English all her life.

PINNACLE OF HUMANITY

In June 1863, Juliette finally separated from her husband and for a while took to living with her parents at Chauny (between Soissons and Saint-Quentin in the north). While there, Renan's *Vie de Jésus* was finally published and caused great excitement throughout Europe, not least in the Lambert household. Dr Lambert considered the publication of this book the most significant event of the latter half of the nineteenth century.[23]

Originally destined for the priesthood, Renan, who had a theory that Frenchness was essentially a 'spiritual principle', lost his faith and put his new conviction into several books, of which the *Life of Jesus* was by far the most influential. The *Life* had the influence it did partly because of its exquisite French but also because it treated Jesus as a historical figure, denied his supernatural acts, presented in a clear manner the scholarship which threw doubts over his divinity, and yet showed him in a sympathetic light, as the 'pinnacle of humanity', whose genius and moral teaching changed the world. At the same time, Renan dismantled the need for churches, creeds, sacraments and dogmas. Like Comte, he thought positivism could be the basis for a new faith. He underlined that Jesus was a moral leader, a great man, but not in any way divine – organised religion had nothing to do with him. Renan's book appealed because it helped people lose their belief in supernatural entities without losing their belief entirely: most people could not go from belief to unbelief in one step. Renan's *Life* was the most famous title published in French in the nineteenth century and it created a sensation in England too. It was part of a movement in France in which intellectual authority was seen as taking the place of the church.[24]

Juliette's appetite for intellectual adventure began to widen her areas of investigation and she started to enjoy the company of two rather distinct sets of colleagues. The figures who were attracted to Mme d'Agoult's salon were aristocratic and elegant republicans concerned with political *reform*, whereas Juliette's other friends in Paris were composed of more radical bohemians and utopians.

Separated now from her husband and living at Chauny, and more and more distanced intellectually from d'Agoult, Juliette was hardly happy. Matters improved when a doctor recommended that she try the south of France as a cure. In next to no time she had formed friendships with the likes of Prosper Mérimée, the romantic novelist and author of *Carmen*, the basis of Bizet's opera of that name, with the philosopher Victor Cousin, whose early thinking about consciousness helped to found the discipline of psychology, and with Jean Reynaud, another eminent follower of Saint-Simon.

From now on, Juliette would spend most of her winters in the south, though she also felt able to return to Paris whenever she wanted. And it was there that Mme d'Agoult said to her: 'Mine will remain the great salon of winter ... and yours shall be the little summer salon.'[25] The adjective 'little' did not go unnoticed. And d'Agoult actually went so far as to send Juliette several pages of notes on how to organise her salon: 'Avoid exchanging confidences ... be modest but not self-effacing ... Appear firm but also tolerant ... be careful to make guests feel that you are more occupied with them than with yourself ...'[26]

In the spring of 1864, Juliette's *salon minuscule* was born, in the rue de Rivoli, with her founding guests being Edmond Adam, a wealthy banker, Edmond Texier, a military historian and wit, Alphonse Toussenel, a naturalist, Napoléon Peyrat, a fiercely anti-clerical historian, and Auguste Nefftzer, editor of *Le Temps*. The salon soon became the centre of republican opposition to the empire. Nefftzer took the stage early on – he was one of the few who saw what Bismarck's true aim was, and that war would come.

In fact, Juliette's salon quickly became a prominent institution in Parisian intellectual life, and more successful than Mme d'Agoult had ever imagined. In consequence, a cloud began to gather over their friendship.[27] As the door to the d'Agoult salon closed, however, another opened. Under the Napoleonic code, Juliette's estranged husband had been able to pocket all her earnings from her books. But in the summer of 1867 he died and her royalties reverted to her.

When her father heard the news about Lamessine, he knew instinctively who his next son-in-law would be. Edmond Adam had originally been a journalist and had been a member of Mme d'Agoult's salon. But he had turned himself into a banker, and made a decent fortune. When Juliette opened her salon, he became one of the founding members. He had shown bravery during the 1848 revolution, trying to restore order on the barricades, and to such effect that the National Assembly awarded him the Légion d'honneur, an honour he refused on the grounds that he could not wear a decoration won in a civil war. [28]

The couple were married within the year. There was one person who objected to the marriage, Mme d'Agoult, who thought Juliette was marrying Edmond on the rebound, saying: 'An intelligent woman should remain free and mistress of her own thoughts.' To which Juliette responded: 'I have greater need of happiness than of freedom.' Mme d'Agoult was offended.

And it was this set of circumstances that brought about the transformation of Juliette's 'minuscule' salon on the rue de Rivoli into a much greater salon on the boulevard Poissonière, to where the couple now moved.

This was also the time when there was introduced to her new grand salon the figure with whom she would be identified as much as with her husband. Edmond was seeing quite a bit of Léon Gambetta, the acknowledged leader of the republican party known as Les Jeunes. Gambetta was from the south, born in 1837 at Cahors, between Limoges and Toulouse. The son of a grocer, he studied as a lawyer but was from the first a fiery student, well read, an orator who enjoyed drinking with the best of them, and a committed hater of the empire.

Gambetta was invited to one of the Adams' Friday evening dinner parties where the fellow guests that night were Jules Ferry, lawyer and creator of the modern French school, Pierre-Jules Hetzel, publisher of Jules Verne, and Louis Nicod de Ronchaud, poet, art historian, a member of d'Agoult's salon, an authority on ancient tapestries and, not least, director of the Louvre. On that first night, everyone was in black tie, except Gambetta who arrived in a 'nondescript' coat and a flannel shirt. He was very embarrassed, but Juliette placed him on her right, and thereafter she taught him how to dress and behave in public, a lesson as he told her he would never forget.

It was not long after this, at the trial of Louis Charles Delescluze, that Gambetta established his fame as an orator. Delescluze was a journalist who had the idea (in 1868, the twentieth anniversary of the 1848 revolution) to build a monument to Alphonse Baudin, one of the leaders of that event, who had been killed by troops on the barricades. Gambetta's argument in the trial was that there are times when it is incumbent on citizens to break the law, when the issues are so important as to make it necessary, and he audaciously drew a parallel between what Delescluze was doing (and the others charged with him) and no less a figure than the emperor himself, who he said had broken constitutional law in his 1851 coup d'état. Gambetta failed to get his client acquitted but it was the daring of his speech that attracted attention, and in Juliette's salon that night there was wild enthusiasm.[29]

Afterwards she and Edmond moved south for the winter, where they established another salon at their house in Bruyères, on the Golfe Juan, where Prosper Mérimée was its *grand homme*.[30] Juliette became very close to Mérimée, who was additionally an archaeologist and translator of Russian writing, and who had a wide circle of friends ranging from George Sand and Empress Eugénie to Louis Pasteur and Charles Gounod.

Juliette had by now published a number of books of a more or less literary kind, but she was more and more interested in – and involved with – politics, and in the general election of 1869 many of her friends were standing as republicans. Gambetta was standing against Émile Ollivier, Mme d'Agoult's son-in-law, so the bitterness between them continued at a higher level. By now, as well as her friendships with Mérimée and Flaubert, Juliette had cemented her relationship with George Sand, and here too Mme d'Agoult plays a part, because, as we saw earlier, Sand turned against d'Agoult and quite badly.

On the day war was declared, 20 July 1870, Juliette was staying with George Sand at Nohant. They both burst into tears when George's son appeared with a drum, announcing the news and shouting '*Vive la France!*' They returned to Paris where the war dominated all discussions in Juliette's salon and where, over the next days and weeks, the news got steadily worse. A great wave of patriotism swept through the country as losses mounted.[31] The word *Dé-ché-ance* began to be heard and chanted – dethronement. On 4 September, Gambetta announced in the *Tribune* (an official news outlet) that Napoleon III no longer ruled France, a republic was declared, and a revolution had passed without the shedding of blood. But the state of the war was still grim.

An outline of the Siege of Paris and the Commune is given elsewhere in this book. But Juliette and her husband and their friends lived through the very worst. To begin with they were better off than most (Edmond was in the cabinet, as minister of munitions) but eventually they too were reduced to eating horseflesh. Her own time was taken up with two organisations, one providing cheap meals for the poor (increasingly difficult), the other finding sewing machines for young seamstresses, so that they could mount their own businesses. By January 1871, she was herself ill and confined to bed.

Throughout the nineteenth century, from Félicité de Genlis and Germaine de Staël until the Franco-Prussian War (and in fact beyond, as we shall see), salons and *salonnières* became steadily more politically minded. The salons acquired more the character of rehearsal rooms for parliament than ante-chambers for the Académie française, while the *salonnières* themselves began to shine beyond the realm of conversation. Though their numbers were small, and though they often published anonymously, or under male names, they started to shine in journalism, fiction and the theatre, in social criticism and politics. They played a particular role in preserving high culture and in bringing different political persuasions together. They were an important ingredient in what General de Gaulle was to call France's 'genius for renewal'.

PART SIX

PARISINE: THE LINEAMENTS
OF FRENCHNESS III

The *Flâneur*, the *Boulevardier*
and the Dandy

In late June 1947, fresh out of Harvard, Stanley Karnow, the American writer, paid $50 for passage aboard a coal freighter bound from Baltimore to Le Havre. After a week's voyage, during which the freighter was diverted to Rotterdam because of a strike at Le Havre, he finally made his way to the Hotel Lutèce in Paris, a cheap and clean establishment in the Latin Quarter, where his upstairs neighbour spent a lot of time mournfully practising the saxophone.

His time was limited so he immediately plunged into a feverish tour of the city. He soon realised, however, that he could not fully appreciate Paris unless he curbed his frenetic pace and turned himself into a *flâneur*. This word – based on the verb *flâner*, to stroll, and/or idle, and/or dream – and its cousin *boulevardier* have no exact equivalents in English and mean, more or less, a stroller but an aimless one, even 'deliberately aimless', coined to emphasise that Paris is *the* city for aimless strolling.[1]

A few years later, Karnow's fellow American writer Edmund White gave his book of reminiscences of living in Paris the title of *The Flâneur*. When he started living in the French capital in the early 1980s, he wrote, there were still knife-sharpeners, glaziers and chimney sweeps strolling the streets of the city, each with his distinctive cry. He made the point that Paris is *meant* to be seen by the walker, despite the fact that it had changed much since the eighteenth century, when it had had 30,000 prostitutes, and 6,000 children were abandoned there every year, and there had been a specialist occupation of *décrotteur*, whose job it was to scrape the muddy boots of the city's inhabitants, so dirty were the streets. And White conceded that Americans above all are ill suited to be *flâneurs*, being 'in too much of a hurry and too keen on self-improvement'.

Flâneur is a term the French are especially proud of and there is now quite a raft of scholarship surrounding this (for the non-French) nebulous concept. Its first usage has been traced back to the early nineteenth century, and while some claim that it was killed off by Baron Haussmann's vast reconstruction of Paris in the middle of the 1800s, others claim that it could not properly exist without the wide boulevards and the associated acres of pavement that Haussmannisation created and which so characterise the city. What is not disputed is that industrialisation came later to France than to Britain or Germany, say, and seems to have been more of a surprise. One effect of this is that the arrival of 'modern life' in France was reflected in wide areas of cultural activity, where the *flâneur* may be said to be at the centre of a number of interlocking features, rather as we saw that the various ingredients of the eighteenth-century French mentality were also interlocked (chapters 16-18).

In many respects, for example, the impressionists painted the *flâneur*'s Paris (think of Pissarro's markets, Monet's *Boulevard des Capucines* and his railway stations, De Nittis's *The Violet Perfumery*, Caillebotte's bridges and *places* and *The House Painters*, Degas's racecourses). In these views, as often as not, they are not only pictures of their subjects, but include people – *flâneurs* – watching the scenes in the paintings. Mary Cassatt's *In the Loge* shows people in the theatre not watching the stage but watching each other. That was part of being a *flâneur*, watching other people. Though Paris was smaller than London or Berlin, it was still a vast cosmopolitan city where the crowd was a new experience – crowds, as we shall see, were the object of study by the new science of sociology, and were suspected of being both a symptom and the cause of the 'degeneracy' of the European races at the time (chapter 37). A final aspect of modernity in the French context was the growth of the consumer society, which found expression in the huge new department stores, the glass-covered arcades (themselves part of the new iron-based technology), and the burgeoning fashion industry that made Paris the capital of *chic*. And of course the wide *trottoirs* of the grand boulevards were made for the pavement café, where so much of Parisian life took place.

An alternative view is provided by James Cannon, who says that the origin of the *flâneur* can be traced to the creation of a zone of non-building land outside Paris in the 1840s, which encircled Paris for more than a hundred years (roughly just inside where the *périphérique* is now). The Zone lay outside the fortified walls and extended for 250 yards of 'no-man's-land' to provide a clear view of approaching enemies. It was said that the 'City of Light' stopped at the Zone, which was soon taken over by gypsies, squatters, rag-pickers and carnival workers (*saltimbanques*), known collectively as '*zoniers*', who lived in shanty towns, caravans and old railway carriages and spawned flea markets, *guinguettes* (open-air cabarets) and *assommoirs* (grog shops). Writers as varied as Hugo, Zola, Huysmans, Brasillach and Céline, the photographer Eugène Atget, and artists such as Van Gogh, Seurat and Raffaëlli were mesmerised by the Zone. Some even saw it as a viable alternative to the hated Haussmannisation of the city. The doings of well-dressed gangsters and pimps, known as *apeches*, were so colourful that there was a daily column in the newspapers devoted to their illegal and sometimes violent activities.[2]

Flânerie, the activity of strolling and looking and (day)dreaming, its importance and its role in modern life, was first identified by the German literary critic Walter Benjamin, in his masterpiece, *The Arcades Project*.[3] This book comprised a series of essays on Charles Baudelaire, where one of Benjamin's main points is that Baudelaire and his work are representative of modernity in a manner that is equalled by no other writer. *Flânerie* is explored in Baudelaire's essay 'The Painter of Modern Life', originally published in *Le Figaro* in 1863 and in his *Paris Spleen* collection of 1869, where he describes exactly what the *flâneur* does. Baudelaire, being a poet himself, conceives of the *flâneur* as a kind of poet whose world is the public places and spaces of Paris. For Baudelaire, the poet/

flâneur can distil aesthetic meaning from the spectacle of teeming crowds that characterise the metropolitan environment. In another of Baudelaire's descriptions of the *flâneur*, in his 1863 essay, he notes that 'the crowd is his domain ... His passion and his profession is to merge with the crowd.'[4]

For Baudelaire's poet/*flâneur*, metropolitan spaces 'are the landscape of art and existence'. He loves to lose himself in the crowd. 'For the perfect idler, for the passionate observer it becomes an immense source of enjoyment to establish his dwelling in the throng, in the ebb and flow, the bustle, the fleeting and the infinite.'[5] This is, of course, a new kind of existence, a new attitude towards life, one not available before the arrival of the crowd.[6] Émile Girardin also recognised this, introducing the *feuilleton*, the occasional article below the fold in his popular newspapers, which often remarked on aspects of city life, cosmopolitan life, crowd life, becoming known as *flâneur* writing. 'The department store is the last promenade for the *flâneur*' in which 'newness is a quality independent of the use value of the commodity'.[7]

Crucially, for Baudelaire, the poet is the individual who *knows* he is a face in the crowd, and this makes him a man apart. 'The observer is a prince enjoying his incognito wherever he goes.' If the poet/*flâneur* could be seen, he would be unable to observe. He is attracted by 'the magnet of the mass' and once he enters a café, he is anxious to be on the move again. Like Dickens, Baudelaire needed street noises to help him work. He disliked Brussels because there were no shop windows, nothing to see, the streets 'were unusable'.[8] In Paris in the Second Empire, the shops didn't close until ten o'clock at night – 'It was the great age of *noctambulisme*'.

Baudelaire makes the poet/*flâneur* the beneficiary of the chance meetings that take place on the city stage and so, importantly, these are not encounters that the poet/*flâneur* chooses. A traffic accident, for example, assembles people who are not defined along class lines.[9] 'They present themselves as concrete gatherings, but socially they remain abstract – namely in their isolated private concerns ... In many cases, such gatherings have only a statistical existence.'[10] 'The practice of self-hood is dependent on the contingencies of spectacles such as crowds' and it is, therefore, and quintessentially, a *restless* identity.

As spelled out in both *Paris Spleen* and 'The Painter of Modern Life', the modern poet is essentially identical with the *flâneur*. The *flâneur* is the man of the public who treats the furniture of the city in a detached way (an attitude which is not quite the isolation and alienation which Baudelaire describes in his other great work, *Les Fleurs du mal*, where the evil is exactly the alienation and anomie described by Durkheim).[11] The end of the nineteenth century was characterised, as we shall see, by a form of neurasthenia, which was held to have several causes, and was known in Paris as '*spleen*'.

Flânerie can be understood, therefore, not only as the observation of the fleeting and the transitory but a realisation that this is the *only* way modern life offers meaning. The *flâneur* is essentially empty, an individual who is in a sense in love with the spectacle of the public. Benjamin contrasted Baudelaire with Hugo. 'Hugo placed himself in the crowd as a *citoyen*; Baudelaire divorced himself from the crowd as a hero.'[12]

The Parisian's Paris: The 'Beat' of the *Boulevardier*

Paris is of course famous for its boulevards but not all of them gave or give their name to the *boulevardier*. This was an insider's term, referring to a relatively small number of very central boulevards between the rue de Caumartin and the rue Taitbout, more familiarly beginning at the Madeleine and extending only so far as the café Tortoni, which was located on the boulevard des Italiens, directly across the street from the Comédie-Française. This central location was, as someone put it, the Parisians' Paris, and anywhere outside this 'beat' was the provinces. It was in this area that politics took place, where the newspapers and the publishers had their offices, where the theatres and a good many of the fashionable shops were located and, perhaps above all, where the most celebrated cafés were to be found. The *boulevardier* was the kind of man (always a man) who knew which café to frequent and when.

The *boulevardier* was well informed without being an intellectual or an aesthete. He kept in touch, says Cornelia Otis Skinner, through magazines such as the *Revue des deux mondes* and *Gil Blas* (which published excerpts from books and short stories) rather than through books themselves (though he always knew what was fashionable, through *Gil Bas*).[13] All this, however, was not quite enough: to be a *boulevardier* of distinction, a man needed wit – and here we return to the matter raised earlier on: the somewhat self-regarding notion that Parisian wit was special, better – sharper – than elsewhere.

The concept of the *boulevardier* also drew part of its identity from the notion of boulevard theatre. Beginning in the last decades of the eighteenth century, both bourgeois theatre and the more popular forms had gravitated to the Boulevard du Temple, which became known as the '*boulevard du crime*' on account of the melodramas and murder stories staged there. This boulevard was a street of theatres but also a place for acrobats and pantomimes. This 'boulevard repertoire' emerged separately from 'straight' theatre at the Comédie-Française, and was reinvigorated during the Second Empire with the addition of vaudeville and the *comédie d'intrigue*.

Given this background, it is no surprise that many of the wittier *boulevardiers* were dramatists and they tended to gather, first, in the café Tortoni, where the leading spirits were Alfred de Musset, Alexandre Dumas and the Duc de Morny. Later, in the 1890s, and despite the widespread Parisian belief that 'a man will change his religion sooner than change his café', the sophisticates moved to the Napolitain, known as the 'Napo'.

The poet Jean Moréas once described the height of 'boulevard enthusiasm'. As he put it: 'You arrived at your café at 1.00 p.m. and stayed until seven. You came back at nine and stayed until 2.00 a.m.' Another literary figure turned up at his favourite café as usual on his wedding day while François Coppée, poet and archivist for the Comédie-Française, described how his wife had fixed up a room in their house to look like a café, complete with rows of bottles and a zinc counter, in a forlorn attempt to keep him at home.[14]

Just as Tortoni's stood opposite the Comédie-Française, so the Napo was opposite the théâtre du Vaudeville, where the clientele were mainly politicians, novelists, journalists, dramatists and drama critics, salted with a smattering of dandies (see immediately below). Paul Bourget and Guy de Maupassant were there, Arthur Meyer of *Le Gaulois* and Léon Blum of *Le Matin*. Among the dramatists and actors were Georges Feydeau, Alfred Capus, Lucien Guitry (father of Sacha) and Tristan Bernard. Among the women were Colette and Sarah Bernhardt.

Feydeau had started out on a newspaper, as assistant to the theatre editor, from which job he was fired for adding his own assessment to an advert for a play. His most popular farces were gloriously silly, though he had a melancholic nature and died in a mental institution, tragically insane. On the way there he had been a handsome, even exquisite man, with a collection of 150 tie-pins which he changed twice a day, and 200 perfume bottles, and some of the first impressionists. He was at the Napo every night for his aperitif and then went on to Maxim's where he had a table for dinner booked every night as well, until at least 2.00 a.m. He joyfully recorded the time he emerged from the restaurant at 4.00 a.m. and, seeing a red streak in the sky, asked a street-sweeper: 'Is that the dawn?' This time the street-sweeper had the last word: 'I don't know, monsieur, I'm not from this district.' Feydeau was so delighted by this answer that he used it in one of his plays. On another occasion, in the presence of a woman he knew to be on the promiscuous side, when she eloquently bragged about her son's devotion to her, adding that 'my little boy is so loving, he is always under his mother's skirts', Feydeau replied: 'He'll meet a lot of people under there.'[15]

Lucien Guitry was a big bull of a man in every way, and he too was a regular at the Napo. One of the greatest actors of his – or any – time (though he also directed), he was largely immobile on stage, believing gesture to be a precious commodity, to be used sparingly. He knew he had a magnetic stage presence and often scorned its absence in others. Like his fellow thespian Noël Coward, he thought that 'work is more fun than fun'. He loved his buffalo hat, says Skinner, which he wore with corduroy trousers, in keeping with his pets, which included an eagle and a small lion.[16] His great roles ranged from Tartuffe to Pasteur but took in friendship as well, and one of his greatest friends was Tristan Bernard.

Bernard, born in Besançon in the same street as Victor Hugo, wrote plays described as 'joyous nonsense based on reality'. He traded on paradox and self-parody. If someone suggested coming to see him, he'd agree. 'Please do, and preferably in the morning. That's when I work.' In his lycée days he had been a notoriously lazy student and on one occasion, when his professor was trying to encourage the class in a maths lesson with the memory that Pascal had fought off his migraines by thinking of geometry, Bernard replied that he fought off geometry by pretending to have migraines.[17]

Once, when a budding author asked his advice about giving his first lecture to a literary group, in particular how he should wind up, Bernard thought for a moment then said: 'Very simple. You pick up your papers, you rise from the reading table, you bow to the audience and then go off on tip-toe.'

'Why on tip-toe?'

'So as not to wake them.'[18]

He had wanted to be a poet and was adept at putting his philosophy into short statements. 'Love affairs are like mushrooms. One doesn't know if they're the safe or the poisonous variety until it's too late.' The theatre that he owned for a short time was named in his honour permanently in 1931.

PEACOCKS AND DANDIES

Baudelaire was also a noted dandy – he described it, says Julian Barnes, as 'the last outburst of heroism in decadent times'. His ideal of the dandy reflected his hatred of the materialism of the bourgeois monarchy, with its motto 'Enrichissez-vous'. He loathed what he saw as a 'money-grubbing, parvenue' world – in effect Balzac's world and the world of the utilitarians and the first socialists, who were intent on preaching that all should work for all. On the contrary, as he wrote at forty, 'it is through leisure that I have grown', adding, 'grown in part to my detriment, since leisure without a fortune increases one's debt and the cares arising from debts'.[19]

In most people's eyes the dominant characteristic of a dandy is his (again, always a him) attention to clothes but, strictly speaking, this is not so. In his history of the dandy, the British author Nigel Rodgers says that 'for him clothes are merely the outward visible form of an inward self-discipline, never to be wholly relaxed' and he makes the point that Beau Brummell, the prototype of the dandy, opted for 'structural tailoring' and an insistence on absolute cleanliness, along with which went 'icy courtesy', charm, poise and 'at times outrageous wit'. It was an attempt to create a debonair aesthetic elite, along aristocratic lines, and an uncompromising independence. Brummell, Lord Byron said, was one of the three great men of the nineteenth century, the others being Napoleon and Byron himself (who placed that self third). True dandies distinguished themselves from mere 'peacocks'.[20]

There had been sightings of peacocks/dandies in France before the nineteenth century – Pascal, as we have seen, had his moments (chapter 2) and Jacques-Louis David had depicted his brother-in-law, M Sériziat, in elegant finery in 1795. In fact, an entire generation – nicknamed *les Incroyables*, the Incredibles – had blossomed after the Terror, when young men had at last been able to dress as they liked after the restrictions of revolution. But again, these were peacocks, not dandies, as was the romantic writer Alfred de Vigny.

The World's Most Elegant Street

The development of the dandy overlapped with that of the café (chapter 8). After 1815 and the Restoration, cafés in Paris expanded in number and in splendour. They acquired mirrors and chandeliers, grander than in the eighteenth century, ornate stucco decors and marble-topped tables. Most important of all, they spread out on to the pavements. The café Tortoni still sold its famous ices and was a notable rendezvous for fashionable people, as were the café Riche and the café des Anglais, all on the boulevard des Italiens. 'This was perhaps the world's most elegant street in the nineteenth century.'[21] The world of the *flâneur* had evolved, even before Haussmann's rebuilding of Paris began in 1853. In Walter Benjamin's words: 'The street became a house for the *flâneur*, he was as much at home among the façades of houses as a citizen was within his four walls ... newsstands were his libraries, and café terraces his balconies from which he looked out.'

The Anglomania in France, after Waterloo and the Restoration, which helped give rise to the dandy, also encouraged associated developments, of which one was the fact that so many returning aristocrats, after years in exile north of the Channel, had acquired a love of horses, of horsemanship and in particular of horse-racing. As a result, in 1833 a group of fourteen young aristocrats got together to form a club, partly to rival the female-organised salons, but also to combine their interests in what, a year later, was known as the Jockey Club, still regarded as one of the smartest institutions of its kind in Paris.[22]

To begin with, dandies were hardly taken seriously – they were acknowledged as elegant, but also 'superficial, egocentric, hardly virile'. Stendhal likened them to comic actors.[23] Nevertheless, the first book on dandyism appeared in France as early as 1830: *Traité de la vie élégante* ('Treatise on the Elegant Life'), written by Honoré de Balzac, no less. He had yet to start on the Comédie humaine and he was writing many magazine articles on fashionable life. In his book – a slim volume – he divided human life into three: the working man's life, the elegant man's life, and the artistic life.[24] Balzac may have had his moments (he once ordered fifty-eight pairs of gloves from Bodiers, Paris's smartest glovers), he may have sought elegance, and valued it, but in truth he was himself hardly in the dandy class, having what was described by one observer as a broad florid face, 'a cascade of double chins' and greasy hair.[25] Delacroix painted several dandies, including himself, dressed in dark brown tails, a huge white cravat and pink shirt.

But by the 1840s, as Anne Martin-Fugier confirms, dandyism had become a 'phenomenon' of fashion. Dandies saw themselves as superior persons, with a very strict way of life, who were a fixture of the boulevards. They attracted attention among other things for the sheer cost of their clothes, one account calculating that the average dandy must spend 94,500 francs annually on his appearance – 20,000 on his hair, 4,000 on shirts, even 1,500 on gloves.[26] Those who managed to convert their 'ephemeral celebrity' into a more durable fame in literature, politics or art were promoted to being 'lions'.

Baudelaire would later dismiss these individuals (save Delacroix, who he revered) as barbarians, 'mere scatterers of horse dung along the boulevards where they walked in their patent leather boots'. In order to follow his 'career' as a poet/dandy, Baudelaire left his stepfather's house as soon as he came into his inheritance and moved into rooms on the Ile Saint-Louis, then a solitary, tranquil village connected to the rest of Paris only by footbridges. His rooms were in the hôtel Pimodan, which was mainly occupied by other artists and literary types. Many creative people met in the rooms of Fernand Boissard, musician, painter, art collector and man of letters, and this was where the *club des haschichins* used to meet at which Baudelaire and Gautier, among others, experimented with the effect of eating hashish in the form of green jelly.[27]

Baudelaire's rooms were high up under a mansard roof where he could see nothing but clouds – helping to give rise to one of his prose-poems about a dreamer who loves nothing in the world but clouds. In these rooms he collected reptiles, paintings (Bassano school pictures, Delacroix lithographs, Japanese prints) and bric-à-brac. His rooms were decorated mainly in red or black, with much gilding, but they were not large, nor the ceilings too high because 'intimate feelings are only collected at leisure in a very restricted space'.[28] 'The dandy', he wrote, 'must aspire to be uninterruptedly sublime. He ought to live and even to sleep in front of a mirror.'[29] Once he had left school, where he was required to wear a uniform, he would know 'every fold' of his clothes.[30]

Byron a Better Model than Napoleon

The day of the dandy was described not only by Baudelaire, but by one of three other great dandies of the late nineteenth century in France. One of these dandies was Robert de Montesquiou, another was Constanin Guys, a painter – and we shall meet both of them soon – but it was the third, Barbey d'Aurevilly, whose diary lets us into their world. Jules Amédée Barbey d'Aurevilly, to give him his full name, was born in 1808 near Cherbourg in Normandy, where he studied law. Like Montesquiou, as we shall see, d'Aurevilly had a high opinion of his own talents, though his early works failed to find a publisher. Instead, he became known for his spirited conversation and for his huge hats with red velvet rims, frock coats tailored to his waist, vast cloaks and trousers edged with purple, silver or gold braid, and cravats of white lace. In May 1885, Edmond de Goncourt noted in his diary that 'Barbey d'Aurevilly was dressed in a skirted frock coat that flared from his hips like a crinoline and wore white woollen trousers that looked like flannel underwear'.[31]

Barbey d'Aurevilly's diary tells us how dandies occupied their days. 'Mornings spent in bed, because one must sleep sometime, chocolate served by a valet, while the recumbent dandy read his letters or whiled away an hour answering one or musing on his fair correspondent. Then an interval of study or reading, interrupted by the daily call of the coiffeur, or the tailor with a new coat, or a friend who asked him to Véfour's for luncheon. Often whole days spent in more or less serious reading until he had to dress for dinner. Visits to bookshops, to a florist, to his favourite glove shop; calls upon actresses, walks on the boulevards or stops at some exhibition. A leisurely dinner unless it was followed by the theatre, and a midnight discussion on politics or the fine arts to end an arduous day. No, not end of it, for this young idler usually read in bed for an hour or more and fell asleep at about two o'clock.'

His ambition was to dominate society through his personality or by a book; in an age of peace Byron was a better model than Napoleon. Barbey never lost sight of his goal, any more than he lost sight of his face and figure in the pier glass of his apartment. On the days when he had to dine out he ate nothing for fear of losing his waistline.

'Equally circumspect were all his rules of conduct. His ideal, according to this diary, was "to be extremely singular in his opinions, but very conventional in his manners, hard even to ferocity in his judgements about things and even more so about persons, but cold even to utter disdain (slaying with words like bullets, dispassionately), grave and intellectual in his morning habits which make his reputation, but a man of the world when he puts on evening dress at night, and making war on pedantry of all sorts – expressing austere opinions in light and mocking words, and trifles in solemn phrases, so that when listening to him, one never knows where one is, – not gay, never laughing except in mockery, laughter being an evident proof of superiority".[32]

In his essay 'The Painter of Modern Life', Baudelaire's focus was on Constantin Guys, as an artist-*flâneur* and artist-dandy. Coming from a well-established naval family, Guys took part in the Greek War of Independence alongside Byron.[33] His preferred media for his light sketches were pen and ink, and watercolours, and he successfully caught the atmosphere and glitter of the new Paris envisaged

and constructed by Haussmann – the carriages in the Bois and along
the boulevards, the opera, the ballet, the finery and elegance of the
clothes, especially those of the women, in Nigel Rodgers's words, a
'detached yet potent sensuality'.[34]

Édouard Manet also became a good friend of Baudelaire. He was
born into a well-off family (his father was a judge), and so he was
never a bohemian or a dandy, though he was always dressed immac-
ulately in a black top hat, black frock coat and cravat, even when
idling in cafés. He can be counted, however, as a *flâneur*. The journalist Antonin Proust, portrayed by Manet in 1877, said this: 'With
Manet, the eye played such a big role that Paris has never known a
flâneur like him, nor a *flâneur* strolling more usefully.' Male clothes
were as much of interest to Manet, and Degas, as female clothes were
to Guys.[35]

THE WORLD'S MOST LABORIOUS SAYER OF NOTHING

'One should always listen to von Weber in mauve.' This comment – somewhere between Oscar Wildean wit and a pretentious
wisecrack – was made by Robert de Montesquiou when he met Sir
William Rothenstein at an all-Weber concert wearing a mauve suit,
mauve shirt and a cluster of pinkish pale violets at his throat. Comte
Robert de Montesquiou-Fézensac was a spectacular snob, a literary
dilettante, a royalist, a self-styled symbolist poet and a sartorial
show-off who, he said, tailored his costumes to suit his moods. When
he wore a scarf his scarf-pins were exotic jewels. On his fingers he
wore a ring set with a crystal that, he said, had been hollowed out to
accommodate a single human tear.

He was descended from the dukes of Gascony, distinguished as far
back as the Crusades, so he said, making him 'prideful but touchy'.
Socially self-assured, he was supremely at home among 'titled women
with literary aspirations'. He was found in all the best salons, aristocratic and intellectual – the Comtesse de Greffhulhe's and Mme
Arman de Caillavet's among others, as well as at Alphonse Daudet's
Thursday dinners and Stéphane Mallarmé's small gatherings up
four flights of stairs on the rue de Rome on Tuesdays. He claimed
to find the Goncourt literary Sundays 'vulgar', despite the exquisite

good taste in that salon, with its Chardins, Bouchers, Gavarnis and Japanese bronzes, and the regular presence of Daudet, Huysmans, Coppée, Clemenceau and Renan.

When Montesquiou entertained himself, the invitations invariably contained a brief note to the effect that 'ladies of society will be present'.[36] His style of conversation was histrionic, a series of more or less elegant gestures with his hands, a series of anecdotes which he, at least, and to judge by his laughter (which Proust imitated), found profoundly funny each time he repeated them, and more a 'one-versation' than genuine dialogue. Jules Renard had something to say about this one-versation: 'It was very refined, very precise, very insignificant.' There was no pleasing Jules, but he may not have been wrong: Gustave Kahn in the *Revue blanche* said Montesquiou was 'the world's most laborious sayer of nothing'.

But, inevitably perhaps with someone so in love with himself, he had his moments, as when he asked Mme Gramont if she hadn't been sprinkling aphrodisiac on her furniture as 'the armchairs seem to want to embrace the small chairs, the library is opening out rapturously to receive the piano'.

He named his house 'The Pavilion of the Muses', decorated in the Oriental style, in red, crimson and pink, each room to fit a mood, and such exotic bric-à-brac as a polar-bear rug and a Russian sleigh.[37] His dressing room, with a full-length mirror, also housed one hundred ties, and a series of erotic male photographs. He collected weird mementoes which he regarded as interesting – the bullet that killed Pushkin, a cigarette once smoked by George Sand, a tear (dried) once shed by Lamartine.[38]

He was in his pomp at the height of the symbolist movement, under the leadership of Mallarmé. His own books, with typically symbolist titles, such as *Bending Reeds* and *The Blue Hortensias*, were brought out in small, expensively bound private editions in satin covers encrusted with jewels in the shape of small animals, such as butterflies. He prevailed on friends such as Forain, Whistler and Helleu to decorate them.[39]

His vanity was prodigious and, says Julian Barnes, fully formed by the time he was twenty; he had a high opinion of himself both socially and artistically. He was, for a time at least, invited everywhere, though his high self-regard did not make him universally popular.[40] He expected always to have pride of place at any dinner he was invited to. He commissioned an inordinate number of portraits of himself, and brushed off the criticism that this inevitably drew, claiming that 'it is better to be hated than unknown'. The best of these is Boldini's 1897 three-quarter-length painting, showing Montesquiou in a mouse-grey suit with satin lapels, white leather gloves, immaculate starched cuffs and a black cravat, matching in colour his sinuous moustache and goatee beard.

Montesquiou met Marcel Proust in a little-known salon, that of Madeleine Lemaire, a flower painter and illustrator among other things, who, according to Proust, 'created more roses than anybody after God'. In her salon she became known for serving delicious little cakes and there is a least the possibility that, together with her Christian name, this helped give Proust the scenario with which he began his great book.[41]

But Montesquiou did not only appear in Proust's work. Before that, before Boldini's superb painting, in 1884 Joris-Karl Huysmans's novel *À rebours* ('Against Nature', or 'Against the Grain') had appeared. Until then, Huysmans, a civil servant in the Ministry of the Interior, had written several realistic novels in the tradition of Zola, all of them sombre and detailed. He had also written sympathetically about the Zone, describing a tavern made of demolition materials, animals grazing on garbage and signs 'forbidding' entry to 'crops' of thistles and brambles. The squalor, to him, had a 'melancholy beauty'. *À rebours* could not have been more different. Huysmans warned Zola that he was changing his style and embarking on 'wild and gloomy fantasy', in which the main character, Jean des Esseintes, was based partly on himself, partly also influenced by Baudelaire and Barbey d'Aurevilly, but the most important model was provided by Montesquiou.[42] Like Montesquiou, Des Esseintes is from a once noble family (and is 'prideful and touchy' about it) and, after a life of extravagance and dissolution in Paris, he retreats to a house in the countryside near Fontenay to devote what remains of his life to aesthetic reflection.

It is the originality of Des Esseintes' surrealist views that dominates the book, interspersed by his recollections of his dissolute

Parisian past, making the need for a plot superfluous. His library consists of mainly symbolist works and decadent fiction, by such authors as Auguste de Villiers de L'Isle-Adam and Barbey d'Aurevilly. He is contemptuous of French romantic writers but applauds the poetry of Baudelaire. At one stage, he has jewellery set into the back of a tortoise, the extra weight crushing the animal's back and causing its death. An entire chapter is given over to smell and in another he envisages a new type of mouth organ in which the musical parts have been replaced by little containers with different flavours, each evoking a different musical instrument: kummel, for instance, evokes the oboe, and crème de menthe the flute.

Huysmans predicted that his weird imagination would be ignored but the opposite was true. Zola was disappointed, but Bourget, Valéry, Whistler and Wilde were all thrilled by it, and Mallarmé was so delighted that he dedicated one of his later poems to Des Esseintes. The book was mentioned in Oscar Wilde's trial and is now regarded as an early example of gay literature.

Montesquiou, once compared to a 'hurricane of daggers', sat 'a hundred times' for Whistler's *Arrangement in Black and Gold* (1891–2), enduring the sittings only by virtue of a 'special cocktail of cocaine dissolved in wine'.[43] He was very close to Sarah Bernhardt and he actually boasted that she was the only woman he had ever gone to bed with and, 'in a tsunami of charm', admitted that after their fling he had 'vomited continuously for a week'.[44]

The dandy, as we have seen, is exclusively a male creature, though Bernhardt came closest as a woman. 'The divine Sarah', as her fans called her, was a bit like Montesquiou in reverse. She wore men's clothing, explored lovers of both sexes (from Charles Haas, the dandified prototype for Proust's Charles Swann, to the little-known impressionist painter Louise Abbéma), 'made love in a hot air balloon and slept in a coffin'. She was as passionate about animals as Montesquiou was about jewels, her menagerie embracing a parrot, a puma, a boa constrictor and a monkey sarcastically named Darwin. In her cross-dressing, she explored a raft of famous 'trouser roles', beginning with Zanetto, the minstrel in François Coppée's *The Passerby* (*Le Passant*, 1869). She went on to stage Hamlet, Judas Iscariot, Lorenzo de Medici, Romeo and Napoleon's ill-fated only son, L'Aiglon (the Eaglet).[45] Montesquiou and Bernhardt were aware of their similarities: in 1874, he commissioned Nadar, the first celebrity photographer, to take pictures of the two of them dressed in matching Zanetto costumes.

Despite Montesquiou never having a hair out of place, and always putting appearances first, Proust was impressed by what he called the comte's 'baroque erudition' and was taken aback by his 'demented grandiosity'. But the master in mauve set about Proust's social instruction into *le monde* with gusto, 'if without mercy'. The putative author of *À la recherche du temps perdu* showed his gratitude with a raft of imaginative gifts – a bluebird in a cage, a bouquet of Liberty ties.[46]

Montesquiou was in too much of a hurry to be a *flâneur* (he described himself as the 'sovereign of transitory things'), and too much of a self-regarding aristocratic insider to be a *boulevardier*, but his collection of clothes, and his *shopping poétique*, as Caroline Weber calls it, made him the consummate dandy of that or any other age.[47]

The Splendours and Spleen of No-Man's-Land

Charles Baudelaire was born in Paris in 1821, the son of a priest who had left the church to work for the state and who died just before his son was six, when Charles moved closer to his mother. Educated at the Lycée Louis-le-Grand, he emerged with a taste for the bohemian life, mixing with artists and poets and prostitutes, through whom – in the latter case – he was to contract the venereal disease from which he never properly recovered.[1] His mother remarried a career soldier who, somewhat later, prevailed on her to take the extraordinary step of mounting a legal action against her son, who had shown a grand taste for profligacy and had dissipated – within eighteen months – almost half the 100,000-franc fortune he had inherited in 1842 when he came of age. This resulted in the imposition of a *conseil judiciaire*, which meant Baudelaire could gain access only to the interest on the money and even then he had to go through a lawyer.[2] Not surprisingly, this resulted in him acquiring an exhaustive fury, and – to many critics – it is Baudelaire's capacity to confront his dark side that made him so powerful as a poet, his 'permanent exasperation' being the force that electrified him throughout.

But it extracted a price: it also made him restless. After he left home, he had more than *seventy* addresses, and he hardly ever settled down long enough to properly deal with his venereal disease. One theory is that he was subconsciously punishing himself for not treating his mother better after his father died.

Baudelaire was an unhappy narcissist, and his achievement was in converting his restlessness into a creative force. Just as he lived in many addresses, so his meetings and friendships with contemporaries of talent – Gautier, Flaubert, Sainte-Beuve, Poulet-Malassis, his publisher, Delacroix, Daumier, Guys, Manet, Wagner – were rarely long-lasting and, more often than not, were raw material for incorporation into his work.

His life was dedicated to writing and, in June 1857, at the age of thirty-six, he published *Les Fleurs du mal*, which was condemned in a matter of weeks as an offence against public morals. He was fined 300 francs and ordered to suppress six poems from the collection. A later edition – generally regarded as the definitive one – was published in 1861. It was condemned, in part, for its poems on lesbian love, its frank sadism, its criticism of accepted morality. There were verses on the ideal in art, on the possibilities of love, on intoxicants and stimulants, on despair and, in 'Parisian Scenes', on the fruits of strolling through the city. Here he invented a new literary form, the prose-poem, prose but where the intensity, colour and concision of the words is such as to emulate poetry. In his approach he blended 'high' and 'low' cultural allusions, in a style that used a 'soaring rapturous cadence of words', in an attempt, as he describes it, to elevate life above 'dim existence' (*'l'existence brumeuse'*).

The collection included three love cycles. The first, the Jeanne Duval cycle, was inspired by his physical love of an exotic woman – Duval was insatiable sexually and at times Baudelaire found her 'like a stinking animal'. She had suffered long years of illness and was actually paralysed when his friend Manet painted her in 1862, and going blind. The second cycle, the Marie Daubrun cycle, was inspired by a love that came in his later years.

The third of the love cycles was inspired by Mme Sabatier, who Baudelaire had met in the late 1840s, and who held a salon he had attended that was populated by writers, painters and sculptors, who all referred to her as 'La Présidente'. Placed on a pedestal, she is described in almost biblical terms – her flesh is 'holy' and 'her scent angelic'.[3] 'Her very presence lights up the way before her.'

In the 'Spleen and Ideal' section, Baudelaire wanders through the city landscape, in a mood of pensive melancholy, only too aware of what has been demolished (by Haussmann) and at the same time apprehensive as to what is to come – the mass experience and its associated social problems. Baudelaire was one of the first to sense this. Another of his poems, 'Les Yeux des pauvres', is set in a pavement café situated at an intersection of a brand-new boulevard, where there is much rubble, but it is also where the city is showing early signs of its future unfinished splendours. The café and its decorations are lovingly described, as are the commodities on offer, and some of the other café-dwellers. The central couple have been walking around Paris and are now having dinner, when they are confronted by a poor man and his children in rags, 'staring at them reproachfully'. Critics have accepted that Baudelaire prefigured Durkheim, Simmel and the Chicago school in highlighting the anomie, social void and social disorganisation of mass crowd-life in the cities that were to come. The café, as he also correctly identified, was the setting for artistic and political provocation (chapter 18).

The main 'flowers of evil' are, Baudelaire says, the *ennui* of modern life, existence being a sort of no-man's-land; the mass experience of the city, where personal qualities are irrelevant and the overwhelming feeling is one of exile, is closer to the 'bad faith' highlighted later by the existentialists. Against the background of Renan's work on Jesus (chapter 31) and the recent insights of Darwin, which together produced in Baudelaire a loss of belief in transcendence, while the vast social changes brought about in Paris by Haussmann had succeeded in driving the working classes from the centre of the city and changed its character, he concludes with the banal/profound thought (juxtaposition being the very epitome of modernity) that the journey through life in the crowd is better than the arrival/conclusion, because the arrival/conclusion is death and that is in fact an ending, not a conclusion.

THE MODESTY OF PROFOUND SENTIMENTS

In the 1850s, over a series of years, Baudelaire wrote a number of poems inspired by one particular woman, who at that time he did not know well, and sent them to her, one at a time, usually with an accompanying letter but in handwriting that was carefully disguised, to preserve his anonymity. The content of the letters only added to the singularity of his actions. Here, for example, is what he wrote on 9 December 1852, which accompanied a poem entitled 'À une femme trop gaie': 'The person for whom these lines have been written, whether they please or displease her, even if they appear totally ridiculous to her, is very humbly *implored* not to show them to *anyone*. Profound sentiments have a modesty which desires not to be violated. Is not the absence of a signature a symbol of this invincible modesty? He who has written these lines in one of those states of reverie into which he is often plunged by the image of one who is their object has loved her deeply, without ever telling her so, and he will *forever* feel for her the most tender sympathy.'[4]

Perhaps only Baudelaire could accompany a poem with a prose-poem in which the contents are so paradoxical. In the poem itself he begins by praising her head, her hair, her 'every way'. By the end, a transformation has occurred, and he has come to resent – as the title suggests – her cheerfulness, her beauty and her sheer vivacity. 'I hate you ... even as I love.' What he makes clear along the way is that the woman's qualities, what attract him to her, contrast too strongly with his own very different nature, in particular his apathy. In a striking metaphor he complains that sunshine and the first hints of spring conspire to make him wish to destroy a flower for what he calls the 'insolence' of nature. And he doesn't end there. In later lines, he allows himself a fantasy-desire in which he creeps up on the woman while she is asleep, bruises her breast, carves a wound in her 'joyous' flesh and infuses his own blood in between the 'lips' of her wound.[5]

Of course, this is a poem, and in the service of art there are no rules. But this was by no means the only poem Baudelaire sent to Apollonie Sabatier accompanied by an anonymous note. Nor was Baudelaire the only writer of note who sent her his verse. Théophile Gautier composed poems inspired by Apollonie, some of which were sexually suggestive, some frankly obscene. And so, although Baudelaire's behaviour was extraordinary enough, what is no less fascinating is the woman who inspired such behaviour.

LA PRÉSIDENTE

Historians are divided on whether Apollonie guessed who was sending her anonymous verses before Baudelaire published *Les Fleurs du mal* in 1857, which contained three of the poems he had sent her, but the chances are that she had a good idea. He was an intermittent member of her salon – which included such figures as Edmond About, Ernest Meissonier, Ernest Hébert, Maxime Du Camp, Gustave Flaubert and of course Gautier himself – so she had enough exposure to mid-century French men.

Apollonie was born Aglaé-Joséphine to Marguerite Martin (later Savatier) of Mézières, in the southern Ardennes, in February 1822. She had exquisite hands and lush copper-coloured hair, with a likeable warm nature, and she was approachable and naturally sexually alluring. A local headmistress offered to take her in at a reduced rate and teach her music, with free piano and music lessons. This drew her to artists' studios and she soon enough became attracted to the bohemian life. This led to a number of affairs with artists, Charles Jalabert among them, all familiar with the demi-monde.[6] None of them had any money but she didn't seem to mind and, more important, neither did her mother.

This carefree life changed when she was twenty-four, in 1846, when she accepted as her protector Alfred Mosselman. Mosselman was Belgian (then a new country, of course), rich and well connected and a patron of the arts. His main love was romantic painting – he frequented the circle of writers and painters who gathered in the apartment of Fernand Brossard at the hôtel Pimodan.[7] This, it will be recalled, was where Baudelaire had rooms and where the *club des haschichins* would meet (chapter 32). It was there that Aglaé first met Mosselman.

Aglaé allowed Alfred to install her in a second-floor apartment at 4 rue Frochot, not far from Notre-Dame de Lorette in an area well known for its kept women (known as 'Lorettes'), and very close to the Nouvelle Athènes café. Her neighbours included the painters Théodore Rousseau and Eugène Delacroix, the composer Hector Berlioz, and the writers Gérard de Nerval, Théophile Gautier and Maxime Du Camp. It was now that she changed her name to

Apollonie. It was her mother's favourite, she maintained, and she felt it more appropriate for a woman 'playing the role of muse to a circle of men'. She also made an incidental but important change to her surname, replacing the 'v' with a 'b'. This cut the connection to '*savate*', which means a used old slipper. She was now Apollonie Sabatier.[8]

Mosselman was a decent mentor to Apollonie, who was more than a decade younger than he, and he had ambitions for her. Soon after she was installed in her apartment, he commissioned a statue of Apollonie from Auguste Clésinger. This was exhibited at the Paris Salon in 1847 where it created a sensation. Until then, Clésinger had had his admirers – Alexandre Dumas *père* and Émile de Girardin among them. But his statue of Apollonie lifted him to the ranks of artistic fame.

He called the piece *La Femme piquée par un serpent*, 'Woman Bitten by a Snake', but no one was fooled. What the work depicted, for all to see, 'was a beautifully formed young woman in the throes of orgasmic ecstasy'.[9] He sculpted a snake wrapped around her foot, to justify the title. But there was no hiding the erotic nature of the statue – Apollonie had a full, rounded, luscious body – and the full-frontal blatancy of the pose was its chief uncompromising feature.

BAWDY TALK

Virginia Rounding, in her entertaining and 'flirty' account of Apollonie's idiosyncrasies, on which this section is chiefly based, quotes this revealing extract from a letter which Gautier wrote to her in October 1850, from Rome: 'President of my heart, This filthy letter, intended to replace Sunday's dirty talk, is long overdue, but that's the fault of the filth and not the writer. Modesty reigns in these solemn but ancient places, and I'm very sorry I can't send you more than this shit-stained and not very spermatic mess ...'[10] As Rounding notes, the reference to 'Sunday's dirty talk' suggests that this letter was intended to be read aloud at one of the regular Sunday evening gatherings which took place at the rue Frochot.

Apparently, it was Mosselman himself who suggested Apollonie held her Sunday dinners on a regular basis. In addition to Gautier, a particular favourite was Ernest Meissonier, painter and sculptor,

famous for his battle scenes and portraits of Bonaparte. As for the
other habitués, Edmond About was a virulently anti-clerical journalist; August Préault, a more romantic sculptor than Clésinger,
rarely missed an evening; Maxime Du Camp was best known as the
much-travelled companion of Flaubert, but he had fought bravely in
Italy with Garibaldi, and was an early enthusiast for the new speciality of photography. Flaubert himself was a regular, as was Henri
Monnier, a lithographer and writer whose name is probably less
remembered now than those of the characters he created in his novels,
plays and even drawings – most of all Monsieur and Madame Joseph
Prudhomme, 'plump, foolish, conformist and sententious', whom
Balzac described as the classic example of the French bourgeoisie.[11]

At the time that Mosselman initiated Apollonie's Sunday evenings,
the first raft of guests decided they should elect a 'president' whose
job it would be to act as, in effect, a master of ceremonies, to help the
proceedings along, and the choice fell on Henri Monnier as the most
senior man present. Gautier added that they also needed a female
president to even up matters, which is how Apollonie became 'La
Présidente', a title by which she was widely known ever afterwards,
though her close friends called her Lile or Lilette.[12]

Apollonie provided an agreeable atmosphere where her guests
could relax, 'say what they thought, and enjoy the company of a
woman who did not expect to be treated with deference merely on
account of her sex'. Meissonier put it this way: 'She had a supreme
talent for attracting famous men about her, and for organising a
salon, in which it was always a pleasure to find oneself. Refined,
subtle, and genial, smiling and intelligent ... For a weary, busy man
it was an exquisite rest and refreshment to find her always the same,
always equable, a true refuge from the cares of life, which she grace-
fully banished for you.'[13]

Charades were very much in vogue and might predominate on
some Sundays. At other times there would be readings. One evening
there was a fancy-dress party and we know that Gautier dressed as
a Turk, Flaubert as a Red Indian 'with a kitchen utensil for a toma-
hawk', Du Camp as a Hindu. Another notable event took place on
27 March 1859, when Gautier had just come back from a long trip to
Russia. He arrived in Paris that very evening and hurried to the rue

Frochot without even going home to change, 'startling and delighting the other guests by his sudden appearance in a fur hat and voluminous overcoat', and showing that some things hadn't changed since Simon Arnauld rushed to Mme du Plessis-Guénégaud's salon two centuries earlier.[14]

Probably the most notable aspect of Apollonie's salon was the bawdy talk.[15] It seems that most members of her gatherings enjoyed the frisson of being able to 'talk dirty' in the presence of a woman who would not pretend to be shocked nor expect it to go any further. In her salon, they could escape their wives' disapproval (several of them were married and others would marry later) and step 'over the borders of respectability and into the demi-monde', but safely because Apollonie retained an aura of unavailability by virtue of belonging to Alfred Mosselman.[16]

In fact, the flirtation may have become too much at times. Here is Gautier yet again, in June 1854, referring to his failure to secure for Apollonie a seat for the first night of a ballet: 'You know I adore you and I'm ready, like a large King Charles spaniel, to lick between your fingers and your buttocks, and your gusset.'[17]

A Secret with a Capital 'S'

La Présidente was not unused to being the inspiration for verse. Gautier, when he could curb his indecent urges, published a poem in the *Revue de Paris* entitled 'Apollonie', in which he waxed lyrical about her name. So, when Apollonie received Baudelaire's first anonymous offering she may merely have smiled knowingly and slipped the lines into her secretaire.

Two months after Gautier's poem in the *Revue*, in May 1853, Baudelaire sent Apollonie a second poem and a second anonymous note. Its subject matter was more explicit, for while Baudelaire refers to her as an 'angel full of happiness, joy and light', elsewhere there is a sense that he hoped the 'angel' will experience 'anguish instead of gladness, hatred instead of kindness, fevers instead of health, and wrinkles instead of beauty'. This poem eventually became 'Réversibilité' in *Les Fleurs du mal*.[18]

Other poems and anonymous letters followed across 1853, 1854 and into 1855 but in June that year the journal *Revue des deux mondes* finally published eighteen poems by Baudelaire, under the title *Les Fleurs du mal*. These eighteen included 'Réversibilité' and two others sent to Apollonie, with the titles 'Confession' and 'L'Aube spirituelle', and his anonymity – if she had never suspected – was exploded.

So far as Apollonie and Baudelaire were concerned, there were no changes to their relationship. He was more taken up with the fact that, when the complete edition of the book was released, it was impounded at the printer's in Alençon and Baudelaire and his publisher charged with offences against public and religious morality.

Two days before the trial was set to begin, on 18 August, Baudelaire sent Apollonie a special copy of his book, bound in green half-morocco. He inscribed it with the words '*À la Très belle, à la Très bonne, à la Très Chère*' on the flyleaf, and wrote another letter, in part of which he told Apollonie that her sister had once laughed in his face and asked if he was still in love with Apollonie and still writing her 'those wonderful letters'. He was distraught but ended by begging her to remember 'that someone is thinking of you, that there is nothing trivial about his thought' and that she was his 'Secret', with a capital 'S'.[19]

After this episode his attendance at her salon began to drop off but he was no less ardent, and at times, Rounding says, Apollonie was no less ardent in return, puzzled that he should be 'terribly afraid of finding yourself alone with me'.[20] At other times he would refer to a letter he had received from her in which, it seems, she had 'offered herself to him'. Apollonie told friends later that they had once gone for a walk arm-in-arm one evening along the terrace of the Tuileries Gardens beside the Seine. In another of his letters Baudelaire refers to 'the scent of your arms and your hair', and she complains about him 'feeling her embraces'. Based on these allusions, some have concluded that she and he slept together at least once, though Rounding is not among their number. As she points out, he was to make clear his extraordinary misogyny in both *The Painter in Modern Life*, where he describes women as 'stupid but dazzling', and *My Heart Laid Bare*, which contains these gems: 'Woman is the opposite of the Dandy. That is why she should be regarded with disgust' and 'Woman is "natural" – that is to say, abominable.'[21]

Whether or not they did sleep together is perhaps beside the point. It does seem clear that she regarded Baudelaire as someone special, and he was to write a later poem which shows that he still, to an extent, carried a torch for her. It is, in its way, one of the more exceptional affairs in history.

After Mosselman died, she became the mistress of the art collector Sir Richard Wallace, whose widow donated his collection to the British nation. Apollonie's own art works (three miniatures) were among those rejected by the 1863 Paris Salon and so were shown in the celebrated Salon des refusés, alongside Manet's *Le Déjeuner sur l'herbe*, in which a voluptuous naked woman in a public spot continued the tradition of outraging *le monde* that had begun with Clésinger's *Femme piquée par un serpent*.

Fumisterie and the Poetics of the Café

If Napoleon III's greatest humiliation was to be his capture by Bismarck during the Franco-Prussian War of 1870–1, his greatest success – although it didn't seem that way to many of his contemporaries at the time – was the mammoth rebuilding project that he and his prefect of the Seine *département*, Baron Haussmann, put into effect. Their aim was to transform Paris into a great modern metropolis so as to rival and even eclipse London, which the emperor had got to know well during his exile. Aided by the imaginative determination of Haussmann, the emperor's government joined together with private enterprise to bring about a massive transformation of the capital's infrastructure – great boulevards were cut through the city, opening up vast vistas, and an elaborate and interlocking system of sewers and drains was installed, which revolutionised the water supply, more or less wiped out the cholera that had been such a scourge, and (somewhat surprisingly) attracted hordes of tourists, having been superbly photographed by Nadar. Five new bridges were built across the Seine, and half-a-dozen others renovated.

The emperor took the project seriously, meeting – we are told – with Haussmann almost every day.[1] Haussmann saw himself, as he put it, as an *artiste démolisseur*, and demolition was certainly one of the things that he was good at. His plans called for – and achieved – the clearing away of much of mediaeval Paris, and which also managed to be home to many of the working classes, who were driven to the periphery of the city. Haussmann's vision made much of the straight line – this aided faster communication and gave the police and military much greater flexibility in tackling uprisings, the new wide boulevards making the erection of barricades – Paris's traditional revolutionary manoeuvre – all but impossible. The rebuilding included four theatres, fifteen churches, seventy schools, six barracks, six town halls and two railway stations, the gares du Nord and d'Austerlitz. On the Île de la Cité most of the old properties were pulled down, to be replaced by new public buildings, with the result that the population there shrank from 15,000 to 5,000.[2]

The emperor and prefect also wanted to transform Paris as a place of relaxation and entertainment and here Napoleon chose to emulate Hyde Park in London, where again his exile had introduced him to an aspect of life – riding – that he thought could benefit Paris. This is how the Bois de Boulogne came about, with its lakes and lawns. The Bois was among the first of the projects to be completed, in 1854, to be followed by the racecourse at Longchamp.

As a direct result of these schemes, thousands of Parisians were forced to abandon their homes in central Paris. The bourgeoisie mainly moved to the outskirts of the city, but the poorer elements were forced into far less salubrious accommodation even further out. The administration was quite frankly interested mainly in making the centre of Paris a jewel for the better off, but this coincided with other unanticipated developments of the nineteenth century, which saw more than 120,000 migrants in the 1850s alone leave the countryside and transfer to Paris, putting terrible pressure on the already overcrowded tenements beyond the glamorous centre.[3]

There was enormous change more generally too. This was when the railways were opening up France, the telegraph was invented, shipping was booming, Pasteur was making his innovations in healthcare. Gaslight had replaced oil lighting in the Paris streets.[4] Many were lit all night and the city was already flirting with electric lighting.

The increasing gap between rich and poor thus became a major element in the politics of the time, with the Orléanists and republicans bitterly divided over the direction the country was taking. These disagreements would not be fully resolved until the Franco-Prussian War had come and gone, but well before that Haussmann's career exploded in disgrace when he was found to have used some highly secretive and unorthodox financing methods (to say the least) that landed Paris, and the emperor, with massive debt.

THE 'INTELLECTUAL CAFÉ'

Not even that, however, could reduce the shine that was beginning to attach to the French capital, the City of Light as it was again becoming known. Here, for example, is *La Chroniqueuse* in November 1859: 'They are all here – England, Russia, Austria, Germany, Italy, Spain, in fact, all the world is represented in a *réunion* in the *salons* of our *élite*; and wealth, that great ruler of us all, lends its aid to magnify and decorate this assemblage of the great and the powerful of all lands. A Parisian *salon* cannot be equalled in this respect, for Paris is the centre of fashion.'[5]

Alongside everything else were two developments that were to build on Paris's – and France's – reputation for a distinctive way of life. These were the café – and in particular the café-concert – and the vogue for department stores specialising in the culture of appearances – that is to say, the fashion business. 'The café-concerts were essentially Baron Haussmann's creation. They grew fat in the free market for eating and drinking which boomed in the boulevards in the 1860s.' According to T. J. Clark's count, by the early 1870s there were at least 145 of them.[6]

We last left the café in chapter 18, in the late eighteenth century, when it was part of the cult of coffee and distinguished as a 'manufactory' of the mind. In many respects, this tradition continued in the last half of the nineteenth century as well. T. S. Eliot, the American-British poet, was to say in one of his works that he had 'measured out his life in coffee spoons'. In much the same vein we may say that the trajectory of modern art in France during what came to be called the Belle Époque can be measured out in cafés. Although some sociologists have expressed doubt that there is such a thing as 'café culture', others – notably the Parisian art historian Gérard-Georges Lemaire – have forged successful careers studying and describing what he calls 'intellectual cafés'.[7]

Throughout the last half of the nineteenth century, and well into the twentieth, the café developed in two distinct ways. On the one hand, cafés remained more or less as traditional institutions, their tables sprawled across the pavements of the great boulevards, where people could idle away the hours, read newspapers and watch passers-by. But they also became increasingly the rallying point – the 'home' in a way, or collective base – of various artistic, literary and musical movements, where painters, sculptors, writers and composers congregated to discuss their work, argue over which direction their art should take, and reinforce one another in their fight for the acceptance of what some critics saw as anything but great work.

It is also important to add that café culture embraced almost everywhere the spirit of *fumisterie* – the hoax, prank or practical joke, what a later age would call 'performance art' – but produced in a spirit of whimsy or irony, to emphasise the inevitable absurdities of life, pointed politically but always attempted in a spirit of gaiety.

The more bohemian, artistic cafés were for the most part spread around the *butte* or hill of Montmartre, though just then *the* place for fashionable cafés was the boulevard des Italiens, '*Les Italiens*' as Parisians called it, where could be found at least six highly fashionable attractions – Hardy, La Maison dorée, Le Cardinal, Le Riche, Le Grand Balcon and Tortoni's, still going strong. In most cases, the waiters in these cafés were young boys, from which the word *garçon* arose.

But the earliest cafés that served as rallying points for painters and sculptors were the Guerbois and the Nouvelle Athènes on the borders of Montmartre, the former at 11 avenue de Clichy and the latter overlooking the place Pigalle on the corner of the rue Pigalle and the rue Frochot, where Apollonie Sabatier had her salon.*

Montmartre was one of the original bohemian areas, quiet in the day, raucous at night. A series of five-storey terraced houses had been built in the 1820s as speculation, affordable by single women who had arrived in the city to work in the new factories or as prostitutes. They were known as 'Lorettes' on account of the nearby church, Notre-Dame de Lorette. Delacroix once caught his breath at seeing a Lorette nonchalantly reveal her long, long legs ('up to the belly button') as she got down from a one-horse carriage.[8]

---

* The impressionist world was rather different from the Barbizon school, which had assembled at Chez Ganne, the village's one and only tavern.

Thursday and Sunday were the favoured days at the Guerbois, Fridays at the Nouvelle Athènes. The Guerbois was noisy and had leather banquettes and marble-topped tables while, according to George Moore, the Irish writer who spent long evenings at the Nouvelle Athènes, that café had glass-panelled doors and a sanded floor. 'In his view, the café was the real Académie des Beaux Arts in Paris, the official one being nothing but a superannuated institution doomed to die.'[9]

Manet was the centre of the crowd who met regularly at the Guerbois, though he wasn't always happy to be associated with other impressionists – Sisley, Monet, Pissarro, Degas, Renoir and Bazille. Zola was a regular, less so his good friend Cézanne, the pioneer photographer Nadar (and balloonist, he was the first person to take aerial photographs), Zacharie Astruc and Louis Edmond Duranty, both art critics, Henri Fantin-Latour and Constantin Guys.

The evenings could be argumentative: on one occasion, in February 1870, Duranty published something in the *Paris-Journal* that Manet took as an insult, challenging him to a duel. Despite friends trying to stop it, the duel went ahead at 11.00 one morning not long after in the forest of Saint-Germain, the duellists 'preparing to defend their honour with cold steel'. In the official account, written by Manet's second, Zola, 'the engagement was short, sharp, and extremely violent'. Both men's swords broke at the hilt, Duranty was slightly cut above his right breast, and Manet declared himself avenged.[10]

Manet was the leader in all ways. Except for Pissarro, he was older than the others, richer, better educated. He was always well dressed, for the most part well behaved though, as the Duranty affair shows, he could be impetuous. His main verbal sparring partners around the café tables were Degas, also well-off and well educated, and Frédéric Bazille, who was reticent in manner but invariably stuck to his implacable opinions. Cézanne was also reticent but did observe on one occasion that the others drank so much – and so late into the night – that it affected their ability to get up in the morning and start painting.[11] It was of course this close fraternity that Zola described in his novel *L'Œuvre*, where most critics think the artist Claude Lantier is a creative amalgam of Manet, Cézanne (who Zola had known since childhood) and the others gathered at the Guerbois and the

Victor Hugo (1802-1885) 'listening
to God'. By Auguste Vacquerie, 1853.
A play on the author's enthusiasm for
spiritualism.

Sarah Bernhardt (1844-1923) by Nadar,
1859. She 'made love in a hot air
balloon and slept in a coffin'.

Auguste Clésinger, 'Woman Bitten By a Serpent', 1847. Otherwise Apollonie
Sabatier in the throes of orgasm.

Jules Barbey d'Aurevilly (1808-1889) in 1881-1882. By Émile Lévy.

Count Robert de Montesquiou (1855-1921) by Giovanni Boldini, 1897. 'The world's most laborious sayer of nothing.'

Interior of the Café Nouvelles Athènes. Jean Louis Forain, 1878.

Yvette Guilbert (1865-1944), by Toulouse-Lautrec, 1894. Star of the Moulin Rouge and other cabarets.

The Palais-Royal in 1843, by William Wyld.

Fall of the Column in the Place Vendôme. Illustrated London News, 27 May 1871.

Interior of the Auberge du Clou, Avenue Trudaine, Montmartre, 1905. Erik Satie was the pianist there for a while.

The Chat Noir cabaret, interior, c. 1900. The pictures on the walls were by the customers.

The Chat Noir cabaret, exterior, c. 1900.

The Artists' Bar, Au Lapin Agile, early 20th century. One of the homes of 'fumisterie'.

Maurice Ravel (right) and Vaslav Nijinsky playing piano at Ravel's home, 1914. They are playing music from Ravel's *Daphnis and Chloé*.

'Les Six' by Jaccque-Émile Blanche, 1921. From left to right: Germaine Tailleferre, Darius Milhaud, Arthur Honegger, Jean Wiener, Marcelle Meyer, Francis Poulenc, Georges Auric (sitting) and Jean Cocteau.

Alice Prin, Kiki of Montparnasse (1901-1953), Man Ray's muse, wearing more clothes than usually pictured. South of France, c. 1925.

Jean Cocteau and friend, in a not-dissimilar pose.

Jeanne Hebuterne (1898-1920), by Amadeo Modigliani, c. 1918-1919.

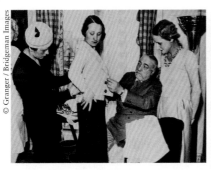

Paul Poiret (1879-1944) fitting a model at his Paris department store, 1933.

Gabrielle 'Coco' Chanel (1883-1971), photographed by François Kollar in her suite at the Ritz Hotel, Paris, 1937.

Sylvia Beach (1887-1962) outside her bookstore, Shakespeare & Company, in Paris, applauds composer Georges Antheil as he enters his apartment by an unorthodox route.

Aimé Césaire (1913-2008), Martinican poet, historian and politician. One of the founders of Négritude.

General Charles de Gaulle (1890-1970) delivering his famous broadcast from London, 18 June 1940. 'An immense vanity for France.'

Philosopher Raymond Aron (1905-1983), photographed by Marcello Mencarini, 1981. He dedicated his life to the renewal of France's self-respect.

Nouvelle Athènes. Another Zola novel, *L'Assommoir*, is about café life too – his very title was Parisian slang for cafés.

Both Manet and Degas were drawn to cafés – and café-concerts – as their subject matter. Degas's well-known painting *L'Absinthe* (also called *Dans un café*) shows a gloomy, isolated, depressed-looking 'Lorette', depicted on one of the Nouvelle Athènes's banquettes. Manet's paintings *La Prune* and *George Moore au café* are set in the Nouvelle Athènes, while Guy de Maupassant described this café in the fifth chapter of *Bel-Ami*.

THE DIVERSE BRANCHES OF THE BEAUTIFUL

Alongside the Guerbois and the Nouvelle Athènes we may put the Chat Noir, founded by Rodolphe Salis in December 1881. This establishment, which would become legendary, in fact had some important predecessors. In the early decades of the nineteenth century, there had been two types of café that were more than cafés. These were the *caveau* and the *goguette*. The original Caveau (1733–43, revived 1759–67) started out as a club of diners who liked to share songs and witty epigrams (Rameau allegedly belonged to this first Caveau). *Goguettes* were more working-class institutions. Another *chansonnier*, Théophile du Mersan, counted 480 *goguettes* in and around Paris in 1845.[12]

Alongside this there emerged the *café chantant*. 'These café-concerts quickly became, in the words of playwright Eugène Héros, "the people's Opéra and its Comédie-Française".[13] It was here that the routine of performances became more or less settled into a more or less standard form: comic genres such as the *pochard* or drunkard, the *gommeux* or eccentric, and his female equivalent, the *gommeuse*, 'usually skimpily dressed', the *diseuse*, 'who declaimed comic texts to music' (Yvette Guilbert was the star here), and the *troupie* or 'bumbling footsoldier'. Visually, they were captured by Toulouse-Lautrec. Eventually, they would evolve into the cabaret.[14]

To begin with a cabaret might be little more than a tavern or corner bistrot. But after artists began gathering at cafés as their base, and as their presence attracted the public, before long the public itself became part of the show – this was bohemia being 'packaged' as entertainment. One such establishment was the Club des Hydropathes. The Hydropathes (literally, those who suffer from the ingestion of water as opposed to alcohol) were 'a band of writers, musicians and hangers-on', the idea being for poets to read their own works, rather than have professional *diseuses* take the credit – and the proceeds. As it happened, the idea took off, so much so that the Hydropathes were forced to move to larger premises and give readings twice a week.[15] They also started to publish their own journal. The Club des Hydropathes led to the Chat Noir when, in November 1881, Salis bumped into Émile Goudeau and told him his new club was about to open. The décor was mediaeval Gothic and on the walls were pictures by his customers.

The idea behind the Chat Noir was that everyone – artists, staff, customers – was perpetually on show, the whole place a continual performance, its underlying ethos being one of 'youth, gaiety, audacity, lyricism, fantasy' in an atmosphere of 'tobacco smoke, thirst, beards and long hair'.[16] Typical fixtures at the Chat Noir were Albert Tinchant, the regular pianist, who provided music for shadow plays, and Alphonse Allais, card-player extraordinaire and humorist who submitted several offerings to the project of another regular, Jules Lévy, who had an idea for an exhibition of 'Incoherent Art', which was, he said, 'dedicated to the works of "people who do not know how to draw".' Lévy himself certainly didn't know how to draw – he billed himself as the world's greatest cornet-player, having allegedly taught himself using only the mouthpiece of the instrument because his family were too poor to afford an entire cornet. For the second exhibition, Allais provided a blank sheet of Bristol (super-white) paper stuck to a wall. This he entitled *First Communion of Young Chlorotic Girls in a Snowstorm*.[17]

To begin with Salis tended the bar while Goudeau held court in the small back room, known as 'the Institut' because it was regarded as 'the site of a fusion between the diverse branches of the beautiful'. Fridays were known as the '*jour chic*' when the better-known clientele read from their works, before an increasingly elegant public. Among those who would read were Guy de Maupassant, Paul Bourget, Frédéric Mistral, Nobel Prize-winner for his efforts to promote the Occitan language, and the singer and comedian Aristide Bruant, who would compose what became their theme song, 'La Ballade du Chat Noir'. Paul Verlaine sent in weekly lines from his hospital bed. In the manner of the time the club published its own periodical.

This being Paris, with alcohol being served, proceedings were not always as quiet as they might have been and after a waiter was accidentally killed, Salis decided to employ a 'bouncer', whom he dressed in the uniform of the Swiss Guard. In turn, this gave him the idea to dress his waiters in facsimiles of the green and gold uniforms worn by members of the Académie française.

THE IMPORTANCE OF BEING ERIK SATIE

On 27 October 1888, the *Chat Noir*, the publication of the cabaret, announced a new innovation in the Parisian entertainment world. This was the birth of the Divan japonais, a new café-concert at 75 rue des Martyrs, which had been bought by a poet, Théophile Lefort. The site had been home to several previous establishments – the brasserie des Martyrs in 1861, the café de la Chanson in 1883 – and now had a vaguely oriental feel.[18]

One of its first shows was a performance of *Au Moulin de la galette*, a one-act operetta by Allais and Jehan Sarrazin, which attracted a glowing review from the *Chat Noir* periodical, not too surprising as the review was written by one 'Sarcey', none other than Allais himself. But the star of the Divan was without question Yvette Guilbert. She normally came on from the Moulin rouge where she was also the star, alongside the *pétomane* Joseph Pujol, and still in the costume she wore at the Moulin. Her repertoire at the Divan was somewhat more risqué than at the Moulin. Here she sang the *chansons* of Bruant and Léon Xanrof in the company of Adolphe Willette, architect of the Moulin rouge, Toulouse-Lautrec, Théophile Steinlen, the Swiss poster artist, and Goudeau. In keeping with the developing tradition, the Divan also produced a publication, *La Lanterne japonaise*, though it didn't last for much more than a dozen issues. The Divan didn't last either.

A not dissimilar fate also befell the Chat Noir, though later. One autumn afternoon in 1903, Dominique Bonnaud, a *chansonnier* and *goguettier*, paid a visit to the Chat and found it deserted.[19] One of the new rallying points was the auberge du Clou (*clou* means 'nail'), among whose colourful characters was the novelist Georges Courteline, a passionate card-player who, between hands, at his table upstairs, told elaborate fantasies and invented what he called an 'idiometer' with which fellow café-dwellers 'could measure their stupidity'.[20]

Satie played the piano at the Clou. In fact, Satie's career could largely be measured out in the cafés where he played – the Chat Noir, the Nouvelle Athènes and the Moulin de la Galette, as well as at the Clou. He was everywhere and he seems to have been everywhere amusingly influential. It was in these cafés that Satie, Ravel and Debussy met and developed their styles, with Satie now given credit for drawing Debussy away from the domineering influence of Wagner and developing his own much lighter, 'more French style' (musical scholars compare, for example, Satie's *Sarabandes* of 1887 with Debussy's *Sarabande* of 1894).[21]

Satie played at the Clou after he fell out with Salis and it was here that he met Debussy. Four years Satie's senior, Debussy was experienced – he had won the Prix de Rome, visited Bayreuth and Moscow and was close to the impressionists, whose art he loved. Debussy inscribed a copy of *Cinq poèmes de Charles Baudelaire*: 'For Erik Satie, gentle mediaeval musician who strayed into this century to give joy to his best friend, Claude Debussy, 27 October 1892.' Their shared dramatic and harmonic ideas would help shape the independence of French music.[22]

It was at the Clou that Satie also met Miquel Utrillo i Morlius (1862–1934), a Catalan engineer and botanist from Barcelona, who had moved to Paris to attend the Institut national agronomique but was quickly seduced by Montmartre, where he formed a small band of fellow Spanish artists that included the painter Ramón Casas and writer/journalist Santiago Rusiñol. They were part of the Spanish art movement of 'modernism' who operated puppet theatres and shadow theatres and published an illustrated weekly. They had started their own club in Barcelona, Els Quatre Gats (The Four Cats), where one Pablo Picasso had designed menus for the cabaret. When Els Quatre Gats folded, Picasso decided to move to Paris. Both Casas and Rusiñol painted Satie in the various cafés.

After the Clou, Satie became the pianist at the Nouvelle Athènes. This was the nineties and the café still attracted painters, writers and musicians, among them an inventor named Pierre-Joseph Ravel, who brought his son Maurice, still in his teens. As his biographer says: 'Ravel never tired of emphasising the decisive character of his meeting with Satie.'[23]

About this time, however, Satie's father died and he inherited a little money and this was when, as Roger Shattuck puts it, he began a life of 'purposeful oddity'. Having been sympathetic to Rosicrucianism – a mystical outfit claiming a hidden order to the world – he now founded a new religion of his own, the 'Metropolitan Church of the Art of Jesus the Conductor', which had hardly any followers though one of them was Henri Gauthier-Villars, a young music critic, who used the pen name 'Willy' and was in fact the husband of Colette. (He would soon be 'excommunicated' by Satie.) At this time, Satie, pursuing a further search for purposeful oddity, ordered a dozen suits in identical grey corduroy, and made several – more or less hopeless – attempts to be elected to the Académie française.

It was now that he met a woman whose career as an acrobat had been aborted by a trapeze accident.

Suzanne Valadon fell back on her 'second string' and had become a professional artist, forming multiple friendships with a succession of great painters, among them Puvis de Chavannes, Toulouse-Lautrec and Renoir, all of whom had painted her, and Degas, who had been the first artist of note to buy her work. Suzanne moved into an apartment next to Satie in the rue Cortot where she painted him as a shaggy-haired bohemian, and he wrote 'musical good mornings' to her. Their passionate relationship spoiled when he took to drink.[24]

Yes, he had a purposeful oddity, but Satie also reflected the ideal of the time of serious whimsy, *fumisterie*, and of making the most of what was there. One of his French biographers, who knew him, wrote that Satie found more pleasure in the company of painters at the Clou. He admitted that he – and Debussy – were trying to do in music what Monet, Cézanne and Toulouse-Lautrec were doing in paint.[25] Satie also mixed with Braque, Derain, Picasso, Léger and Brancusi.

In 1897, the Chat Noir closed and Satie lost touch with this world for years, setting off on a decade of 'isolation and hibernation', locked away in his lodgings in Arcueil, still in the country at that time. Satie's hibernation lasted until 1910, when we shall catch up with him again.

THE IMPRESARIO OF MODERNISM: A STROLL WITHOUT END

A painting by Augustin Grass-Mick (1873–1963), a friend of Toulouse-Lautrec and Verlaine, shows Satie at yet another café, the Lapin agile, listening as Frédé, the owner, plays his cello. The Lapin agile, aka the Lapin à Gill or Là peint A. Gill – maintaining the whimsy – was the Montmartre cabaret that succeeded the Chat Noir around the turn of the century. No less than Salis at the Chat Noir, Frédé was part of the show, as indeed was Lolo, 'his unhouse-broken donkey'. Lolo was the subject of a celebrated *fumisterie* inspired by the novelist Roland Dorgelès, in which a canvas, brushed entirely and only by Lolo's tail, was hung in the Salon des Indépendants with the title *And the Sun Went Down over the Adriatic*. Dorgelès added the signature 'Joachim Raphael Boronali', and the work attracted no little praise, even from professional critics.

As Satie had acted as a lightning rod for the cafés in the Paris of the last years of the nineteenth century, so Guillaume Apollinaire fulfilled the same role in the early years of the twentieth. Of Polish extraction, a poet and art critic, coiner of the term 'surrealism', in 1903 he encountered three different groups of artists in Paris and their associated cafés.

In the winter of 1903–4 he was introduced to the Criterion café opposite the Gare Saint-Lazare by Jean Mollet, a literary memoirist and editor (known variously as 'Baron', 'the Magnificent' or 'Satrap').[26] This café had already featured in at least one celebrated novel, for it was in this establishment that Des Esseintes, the central figure in Huysmans's *À rebours* (chapters 32 and 37), ended his trip to England. At this café, Apollinaire and Mollet found Picasso – then twenty-two and on his fourth trip to Paris – conversing with a raft of hangers-on. Apollinaire and Picasso hit it off and, for their next meeting, Picasso brought along his friend Max Jacob. Jacob was a writer and critic, with whom at one point the painter shared a room, and who he had met at Ambroise Vollard's art gallery (Vollard being Cézanne's and Renoir's dealer, among others). Jacob's impressions of Apollinaire at that first meeting were vivid: 'He was an imposing young man with a deep chest and heavy limbs ... He changed in an instant from childlike laughter to pale gravity. The three of us left together and Guillaume carried us off for a stroll which never came to an end ...'[27]

At roughly the same time, in Chatou, a suburb of Le Vésinet, west of Paris, surrounded by a loop of the Seine, Apollinaire met a separate group of painters – separate just then anyway – centred around Maurice de Vlaminck and André Derain, both of whom were enthusiastic health freaks, as we would say – Vlaminck, for instance, had once been a bicycle racer. The two painters had met one day while painting the same landscape and had become keen friends. They introduced Apollinaire to their hang-outs – which were mostly disreputable bargemen's cafés, hashish dens or brothels. They played cards and drank but carried on conversations about painting and aesthetics that overlapped with what Apollinaire was hearing among Picasso and Jacob.

What they also had in common was that they all worked hard and consistently – they worked hard before playing hard at the Lapin agile and the *cirque* Medrano, once a week crossing town to the Closerie des Lilas, 'where Paul Fort's new revue *Vers et prose* held its wild soirees'.

The presence of Henri Monnier and Alphonse Allais was part of the general background here, together with that of Alfred Jarry (chapter 37), another notorious prankster. His 'pataphysics' was almost a formalised *fumisterie*, using ironic absurdities to point up uncomfortable truths. This matters because Apollinaire introduced Picasso to Braque and there has always been an undercurrent of feeling that cubism, which began at this time and in these circumstances, was an elaborate hoax before it became serious. (Braque was also friendly with Satie.) Certainly, the Lapin agile, the true salon of this new art, was no stranger to serious whimsy. Maurice Princet, an articulate professional mathematician, had input into this group, which may have helped give rise to cubism.

The weekly meetings at the Closerie des Lilas were the third group that Apollinaire discovered and publicised in his role as self-appointed 'impresario of modernism'. The Closerie was important insofar as it was situated on the boulevard de Montparnasse, and was one of the locations by which the 'avant-garde' began its switch from Montmartre across the river to the Latin Quarter.[28] The Closerie had in fact begun life as the Bal Bullier and had been the home of a group of painters originally known as 'les intransigeants', arising in the atelier of Charles Gleyre and comprising Bazille, Renoir, Monet and Sisley, who would eventually become the impressionists – it was, in effect, an alternative base to the Nouvelle Athènes. The Bullier changed its name in the 1860s, forming one of another series of 'intellectual' cafés, known as the 'Montparnos', in the boulevard du Montparnasse, that also included the Dôme, the Rotonde, the Select and the Coupole.

Apollinaire had his ear to the ground. After the First World War, as we shall see, the tradition of the intellectual café continued, but not in Montmartre. The switch to the Latin Quarter was now complete.

Chic: The Parisienne as a Work of Art

In 1846, when Baudelaire first referred to 'chic' as 'that strange and awful word of modern invention', we may take it that *chic* then was not what *chic* would become or means now. It may have had German overtones, deriving from *Geschick*, meaning 'skill', possibly taken from tailors' argot. And it took a while to change. Nestor Roqueplan was in some ways a typically colourful nineteenth-century figure with a lot of strings to his bow. He was, at various times, editor-in-chief of *Le Figaro*, fighting a duel with one of his readers who objected to something he had written (he was wounded), an amateur magician, a director of four theatres, including the Paris Opera, and a dandy who invented the silk braid trim on trouser seams. In other words he was, by our standards, somewhat chic himself. In 1865, he too wrote that 'the word *chic* is ugly'. He did go on, however, to record a multitude of near-synonyms which suggest that its meaning was indeed beginning to change. Although he personally found the term ugly, he conceded that 'taste, distinction, fashion and elegance are all rolled into chic'. This coincided with the fact that the mid-1860s was the period when the new department stores were opening in Paris, which Zola would make so much of in *Au Bonheur des dames*.[1] And so, by the turn of the century, Octave Uzanne, bibliophile and a frankly nationalistic fashion writer, 'took it for granted that *chic* was a high compliment' and, moreover, that 'the supreme *chic* (there is no other word)' was the special gift of the Parisienne.[2]

Paris, it has been often enough said, was the capital of the nineteenth century. Whether other nations might argue that London or Berlin or Vienna could rival Paris on that score, no one would seriously contest that Paris was the capital of fashion. Chic, says Ruth Iskin, had become a national trait 'reflecting a superior French taste'. This transformation, as several historians have pointed out, was the product of mass consumption that characterised the second half of the nineteenth century.[3]

There was in truth more to it. In 1877, when the royalist-inclined president, Patrice de Mac Mahon, had dismissed the frankly republican prime minister, Jules Simon, and created a crisis, the ultimate result, later in the year, when the dust had settled, saw a parliamentary system prevail over a presidential one, which was seen as confirming the 1875 constitution. This basically paved the way for a bourgeois nation rather than an aristocratic one and helped to determine the longevity and legitimacy of the Third Republic (until 1940). And this – and perhaps it could happen only in France – had an aesthetic dimension. As Lisa Tiersten puts it: 'In a nation deeply invested in its reputation for aesthetic refinement, the presumption of bourgeois vulgarity sparked concern in diverse quarters. Middle-class elites and their critics alike thus feared that the entrenchment of a bourgeois republic in 1877 had put France's aesthetic patrimony in jeopardy from which it threatened to squander that inheritance.'[4] The phenomenon of the chic Parisienne, she says, arose from this perceived threat.

This is a topic which – again – shows the interlocking nature of French history. We have already noted how impressionism was and is a *flâneur*'s art. But it was also, in many ways, the art of chic. For Baudelaire, the painter of modern life – who is a *flâneur* – is also a connoisseur of feminine fashions, who keeps up to date with the latest seasonal changes. 'If a fashion or the cut of a garment has been slightly modified, if bows and curls have been supplanted by cockades, if *bavolets* have dropped a fraction towards the nape of the neck, if waists have been raised and skirts become fuller, be very sure that his [the impressionist painter's] eagle eye will already have spotted it from however great a distance.' 'The chic Parisienne', says Iskin, 'became as predominant in avant-garde paintings as she was in the print media.'[5] Most of the impressionists featured modern dress in their works – Manet, Degas, Monet, Renoir, Morisot, Cassatt (Pittsburgh-born but settled in Paris) – displayed at fashionable venues, at the races, various resorts, the opera, the theatre, the cafés, the gardens and the boulevards (Berthe Morisot and Mary Cassatt both bought their clothes at Worth's; the latter also modelled for Degas).

The rue de la Paix was known as the most popular place for high-class *flânerie* in the Paris of the Third Republic. On an afternoon, the coupés and the victorias of the *haute-couture flâneurs* were drawn up in double and triple file in front of Worth's, Virot's, Doucet's and the other studios. Degas was among them and, said Paul Gauguin, he went 'into ecstasies before the milliners' shops on the rue de la Paix'. Manet was little different: we know he also spent a day of 'ecstasy' in front of the fabrics of leading dress-designers.[6] He pleaded with one lady friend to give him her fur coat once she had finished with it so he could paint it, referring to it as 'the stuff that dreams were made of'.[7] The chic Parisienne – always a Paris*ienne* – became a stereotype of fashion and femininity, of the consumer economy and, no less important, of the cultural superiority of France.

Parisiennes had no doubt of their superiority. Here is Emmeline Raymond, the publisher of a fashion magazine: 'Fashion is French simply because it cannot exist without the Parisienne ... A Parisienne always admires herself, whatever she does, and always accepts without examination the flattering superlatives of which the Parisian tongue is composed.' Elsewhere she noted that 'the Parisiennes are women, but they are more so than all other women,' which implies 'not only the Parisienne's feminine superiority but also France's superiority over other nations'.[8] Léon Gozlan, novelist and columnist on *Le Figaro*, agreed, writing as early as 1852: '[The Parisienne] is the shining justification of the superiority of France over other nations.'

This longing to be always number one might be tiresome except that in this case it so obviously paid off. Impressionist paintings such as Monet's *Woman in the Garden* and *Woman with a Parasol*, Caillebotte's *Paris Street, Rainy Day*, Renoir's *La Parisienne*, Cassatt's *Woman with a Pearl Necklace* and *The Cup of Tea*, Morisot's *Before the Theatre*, Manet's *Spring* and *In the Conservatory*, and Degas's twenty-two paintings of milliners, are each magnificent renderings of chic, with not a bow, or a ribbon or a hat-pin out of place. In fact, in many impressionist paintings the costumes are the primary focus of attention.[9] Degas helped introduce the shop window into art while George Moore considered that inanimate commodities were a new form of still life.[10]

A FEMALE CITY

The significance of the way Paris was transformed into 'a female city', as Lisa Tiersten puts it, is underlined by the fact that the number of couturiers in the city rose from 158 in 1850 to 684 in 1872 and 1,636 in 1895.[11] By the 1880s, there were a hundred fashion journals in Paris, a good number selling at least 100,000 copies.[12] Fashion posters reached their heyday in the 1890s, when Georges Seurat collected them and closely studied in particular Jules Chéret's striking works. He was the most prolific poster artist of the century, helping to shape impressionism.[13]

No less striking was the fact that only 37 per cent of the couturiers' clients were French. Jean-Philippe Worth, son of the leading designer Charles Frederick Worth, the English-born 'father of haute couture', boasted that 'the City of Light became the chief source of supply for the civilised world', adding that the chic Parisienne 'became so renowned in time for her instinct for sartorial beauty that a gown that did not come from Paris was not considered, as women insisted they must have a French model'.[14]

It was widely appreciated that one could learn a lot simply by *being* in Paris and behaving, more or less, as a *flâneuse*, entering department stores and looking at shop windows so as 'to know what was happening'.[15] Baudelaire drew attention to what he called the 'incognito gaze', looking at things without drawing attention to oneself, and etiquette books also advised that gazing should be 'non-confrontational'; the *flâneuse* 'avoids looking people in the eye' and so retains the freedom to move about as she wishes.

A painting by Henri Gervex, *Cinq heures chez Paquin*, shows the House of Paquin at five o'clock in the afternoon, when twenty-one women, and four men, are examining clothes, but it is also clear that this is a social scene, where women are catching up on the gossip at the same time as observing more or less unobtrusively who is wearing what, who is buying what, who is trying on what. This is fashion as a way of life where chic was 'said to regulate the unrestrained individualism and dangerous desires ascribed to the female consumer, turning her on the one hand into a virtuous citizen, and on the other into a refined connoisseur of goods'.[16]

This restraining influence of chic was important because there was no shortage of people who feared that the modern marketplace was dangerous 'precisely because it provided women with the kind of financial and psychological independence that undermined their supporting, independent roles within the family'. The spaces and rituals of the modern marketplace, it was also held, offered a whole new range of possibilities for 'feminine posing'.[17]

The 'deep background' to this is that, in the aristocratic society of the *ancien régime*, taste was defined by the connoisseur's knowledge-based and therefore *disinterested* relation to art and the world of goods. This was felt to be the perquisite of aristocracy, and unavailable to the bourgeoisie.[18] One consequence of this, which links forward to chapter 37, is that the bourgeois woman in late nineteenth-century France stood at the centre of narratives of decline and degeneration. 'For many, her lack of taste threatened to ravage France's aesthetic reputation and, in so doing, to drive the nation to the brink of economic ruin.'[19]

This may be going a bit far, but it does help to explain the emergence of what Tiersten calls 'marketplace modernism', in which taste shifted from the eighteenth-century idea and ideal of the *passive recognition* of beauty, into an attitude where the consumer was herself an artist, where commodities were art objects, where consumption was itself an artistic enterprise. And so chic involved the *active creation* of beauty. Moreover, it was held that not only could taste be learned but it could be achieved via the marketplace, by observing what was happening, by being, in effect, a *flâneuse*. To be chic was to be part of an aesthetic elite.[20]

Balzac, Zola and the impressionists all realised that women's relationship with goods was changing. The age of the department store – partly brought into being by Haussmann's 'improvements' – was also characterised by new kinds of commercial space, new rituals of selling and buying and a new middle-class clientele. The department store was, on this analysis, a self-enclosed feminine metropolis. Catholic conservatives fulminated against this new world, but it was far too seductive for them to make much headway.[21] 'Crossing the threshold of the *grand magasin*, the *flâneuse* became a browser, with no obligation to strike up a conversation with sales personnel or other customers or even to make a purchase. [The 'incognito gaze' again.] She could continue her urban promenade unmolested through the vast spaces of the department store, circulating freely, a spectator rather than a participant.' The woman who simply fondled the goods, or stroked them, without buying, was even given a name – '*palpeuse*' – which had erotic overtones. This environment, some thought, was dangerous because it aimed 'to envelop Frenchwomen in an atmosphere of desire'.[22] The French for window-shopping, *lécher-vitre*, literally to lick the window, also contains an erotic element, which went alongside the widely held conviction that sales assistants in department stores were sexually available.

And alongside all that went the idea that the department store was an aspect of – or a contributor to – degeneration, one form of 'urban pathology'. Women shoppers were, in the words of one journalist, 'afflicted with new styles of neurosis'. Gustave Le Bon held that the department store was a breeding ground for revolutionary ideas.[23]

SATELLITES OF RADIANCE

These fears about commercialisation and the aesthetic decline of Paris need to be understood against the historical role of taste in defining Frenchness, which went back, as we have seen, to at least the middle of the eighteenth century and its 'frenzy for fashions' (chapter 17). 'For most commentators of the era, France's status as a world power was inseparable from its reputation as an arbiter of taste.' One journalist argued that art was 'the most indisputable of French glories' and that women's fashion was its 'most delicate and exquisite branch'. The aristocracy's use of clothing, décor and connoisseurship to express a 'caste identity' had created in effect an 'aesthetic caste', which meant that, in comparison with Germany, say, or England, the French bourgeoisie 'retained a sense of cultural inferiority vis-à-vis the nobility ... a deficit of critical importance'.[24]

In 1877, the French bourgeoisie had achieved full political power but not yet in cultural terms – this was the crucial displacement. This is one reason why, for a time, the department stores were held to be 'enemies of beauty' by offering goods that were below standard, according to traditional (aristocratic) levels. It was held that women – in particular Parisian women – possessed an innate aesthetic instinct but that it had not yet been realised in the bourgeoisie. 'A woman without taste ... does not know how to speak ... to dress, to maintain her household, to raise her children, to receive visitors ... in the appropriate fashion.' This 'moral malaise' was regarded as a byproduct of the advent of a republic.[25]

In the years after 1877, however, a different sort of change began to come about. 'To be chic is to be an artist,' wrote Marguerite Herleroy in the magazine *Femina*. Another historian observed a 'widening cult of art' in these years, 'a seismic cultural shift in the constitution of self and social identity'. Taste was coming to be seen as an essential way to assert 'individual distinction' and the meaning of the chic Parisienne began to take on the aura of 'taste and moral probity', assuaging status anxiety, says Lisa Tiersten, and again bolstering 'the nation's reputation for aesthetic superiority'.[26]

The meaning of chic was now totally transformed: both consumption and the female consumer were valued. The everyday contained opportunities for heroic experience, and that sensory experience was the basis of knowledge. The self was a work of art.

With this came an explosion in etiquette books, one of which claimed: 'The sphere of a pretty woman does not end with the last fold of her skirt. Her apartment, her carriages, her receptions, and her friends are like satellites of her personal radiance ...'[27]

There were held to be three aspects to chic, epitomising a new psychology. The first was a new importance attached to personality, in the sense of a unique aspect of individuality. Second was the idea that personality was mutable, it was not a set constellation of character traits but could be developed. Finally, chic came to mean a *general* ability of improvisation and not some finite code of conduct. Chic meant being a master/mistress of oneself.[28] It was, as Barrès phrased it, echoing Baudelaire, a form of heroism. Chic was also fuelled by the fact that, in Haussmann's new Paris, neighbourhoods were more segregated by class and it was only in the commercial centre that the different layers of the bourgeoisie could meet on the same stage and, as it were, compare notes.

ARTISTIC SNOBBERY AND SELF-IMPROVEMENT: LIVING AESTHETICALLY

Against this background, the newly chic bourgeois woman was encouraged to take a greater interest in the arts, so much so that 'artistic snobbery' began to flourish as an aspect of 'self-improvement'. Women were encouraged to 'live aesthetically' in a way in which their 'inner sensibility' might be expressed in their external chic.[29]

This applied no less to interior decoration – a woman's living circumstances were as much an expression of chic as were her clothes. In this way, 'the ideal Parisienne imagined by commercial media was an artist-consumer for whom the market was a creative sphere in which she cultivated and expressed her aesthetic and moral sensibility'. It was even said that there was 'a new feminine duty – to consume French fashion'.[30]

In the research for her book on Paris chic, Lisa Tiersten unearthed the full publishing records of no fewer than sixty periodicals given over to the subject, some of which, in addition to clothes and interior decoration, highlighted the areas of the city where it was chic to be seen. The 'education of the eye' became one of the main aims of these periodicals, again attaching a feeling of high seriousness and grandeur to what was essentially shopping. Art lessons, it was held, would help the aspiring chic woman to improve her colour-coding, and help in matching furniture to carpets and wallpaper, for example. This was so because 'the superiority of France in fashion derives from its long Parisian tradition of taste in all artistic professions'. Arsène Houssaye, novelist, editor of *L'Artiste*, administrator of the Théâtre-Français, declared it the 'duty' of the chic Parisienne to pay a 'monthly visit' to the studio of established painters. In 1881, the Comtesse de Verrasques likened the Parisienne at her toilette to the artist painting a self-portrait.[31]

The specifically stated goal of the periodical *L'Art de la mode* was to 'elevate it [*la mode*] to the same stature as the subject of art'.

Octave Uzanne, again, argued that the imagination of fashionable women had changed the very course of modern art.[32]

Much the same arguments applied with the chic interior. The bourgeois home did not have much in the way of inherited furniture or paintings, and so, according to critics, also had little in the way of memories, but that simply left the modern woman 'free' to build – create – her own environment. Decoration, as we have seen, had once been a male preserve, right up until the early nineteenth century. But now women were reminded of the dominance of French taste in the field of design and master craftsmen. Along with this, the chic modern woman was encouraged to look upon herself as a 'collaborator' with decorators; they were not merely clients.

However, their status as 'artist-consumers' was not always recognised by modernist artists themselves, who had a vested interest in maintaining a firm distinction between 'high' art and merely 'decorative' art, and this, to an extent, kept women in a subordinate aesthetic position.[33] Some 'experts' went along with this by treating women as works of art rather than as artists. This was implicit, Tiersten says, in the advice given to bourgeois women – for example, that in their choice of fabrics in the home, or for their clothes, they should limit themselves strictly to colours 'that blended with their hair-colour and skin tone … Use your rugs and curtains to dress yourself.' Or: 'Your salon, Madame, is nothing more than a frame to set you off.' Clothing, it was also said, could make a woman into a 'living poem'.[34]

Overall, then, the chic woman in the last half of the nineteenth century in France had a powerful social identity. By the 1890s the pairing of economy and elegance had become a defining aspect of the Parisienne, and had even achieved a moral dimension, chic being regarded as a form of discipline which made a contribution to the social good, creating an 'imagined community' of taste to which all had equal access. At the same time it preserved France's reputation. 'The French woman is still the queen of the world', was the verdict of a Bon Marché catalogue in 1912.[35]

Given the thrust of this chapter, one can see why, in October 2021, when Condé Nast, the American owners of *Vogue Paris*, ruled that the name of the French capital should be dropped from the title, the French were outraged. *Le Figaro* regretted the imposition of 'Anglo-Saxon values'.[36]

PART SEVEN

Defeat, Decadence, Dazzle

'All Progress Depends on France Remaining Intact'

On Friday 22 May 1885, four months after an immense state banquet to celebrate his eighty-third birthday, Victor Hugo died. His remains lay in state for twenty-four hours on top of a mammoth urn which filled the Arc de Triomphe and was guarded in half-hour shifts by young girls and boys in ancient classical Greek garb. The 'endless' processions across Paris the next morning comprised several brass bands and every political and literary figure of the day and resulted in several deaths in the press of the multitude, before Hugo's final entombment in the Panthéon. 'By this orgiastic ceremony', says Roger Shattuck, 'France unburdened itself of a man, a literary movement, and a century.'[1]

Paris at the time, he adds, was like no other place in the world and 'even in retrospect her physical presence demands the feminine gender'. Baron Haussmann's plans for opening up the almost mediaeval city had been virtually completed and the capital, Shattuck concluded, had become a stage, 'a vast theatre for herself and all the world'. It was this theatrical aspect, this 'light-opera atmosphere', which gave what would be called the Belle Époque its defining flavour.[2] 'Street cleaners in blue denim, gendarmes in trim capes, butchers in leather aprons, coachmen in black cutaways, the army's crack chasseurs in plumes, gold-braided and polished boots – everyone wore a costume and displayed himself to best advantage.' It was the era of gaslights and horse-drawn omnibuses, of *cordon bleu* cooking and campaigning feminists. The waiters in Paris cafés 'downed spoons' and went on strike for the right to wear beards. 'You were not a man or a republican without one.'[3]

The Belle Époque 'lay across 1900 like a blast of night colour'.[4] Paris was again setting the fashions in dress, the arts and, as we have come to expect, the pleasures of life. Upper-class leisure, not burdened by the exigencies of work, produced a way of life reminiscent of the eighteenth century: pompous display, frivolity, hypocrisy, cultivated taste, 'relaxed' morals. 'The only barrier to rampant adultery was the whalebone corset; an errant wife, when she returned to her coachman, had to hide under her coat the bundle of undergarments her lover had been unable to replace.' And the 'king of couturiers', Paul Poiret, with Coco Chanel's help, would soon put an end to the corset as well. 'Meals had acquired such epic proportions that an intermission had been introduced by way of a sherbet course between two fowl dishes.'[5]

Artists sensed their moment. It was a time when there had never been so many 'isms'.[6] The café was at its height, partly at the expense of the salon, says Shattuck, though – as we shall see – yet another forecast of its disappearance was premature.

ERASING THE EXPERIENCE OF DEFEAT

What is extraordinary about this colourful picture is the date: 1885. The French Revolution – probably correctly – is usually highlighted as the most important period of modern French history. But the half-century 1870–1919 – from the Franco-Prussian War to the end of the First World War, and even beyond – runs it close. France's defeat at the Battle of Sedan in 1870, when Napoleon III was captured, to be followed by the Siege of Paris and the Commune, ranks as one of the country's most humiliating capitulations, easily on a par with its defeats in the Seven Years War and at Waterloo, and the Vichy collapse of 1940. But, by Hugo's death, merely half a generation after the siege and the Commune, Paris had recovered sufficiently to be once again regarded as the centre of civilisation, rather than Berlin, say, or Vienna, or London. It was, arguably, the greatest – and swiftest – turnaround in history, the greatest of France's recoveries.

What is also interesting about this picture is that while none of the above is, strictly speaking, inaccurate, it is as ever wise not to overstate the picture or ignore other incompatible developments. And there was no shortage of such incompatible evidence. This was a time in France when a great many more serious souls worried that society – French people – far from leading the way, were showing signs of degeneration, decadence, corruption. There was no short-age of people who took the view that the catastrophe at Sedan, the surrender of the emperor and the humiliating bloody horrors of the Commune flagged up the possibility – even the probability – that France was becoming a nation of inferior individuals, suffering a debilitating plague of suicide, mental instability, venereal disease and a falling birth rate. From the vantage point of the twenty-first century, we can laugh off the incommensurability of this juxtaposition, but it was real enough at the time.

And it is not hard to see why. As early as 1868, Lucien-Anatole Prévost-Paradol, the French ambassador in Washington, had raised the alert about what he saw as the changing nature of his coun-trymen, when he published a book, *La France nouvelle*, in which he depicted France and Prussian Germany as two trains speeding towards an inevitable head-on collision.[7] The most worrying element, he said, was Germany's nascent nationalism. This was all-important, Prévost-Paradol said, because should France come out on top in the collision, that would only make Germany even more nationalistic. If Germany were to win, however, defeat would confirm the end of France as a world power. The only way to get around the predica-ment of impending obscurity, he argued, was to aggrandise France through imperial expansion into Africa, with Algeria as the base from which to launch this new theatre of operations.

Despite being decades in the past, Wolfgang Schivelbusch argues that Prévost-Paradol's pessimism was but one example of a delayed reaction to the earlier parallel French collapse of 1814–15. He bases this view on the fact that, far from being acknowledged as a national trauma, the Waterloo defeat had been dismissed as the personal failing of Napoleon. At the time, many people had been worried that Napoleon's fall marked the beginning of France's slump into second-rate power status, dropping behind, in particular, Britain,

America, Russia and Germany. Because Napoleon had been sacrificed – to France's great relief – the nation felt that it was untainted by defeat, despite the awkward fact that it had been occupied by an enemy 'for the first time in 400 years'. Also relevant was the fact that the nation had been beaten by a coalition. France could still feel itself superior to smaller fry.[8]

The Franco-Prussian War of 1870–1, despite its brevity, was divided cleanly into three distinct phases. The first lasted from the Second Empire's declaration of war on Prussia on 19 July 1870 until Napoleon III's surrender and capture at Sedan seven weeks later, on 2 September. This brought about the fall of the Second Empire and the hurried declaration of the Third Republic only two days later. A month or so on, the second phase began when the provisional government failed in its effort to negotiate an emollient peace settlement, originally envisaged as similar to that of 1814, a miscalculation that resulted in the Prussian siege of Paris. Surrounded by Prussian forces, the republic did its best to resist via a *levée en masse* that endured until 28 January 1871, when the provisional government finally had no option but to surrender. Just over a month later, in March, following the acceptance of German terms, which included the amputation of Alsace-Lorraine, native inhabitants of the French capital took up arms in what Karl Marx termed 'the French Civil War' and is more generally known as the Paris Commune uprising. This lasted until May and was hardly less murderous than the Prussian war itself. While 80,000 French were slaughtered in the Prussian war, 30,000 died in the Commune.[9] No wonder this was described as the *année terrible*.

Victor Hugo was just one who saw the German invasion of the late summer and autumn of 1870 as a repeat of 1792, when the Austro-Prussian invasion was halted at Valmy. But of course this carried the implication that France would ultimately triumph. This had in fact been expected on 1 September 1870, just a day before Sedan, when the German advance on Paris was reported in the *Revue des deux mondes* not as an emergency but as 'a welcome wake-up call for a nation spoiled by too many quick and easy victories'. A similar denial of reality was reflected by Paul Leroy-Beaulieu, a professor of finance. 'After we have repelled the enemy and dictated a glorious peace on our own terms, the patriotic work will begin in earnest.'[10]

The abrupt rupture of Sedan put paid to these expectations. Yet as Schivelbusch terms it, the news of France's crushing defeat 'produced an astonishing capacity among the citizenry to invent an alternate, more comforting reality'. Within hours, he says, before national malaise could set in, the revolutionary past was being replayed. 'A Parisian mob disrupted the meeting of the *corps législatif* on the afternoon of September 4 and joined republican delegates under the leadership of Leon Gambetta in marching on the Hotel de Ville. There Gambetta assumed the role of Danton by proclaiming the republic.' And, he adds: 'The crowds were not just following the models of 1789, 1792, 1830 and 1848; they had become the very reincarnation of those earlier events.' His point is that the re-enactment of revolution was a 'triumph that erased the experience of defeat'. Once again, as in 1815, only a Napoleon had been defeated, not the nation, 'and the shame of Sedan disappeared with him into a German prison'. The establishment of a republic guaranteed ultimate victory.[11] France even put forward a peace involving a return to the *status quo ante* and was astonished when the German response was – to put it mildly – lukewarm.

Gambetta was traditionally French. He warned on the evening of 3 September that 'in no case should the republic be held responsible' for the French defeat at Sedan. But his decision to declare a republic so soon after defeat was an effort to adjust to popular pressure. The defeat was clear enough but, says Schivelbusch, the war was too 'young' in the public mind to be fully absorbed. Sedan had undermined French complacency, but it had not yet destroyed their appetite for a fight.

This continuation of revolutionary rituals which had followed the triumphal proceedings of the First Republic in 1792 were no more than 'ghosts', says Schivelbusch. France had suffered yet another defeat and one which this time could not be laid at the door of 'a deposed tyrant', who could not answer back. The burden was too much and this, he says, is why the nation split into two – Paris and the provinces.

DROWNING IN BLOOD

After the Sedan defeat, the capital declared itself ready to carry on the fight, showing that the battles of 1848 were still remembered, and that these memories still had force. And so the Paris Commune became 'the first great modern battle between the classes'.

The division was heightened by the 'decapitulation' of the capital by Adolphe Thiers, despite the key roles he had played in the revolutions of 1830 and 1848, and the fact that he was elected as president of the Third Republic. It was he who orchestrated the moving of the National Assembly to Versailles and it was this strategy that heightened the division within the nation and made subsequent events even worse.[12]

Nor was it helped by the plight of the army. This was one institution above all others whose self-confidence had been dramatically shaken by Sedan, and it could not erase the shameful fact that it had failed to win a single battle, that its only actions had been retreats and that it had surrendered not once but twice. It had failed to prevent the siege of Paris or to break through the German lines around the city. This was hardly a distinguished achievement, but worse was to come. The army could only stand and watch as a heroic resistance was sustained by civilians led by Gambetta and the 'soon-to-be legendary' fighters of the *francs-tireurs* (irregular forces, organised outside the regular army). To quote Schivelbusch again: 'It would be difficult to imagine a more thoroughly defeated, demoralised and generally despised force than the French army after its final capitulation in January 1871.'[13]

The officer corps were demoralised most. This helps account for the fury they showed in overcoming the Commune. In contrast to the lower ranks – who transacted their business with mechanical efficiency – the officers threw military ethics to the wind and 'did everything to ratchet up the level of violence'. Their motivation, clearly enough, was to wipe out their own shame.[14]

Here are the remarks about these events by Louise Colet, Flaubert's lover, soaked in sarcasm: 'Decked out from head to toe in medals, the officers celebrate themselves. Ovations, embraces, laurels. As though they had conquered Berlin.' She was not alone in thinking that the Commune was a laughing stock and a target for derision 'for the entire world'. Others saw the Commune as a heroic and radical deed. This too divided the nation and kept the wound fresh. The trauma would continue to divide the people for years, and played a major role in the Dreyfus affair (chapter 37).[15]

An Oratorio of Martyrdom

Another complicating element in all this is the fact that hostilities had begun against Prussia but the defeat was inflicted by Germany. France had always rather high-handedly regarded Prussia as less a state than, as Schivelbusch puts it, 'a gigantic factory whose capacity for producing *hommes machines* may have been impressive but whose utter lack of soul and inability to bring forth *hommes libres* was thoroughly alienating'. Moreover, Prussia's collapse in the face of Napoleon I back in 1806 had confirmed how inferior it was to the 'superior vitality' of France.[16]

After Sedan, that comforting fiction went out of the window. French barbs, by tradition aimed at Britain, were now redirected at Prussia. Indeed, in what one might call an embarrassment of riches, English mercantilism and Prussian militarism became parallel scourges, both dismissed for their 'calculating coldness, heartlessness, methodicalness, lack of grace, fighting spirit and heroism'.[17]

At this crucial point, Victor Hugo had, he said, three fundamental convictions. First, that humanity had found its 'ultimate expression' in republican France. Second, that French republicanism was without doubt 'the highest cause of humanity'. And third and most striking, that the unification of Europe could only be conceived as 'an extension of the French republic'. 'He became the choirmaster of France's oratorio of martyrdom', as Schivelbusch grandiosely puts it. 'Like ancient Greece and Rome,' Hugo wrote, 'France today is civilisation and a threat to France is a threat to all ... Should the *unthinkable* transpire, and France be defeated, it would be a sign of how far humanity has sunk ... Saving Paris means more than saving France: it means saving the world. For Paris is the heart of humanity, its holy city, the capital of civilisation.' And finally: 'France is not just France but the world, and all progress depends on France remaining intact.'[18]

As Schivelbusch, again, phrases it, Hugo was saying: 'Victor beware ... Nations tend to slip on the blood they have shed.' In saying this, he became the vehicle through which the new nationalists spoke.[19]

THE COLLECTIVE UNCONSCIOUS OF REVENGE

Looking backwards, Schivelbusch has seen – and made much of – the parallels between 1870–1, 1814–15 and 1763, the defeats of France at Waterloo and in the Seven Years War, and he is not alone. Both Karine Varley and Robert Gildea have argued that 'because of its history of humiliation on the battlefield, France has developed a political culture centred on concepts of greatness and honour'.[20]

Varley draws attention in particular to the village of Bazeilles, tenaciously defended by marines 'to the last cartouche', in the face of overwhelming Bavarian force, in which 400 houses were burned down and civilians massacred. Within a few years of the war ending, however, national perceptions of Bazeilles shifted from images of martyrdom towards notions of resistance. The 'endless' depictions of the war, Varley says, sought to perpetuate memories of the defeat as a spur to action.[21] *Les Dernières Cartouches* ('The Last Cartridges'), a painting by Alphonse de Neuville set in Bazeilles, won instant acclaim in the Salon of 1873. The forty-two soldiers buried at Héricourt had on their memorial the inscription 'THEIR DEFEAT IS A VICTORY'.[22]

In other contemporary works, Varley points out that Germans were portrayed as barbarians and the French as 'enlightened, civilised, audacious and physically diminutive'. The anthropologist Jean-Louis Armand de Quatrefages singled out the Prussian 'race' as primitive and savage, while claiming that the French, British and (other) German peoples were endowed with a superior intelligence. Zola, on the other hand, had no doubt that the French defeat was due to its decadence and the weaknesses of the Latin race.[23]

In much the same vein, Bertrand Taithe observed that, in France, the defeat in the Franco-Prussian War 'reached deeper meaning than any before 1870' and that over 7,000 books were published on the subject before 1900.[24] While the Germans celebrated Sedan Day, the French marines (still) have Bazeilles Day celebrations. Taithe adds the view that the 'orgy' of violence in the bloody week 'illustrated the cultivation of hatred against one's own shortcomings in the previous collective humiliation'. But economic and *Annalist* historians came to the view that the war had relatively little impact on the structures and vitality of French society. At the same time, the search for an elusive scapegoat invariably settled on the Jews and was part of the 'deep background' to the Dreyfus affair some decades later.[25]

These were not just defeats but humiliations which settled into *revanche*, a specifically French form of revenge which, Schivelbusch maintains, conformed to a 'political religion'. What he means by this is that, rather than being a 'hot feeling', *revanche* is an agreement among the political classes – but the public too – in which revenge becomes a sometimes unspoken but ever-present cohesive factor, in effect a collective unconscious, uniting the nation. After the Seven Years War, for example, as we have seen, the American War of Independence was valued as an indirect way of righting the wrongs of 1763. In the wake of 1870–1, the next stage of the process was the re-establishment of an equilibrium.[26] *Revanche*, in French, Schivelbusch maintains, carries a 'double sense of revenge and peaceful re-establishment of an equilibrium'. It even echoes the Fronde, when personal honour was the only thing left to the aristocracy. Following Sedan and the Commune, the feelings of *revanche* were a way of maintaining equilibrium and honour. The enthusiasm for Joan of Arc, which now blossomed, and the *Song of Roland* – heroising defeat – both served a similar cohesive purpose.

The underlying belief in all this was that defeat 'was an accident that would soon be corrected'. And, as the next chapters will show, it was. The various phases of *revanche*, identified through the successive leaderships of Paul Déroulède, Georges Boulanger and Maurice Barrès, and the intuitive philosophy of Henri Bergson, whose *élan vital* emphasised contingency and creativity, in the event carried the day, not least with Charles de Gaulle, as we shall see.

As the nineteenth century came to a close, and with its (relatively modest) adventures in imperialism, France had turned the corner and was making advances. Showing what de Gaulle would call its genius for renewal, France was again at the forefront of nations – in physics, medicine, psychology, technology, industry, art and literature, in automobile and aircraft competitions, and in film. Not least, it was fixated, as it had always been, on quality not quantity. In the wake of military humiliation, the yearning for grandeur had brought about a convincing – and really quite rapid – turnaround in France's fortunes.

'Vegetations of the Sick Mind'

The conviction that mankind was afflicted by degeneration – one of the conditions that gave rise to spleen – was in fact spread right across Europe at the time, though several of the leading advocates of this view were French. For some, the process had begun with the Revolution, which had 'bequeathed' a pathology on the nation. Hippolyte Taine, in his history of the Revolution, especially his volume on the Jacobin conquest, claimed to identify 'the morbid germ which entered the blood of a diseased society [and] caused fever, delirium and revolutionary convulsions'.[1]

Medico-psychiatric terminology came into use – again not surprising as France was among the leading nations in this discipline. Attention focused on the prevalence of certain groups (cretins, criminals and the insane) who – it was worried – were becoming more common. The *demi-monde*, though colourful when looked at from one point of view, could also be seen as threatening from another standpoint. The wide reach of prostitution (a byproduct of poverty) and the associated spread of venereal disease – also common among the *demi-monde* – was yet another cause for alarm. Several prominent writers succumbed to venereal disease – Baudelaire, Maupassant, Daudet, Jules de Goncourt. This was overlaid with racial feeling, that the peoples of eastern and southern Europe were especially susceptible to the vices of degeneration, and there were growing calls for these pathological entities to be removed from social circulation.

France in the late nineteenth century was notable for having a number of prominent racial theorists. Modern 'scientific' racism stems from three factors. One, the Enlightenment view that the human condition was essentially a biological state (as opposed to a theological state); two, the wider contact between different races brought about by imperial conquest; and three, the application and misapplication of Darwinian thinking to the various cultures around the world.

One of the early propagators of biological racism was Julien-Joseph Virey, a French doctor from Langres (Diderot's hometown), who addressed the Parisian Académie de médecine in 1841 on 'the biological causes of civilisation'. Virey divided the world's peoples into two. There were the whites, 'who had achieved a more-or-less-perfect stage of civilisation', and the blacks (the Africans, Asians and American Indians) who were condemned to a 'constantly imperfect civilisation'. Virey was deeply pessimistic that the 'blacks' would ever achieve 'full civilisation', pointing out that, like white people, domesticated animals, such as cows, have white flesh, whereas wild animals – deer, say – have dark flesh. This didn't square with science even then (it had been known since the sixteenth century that, under the skin, all human flesh is the same colour) but for Virey this basic difference accounted for all sorts of consequences. For example, he said that 'just as the wild animal was prey to the human, so the black human was the natural prey of the white human'. In other words, slavery – far from being cruel – was consistent with nature.[2]

One new element in the equation was the development in the nineteenth century of racist thinking *within* Europe. A key name here is Arthur de Gobineau, born in Haiti and someone who always feared he might have black blood. In *On the Inequality of the Human Races* (1853–5, i.e. before Darwin and natural selection), he claimed that the German and French aristocracy (and note that he was a *self-appointed* aristocrat) 'retained the original characteristics of the Aryans', the original race of mankind. Everyone else, in contrast, was some sort of mongrel. This idea never really caught on, but more successful was the alleged difference he claimed to find between the hard-working, pious – even joyless – northern Protestants, and 'the languid, potentially passive and potentially despotic Latins' of the Catholic south. Not surprisingly perhaps, many northerners could be found who became convinced that the northern 'races' – the Anglo-Saxons, Russians and Chinese – would lead the way in the future. The rest – including France – would form the 'dying nations' of the world.[3]

This reasoning was taken to its limits by a third Frenchman, Georges Vacher de Lapouge (1854–1936). Lapouge, who had been a student at Poitiers, where he investigated ancient skulls, believed that races were species in the process of formation, that racial differences were 'innate and ineradicable' and that any idea that two sets of people could integrate was contrary to the laws of biology. For Lapouge, Europe was populated by three racial groups, *Homo europaeus* – tall, pale-skinned and long-skulled (dolichocephalous), *Homo alpinus* – smaller and darker with brachycephalous (short) heads, and *Homo mediterraneus* – long-headed again but darker and shorter even than *H. alpinus*. Lapouge regarded democracy as a disaster and believed that the brachycephalous types were taking over the world. He thought the proportion of dolichocephalous individuals was declining in Europe, due to emigration to the United States.[4]

Max Nordau (1849–1923), like the sociologist Émile Durkheim, was the son of a rabbi. Born in Budapest, he spent most of his life in Paris, partly working as a foreign correspondent for Hungarian and German newspapers. His best-known book was the two-volume *Entartung* ('Degeneration'), which, despite being 600 pages long, became an international bestseller. Nordau was convinced there was 'a severe mental epidemic; a sort of black death of degeneracy and hysteria', which was affecting Europe, sapping its vitality, and was manifest in a whole range of symptoms: 'squint eyes, imperfect ears, stunted growth ... pessimism, apathy, impulsiveness, emotionalism, mysticism, and a complete absence of any sense of right and wrong'. Everywhere he looked there was decline. The impressionist painters were the result, he said, of a degenerate physiology, nystagmus, a trembling of the eyeball, causing them to paint in the fuzzy, indistinct way that they did. In the writings of Baudelaire, Wilde and Nietzsche, Nordau claimed to find 'overweening egomania', while Zola had 'an obsession with filth'. Nordau believed that degeneracy was caused by industrialised society – literally the wear and tear exerted on leaders by railways, steamships, telephones and factories. When Freud visited

Nordau he found him 'unbearably vain' with a complete lack of a sense of humour.[5]

Darwinism was relatively slow to catch on in France, where Émile Blanchard managed to block the great man's election as a corresponding member of the French Academy of Scientists on the grounds that his studies were unscientific and that in any case his idea of evolution was hardly original. But once France did generate Darwinist scientists, it soon had its own passionate social Darwinist. In her *Origine de l'homme et des sociétés*, Clémence Royer took a strong social Darwinist line, regarding 'Aryans' as superior to other races and considering even that warfare between them was inevitable 'in the interests of progress'.[6]

THE THREAT OF MODERNITY

But it wasn't only racism that was felt to be a cause of degeneration. At the same time, and more broadly, there were worries that modernity itself – the very existence of great urban entities with masses of people living cheek by jowl, the speed of modern life, railways, motor cars and, eventually, aircraft – was in some senses unhealthy. As Daniel Pick put it in his book on degeneration: 'The modern world, as seen through the eyes of a Taine, a Zola or a Gustave Le Bon, was bound up in an ambiguous biological and cultural regression, involving, among other things, the threat of mass politics, anarchism, the vexed question of the enfranchisement of women, and of the crowd's potential eruption, and regression at the behest of morbid, excitable leaders.'[7]

One particularly excitable idea bound up in this miasma was the extent to which the predicament could be understood as science or in more humanistic ways. It was felt that the critical and dystopian novels of Émile Zola, whose massive twenty-volume Rougon-Macquart series of titles sought to chronicle the degeneration of one sprawling family over decades, were unhelpful, pretending to a science that had not yet found its feet.

Zola himself also divided the doctors on the reality and nature of degeneration. In the Rougon-Macquart series, he thought that he was doing more than write a fictional chronicle; he believed his observations had the status of science, but Dr Henri Martineau, in his book *The Scientific Novels of Émile Zola*, was highly critical of Zola's 'pretensions', condemning his 'incredible fatuity'.

THE POST-HAUSSMANN CROWD CIVILISATION

Zola, then, was widely accused of 'dabbling' in medical science and so was Gustave Le Bon. True, he was trained as a medical doctor and had a close interest in anthropology, another field where France led the way in the nineteenth century. But Le Bon was also a noted misogynist and attached unreasonable importance to the new science of craniometry, where his results conveniently found that men's brains were bigger than women's and 'civilised' brains larger than those of 'savages'.[8]

Le Bon attended lectures by the neurologist Jean-Martin Charcot and considered that his studies of hysterics confirmed a process of decline in the French race. Gustave's particular interest was the crowd, in his view a new phenomenon in the vast urban spaces created by Haussmann, and he held that it amounted to a 'psychopathology of history', the crowd an inevitable aspect of regression. Le Bon thought that mere denunciations of modernity were futile, that France had entered the era of 'crowd civilisation' and that 'the very act of gathering in a group' amounted to nothing less than a moral ('evolutionary') decline. Like Taine before him, he thought that revolutionary violence in general, and the French Revolution in particular, epitomised that decline and he warned against a 'repetition compulsion' of one revolution after another, as had been happening above all in his own country in 1830 and 1848.

The early 1870s – the immediate wake of war and the Commune – brought a veritable avalanche of titles revealing this mood: *La Fin du monde latin!*; *Les Premières Phases d'un décadence*; *Des causes de la décadence française*; *La Chute de la France: République ou décadence?*; *La France dégénérée*. At that stage, what particularly exercised some French, as mentioned above, was the fact that the defeat in the Franco-Prussian War had involved defeat to a single opponent, not a coalition, as at Waterloo. This was *the* crucial indicator of decline.[9]

Émile Durkheim found a different metaphor to explain what was happening, though his verdict was much the same. He thought that societies embodied 'collective forces' or 'social currents', much in the manner of electricity or thermodynamics, itself a new science, dating from the 1850s, and his main concern was whether 'hereditary pathology' was itself just such a social current which could explain what was happening. In this changing world, different aspects of society were brought together to predict disaster. For example, the growth of venereal disease and prostitution was seen against the declining birth rate as a 'degeneration' of motherhood, to be put alongside hereditary pathology, doubling up the dire consequences.

At the political level there was the same troublesome idea – national defeat in battle was underscored, and perhaps overlapped with, alcoholism, crime and other forms of depravity, which might – would – interfere with recovery. The relatively new science of statistics was used both to flag up the problem and, in offering what was in fact a spurious specificity, to suggest that a lid could be kept on the problems. For example, it was 'discovered' that out of every 100 male participants in the March 1871 insurrection, during the Commune, twenty-five were recidivist criminals. Likewise, it was held that twenty-five out of every 100 women were prostitutes, both conveniently neat, round numbers.[10]

Politicians from Charles Maurras and Maurice Barrès to Georges Sorel were convinced that France was suffering decadence, and this was due, somehow, to 'racial debasement'. Barrès was the bleakest, arguing that France should acknowledge what he termed 'the law of eternal decomposition'.

THE RISE OF PSYCHIATRY

One effect of this cultural context was the rise of psychiatry, which became almost a chic activity, as it would be much later in mid-twentieth-century Manhattan. This too was reflected in the work of Zola where, in his novel *L'Assommoir*, Valentin Magnan, the psychiatrist, becomes a very fashionable doctor, specialising in the various aspects of hysteria, depression and the other illnesses of the day. Zola gives Magna his own theory of *dégénérance*.

This was reflected in the real world in a celebrated series of Tuesday lectures given by Jean-Martin Charcot at the Salpêtrière hospital, attended by many of the fashionable Proust prototypes that are the subject of chapter 39, and at his salon and the great dinners he gave for a wide array of politicians, scientists and artists, including Freud. (In his lectures, Charcot argued that hysteria was more common among women and Jews.) Furthermore, as Daniel Pick again points out, France had a special understanding of evolution, never having totally conceded the Lamarckian view 'which assumed the reproduction of acquired characteristics'.[11] This reinforced the idea that environment was the key element in degeneration.

On the other hand, Abbé Ernest Dimnet, a philosophically minded priest, author of the popular *Art of Thinking*, put the blame for degeneracy squarely on the anti-clerical mood of France in the last half of the century and in particular the works of such writers as Zola and Mallarmé. The positivist views of Saint-Simon and Comte were also under attack, Henri Bergson arguing that 'scientism' was unable to help people reach their 'inner selves' or capture the mystery of life forces, which prevented alienation.

THE 'DECADENTS'

One group of individuals – not doctors, sociologists or anthropologists – who had no doubt about decadence and degeneration was a set of writers born around 1860 who shared a similar vision of existence and art, who contributed to a small number of periodicals and who embraced with enthusiasm a number of older writers who they knew, imitated, and sometimes collaborated with. They were known as the 'decadents'.

The term 'decadence', says the biographer of Rachilde – one of the leaders of this group – signifies, on the one hand, a 'distillation of a broad generational mood', a sense of decay, decline or world-weariness that is found originally in the work of Baudelaire and Flaubert. A later generation took in Barbey d'Aurevilly (1808–89), who helped to elaborate the themes and aesthetics of decadence with (among other texts) *Les Diaboliques* (1874), and Auguste de Villiers de L'Isle-Adam (1838–89), who published the 'decadent' *L'Ève future* in 1886, while Catulle Mendès produced *La Première Maîtresse* in 1887. The poet Paul Verlaine (1844–96) wrote verse 'some of which reads like a decadent manifesto'.[12]

But the two decadent writers we shall make most space for are Joris-Karl Huysmans and Marguerite Eymery, better known as Rachilde. Huysmans's *À rebours* has been described as 'nothing less than a love affair with degeneration', making it perhaps the quintessential decadent novel. The central character, Des Esseintes, is born into an aristocratic family of some standing, but he is presented as the last 'survivor' of a line that has been steadily degenerating for at least 200 years, 'dissipating its strength, impoverishing its stock'.[13] By the time of the novel's action, in the late nineteenth century, the end of the 'ancient house' is near. Des Esseintes, whose childhood was blighted by ill-health, is, in his young adulthood, highly strung, showing the nervousness so characteristic of the time. Not only is he anaemic, he suffers from chlorosis (also iron deficiency, then believed to have a neurotic origin), is 'depraved and effete' in his tastes in equal measure, enjoys a life of dissipation, and is 'obsessed by a desire to preside over a supremely refined debauch'.

He goes so far as to seek medical assistance about what he perceives to be a growing fatigue and lethargy. The medico-psychiatric advice he receives is to lead a quiet life but in the Paris of the Belle Époque that could never last and before long he has drifted back to his old ways, wallowing in 'unnatural love affairs and perverse pleasures'. Among the more outré episodes of the book is a funeral banquet which Des Esseintes gives 'in honour of his lost virility' and where everything in the banquet and its surroundings is – suitably enough – black: Russian rye bread, caviar, Turkish olives, 'sauces the colour of liquorice and boot polish'. black pudding from Frankfurt; the room and garden are lined with black. Zola was put out. Huysmans had once been part of his Medan group (Zola's house about 25 miles from Paris, where he frequently hosted Cézanne, Manet, Maupassant, Daudet and others), and the great novelist thought Huysmans was betraying the spirit of naturalism. He concluded: '[With Baudelaire] he has finally reached those districts of the soul where the monstrous vegetations of the sick mind flourish.'[14]

Meanwhile, a transformation had occurred. Initially, decadence had been a term of abuse, coined by Paul Bourget (1852–1935), novelist and critic (nominated five times for the Nobel Prize), in his *Essays in Contemporary Psychology* (1883), a study of other writers, where he deplored his contemporaries' 'decadence' or 'mortal weariness with life, and bleak perception of the vanity of all effort'. But, to the decadents, this very idea was the ideal. The group comprised also Alfred Vallette (a future editor of the *Mercure de France*, a symbolist review), Jean Moréas, pen name of Yannis Papadiamantópoulos, a Greek poet, Paul Verlaine and Rachilde. All wrote for Anatole Baju's combative *Le Décadent*, founded in 1886.[15]

The decadent worldview was uncompromising: the heroes of its works consider both science and the naturalistic world of Zola, and that of *le monde*, to be tedious and contemptible, and their response is to 'retreat into art', into self-enclosed artificial surroundings marked by 'works of art, hothouse plants, synthetic perfumes and memories'. 'Artifice', says Diana Holmes, 'seems to Des Esseintes the distinctive work of human genius.'

Underpinning this, the decadents have no appetite to change the imperfect world we see about us. 'Where the republicans understood civilisation as striding forward toward increased prosperity, knowledge and happiness, the decadents saw only a civilisation in decline. They themselves were outsider heroes, representing the last gasp of a brilliant creativity that preceded the total victory of the barbarian hordes.'[16]

After Huysmans, the most interesting figure was Rachilde, not least, says her biographer, because of her capacity for self-dramatisation, which helped generate more than one myth about her. Marguerite Eymery was born on 12 February 1860 in her family home of Le Cros, near Périgueux in south-west France, and she would live to be ninety-three, spending her life at first under the Second Empire and then most of it under the Third Republic.

Like Germaine de Staël, she idolised her father, a soldier, one of whose abilities, she always said, was that like an eagle 'he could look straight into the sun'. He was a skilled horseman who taught his daughter the same ability, something which proved a great help later on when, as a journalist, she was able to keep up with the cavalry, unlike her colleagues, so giving her an advantage in her written accounts of military manoeuvres. At school she was a 'tomboy', liked wearing trousers and fought with the boys.

When she was fifteen, she became engaged – much against her will – to one of her father's fellow officers. As part of the preparations for the engagement dinner, her parents – without telling her – drowned all her pets in a large pond by the house. Marguerite took this hard, tried to stop it and, in doing so, she herself nearly drowned, an episode that might have been a suicide attempt.[17] The engagement was called off.

Marguerite began writing as a journalist and early on formed the ambition to be self-sustaining from her pen. She acquired the name 'Rachilde', according to her own later account, because her parents and grandparents had become believers in the fashionable pastime of spiritism and would hold 'interminable' séances.[18] Dismissive of these activities, Marguerite – then aged sixteen – planned a hoax in which a spirit manifested itself by knocking on the table and revealing that he was Rachilde, a sixteenth-century Swedish aristocrat, who told them that they had all lived earlier lives, including Marguerite, who had in fact lived as Rachilde himself.

Though she was still living at home, her confidence as a journalist was growing, her works being accepted in an ever-wider array of periodicals, and it was boosted further when, in 1875, she sent Victor Hugo one of her stories, 'Le Premier Amour', and he actually replied.[19] She then found employment in Paris with her cousin, who worked on a conventional (rather than feminist) magazine, *L'École des femmes*, writing a range of pieces, not excluding fashion (for example, a recipe for dyeing lace).

The literary lions of the time included Hugo, her early hero, Zola, to whom she was introduced by Catulle Mendès, and Villiers de L'Isle-Adam. For a time she was young and unknown in Paris, but she did benefit from the fact that her family were reasonably well off and well connected in the literary and publishing world. Writing for *L'École des femmes* gave her more introductions, and the salon which her mother had taken to holding every week in her new apartment on the elegant quai de Bourbon also helped Marguerite into society. It was here, she tells us in a memoir, that she first met Maurice Barrès.

Barrès was a novelist and journalist who became a politician, and whose ideas went through various changes. He was educated at the lycée in Nancy, in the east of France, and this conditioned his later outlook on politics and revanchism, and though he became a fervent nationalist, his psychology was complex and not entirely stable.

At the time Rachilde met him he was best known as the author of a three-volume tract, entitled *The Cult of the Self*, advocating that the way to psychological freedom was via the senses. He would go on to compose another three-volume work, *The Uprooted*, which explored the sources of national energy, the cult of the earth and the dead.

Barrès was not the only famous personage Rachilde met just then. Catulle Mendès was a celebrated novelist and well known as a womaniser, for spending a month in jail for one of his works and for his libretto for Emmanuel Chabrier's opera *Gwendoline*. Rachilde decided against becoming his mistress (she said she didn't want to be one of his 'crumpled flowers') but, says her biographer, the 'conflict between attraction and strategic self-defence affected her deeply'. Her legs were paralysed for two months.

It was in recovering from this ailment that she discovered a group of kindred spirits, when she paid a visit to a famous Parisian café, the café de l'Avenir, where 'she heard a group of neurotics talking like herself, but *more level-headed than she was*'. This group – where she was gradually accepted – comprised Albert Samain, Paul Adam, Jean Moréas, Felix Fénéon, Jean Lorrain, Laurent Tailhade and several others who met in the Latin Quarter, as often as not at the Cabaret de la Mère Clarisse.[20] These were the decadents.

MADEMOISELLE BAUDELAIRE

Out of this milieu, in 1884 Rachilde suddenly achieved notoriety. The immediate spur was the usual one, a mix of the desire for fame and an equally pressing desire to escape poverty (since she had made herself independent of her family). She said later that she decided she had two choices: 'to throw herself into the gutter or ... to write within a fortnight a truly shocking work'.[21] The result was *Monsieur Vénus*, a story about a cross-dressing female aristocrat, Raoule de Vénérande, who, in order to escape the *ennui* of her tradition-bound existence, takes as her 'mistress' a beautiful working-class boy, and makes of him a malleable, feminised object of pleasure. The book was helped by being published with a preface by Barrès, which was entitled 'Mademoiselle Baudelaire' and alluded to the paradox that lay between Rachilde's youth and innocence and her 'scabrous imagination'.

The book, a huge *succès de scandale*, was published first in Brussels, the traditional route for outré books, so that the author could be prosecuted – and convicted and sentenced – in her absence and safety, which offered unrivalled publicity. On cue the Paris courts ordered that all copies be sequestered and Rachilde only managed to hang on to her own by hiding them.[22] The whole business earned her both the notoriety she felt was necessary to push through the decadent message, and enough funds to escape immediate poverty.

Rachilde now became a well-known fixture in the haunts of bohemian Paris. She capitalised on this by starting to dress as a man. This was not as easy then as it is now. In fact, she was required to apply to the prefect of Paris for his official permission, since the practice was seen as threatening to public order. She also cut her hair short.

She was moving closer to the heart of the decadents. Paul Verlaine, afflicted by his addiction to alcohol and in declining health, stayed for a time in her apartment, with Rachilde moving out of her bedroom and lodging with her mother nearby, while looking after the poet during the day. This is also when she met Alfred Vallette, a more down-to-earth character than some of the other decadents, who was remarkable in his day for treating women as complete equals, and who developed a genuine affection for Rachilde, to the extent that, despite part of her preferring to live alone as a man, they were married in 1889. The marriage endured, right up until Vallette's death in 1935. Six months after the wedding, a daughter – Gabrielle – was born, their only child.

The other fruit of the union was a journal, the *Mercure de France*, which lasted until 1965, and was edited for many years by Vallette and Rachilde. The first number was dated 1 January 1890, just as Paris prepared to celebrate the centenary of the Revolution, and advertised France's restored self-confidence with the building of the Eiffel Tower and the first *exposition universelle*. In some ways, the *Mercure* was a family business – Vallette dealing with the editing and production, while Rachilde's role was reviewer and star author, but also hostess, for she now held a salon above the premises. Her salon had in fact begun earlier, in the days of poverty and scandal in the rue des Écoles. Her weekly gatherings, moving with her to the *Mercure* premises, would continue until 1930, with a break during the years of the First World War. The Tuesday salons were not just for conversation but also offered the opportunity to attract and evaluate new contributors to the journal.

She always claimed later that she was little more than 'a tea-pourer' at these gatherings, 'saying little and listening a lot'. Oscar Wilde was apparently taken aback to find that the author of *Monsieur Vénus* was 'an enigmatic creature in a black woollen dress ... inexplicably bourgeois'. Jules Renard told a different story, describing her as receiving guests in 'a fiery red blouse ... her hair cut like a boy's and her eyelashes like long pen-strokes in black ink'.[23]

Her most famous protégé, who attended her salon regularly, was Alfred Jarry. Small and hirsute, when he met Rachilde he had already – a bit like Baudelaire – worked his way through his inheritance, spending it on alcohol. Though invariably poorly dressed, he had a 'magnificent eloquence' that mingled 'great erudition with wildest flights of fantasy'. Rachilde found his drinking hard to take but she had no doubt about his wild flights of imagination.[24]

Jarry's most famous work, the play *Ubu Roi*, was performed initially in December 1896 at the théâtre de l'Œuvre and the entire *Mercure* crowd were there, to witness Père Ubu's opening word, '*Merdre!*'* produce such a scandal (laughter, anger, indignation) that proceedings could not continue for fully fifteen minutes.[25] This *succès de scandale* was much like Rachilde's own with *Monsieur Vénus* in that it ensured income for Jarry to maintain his absinthe habit, until it could no longer be hidden that 'Père Ubu' was drinking himself into the grave. Nonetheless, he managed to attend Rachilde's Tuesdays until the very end. He died in hospital in 1907, writing in one of his last letters that he intended to be buried in a mauve shirt, mauve being the colour of the covers of the *Mercure*.

---

* *Merdre* is French for 'shit' with the second 'r' added, which has provoked endless speculation as to why.

Rachilde's salon fostered a lot of new talent. Outside that, for her own part, her novels – mostly but not always set in Paris in her own time – were composed equally of social commentary and satire: *Nono* makes fun of provincial politics, *À mort* ('To the Death') satirises self-consciously fashionable bourgeois Parisian salon society, and *L'Animale* takes on small-minded bourgeois culture.

At one point, and for a time, the decadents' political stance overlapped with anarchism. Their desire to challenge the formal conventions governing art (for example, the rules of poetic versification challenged by the symbolists' use of free verse) paralleled in a way the anarchists' longing to extricate society from hierarchy and oppression. Between 1892 and 1894, there was a spate of anarchical acts of violence which threatened national institutions. The Chamber of Deputies and a barracks were bombed and figures of authority (a judge, and in June 1894, Sadi Carnot, president of the republic) were assassinated. Many artists and writers were impressed, moved by the 'romantic individualism' of the solitary perpetrators.[26]

Rachilde's life was transformed by the First World War. The *Mercure* ceased publication, though it resumed afterwards. Her salon was discontinued, though it too was resurrected in 1919. The war would change the sexual balance in France, with so many men killed, and it would also enable women to take a more prominent role in many different career specialities, so that feminine self-confidence underwent a major transformation. Rachilde was never the most earnest of feminists but after the war she did attend feminist gatherings at Natalie Clifford Barney's 'Temple of Friendship', which was also attended by Emmeline and Christabel Pankhurst.

Rachilde's book on the 1914–18 war, *Dans le puits, ou La Vie inférieure* ('In the Well, or Life below Ground', 1918), part diary, part narrative, reflected her horrors of the war and to what extent it was 'worth' it, and contrasted her own withdrawal from public life with the self-seeking of other, more combative feminists. She would later write another account of her reactions to the Second World War, and the Vichy government. The fiery young woman of the *fin-de-siècle* had by then become the solid, respectable, middle-aged writer who people either looked up to or thought was old-fashioned. But her Tuesday salons continued until 1930, when she was seventy.[27]

'THERE IS NO DREYFUS AFFAIR'

We should not overlook the fact that, by the time of the Belle Époque, a deeper context was taking form. In place of the 'jumbled patchwork' of states that had occupied central Europe for centuries, the nineteenth century saw two massive powers coming into being – unified Germany and unified Italy.

The other European nations responded to this with what Hagen Schulze has called 'patriotic regeneration'. This was especially true in France, for example, where the entire education system was placed in the service of the nationalist cause. The teaching of history and national politics was to be the cause of national regeneration after revolution and repeated defeat. The most obvious – one might say the most lurid – example of this was G. Bruno's *Le Tour de la France par deux enfants: devoir et patrie*. This was the story of a fourteen-year-old boy, André Valden, and his brother Julien, aged seven. The story is set in the wake of the Franco-Prussian War after the two boys have been orphaned and stranded in their hometown of Phalsburg, which has been annexed by Germany. They escape and journey throughout France, in the course of their adventures ultimately finding a new home in the country which, thanks to those adventures, they now see in all its glory.[28]

Another example of the fervent nationalism of the times is that while Jules Ferry (1832–93) was education secretary every classroom was required to display a map of France with Alsace and Lorraine shown surrounded by black mourning crêpe. Jules Michelet (1798–1874) wrote about France as the 'pontificate of modern civilisation', meaning that it was the pioneer of the modern enlightened state: 'The French idea of civilisation had thus become the very core of a national religion.' (The *Marseillaise* was adopted as the national anthem in 1879.)

The downside to this outbreak of nationalism was yet more racism, anti-Semitism being especially virulent in France and Germany. This partly had to do with the envy of Britain: the French and German empires were so small, compared with the British, that the view formed, as Paul Déroulède, founder of the League of Patriots in France, put it, that 'we cannot hope to achieve anything abroad before we have cured our domestic ills'. And there was no doubt who was internal enemy number one – the Jews.

In 1886 Édouard Drumont published *La France juive*, a 'concoction' of Jewish life and customs which, though crude and clumsy, became an instant bestseller. It turned out to be the prelude to a wave of anti-Semitism in the country, culminating in the Dreyfus affair, when a Jewish officer was falsely accused of being a German spy.[29]

The affair is too well known to need more than a brief restatement here, but what stands out, in any re-examination of the course of events, is the virulent reluctance of the anti-Dreyfusards to consider, and reconsider, the evidence in his favour. The fact is that more than anti-Semitism was at stake – in particular the honour and prestige of the army, which had suffered such a humiliating series of defeats in the Franco-Prussian War, and in the siege of Paris and the succeeding Commune, where it had been put to shame in its vindictive behaviour and had suffered by comparison with the *francs-tireurs*.

This helps to partly explain the showy nature of Dreyfus's degradation, when the emblems of rank were torn from his tunic and his sword broken. It helps to partly explain why, when Colonel Marie-Georges Picquart, head of the army's Intelligence Service, who had taught Dreyfus at military school, began to suspect Major Ferdinand Esterhazy, he – Picquart – was posted to Tunisia. It helps to explain why, when Picquart, on a short leave from Tunisia, caught the ear of a lawyer who in turn persuaded a prominent politician, Auguste Scheurer-Kestner, to approach premier Jules Méline, no one at the top wanted to have anything to do with the case, Méline telling the Chamber in 1897: 'There is no Dreyfus affair.'

Opponents of Dreyfus maintained it was all a Jewish plot to bring the army into disrepute and 'weaken the nation'. The *amour-propre* of the army also helps explain why, when Esterhazy was finally brought to trial in 1898, he was quickly acquitted. The aim was a cover-up, as it was when Zola published his famous article in *L'Aurore*, 'J'accuse'. He was supported by a raft of intellectuals, including Anatole France and Marcel Proust, but they were relatively few – according to Robert

Gildea, out of fifty-five daily newspapers in Paris that were published
at the time of Zola's polemic, forty-eight were anti-Dreyfusard. It
explains why, even as Zola went into exile in Britain to escape imprisonment, a Ligue anti-sémitique, 'composed mainly of butchers' boys
from the abattoirs of La Villette', came into being, quite openly.[30] In
elections that year, twenty-two notable anti-Semites were returned
and pro-Dreyfus candidates lost their seats. It explains why, when
suspicion shifted from Esterhazy to Colonel Hubert Henry, also of
the Intelligence Section, he slit his throat rather than face trial. The
fact is: it was felt in many quarters that defeat for the army hierarchy
in the Dreyfus affair would be a humiliation too far for the French
military. It explains why the retrial of Dreyfus, when it eventually
took place in 1910, had to be held outside Paris. Had he been acquitted, the army top brass would have been liable to prosecution for
obstruction of justice, which – it was feared – might have triggered
a coup d'état. It also explains why Dreyfus was convicted again,
though 'with extenuating circumstances', which opened a way to a
pardon, not at all what the Dreyfusards wanted – they must not be
allowed victory. And it explains why, eventually, all involved in the
affair were amnestied.

THE SOIL AND THE DEAD

Nationalism reached its ultimate form at the turn of the century
in Maurice Barrès's trilogy *Le Roman de l'énergie nationale*
(1897–1903). Barrès's idea was that the cult of the ego was the
main cause of the corruption and degeneration of civilisation. 'The
nation ranked above the ego and had therefore to be regarded as the
supreme priority in a man's life. The individual had no choice but
to submit to the function assigned to him by the nation, "the sacred
law of his lineage", and to "hearken to the voices of the soil and the
dead".' As Hagen Schulze has rightly pointed out, nationalism, the
idea of a nation, which at the turn of the nineteenth century had
been seen as a form of utopia – as a natural political and cultural
entity – had become by the turn of the twentieth century a polemical factor in domestic politics. 'It no longer stood above the parties
uniting society, but itself turned into a party and divided society.'[31]

The consequences, more bitter in France even than in Germany at the time, were to prove catastrophic, leading to the First World War and the Versailles Treaty that came out of it, which led in turn to the Second.

'The Old Brilliance Revives'

In 1871, when the Duc d'Uzès, the highest-ranked nobleman in France, congratulated Adolphe Thiers, the bourgeois statesman, on becoming the Third Republic's first president, Thiers couldn't help himself and let slip: 'Oh, but Mme Thiers would much rather be a duchess.' A quarter of a century later, the novelist Jules Renard revealed that little had changed even then. 'Since the Revolution,' he wrote, meaning the 1789 revolution, 'our republic hasn't made a single step towards [equality] or liberty. It's a republic where all people care about is being invited to [Mme] Greffulhe's.'[1]

There is of course an irony here, a profound one. At the very time some French thinkers (Le Bon, Bergson, Morel) were devoting their attentions to what they saw as decadence and degeneration, intellectual and artistic life in France was blossoming. During the years that lay across 1900, from the death of Victor Hugo to the First World War, there were probably more salons in Paris than at any other time, more than in the *ancien régime*, more than in the First Empire, more than in the Restoration, more than in the July Monarchy, and very probably more than in the Second Empire. Not all of the women could claim the solid achievements of Marie du Deffand, Germaine de Staël, Marie d'Agoult, Juliette Adam or Rachilde. In fact, several of them were highly bred socialites whose salons were a luxurious mix of social glitter and intellectual polish, who were known as much for their poise as for their ideas, and alongside them was a second, small group, who were artistically and/or intellectually gifted but were also homosexual.

Caroline Weber, in her investigation of the Parisian women on whom Proust based the Duchesse de Guermantes in his great work, À la recherche du temps perdu, quotes from an article he published in Le Gaulois in September 1893, titled 'The Great Parisian Salons'. In fact, it was a brief history of salons as well. 'Salons', he wrote, 'used to play the role the clubs play now; they were places where people talked about everything, from literature to politics. It was in salons that reputations were made or new ideas came under fire ... Today, the most esteemed closed salons in Paris are those of the Duchesse de Noailles, the Dowager Duchesse de Mortemart ... the Dowager Duchess de Maillé; the Duchesse de la Trémoïlle; the Duchesse d'Avarny; Comtesse Aimery de La Rochefoucauld; the Comtesse Greffulhe; the Marquise de Lévis; Mme Standish; the Marquise de Montboissier; the Comtesse de Croix; and the Comtesse de Gramont d'Aster.'[2] All those titles – duchesse, dowager duchesse, comtesse – rather give the game away. Proust, as the world knows, was an inveterate snob, and in this case he went on to list yet more salons, led by five princesses, two duchesses, six comtesses, one marquise and one baronne. None of these, save one, will feature in our story.

Proust's account reinforces the notion that the number of salons in Belle Époque Paris was huge, that such a way of life was far from dead, but it also shows where the idea that the salons were 'trivial' comes from. The salon was still a very attractive way of life, but some of its more worthwhile features were being taken over, as we have seen, by clubs and cafés.

THE IRON OF DEFEAT

Once the siege and the Commune were over, Juliette Adam recorded that it took the best part of a year before 'the old brilliance revived', and that the first sign was when Parisian women began to care again about their clothes.[3] It was now that her Wednesday and Friday dinners resumed, in which the main topic of conversation was still Léon Gambetta's speeches.

Juliette's relationship with Gambetta went through three distinct phases. During the war she regarded him as 'the incarnation of national defence'. After the defeat he was for her the man of revanche.

Finally, when he didn't share her intense concern for *revanche*, she became disappointed with the man who had once been her hero.

Where Juliette and Gambetta disagreed was over the presence of an elite in society. She had an idea of democracy as the Athenian elitist kind, where she and people like her would use their education to the benefit of all, whereas Gambetta thought there should be no elite – 'the masses were to guide and govern themselves'.[4]

Juliette would, for most of the life that remained to her, be obsessed by *revanche* – 'the iron of defeat entered into her soul'. And it was to keep this idea alive that she launched what was her greatest achievement, a new periodical, using money her late husband had left her: this was the *Nouvelle Revue*. This, plus her revitalised salon, now became a 'lobby' to the Chamber of Deputies, in which the strength of France was the main – the overriding – concern, where it was felt that the German Empire 'was suffocating in central Europe', and therefore always likely to want to break out.

Juliette's main view of foreign policy was to form an alliance with Russia and never to form one with Great Britain. Right up until the First World War, Juliette was dead set against Perfidious Albion.

Now was when she began to part company with Gambetta. One reason was because he favoured more colonial adventures, which she felt accorded too much with Bismarck's ideas, in that if France concerned itself with new colonies it would forget Alsace-Lorraine, and because Gambetta – who was now putting on weight and enjoying the luxuries of life that he had not been born to – actually favoured another salon, that of La Païva. Juliette was one of those who felt that the Russian-born La Païva, originally Esther Lachmann, the 'queen of kept women' and a notable collector of jewels, was one of Bismarck's spies. She was disappointed too when Mac Mahon fell in 1877 and Gambetta, instead of becoming president of the republic, accepted a lesser role as president of the council, and – arousing great opposition – appointed as minister of public worship Paul Bert, a well-known agnostic. By the time Gambetta died in 1882, he and Juliette were estranged.[5]

With her antipathy to everything 'Gothic, Teutonic and mediaeval', she was determined to bring about an 'Athenian republic' in France. She attracted to her pages a raft of new versifiers, who included

François Coppée, Sully Prudhomme, José-Maria de Heredia, a Cuban-born poet, Daudet, Baudelaire, Villiers de L'Isle-Adam, Anatole France and Leconte de Lisle. When she could, Juliette liked to draw away from politics in her salon, and retreat into her Athenian republic.

Prudhomme and Leconte de Lisle were both members of the so-called Parnassian movement (the Greek aspects of which appealed to Juliette), which was a reaction to the overblown and sentimental excesses of the romantic movement, their verse being restrained and technically precise, though it didn't eschew more ambitious philosophical ideas. Two of Prudhomme's most well-known works are 'Justice' and 'Happiness', the latter about the links between love and knowledge. He was awarded the first Nobel Prize in Literature in 1901. Juliette's own best novels – *Laïde*, *Grecque* and *Païenne* – all have Hellenic themes and sympathies, and were warmly praised by Jules Lemaître, who had followed Sainte-Beuve as France's most respected literary critic.[6]

At this time too there was a further change to the make-up of her salon, where she welcomed more painters, such as Édouard Detaille, famous for his meticulous military paintings, appointed the official painter of battles, and Carolus-Duran, a pupil of David, a follower of Courbet and a colleague of Fantin-Latour, with whom he dined once a month to eat Japanese food. Carolus-Duran became known for his many portraits of fashionable Belle Époque society.[7]

When she initially had the idea for the *Nouvelle Revue*, one of the first persons she confided in was Flaubert, whom she had known for years, being introduced via George Sand and the Goncourt brothers. He didn't relish the idea of writing articles for her, scribbling, as he put it, 'by the yard', but he did say that once he had finished *L'Éducation sentimentale*, he would send her his next book, *Bouvard et Pecuchet*, which he himself described as a sort of 'encyclopaedia about knowledge'. The book tells the story of two copy clerks, Bouvard and Pecuchet, one of whom inherits a fair amount of money, enabling them to retire to a farm they buy and use it as a base to inquire into every form of knowledge, rarely – if ever – actually reaching a conclusion as to what knowledge is ascertainable and, more to the point, useful. It was, in fact, Flaubert's way of laughing at the nineteenth century's obsession with science, classification and measurement.

Juliette's salon and the *Revue* both shared her obsession with *revanche* as she undertook to show that France, though defeated militarily, was – when it came to literary, artistic and scientific vigour – the 'most superior country anywhere'.[8] For twenty years of her life – still signing her work 'Juliette Lambert' – she lived through the *Nouvelle Revue*. When people marvelled at her workload, she would reply that she preferred 'to wear out than rust out'.[9]

As the war approached, she didn't much like what she saw. The art of conversation, she was convinced, was dying. 'When I begin to talk in a modern drawing-room,' she once said, 'I am told to be silent because I am interrupting a game of bridge, or because someone is going to dance the tango.' And she found that the 'dull weight' of the Germanic spirit then permeating French intellectual society 'had extinguished the sparkle of French talk, had blunted the rapier of French irony'.[10]

Between 1902 and 1910, she published seven volumes of her *Souvenirs*, in which the events of 1870–1 figure large. She thought France was too centralised, that the nation's regions were a source of energy and creativity, and she remained, as she put it to her biographer, 'an ardent feminist'. So she was pleased when, at the outbreak of fighting, certain artillerymen of the 21st Army Corps, serving at the front, had the felicitous idea of naming one of their guns 'Juliette Lamber' to mark the spot where the first Frenchman was killed in the war, a war which would of course lead to the return of Alsace-Lorraine to France.[11]

Proust's Prototypes

No one could have been more different from Juliette Adam than Mme Aubernon and, in fact, from what one reads about her, it is a wonder she ever had a successful and intellectually stimulating salon. She was more of a schoolmistress than a princess, or a goddess, and she ruled her salon with the proverbial rod of iron but in the form of a small silver bell which was rung whenever anyone dared to speak out of turn, or when asked to contribute. No side-talk was allowed at her table, and only one person was permitted to speak at any one time.

Born Euphrasie-Héloïse-Lydie Lemercier de Nerville, she lived and entertained in the place de Messine (a few blocks from the Gare Saint-Lazare), where all guests were expected to be brilliant and to be listened to 'with the attentive respect an audience pays to a violin virtuoso at a concert'. She herself would select the subjects for discussion and give someone the floor until she felt they had begun to repeat themselves, when she would ring her bell and take the subject round the table one by one. It sounds awful and, certainly, some of her newer, less experienced guests could be – and were – intimidated, including one young woman who turned up late (already a sin) and was asked to contribute immediately to the discussion, which that night was adultery. 'I'm so sorry,' said the flustered young woman, 'tonight I have only prepared incest.'[1] On another occasion, Ernest Renan was overheard indulging in side-talk. The bell was rung, and the table fell to silence. Fixing Renan with her steely glint, Lydie intoned: 'Our illustrious friend is expressing some valuable ideas which I am sure we will all want to hear.' Renan blushed and replied meekly: 'I was just asking for another helping of peas.'[2]

She was a woman of Rubensesque stature, who preferred to dress in pastel shades with ribbons in her hair, insisting that such gaiety overcame gloom. And she could – and did – talk for hours on end. After a few short years of hardly happy matrimony, her husband Georges, a councillor, had given up and exiled himself as far away as possible and still be in France – in Antibes. She did not find pretty women to her taste, feeling that their advantages distracted menfolk from more serious matters. When one of these young ladies came to her for advice on how to run a salon, Lydie dissuaded her with the words: 'Don't try! You have too luscious a bosom to keep the conversation general.'

She still sounds awful, as embarrassing as she was rich, but this can't be the complete picture because her salon lasted for years on end and became known as one of the most exclusive and 'the most reputed' in Paris – there must have been *something* to her.[3] That something may have been her sheer appetite for following all the trends in literature, drama and the arts. During the years when the Russian writers Tolstoy and Dostoevsky took Paris by storm, she was assiduous in cultivating them, as she was with Ibsen when the fashion for his plays was at its height. She staged several of Ibsen's plays in the large hall of her house, which she christened the théâtre de Messine.[4]

Henri de Régnier, symbolist poet, never made the grade – 'He dines badly,' she said. But she welcomed Paul Bourget, Jules Barbey d'Aurevilly, Leconte de Lisle, Ferdinand Brunetière, editor of the *Revue des deux mondes*, Jules Lemaître and Anatole France, until Lemaître was 'stolen' by Mme de Loynes and France was taken off by Mme Arman de Caillavet.[5]

But Mme Aubernon's real star – who she hung on to – was Alexandre Dumas *fils*. It was mainly in his honour that she organised her dinners, concerts and 'theatricals'. Dumas's second publication, *La Dame aux camélias*, took Paris – and then the world – by storm, appearing in 1848 and only five years later as Verdi's opera *La traviata*. Not only was there quite a to-do over staging the play in the first place, but the traditional French game of trying to guess/prove who the real-life 'prostitute with a heart of gold' was has proved endlessly entertaining down the years, with at least seven books devoted to the subject. Named as Marguerite Gautier in the book, she was in fact Alphonsine Plessis, from Normandy, who changed her name (as many courtesans of the day chose to do) to Marie Duplessis. In a very romantic touch, she really was the daughter of a prostitute and a priest, who abused his wife because he had wanted a son. With her background, and beauty, Alphonsine had precocious sexual experiences, met all manner of men, some of whom paid for her piano and dancing lessons, and at one point she became so expensive that seven members of fashionable Paris clubbed together to purchase her favours collectively since no one could afford her on his own.[6]

Although she had some *amants de cœur*, people she slept with out of affection, rather than for money (of whom Dumas was one, but allowed to visit her only between midnight and 6.00 a.m.), her heart wasn't entirely made of gold: she was an inveterate liar and gambler, was reduced to pawnshops on at least nineteen occasions and could be – was – coarse of speech.[7] Shortly after he had separated from Marie d'Agoult, Franz Liszt was a guest at a number of soirées she held at her rooms in the boulevard de la Madeleine. She fell for him and wanted to accompany him on tour, but he cleverly dissuaded her.

Having lost Lemaître and Anatole France, Mme Aubernon was anxious to hold on to Dumas. 'Dumas is never as witty with others as he is with me,' she would insist.[8] Dumas's other works included the play *Le Demi-Monde*, a phrase he is said to have invented, and a novel, *L'Affaire Clemenceau*, about a virtuous husband who kills an unfaithful wife and then pleads his case in court. There was more to the context than that, though, for Dumas used this case to highlight the strikingly different legal status between men and women in nineteenth-century France.

Second only to Voltaire

Just as Mme du Deffand had taken on Julie de Lespinasse as a protégée, so Mme Aubernon took on Mme Arman de Caillavet ... with much the same embarrassing result. Mme Arman de Caillavet was equally as strong-willed as her mentor and had a sumptuous house on the avenue Hoche (north-east from the Arc de Triomphe). She was more graceful and flirtatious than Lydie Aubernon, less demanding of her guests, and before long there were defections. Jules Lemaître led the way, followed by Victorien Sardou and Anatole France. Mme Arman de Caillavet devoted her life to 'creating' Anatole France.

Born Léontine Lippman into a rich Jewish family, she seems to have been altogether more agreeable than Mme Aubernon. Alexandre Dumas *fils* was just one who was far more relaxed in her presence, on one occasion writing to her: 'I am very happy to have your delightful letter and I kiss the hand that wrote it. If the other hand is anywhere about, I kiss it also.'[9]

Her salon was lively, liberal and though mainly literary was not without its politicians – Raymond Poincaré (three times prime minister and later president), Jean Jaurès, leader of the Socialist Party, and Georges Clemenceau, 'with his tufted eyebrows, prominent cheekbones and Asiatic appearance'. Not as formidably formal as Mme Aubernon, Mme Arman de Caillavet included her own son in her salon, who brought his friends, one of whom, with 'big sad eyes', was Marcel Proust. Pierre Loti, a bit of a dandy (as shown in his portrait by Henri Rousseau) and with a mesmerising speaking voice, would describe his travels in the French navy to Tahiti, British India, Constantinople and north Africa (Cairo, Fez).[10]

Mme Arman de Caillavet's Wednesday salons were small compared to her Sundays, when there might be a hundred guests, when there might be concerts or theatricals, as the phrase went, the plays usually being the work of the best boulevard playwrights – Alfred Capus, Georges Feydeau, Tristan Bernard – with Reynaldo Hahn at the piano.[11]

Above all, Léontine's main purpose in literary life was her support for Anatole France, who she felt was second only to Voltaire as an author and a thinker. This was going a bit far, but they did become lovers so perhaps the exaggeration is permissible. Léontine turned into a combination of secretary, research assistant and travelling companion for France, taking him to places he would never have gone to on his own, translating papers for him (she was an accomplished linguist), writing articles and parts of his books under his name, discovering new areas of erudition for him, even cleaning him up sartorially, as a result of which he produced far more than he would otherwise have done. It was generally recognised that Léontine was responsible for France's admission to the Académie française and, albeit long after she was dead, being awarded the Nobel Prize. It has also been generally accepted that France was the model for Bergotte in Proust's *In Search of Lost Time*.[12]

France was always a bookish man, being the son of a bookseller and for a while librarian to the Senate. In his books, he wrote about crime and the place of crime in French society. He poked fun at mystical belief and in *Penguin Island*, for example – one of his most imaginative works – he looks at penguins transformed into humans after a short-sighted *abbé* baptises the birds. In *The Gods Are Thirsty*, he writes ironically from the point of view of a follower of Robespierre, exposing the psychology of fanaticism.

France is now rather less well remembered than Voltaire but that may be unfair. He wore his learning lightly – learning in large part derived through Léontine – but his books tackle serious issues of nineteenth-century France: religion, revolutionary fervour, political passion in general, in a more light-hearted way that many of us, perhaps the French especially, feel does not live up to the weight of the subject. He eventually grew out of Léontine's attentions, but he would not have achieved what he did without her.

LA DAME AUX VIOLETTES

Eugène Emmanuel Amaury Duval's portrait of Jeanne Detourbey, Comtesse de Loynes, shows a stunningly beautiful, beautifully dressed, beautifully coiffed woman, her dark hair parted in the middle, with long delicate fingers and penetrating eyes, staring straight out at the viewer, artfully poised, fully aware of the effect she is having. By all accounts she was one of the most feminine of *salonnières* in *fin-de-siècle* Paris, with whom countless men fell in love. She was known, not without irony, as '*La Dame aux Violettes*' on account of the colour of her eyes. She was rumoured to have been the inspiration for Flaubert's *Salammbô*, his novel set in Carthage.

Born into modest means in Reims (at one point she was a bottle-washer in a champagne house) it did not take her long to acquire a series of well-heeled and well-known lovers – Émile de Girardin, Prince Napoleon, son of King Jérôme and brother of Princesse Mathilde, Alexandre Dumas *fils*, and for a brief while Flaubert.[13] An early lover was killed in the Franco-Prussian War but the second – and greatest – love of her life didn't strike until she was well past fifty. Like Princesse Mathilde, she was close to Sainte-Beuve, Renan, Gautier and Taine, and like the Princesse de Polignac (chapter 40) she courted Gounod and Massenet. What set her apart was her political taste, ranging from Georges Clemenceau to Paul Déroulède, who were invited on different days.[14]

Victorien Sardou was another frequent guest on Fridays. His early efforts at drama came to nothing after a variety of misfortunes – theatre managements changed, producers died, one play that *was* produced was attributed to someone else. He finally made it after falling ill with typhoid and being cared for by a woman living in the same premises who knew someone with her own theatre. Among his many plays were *Fédora*, which made the fedora hat fashionable, *La Haine* – a clever study of how hatred can turn to pity, and then to love – and three plays on the French Revolution, *Les Merveilleuses*, *Thermidor* and *Robespierre*. Sardou also revived the Napoleonic era with *La Tosca*, which became even more famous after Puccini turned it into an opera. Many of Sardou's plays were written at the height of his affair with Sarah Bernhardt, who he felt was also the greatest interpreter of his ideas. They were known as 'The Two S's'.

Mme de Loynes's conversational skills, according to one biographer, lay in her knowing what her guests did and did not want to talk about. For example, Leconte de Lisle, the Parnassian poet, was much more interested in gardening, while Louis Pasteur liked nothing better than to talk about the mysteries of Catholicism rather than anthrax. Many artists, she knew, would rather talk sex than art.[15]

But the centre of her life, and her salon, was Jules Lemaître, a drama critic whose *feuilletons* of contemporary authors were much admired for their character penetrations, and probably the highest point was reached on 16 January 1896, when he was received into the Académie française. He was Mme de Loynes's last lover and she had worked hard to help him gain entry to the academy at the relatively young age of forty-three. ('His April contrasting sharply with the

December of the other members,' as someone laboriously put it.) This was ten years after they had met, he at thirty-three, she close to fifty.

They had met at a masked ball given by Arsène Houssaye, director of the Théâtre-Français, who gave lavish parties where he invited the leading cocottes of Paris. Léontine and Jules had spent two hours talking and she invited him to call on her the next day, which he did, finding Maurice Barrès there, with the playwright Ludovic Halévy, Boni de Castellane, politician and 'taste-maker', and Ernest Renan. This set, later, were mildly perplexed by the Loynes–Lemaître ménage and not everyone was entirely convinced. 'Jules Lemaître', droned Henry Becque, another playwright, 'is now working in demolition.' The comtesse didn't care: 'I am rewarming myself with his youth.'[16]

But, sad to say, the advent of Lemaître into her salon meant that, when it came to the Dreyfus affair, it was anti-Dreyfusards who gathered around Mme de Loynes's splendid table. The Ligue de la patrie française was largely formed in her salon and Lemaître was chosen as president. Once a bourgeois liberal, and a republican, he had become reactionary due partly to a fear of degeneration in France (chapter 37) and to a number of scandals implicating the government, including the Panama scandal, in 1892, when members of the government took bribes to keep quiet about the failed attempt to build the Panama Canal, causing droves of investors to lose everything. He thought he saw the hand of Jewish financiers in the sordid details and the Ligue grew in numbers, with the meetings of its leaders all taking place in the Loynes salon. With her death in 1908, as one observer put it, 'the thunder of political strife echoed no longer within these gracious walls, and when at last she died it seemed as though a peculiarly French tradition of culture had passed away for ever'.[17]

A LOVE OF BOOKS WAS A CHARACTER FLAW

In Search of Lost Time, or *Remembrance of Things Past*, by Marcel Proust, is without question one of the most famous novels in history. At seven volumes and thousands of pages long, it may also be one of the least read all the way through. Its contents are considered in other chapters of this book. Here we need to examine it in a different way. Since the book is so long, and so detailed, a type of literary game has developed, as critics and fans attempt to discover which real people of Belle Époque France are depicted in its pages. We have already seen in passing that such figures as Robert de Montesquiou and Anatole France have been canvassed as Proust's prototypes. One of the latest attempts to play this (serious) game is by another female American academic who has devoted her considerable energies to sorting out just who was who in the Proust pantheon, with a concentration on the main female *salonnière*, the Duchesse de Guermantes. This is Caroline Weber, professor of French and comparative literature at Barnard College, Columbia University, in *Proust's Duchess: How Three Celebrated Women Captured the Imagination of Fin-de-Siècle Paris*.[18]

At the beginning, Professor Weber reminds us that Proust's world was an anachronism, in some ways an embarrassingly hereditarily still-privileged society left over from the *ancien régime*, but one which continues to hold an 'inexhaustible fascination' for their compatriots. As she spells it out, the Duchesse de Guermantes – for Proust the best example of the aristocratic high life – was based on three 'grandes dames who together constituted his dream of patrician elegance and grace'. These women – Geneviève Halévy Bizet Straus, Laure de Sade, Comtesse Adhéaume de Chevigné, and Élisabeth de Riquet de Caraman-Chimay, Comtesse Greffulhe – were famous in their lifetimes, with Élisabeth Greffulhe receiving so much fan mail that her archives contain a file marked 'Homages and Appreciations from People I Don't Know'.[19]

Proust's book chronicles the decline and fall of an aristocratic ideal and Weber doesn't pull her punches, showing how the three women embraced a worldview descending all the way back to Louis XIV that favoured appearance and form over authenticity and substance, the culture of appearances (chapter 17) remaining a 'shibboleth'. They ignored their children, they were avid gamblers, women were in thrall to their husbands and as a result they often had a dearth of sexual awareness. 'A love of books was seen as a character flaw.' They had baby names for one another. The Comte Greffulhe had royal blood in his veins, his great-grandfather being a love-child of Louis XV, which meant he was referred to as 'Demi-Louis'.[20] Laure de Sade had no royal blood, but she was nonetheless proud of being descended from that notable pornographer the Marquis de Sade.

They would change their costumes seven or eight times a day, and as someone said of Mme Greffulhe, 'it was no laughing matter to be the most beautiful woman in Paris'.[21] In fact, it was a world where, as someone else observed, 'being beautiful and being ugly make women into two completely different sexes'.[22] Their artistic taste was suspect – they preferred fashionable society portraitists such as Federico de Madrazo and Paul Helleu to Sargent or Toulouse-Lautrec. And they could be virulent anti-Semites and bigoted. The Prince de Sagan once thought he was being poetic when he compared a starry night sky to 'a Negro suffering from smallpox'.[23]

At the same time, each of these women had a salon, membership of which was a complex amalgamation of social cachet, creativity and privilege, not always the model we have been focusing on. Proust attended the Straus salon from 1889, when he was always placed – as he admitted – in the worst seat. He had a relationship with Mme de Chevigné from 1892 but she didn't introduce him to any of her *mondaine* friends for years. By 1900 he filled a space in her box at the opera and became a 'toothpick', someone brought in after dinner.[24]

Laure de Sade, Comtesse de Chevigné, was known more for her strawberry-blonde hair, her chain-smoking and her charms than her intellect, but men were so entranced that a once-a-week salon was not enough and many of them insisted on visiting her every day.[25] Always dressed in Worth or Doucet, she had perfected the art of being seen and, like Geneviève Straus, was 'a tireless social butterfly and a shameless coquette'. The stars of her salon were performers – Yvette Guilbert, Hortense Schneider and Réjane. And she was a keen aficionada of the nightlife of Montmartre, in particular the Chat Noir. Maupassant described himself as a 'rabid fan', incorporating her into *Bel-Ami* (1885), his second novel, about the rise and rise of a disreputable journalist, which put him on the map.[26]

Geneviève's salon was more substantial than Laure's, partly – but not entirely – on account of her marriage to composer Georges Bizet. Music was in her veins because Georges – a big bear of a man – was a student of Geneviève's father, Fromental Halévy, himself the son of a cantor, who had been admitted to the Conservatoire at the age of ten, where he became a pupil of Luigi Cherubini. Halévy had not found success easy to come by and had served as chorus master at various theatres, including the Opéra, until his very grand work, *La Juive*, made him a household name (even Wagner admired the composition, despite its subject). The Halévys were a colourful, educated and creative family. Fromental's wife, Léonie, sister of Eugénie Foa, a French novelist, became an accomplished sculptor, while his brother Léon was a historian and *his* son, Ludovic, was the librettist for Jacques Offenbach's *Orpheus in the Underworld* and Bizet's best-known work, *Carmen*.

Bizet was not the normal top-hatted Parisian type, being partial to sailor suits and straw hats. On the chubby side (he was always nibbling madeleines), his subdued but elegant dress belied his high temper.[27] Much influenced by Gounod, his first well-known composition, *The Pearl Fishers*, contained some beautiful, haunting melodies, in particular the 'Friends' Duet' where the tenor's and baritone's arias entwine each other.

A year after Geneviève and Georges had been married, in 1869, Bizet fought in the Franco-Prussian War as a soldier in the National Guard (as did Saint-Saëns, while Massenet and Fauré were infantrymen). Bizet didn't stop composing during the war, producing *Jeux d'enfants* and starting to conceive *Carmen*, which he took from a story by Prosper Mérimée. The new elements in the opera were in the characterisation, telling of the disintegration of a soldier and a woman who, whatever else happens to her, is always true to herself, and spurns promiscuity, despite many opportunities, refusing to employ her charms in that way. Bizet's aim in the music was to depict life as it is, not idealised. He himself thought it was a flop at first and as a result suffered a psychosomatic illness. Yet Wagner, Tchaikovsky and Brahms all thought highly of it.

The couple formed the centre of a lively group. Degas was a neighbour and dropped by almost every day, sometimes with his mistress, Hortense Howland. Others included Ivan Turgenev, Georges's fellow composers Berlioz, Massenet and Gounod, and the painters Gustave Doré, Gustave Moreau and Pierre Puvis de Chavannes.[28] The 1870–1 war put an end to everything. During the hostilities, Geneviève suffered a nervous breakdown.

After the war the relationship between the Bizets declined. He was now hard at work on *Carmen* and she, to begin with, became hostess to a large cast of 'bohemians', as she put it, whom she encouraged to drop by whenever they felt like it, for gossip, cards and company, she as often as not dressed more suitably for the boudoir than the drawing room. Later, as her relationship with Bizet continued to falter, Geneviève took off for Bougival, a small hamlet about 10 miles west of Paris, on the Seine, which was now home to Dumas *fils*, Turgenev and a whole raft of painters – Renoir, Sisley, Monet, Morisot, and also Élie Delaborde, with whom she soon had an affair. A piano virtuoso, his playing was so seductive that people had turned out to hear him even during the siege of Paris.

It was after what Bizet thought was the failure of *Carmen* that he too escaped to Bougival, where he went swimming in the Seine with Delaborde, which, given his deteriorating condition, some historians have speculated was a suicide attempt. Not long after the swimming excursion he slipped out of consciousness.[29]

Geneviève enjoyed her status as the Widow Bizet. She went on to marry Émile Straus, an eminent Jewish lawyer, thought to be the illegitimate son of Baron James Rothschild. She also had an affair with Maupassant, at the time that he was riding high on the success of *Bel-Ami*, which had been reprinted thirty-seven times in four months.[30] Maupassant, who was one of 300 French artists who had signed a petition against the Eiffel Tower, was not at first drawn to Geneviève's Semitic looks but he liked her world.[31] As well as introducing him to society, she also provided him with material, Geneviève's flirtatious nature finding its way into *Strong as Death*, with its picture of the main character 'made of sunshine and mourning'.[32]

SHE WHO WOULD BE QUEEN

By all accounts, the third model for the Duchesse de Guermantes, Élisabeth Greffulhe, had 'high-cultural pretensions', which she believed set her apart from the rest of the *gratin*, and was more than anything concerned with appearances. As a result, she was lampooned repeatedly in the press and compared sarcastically to Mme de Pompadour and Marie Antoinette, where her 'picturesque lateness' at balls was judged as seriously irksome. Many of her own writings, some in a secret code, were nothing but flattering descriptions of herself. Proust was dismissive. 'Like rouge,' he quipped, her cultural pretensions allowed her to 'look good from across the room but they would never qualify her to be a real friend to a man of genius'.[33]

There were other salons in the years of the Belle Époque – those of Judith Gautier, Marguerite Charpentier (whose guests included at least six major impressionist painters), Emmanuela, Comtesse Potocka, Marie Trélat, Mme Bertin, Nina de Callias, Mme de Chimay, Diane de Beausacq, Mme Chambost, Mme de Brantes, Mme Edouard André (Nellie Jacquemart) and many, many more.

As ever there were critics. One of the loudest complaints came from Julien Benda, a novelist who would turn into the scourge of French intellectuals after the First World War. Between 1900 and 1914 he had been a member of the salon of his cousin, Simone Benda, an actress of talent, whose fellow salon members included Charles Péguy, Jean Cocteau and Alain-Fournier, the latter also being her lover.[34] But Benda was scathing. Salons, he said, no longer attracted the greatest wits, the most glorious literary types, the great editors of newspapers; the spirit had entirely gone out of them. The salons now, he insisted, were superficial, confused as to purpose, full of boring gossip between mediocrities. There was little insight into the psychology of the times, no discussion of metaphysics, the language routinely used was lacking in precision, full of gratuitous crudities and political cliché. The salons, he concluded, were dying and could no longer contribute to the intellectual quality of life in France, though he did single out and congratulate Mme Chambost and Mme de Balcourt for running two of the first 'academic' salons.[35]

Benda somewhat overembellished his argument. The Chambost and Balcourt salons did not catch on, whereas Juliette Adam's and Winnaretta de Polignac's salons would last for years, and Benda does not seem to have been aware of the salons of Rachilde, Natalie Clifford Barney, Misia Sert or Anna de Noailles, all of whom continued to attract serious artists and writers and politicians for decades beyond the First World War.

As others had previously pointed out, the advent of mass-circulation newspapers (courtesy of Émile de Girardin) meant that 'new opinions arrived every morning'. Another change was the development of lunch and dinner clubs, which, in an echo of what happened on the eve of the Revolution, were mainly – if not entirely – all-male affairs. Their tendency to be all-male must mean that, for some at any rate, the traditional female-organised salons were no longer entirely adequate.

Anne Martin-Fugier has looked at two of these in more detail than the others. They were the dinners at Magny's and the *dîners Bixio*. The first of these was organised by Paul Gavarni, the illustrator for *Le Charivari*, and François-Auguste Veyne, a doctor friend to Sainte-Beuve, known to all the 'bohemians' of Paris. He suggested they meet every fortnight at Magny's, a restaurant mentioned in the *Guide Joanna*, the *Guide Michelin* of its day. Other members of the club were Gautier, Nefftzer, Marcellin Berthelot, the famous chemist and, later, minister of foreign affairs, Taine, Sand, the Goncourts and Turgenev. According to Martin-Fugier, evolution was one of the main topics of conversation, and why modern love was so melancholic; on another occasion Taine placed Musset above Hugo, to the fury of some of his fellow diners; at other times Sainte-Beuve preferred Diderot to Voltaire, Candide being condemned as an 'idiot'. On yet another occasion, she says, 'Renan and Taine horrified the Goncourt brothers by putting La Rochefoucauld above La Bruyère'. Renan declared Pascal the first writer of the French language, 'upon which Gautier cried out with the worst obscenity imaginable'. The club's later members included Gambetta, a keen fan of Rabelais apparently.[36]

The *dîners Bixio* were not called that until the founder, Alexandre Bixio, a banker friend of Marie d'Agoult, died, in 1865. In this case twenty people met on the first Friday of the month, to discuss letters and politics, though the club's membership did include Auguste Villemot, a mathematician as well as an editor, and Léon de Maleville, from the commission on historic monuments. Alexandre Dumas *père*, Fromental Halévy and Prosper Mérimée were other members. The meetings were held at the café Brébant then, from 1892, at the café Anglais. Raymond Poincaré, the doyen of the group, was elected in 1898, other members by then including Paul Bourget, Henri de Régnier, the symbolist poet, Charles-Marie Widor, the virtuoso organist, Maurice Barrès and Marshal Foch.

These dinners were serious, says Martin-Fugier, though elections were subject to vote by, of all things, haricot beans. White beans meant the candidate was acceptable; one red bean and he was excluded.[37]

Of course, artists, writers, politicians and even philosophers all over the world meet up to swap ideas, to make friends, to tell stories, jokes and lies, to enjoy the pleasures of the table, to avoid work, to fall out, make up, support one another, attack one another, and go home slightly the worse for wear. But it is only in France – or especially in France – that this sociability (a word the French use a lot) is so formalised, so assiduously recorded, so much a part of the nation's (somewhat self-satisfied) self-image. Where conversation, language, words and writing are so lovingly cherished.

In his book on intellectuals, the distinguished American sociologist Lewis Coser argued that in order to produce new ideas, intellectuals need an audience, 'a circle of people to whom they can address themselves and who can bestow recognition', and that they require regular contact with their fellow intellectuals where they can 'evolve common standards of method and excellence, common norms to guide their conduct'. He identified throughout history eight institutional settings which incubate intellectual activities: the salon, the coffee house, the scientific society, the monthly or quarterly review, the literary market, the political society, Bohemia and the little magazine. The salon, he said, had come first.[38]

The Crossroads of French Musical Life

A rguably the most distinguished *salonnière* of all time was not anyone in the seventeenth or eighteenth centuries but someone whose salon flourished long after many historians have said that the salons were dead. The extraordinary life of Winnaretta Singer, Princesse de Polignac (1865–1943), has been chronicled by Sylvia Kahan, whose 2003 university press biography of the princess, all 547 pages of it, sums up her life in three revealing statistics. Between May 1888 and July 1939, on the eve of the Second World War, no fewer than 165 musical performances were produced in her salon, including the first performance of works by Stravinsky, Ravel, Debussy, Falla and Poulenc. During that time, twenty-nine musical compositions were either commissioned by her or dedicated to her (by Fauré, Ravel, Stravinsky, Milhaud, Weill and Satie). And among the 561 individuals whom Kahan identifies as having graced her evenings, we may include Sir Thomas Beecham, Giovanni Boldini, Nadia Boulanger, Jean Cocteau, Serge Diaghilev, Gabriel Fauré, Jean-Louis Forain, Jean Giraudoux, Paul Helleu, Vincent d'Indy, Jeanne Lanvin, Serge Lifar, François Mauriac, Elsa Maxwell, Darius Milhaud, Anna de Noailles, Raymond Poincaré, Cole Porter, Marcel Proust, Léon Renault, Arnold Schoenberg, Igor Stravinsky, Violet Trefusis, Paul Valéry, Siegfried Wagner and Edith Wharton.[1]

There was, according to another of her biographers, something intimidating about Winnaretta Singer. For her fourteenth birthday, she had rejected her mother's offer of a watch from Boucheron or a fan decorated by Arthur Chaplin, who specialised in flower images, and said instead that she would much rather her mother organise a live performance of Beethoven's Fourteenth Quartet, then a relatively new – and hardly familiar – part of the musical repertoire.[2]

She was the second of six children borne by the Duchess of Camposelice to her first husband, Isaac Merritt Singer, the creator of the Singer Sewing Machine Company of New Jersey. And she was his *twentieth* child – in all he would father twenty-four children from two legal and three common-law marriages. Before he founded his company, Singer had been a strolling player, so she had music in her genes. There was also generosity in her genes. Her father, who had fought in the American Civil War, later donated 1,000 sewing machines to the army.[3]

He was also an incurable womaniser, who had had affairs – and not a few children – all over America and, as he started to amass enormous wealth, several of these women chose to mount claims against him. He paid some of them off, but the allure of Europe grew in his eyes and in 1861 he took ship. He found France much to his taste.

This was the decade when the weakness of Napoleon III's foreign policies was emerging and no matter how much intrepid gaiety there was – and there was plenty – the real change was that, under the emperor, money was becoming an ever-increasing determinant of social status. On this basis, Singer had no difficulty in fitting into the better – if not the very best – levels of Paris society. In such a world a womaniser could hardly avoid meeting a new beautiful young lady, in his case Isabella Boyer, many years his junior, who, before too long, found herself pregnant. He took Isabella back to America where they were married and, on 8 January 1865, Winnaretta Eugénie was born. She spent only two years in America. In 1866, the Singers returned to France and moved into a spacious apartment on the boulevard Malesherbes, at the heart of Haussmann's newly reconstructed Paris.

Aware of the deteriorating relationship between France and Bismarck's Prussia, Singer took the precaution of buying a house in London. And when his health began to fail, and because the south of France was for the moment out of the question, he bought another house on the 'English Riviera', at Paignton on the south Devon coast.

This is where Winnaretta grew up until she was ten, when Isaac died in 1875.[4]

In 1878, with the Franco-Prussian War well over, and with the 1877 crisis resolved between President Mac Mahon and Jules Simon, a moderate republican (chapter 35), Isabella took the family back to Paris. Not long after, she met Victor Nicolas Reubsaet, of the Luxembourg nobility, and in time became first the Vicomtesse d'Estenburgh and then, after the vicomte had discovered some long-lost papers verifying a long-buried ducal title held by his ancestors, she became the Duchess of Camposelice.[5] Not long after she bought a sumptuous house at 27 avenue Kléber and opened a salon which became an active centre of musical activity. At the age of thirty-six, and the mother of six children, she was still beautiful, a fact recognised by the sculptor Frédéric Bartholdi, who – so family legend has it – was just beginning his famous work, *La Liberté éclairant le monde* (better known today as the Statue of Liberty). Sylvia Kahan says that there is a remarkable resemblance between Miss Liberty and the young Winnaretta Singer.[6]

Winnaretta revelled in her mother's musical salons despite the fact that she felt her mother had moved on from her father rather too quickly. But the duke and new duchess do seem to have been fond of each other and had a shared interest in their love of music. In conjunction with her new husband, Isabella was forming a remarkable collection of stringed instruments – including Stradivarius and Guarnerius violins, violas and cellos.[7]

Though surrounded by music, in her early teens Winnaretta also discovered the teeming art world of Paris and her mother agreed that she could learn to be a painter. Winnaretta was sent to the studio of Félix Barrias in the rue de Bruxelles, where she did well. More than that, at the end of the 1870s she discovered the Salon des refusés, and was immensely moved by the works of Manet, Sisley, Boudin, Monet and the others. During her teens, Manet became an object of hero-worship for Winnaretta and she was heart-broken when he died in 1883 (two months after Wagner, another hero of hers). But then, to her surprise, Barrias took the opportunity to move into Manet's studio and this offered her the opportunity to speak with her hero's concierge.

Manet's influence was strong in her own paintings which she produced after his death, and which were of such a quality that they were accepted by the Salon des refusés over a number of years. Another sign of their excellence is that, some years later, the well-known dealer Bernheim Jeune sold one of her paintings *as* a Manet. She also learned the piano, studying under Émile Bourgeois, a rehearsal accompanist at the Opéra-Comiques.[8]

Winnaretta's list of friends in the art world began to grow. She was appreciative of the work of Berthe Morisot, Manet's sister-in-law, and she was taken to Degas's studio by a friend who was also receiving tuition from Barrias and who was having her portrait painted by the impressionist. Winnaretta became friendly with Jean-Louis Forain, the impressionist lithographer and etcher and one of those who took part in the great debates at the Nouvelle Athènes café. He was so impressed by her knowledge of art and the art world that he arranged a position for her as translator for the Louvre's English version of its catalogue.

It was around now that she first met Gabriel Fauré, the first of the great French composers whose careers she was to encourage and influence and who all became good friends. Fauré's family mixed with her mother's in Normandy in the summer.[9]

Born in Paniers in 1845, when Mendelssohn, Chopin and Schumann were still alive, Fauré lived through romanticism all the way up to Wagner and the post-romanticism of Brahms and Mahler, dying well into the twentieth century in 1924. He did not attend the Conservatoire, one of the few French composers not to do so, but instead studied at the École Niedermeyer, where he was taught by Saint-Saëns, who introduced him to the whole range of music then being written. Fauré left the École when he was twenty, winning first prize not just in composition but in piano, organ and harmony. He fought in the Franco-Prussian War, returning afterwards to the Niedermeyer as professor of composition, and became organist at the Madeleine.[10] Later he became deaf and suffered disorders of pitch but worked on through his disability.

Winnaretta's mother also took her to Bayreuth, which would become an annual pilgrimage. On one occasion, they stopped off at Munich when a production of the *Ring* cycle was being prepared and

Winnaretta encountered Vincent d'Indy in the café Maximilian opposite the theatre. He was the second great French composer she formed
a strong friendship with. D'Indy's music is little performed today but
in his lifetime he was very much in the swim, friendly with Bizet and
Massenet, and Brahms, who he visited in Germany. And he was an
excellent teacher – of, among many others, Honegger, Milhaud, Satie
and Porter. His music drama *La Légende de Saint Christophe* is well
known to music buffs – for being performed only once.

MUSIC AND CONVIVIALITY

In the fullness of time, and in the familiar custom of the time, a husband was found for Winnaretta. Prince Louis de Scey-Montbéliard
was the first of Winnaretta's two prince-husbands. The marriage took
place in July 1887 – Winnaretta was pleased, or relieved, at least to
begin with, because the marriage released her from the suzerainty of
her mother. Her happiness – if happy she ever was – was short-lived.
It soon became clear that the prince was capable of great cruelty and
after five years of awkward dealings with the Catholic Church, in
1892 the marriage was annulled. In truth, the prince's behaviour was
not the only factor leading to annulment. Probably equally important
was the fact that Winnaretta had developed strong lesbian proclivities and was unable and unwilling to fulfil her marital obligations.

Notwithstanding all that, her marriage changed her life in that it
gave her social standing: at twenty-two, she was much more socially
acceptable as a married woman, and as a princess she was now
invited to the best-known salons of the day, including that of Lydie
Aubernon.[11]

Just then, the music salons in Paris had never been more popular
or more numerous.[12] Sylvia Kahan assures us that the prevalent view
that 'salon repertoires and performances were not "real music" or
"real concerts" does not hold up under scrutiny'. Most of the salon
recital programmes consisted of major works from the standard repertoire by major composers – Schumann, Wagner, Mozart, Beethoven
and J. S. Bach. Among nineteenth-century French composers, the
most-performed pieces were those of Saint-Saëns, Massenet, Fauré
and Ambroise Thomas, director of the Conservatoire. Moreover, the

performers who appeared in the salons were often of great renown themselves. 'Many of the greatest artists of the capital devoted a significant amount of time of their professional lives to performances in the salons; these venues were perceived as important stepping stones to greater visibility in the public sphere. Composers, too, aspired to have their pieces performed in private gatherings, as important contacts could be made. Saint-Saëns, Fauré, Debussy and Ravel were among those who came to the public's attention in part because of their participation in salon culture.'[13] Nor was it at all unknown for hostesses – or their husbands – to be the main musical attraction.

According to Kahan, composer-singer-pianist Reynaldo Hahn was doing his military service when Winnaretta first met him and he would change out of his uniform before settling down to play, often until long after midnight.[14] Hahn was a former student (and possibly a lover) of Saint-Saëns.

A handsome Venezuelan, he had arrived in France at the age of three and later became naturalised. Yet another musical child prodigy, he had made his debut at another salon, that of Princesse Mathilde, singing songs by Offenbach. He entered the Conservatoire at the age of ten, and studied under Gounod, Massenet and Saint-Saëns. Immensely talented in a wide range of activities – he was a theatre director, critic (for *Le Figaro*) and conductor besides his song-writing – in two later biographies he is described as *the* musician of the Belle Époque. Very friendly with Proust, who he met alongside Winnaretta in the salon of Madeleine Lemaire, he set to music verses by Hugo and Verlaine.[15]

FRIVOLITY AS AN END IN ITSELF

Winnaretta opened her own salon not long after her marriage, where her taste for the avant-garde showed itself immediately. What was avant-garde then would not strike us as revolutionary now. But the tunes of Debussy and the sparkling piano settings of Emmanuel Chabrier were dismissed by the (conservative) mainstream – Saint-Saëns, Massenet and Ambroise Thomas – as virtually unlistenable to. Yet, along with Fauré, Chabrier became a major figure in Winnaretta's musical circle.[16] It appealed to her that he was a friend of both Manet and Verlaine and collected paintings she liked (forty-eight impressionists were auctioned after his death). 'Short and stout', Chabrier would play entire acts of operas before dinner at Winnaretta's, singing all the parts himself.[17]

In musical terms his masterpiece is *Le Roi malgré lui*, which is typical in that Chabrier's aesthetic was to be *serious* about being light and amusing, embracing to the full the notion of frivolity as an end in itself, in some ways an idea that epitomised the Belle Époque (the *fumisteries* in café-concerts, for example). Chabrier is best known for his opera *Gwendoline*. Very influenced by Wagner, he had a day job in the Ministry of the Interior and composed in his time off. When he got to know Winnaretta he had just completed *Gwendoline*, a tragedy in which the English daughter of a Saxon king, betrothed to the leader of Viking invaders as part of a plot to kill him, falls in love with him instead and kills herself after her father slaughters the invader. A typically complex, highly wrought, highly interwoven plot, its libretto was by Catulle Mendès. Winnaretta helped Chabrier to have this work performed. It had been staged in Brussels but nowhere else, so Winnaretta arranged two performances in her salon, the second of which was performed by a chorus of twenty-four well-known soloists from the Paris Opéra. At the performance, Fauré played the harmonium and André Messager, a well-known conductor, as well as a composer, who had also written a ballet, was on percussion, together with Vincent d'Indy. The conductor that night was Gabriel Marie, a composer who specialised in works for piano and strings. Setting the seal on the event, in the audience was Tchaikovsky. So that made six composers in the salon all at once.[18]

A warm friendship emerged between Chabrier and Winnaretta and they often played duets together and, as he was much influenced by Wagner, she took him to Bayreuth, where they heard *Parsifal*, which, at that time, had scarcely been heard anywhere else. She was very upset when, at the beginning of the 1890s, Chabrier began to show symptoms of manic depression, and slumped into melancholia prior to his relatively early death in 1894.

Through Chabrier she met and formed friendships with Léo Delibes, Jules Barbey d'Aurevilly, Paul Bourget and, in the salon of Mme Aubernon, she met the Comte de Montesquiou (chapter

32). They became good friends, though they would later fall out spectacularly.

Delibes is now known mainly for three pieces of music, his opera *Lakmé*, and his ballets *Coppélia* and *Sylvia*, though there was much more to him than that. He had a very musical childhood, partly because as a boy he had an excellent singing voice, being a chorister at the Church of the Madeleine and at the Paris Opéra, where he sang at the premiere of Meyerbeer's *Le Prophète*. He was admitted to the Conservatoire at the age of twelve.

Later, he composed many comic operas for Jacques Offenbach's theatre, was chorus master at the Opéra and inspector of schools. So he had a lot to offer Winnaretta, though in the end it was his ballet music that set him apart. He never wanted to be typecast as a ballet composer but here is what no less a figure than Tchaikovsky had to say about *Sylvia*: 'The first ballet in which music constitutes not just the main, but the sole interest. What charm, what grace, what melodic rhythm and harmonic richness. I was ashamed. If I had known this music earlier, then of course I would not have written *Swan Lake*.'[19] 'Melody', 'grace', 'sparkling', 'colourful', 'wit' and 'lightness' are the words most often associated with Delibes's music, along with 'characteristically French', which sums him up.

Robert de Montesquiou was helpful when Winnaretta bought a new house at the corner of the avenue Henri-Martin and the rue Cortambert and began to rebuild it on a grand scale. A young but already renowned architect, Henri Grandpierre, was engaged to do the job and he introduced her to Paul Helleu, whose fine pen made him not only a painter but a virtuoso engraver. He agreed to collaborate on the interior decoration but only after she had bought one of his paintings. Her first commission from him created not one but two scandals because it contained portraits 'of all her closest women-friends'. Paris, Michael de Cossart says, was divided over which was the greater scandal, the identity of the women, or the fact that Helleu had agreed to destroy the plates afterwards, so Winnaretta could own a unique work of art.[20]

Montesquiou also helped her with her music. He was close to Fauré, it being his suggestion that the composer set the words of Verlaine to music, which had started a new phase in Fauré's work.

And that is how *Clair de lune* came about. After Fauré reworked it, the first performance was given at Winnaretta's salon. At the same time, Fauré was developing amorous feelings for Winnaretta. He wrote a number of quite passionate letters over the years, but it is surprising he persevered.[21]

She also formed a friendship with a fellow American expatriate, John Singer Sargent (no relation), who had studied in Paris under Carolus Duran but had left for London after the storm of protest that had greeted his '*très décolletée*' portrait of Mme Pierre Gautreau, the American-born wife of a French shipping magnate. He was a friend of Monet at Giverny, and he agreed to make a portrait of Winnaretta. This, a full-length work, was very impressive and it was during the sittings that Sargent interested her in Italian civilisation. This would eventually lead to her love affair with Venice, where she would buy a palazzo, to which she invited Fauré and where he wrote more of his settings for Verlaine's verses.

In 1891 Winnaretta began to form a new friendship with Comtesse Élisabeth Greffulhe, who hosted probably, after Mme Aubernon, the most exclusive salon in Paris at the time, if not the most intellectually distinguished. Born in 1860, making her of similar age as Winnaretta, she was very beautiful if not very rich, at least to begin with. Her father was Joseph de Caraman-Chimay, a Belgian diplomat, and her mother had been born Marie de Montesquiou, a talented pianist who had studied with Clara Schumann and played chamber music with Liszt.[22] Her parents had found a husband for her, Vicomte (later Comte) Henry Greffulhe, eleven years older than she and sole heir to a substantial fortune. The marriage was not a success, however, and, in the French way, Élisabeth soon chose to make a life of her own, helped by Robert de Montesquiou, who was her cousin.

She instituted quite a grand salon on the rue d'Astorg, where she attracted artists, writers, politicians and musicians. Always a little haughty, and always dressed in Worth or Fortuny, her salon became known for its exclusivity and inaccessibility, making an invitation very sought-after. She herself studied the relatively new speciality of photography with the caricaturist-turned-photographer Nadar.

By now, 1892, Winnaretta was beginning to be noticed for her 'increasingly avant-garde salon', and she took care to attend all the main cultural events of Paris. But then her annulment came through from the Vatican and, while it was welcome, it also posed a problem as to what she should be called: she was no longer a princess. This is when Élisabeth and Montesquiou stepped into the breach. They found for her what they believed was 'a perfect match', not least because he was in fact another prince, Edmond de Polignac. He was witty, he was artistic, with cultured tastes and he came from an old aristocratic family. Best of all, he was 'notoriously' homosexual, so he would not 'trouble' her in the bedroom.

Once they were married, a rapport of mutual respect soon developed. This is not so surprising because, although he had first been intended for the navy, Edmond had developed a passion for music, was accepted at the Conservatoire, won first prize for composition and, in an opera contest, came fifth where Bizet came seventh. 'Even Wagner sought out Edmond and told him he was impressed by some of his compositions.'[23] Edmond was nothing if not original. He invented new scales, and there is some evidence that his views about tonality and rhythm influenced Satie and Debussy.

And Edmond was just as sociable and in the swim as his new wife – he posed as a dandy for Tissot's *Balcon du cercle de la rue Royale* (1868), he was a natural friend of Montesquiou, and through Sargent he was introduced to Henry James, who in turn introduced him to Whistler, who showed him his Peacock Room.[24]

As Winnaretta's biographer puts it, they took an almost child-like pleasure in each other's company from the beginning. This was despite the fact that she had a very un-French voice. Although totally bilingual, she spoke both languages slowly, 'between her teeth'. And she still pursued any impressionist painting that came on the market. In May 1895, when Monet put up twenty canvases at Durand-Ruel's, Winnaretta carried off the rose version of his Rouen Cathedral series.[25]

In 1900–1, however, Prince Edmond began to ail. One of the last evenings he attended was a dinner organised by Proust to try to reconcile differences which the Dreyfus affair had brought about between former friends.[26] To an extent, the dinner was a success – at least it was insofar as Léon Daudet, one of the more vicious anti-Semites, actually sat next to the daughter of a Jewish banker and kept his tongue under reasonable control. But in fact the 'affair' still had some way to run before it was finally settled, and perhaps 'settled' is not the right word. Edmond died that August.[27]

Winnaretta had taken care to create a variety of projects to help her through her grief but Edmond left a bigger hole than, perhaps, she was expecting, and it took her a while to find something truly satisfying. But she eventually managed it when she reread *Walden*. Her father had instilled in her an interest in American literature, and she now conceived a plan to translate the work into French.[28] News of Winnaretta's translation began to spread among their friends but it didn't reach Proust at first and when it did their friendship took a knock. At a dinner, she happened to remark that she had just finished a translation of Henry Thoreau's major work. Proust was dismayed because he too was an enthusiastic reader of American literature and he had been planning just such a task himself. She had made her translation on and off during her travels, but it was a professional job, so much so that when she showed it to Constantin de Brancovan, editor and publisher of a new periodical, *La Renaissance latine*, he quickly offered to publish it.[29] The first instalment of her translation appeared in December 1903 and another the following month, being well received and sparking a lively interest in Thoreau's approach to life in such French authors as André Gide.

THE FASHION FOR LESBIANISM

In any sexual history of the modern world, the years around the turn of the twentieth century stand out as a curiosity. In 1902, not so long after Oscar Wilde's release from prison in 1897 and his death in 1900, Europe was rocked by the arrest of Baron Jacques d'Adelswärd-Fersen for, as Michael de Cossart puts it, 'taking too much interest in schoolboys from the Lycée Condorcet'. A few years later, in 1907, the Kaiser's favourite *Fürst*, Philipp zu Eulenburg, and his friend, no less a personage than General von Moltke, adjutant to the Kaiser and commander of Berlin, survived criminal prosecution for homosexual activity though in both cases their careers were ruined.

Again as Cossart put it: 'Throughout Europe the homosexual fraternity received a shock to its system.'[30]

Strangely, though, and this is why these years were so odd, lesbianism appeared untouched by these events. In fact, it is not untrue to
say that lesbianism 'became almost fashionable' across all elements
of society.[31] This was when Colette abandoned her unfortunate
husband Willy, whom she had anonymously supported for years,
and appeared in public, and on stage, with 'Missy', the Marquise
de Belbeuf.[32] Colette openly wore a bracelet which read: 'I belong
to Missy.' And it was in this wider, more general atmosphere that
Winnaretta met another intimidating lesbian.

Ethel Smyth was British and a composer. Born in 1858, her
most important composition until that point was her Mass in D,
performed in the Albert Hall in 1893. But that and her other compositions enjoyed success and were heard in Dresden, Covent Garden
and the Metropolitan Opera in New York.

The two women hit it off from the start. Winnaretta liked the
fact that Ethel was very friendly with Bruno Walter, the conductor,
pianist and composer. Winnaretta and Ethel soon became lovers,
but they were both too intense, too much alike – too wilful and
controlling – for a relationship to be sustained. In any case, no
sooner had the relationship with Ethel come about than Winnaretta
conceived another passion, this time for Baroness Adolph de Meyer.
Born Olga Alberta Caracciolo, and reputed to be the illegitimate
daughter of Edward VII, she had her own salon in London, and it
was with Olga that Winnaretta had her first real relationship since
Edmond's death.[33]

Not that she was cut out to be faithful even now. While still
seeing Olga, she struck up another new relationship with another
foreign woman she actually met in Olga's salon. This was a young
American painter named Romaine Brooks. Then there were two
young American poets, Natalie Clifford Barney and Renée Vivien,
who settled in Paris in the early 1900s. Renée died in 1909 after
a life of extremes, not least in terms of the amount of alcohol she
consumed, but Natalie lived on for another six decades, occupying
her *temple de l'amitié* on the rue Jacob, at one stage with Anna de
Noailles. Gertrude Stein arrived later in the decade and would soon

be surrounded by creative artists and aristocratic lesbians in more or less equal numbers.

Winnaretta stood out among this group by not standing out, though she was known from time to time to have shared the role of 'High Priestess of Lesbos' in Paris.[34] Despite what Michael de Cossart calls her 'grim discretion', many people in Paris realised that Winnaretta 'hovered on the sado-masochistic fringes of the Lesbian world'. In the *romans-à-clef* of the time – and as ever, since Mme de Scudéry invented the genre, there was no shortage of them – she was depicted, in fictional form, as dressing in masculine attire and whipping a girlfriend. In real life, there was rather more drama. At one point she had a passionate affair with a younger married woman, who was unable to cope with the emotional intensity and committed suicide. Mortified, Winnaretta took herself off to the countryside, and tried to kill herself. Her friends were astonished at her uncharacteristic loss of self-control.[35]

She was still close to Fauré and Debussy, who still played their latest compositions in her salon, and she also helped introduce the music of Reynaldo Hahn to the public, in particular his musical settings of poems by Verlaine and Robert Louis Stevenson, in which Reynaldo was often both singer and pianist. She had patched things up with Proust and it was about now that he attended a musical salon that he would describe so well in his great book.

Between, roughly, 1906 and 1914 the lineaments of what would come to be called modernism appeared.[36] Artists from everywhere were attracted to Paris, Vienna and London, more or less in that order. In Paris André Gide founded the *Nouvelle Revue française*, a new periodical featuring such writers as Paul Valéry and Guillaume Apollinaire. Ravel and Satie, now mature, produced their most innovative sounds. After 1907, the century's newest medium – film, a French invention by the Lumière brothers – became more widely established as the Pathés, another set of French brothers, and the industrialist Léon Gaumont started to erect cinemas all around Paris. Another arrival was Jean Cocteau.

The 'gadfly' Cocteau graduated from the Lycée Condorcet (the most prominent after Louis-le-Grand) to make his mark on everything from painting to literature to opera. Much as Proust had done a decade or so earlier, Cocteau grasped that an introduction into the prestigious salons, 'where the hostess was always on the look-out for the next young "genius", would help smooth the path toward artistic renown'. He managed to contrive his first luncheon invitation in 1908. His entrance was carefully stage-managed, with him declaring that 'he had just come by foot from the Luxembourg gardens where he had awaited spring, with whom he had a rendez-vous'. He then 'executed a glissando across the polished floor'.[37]

Despite his range of talents, he was almost outshone by Anna de Noailles, who frightened him, he said, because – as he soon found out – her facility with words was greater even than his own. He noticed that she was surrounded by women 'longing to hear her', and it didn't escape him either that even the servants hid near the doors to hear her speak. He too was carried away.

Anna Elisabeth de Brancovan, as she was born, had an almost unrivalled romantic background, her parents being an amalgam of Romanian and Greek aristocracy. Her mother was brought up in Istanbul and London, and was the dedicatee of several works by Ignacy Paderewski, the Polish composer. Anna herself was (well) educated at home, becoming fluent in English and German as well as French. The family spent their winters in Paris and their summers at an estate near Évian on the south shore of Lake Geneva. When she married Comte Mathieu de Noailles in 1897, at the age of twenty-one, they became one of the most fashionable couples of the Belle Époque.

Very beautiful, in a dark, gypsy sort of way, thanks to her Romanian background, she was painted by Ignacio Zuloaga, Kees van Dongen, Jacques-Émile Blanche, Jean-Louis Forain and Philip de László, and sculpted by Rodin. Although she published three novels, she was best known – and most admired – for her poetry, which was rooted in the loss of her father at the age of ten. In the midst of her grief, she had discovered Victor Hugo's Les Contemplations, written in 1856 and dedicated to his drowned daughter, Léopoldine. In this work Anna discovered a language that enabled her to express her-self and overcome her feelings through art. This led, in time, to her first collection of poems, Le Cœur innombrable ('The Innumerable Heart', 1901), which was a great success, followed by several other collections of which *Les Éblouissements* ('Dazzling') had the greatest impact.

In 1903 she had begun a long and 'tormented' friendship with Maurice Barrès which lasted until his death in 1923. However, from 1911 on she hardly left her home, suffering from health problems that required her to receive her friends at her bedside. Besides Barrès, Cocteau and Winnaretta, those friends included Colette, Frédéric Mistral, Rainer Maria Rilke, Paul Valéry, Pierre Loti and Max Jacob. After the First World War her genius was recognised when she became the first woman to receive the high rank of commander of the Légion d'honneur and the Grand Prix de littérature from the Académie française. Never quite getting over her obsession with death, her last collection of poems, published in 1927, bore the title *L'Honneur de souffrir*, 'The Honour of Suffering'.[38]

DIAGHILEV'S MUSE

Amid these 'Banquet Years', to use Roger Shattuck's phrase, there arrived a charismatic young Russian who would provide Winnaretta with one of her crowning achievements. No less than Cocteau, Serge Diaghilev became a frequent guest in her salon, but unlike Cocteau he was interested in more than conversation because her evenings were the crossroads of French musical life. Degas had once remarked that at Winnaretta's, talent was welcomed without a tailcoat, but Diaghilev was an inveterate snob, and went to her salon to meet potential backers.

And so it was that, at her salon on 4 June 1908, the subject of a full season of Russian ballet and opera was first mooted. The French impresario Gabriel Astruc, already famous for taking calculated risks and launching Artur Rubinstein, Wanda Landowska and even Mata Hari, mentioned Diaghilev's idea to the Grand Duchess Vladimir, the morganatic wife of Tsar Nicholas II's great-uncle. She approved and they set about raising 250,000 francs. The list of possible backers included the Comtesse de Chevigné, the Marquise de Ganay, the Comtesse de Castellane, and Misia Edwards, soon to be the wife of José Maria Sert.

The following May Diaghilev produced a programme with a list of names from the Mariinsky theatre in St Petersburg that were then unknown but would not remain so for long. The story of Diaghilev and the Ballets Russes, and their transformative effect on artistic modernism, rates as one of the most colourful and dramatic episodes in French – European – cultural history. Winnaretta's role in this chapter of events can hardly be exaggerated. Serge Lifar, the dancer and choreographer, and pupil of Bronislava Nijinska, who was to write the first biography of Diaghilev shortly after his death, confirmed that Winnaretta was 'nothing less than Diaghilev's muse'.[39]

The first night, 19 May 1909, showed the splendid vision that Diaghilev sought. The boxes and the balconies of the théâtre du Châtelet had been swamped in crimson velvet, setting off Alexandre Benois's exotic scenery and costumes, and the brilliant dancing of the company, which in total comprised no fewer than 250.[40] That night the production included *Le Pavillon d'Armide*, inspired by a Théophile Gautier story, the Polovtsian Dances from Borodin's *Prince Igor*, and the one-act ballet *Les Sylphides*. The dancing of Tamara Karsavina and Vaslav Nijinsky, the latter making his Paris debut, set audiences alight. Anna de Noailles was there and would later report: 'I didn't quite believe in the revelation I had been promised by certain initiates; but right away I understood that I was witnessing a miracle.'[41]

Winnaretta was fascinated by Diaghilev and this fascination would lead to their greatest collaboration. But before that, and in the meantime, her private life was stabilising. Her ardour for Romaine Brooks had cooled and Romaine, for her part, had found her own stability with Ida Rubinstein and Natalie Clifford Barney. Winnaretta turned to Olga de Meyer. Her personal life was still more or less discreet, far more so than that of her brother, whose passionate affair with Isadora Duncan was the talk of Paris.

But it was her relationship with Diaghilev – and later, through him, Stravinsky – that really shows her in full-throttle mode. Nor should it be overlooked that, to an extent, Diaghilev repaid the compliment by staging works by her friends – Hahn's *Le Dieu bleu*, a ballet based on a libretto by Cocteau, Ravel's *Daphnis et Chloë* and a creation by Nijinsky set to Debussy's *Prélude à l'après-midi d'un faune*. Without Winnaretta it is very doubtful these works would have been staged as they were.

She formed a firm friendship with Stravinsky and they met in Rome more than once, when he was working on the follow-up to *Le Sacre du printemps (The Rite of Spring)*, and what Diaghilev wanted to be 'the first Russian' ballet (because until then Russian choreography had used mainly French and Italian practices). This was *The Firebird*, which Stravinsky wrote in six months and which, when premiered on 25 June 1910, created another sensation, in many people's eyes being Diaghilev's most successful achievement of the 'total work of art', a brilliant integration of music, dance and visual elements.

Sylvia Kahan says that through her friendship with Stravinsky, Winnaretta was brought into the midst of Diaghilev's coterie, and it was there that she met Mrs Alfred Edwards, née Misia Godebska, a young woman of Polish descent, who had first been married to Thadée Natanson, editor of the arts periodical the *Revue blanche*, to which Proust, Félix Fénéon, Léon Blum and Octave Mirbeau were contributors, and which had stood up for Dreyfus during the 'affair'. Misia had divorced Natanson to marry Edwards, the wealthy owner of the daily *Le Matin*. She later left him and started living with the Spanish painter José Maria Sert, who she would eventually marry. Misia was painted even more times by prominent artists than was Anna de Noailles – Vuillard, Bonnard, Toulouse-Lautrec, Renoir and Redon. Winnaretta liked Sert, who specialised in murals, and she asked him to show some of his work in her atelier.

But of course all these welcome developments were overshadowed by the first performance, on 29 May 1913, of Igor Stravinsky's ballet *The Rite of Spring*, where Nijinsky's 'coarse-grained' choreography caused a riot so bad that the dancers were forced to stop and the orchestra was reduced to silence. Winnaretta was at the first night and was gratified to see that, by the end of the season, the performances gradually won approval.[42]

She was still fond of Fauré and attended the Paris premiere of his first full-length opera, *Pénélope*. The opera helped establish the new théâtre des Champs-Élysées.

Winnaretta, while not blind to politics and political developments, never saw them as central to her concerns or passions. But with the approach of the First World War, she could not keep completely on the sidelines. In spring 1912, Christabel Pankhurst fled from England to Paris and for the next two years, under the name of Amy Richards, she held court in a flat she occupied in the avenue de la Grande Armée. She was a good friend of Ethel Smyth, who, of course, introduced her to Winnaretta, and through her Pankhurst met many women interested in the suffragette cause.[43]

As the world descended into chaos, Winnaretta gave ever more lavish soirées, but nothing could hide the fact that many of the habitués in her salon could only talk politics – what Austria was doing, where Bulgaria stood, how Germany was reacting, where lay the sympathies of the various grand European families whose members mingled in her rooms.

She did her best to keep up the old, familiar, reassuring rhythm of life. At Christmas 1913 she went to Venice with old friends who included Henri de Régnier, Paul Bourget and Princesse Ruspoli, where they ate 'two enormous plum puddings'. During the visit Bourget and Régnier stood at a window of the Palazzo Polignac watching the dawn come up. Régnier remarked on the smooth red-coloured waters of the canals and turned to Bourget: 'One must clasp these moments to the heart . . . and plant a forest of memories. Disillusionment will never be able to penetrate it.'[44]

When war was declared, Winnaretta was staying with friends in Surrey. Like many others, she didn't grasp at first the disillusionment that would engulf all of Europe.

PART EIGHT

'Life Is What We Win'

Miracle, Mutiny, Mourning, *Mondains*

In early August 1914, only days after the First World War began, André Gide hurried back to Paris by the last available civilian train, when he heard one of the railwaymen call out, 'All aboard for Berlin!' This put him in good spirits. Three days on, he wrote, 'the wonderful behaviour of the Government, of everyone, and of all France ... leaves room for every hope. One foresees the beginning of a new era: the United States of Europe bound by a treaty limiting their armaments.' Limiting their armaments? Little did he foresee what everyone else failed to foresee.

For most Frenchmen the *sine qua non* of such a hopeful future was of course the return of Alsace-Lorraine. The provinces were never as bellicose as the capital, or Proust as Gide. Proust was disqualified from fighting because of his chronic asthma and he was more concerned to find a publisher for *À la recherche du temps perdu*.[1] Among those to join the fighting at the first chance were several members of the Dreyfus family, in particular Alfred's son, Pierre, who fought in the early skirmishes as a corporal, then – through Verdun, and with fifty-four days on the Somme, where he was gassed – he was promoted five times, ending the war as a captain with a hero's Croix de guerre and Palm. Alfred himself was eventually allowed to take part – despite being too old (he was fifty-five) – and performed as a gunner in the catastrophic Nivelle offensive of 1917, when a plan to break through the German lines, with an anticipated loss of 13,000 men, turned into a rout with 128,000 casualties.[2]

When Gide had heard the raucous cries 'To Berlin', whether he knew it or not, it was an echo of similar cries forty-four years previously and, had he known it, the underlying situation was just as dire. At one level, morale in the French army was high – it had recovered from the humiliation of Sedan and the Dreyfus affair very well. (On mobilisation the rate of defection had been anticipated to be 13 per cent, but in fact was less than 1.5 per cent.) Underneath that, however, the more prosaic truth was that, in August 1914, the French army possessed but 300 heavy guns, whereas the Germans had 3,500.[3] The outdated fashion of French thinking was exemplified by the way they went to war in bright red and blue uniforms, despising the Germans for their *feldgrau*, field grey. In the early fighting the French showed supreme courage, but the German artillery laid waste to vast numbers, so that the killing fields were covered in red and blue uniforms and dead horses.

In the first appalling weeks of August it seemed as if the Schlieffen plan could not fail to succeed. The stables of Chantilly (35 miles from Paris) had been breached by German outriders.[4] But then French intelligence captured a haversack taken from the corpse of a well-placed German cavalry officer which contained a bloodstained map disclosing the lines of advance – south-eastwards, in other words away from the capital. General Joseph Joffre, commander-in-chief of the French forces on the Western Front, had anticipated having to sacrifice Paris but he now grasped that the Germans were not headed there but were wheeling behind the French forces in the east, in the hope of trapping them up against the border with Switzerland. This meant, as Joffre realised, a fight on the Marne. Which is exactly what happened with the incredible help of 600 red taxis ferrying soldiers across the intervening countryside, each carrying five soldiers, twice a day.

The resulting 'Miracle of the Marne' was a much-needed psychological victory. It may, in fact, have been *the* decisive victory, because many historians, then and later, came to feel that Germany lost the initiative – and the war – on the Marne. But it was not conceded more generally for decades and it is not hard to see why. France had lost 300,000 men, wounded and missing, and no fewer than 4,778 officers, a tenth of its officer strength. Because of the efficiency of French censors, however, these devastating figures were not released for years. At least, that is what we are told, but there was and is no hiding the fact that France had lost Lille, Valenciennes, Arras, Amiens, Cambrai, Laon, Soissons and even Reims – some 12 per cent of its territory, more than 16 per cent of manufacturing and 20 per cent of its wheat. And of course it had not regained Alsace-Lorraine.[5]

The most important thing, however, was that, for now, the country was saved, the government could return again to Paris, and another of France's great recoveries was under way – for a time. Jean Cocteau was able to write, without fear of contradiction: 'France equalled Civilisation! Germany, Barbarism.'[6]

As the world now knows, the carnage of the First World War was unprecedented. The Battle of Verdun, which followed fifteen months after the Marne, was in some ways very different. Like the earlier engagement it was a victory – but it didn't feel like it, either then or even on reflection. This is what Churchill meant when he called the victory 'ambiguous'.

The Germans struck first, on 21 February 1916, not initially to capture Verdun but to 'bleed white' the French army by forcing it to fight to the death for its linchpin. The French were surprised and unprepared and were to suffer 400,000 casualties across a 15-mile front, the Germans very nearly as many. General Philippe Pétain would be brought in as a saviour but the fighting lasted ten months, making it the longest battle in history as well as the worst to that point. It was a major mistake of the Germans and an incredible victory for the French but culturally – and this is what mattered in the long run – it scarcely felt like it.

Its negative effects were two-fold. In the first place, there was the sheer scale of the losses and its effect on morale. The extent of those losses became known in Paris and, despite censorship, a serious malaise developed about the psychological state of the army. Some in the ranks began singing revolutionary songs from Russia, others beat up the military police and uncoupled engines to prevent trains leaving for the front. Officers who tried to intervene were attacked, mutinies broke out and, on 3 May, less than three months into the battle, the 21st Division, which had endured some of the worst losses on the Marne, refused to fight. The most senior offenders were shot or sent into exile. 'But unit after unit followed the 21st and over 20,000 men deserted ... By June the mutinies had spread to half the French Army; at one point there was not a single reliable division standing between the Germans at Soissons and Paris.'[7]

The full details of these mutinies have hardly ever been fully released, although André Loez, in his book on '*les refus de la guerre*' provides a table of mutinies showing they peaked in early June 1917 and a map which shows they stretched from Soissons to Nancy and beyond, nearly 200 miles. He concluded that the mutinies were as much due to the inequalities that existed within the French army as to the exigencies of war itself.[8]

Worse, back in Paris there were rumours of profiteering, espionage, treason and defeatism, turning the nation against itself.[9]

The second aspect of Verdun that interests us is its effect on French thinking, because during the fighting one of the Frenchmen captured was an officer by the name of Charles de Gaulle. He had arrived there with his regiment on 25 February, four days after the Germans had unleashed 'the most intensive bombardment in the history of warfare'.[10] On 1 March his regiment was ordered to relieve another in the village of Douaumont, but he was sent on ahead to reconnoitre the position his regiment was intended for. Here he identified a dangerous gap in the defences between his regiment's new location and the next, to the right.

At dawn the following day, just as the regiment was settling into its trenches, the Germans attacked, from the front and through the gap de Gaulle had identified. By the end of the day, his company had been all but wiped out. He himself was believed to have been killed and Pétain signed a posthumous citation commending him for bravery in the field. A few days later, it became clear that he wasn't dead. He was a prisoner of war for thirty-two months in six separate camps, but mostly in a fortress near Ingolstadt in Bavaria.[11] De Gaulle tried to escape five times. On one occasion, he took picric acid, which mimics the symptoms of acute hepatitis, and this brought about his transfer to the sanatorium, from where he managed to flee, covering roughly 80 miles towards the Swiss border before he was apprehended. At 6 foot 5, he was hard to disguise.

Apart from the solitary confinement imposed after his escape attempts, he did not have a hard time of it, sharing quarters with five others and receiving food parcels from home. He was able to exercise and took care, as he later wrote, 'to dominate oneself perpetually ... The advantage of being a brilliant conversationalist is not worth anything compared to the capacity to retreat into oneself ...'[12] In his letters home to his mother, he returned again and again to the 'inexpressible sadness' caused by the humiliation of capture and refused her request for a photograph because he did not wish anyone to see him as a prisoner.

But he did use the prison library to embark on a wide range of reading – Wagner, Rodin, Heraclitus, Tocqueville, Bergson, Zola, Stendhal, Flaubert. Julian Jackson, in his recent biography of de Gaulle, says he comes across 'as an earnest and well-read but also rather conventional and priggish young man'. Jackson found that the lectures de Gaulle gave while a prisoner offer a better perspective about his views on military life and life in general, in particular using the insights of Bergson and Émile Boutroux, who he felt had given new life to the spiritual side of French thought. Boutroux (1845–1921) and Bergson (1859–1941) were both still very much alive and both were widely read philosophers who attacked the positivist view of the world that all phenomena could be explained by determinism and rationalism. Boutroux in particular stressed the importance of contingency and indeterminacy.[13] In his lectures, de Gaulle linked Boutroux to Pascal and what Pascal called 'judgement', 'that is to say the importance of the heart and soul in thinking about the world'. And he went on to say that military leaders – and by implication other leaders as well – should have 'minds capable of synthesising, that is to say the ability to generalise, capable of distinguishing the essential from what is accessory'.[14]

But there was always the unavoidable fact of his capture and his 'indescribable regret at not having played a greater role. I think that for the rest of my life – whether it be long or short – that regret will not leave me.'[15]

THE SUBORDINATION OF SCIENCE TO LITERATURE: THE CLASSICAL REVIVAL

De Gaulle was by no means alone in France in his scepticism of positivism.[16] In 1901, Jacques Maritain, the son of Paul Maritain, a prominent Parisian lawyer, and Geneviève Favre, daughter of the French statesman Jules Favre (a leader of the Republicans in the National Assembly of the Third Republic in 1870), met Raïssa Oumansoff, a fellow student at the Sorbonne and the daughter of Russian Jewish immigrants. The couple fell in love but to begin with their relationship was dominated by what they both felt was a 'spiritual aridity' in French intellectual life. Their professors at the renowned institution, many of them scholars of great distinction, had – to an extent – been responsible for the crisis because they were wedded to relativism and scepticism, convinced that only the physical sciences could provide insights into reality, which, in the manner of positivism, must always be 'tentative' and 'provisional'. 'Beyond what the scientists could unearth, there lay only the impenetrable void.'[17]

This did not satisfy the nineteen-year-old Jacques one bit, or Raïssa, a year his junior, and, one day in the Jardin des plantes, the young couple concluded the type of pact that only young couples enter into – a suicide pact – in which they vowed to kill themselves unless, before the year was out, they could find 'some answer to the apparent meaninglessness of life'. As it happened, at the suggestion of one of Jacques's friends – the poet and religious thinker Charles Péguy – the couple were exposed to the lectures of Henri Bergson at the Collège de France. Bergson was at the time lecturing on his theory of 'creative evolution'. In this theory he gave a prime role to spiritualism and 'vitalist intuitionism', which, he said, endowed man with the free will to 'intuit' basic reality; he disparaged intelligence; and, among other things, and despite the fact that Bergson was himself Jewish, he offered support for Christian mysticism in defence of the philosophy and theology of the Catholic faith. All thoughts of suicide were forgotten and Jacques and Raïssa went on to have distinguished careers, in which they explored what they termed 'intellectual spirituality', which they felt was most clearly exemplified by a study of Christian saints, in particular St Thomas Aquinas, whose life and work the couple studied at Heidelberg.

DEGREES OF KNOWLEDGE

In particular, in the theory's most developed form, Maritain maintained that there are 'degrees of knowledge'. He accepted that modern physical science is one of the major conquests of the human spirit but argued that the physical sciences are not the only valid forms of knowledge – other forms of 'authentic knowledge', as he put it, include metaphysical philosophy, supernatural theology and, 'in some respects the most precious of all', mystical knowledge. Freedom, natural rights, social justice and the cultivation of the fine arts are to be encouraged and promoted, he said, as ends in themselves, not means for achieving after-life bliss. But they were not the absolutely final ends of human life. 'Too many of the "moderns" had turned proximate ends into ultimate ends.'

This path would take Jacques and Raïssa Maritain through much of the twentieth century (she died in 1960, he in 1973), and to world-wide acclaim among the religious, and helped fuel a French scepticism towards science that extended throughout the twentieth century. But their arguments were especially relevant during the dark years of the First World War where, in France, there was yet another return to the old battle of the ancients versus the moderns, only this time with much greater bitterness and importance to the divide.

The ever-present background to this dispute was the nature of the crushing defeat France suffered in the 1870–1 war at the hands of the Prussians, together with the highly technical nature of the war in the eastern borders of France in the 1914–18 conflict. Both Ernest Renan and Louis Pasteur argued that Prussia's advantage on the battlefield was grounded in the education offered in its classrooms, in particular the instruction offered in the sciences. As the latter put it: 'For more than fifty years, while the French had absorbed themselves in searches for the perfect political system, the Prussians had invested heavily in scientific education and its coordination with industry.' Furthermore, as Martha Hanna outlines the picture, in her book *The Mobilization of Intellect*, the great prestige of nineteenth-century French education derived from the 'disinterested, distinctly nonutilitarian character' of its classical culture, so that anything that smacked of 'vocationalism' was abhorrent to those who considered themselves caretakers of

France's great tradition, a tradition that insisted on the subordination of both science and history to literature.[18]

Reforms to the curriculum, to make it more modern, introducing more science, mathematics and modern languages, had been pushed through in 1902, but even before that opposition had shown itself. In 1895, Ferdinand Brunetière, writing in the *Revue des deux mondes*, after a visit to the Vatican, railed against the 'bankruptcy of the sciences' and challenged the belief that 'everything true could be discovered by reason and catalogued by science'. Empiricism alone, he insisted, was not an 'adequate epistemological foundation' for understanding humanity. He was by no means alone in his view, and in the background, of course, and adding to the urgency of the situation, were the fears that France in particular was decadent, that being one reason for the disaster of 1870-1. This being France, the predicament was politicised. Action française – the extreme right-wing and monarchical movement – took up the 'anti-science' assault by arguing that the analogy between science and democracy – that it was open and transparent, and moved ahead by calm and reflective agreement – was false also.

Whereas the modernisers wanted to get rid of the classical tradition in French education, the Ligue pour la culture française, formed in May 1911, was established specifically to 'defend the study of the classics compromised by the most recent reforms in secondary education', stressing that a 'compulsory classical education' provided the best foundation for future scholarship *'in all disciplines'*. (Italics added.) The Ligue called upon parliament to reinstate 'a unified, single curriculum that would require instruction in Latin and Greek throughout the first six years of a [seven-year] lycée education'.[19]

THINKING UNDER FIRE

At this distance, there is something unreal about the debate. With tanks and aircraft being used in warfare for the first time in the First World War, with new forms of explosives, poisonous gases and guns of unprecedented power and range, it was more than ever obvious that scientific precision and industrial organisation were of profound importance. Yet the dispute was also typically French. One anonymous author, writing as 'Brutus' in *La Grande Revue* in early 1915, argued that only by reinforcing the efforts of the combatant army 'with the reflections of reason could the French intelligentsia remain true to itself and to an honourable French tradition, dating from the Revolution, of "thinking under fire"'.[20] While the troops at the front were protecting 'eternal France', he said, non-combatants needed to keep that eternal France alive by continuing its intellectual life as far as possible uninterrupted. Jacques Maritain himself quickly joined in. Now in his mid-to-late thirties, and much more accomplished, he was one of many scholars who gave lectures for public benefit, in which he argued that German philosophy was in fact responsible for German militarism.

This debate was exacerbated by the publication, on 13 October 1914, ten weeks or so into the war, of 'An Appeal to the Civilised World'. Intended for distribution to neutral audiences, this was a statement by ninety-three of Germany's most distinguished men of letters and science (Gerhart Hauptmann, Max Liebermann, Fritz Haber, Max Planck, Max Reinhardt, Wilhelm Röntgen) in defence of German *Kultur*. The French responded quickly and, as it were, with all guns blazing, in particular countering the German claims that its soldiers had committed no atrocities. In his presidential address to the Institut de France, delivered two weeks later on 26 October, Paul Appell, the mathematician, argued that the war had brought into play 'two opposing conceptions' of human civilisation.[21] Appell said – and this is something Bergson agreed with – that Germany embodied 'impeccable organisation, lengthy, systematic detailed preparation ... and the practical application of the most recent scientific discoveries'. But beyond its material organisation was a disturbing truth: Germany appeared to hold that 'Force, when organised and disciplined to perfection, creates Right, and is superior to all else: to the Truth, to treaties, to oral commitments, to the idea of fraternal freedom, and to respect for Humanity and its works'. Bergson put it more pithily, describing the German approach as 'scientific barbarism'.[22]

Intellectually, for the French in the context of war, there were three things to be settled during the course of hostilities. One, was there anything of the German cultural tradition which remained worthy of respect, for example the thought of Kant? Two, was France truly special in being both 'the eldest daughter of the church' *and* the modern heir of Greece and Rome, as she had always maintained? Three, to what extent was science a product of German *Kultur* or was it more rooted in the philosophical traditions of France and Great Britain?[23]

These debates might seem typically French in being overly intellectual and abstract but in fact in the dark war years, when discipline, obedience and self-abnegation became civic virtues essential to the nation's survival, as Martha Hanna puts it, the French warmed to the regulated moral and aesthetic order of classicism. She shows that, surprisingly, in art, theatre and public oratory there was a marked classicist revival in France. 'The cultural and political principles of Greece and Rome – rationalism, the rule of law, and the autonomy of the individual – were, in this view, the classical precursors of liberty, progress and international peace. Greece had bequeathed to France a legacy of individual liberty predicated on the essential rationality of all individuals; Rome had taught reverence for the rule of law and republicanism; and Christianity, the final element in the French classical equation, preached universal brotherhood. When combined, the Graeco-Roman and Christian traditions gave rise to the famous fundamental principles of French republicanism: Liberty, Equality, and Fraternity.'[24]

The revival was evident. For example, Corneille, 'almost ignored in peacetime, came to dominate the Parisian stage'. Moreover, there was a 'compatibility' between classicism and the 'culture of bereavement'. Classicism revived, Hanna says, because it offered the French a positive cultural paradigm, 'through which they could come to terms with their suffering and not be overwhelmed by it'.[25] It allowed them to transcend private bereavement by drawing inspiration from their dead.

The classical tradition also enjoyed a comeback in the schools of France and parents urged their sons to opt for classical education. In contrast, modernists denigrated classical culture as elitist, archaic and insufficiently practical, concerned only with the disinterested pursuit of *culture générale* and failing to teach practical skills necessary to the modern world.[26] Classics, Hanna says in a striking phrase, were suited to a nation in mourning, and this was, to an extent, underlined by the Académie française, which restricted almost all its literary awards to front-line troops, meaning that most of those awards were bestowed posthumously.[27]

PEDAGOGY OF DEFEAT

At that time, it was customary for the permanent secretary of the Académie to report the results of literary competitions at a public meeting scheduled for the end of each year. The secretary just then was Étienne Lamy, a political historian originally from the Jura. He thought that the war had saved France from the moral and social disorder of the prewar era, that there had been a return to the seventeenth-century spirit of classicism – orderly and obedient, disciplined and dutiful, which in the nineteenth century had succumbed to the allure of individualism. In December 1915 the Académie awarded prizes to seventy-eight writers and scholars killed in the first years of the war, and Lamy addressed the literary merits of each one. These, he reminded his countrymen, had helped eradicate a divide that for generations had separated '*la France de la pensée*' from '*la France du courage*'. 'Only when men of intellect imitated their classical forebears and fought side-by-side with career soldiers was France able to transcend this artificial and debilitating division.'[28]

Lamy was joined by René Doumic, a historian of literature, who also advocated that France 'return home' to its classical education. His major essay was actually entitled 'Retour à la culture française', in which he specifically argued that a classical education should not ignore history or the sciences but that the study of both should be subordinate to that of literature. The pursuit of science, he said, had 'contaminated' French education. And he went further, arguing that the modernisation of French education after 1870 was part of a 'pedagogy of defeat' and that it was 'no longer appropriate to perpetuate the domination of the enemy in the school curriculum'. All vestiges of German influence should be repealed, he said.[29] The nation could only survive if it could return to classical culture, in which Latin was indispensable. Others argued that one could not be fully fluent in French without a grounding in Latin.

In like vein, in February 1915 the Faculty of Letters at the Sorbonne held an assembly to celebrate Latin culture, with 3,000 in attendance including guests from independent countries, in which the message was that all these people were direct descendants of Greece and Rome, and French philosophy was presented as more universal than merely French, the argument being that true philosophy could not be French or German, but that it was available to anyone 'endowed with reason'.[30] The composer Vincent d'Indy lectured to the effect that French culture was little more than Latin culture 'that honoured clarity, logic and balance', that Molière and Racine, Descartes and the architectural splendours of Versailles and Jesuit pedagogy were classical accomplishments that suggested France should seek to recapture the spirit of the seventeenth century.[31] At the Collège de France, Bergson actually went so far as to question the utility of science, suggesting it provided little 'that was essential to the war effort'. He maintained that the war would be won through the 'moral superiority' of the French army, that the quality of its materiel was of 'secondary importance'.[32]

The Academy of Sciences, on the other hand, affirmed that science was really a French and British idea, but unacknowledged as such, and implied that the Germans had in fact 'stolen' the basic conception without due acknowledgment. What separated out French science was the spirit of 'finesse', by which was meant a cross between imagination and intuition, in contrast to the 'dead hand' of German rational thoroughness. Maritain even said that relativity theory lacked a fundamental 'Pascalian finesse'.[33]

Underneath all this, of course, was a feeling in France that the nation had lost its edge after 1870. This helps explain the publication of an anthology of essays proclaiming the vitality of France's accomplishments, published in 1916 under the title *Un demi-siècle de civilisation française 1870–1915* (Poincaré, Widor and Doumic being among the compilers), in which it was claimed that France had quietly made more progress, and more discoveries, 'than any other country in the same period'.[34]

The overall effect of these arguments and surveys, says Martha Hanna, was to 'bestow' on France during the war years an unprecedented authority in the cause of 'cultural conservatism', leading to the emergence of an 'intellectual nationalism'.[35] This intellectual nationalism was part of the background that would cause Georges Clemenceau to drive such a hard bargain at the Versailles Conference after the First World War armistice, where it was also argued, improbably, by certain French intellectuals, such as Maurice Barrès, that the successful amalgamation by the Germans of their science and industry was really no more than an idea of French origin, that 'Descartes, Colbert, and Bonaparte had all advocated the development in France of a closer association between science and industry'. Therefore, 'the secret of German power', argued Barrès in 1920, '[was] nothing other than the ancient secret of French grandeur'.[36]

Intellectual nationalism proved to be a double-edged sword. After the war, says Hanna, French scientists, convinced of the intellectual superiority of French scholarship, 'isolated themselves from other nations, failed to keep pace with new developments, and took comfort in past accomplishments. Professor Maurice Caullery of the University of Paris conceded as much in 1933 in a speech to an American audience on the importance of French contributions to science. As the war essayists had done, he insisted that "France had played one of the most important parts in the building up of modern science as a whole". But he acknowledged that French science had excelled in fundamental abstract discovery, rather than patient, concrete application.'[37]

THE DISTINCTIVE INTELLECTUAL CLIMATE OF THE LATIN QUARTER

That reference to abstract discovery also brings into view the work of the Chicago sociologist Terry Nichols Clark, who makes a number of astute observations about French – and especially Parisian – intellectual life, and how it differs from that elsewhere.[38] This difference, as we have just seen, was especially marked during the First World War and the years immediately beforehand.

Clark makes in essence three main points. One is that the Latin Quarter of Paris – the Left Bank, where the Sorbonne, the Institut de France and the Collège de France are located, where the main cafés are situated, and where many of the salons were to be found – produced a distinctive 'Latin Quarter intellectual climate', a sort of 'cloister' that dominated cultural life, and one that could be at times quite 'faddish'. He says that there were two main configurations of thought in the Latin Quarter throughout the nineteenth century and into the twentieth – to which he gives the names 'cartesianism' and 'spontaneity'. Both, he says, were deeply rooted in French culture and each generated a reaction against the other.

'Cartesianism was identified with order, hierarchy, authority and the bureaucratic institutions exemplifying the *esprit de géométrie*: the state, the military, and the university. Laying claim to the Enlightenment heritage, seeking to realise the ideal of *raison*, the bourgeoisie was the social group most identified with cartesianism.' Spontaneity, on the other hand, which celebrated a glorification of personal invention and romantic subjectivism, was to be found in the highest social strata. 'From the prowess of medieval battle, to the romance of courtly love, to the indulgences of the salons ran a tradition which sneered at the cartesianism of the bourgeoisie ... The romantic nationalism of a Chateaubriand, by the end of the nineteenth century, could merge with the anarchistic tendencies of students in street fights of the Action Française ... these antagonisms between cartesianism and spontaneity found particularly sharp expression in the bookstores, lecture halls, and streets of the Latin Quarter.'[39]

THE LEADING ROLE OF THE LITERARY INTELLECTUAL

The lycées, which in those days (though not today) comprised seven years of secondary education, were the linchpin of the system, says Clark, rather than the universities, and they offered two main subjects – letters and science, there being little demand for more specialised subjects. The growth of knowledge took a back seat to what, he says, 'was referred to with no little provincialism as *la culture générale*'.[40]

One result of this – and it is Clark's second point – was that a constant throughout most of the nineteenth and early twentieth centuries was the leading role of the literary intellectual.[41] 'An appeal to general ideas and some literary accomplishments were sufficient qualification to speak on almost any issue.' Intellectual reviews and newspapers were continually founded which featured prominent contributions from 'generalising literary intellectuals'. Such journals dominated the cultural landscape, especially that of the Latin Quarter.[42] He goes on: 'The role of the generalising rhetorical stylist dominated the Faculty of Letters in the days of Victor Cousin and Francois Guizot, who would draw sizeable audiences from the boulevards.'

From 1880 *some* specialisation was introduced, in letters, philosophy and history, but a common section was still required, 'including written examinations in French and Latin, and oral French, Latin, and Greek "explications"'. In another examination, for teachers, candidates were given a lecture topic to work up in just one day.[43] The result, Clark notes, was that 'superficial but polished articulateness was rewarded and came to be seen as distinctive'. Furthermore, with almost no examination of students even attending class at the Collège de France, 'many professors presented polished lectures to appeal to the general public'.

At the lycées, the basic curriculum in letters was built around the classics – each week students would have three hours of Latin, three of Greek, and two hours each of literature, history and philosophy. There was still a concern to produce *literate generalists*.

Academics could be divided into three types. There were the *érudits*, researching into esoteric subjects, such as ancient languages, the *universitaires*, who held senior positions in the Sorbonne or the Collège de France, or in provincial universities, and the *mondains*, the accomplished speakers who captured the interest of the general non-academic public. At the Collège de France, literary critics like Sainte-Beuve, historians like Michelet and philosophers like Bergson fitted this mould. All wrote prolifically but unlike the *érudits*, the *mondains*' books sold well with the general public. They also wrote frequently for general intellectual and even popular magazines and newspapers, serving as critics of plays and bestselling books, debating political issues, and acting generally as arbiters of the *goût public*. The *mondains* remained outside the *école normale* and Sorbonne circuit of traditional *universitaires*. They tended to be of a higher social background than the *universitaires*, and self-taught in certain areas. Often, they had not completed the full sequence of university degrees. In style they were more spontaneous than cartesian. For such writers as these, membership of the prestigious Académie française was important – it could influence the sales of their books.[44]

Clark's third observation is that French academic life centred around the 'cluster', a cluster being a group of scholars gathered around a 'patron', an intellectual 'star', a leader of a certain school of thought, often disdainful of rival schools, who would arrange appointments for his disciples, often in provincial universities, who would then await their 'turn' to be called to the capital and take over when the patron retired or died. The fortunes of the patron, however, could be affected by the changing intellectual climate of the Latin Quarter, and this, Clark argues, is partly responsible for a particular quality of French cultural life – what he sees as the coexistence of brilliance and mediocrity. The patrons also tended to be generalists. The chief negative effect of the cluster, Clark felt, was to discourage the development of professional associations, since patrons were unwilling to concede their 'starring' roles. Such Latin Quarter institutions as the café, the bookshop and the little magazine linked the specialised fields with French general culture.[45]

Professor Clark identifies characteristics of French culture that readers of this book may have begun to notice, and which may also relate to the salons. This is the predominance of literature in French intellectual life. This is not to say that French music or painting or science are lacking. But it is true to say that the generalising literary intellectual is more of a feature of the French way of life than that of other nations and that, as Clark also points out, student heroes are more likely to be a Gide or a Barrès than a Comte or a Pasteur. It is a fair question as to how much the salons are part of the reason for this.

Although we have good evidence for several scientific salons – Mme Lavoisier's, the gatherings at Arcueil centred around Berthollet and Pierre-Simon Laplace, the famous polymath, the salons of Georges Cuvier and Jean-Martin Charcot, and we know that Baron d'Holbach's coterie didn't shy away from discussing scientific subjects – for the most part it is a fair assumption that in most salons, although astronomy seems to have been a popular subject, and sometimes archaeology, literature, philosophy, history, politics and music were far more so, not least because the coinage of writers was and is words, and the currency of the salons was conversation. Although

Freud was briefly a guest in Charcot's salon, the other members were wordsmiths like Daudet, Prudhomme and Mistral. Arguably, the salons helped to create the 'climate' of the Latin Quarter, alongside the cafés, bookshops, colleges and universities and three or four of the best lycées. They also played a role in maintaining the enthusiasm for the return to classicism in the First World War which so set the French apart.

Importantly, the classical, conservative, intellectual nationalism that won out during the First World War was, to an extent and revealingly, still extant by the time of Vichy France. In Vichy, Latin was still required of most boys at school, and the administration imposed upon its adolescent women 'a consciously domestic curriculum'.[46]

In November 2021, Jean-Michel Blanquer, education minister, said that Latin and Greek were to be introduced in professional lycées, where sixth-formers study vocational courses to train them for jobs in places such as restaurants, factories, beauty parlours and garages. He said that his aim was to underline and strengthen Latin and Greek at a time when they were under threat 'from American left-wingers denouncing them as the fount of racism'.

A Revolution in Kissing:
The Landscape of Sex in Paris

When the celebrants of Armistice Day paraded in Paris, they were only too aware that 1.4 million Frenchmen had been killed in action, a higher proportion than for any other of the combatant nations. Taking civilian deaths into account, the nation had lost 7 per cent of its population. While Germany was still fairly intact, French public debt had increased from 33.5 billion francs to over 219 billion, plus 33 billion owed abroad.

But, beginning with the Versailles Peace Conference, Paris once again became the centre of world affairs.[1] The palace was chosen ostensibly because it was said that if Germans were seen in the centre of the capital it might cause a riot, but the real reason was the 'pleasing historical congruence' of making the enemy sign at the scene of his triumph – and France's all too well-remembered humiliation – forty-eight years earlier. The German representatives were put up at the hôtel des Reservoirs, where, in 1871, the French peace commission had been forced to reside while suing for peace with Bismarck. And although there was no shortage of troops in Versailles – quite the opposite – the Germans were made to carry their own luggage (and were stoned by the local inhabitants).[2]

As Alistair Horne sees it, a kind of false cheer reigned through much of the 1920s and 1930s in France. It was seen in the music halls and the songs of Maurice Chevalier, 'the self-proclaimed ace

French lover' (and future collaborator in the Second World War) and his jaunty lyrics to 'Dans la vie faut pas s'en faire' ('In Life You Mustn't Worry'). In art Dadaism had already begun, with its self-consciously assertive move against the 'perpetual spring' of impressionism, to be succeeded by surrealism, the self-declared 'enemy of reason', which had begun, appropriately, in a wartime psychiatric hospital where shell-shocked *poilus* had been treated by the poets André Breton and Louis Aragon. The 1920s in Paris were, for many, '*les années folles*', 'the crazy years', 'the years of illusion', 'the smiling 1920s', in which the whole world wanted to come to what was again the City of Light. It was yet another amazing recovery, after the ravages of war.

Not a few artists, writers, actors and musicians had served in, and/ or been killed or injured in the war (Apollinaire, Derain, Braque, Gaudier-Brzeska, Masson, Ravel, Auric, Poulenc, Clair, Giraudoux, Barbusse, Chevalier, Léger – a stretcher-bearer at Verdun, gassed on the Aisne – while Cocteau served as a driver in Misia Sert's private ambulance corps, in a uniform designed by Coco Chanel). The interruption to cultural life was, however, in the circumstances, nowhere near as bad as it had been across the 1870–1 imbroglio. Cocteau's one-act ballet *Parade*, with music by Satie and sets and costumes by Picasso, and directed by Diaghilev, had premiered in May 1917.

Picasso also designed the sets for Stravinsky's *Renard*, which opened on 18 May 1922, and it was at a party after the first night, in honour of Diaghilev, where Picasso was also present, that Marcel Proust first met James Joyce. Afterwards Proust gave Joyce a lift home in a taxi, and during the journey the drunken Irishman made it clear that he had never read a single word Proust had written. Proust was very offended and took himself off to the Ritz, where he would always be fed, however late.[3]

ODÉONIA

Joyce's insult was unbecoming. At the time of his death later that year, Proust's reputation was high. Now, however, some critics argue that his achievement no longer merits the enormous effort. For others, *À la recherche du temps perdu* is still one of the outstanding achievements of modern literature, 'the greatest exploration of a self by anyone, including Freud'.[4]

James Joyce, Proust's unpleasant taxi companion, was better company with Sylvia Beach, an American bookseller he had met in 1920, who in turn was friendly with – and a sometime lover of – a French bookseller, Adrienne Monnier. Both had bookshops on the rue de l'Odéon, which crossed the boulevard Saint-Germain. Beach's bookshop was called Shakespeare & Co., selling mainly English-language titles, and Monnier's was La Maison des amis des livres, selling French-language books. The shops were virtually opposite each other – Beach called the street Odéonia and Joyce labelled it 'Stratford-on-Odéon'.[5] Each loved literature and literature-makers and, like Natalie Clifford Barney (see below), enjoyed introducing one culture to the other.

Adrienne had arrived in Paris during the First World War and bravely opened her premises when rents were low and, to be fair, many male bookshop-owners had been called up. She was of peasant stock from Alpine France, her father a postman, sorting letters on the night-train heading south from Paris. When he was injured in a railway accident at Melun, he received an insurance settlement and Adrienne used some of it to start her business. She also used the shop's premises as a base for a small number of literary journals and in this way befriended – and defended – some of France's greatest writers, among them Valéry, Apollinaire, Rachilde, Gide, Romain and Léon-Paul Fargue, who she had met during the war and stopped by most afternoons. Janet Flanner, the *New Yorker* correspondent in Paris, compared the two women: Mlle Monnier, 'buxom as an abbess', placidly picturesque in the costume she had prematurely adopted, consisting of a long, full, grey skirt, a bright velveteen waistcoat and a white blouse; and slim, jacketed Sylvia, 'with her schoolgirl white collar and a big coloured bowknot'.[6]

At first, Adrienne invited Sylvia to her bookshop to hear Paul Valéry, in French army uniform, read his anti-war poem 'Europe'. After the war ended it was Adrienne who suggested Sylvia open a French-language bookshop in London or New York. When she looked into it, Sylvia found the rents in both cities prohibitive, so turned the idea on its head and opened an English-language bookshop in Paris.

An early customer was Gertrude Stein, who eventually became one of Sylvia's 'bunnies', a word she coined from the French for 'subscriber' – *abonné*. To begin with, to help Sylvia survive, bunnies paid a fixed sum for two years to help out and received a book a month.

When it proved impossible for Joyce to publish *Ulysses* either in Britain or America (or anywhere else) Sylvia stepped into the breach, and also persuaded customers/authors like Hemingway to smuggle copies of the banned book into the United States. Excerpts from Joyce's book had been read in Monnier's bookshop. Adrienne and Sylvia were also drawn to the visual arts as well as literature and, since Louis Aragon and André Breton were habitués of one shop or the other, they were present at the birth of surrealism.[7] But first we need to consider two other customers/authors of Odéonia: Jean Cocteau and André Gide.

THE LAST WORD IN AVANT-GARDISM

Immensely multi-talented, Cocteau was a poet, playwright, novelist and designer; he could make excellent sketches in pen and ink and, finally, he became a filmmaker, recognising early on the promise of that new medium. After its debut, his one-act *Parade* was turned into a full-blown production, with additional material from Francis Poulenc and Maurice Ravel. Cocteau also had a great influence on Les Six because they too took their colour from *Parade*, after which a group of young musicians gathered around Satie – if Cocteau was their intellectual leader, Satie was their spiritual guide. The composers were Arthur Honegger (Swiss), Georges Auric, Louis Durey and Germaine Tailleferre, joined later by Poulenc and Darius Milhaud. 'We were tired of Debussyism,' wrote Poulenc, 'of Ravel. I wanted music to be clear, healthy and robust – music as frankly French in spirit as Stravinsky's *Petrushka* is Russian. To me, Satie's *Parade* is to Paris what *Petrushka* is to St Petersburg.'[8]

The approach of Les Six was to achieve an intermarriage not just of the old and the new but of the high and the low. 'One did not write symphonies. Instead, one wrote foxtrots, satires, burlesques, short pieces, dance music.' In practice, only two of the six found enduring fame in the repertoire and they both happened to be French – Milhaud and Poulenc. Milhaud, always industrious, produced a variety of polytonal pieces, such as *La Création du monde* (1923) and *Le Bœuf sur le toit* (1919; the prewar bar of that name was still going strong), which were 'spicy, clever, and dissonant', shocking the bourgeoisie. This was 'the last word in chic avant-gardism'. But eventually shock after shock paled and today they are little heard. In contrast, Poulenc, always more conservative than the others, and regarded – to begin with – as a bit of a lightweight, 'a musical soft-shoe man', started at the back of the group but began to grow, developing as a writer of songs, if not grander, bigger conceptions, until many placed him on a par with Fauré and Debussy.[9]

Cocteau's best-known books of this time were *Les Enfants terribles*, written when he was undergoing treatment for opium addiction, followed by *Opium: Journal of Drug Rehabilitation* (1929), actually illustrated by his own pen and ink drawings, in between more general thoughts and reflections on the world at large. No less original and enjoyable was his play *La Voix humaine*, which involves one woman on stage, alone, speaking into a telephone for more than an hour. The man on the other end is her lover who, we learn, is about to leave her.[10] It has turned out to be his most copied work – for example, Poulenc's opera with the same title, Gian Carlo Menotti's opera *The Telephone*, and Roberto Rossellini's much later film version in Italian, *L'Amore*. Cocteau's other books of that time were *The Blood of a Poet* and *Le Livre blanc* (1928), in which he discussed his homosexuality.

Homosexuality was one of the links Cocteau had with Gide and in fact, as we shall see, homosexuality – male *and* female – was an important component of the Paris scene in the crazy years, and made it exceptional, simply because it was acceptable there when it was much less so elsewhere.

'NEVER REMAIN THE SAME'

Gide was two decades older than Cocteau and besides being a Protestant had been raised by a strong – even domineering – mother. He had married a childhood acquaintance, also a Protestant. But Gide also had paedophiliac tendencies, something that not even his most advanced friends could tolerate, and this made him – combined with being an only child – somewhat secretive. He admired his wife, and made her the heroine of two novels, *Strait Is the Gate*, about the conflict in a young woman torn between asceticism and her sensual yearnings, and *The Immoralist*, where the protagonist, Michel, travels through Europe and north Africa with the intention of letting his passions run free, including the lure of Arab boys, while neglecting his wife, who dies of TB. The book is in essence an attempt by Michel/Gide to convince others – and himself, of course – of where integrity lies. Is paedophilia a sensibility too far? All his life, Gide explored the idea that every individual has a duty to discover their true inclination – this is why his homosexuality was central to who he felt himself to be, leading to a course of action of which society may disapprove.[11]

Gide's poor eyesight had removed him from fighting in the war and he started a centre for Belgian refugees. That eventually dried him up, he felt, but in 1917 he met and fell for Marc Allégret, the son of a friend of the family, who was studying in Cambridge. Until that point, Gide had pursued mainly boys in public baths, and discreetly so, out of respect for his wife (and the law), but with Marc all that changed. When she found out, his wife burned the letters he had written her, which profoundly shocked Gide. In his shock he turned to Maria Van Rysselberghe, sophisticated and understanding but also conveniently separated from her husband, the Flemish painter Théo Van Rysselberghe. There then followed a curious – almost unique – moment, when Maria happened to mention that her daughter Élisabeth, who had been close to the English poet Rupert Brooke, killed prematurely in the war, had always regretted not having a child. This was the set of circumstances which led Gide to propose that he father Élisabeth's child without any intention, on either part, of getting married. This unusual proposition worked and, in turn, Gide set up a very unusual *ménage à trois* in Paris with Maria in one room of the apartment and Marc in another.[12] Élisabeth and Catherine, her daughter with Gide, were regular visitors.

And it was from this flat that Gide ran the *Nouvelle Revue française*, the literary monthly he had founded before the war and which, despite turning down Proust's masterpiece (which Gide later apologised for), was now the leading outlet for many promising young writers. The main philosophy was 'never remain the same', 'dare to be yourself', which of course overlapped a lot with sexual freedom.

THE PICASSO OF FASHION; WELL-DRESSED MINDS

We noted earlier that, following the siege of Paris and the Commune, life went back to normal only when women began again to take an interest in fashion, and this was also true in the wake of the First World War. Paul Poiret, master couturier and sometimes referred to as the 'Picasso of fashion', had come up with some sumptuous post-war dresses with high waists and hems raised daringly just above the ankle. Though popular to begin with, fashions quickly changed to a more severe look, in which dresses fell in a straight line past a waist that had dropped to the hips, and hair was likewise cropped severely short, leaving the nape of the neck clear. All of this went with a transformation in cosmetics, in which the most important innovation was lipstick. Revolutionary here was the innovation of the chemist Paul Baudecroux, who, using orchid extract, invented a long-lasting *rouge à lèvres baiser*, with which women daringly 'could kiss without leaving a mark', perfect for mistresses and courtesans. Coloured nail varnish came in, the more coquettish had false eyelashes to make the most of, and a new form of salon – the *salon de beauté* – became the rage. Colette set the fashion for slimming by rowing on the Seine and she was also one of the first to *se faire remonter le visage*, have a facelift.[13]

In this feminine world, the Princesse de Polignac's musical salon was still going strong. Salon life had not died out with the war, but it had mutated and a new breed of the form was on the rise.[14] Comte Étienne de Beaumont held the most celebrated of these new-style gatherings. He was an almost impossibly elegant man, famous for a series of masquerade balls, but he also wrote the libretto for an opera by Léonide Massine, staged Paris's first jazz performance, using American soldiers, employed a raft of avant-garde artists to decorate his apartment and helped Cocteau present *Le Bœuf sur le toit*. Another new salon was that gathered around Charles and Marie-Laure de Noailles, who, again under Cocteau's role as social impresario, became what they called 'godparents' to a generation of young surrealists – Paul Éluard, André Breton, Max Ernst, Man Ray, Jean Arp and Luis Buñuel.[15]

Immediately after the war a new salon had been launched by Jacques Bousquet and his wife Marie-Louise. Jacques was a screenwriter who made a number of films in several language versions, as was popular in the early days. His wife, the chain-smoking, bird-like Marie-Louise, was a fashion journalist, later to become Paris editor of *Harper's Bazaar*. Their Thursdays at the place du Palais-Bourbon brought together Picasso, Aldous Huxley and, eventually, Carmel Snow, later to be an editor at *Vogue* but then at *Harper's Bazaar* and famous for her idea that fashion magazines should be homes for 'well-dressed women with well-dressed minds'. Their salon, a notorious collaborationist enclave in the Second World War, would last until 1966.

But the Princesse de Polignac continued to outshine most of these new salons with her largesse, as if the war had never happened. She identified the new 'people's poet', Léon-Paul Fargue – Adrienne Monnier's discovery – whom she likened to François Villon as 'eloquent, truculent and original'. He was by then the melancholic poet-in-residence at the Bœuf sur le toit, and was also in the ambit of Rachilde. Through him the princess added poetry readings and literary lectures to her salon activities.

The princess had a ten-year affair with Violet Trefusis, daughter of Alice Keppel, one of Edward VII's many mistresses – Edward was possibly Violet's father – and in turn a lover of Vita Sackville-West. The princess's friendship with Colette endured, although the latter's open sandals and bright red toenails were not really Winnaretta's style, as did that with Anna de Noailles, who, she noted, still perceived any silence 'as an invitation to fill it'. Colette got on so well with Ravel that they cooperated on an opera.[16] Winnaretta translated some of President Calvin Coolidge's speeches into French – he had formally authorised her to do so.[17] Winnaretta, Coco Chanel, Colette, Anna and Misia Sert formed a powerful – and stylish – group, who sometimes had dinner together with no men present, sitting cross-legged on the floor.

The arrival in Paris of musicians of the calibre of Vladimir

Horowitz, Artur Rubinstein and Paul Hindemith prompted the princess to introduce a new form of salon – her 'piano Fridays'. But she was no longer narrowly musical and engaged Le Corbusier to design the building for one of her charities – the Salvation Army. Her Russian friends in Paris had now expanded to include Nabokov.

At roughly the same time Winnaretta came into contact with Nadia Boulanger, who agreed to give her some lessons on the organ, and this led to perhaps the last great relationship of her life. Boulanger was the teacher of a wide range of composers, but she also took over the running of the practical side of Winnaretta's salon. It was a non-sexual relationship but immensely satisfying, as Nadia chose the music, hired the musicians, and arranged rehearsals and payment. 'Winnaretta's relationship with Boulanger was chaste; in place of sex, they had a salon.'[18] Everything seemed fine until, in 1934, with her generosity a legend in the musical world, she began to receive requests for help from increasing numbers of German Jewish musicians.

THE LEFT BANK OF LESBOS

As we have seen, Winnaretta always tried to be discreet as regards her sexuality. That did not apply to two other women on what William Wiser aptly calls 'the Left Bank of Lesbos'.[19] Natalie Clifford Barney, he says, was the most uninhibited of the Sapphic muses. Born in Dayton, Ohio, in 1876, she was to become a legendary figure in France, known for her writings (verse, drama, fiction, essays) and for being written about and for her international salon. 'Never as attractive as her many conquests, Natalie was nevertheless an attraction – to men as well as to a veritable harem of women – her great mass of hair held loosely with pins, and liable to flow freely as the pins fell.' Her favoured colour was white – Lanvin and Schiaparelli in her case – a white fox fur cast nonchalantly over her shoulder.[20] Jeanne Lanvin had begun as a milliner in 1889, before expanding into fashion more generally, but she was rather overshadowed by the exotic and intoxicating Schiaparelli. Elsa Schiaparelli wasn't French, but Italian, born in Rome to a very artistic and learned family (she numbered noted astronomers and Egyptologists among her relatives). Very friendly with Dalí, Cocteau, Duchamp and Giacometti, and encouraged by Poiret, her designs were especially innovative – during Prohibition in the United States, she designed one dress with a hidden pocket for a whiskey flask; she also introduced avant-garde fashion to Wimbledon whites.

Natalie was an unswerving lesbian, 'flamboyant in her unorthodoxy'. She went riding every morning in the Bois de Boulogne, dressed in male clothing. Like Winnaretta Singer, Natalie 'was as French as an American can be', perfectly bilingual, her love poems being written in French for she was happier in that language than in English. Her money came from the railway carriages that her family manufactured. Natalie attracted French writers to her salon until the wave of Americans arrived in Paris in the early to mid-1920s.[21] Ezra Pound, James Joyce and Virgil Thomson all became friends of hers, but so too were Renée Vivien, Mata Hari, Colette, Anatole France, Henri Barbusse, Pierre Louÿs, Paul Valéry, Remy de Gourmont, Philippe Berthelot and Paul Poiret.

Most French probably remember the name Philippe Berthelot more than Natalie's other *intimes*. The ideal diplomat, he was the son of a world-class chemist, Marcellin Berthelot, who had been one of the explosives experts during the siege of Paris. Philippe's first interest was poetry and he contributed articles to *La Vie parisienne* and *La Grande Encyclopédie* before joining the foreign office. Needing but four hours' sleep a night, he was as multi-talented as Cocteau, but in a different way. He and his wife, an artist's model, had their own fashionable salon where they entertained writers and artists in a room decorated with Chinese porcelain and lacquer and angora cats – Colette called him 'Seigneur Chat'. But it was in the wake of the Versailles Peace Conference that Berthelot came into his own.

A committed elitist, and convinced that only French civilisation mattered, it was Berthelot who proposed that a series of new states should be established in the wake of war, based on the principle of national self-determination – which is how Czechoslovakia, Yugoslavia and Lebanon were conceived and came about. Philippe shared many of Natalie's tastes and enjoyed her staged 'Sapphic pageants', transvestite playlets in front of a mock Greek temple, the Temple à l'Amitié, to evoke the isle of Lesbos. 'To a mixed audience Paul Valéry might read his *La Jeune Parque* or Colette preview her 1922 play *La Vagabonde*, with Paul Poiret playing opposite her.' (*La Vagabonde* was in fact first performed in Natalie's salon.)[22] To begin with only tea and cake were served, but Natalie gradually relaxed the rules.

Natalie was a high-minded poet and literary individual, but she was also, she claimed, the lover of over forty women and her salon, unlike others, was explicitly a place of sexual rendezvous. Among her liaisons, according to her *Souvenirs indiscrets*, was Liane de Pougy, whom she first saw riding in her carriage in the Bois. Liane was one of the best-known *grandes horizontales* and Natalie said she was determined to 'save' Liane from 'degradation at the hands of men'.

Known as '*Notre courtisane nationale*', with a skin like 'a flawless white camellia', Liane married a naval officer at the age of nineteen but soon sued for divorce. Whereupon the ungracious officer unloaded two bullets into her shapely thigh, 'where they lodged without further damage'.[23] Ever after, her lovers were invited to feel the bullets, an offer most found irresistible. Liane performed at the Folies-Bergère, once dressed as a spider caught in a web of pure gold wiring. At one point a man in the audience reportedly offered her 86,000 francs just for the privilege of seeing her naked. Since his heart wasn't in the best shape, a raft of his friends wrote him a collective letter urging him not to endanger his life – and their friendship – by going through with this dangerous exercise. It does not come as much of a surprise, therefore, to find that Natalie's plan for rescuing Liane from her wayward life didn't work out. Liane put all the details of their steamy affair into her own novel, *Idylle saphique*.[24]

Another of Natalie's liaisons was with Renée Vivien, a French name for a British writer, who escaped to Paris as soon as she could, also, like Natalie, preferring French to English. A passionate poet, Vivien showered Natalie with jewellery and Lalique glass, but was upset by her promiscuity and turned to another prominent Parisian lesbian, Baronne Hélène van Zuylen, a French Rothschild. Colette's *Pure and Impure* (which she considered her best book) was an examination of the range of sexual activity, and featured Vivien as one of the subjects. Natalie enjoyed a liaison with Ida Rubinstein while she was dancing for Diaghilev and with Romaine Brooks, also American, a painter who had been born in Rome and had, before the war, enjoyed a liaison with none other than the Princesse de Polignac.

Romaine painted Natalie many times, but Natalie was often painted in words, being the model for Evangeline Musset in Djuna Barnes's *Ladies Almanack* and for Valerie Seymour in Radclyffe Hall's long-suppressed *The Well of Loneliness*, in which Hall was rather dismissive of the salon, arguing that it was 'more conspicuous for homosexuality than for talent'.[25] Dolly Wilde once appeared at Natalie's Friday meetings dressed as her uncle Oscar and she too fell in love with her. She also found her promiscuity a burden – Dolly tried to slit her wrists on Natalie's account.

As a confirmed feminist, Natalie started her own academy to rival the male-dominated Académie française, which she called plainly the Académie des femmes, and which she used to offer support to literary women. Ezra Pound was not especially flattering about Natalie's verse and this may be why she once quipped, 'My only books / Were women's looks', and spent more energy on her *intimes* than on writing. Other French figures in her salon included Anna de Noailles, the cubist painter Marie Laurencin, bisexual and shared at one point between Apollinaire and Natalie. Gertrude Stein, yet another American lesbian, had her own rival salon, but the rivalry was not especially intense. Both had a passion for chocolate and would together visit Antoine Rumpelmayer's tearoom in the rue de Rivoli for *mousse au chocolat*.[26]

A Skill for Marrying Money

Just as Nadia Boulanger was known for the many notable composers she taught, so Misia Sert was known for the many artists who painted her – Vuillard, Bonnard, Toulouse-Lautrec, Renoir, Redon. She too was one of those impossibly romantic figures from the *années folles*. She was born Maria Godebska in 1872 in Tsarskoye Selo, the imposing imperial residence outside St Petersburg, where her father Cyprian, a noted Polish sculptor, was working on the elaborate reconstruction of a royal building.

Misia – the Polish diminutive for Maria – grew up in a household no less musical than Boulanger's (Liszt was a family friend) and became herself a gifted pianist. In Paris, she studied under Fauré, who was impressed enough to describe her as a prodigy. She was to marry three husbands, the first of whom was her cousin Thadée (Tadeusz) Natanson, a bohemian figure mixing in intellectual circles and strongly Dreyfusard. The Natanson home on the rue Saint-Florentin boasted a salon with a familiar roster of guests which included Léon Blum, Proust, a raft of impressionist and post-impressionist painters, Debussy, Mallarmé and Gide. Natanson was particularly taken with the Nabis (Bonnard, Vuillard, Maillol, Denis), who followed Gauguin's maxim to paint in flat, pure colours, away from the impressionists and who, to an extent, were influenced by symbolism. It was not a movement which lasted but, in its heyday, Natanson brought out the *Revue blanche*, in which Misia as often as not was on the cover.

The review didn't last and to stave off disaster Natanson turned for help to Alfred Edwards, owner of Paris's biggest-selling paper, *Le Matin*. Edwards agreed but on one remarkable condition. He was in love with Misia and for Natanson to have the money he had to give up his wife. Natanson swiftly agreed and Misia and her second husband set up home in the very fashionable rue de Rivoli, and the salon reassembled. Once again, musicians were central. Ravel dedicated *Le Cygne* and *La Valse* to Misia; she herself accompanied Enrico Caruso on the piano when he was in town.

It was an idyll, but it didn't last either, and they were divorced in 1909. She didn't marry again for quite some time, not until after the First World War, when she met the Catalan painter José Maria Sert. And so, for yet another time, her salon reassembled. In the fashion of the times, the Serts' life was almost a return to libertine days, with much sexual abandon, added to now by drug abuse. At one point, José became involved with Roussy Mdivani, a beautiful woman from the Russian Mdivani family, known as the 'Marrying Mdivanis' for their 'skill in marrying money'. Misia responded in the way we have come to expect of Parisian women of the epoch – she too made advances to Roussy.[27]

Misia's other conquest – if that is the right word – was Coco Chanel. Gabrielle Bonheur ('Happiness', 'Good fortune') Chanel, with her 'flat chest and too-thick ankles', had a mixed itinerant life before she settled down as a prolific fashion designer, credited with 'liberating' postwar women from the corset. Her mother was a laundrywoman and her father a street pedlar in Saumur, so she was sent with her two sisters to a convent-orphanage where, among other things, she learned to sew. That led to employment as a seamstress, but she also sang in cabarets, which is where she may have first been called 'Coco'. Her life began to take off only when she met, first, a French ex-cavalry officer and heir to a textile fortune, and then one of the cavalry officer's friends, an aristocratic English soldier. These military men – competing for her body, as she later put it – helped her get started in the fashion business.

She began as a milliner in 1910, not in Paris but in Deauville, a fashionable summer playground on the English Channel. But she soon branched out after a famous actress, another Gabrielle – Gabrielle Dorziat – wore her hats in a successful play in 1912. From Deauville, Chanel moved on to Biarritz, another playground of the rich, near the Spanish border, and then eventually to Paris where, by 1927, she had five outlets in the rue Cambon. Her other innovation was to change perfumes from the heavy and expensive animal and flower oils, and to persuade a leading Grasse perfumer, Ernest Beaux, to start synthesising aldehydes. She asked him to try out ten possibilities and settled on the fifth: Chanel No. 5 was born.[28]

Like Misia, and like the Princesse de Polignac, Chanel met and indemnified both Diaghilev and Stravinsky against financial loss for performances of *The Rite of Spring* and she also designed costumes for the Ballets Russes, working with Nijinsky. (Misia had also rescued *Petrushka* when 4,000 francs had been needed at the last minute, to prevent repossession of the costumes.) Chanel's relationship with Misia was to endure for decades, partly helped by their both being convent-educated and both being habitual users of cocaine (Chanel needed to inject herself every day).

Colette had a better upbringing than Chanel, but she too was another member of what we might call a very creative set of sexually adventurous women. And she too was a Gabrielle, her real name being the very pretty Sidonie-Gabrielle Colette. She was from Burgundy, where her father was a tax-collector and a hero of the Franco-Prussian War. Her early professional life had its share of scandal. In 1893 she had married Henry Gauthier-Villars, a writer and publisher known by his pen name, Willy. She wrote four novels which she published under his soubriquet – coming-of-age stories of the same young girl, Claudine. Colette always said she owed a lot to Willy for setting her on a writer's career, but this is not how others saw it. He was a notorious libertine and introduced Colette to all that the Paris literary-bohemian-sexual world had to offer.[29] The trade-off was that her books were published under his name, one consequence being that for several years he swallowed all the royalties.

Willy was fourteen years older than Colette, and disparity in age was an issue that distinguished her life, too. After she divorced him, she married Henry de Jouvenel, editor of *Le Matin*, and three years younger. She divorced *him* in 1924, partly on account of her affair with his stepson, thirty-one years her junior. This age disparity was reflected in her novel *Chéri*, about a love between an older woman and a much younger man.

While she was married to Willy, she started an acting career, at times playing Claudine in sketches taken from her own novels. The role of women in a male-dominated society was the subject of her novel *La Vagabonde*. She kept up the lesbian theme in having an affair with Mathilde de Morny, the Marquise de Belbeuf, a fellow actress known as 'Missy', who sometimes appeared on stage with Colette. On one occasion, in a pantomime, the couple kissed, causing such a fuss that they had to give up living openly together. Colette finally achieved a semblance of stability when she married Maurice Goudeket, though even here age was a factor – he was sixteen years her junior. In addition to *Chéri*, her novel *Le Blé en herbe* also deals with love between a woman getting on in years and a much younger man – she would never let up on the way French society treated women. She continued to write throughout the interwar period and in 1944 would publish *Gigi*, where again the heroine is a fifteen-year-old ingénue being groomed for courtesanship.[30]

All these women achieved prominence in a postwar world where females outnumbered males by seven to five. Politicians, however, refused to consider the obvious – electoral reform – for one old-fashioned reason: the church. Traditionalists held the condescending view that, in principle, women – if given the chance – would vote as their *curés* told them to. There was a mild movement of suffragettes in France, but nothing like in Britain. The French approach to reform was summed up in one word – '*douceur*'.[31]

Shell Shock, Surrealism and
the Seventh Art

Among the early regulars at Adrienne Monnier's bookshop were two men who had met during the war when they were both medical orderlies. André Breton and Louis Aragon would be responsible for creating one of two major developments in the visual arts in postwar Paris: surrealism and film.

Paris still retained its exceptional status as a magnet for artists. Consider this list of just some of the 10,000 or so painters or sculptors who have been identified as living in the French capital in the post-First World War years: Salvador Dalí, Juan Gris and Joan Miró (all from Spain), Alberto Giacometti (Italian-speaking Switzerland), Paul Klee (German-speaking Switzerland), Le Corbusier (architect, French-speaking Switzerland), Max Ernst (Germany), Constantin Brancusi (Romania, who had walked to Paris), René Magritte (Belgium), Tsuguharu Foujita (Japan), Jules Pascin (Bulgaria), Marc Chagall (Russia), Chaïm Soutine (Lithuania) and Moïse Kisling (Poland), not forgetting that other Spaniard, Picasso, who had been there since well before the war.

Breton had originally intended to be a doctor, and he and Aragon met on the wards of the Val-de-Grâce mental hospital in the southern part of Paris and discovered a shared love of literature. Both from modest backgrounds, they quickly became friends, united also by a shared feeling for works by Picasso, Braque and Matisse, reproductions of which they pinned above their beds in the dormitory, much to the derision of their other colleagues.[1] In the hospital they became aware that some of the shell-shocked patients would express themselves in disjointed phrases or would keep repeating certain images they had seen in war and which obsessed them. The hospital doctors at Val-de-Grâce made use of some of the theories of Pierre Janet which both prefigured and echoed Freud's ideas about the unconscious, and at times hypnosis was used.

Breton in particular was drawn to this because he too sometimes found that incongruous words and images would obsess him, when he was unable to rid such thoughts from his mind. In this way, he began to wonder whether the sane mind could also express itself in what would normally be called irrational ways, when in fact it was the unconscious speaking, having been disturbed by the disastrous events of war. Breton was a serious man, who would make it his business to meet Freud in 1921, but he was drawn in particular to one patient who lived entirely in his own world. The man had been in the trenches but had become convinced he was invulnerable. He thought the whole world was 'a sham', played by actors who used dummy bullets and stage props. So convinced was he of his vision that he would show himself during the fighting and gesture excitedly at the explosions. The miraculous inability of the enemy to kill him only reinforced his belief.

It was the 'parallel world' created by this man that had such an effect on Breton. For him the patient's madness was in fact a rational response to a world that had gone mad, a view that was enormously influential for several decades in the middle of the century. Dreams, another parallel world – a route to the unconscious as Freud said – became for Breton the route to art. For him, art and the unconscious could form a 'new alliance', realised through dreams, chance, coincidence, jokes – all the things Freud and, to an extent, Janet – were investigating. This new reality Breton called *sur*-reality, a word he borrowed from Guillaume Apollinaire, who had described Cocteau's ballet *Parade*, already referred to, as *'une espèce de surréalisme'*.[2]

In truth, surrealism owed more to what its practitioners *thought* Freud meant than to what he actually wrote. Few French and Spanish surrealists could read Freud's works as they were still only available in German (though a book on psychoanalysis in French had been published in Paris in 1914). Breton's ideas about dreams, about neurosis as a sort of 'ossified' form of permanent dreaming, would almost certainly have failed to find favour with Freud.

Breton began experimenting with these ideas with another poet friend, Philippe Soupault, with whom he would spend hours pronouncing aloud disjointed phrases and images they were haunted by, to see where they led.[3] Breton thought he could indeed discern an order in what came out and published his findings as 'Champs magnétique' in 1919 in a new journal he had founded himself, with the ironic title *Littérature*. Although its title was ironic it did serve to attract various other talents to Breton and Aragon, among them Marcel Duchamp. Born in Normandy, from a family of artists, he had decamped to New York in 1915, and had shocked the world by exhibiting a urinal as a 'Fountain'. Another newcomer was a young Romanian, Tristan Tzara, who – with Jean/Hans Arp, an artist from Alsace, then still part of Germany – had founded a militant radical artistic movement known as Dada, dedicated to ending war for all time by wholesale reformation of society. Dada had spread to Berlin but petered out after that and Tzara had migrated – like so many others – to Paris.

Breton and Aragon got on well with Tzara and started organising musical and theatrical events. They also consulted Paul Valéry, a good friend, who had suggested *Littérature* and also found Breton a job proof-reading for Gallimard, the publisher, an early task being to visit Proust in his famous cork-lined apartment where he was asked to read aloud proofs of *Sodome et Gomorrhe*.

Aragon, who was never as extreme as Breton, or as communist-minded, made his early contribution by reviving the old custom of the *flâneur*. He liked to browse the backstreets of the city, he liked sitting in cafés and reading, all as a remedy for what he still called Paris spleen, publishing *Le Paysan de Paris* in 1926. This work celebrated unfamiliar quarters of the city with its small eclectic shops – one offering carved pipes, another walking sticks with unusual handles; elsewhere he describes an accordionist who, when his instrument unfolds, displays the word 'PESSIMIST'. Aragon watches prostitutes trawling for customers and other women trawling for husbands. He persuades a café-owner to let him hide in the ladies' room so he can give an account of what women 'really' get up to.[4] His account is surreal in its juxtaposition of very different activities cheek by jowl with one another.

The poet Paul Éluard joined the group, invited because of his exquisite anti-war verse, and he held the agreeable view that 'God manifests himself in beautiful women'. He had married a beautiful Russian-born woman, Gala Diakonova, while they were both being treated for TB in a Swiss clinic. Like many passionate affairs, this one burned out – to the point where Gala left Éluard, ending up in another steamy liaison, this time with Salvador Dalí.[5]

THE UNCENSORED SELF

Though surrealism started out as a movement of poets, led by Breton, Éluard and Aragon, it was the painters who were to achieve lasting international fame. Gala knew what she was doing.

Max Ernst was the first artist to join the surrealists, in 1921. He claimed to have often hallucinated as a child, so was predisposed to this approach. Joan Miró, the son of a goldsmith, was paralysed when he first arrived in Paris – he said he was 'intellectually paralysed', the shock of Paris being too much.[6] He met the surrealists through the painter André Masson, who lived next door to him. Masson had fought in the war, emerged 'shattered' and undergone a long treatment at none other than Val-de-Grâce.

Juan Gris, Yves Tanguy, Giorgio de Chirico ... all fitted the postwar surrealist scepticism of rationality, which many believed – or affected to believe – had brought about the disaster of the First World War.

René Magritte (1898–1967) took ordinary subjects – a bowler hat, a pipe, an apple, an umbrella – and made extraordinary things happen to them (he himself often wore a bowler). In the summer of 1929, he and his wife had a working holiday with Paul and Gala Éluard. In the interim, she had had an affair with Max Ernst but then returned to Paul. Also there, however, was another Spaniard, a very thin and sleek Catalan, with protuberant dark eyes – Salvador Dalí. Dalí fell for Gala and persuaded her he was a genius. She helped arrange an exhibition of his work, as did Picasso, who was not a surrealist, but did know Gertrude Stein, who became one of his backers.

Gala eventually married Dalí and the relationship happily lasted, despite the fact that Dalí was impotent and incapable of sexual intercourse. That being the case, Éluard, who was still in love with Gala, was allowed to sleep with her from time to time.

Though Dalí would become the best-known surrealist, he was, in fact, a rather late arrival in Paris. After Picasso, he became the most famous artist of the twentieth century, though this is not the same as saying he was the second best. It had more to do with his extraordinary technique, his profound fear of madness, and his personal appearance – his staring eyes and handlebar moustache, adapted from a Velázquez portrait of Philip IV of Spain. Dalí remained a surrealist. Though much of his work has since been dismissed, usually as 'meretricious', he took himself jovially seriously. He had a sign on his bedroom door: 'Poet at work'. His favourite exercise, he said, was going up in a lift.[7]

Musical Beds

It is worth pointing out that surrealism – and the Parisian art world of that time – was, exceptionally, almost as well known for the artists' models and companions as for their paintings. Anna de Noailles and Misia Sert have already been introduced. Alice Prin, known as Kiki of Montparnasse, could be found every night at the Dôme café, caressing a small white mouse, chained to her wrist. She was able to draw, up to a point, but she was photographed countless times, usually in the nude, and modelled for 'scores' of artists, including Soutine, Foujita, Picabia, Breker, Cocteau and Kisling, as well as playing 'musical beds' with one or the other, and at the advanced age of twenty-eight wrote her memoirs.[8] The English translation was banned in the USA.

A not dissimilar figure was Lucie Badoud, a buxom farmer's daughter, who read a description by Apollinaire of the Rotonde café in Paris, and lost no time going there, where she fell for Foujita (part of his attraction was that he had a large bath with hot running water).

His portrait of her was a great success at the 1924 Salon d'automne, where she is shown on snow-covered ground with a big black dog. Foujita, who, like Juan Gris, was mad about dancing and took lessons from Isadora Duncan, nicknamed her Youki, Japanese for 'rose snow'. She became Foujita's third wife but later left him and married the surrealist poet Robert Desnos.[9] More musical beds.

Other women who were part of this scene include Jeanne Hébuterne, generally described as the common-law wife of Amedeo Modigliani, but also a painter in her own right, and Fernande Barrey, who started as a prostitute but became a model for Modigliani and Soutine and also for Jean Agélou, a canny specialist in erotic photography. She too turned to painting.[10]

And then, of course, there were Picasso's models/muses/mistresses/wives. In 1917 the painter had accompanied Cocteau to Rome where Stravinsky was preparing *Parade*, for which the painter had agreed to design the costumes and sets. There he met and fell in love with a young Russian ballerina, Olga Khokhlova, as beautiful and lithe as only a ballerina can be. But she was heavily chaperoned, and disciplined, and old-fashioned, and Russian, and she would not sleep with him outside marriage. This was a new predicament for him – throughout the war until that point he had had no fewer than three mistresses. But Olga was as strong-willed as he, and she won. In addition to marriage, she wanted a social position in Paris and Picasso had to call on Misia Sert to introduce Olga to *le tout Paris*.

The effect on Picasso's art was marked. When his wife gave birth to a son, Paulo, Pablo's style turned more classical, even Romanesque in a way, with the boy sometimes dressed as Pierrot, sometimes as a child amusing itself. The subject matter – and the style – was totally unlike what had gone before.[11]

But, this being Picasso, in 1924, outside a Métro station, he saw a young girl he could not resist. Just seventeen, Marie-Thérèse Walter became his mistress inside six months. Unlike Olga she was sporty, not especially forceful or intelligent, and above all submissive. And so now, in a series of etchings, a new sensuality could be seen in Picasso's work. Marie-Thérèse is asleep, on the beach, nude in front of a mirror – again it is a new style which, as much as anything, told Olga what was afoot. She began to make scenes – and this too

was a third new style shown in his work, when he started representing woman as ugly, spiteful, bitter, in one case a heap of misplaced
limbs.[12] This was woman as entrapper, as snare, as possessive bitch.
Olga as ogre. In 1935 she left him, taking Paulo with her. A year later
the Spanish Civil War broke out and he had yet another new subject,
and another new style.

After the First World War, the art in the City of Light was as fertile
as ever, no less outrageous than at other times, colourful, fantastic,
above all coruscatingly imaginative. But, save for a handful (Masson,
Léger, Tanguy, Breton), it was Parisian but it wasn't really French. The
post-First World War art of Paris was part of French civilisation – and
French history – without really being part of the French mind.

THE SILENT PRINCE

On the other hand, the French mind found a fertile outlet as one of
the pioneers of cinema, what was known in Paris as the 'seventh art',
to include still photography as well. In fact, still photography came
of age in 1927 with the debut of the very first Salon indépendant
de la photographie. In moving pictures, France wouldn't always be
able to resist the onslaught of Hollywood, but in the late 1920s and
early 1930s, French filmmakers still proved exceptionally creative.
To begin with, people like Cocteau and Anna de Noailles worked
in early film, often being financially supported by the Comte de
Beaumont. Cocteau's *The Blood of a Poet* is a surrealist work and
this link between surrealism and early photography/film is often
overlooked.

In early film the names to conjure with in France are René Clair
and Abel Gance. Like the still photographers, Clair was part of the
art set, mixing in particular with Francis Picabia (who had a salon
of sorts) and Erik Satie. Tall and thin, he was drawn into film by
accident when a friend asked him to accompany her to a theatre
where a silent film was being made and a 'prince' was required. The
director took to Clair, dressed him as the prince, added make-up
and instructed him to repeatedly kiss the females in the film. Clair
so enjoyed the experience that thereafter he tried his hand at various
short silent films, many of them with a surrealist theme, because

such themes – in an age of silent movies – attracted the eye. In one he filmed a hearse being pulled by a camel – he saw the comic possibilities immediately. In another, Paris came to a standstill because of a mysterious ray produced by a scientist.[13] In silent films, movement is more important than in films with sound.

But when sound came along, in 1928, Clair started telling more sophisticated stories, and he also realised that film was a much more demotic medium than painting, and that protagonists did not always need to be stars, not then anyway. His two most successful films were *Sous les toits de Paris* (1930) and *À nous la liberté* (1931). The first tells the story of a street singer set against a background of petty theft, wrongful arrest, escape and – what films would fall in love with – a chase. In *À nous la liberté*, two prisoners sharing a cell try to escape. One gets away but the other doesn't. The escaped prisoner becomes a successful factory-owner whereas the other becomes a worker in ... the same factory. Trouble erupts and at first the two men are on opposite sides. But as the industrial troubles deepen, the two men are drawn together and together they take to the open road. In summary it sounds contrived, but it was cleverly told and not too sentimental.[14]

Abel Gance could play the piano and the violin and thought these skills would help him become an actor, but he failed to get into the Conservatoire, and took a job in Brussels writing film scenarios. He remained there during the First World War because he suffered from TB and was exempt from military service. After the war he returned to Paris and moved into making films. One of his first efforts was *La Roue*, about railways, with sets being designed, suitably, by Fernand Léger. The story begins with a catastrophic train crash, after which the engine-driver discovers and adopts an orphan girl, Norma, with whom – to his horror – he discovers he is falling in love. He confides in a 'friend' who turns on him and blackmails him, threatening that he will tell the world unless the train-driver lets him marry the girl. This happens but the marriage is unhappy and, later, the driver's own son falls for Norma. This provokes a fight between the son and the 'friend', when both are killed. At the end the driver starts to go blind and is looked after by Norma. It is a good story, the only problem being that it lasts seven-and-a-half hours.

The same problem afflicts Gance's other masterpiece, *Napoléon*, which is almost six hours long. For many it is the greatest silent film ever made, the ending being displayed on three side-by-side screens. It was intended as a monument to France's recent 'four years of heroism', recalling the first consul's heroic acts against international opposition and his – and France's – pride in victory. During the making of the film, which took three years and ran across the general strike of 1926, Gance signed on several hundred strikers at the Renault car factory, exhorting them to put aside their 'petty' personal considerations in order to do justice to the immensity of the theme. The film doesn't have a conclusion or climax, it just stops. Gance had run out of money.[15]

J'Accuse is not about Zola's great campaign but uses the phrase to condemn war, as Zola condemned the army. It is a powerful anti-war film, in which the main protagonist, François, and the man who is his wife's lover, Jean, serve in the same battalion at the front. Édith, wife of one and mistress of the other, is sent to Lorraine for safety but is captured, raped by Germans and gives birth to a half-German child. When the men return on leave, and the truth comes out, instead of fighting, which everyone fears, the two men return to the front. One, François, is killed, the other, shell-shocked, is driven mad. Jean returns home and, in a very moving scene, reads the poems he has written to the villagers, as the dead rise up from their graves and face their living relatives. Then they return to their graves and Jean dies.

Jean Renoir, second son of the impressionist painter, served in the war and was invalided out after being shot by a sniper. After trying pottery and acting, he began making films, silent ones at first, but his masterpiece was *La Grande Illusion*, set in a German camp for French prisoners of war. The prisoners are a social mix of working class, aristocrat and Jew. The commandant of the camp is a German aristocrat and the two noblemen discover a set of shared values. Rather than being anti-war, Renoir's film is anti-nationalism.[16]

Julien Benda was no fan of the surrealists, or of Henri Bergson, or of the celebrity glitter of 1920s Paris. Independently wealthy, intensely serious, as we saw in an earlier chapter, he was an essayist of distinction who was, like Paul Bourget, nominated for the Nobel Prize several times without winning, though his collection of writings on the Dreyfus affair had won many accolades. In 1927, however, he published his best-known and most influential book, a slim volume called *The Treason of the Learned*. The learned or *'clercs'* of the title were French and German and this adds something to his argument, in that he wasn't being narrowly nationalistic, something unusual for the time and part of his main point.

Benda (1867–1956) came from a once-prosperous Jewish Parisian family, whose firm had gone bankrupt during the First World War. A prolific author, of some fifty books, he was one of the defenders of Alfred Dreyfus and saw himself as a supreme rationalist in the French tradition, setting himself decisively against the 'intuitionism' of Bergson and others like the surrealists. Benda's main argument in his book was that the nineteenth century had seen the growth of political passion out of all proportion to anything that had gone before. The emergence of a bourgeois class, he said, had spawned the sobering development of class hatred and a rise in nationalist sentiment, which he put down to democracy.[17] Not least, the intensifying of Jewish nationalism had spawned a corresponding spread of anti-Semitism. Benda's further argument was that political passions had become much more fervent in the nineteenth century, but in particular *national* passions, 'not only as regards their material existence, their military power, their territorial possessions, and their economic wealth, but as regards their *moral* existence. With a hitherto unknown consciousness (prodigiously fanned by authors) every nation now hugs itself and sets itself up against all other nations as superior in language, art, literature, philosophy, civilisation, "culture". Patriotism is today the assertion of one form of mind against other forms of mind.'[18] It was, he added, impossible to overstress the novelty of this form of patriotism in history, which was inaugurated in Germany in 1813, and came to embody three ideas – the movement against the Jews, the movement of the possessing classes against the proletariat, and the movement of the champions of authority against the democrats.[19]

INTELLECTUALS INFERIOR TO SOLDIERS

Most of all, though, Benda saw a change in the behaviour of intellectuals, creative people, scientists and philosophers. Before the nineteenth century, he said, people of the character of Leonardo da Vinci, Goethe, Erasmus, Kant, Thomas Aquinas, Kepler, Descartes, Roger Bacon, Pascal and Leibniz 'set an example of attachment to the purely disinterested activity of the mind and created a belief in the supreme value of this form of existence'. But now, he said, it was different, very different. 'Today, if we mention Mommsen, Treitschke, Ostwald, Brunetière, Barrès, Lemaître, Péguy, Maurras, d'Annunzio, Kipling, we have to admit that the "clerks" now exercise political passions with all the characteristics of passion – the tendency to action, the thirst for immediate results, the exclusive preoccupation with the desired end, the scorn for argument, the excess, the hatred, the fixed ideas.' In descending to the level of the rest of the public, Benda thought these men were acting not like Socrates or Jesus, but like the mob.

Benda was anxious to show that this betrayal had occurred not just in France. His chief focus was the French, but he extended his arguments from France to Germany, Italy, Britain and America, more or less in that order, and he thought that German intellectuals had been especially culpable in the First World War, particularly in regard to the 'Manifesto of the Ninety-Three' (chapter 41). 'We know how systematically the mass of German teachers in the past fifty years have announced the decline of every civilisation but that of their own race, and how in France the admirers of Nietzsche or Wagner, even of Kant or Goethe, were treated by Frenchmen ...'

Although he excoriated his fellow French in this regard, Benda did argue that it was the German intellectuals who had 'led the way in this adhesion of the modern "clerk" to patriotic fanaticism'. He thought that it had begun with Lessing, Schlegel and Fichte, who were 'organising in their hearts a violent adoration for "everything German", and a scorn for everything not German. The nationalist "clerk" is essentially a German invention.' In making this innovation, he added, Germany made this species necessary to all other nations.[20]

And although he targeted novelists, dramatists and artists, he

reserved particular venom for historians. '"A true German historian", declares a German master, "should especially tell those facts
which conduce to the grandeur of Germany."' And the philosophers
were hardly better, he insisted. 'Fichte and Hegel made the triumph of
the German world the supreme and necessary end of the development
of Being . . .'

The most important impact in all this, Benda thought, was that the
military life and war, fought inevitably with nationalist aims in mind,
became attached to morality rather than utility. Courage, honour
and harshness came to be extolled by the learned – even, in the case
of Nietzsche, cruelty. ('Every superior culture is built upon cruelty.')
Another cult – the cult of the will – had arisen, supported by everyone
in Germany 'since Hegel' and by a large number in France 'since de
Maistre', the monarchist late eighteenth-century philosopher who
argued that France's godlessness had caused the French Revolution.

All this, said Benda, was in the ascendancy, whereas the passion
of the learned to *understand*, the desire to be universal or objective,
had, since Sorel and Nietzsche, been derided. Several French writers
had insisted, he noted, that people interested in purely intellectual
things were 'inferior to soldiers'. For him, this had all amounted to a
'prodigious' decline in morality, a contempt for the 'true clerk' whose
joy 'comes from the exercise of thought and who disdains sensation,
particularly the sensation of action'.[21]

He concluded by saying that the battle was over. 'Today . . .
humanity is national. The layman has won . . . The man of science,
the artist, the philosopher are attached to the nation as much as the
day-labourer and the merchant.' And then, on page 145 (and remember this was first published in 1927): 'This humanity is heading for
the greatest and most perfect war ever seen in the world . . . I can well
imagine a future war when a nation would decide not to look after
the enemy wounded, a strike when the bourgeoisie would make up
its mind not to support hospitals for the benefit of a class which was
ruining it and anxious to deny it . . . And History will smile to think
that this is the species for which Socrates and Jesus Christ died.'[22]

In retrospect, the 1920s would come to be seen as – yes, crazy, but
also a productive interregnum before a deluge of anti-war literature
and art broke out across the years of global depression.

Solitude, *Négritude* and Other Half-Way Houses

B enda looked back with acerbic clarity and his prognostications were to prove no less valid in the long run. But, as the new decade was ushered in, few of his countrymen saw what he did. They were too concerned with more immediate matters.

Politically, the story of the 1930s in France can – for once – be told succinctly in statistics. It was a disappointing decade. Between 1928 and 1934, industrial production dropped by 17 per cent. Between 1929 and 1936, average income fell by 20 per cent. By 1935 there were 800,000 unemployed out of a population of 40 million. Between 1932 and 1939, France had nineteen governments, making use of eleven prime ministers, meaning that the average life of an administration was roughly four-and-a-half months. In the early 1930s, France could mount an army of 184,000 'effectives', whereas the equivalent figure in Germany was 464,000. At the Armistice there had been 26 francs to the pound; by 1926 that had sunk to 220. The franc was to be devalued three times, in June 1936, January 1937 and again in 1938.[1]

These off-colour figures were fertile ground for the communists – in none of the other victorious countries did the Russian October Revolution have so many sympathisers as among the French, striking a chord with the memories of 1789, 1848 and, most of all, the Commune of 1871, where the brutality of the way the Communards had been put down was still a sobering memory. In early February 1934, just after the fall of yet another government, in office for two months and four days, a group of nationalist right-wingers, 'sickened by France's retreat from *grandeur* since 1919 ... united to march on the assembly'. Some 40,000 demonstrators turned out, 16 were killed, 655 were wounded and so were a thousand policemen. In June that year there were no fewer than 12,142 strikes, two-thirds of them sit-ins.[2] These unhappy self-conscious, self-centred times were well reflected in the literature and philosophy of the decade with their focus on pessimism, impoverishment, incertitude, limits and disappointment.

A Retreat from Sociability

Doctor, linguist, 'shagger of showgirls', noted anti-Semite, Louis-Ferdinand Céline is also regarded by many as the greatest French prose stylist of the twentieth century, despite the scandals and controversy that still dog his memory. That scandal/controversy began in 1932 with publication of his book *Journey to the End of the Night*, a vast, partly autobiographical narrative of jaundiced lyricism, following the protagonist Ferdinand Bardamu all over the world, as he collects disparate dangerous and traumatic experiences in what traditional types might call a remake of *Candide*.

The book begins in the First World War (where Céline was a soldier), then travels to the African colonies and the industrial wasteland of Detroit, where Bardamu works in a Ford car factory, before returning to Paris. The book is vulgar, sarcastic, mordant, sneering, above all sardonic and cynical, what the French call *narquois*.[3] It is hardly *Candide* but in the course of the book's four parts, Bardamu experiences – wherever he turns – the misery and emptiness of existence. He is wounded in war, undergoes the brutality of the colonies, contracting a tropical disease, and is ferried by hospital ship to the United States, where he is bored and forms an unsatisfying relationship with a prostitute. Back in France, Bardamu lives in and around the Zone on the edges of Paris (chapter 32), dealing with mad and tubercular patients, who suffer in both material and moral squalor, being both poor and untreatably grasping and greedy. (Céline himself, as a young man, set up his first practice on the edge of the Zone.) Bardamu's final move is to a psychiatric hospital in Paris, where the physician superintendent himself goes mad. The solitude, lassitude, self-obsessions and degradation are unremitting, save perhaps for the wit that breaks through the cynical sarcasm now and then.

Many have found the book irresistible, though French people have been known to refuse to read it on account of its crude anti-Semitism (and, it should be said, the author's behaviour in the Second World War, to which we shall return). Set mostly in the First World War and the 1920s, it looked back but, with the benefit of hindsight, its title especially invites us to look forward. And certainly, after the colour, splendour and roaring music of the 1920s, especially in Paris, the 1930s in France were a serious, even sombre decade, not devoid of achievement but overall well meriting description as 'the locust years', the 'most sustained period of wilful blindness'.[4]

'No One Can Fully Explain Humankind'

One of the more serious-minded figures in Paris in those years was the Russian Alexandre Kojève. His family was well connected – he was Kandinsky's nephew and he studied philosophy in Heidelberg with Karl Jaspers. But then he came under the influence of Heidegger and Marx, and another Russian and another Alexandre, Koyré, a historian of religion who had studied under Edmund Husserl and David Hilbert, the eminent mathematician, at least until Husserl took exception to Koyré's dissertation and the young man decamped to Paris. There he studied with Bergson and Léon Brunschvicg, before joining the French Foreign Legion and undergoing a distinguished war. After the war, and after he had completed his doctorate, Koyré took up teaching at the École pratique des hautes études (EPHE). This set a pattern that Kojève was to follow. After Koyré left to teach in the Middle East, Kojève replaced his fellow countryman at the EPHE as lecturer on Hegel.[5]

Just as Jacques Maritain had travelled to Germany and discovered Aquinas there, and felt that France could benefit from his ideas, so Kojève also travelled to Germany where he discovered Hegel and became convinced that France could benefit from a closer associa-tion with *his* ideas. There *are* certain parallels between Aquinas and Hegel, though they were of course very different in many ways. What both had in common was the idea that knowledge – more knowledge, new forms of knowledge – could not but help add to the grandeur of existence and help show the way forward, help reveal the true purpose of history, that the point of life was the progressive discovery of ourselves and the context.

Like the École normale supérieure, the EPHE is one of France's *grandes écoles*, prestigious higher centres of learning, in this case of religious studies, history, cultural affairs and earth studies, whose famous alumni include Jean-Martin Charcot, Marcellin Berthelot, Paul Broca and Joseph Halévy. Established in 1868 under Emperor Napoleon III, its main aim – following the German universities – was to promote *practical*, research-based learning and the relationship between learning and power structures.

The *grandes écoles* in France are a system special to it. They are – relatively speaking – small schools, very elitist and self-regarding, separate to and parallel with the universities, and designed to help establish and maintain the governing/administrative class in France. Students attend preparatory schools for two years beforehand and, in some cases, receive a salary while doing so, on the understanding that, if they qualify, they will work for the state for the first ten years of their career. They are another reason why learning has a higher social cachet in France than elsewhere.

Kojève would become as important an influence in France, in terms of political philosophy, as Maritain was in terms of religious philosophy. Among Kojève's well-known students were Jean-Paul Sartre, Maurice Merleau-Ponty, Georges Bataille, Jacques Lacan, André Breton and Raymond Aron. Kojève's underlying argument was that Western civilisation and its associated democracy had triumphed over every alternative (self-regarding and narrow in itself in view of what was happening then in Germany, Russia and Italy, and in Spain from 1936 on) and that everyone would be bourgeoisifed.[6]

This way of thinking began, as perhaps it was bound to do, with the successive disasters and catastrophes of the First World War, the terror and purges in Stalin's Russia, the stock market crash and the ensuing depression, and the Spanish Civil War and its horrors, such as the bombing of Guernica. Against this enervating background, Kojève, Koyré and Bataille in particular, following Heidegger, found traditional atheism – replacing God with man, history, nations and states – as a 'sinister impoverishment'. They were also at pains to point out that their ideas were an 'anti-humanism'. Humanism, they went so far as to say, had led to fascism. What they meant by this was that humanism, even atheistic humanism, carried with it the idea that man was an end, a fixed end, a form of unchanging perfection already created. For them, this was manifestly untrue – man is still in the process of being formed, and it was the very idea that we (mis)understand what man *is* that had led to the catastrophes, as the dictators and other politicians tried to force man into a set mould. 'Neither Marxists nor Capitalists nor humanists ... can fully explain mankind.'[7]

THE LIMITS TO WHAT WE CAN KNOW

Kojève *et al.* were much influenced by science, by what was then recent science, in particular physics, mathematics and anthropology. Science in general they thought had impoverished us because 'completeness' is inherent in scientific and mathematical thought – this is where the idea of 'perfection' had come from in the first place (in the Enlightenment). But the more recent findings of physics and mathematics – in particular, Heisenberg's uncertainty principle – had shown that we are not separate from nature, that the very measurement of the 'outside' world is affected by our presence, and in any case, as Kurt Gödel had shown, there are logical limits to what we can know. Moreover, Kojève argued, there is no such thing as Nature, with a capital 'N', there is no *fixed* nature because science is always advancing our grasp of what nature consists of – incertitude is endemic. On top of that, the discoveries of anthropology show that there are very great differences between peoples, not least in their understanding of God. Therefore, there is no such thing as Being in the abstract (this was Heidegger's point); to *be* exists only at a specific time and a specific location, we can only understand ourselves via the *immediacy* of the concrete, meaning there is no 'pure', privileged long-term perspective on 'life'. In the disappointing decade, this view drove people in on themselves.

And what follows from this, they said, is that we can have no access to transcendence. We cannot step back from the world, as

Heidegger said, with Kojève and the others following; man cannot be 'outside' the world in some way, meaning that transcendence is simply not available. There is no teleology, no direction to the world. The aim of life, one aim among others, is – as Péguy and Maritain also said – to surpass oneself, but even here no generalisations are possible because no generally agreed direction can exist *even in principle*, because humans cannot transcend their subjectivity – philosophically, subjectivity is a central limit to life. All we can hope for, as Emmanuel Levinas (a Lithuanian-turned-Frenchman) put it in a useful neologism, is 'excendence'.[8] And so, as Paul Valéry had said before him, we are condemned to live as solitary individuals within limits and therefore with disappointment.

'NOTHING CAN BE KNOWN BEYOND ACTION'

Though he shared many of the ideas of the existentialists, André Malraux was not really a physical part of the intellectual circuit considered above. He was much more a man of action, travelling to Cambodia and China in his twenties and, while he was in the former country, being arrested for removing some antiquities. His sentence was later revoked but that didn't stop him being critical of the French colonial authorities. In 1930 his father, a banker, committed suicide after the stock market crash. In the mid-1930s Malraux fought in the Spanish Civil War. He also found time to write, his 1933 book *La Condition humaine* winning the Prix Goncourt.

His background was important for his philosophy, which, despite his different lifestyle to the other intellectuals of Paris in the 1930s, nonetheless would in time form part of the canon of what later came to be called existentialism. He accepted that we can have no preconceived idea of man, that 'existence precedes essence' – the founding mantra of existentialism, the first of two distinctive French philosophies of the twentieth century (the other being postmodernism, see chapters 47–8) – and that therefore there is no 'model existence' we can aspire to. Instead, he said, we must aspire to two things: for our lives 'to leave a scar on the face of the earth'; and for our actions to be conducted with other people – 'common action is a common bond'. Life is not sacred, he argued, it is not a possession, but 'an instrument

of value only to the extent that it is utilised'. Malraux thought that
the then fashionable obsession with an 'inner world, the inner life',
was a red herring. He had discovered a different mentality in China.
'The China man, for example, does not conceive of himself as an
individual, the notion of "personality" is foreign to him. The Chinese
feel themselves far less distinct from others and from things than does
the Westerner.'[9]

If there is no direction to life, Malraux decided, then its only
meaning 'must lie in its intensity'. And intensity is determined by
action, from which it follows that the only plan the world will ever
have for us is the one 'we temporarily force upon it' – nothing must be
accepted without a fight, limits must be challenged, the 'constant criticism' of the proto-existentialists. This also meant a refusal to accept
all forms of order, order such as one's position in society, the apparent
order in personality – never accept that you are one type of person or
another, everything is always changing. Malraux agreed with Gide
that there is nothing beyond the immediate, no understanding apart
from experience, that what is not available to sensation does not exist
and that therefore nothing can be known beyond *action*. This is what
La Condition humaine is about.

For Malraux, the real dilemma was this: if action – the decisions we
take and the movements we make – is to remain 'pure', pristine, then
how can we account for other people? In a sense, action and solitude
go together; the immediate experience of action – its very intensity –
distances us from others. And this gives rise to the famous statement:
'Love is not a solution to human solitude; it is a refuge from it.' This
may be extended, to say that there are no solutions to the mysteries
of life, only (temporary) refuges from the constant struggle. Indeed,
Malraux goes so far as to say that intercourse with other people can
never be a satisfactory cure for solitude – only feeling that we have a
reason for being on earth can do that, but metaphysics and religion
he dismisses as no more than irrelevant 'half-way houses'. If we are
to lead an intense life through action, solitude is the inevitable price
we pay.[10]

Malraux thought – and acted – according to his belief that the
universe is not a riddle to which we must find the key, but in fact that
the universe has nothing to conceal from us. We must explore it as

intensely as we can, trying as best we can to both enjoy the experience and *observe ourselves experiencing it.* If we need a metaphor by which to live, we should be like modern artists, creating something which is its own justification and which others will only understand incompletely. Understanding, as Gödel said, has its limits; it is another half-way house.

A Great Negro Cry … Nourished with White Decadence

The years 1929 to 1939 saw the birth and far-reaching influence of a very unusual and internationally minded salon in Paris, one animated by the black hostesses Paulette Nardal (1896–1985) and her sister, Jeanne (1900–93), and which was to become known in later generations either as the Salon de Clamart, after the area of southern Paris where Paulette lived, or, more specifically, as the Négritude Salon. Paulette and her sister, whose great-grandmother had been born into slavery but was freed in 1850, were two of seven daughters of a flute-playing construction engineer and his wife, a piano teacher, in the French West Indian island of Martinique, where their home was a salon for musicians. After graduating from school both Paulette and Jeanne chose to continue their education in Paris, becoming the first black students to enrol at the Sorbonne, where Paulette wrote her thesis on Harriet Beecher Stowe, the American white anti-slavery activist.[11]

In October 1931, Paulette and Jeanne helped to found a bilingual (French and English) journal, the *Revue du monde noir,* together with their cousin Louis Achille, Louis Jean Finot, a sardonic writer whom Jean-Paul Sartre was to praise for the vigour of his characters, Léo Sajous, a Haitian academic, and Clara Shepard, an African-American teacher and translator. Another early influence was Claude McKay, a black American writer whose early novel, *Banjo,* was set on the waterfront in Marseilles and was first published in Paris in 1931. Through the Americans, Paulette and Jeanne – and two other sisters, Andrée and Alice, who had followed them to Paris – came under the influence of the Harlem Renaissance, which itself had been sparked by the return of black soldiers from the First World War in the expectation of a better world they had fought for.

The *Revue du monde noir* lasted for only six issues and afterwards Paulette began working for a Senegalese deputy in the French
National Assembly and was involved in the political movements that
followed the 1935 Italian invasion of Ethiopia. In her journalism she
worked for other black publications, *France-Outremer*, *Le Cri des
Nègres*, the *Dépêche africaine* and *L'Étudiant noir*. In particular,
she wrote about black arts and culture. Jeanne helped to found the
Dépêche africaine.

But it was in the sisters' salon, held on Sundays at 7 rue Hébert
in the fourteenth arrondissement, that, arguably, they exerted the
most influence. Two early guests were René Maran and Alain Locke.
Like the sisters, Maran was born in Martinique, though of Guianese
parents. He accompanied his father, who was a diplomat, to Gabon
in central Africa and was then educated in Bordeaux before entering
the colonial service himself. His first book, *Batouala*, which was
read in the Nardal salon, was inspired by these experiences and
swept the Goncourt Prize in 1921, the first book by a black author
to win the award. Alain Locke, a graduate of Harvard, was the first
African-American Rhodes scholar at Oxford, and he also attended
the University of Berlin and the Collège de France in Paris, where he
studied philosophy. He was the editor/compiler of *The New Negro*,
a landmark in black literature and a central element in the Harlem
Renaissance, and he stood for the view that 'modern Negro art was
not to be viewed as merely an extension of African art but, rather, as
an expression of contemporary racial temperament'. This too was a
central element in *Négritude*.[12]

If these individuals, extending the limits of black life, helped
to inspire the Nardal sisters, the sisters in turn inspired the trio
who between them combined to formulate the basic ingredients of
Négritude. Indeed, the relationship was even more direct than that:
Léopold Sédar Senghor apparently fell for Andrée, the prettiest of
the sisters and a gifted pianist, though the family was against the
match, and Léon Gontran Damas married Isabelle Achille, daughter
of Louis Achille, the sisters' cousin.[13]

It was discussions in the Clamart salon that inspired Aimé Césaire,
Senghor and Damas to explore the aesthetics, politics and epistemology of Négritude, a concept that came into being around 1935. In

Paulette's final essay in the last issue of the *Revue du monde noir*, she outlined '*l'éveil de la conscience de race*', 'the awakening of race consciousness'. Senghor in particular was close to Maran, who, he said, also 'prepared the way to Négritude for us ... after Maran no one could ever make Negroes live, love, work, cry, laugh, or speak likes Whites again'.[14] Senghor had arrived in Paris from Senegal in 1928 to prepare for the entrance exam for the École normale supérieure at the Lycée Louis-le-Grand, where Césaire arrived two years later from Martinique. Originally from French Guiana, Damas had been sent to school in Martinique where he became friendly with Césaire. It was the Nardal sisters who introduced this close-knit group to visiting Americans.

Négritude was born of the solitude and limits to life that many black people felt in a white Europe and, in order to cope with that predicament, became a collective attempt to explore if there was such a thing as black culture. It was also driven by several other resentful impulses, one being to overcome the experience of slavery, and the 'displacement' that had brought about ('the belly of a slave ship is my heritage' as Césaire wrote). Another was to counter the way Picasso and other modern artists had appropriated African culture (in *Les Demoiselles d'Avignon*, for example) and the paternalistic accounts by the anthropologist Lucien Lévy-Bruhl in such books as *Primitive Mentality* (1922) and *How Natives Think* (1926) and, later, Father Placide Tempels's *Bantu Philosophy*. A third impulse was the embarrassment felt by Creoles of the Caribbean who considered themselves, then, to be the vanguard of black people, and who looked down on Africans as less civilised. Fourth was the opposite view, that the Caribbean peoples had grown up in a society 'nourished with white decadence'. And a final impulse was the feeling that African-Americans were too turned inward, 'so as to avoid reprisals from their white countrymen' and so, despite the Harlem Renaissance, weren't wholly themselves, their individuality compromised.

Was there a 'Negro spirit' (the phrase used at the time) that transcended these differences, asked this group gathered at the Nardal salon, was there such a thing as African civilisation that would unify the Negro experience and not 'ape Europe' (as, perhaps, the salon itself was doing)? The answer would take time to emerge, Césaire arguing that, through their distinctive traditional religions, Africans harboured numerous 'witch doctor secrets' in their soul, that such phenomena as totemism and magical thinking could be fused into a 'great negro cry until the foundations of the world shall tremble'. But, being in Europe, they were also influenced by Herder and Bergson, in particular Herder's idea of the importance of folk arts and religions, and Bergson's distinction between intellect and intuition (Césaire talked of an 'Afro-Bergsonian epistemology'). Intuition, Bergson claimed, flourished in solitude and knew no limits, least of all scientific ones.

For Senghor the central idea of Négritude was that the Negro was a distinctive 'force' in the world and that the purpose of force was to increase. Moreover, this force was especially evident in art – in animism and rhythm, for example, what he identified as 'the negro style', the 'negro way of knowing'. Jeanne Nardal wrote that rhythm was 'the "sovereign" master of black bodies', and Césaire had his notion of a 'spirit of the bush'.[15]

Essentially, the argument boiled down to Dionysian black culture versus Apollonian white, the idea that rhythmic and emotional Negro art was a vital response to 'the mechanistic and dehumanising philosophy that produced and was produced by modern Europe'.[16] At the same time, Senghor and Césaire both appreciated that blacks had to live in the modern world, 'live within history', and so they must assimilate to the dominant culture – Dionysus has to live with Apollo and so could never be more than a half-way house.

Négritude was criticised by French Marxists, Sartre especially, for placing race ahead of class and art ahead of economics. Poetry, Sartre said, was too solitary, too personal and too inward, to ever match the collective, sociable achievements of politics.

'MAN HAS NO INTERIOR'

Though he is best known, generally speaking, for being a pioneer aviator and for his novella *The Little Prince* (translated into no fewer than 250 languages), Antoine de Saint-Exupéry won several literary prizes, in France and the United States, and would fight as part of the Free French Air Force in north Africa in the Second World War (despite being wildly over age). His books would earn the distinction of being banned in both occupied France and free France (he was very suspicious of de Gaulle). Famously, he disappeared on a reconnaissance flight over the Mediterranean in July 1944.

His much earlier book *Vol de nuit*, which appeared in 1931, was arguably a much better effort. Despite his literary prizes, Saint-Exupéry had no especial fondness for men of letters – like Malraux he believed in action. 'The role of spectator has always been my bugbear. What am I if I do not take part?' Because the universe is not rational, he said, 'it reveals itself to action and not to thought'.[17] And like Malraux, Saint-Exupéry believed that 'man has no "interior" considered either as a depository of "innate" truths, as a receptacle for facts acquired by perception and reason or as a set of clearly defined characteristics'. He agreed with Malraux and, as he showed with his character Robineau in *Vol de nuit*, 'neither action nor individual happiness allow of being shared'. For him, throughout history there have been two means of responding to the 'spiritual dry rot' of bourgeois society – love and religion. 'To love, to love and nothing else – what a dead end!"[18]

Contemporary religion, Saint-Exupéry claimed, is unsure of itself, of the message it brings, or the light it offers, and so is unbelief. '[Jacques] Bernis [a character in *The Aviator*] enters a church to listen to a sermon which seems to him a cry that has long since ceased to expect an answer.' This, for Saint-Exupéry, is the wrong way to look at the world, to expect an answer to a question. Life is not what we possess, he is saying, but what we *win*. In his book *Pilote de guerre* (1942), he says: 'Anguish is due to the loss of a real identity, and it is only through action that identity may be regained.' And he admits this is based on his own experience. In the lull before his sortie to Arras, he felt he was awaiting an 'unknown self' which he sensed was 'coming towards him from outside, like a phantom'. By the time his mission was completed, his 'unknown self' was no longer unknown; he had discovered a little more of who he was *through his deeds*. 'Humanism', he liked to say, 'has taken too little notice of deeds.' Being cultured is not to be achieved by contemplation, but by being enriched by action, *doing*. 'There is no existence that is not contact with things.'

And 'life', moreover, is not one thing. We are constantly redefining what it is by our actions, our deeds. Saint-Exupéry's ideal on this score – his model – was not a great writer or philosopher, but (simply) Hochedé, a fellow pilot during the war. Hochedé had no real inner life, Saint-Exupéry tells us, he was 'pure existence' in that his acts and his identity were one. Saint-Exupéry said he experienced this himself briefly, just once, when he was over Arras where, in the thick of enemy fire, 'you are lodged in your act ... Your act is you ... You no longer find anything else in you.' This individual completeness, without the need for anyone else, was, for him, transcendence. 'Hochedé ... would not know how to throw any light upon himself. But he is constructed, he is complete ... We usually think of an "accomplished" man as one who has somehow found time to bring to perfection both his mental and physical activities, who is both philosopher and peasant, or statesman and soldier. Hochedé, however, has no "inner" life, yet he lacks for nothing; for what really exists, exists in things exterior to us and comprehensible in themselves.' As Malraux said, so Saint-Exupéry agreed: we gain personal fulfilment by doing rather than by thinking. 'Happiness is the "warmth of acts"; a civilisation rests upon what it exacts from its people, not what it furnishes them.'[19] Solitude is by definition a half-way house, but it is all there is.

A Surrender to Defeatism

Each of these writers – the philosophers no less than the novelists – was concerned with identifying and extending what we might call both the grandeur and the limits of existence but, in the context of the 1930s, the locust years, the emphasis was more on the solitary nature of experience rather than the traditional French interest in sociability. No one could avoid being aware of the fragility of civilisation, and that the France of the 1930s was anything but healthy. Solitude and Négritude were surrounded by lassitude and incertitude. Half-way houses were as much as people could hope for.

To return to the context, in 1936 France was paralysed by sit-in strikes, affecting – and here again the figures mentioned above do not lie – no fewer than 12,000 enterprises, including a raft of companies making weapons. The strikes did, it is true, bring about the biggest single advance in industrial relations in France: workers were guaranteed compulsory collective bargaining and annual paid holidays, a forty-hour week and an immediate rise in wages of between 7 and 15 per cent. Even so, the strikes continued, governments continued to fall, and Hitler occupied the Rhineland. France did not act.

Also, thanks to the agreement brought about by the sit-in strikes, France discovered leisure. Between 1936 and 1938 the number of bicycles there rose from 7 million to 9 million. Yet there were dark clouds in this silver lining too: as leisure use increased, this rather vitiated the communist aim of bringing high culture to the masses, while industrial production continued to stagnate and worse – its level in 1938 was 25 per cent below the 1930 level, whereas the equivalent figure in Germany was an increase of 30 per cent.[20]

Many historians now believe that the Rhineland incursion was the crucial episode in the approach to war, not Munich. Had France acted and been able to resist the incursion, Hitler would not have found it so easy to have his way in Germany. But, as on the eve of the Franco-Prussian War, France was not prepared to look reality in the face. Instead, in the Paris of the 1930s, intellectual life – as these examples show – was both grandiose and yet self-centred. As one observer put it: 'The energy that might have been directed abroad was turned inward.' In October 1938 when the American journalist William L. Shirer, who was based in Berlin, visited Paris, he was appalled by what he found. It was sick, he said, 'a frightful place, completely surrendered to defeatism with no inkling of what has happened to *France* ... Even the waiters, the taxi-drivers, who used to be sound, are gushing about how wonderful it is that war has been avoided, that it would have been a crime, that they had fought in one war and that was enough.' The Germans, he added, had also fought in one war, but in no way did they share the French sentiment.[21] Was it the case, as someone said, that 'French unhappiness might be caused by too much thinking?' The journey to the beginning of the night was well under way.

For Paulette Nardal that journey was especially perilous. In early September 1939, when the Second World War was declared, she was actually back home in Martinique working on a screenplay for a film commissioned by the French minister of colonies. Despite the war, she fearlessly headed back to Paris and on the thirteenth of the month boarded the SS *Bretagne*. As the ship neared the English coast the *Bretagne* was torpedoed by German submarines. The attack lasted throughout the night but then a British destroyer appeared to pick up the survivors. The destroyer had itself been hit during the hostilities so that passengers had to use knotted ropes to transfer between ships. In the middle of continual fire, Nardal, then forty-four, took three attempts to get across from one ship to the other, and at the last minute she was required to jump. The jump saved her life but owing to the fact that the edge of the destroyer had been damaged in the fighting, when she landed her left leg was very nearly separated from her body. She was forced to remain in hospital in Plymouth for eleven months, hovering between life and death for three of them. She had lost everything and was left permanently disabled.

In July 1940, Louis Achille, her cousin, by now a professor at Howard University in America, cabled her the money necessary for her return home. When she arrived, after a second crossing of the Atlantic in wartime, it was to find Martinique taken over by Vichy rule. Once there, she risked arrest by giving English lessons to locals who wanted to escape to nearby Anglophone islands to join Charles de Gaulle's Free French. When the island was liberated, she started another salon.[22]

The Collaboration of Culture and the Culture of Collaboration

On the morning of Friday 14 June 1940, Sylvia Beach was waiting with Adrienne Monnier in the latter's fourth-floor apartment in the rue de l'Odéon. Odéonia, as their tiny empire of bookshops had been christened all the way back in the First World War, still existed, twenty years on, and Adrienne's window still commanded a clear view to the north, where their tiny lane led into the boulevard Saint-German and its leafy chestnut trees. As she watched, a column of German trucks and motorcycles suddenly came into view, and then an 'endless procession of motorised forces: tanks and armoured cars and helmeted men seated with arms folded . . . all a cold grey, and they moved to a deafening roar'. As the two women watched, tears were streaming down their cheeks.[1]

Odéonia had survived the interwar years, but only just. The depression had hardly helped but writers such as Gide, Valéry, Maurois and Duhamel had formed a subscription company along the lines that Gertrude Stein had dreamed up earlier on. By 1940, however, many of their stalwarts – Man Ray, James Joyce, Gisèle Freund, the photo-journalist who portrayed so many artists and writers – had escaped to the safety of the south or Switzerland. Adrienne had been hiding the Hungarian-Jewish, anti-Nazi, anti-Soviet Arthur Koestler in her apartment until documents could be forged to help him escape. Most of the people Sylvia and Adrienne mixed with were anything but collaborators, including Paul Valéry, then sixty-nine, who, when

Henri Bergson died in January 1941, was chosen to deliver his eulogy. Bergson, who was eighty-one when he died, had been considering converting to Catholicism – but, seeing the anti-Semitism that was sweeping Europe, France included, he decided he could not abandon the persecuted. It was also reported that he died from a cold contracted when he was standing in line to register his Jewish status, as then required by law. His registration read: 'Academic, Philosopher, Nobel Prize Winner, Jew.'

A BROTH OF HATRED

The literature on the imagination of France and the French during the exceptional circumstances of occupation in the Second World War is copious, in French, English and German sources, as well it might be, given the at times disgraceful way that the Germans treated the French and the French – some French – treated their fellow countrymen and women. (See the notes for some book titles.)

In his very tart account of intellectual and artistic collaboration during the Occupation of France, Frederic Spotts divides his account very simply into two hemispheres, those who did what the Germans asked of them, and those who had the 'morals, wit or balls' to resist. This distinction is – and will always be – a major element of French history.

'The true France was not at Vichy, the true France never collaborated.' This was President Sarkozy as late as May 2008, on the anniversary of the end of the Second World War in Europe. Everyone knows that these sentiments are ludicrous. At least de Gaulle had the honesty to admit that the events to be recounted amount to a 'dull pain in the depths of our national consciousness'.[2] Spotts observes that France's greatest psychological need in the wake of the 'ignominious debacle' of 1940 and all that followed 'was to regain a sense of self-respect – the very *honneur* and *gloire* that de Gaulle invoked in his broadcasts from London'.

'France was not defeated on the artistic front,' insisted Louis Hautecœur, head of the Académie des beaux-arts in the summer of 1940. 'Our architecture, our painting, our sculpture, our music continued to arouse admiration.' This somewhat misses the point when

Hitler was on record as being ardent in his intention to show the German cultural supremacy over the French as a challenge to their self-confidence and to weaken their sense of national identity. After the war the German ambassador in Paris during the Occupation claimed baldly that 'it would be extremely difficult to name any notable French artist who had not supported collaboration'.

It is of course easy – perhaps too easy – for those who did not undergo occupation to criticise the behaviour of those caught up in these events. At times, as Gilles and Jean Ragache remind us, people 'lived in the very real fear that the Occupation would last a century'.[3]

To begin with, though, it wasn't like that. In London, theatres and concerts and cabarets were closed immediately at the start of hostilities, and parks were disfigured by the digging of trenches. In Paris theatres stayed open, as did cafés and restaurants, and the races reopened after a short closure. Simone de Beauvoir could be found at the café de Flore after her teaching job at a lycée. Everyone, as she said, was waiting. They didn't know what for, but they were waiting.

Painters were assigned to camouflage units, Henri Cartier-Bresson and Jean Renoir to film units. In the *drôle de guerre* painters were allowed time off to return to their studios and continue work. Maurice de Vlaminck remarked that, if the First World War was a cubist war, the Second was a surrealist war. There certainly were surreal moments. On 25 May 1940, as the Belgian army was capitulating and Dunkirk was being encircled, in Paris audiences were filling the opera house to capacity for Darius Milhaud's new work, *Médée*.

Paris fell after only thirty-five days of fighting in 'one of the most shocking events of the Second World War'.[4] Many artists and intellectuals managed to flee, and some managed to escape France altogether, thanks to Varian Fry's US-funded Emergency Rescue Committee, set up partly on the initiative of Eleanor Roosevelt, which identified and paid for selected talents to be secretly ferried over the Pyrenees to Lisbon, and on to a boat to the United States.[5]

In the early days, German soldiers were instructed to be friendly and inoffensive but on top of that the Germans had an interest in Parisian cultural life returning to the *status quo ante* as soon as possible, to help create the impression that everything was normal, though British and American films were banned. By 1942 there were hundreds of nightclubs and cabarets back in business in Paris, as were the brothels where occupier and occupied met, frequenting the same *horizontales*. One brothel posted a sign in summer 1940: 'Business as usual from 3.00 p.m.' A sexology of collaborationism wasn't published until 2008 but it was then revealed just how much sex between occupiers and occupied had taken place.[6]

The 112 was the most soigné of the nightclubs, and here Sacha Guitry, Maurice Chevalier and Fernandel mixed with Germans. 'The population easily accepted the Occupation. Paris had never been so brilliant culturally,' said Véronique Rebatet, wife of Lucien Rebatet, an extreme right-wing journalist who had worked for *Action française* and then joined *Je suis partout*, an equally collaborationist publication. Across the river, the Deux Magots was very anti-German and their officers stayed away, but at the café de Flore Picasso, Sartre, Beauvoir, Éluard, Camus and others periodically had their 'fiestas' or else held play-readings, with Barrault, Braque, Lacan and Bataille in the audience. 'Paris was more well-read and less prudish than Vichy.'

People still quarrelled over ideas but running through the disagreements was a mix of Anglophobia, anti-Semitism, anti-communism, homophobia and a virility cult that took its strength from what Spotts calls a 'broth of hatred'. Long-pent-up feelings festered from the sheer shame of the defeat. Simone de Beauvoir said that whatever they might enjoy at the Flore, she felt she was living in a gigantic prison.

Many collaborators were not sudden converts to fascism – they had been imbibing the idea for some time. Journalists like Robert Brasillach had even been pan-Germanists for years. In some ways the years of preparation were uncanny. Otto Abetz, the German wartime ambassador in Paris, was drawn to Hitler early on. Interested in the cultural impact of war, he had been in France in the 1930s where he had studied French aesthetics and culture and identified a number of sympathetic individuals who could help 'when the time came'. In fact, he had 'researched' the subject to such an extent that he had been expelled by the government. For his German staff he deliberately chose individuals who felt the German defeat in 1918 as a humiliation. His main point on arrival in Paris was to encourage the French to acknowledge German cultural superiority.

THE OTTO LIST

On the one hand, German propaganda was keen to encourage at least the idea that cultural activity in France should continue, to appear reasonable and cultivated. The problem with this was that the Germans couldn't help themselves, so that anything having to do with Jews, Freemasons, communists or British or American culture was forbidden. In addition to which they had quite a hefty machinery for ensuring they got their way, which was hard to overlook or ignore. Censorship offices called *Staffeln* were established in a variety of cities. Art exhibitions in private galleries and museums were inspected, theatre programmes, concerts and operas were regulated. A central office held weekly meetings to outline to newspaper editors the way their publications should 'cover' various issues. It employed some 30,000 informants, known as *mouches*, or 'flies'.[7]

But there were plenty of French all too ready to write what was wanted of them by their new masters. The *ultra-collabo* press consisted of *Je suis partout* ('I Am Everywhere'), popularly known as *Je chie partout* ('I Shit Everywhere') and later, near the end, as *Je suis parti* ('I Have Left'). Others were *Au pilori* ('To the Scaffold') and *Gringoire*, a publication of the traditional Catholic right.

Je suis partout had been launched in 1930 by Jean Fayard, a writer of fiction and non-fiction, a member of the Fayard publishing house and a winner of the Prix Goncourt. It was extremely right-wing, its journalists including the bow-tie-wearing Lucien Rebatet and the historian Pierre Gaxotte, and was heavily influenced by the ideas of *Action française*, supporting Franco in Spain, Mussolini in Italy and Oswald Mosley in London. In its anti-Semitism it had made much of the Stavisky affair, a financial scandal in 1934 involving a Russian Jew, Alexandre Stavisky, who died in mysterious circumstances, provoking right-wing demonstrations, in which fifteen were killed, events which may have been intended to provoke a coup d'état. *Je suis partout* violently opposed the Popular Front government of (the Jewish) Léon Blum in 1936 and, not long before war broke out, the paper was banned. It reappeared in 1941, calling loudly for the persecution of Jews and left-wingers. *Je suis partout* ran a weekly column entitled 'Partout et ailleurs' ('Everywhere and Elsewhere'),

revealing the identities and addresses of people not considered 'altogether reliable'.[8]

Far more problematic, in retrospect, was *Comœdia*. This was an old
French periodical, a weekly arts and literature publication with a not
undistinguished history, though it had closed in 1937. Abetz revived it
and appointed René Delange, a well-regarded journalist (well regarded
before the war) as editor. He attracted a lot of distinguished writers,
including Henry de Montherlant, precocious essayist and dramatist,
Jean-Louis Barrault, the famous mime-actor, and the Swiss composer
Arthur Honegger. Sartre himself wrote a piece on *Moby-Dick*, there
was a report on Saint-Exupéry's return to France from America,
before he left for Algiers, and an interview with Paul Valéry. These
were first-rate names. *Comœdia* didn't indulge in the crude manoeuvres of *Je suis partout*, but it *was* financed by the German Occupation.
Sartre and Valéry were warned off and saw the light.

Worse was the early decision by French publishers, led by Bernard
Grasset but including the Gallimards – two of the hitherto most distinguished houses – to censor themselves, offering, off their own bat,
to 'respect the rights of the victor' in anything they might publish,
even going so far as to say they would be 'eliminating undesirable
works' which 'in any way whatsoever [might] damage German prestige or interests'. The list of proscribed books – the first list – which
was published in September 1940 and became known as the 'Otto
List' after Abetz's first name, was in fact produced by the French
publishers themselves, anticipating what the Germans would want
proscribed.[9] One title on the list, incidentally, was *Mon Combat*, a
French translation of a book by a certain Adolf Hitler. Frederic Spotts
is suitably pointed about this: 'Perhaps the ban was not quite so ridiculous. If they read it, the French would know that Hitler despised
them and admired the British.'[10] Two more expanded lists would be
published, in July 1941 and May 1943.

A MACABRE CULTURAL DANCE

The man in charge of book censorship in Paris was Gerhard Heller,
who arrived in November 1940 on his thirty-first birthday. He had
been an early member of the Nazi Party, since well before the time it

was necessary to join if one wanted advancement. He had also studied in Toulouse on a scholarship.

He was a great favourite of the five *salonnières* who dominated collaborationist social life in Paris between 1940 and 1944. These included the three Maries – Marie-Louise Bousquet, editor of the French *Harper's Bazaar*, Marie-Blanche de Polignac, heiress to the Jeanne Lanvin fashion house, and Marie-Laure de Noailles, the interwar muse of the surrealists, plus Mme Boudot-Lamotte, on the rue de Verneuil, where one evening in February 1942 *le tout Paris intellectuel* listened as Jean Cocteau read his new play, *Reynaud et Armide*. The most remarkable salon of the Occupation, however, was that of a striking woman, Florence Gould, San Francisco-born of French parents and arguably the worst of them all. It was these salons that allowed the two sets of elites to meet in agreeable surroundings.[11]

Gould had moved to France after the 1902 earthquake in California where, following boarding school with her sister and a swift marriage and divorce, she became a singer and drew the attention of Frank Jay Gould, described as 'the seriously rich son of a corrupt American railway mogul', a background not too dissimilar to Natalie Clifford Barney's. The couple had several houses, one on the Riviera, where they helped turn Cannes into the capital of the Côte d'Azur, one in the spa town of Vichy, and a grand house in Paris, just off the Étoile at 129 avenue de Malakoff, to which Florence moved in 1942, after living in the hôtel Bristol.

During the Occupation, she began by sending food packages to French soldiers and volunteering as a nurse in a Paris hospital but then, aged forty-five, she took to inviting friends for lunches, teas and dinners at the Bristol. She also attended Marie-Louise Bousquet's salon, until it was suggested that she hold her own. This began at the hôtel Bristol but transferred to the avenue Malakoff, held every Thursday. Ernst Jünger, author of the First World War novel *Storm of Steel*, was a regular, much taken by her vivid green eyes, often hidden behind dark glasses. Rumoured to be one of her many lovers, he was working just then in intelligence, on the invasion of Britain (Operation Sea Lion) and then had a cushy job reading intercepted letters.[12] He was impressed by Florence's ability to be with powerful people (she realised the trick was to be 'never afraid'). Another

regular early on, besides Heller, was Helmut Knochen, fanatical head
of the Gestapo in Paris and a protégé of Reinhard Heydrich, architect
of the Holocaust. Knochen's responsibility was the rounding up of
French Jews and blowing up synagogues (he destroyed seven).

On the surface, Gould's salon was of the literary kind, other guests
including Jean Paulhan, a secret resistant, Comœdia's editor-in-chief
René Delange, Sacha Guitry, Jean Giraudoux, playwright and novelist, and the decorator Christian Bérard. But there was really no hiding
the fact that it was partly a political gathering, based on Nazi sympathies, Anglophobia, anti-Semitism and hangers-on. It was partly
that Florence offered sumptuous feasts with unmatched black-mar-
ket food and wine. And though the subjects of discussion ranged
through literature, business, politics, food and art, the Thursdays at
129 avenue de Malakoff were also partly 'juxtapositions of love and
hate; collabo and résistant; rampant sexuality and closet homosexuality ... entwined in a macabre cultural dance'.[13]

One of the guests she took a shine to was Marcel Jouhandeau,
Catholic closet homosexual, who had released Le Péril juif in 1938,
basically four anti-Semitic articles he couldn't get published in the
newspapers, aimed at Léon Blum and his Popular Front government.
The salons had begun on Thursdays in April 1942 because that was
the only day Jouhandeau could get free from teaching at his lycée.
Gould had taken a liking to this 'unprepossessing' man, despite
his scrawny build and unbecoming beard which hid – but did not
hide – his harelip. The others present at that first encounter included
Marie-Louise Bousquet, Pierre Benoît of the Académie française,
the novelist Marcel Arland, Jean Paulhan, director of the Nouvelle
Revue française, Marie Bell and Arletty, the actress and singer.[14]
Camus's biographer says he and Sartre and 'the left bank crowd'
always rejected invitations from Gould.

Conversation was encouraged by the fact that Gould was an
avid art collector and her apartment was decorated in priceless
works – unguent boxes and lachrymatories from Egyptian tombs,
impressionist paintings bought from Wildenstein (whose gallery had
been 'Aryanised'), illuminated manuscripts and mediaeval engravings. More than one guest – Marie Laurencin, for example – later
confessed to attending mainly because the food was so good.[15]

The French writer Claude Mauriac, journalist son of Françoise Mauriac and later secretary to Charles de Gaulle, referred to one of her parties in his memoirs. He confessed to Hervé Le Boterf that he was 'stupefied to be shaking hands with one of those [German] officers whose contact I find so repugnant on the Metro ... The champagne and the atmosphere of sympathy and youth made everything too easy.'[16]

She did try to corral Céline into her gatherings, but he played hard to get, despite the fact that Gould money financed a sexual diseases clinic that Céline was associated with as a doctor. And on one occasion she was forced to go to him, not the other way around, 'taking her dinner with her'. Céline was part-scathing and part-respectful. 'She was absolutely insistent on buying my manuscripts,' he said later. 'I refused, not wanting to owe anything to an American multi-millionairess. In her rush to leave one evening she was drunk and it was dark and she slipped on the steps at the bottom of the staircase and broke her leg.' He did not visit her in hospital though he did say later that he had some respect for her, describing her as 'amazing and not stupid, a snob'. Later still he added: 'She was enormously compromised with the Luftwaffe – where she had at least three young lovers and was very much at home in the German military headquarters.'[17]

Behind her back, Jünger and Heller would joke about her and her money. While Sylvia Beach and some 3,000 British and American civilians now languished in the internment camps, Gould remained free even to pass back and forth between the occupied and unoccupied zones, an unheard-of privilege.[18]

During the course of the war, Gould's salon flourished. In the summers it transferred to Juan-les-Pins, where she would entertain Matisse. Jouhandeau was eventually replaced as her co-host/master of ceremonies by Robert Denoël, Céline's publisher. Among her many lovers – and rumoured lovers – was Ludwig Vogel, an engineer who worked for Focke-Wulf, which made fighter planes for the Luftwaffe, who took her to Germany twice to view the company's main factory, Florence travelling each time under an assumed name. She was well informed – Jünger in his memoirs reports that it was Florence who told him that Mussolini had resigned.[19] Colette was also often there with her husband.

Remarkably Florence and her salon seemed unaffected by the fact that America was at war with Germany, though she did have to part with some of her art when the Einsatzstab Reichsletter Rosenberg, the Nazi art police, found some valuable pieces during a search for weapons at her house in the south. A deal was done with Göring. She also suffered a scare when her husband – living all the time in the south – was investigated for being Jewish. But that too was resolved.

Throughout the war she was seen all over Paris in social settings and even visited the studios of Picasso, Braque and Dubuffet, the latter being invited to her salon, where he painted several of her guests.[20]

Despite all this, and despite the fact that Florence left no written record of her own, Alan Riding, in his account of cultural life in occupied Paris, says, somewhat surprisingly, that there was 'never any suggestion' that she herself ever expressed pro-German or anti-Jewish opinions.[21] And she never had her head shaved, like so many other women during the *épuration*, possibly because she made a timely donation to the resistance movement. Riding says that, in fact, her lunches resumed after the Liberation, 'now with occasional American guests, as if the war had been no more than a passing storm'.[22] Even in late 1945, just six months after the end of the war, Heller received a letter that, he recalled, read: 'Come quickly, the Thursdays await you.' It was signed by Florence, Paulhan, Léautaud, and Arland.

Heller took his time to respond, and it was not until 1981, forty-six years after the war, that he finally got round to publishing an account of those years, as *Un Allemand à Paris*. Very possibly he had waited so long until all other survivors from those years had died and could not contradict him. In his book, he shows himself as something of a *boulevardier*, dwelling on the salons of both Marie-Louise Bousquet and Florence Gould. He found Florence 'beautiful, great, with chestnut hair; a very attractive woman in her thirties; she had a great knowledge and a great love of literature'. In fact, Gould admitted, in her self-confident irritating way, that she knew little about books but a lot about authors – 'all writers are cocottes,' she said.[23] Heller identifies some of the 'arch-collabos', the names France would like to forget: Marcel Arland, founder of the Dadaist newspaper *Aventure*,

Jacques Benoist-Méchin, journalist and historian, graduate of the Lycée Louis-le-Grand, Abel Bonnard, poet and politician, Pierre Drieu La Rochelle, Alfred Fabre-Luce, founder of the political weekly *Pamphlet*, Jacques Chardonne and Robert Brasillach. Heller claims that François Mauriac agreed to make several textual changes to one of his novels in return for him increasing the print-run and that Roland Dorgelès, author of *Wooden Crosses*, refused to delete the word *boche* from the text and so the book was not given a licence. (*Caboche* in French means 'cabbage', but the term may also derive from '*alboche*', meaning 'wooden head'.)[24]

Heller made much of the 'fact' that during the Occupation more books were published in France than before the war, and more than in Britain and America. He had nothing to say about quality control.

A CULTURAL SUPERIORITY COMPLEX

A truer picture of what the Germans were about can be seen from the work of Karl Epting, in charge of the German Institute, which had looked after student exchange before the war. After the invasion, Epting's job was quite simply to destroy the French 'cultural superiority complex'. As he told an audience 'to their faces' in a speech: 'French intellectuals must give up the idea of being world leaders ... They must not pretend to speak in the name of principles valid for every country and they should not try to spread these principles beyond France.'[25] Attending events at the German Institute 'became a critical gauge of a person's attitude toward the Occupation'. Among those who did attend were Serge Lifar, Jean Giraudoux, Alfred Cortot, Robert Brasillach, the sculptor Charles Despiau, Louis-Ferdinand Céline, Jean-Louis Barrault, José Sert, Henry de Montherlant and Jean Cocteau. After the course of the war changed, Epting stayed on as long as he could and tried to entice the collaborators to leave with him. Some – Bonnard, Rebatet, the pianist Lucienne Delforge and Jean Hérold-Paquis, propaganda journalist and author of *L'Angleterre comme Carthage* ('England like Carthage'), that old, that very old charge – did go with him. Others – Drieu, Brasillach, Germaine Lubin, an opera singer, Lifar – refused. Still others went – like Céline – but not with him.

Artists were, for the most part, left unmolested. André Breton thought it was important for the spirit of France for art to continue but, to be candid, it was much harder for painters to paint anti-German art than it was for writers to come up with anti-German stories. Matisse, Bonnard, Rouault and Picabia painted on in the unoccupied zone. Artists ignored Vichy and Vichy ignored them.

A SHAMEFUL PEACE

The life of Jean Cocteau during the war years was not noticeably different from his life at any other time. He continued to do his best to be an *enfant terrible*, admired, irritated and mocked by a whole slew of contemporaries from Gide to Picasso to Chanel, who admired his elegance and the range of his talents but also managed to feel that his achievements were somehow overrated. Frederic Spotts has two phrases about Cocteau that usefully sum him up. One, that life was a party and he was the life of it. And the other was in his record of the war years in which he said 'Long live the shameful peace', the title Spotts gave to his book on the culture of collaboration.

Cocteau could write this with heartfelt feeling because, among all the other things he did and did not do, he still kept company with the *grandes dames* of Paris, the great hostesses. Throughout the war, his social life was hardly affected – he still dined at Le Grand Véfour, La Tour d'argent and Maxim's and with Picasso at Le Catalan. The Vicomtesse de Noailles – herself compromised as the bedmate of a Wehrmacht officer – remained one of his favourites. 'Such a comfort it was to visit her!' Cocteau was in any case well connected – François Darlan, commander of the navy and premier from February 1941 to April 1942, was his cousin. Many of the leading *collabos* of the theatre world were his regular dining partners. At least once, he turned up at what he termed Florence Gould's 'Nazi coterie'.

Whatever unpleasant side to him there was, it cannot be denied that he was immensely creative, even under occupation. He made one faux pas when he reviewed Arno Breker's exhibition in May 1942, which drew a raft of criticism from people he either admired or whose admiration he would have liked – people such as Paul Éluard. But he also organised an exhibition of his own drawings, did the décor and costumes for a Feydeau farce, produced a version of *Antigone*, with music by Milhaud, and arranged a reprise in 1942 of *La Machine à écrire*, first performed in 1938.[26] He produced a love story, *Renaud et Armide*, and turned *Tristan and Isolde* into modern garb as *L'Éternal Retour*, a very successful film.

And yet ... and yet ... he was constantly comparing Hitler to Napoleon. Hitler, he thought, had not only Napoleon's gifts as a warrior but also Talleyrand's as a diplomat: 'With Hitler we have a poet who rises above the mentality of these little men.' He dismissed Churchill as a drunk 'weeping over the abdication of Edward VIII'.[27] Once the Liberation was under way, a notable feature of his reaction was that he decried the presence of British and American forces in Paris much more aggressively than he had ever criticised the German military: 'The organised disorder of the Americans contrasts with the style of German discipline.'[28]

He looked on the *épuration sauvage* with equal disdain, likening the 'caprice' of the crowd to that of the Gestapo. He was as upset that the guilty went unpunished as he was that artists were being selected for show trials. He was equally dismissive about the Resistance, realising that far more people claimed to have been in it than can ever have been the case and that a sort of game had begun. He was certainly right about that. As Sudhir Hazareesingh – among many others – has said: 'This reinvention of the French as a "nation of resisters" was de Gaulle's durable legacy transforming the Lavissean ideal of French greatness ... into a new myth of Gaullian *grandeur*.'

Towards the end of 1944 Marie-Laure de Noailles gave a party 'at which the guests made fun of songs of the Liberation by caricaturing them'. As Cocteau noted, such cavorting would have been impossible even two months earlier. Picasso had his number. Cocteau had contracted a skin ailment. 'Don't shake hands with Cocteau,' Picasso advised friends. 'He's suffering from a nasty skin disease – something he caught from the Germans during the war.'[29]

Some historians have spoken of the Occupation of Paris as a 'golden age' of the theatre. There certainly were a large number of plays mounted – more than 400 according to some accounts – but is the sheer number any guide? A lot were revivals, people had little else to do, British and American films and books were banned and given the grimness of the Occupation, is it really so surprising that theatre should do so well?

As soon as the armistice was signed in 1940, Guitry, who was in the south of France at the time, hurriedly returned to Paris and put himself 'at the disposal' of the Wehrmacht authorities. As happened to others, he was accused of being Jewish and in his case the matter was referred to Berlin. If that matter was settled to his satisfaction, much less so was the fate of one of his plays which he wanted performed, an operetta called *Le Dernier Troubadour*. This was set in an early fifteenth-century, English-occupied Paris before its liberation by Joan of Arc. The parallels were fairly obvious to anyone and, not surprisingly, the Germans wouldn't allow it to go on. He should have known this. Censorship of the theatre was a tricky business, mainly because it wasn't just a question of the raw text, as with books, but of the delivery of the lines, which could use nuance, add sarcasm and so on.[30] So the censors not only read the scripts but attended rehearsals.

In the early years of the Occupation, Guitry comprised part of a group – Cocteau, Arletty and the actress and singer Alice Cocea were others – who 'radiated glamour' to the theatre set and, more to the point, attended glittering social occasions at the German Institute or other gatherings hosted by, for example, Reichsmarschall Göring. Guitry also penned a tribute to Pétain, *De Jeanne d'Arc à Philippe Pétain: 1492–1942*, arguing without a blush that French civilisation had culminated in Pétain, who sent him a note of thanks.

Conceivably, more people knew about Guitry outside France than inside. On 24 August 1942 *Life* magazine published a 'Blacklist' of French people condemned by the Resistance for collaborating. Among the artists included were Guitry, Maurice Chevalier and the risqué comedienne and Folies-Bergère star Mistinguett.[31]

Among the charges against Guitry was that he had a statue of Hitler in the foyer of his theatre, his curious defence being that it was a statue of his father, 'who looked like Mussolini'. On another occasion Paul Léautaud wrote in his diary that he had turned up at Maxim's one day, to find a display of 'fourteen German officers' hats and one civilian hat' outside a private dining room. When Léautaud inquired, the maître d'hôtel whispered: 'It's Monsieur Guitry, who is giving lunch to German officers.'

As in so many cases, however, the paperwork against Guitry was inconclusive, mainly because much of it had been spirited back to Berlin, or destroyed, and, in 1947, the court found he had no case to answer. His reputation, however, never recovered. His old friends – Paul Valéry, Colette and others – shunned him.

While the views of the Resistance are not to be neglected, Guitry was allowed back into the Paris theatres in 1948 and, when he died, in 1957, aged seventy-two, more than 10,000 people turned up at his funeral. They didn't know then what we know now. In August 1939, barely two weeks before war broke out, he visited London and smuggled with him a replica Enigma machine which the Polish secret services had 'acquired' from the Germans.[32]

It would be neat, and convenient, to say that with the end of the Second World War, and the unfortunate collaboration of so many prominent salons during the Occupation of Paris, the very phenomenon of the salon came to an end. That was not the case. Four of the collaborationist salons lingered on, until their hostesses died, Marie-Blanche de Polignac in 1958, Marie-Laure de Noailles in 1970, Marie-Louise Bousquet in 1975, and Florence Gould not until 1983. She survived a number of investigations into her links with the Nazis, not least by the FBI, to be honoured by the first-ever private party at New York's Metropolitan Museum.

But if there will always be a shadow over the memory of Florence Gould, it is eclipsed by that of Edmée de La Rochefoucauld, perhaps the last great *salonnière*, who was as accomplished as any of the other women in this narrative. She had a glittering childhood which led to an equally golden maturity.

Born in April 1895, her father – count Edmond de Fels – was a diplomat, a director of the *Revue de Paris* and an authority on eighteenth-century architecture, who introduced her to the philosophies of Kant and Fichte. During the First World War Edmée lost a brother and a suitor but in December 1917 she married count Jean de La Rochefoucauld, who would become the thirteenth Duc de La Rochefoucauld on the death of his father in 1926. They would have four children, one of whom, Solange, would also become a distin-guished writer.

Edmée, despite her glittering youth and brilliant society marriage, was to become a woman of wide-ranging intellectual interests and achievements.[33] From 1927 on, she became a director of the Union national pour les votes des femmes, campaigning for the vote for women in France. Always highly intellectual, and always 'well turned out', she reported from the Spanish Civil War and later branched out into literature, philosophy and poetry. No less a figure than Abel Bonnard, the noted collaborator, encouraged her to publish her poems, which she released, in the manner of salonnières down the ages, pseudonymously, under the name Gilbert Mauge.

In her mature years her twin interests were feminism – Edmée was the president of the jury for the Prix Fémina – and, as time went by, and her interests in politics faded, after the Second World War, she built up a body of work on literary and philosophical subjects. Besides her biography of Anna de Noailles, she wrote books on Paul Valéry and Léon-Paul Fargue and, among other works of philo-sophical morality, Le Voyage dans l'esprit (1931), Les Moralistes de l'intelligence (1945), Pluralités de l'être (1957) and De l'ennui (1976). Between 1982 and 1989, two years before her death, she published three volumes of memoirs, Flashes, which some have said have a style similar to Pascal's Pensées.

In her book Femmes d'hier et d'aujourd'hui (1969) she had chap-ters on female poets, novelists, dramatists and moralists and on the political role of women as revealed by their writings. She sought to bring out from obscurity names such as Céline Arnauld, Louise de Vilmorin, Zoé Oldenbourg and such seventeenth-century figures as Jeanne de Schomberg, later Mme de Liancourt, who was both a mor-alist and a garden designer, and who Edmée equated with Le Nôtre (who designed the gardens at Versailles for Louis XIV) and put on a par with Mme de Scudéry and Mme de Sablé. She also had a chapter on Salic law, the best-known tenet of which is the exclusion of women from the inheritance of thrones. Edmée was therefore an impressive Frenchwoman in her own right, but also an enthusiastic historian of French women who had preceded her.

Her salon was held at her hôtel in the place des États-Unis, attended by *le tout Paris* but where among her favourites could be found André Maurois, Paul Morand, Jules Romains, André Malraux, the painter Georges Mathieu and Marcel Griaule, a pioneer ethnologist famous for his studies of the Dogon people in Mali. Hugo Vickers, biographer of royalty and of Cecil Beaton, recalls attending Edmée's salon in October 1978, where he found 'lots of very ancient academicians tucking into tiny sandwiches for all they were worth'. Like several salons before hers, Edmée's was known as 'the antechamber of the Académie française'. She herself failed to be elected in 1983, but that didn't slow her down – she published her last book at ninety-four. She died in 1991, aged ninety-six, and in 2000 the Prix Edmée de La Rochefoucauld was established, the annual award being given to what the judges regard as that year's most distinguished first novel.[34]

PART NINE

Post-Vichy France and the Anglosphere

Anti-Americanism and *la Famille Sartre*

Intellectual life in Paris experienced a resurgence in 1944, pre-cisely because the city had been occupied. Many books had been banned, theatres censored, periodicals closed; even conversation had been guarded. The paper shortage had ensured that books, newspapers, magazines, theatre programmes, school exercise books and artists' materials were in short supply. Sartre apart, this was the age of André Gide, Albert Camus, Louis Aragon and all the formerly banned American authors – Hemingway, Steinbeck, Wilder, Runyon. Nineteen forty-four became known as the year of *Ritzkrieg*: though the world was still at war, Paris had been liberated and was inundated with visitors. Hemingway visited Sylvia Beach – Shakespeare & Co. had closed down, but she had survived the camps. Other visitors, staying at the Ritz hotel, included Marlene Dietrich, William Shirer, William Saroyan, Martha Gellhorn, A. J. Ayer and George Orwell. Simone de Beauvoir talked about 'Paris in the Year Zero'.[1]

Sartre, who had been in the army, interned in Germany, and a member of the Resistance, saw the postwar world as his moment, and he wanted to carve out a new role for the intellectual and the writer. Born in Paris in 1905, Sartre grew up in comfortable surroundings with sophisticated and enlightened parents who exposed their son to the best in art, literature and music (his grandfather was Albert Schweitzer's uncle). He attended the Lycée Henri IV, one of the most fashionable schools in Paris, and then went on to the École normale supérieure.

Initially he intended to become a poet, Baudelaire being a particular hero of his, but he soon came under the influence of Marcel Proust and, most important, Henri Bergson. 'In Bergson,' he said, 'I immediately found a description of my own psychic life.' Other influences were Edmund Husserl and Martin Heidegger, Sartre's attention being drawn to the Germans in the early 1930s by Raymond Aron, a fellow pupil at the same lycée. Aron, best known for his 1955 book *The Opium of the Intellectuals*, which inverted Marx's claim that religion was the opium of the people and argued that French thinkers were too in thrall to the German political philosopher, had just returned from studying with Husserl in Berlin. It was Husserl's theory that much of the formal structure of traditional philosophy is nonsense, that true knowledge comes from 'our immediate intuition of things as they are', and that truth can best be grasped in 'boundary situations' – sudden, extreme moments, as when someone steps off the pavement in front of an oncoming car. Husserl identified these as moments of 'unmediated existence'.[2]

Sartre followed Aron to Berlin in 1933, apparently ignoring Hitler's rise. For Jean-Paul, following Heidegger, man was alone in the world and gradually being overtaken by materialism, industrialisation, standardisation, Americanisation. Life in such a darkening world, according to Sartre, was 'absurd' (another famous coinage). This absurdity, a form of emptiness, Sartre added, produced in man a sense of 'nausea', a new version of alienation and a word he used as the title for a novel he had published in 1938, *La Nausée*. One of the protagonists of the novel suffers this complaint, living in a provincial bourgeois world where life drags on with 'a sort of sweetish sickness'. Most people, says Sartre, prefer to be free but are not: they live in 'bad faith'.[3] This was essentially Heidegger's idea of authenticity/inauthenticity, but Sartre, owing to the fact that he used more accessible language and wrote novels and, later, plays, became much better known as an existentialist. Although he became more optimistic after the war, both phases of his thinking are linked by a distaste for the bourgeois life. He loved to raise the spectre of the surly waiter, whose surliness – *La Nausée* – existed because he hated being a waiter and really wanted to be an artist, an actor, knowing that every moment he spent waiting was spent in 'bad faith'. Freedom could only be found in breaking away from this sort of existence. Although it felt new, this hatred of the bourgeoisie, as we have seen, went all the way back in France to Rousseau.

Sartre's aim, as a philosopher, was still the creation of *l'homme révolté*, the rebel, whose aim in turn was the overthrow of the bourgeoisie; but to this he now added an attack on analytic reason, which he described as 'the official doctrine of bourgeois democracy'. Sartre had been struck, in wartime, by the way an individual's sense of isolation had disappeared, and he now felt that existentialism should be adapted to this insight – that action and choice (the interwar ideas of Malraux and Saint-Exupéry) were the solution to our predicament (here again, the culture of defeat is proving fertile). Philosophy, existentialism, became for him – in a sense – a form of guerrilla war in which individuals, who are both isolated souls and yet part of a joint campaign, find their being.

With Simone de Beauvoir and Maurice Merleau-Ponty, Sartre (as editor-in-chief) founded a new political, philosophical and literary journal called *Les Temps modernes*, the motto for which was 'Man is total: totally committed and totally free'. This group in effect joined the long line of thinkers – Bergson, Spengler, Heidegger – who felt that positivism, science, analytic reason and capitalism were creating a materialistic, rational but crass world that denuded man of a vital life force. In time this would lead Sartre to an equally crass anti-Americanism, but to begin with he declared in his *Existentialism* (1946) that 'man is only a situation', another of his seminal phrases. Man, he said, has 'a distant purpose', to *realise* himself, to make choices in order to *be*. To do so, he has to liberate himself from bourgeois rationality.[4]

There is no doubt that Sartre was a gifted phrase-maker, the first soundbite philosopher, and his ideas appealed to many in the postwar world, especially his belief that the best way to achieve an existential existence, the best way to be 'authentic', was to be *against* things. The critic, he insisted, has a fuller life than the acquiescer. (He refused, later in life, the award of the Nobel Prize.) It was this approach which led him in 1948 to found the Revolutionary Democratic Association, which tried to lead intellectuals and others away from the obsession that was already dominating their lives: the Cold War.

Sartre was a Marxist – 'It is not my fault if reality is Marxist' is how he put it. But in one important regard he was overtaken by the other member of the trinity that founded *Les Temps modernes*. Maurice Merleau-Ponty had also attended Kojève's seminar in the 1930s and he too had been influenced by Husserl and Heidegger. After the war, however, he pushed the 'anti' doctrine much further than Sartre. In *Humanism and Terror*, published in 1947, Merleau-Ponty welded Sartre and Stalin in the ultimate existential argument. His central point was that the Cold War was a classic 'boundary situation', which required 'fundamental decisions from men where risk is total'. Successful revolutions, he claimed, had not shed as much blood as the capitalist empires, and therefore the former were preferable to the latter and had a 'humanistic future'.[5] Stalinism, for all its faults, was a more 'honest' form of violence than that which underlay liberal capitalism. Stalinism acknowledged its violence, Merleau-Ponty said, whereas the Western empires did not. In this respect at least, and incredible as it may seem, he concluded that Stalinism was to be preferred.

Existentialism, Sartre and Merleau-Ponty were, therefore, the conceptual fathers of much of the intellectual climate of the postwar years, especially so in France. When people like Arthur Koestler (hidden for months by Adrienne Monnier) – whose *Darkness at Noon*, exposing Stalinist atrocities, sold 250,000 copies in France alone – took them to task, they were denounced as liars. Then Sartre *et al.* fell back on such arguments as that the Soviets covered up because they were ashamed of *their* violence, whereas in Western capitalist democracies violence was implicit and openly condoned. Sartre and Merleau-Ponty were one factor in France having the most powerful Communist Party outside the Soviet bloc (in 1952 *Les Temps modernes* became a party publication in all but name), and their influence did not really dissolve until the student rebellions of 1968.[6]

Their stance also led to a philosophical hatred of America (in 1955 the communists waged a campaign to prevent English being taught in secondary schools), which had never been entirely absent from European thought but now took on an unprecedented virulence. In 1954 Sartre visited Russia and returned declaring that 'there is total freedom of criticism in the USSR'. He knew that wasn't true but felt it was more important to be anti-American, then going through its McCarthyite anti-communist turbulence, than critical of the Soviet Union. This attitude persisted, in Sartre as in others, and showed itself in the philosopher's espousal of other Marxist anti-American causes: Tito's Yugoslavia, Castro's Cuba, Mao's China and Ho Chi Minh's Vietnam. Nearer home he was of course a natural leader for the protests against France's battle with Algeria in the mid-1950s. It was this support that led to his friendship with the man who would carry his thinking one important stage further: Frantz Fanon.

LA CATHÉDRALE DE SARTRE

France, as we know, lays great store by its intellectuals. Streets are named after philosophers and even minor writers. Nowhere is this more true than in Paris, and the period of the Second World War was the golden age of intellectuals (in his monumental *Le Siècle des intellectuels*, Michel Winock divides his account into 'the Barrès years', 'the Gide years' and 'the Sartre years'). During the Occupation the intellectual resistance had been led by the Comité national des écrivains, its mouthpiece being *Les Lettres françaises*. After the Liberation the editorship was taken over by Louis Aragon, the surrealist-turned-Stalinist. His first act was to publish a list of 156 writers, artists, theatre people and academics who had collaborated and for whom the journal insisted on 'just punishment'.[7]

The various groups of intellectuals each had their favourite café, in true Parisian style. Sartre and Beauvoir used the Flore at the corner of the boulevard Saint-Germain and the rue Saint-Benoît. Sartre arrived for breakfast (two cognacs) and then sat at a table upstairs and wrote for three hours. Beauvoir did much the same but at a separate table. After lunch they went back upstairs for another three hours. But after Sartre became famous, he received so many telephone calls at the café that a line was installed solely for his use.

The brasserie Lipp, opposite, was shunned for a while because its Alsatian dishes had been favoured by the Germans (though Gide had eaten there). Picasso and Dora Maar used Le Catalan in the rue des Grands-Augustins, the communists used the Bonaparte on the north side of the *place* Saint-Germain-des-Prés and musicians preferred the

Royal Saint-Germain, opposite the Deux Magots, Sartre's second choice. But in any event, the existential life of 'disenchanted nonchalance' took place only between the boulevard Saint-Michel in the east, the rue des Saints-Pères in the west, the *quais* along the Seine in the north, and the rue de Vaugirard in the south: this was '*la cathédrale de Sartre*'.

In those days, too, many writers, artists and musicians did not live in apartments but took rooms in cheap hotels – one reason why they made so much use of café life. The only late-night café in those days was Le Tabou in the rue Dauphine, frequented by Sartre, Merleau-Ponty, Juliette Gréco, the *diseuse* (a form of singing, almost like speaking), and Camus. In 1947 Bernard Lucas persuaded the owners of Le Tabou to rent him their cellar, a tube-like room in which he installed a bar, a gramophone and a piano. From then on Saint-Germain and '*la famille Sartre*' were tourist attractions.[8]

Few tourists, however, read *Les Temps modernes*, the journal that had been started in 1945, founded by Gaston Gallimard and with Sartre, Beauvoir, Camus, Merleau-Ponty, Raymond Queneau and Raymond Aron on the board. Simone de Beauvoir saw *Les Temps modernes* as the showpiece of what she called the 'Sartrean ideal'. Paris at the time was in the middle of another intellectual resurgence, not just in regard to philosophy and existentialism. In the theatre, Jean Anouilh's *Antigone*, Camus's *Caligula* and Sartre's own *Huis Clos* had appeared in 1944, Giraudoux's *Madwoman of Chaillot* a year later. Sartre's *Men without Shadows* appeared in 1946.

Exciting as all this was, the climate of *les intellos* in Paris soon turned sour thanks to one issue that dominated everything else: Stalinism. France had a particularly strong Communist Party, but after the centralisation of Yugoslavia, in the manner of the USSR, the communist takeover in Czechoslovakia, and the death of its foreign minister, Jan Masaryk, many in France found it impossible to continue their membership of the PCF, or were expelled when they expressed their revulsion. A number of disastrous strikes in France also drove a wedge between French intellectuals and workers.

Two things followed. In one, Sartre and his '*famille*' joined in 1947 the Rassemblement démocratique révolutionnaire, a party created to found a movement independent of the USSR and the United States.

The Kremlin took this seriously, fearing that Sartre's 'philosophy of decadence', as they called existentialism, could become 'a third force', especially among the young. Andrei Zhdanov, we now know, saw to it that Sartre was attacked on several fronts, in particular at a peace conference in Wrocław, Poland, in August 1948, where Picasso too was vilified. Sartre later changed his tune on Stalinist Russia, arguing that whatever wrongs had been committed had been carried out for the greater good. This tortuous form of reasoning became ever more necessary as more and more evidence was revealed about Stalin's atrocities.[9]

But Sartre's continuing hatred of American materialism kept him more in the Soviet camp than anywhere else. This position received a massive setback in 1947, however, with the publication of *I Chose Freedom*, by Victor Kravchenko, a Ukrainian engineer who had defected from a Soviet trade mission to the United States in 1944. This book turned into a runaway success and was translated into scores of languages. It was the earliest first-person description of Stalin's labour camps, his persecution of the kulaks and his forced collectivisations.

In France, due to the strength of the Communist Party, no major publishing house would touch the book, but when it did appear it sold 400,000 copies and won the Prix Sainte-Beuve, a new literary prize with Raymond Aron and Raymond Queneau on the jury. The latter was an editor at Gallimard, who would become famous for his novel *Zazie dans le Métro*. Kravchenko's book was attacked by the Communist Party, and *Les Lettres françaises* published an article by one Sim Thomas, allegedly a former OSS officer, who claimed that the book had been authored by American intelligence agents rather than Kravchenko, who was a compulsive liar and an alcoholic. Kravchenko, who by then had settled in the United States, sued for libel.

The trial was held in January 1949 amid massive publicity. *Les Lettres françaises* had obtained witnesses from Russia, with NKVD help, including Kravchenko's former wife, Zinaida Gorlova, with whom, he said, he had witnessed many atrocities. Since Gorlova's father was in a prison camp, her evidence was naturally tainted several times over. Despite this, faced by her ex-husband in the witness box, she physically deteriorated, becoming 'unkempt and listless'. She was eventually taken to Orly airport, where a Soviet military aircraft was waiting to fly her back to Moscow. 'Sim Thomas' was never produced; he did not exist. The most impressive witness for Kravchenko was Margarete Buber-Neumann, the widow of the prewar leader of the German Communist Party, Heinz Neumann. After Hitler achieved power, the Neumanns had fled to Soviet Russia but had been sent to labour camps because of 'political deviationism' where Heinz was executed in 1937. After the Molotov–Ribbentrop non-aggression pact, in 1940, Margarete had been shipped back to Germany and the camp at Ravensbrück. So she had been in camps on both sides of what became the Iron Curtain: what reason had she to lie?

The verdict was announced on 4 April, the same day that the North Atlantic Treaty was signed. Kravchenko had won. He received only minimal damages, but that wasn't the point. Many intellectuals resigned from the party that year, and soon even Camus would follow. Sartre and Beauvoir did not resign, however. For them, all revolutionaries had their 'terrible majesty'.[10] The hatred of American materialism outweighed everything still.

BOURBAKI AND BIRDSONG

After the war, Paris seemed set to resume its position as the world capital of intellectual and creative life, the City of Light it had always been. Breton and Duchamp were back from America, mixing again with Cocteau. This was the era of Anouilh's *Colombe*, Gide's *Journals* and his Nobel Prize, Malraux's *Voices of Silence*, Alain Robbe-Grillet's *Les Gommes*. It was again, after an interlude, the city of Édith Piaf, Sidney Bechet and Maurice Chevalier, of Matisse's *Jazz* series, of major works by the *Annales* school of historians, considered later on, of Frantz Fanon's *Black Skin, White Masks*, of Jacques Tati's *Mr Hulot's Holiday*, and of the new mathematics of 'Nicolas Bourbaki', a collective pseudonym for a remarkable group of mathematicians, formed in the interwar years to repair French mathematics, which had been decimated by losses in the First World War. Named in honour of a mathematically minded French general of the nineteenth century, the group of about a dozen members held private meetings to work up new methods of analysis, and was yet another example of the extraordinary intellectual sociability of the French.

In serious music it was the time of Olivier Messiaen, who, on the contrary, was splendidly individualistic. Far from being an existentialist, he was a theological composer, 'dedicated to the task of reconciling human imperfection and Divine Glory through the medium of Art'.[11] Messiaen detested most aspects of modern life, preferring the ancient grand civilisations of Assyria and Sumer. Much influenced by Debussy and the Russian composers, his works sought to create timeless, contemplative moods, and although he tried serialism, he frequently employed repetition on a large scale and – his particular innovation – the transcription of birdsong. In the decade and half after the war Messiaen used adventurous new techniques (including new ways of dividing up the piano keyboard), birdsong and Eastern music to forge a new religious spirit in music: *Turangalîla* (Hindu for 'love song', 1946–8), *Livre d'orgue* (1951), *Réveil des oiseaux* (1953). Messiaen's opposition to existentialism was underlined by his pupil Pierre Boulez, who described his music as closer to the oriental philosophy of 'being' rather than the Western idea of 'becoming'.

And yet, despite all this, the 1950s would witness a slow decline in Paris, as the city was overtaken by New York and, to a lesser extent, by London. It would be eclipsed further in the student rebellions of the late 1960s. This was as true in painting as in philosophy and literature. Alberto Giacometti produced some of his greatest, gauntest, figures in postwar Paris, the epitome for many people of existential man. And Jean Dubuffet painted his childlike but at the same time very sophisticated pictures of intellectuals and animals (cows mainly), grotesque and gentle at the same time, revealing mixed feelings about the earnestness with which the postwar Parisian philosophical and literary scene regarded itself.[12]

The decade after the end of the Second World War was the last great shining moment for the City of Light. Existentialism had been invigorated and was popular in France because in part it was a child of the Resistance, and therefore was yet another example of fertile recovery after defeat and humiliation. Sartre apart, Paris's final glory was delivered by two men and one woman who together comprised the last great throw of modernism. This was the last time high culture could be said to dominate any major civilisation.

'God Was Hollow'

Camus was a *pied noir*, born in Algeria. A journalist and philosopher whose father had been killed in the First World War, he was raised in poverty and never lost his sympathy for the poor and oppressed. Briefly a Marxist, he edited the Resistance newspaper *Combat* during the war. Like Sartre, he too became obsessed with man's 'absurd' condition in an 'indifferent' universe, and his own career was an attempt to show how that situation could (or should) be met. In 1942 he produced *The Myth of Sisyphus*, a philosophical tract that first appeared in the underground press. His argument was that man must recognise two things: that all he can rely on is himself, and what goes on inside his head; and that the universe *is* indifferent (as the members of d'Holbach's coterie had argued), even hostile, life is a struggle and we are all like Sisyphus, pushing a stone uphill, and if we stop, it will roll back down again. This may seem – may indeed be – futile, but it is all there is.

'We were born at the beginning of the First World War. As adolescents we had the crisis of 1929; at twenty, Hitler. Then came the Ethiopian War, the Civil War in Spain, and Munich. These were the foundations of our education. Next came the Second World War, the defeat, and Hitler in our homes and cities ... Now that Hitler has gone, we know a certain number of things. The first is that the poison which impregnated Hitlerism has not been eliminated; it is present in each of us ... Another thing we have learned is that we cannot accept any optimistic conception of existence, any happy ending whatsoever. But if we believe that optimism is silly, we also know that pessimism about the action of man among his fellows is cowardly.'

Camus delivered these words in 1946 at Columbia University in New York. His first novel, *L'Étranger* ('The Stranger' or 'The Outsider'), was published in 1942, and in it Meursault, the main character, has killed a man and is scheduled to be executed, pondering Camus's central concern, the 'absurdist' position that a life that can seem so important to him (his own) can have so little meaning in the wider scheme of things.[13]

He moved on, to publish *The Plague* in 1947. This, a much more accessible read, starts with an outbreak of bubonic plague in an

Algerian city, Oran. There is no overt philosophising in the book; instead, Camus explores the way a series of characters – Dr Rieux, his mother or Tarrou – react to the terrible news, and deal with the situation as it develops. Camus's main objective is to show what community does, and does not, mean, what an individual can hope for and what he or she cannot – the book is in fact a sensitive description of isolation. And that of course is the plague that afflicts us. Camus had created a work of art out of absurdity and isolation, a return in some ways to the predicaments and anxieties explored between the wars. Like Valéry he was saying that disappointment is a fact of life.[14] He received the Nobel Prize in Literature in 1957 but was killed in a car crash three years later.

Jean Genet – Saint Genet in Sartre's biography – introduced himself one day in 1944 to the philosopher and his consort as they sat at the café de Flore. He had a shaven head and a broken nose, 'but his eyes knew how to smile, and his mouth could express the astonishment of childhood'. His appearance owed not a little to his upbringing in reformatories, prisons and brothels, where he had been a male prostitute. Genet's future reputation would lie in his brilliance with words and his provocative plots, but he was of interest to the existentialists because as a homosexual and criminal he occupied two prisons (psychological as well as physical) and, in living on the edge, in boundary situations, he at least stood the chance of being more alive, more authentic, than others. He was also of interest to Beauvoir because, being homosexual and having been forced to play 'female' roles in prison (on one occasion he was a 'bride' in a prison ménage), Genet's views about sex and gender were quite unlike anyone else's. Genet certainly lived life to the full in his way, even going so far as to desecrate a church to see what God would do about it. 'And the miracle happened. There was no miracle ... God was hollow.'[15]

In a series of novels and plays Genet regaled his public with life as it really was among the 'queers' and criminals he knew, the vicious sexual hierarchies within prisons, the baroque sexual practices and inverted codes of behaviour (calling someone a cocksucker was enough to get one murdered). But Genet instinctively grasped that low life, on the edge of violence, the boundary situation par excellence, evoked not only prurient interest on the part of the bourgeois but deeper feelings too. It opened a longing for something, whether it was latent masochism or latent homosexuality or a sneaking lust for violence – whatever it was, the very popularity of Genet's work showed up the inadequacies of bourgeois life much more than any analysis by Sartre or the others. *Our Lady of the Flowers* (1943) was written while Genet was in Mettray prison and details the petty but all-important victories and defeats in a closed world of natural and unnatural homosexuals. *The Maids* (1947) is a play ostensibly about two maids who conspire to murder their mistress. However, Genet's insistence that all the roles be played by young men underlines the play's real agenda, the nature of sexuality and its relation to our bodies. By the same token, in *Blacks* (1958) his requirement that some of the white roles be played by blacks, and that one white person must always be in the audience for a performance, further underlined Genet's point that life is about feeling (even if that feeling is shame or embarrassment) rather than 'just' about thought. As an erstwhile criminal, he knew what Sartre didn't appear to grasp: that a rebel is not necessarily a revolutionary.[16]

LA GRANDE SARTREUSE

'*La famille Sartre*' was the name given to the group of writers and intellectuals around the philosopher/novelist/playwright. This was not without irony, certainly so far as his chief companion, Simone de Beauvoir, was concerned. The couple had met in 1929 at the Lycée Janson de Sailly, where Beauvoir took courses to become a trainee teacher (together with Maurice Merleau-Ponty and Claude Lévi-Strauss). She easily attracted attention to herself by virtue of her exceptional cleverness, so that she was eventually accepted into the elite intellectual *bande* at the school, led by Sartre. This began the long-term and somewhat unusual relationship between these two – unusual in that no sooner had they begun their affair than Sartre told Beauvoir he was not attracted to her in bed. This French *galanterie* was less than flattering but she adjusted to the situation and always considered herself his main companion, even to the extent of helping him to procure other lovers. For his part, Sartre was generous, supporting Beauvoir financially (as he did several others) when his early novels and plays proved successful.[17]

Sartre and Beauvoir were always irked by the fact that the world viewed them as existentialists – and only as existentialists. But on occasion it paid off. In spring 1947, Beauvoir left France for America for a coast-to-coast lecture tour where she was billed as 'France's No. 2 Existentialist'. While in Chicago she met Nelson Algren, a writer who insisted on showing her what he called 'the real America' beyond the obvious tourist traps. They became lovers immediately (they had only two days together), and she had, she later admitted, achieved her 'first complete orgasm' (at the age of thirty-nine). Despite her dislike of America (a feeling she shared with Sartre), she considered not returning to France. As it was, when she did return, it was as a different woman. Until then she had been rather frumpy (Sartre called her 'Castor', meaning 'Beaver', and others called her *'La Grande Sartreuse'*). But she was not unattractive, and the experience with Algren reinforced that.[18]

At that stage, nothing she had written could be called memorable (articles in *Les Temps modernes* and *All Men Are Mortal*), but she returned to France with something different in mind that had nothing to do with existentialism, a book that investigated the situation of women in the postwar world. Beauvoir seems to have been precipitated into the project by two factors. One was her visit to America, which had shown her the similarities – and very great differences – between women in the United States and women in Europe, especially France. The second was her experience with Algren, which highlighted her own curious position vis-à-vis Sartre. She was in a stable relationship; they were viewed by all their friends and colleagues as a 'couple'. Yet they weren't married, they didn't have sex, and she was supported by him financially. This 'marginal' position, which distanced her from the situation 'normal' women found themselves in, gave Beauvoir a vantage point that, she felt, would help her write about her sex with objectivity and sympathy.

At the same time, she was reflecting something more general: 1945 was the year women could first exercise the right to vote in France, and her book appeared at almost exactly the time Alfred Kinsey produced his first report on sex in the human male. Beauvoir began her research in October 1946 and finished in June 1949, spending four months in America in 1947. She then went back to *la famille*

Sartre, the work a one-off, at a distance from her other offerings and, in a sense, from her. Years later a critic said that she understood the feminine condition because she herself had escaped it, and she agreed with him.[19]

Beauvoir relied on her own experience, supported by wide reading, and she also carried out a series of interviews with total strangers. The book is in two parts – the French edition was published in two volumes. Book 1, called *Facts and Myths*, provides a historical overview of women and is itself divided into three. In 'Destiny' the female predicament is examined from a biological, psychoanalytic and historical standpoint. In the historical section women are described, for example, in the Middle Ages, in primitive societies and in the Enlightenment, and she closes the section with an account of present-day women. She examines the treatment of women in five (male) authors: Henry de Montherlant, D. H. Lawrence, Paul Claudel, André Breton and Stendhal. She did not like Lawrence, believing his stories to be 'tedious', though she conceded that 'he writes the simple truth about love'. On the other hand, she felt that Stendhal was 'the greatest French novelist'. The second volume, or Book 2, is called *Women's Life Today* and explores childhood, adolescence, maturity and old age. She writes of love, sex, marriage, lesbianism. She made use of her impressive gallery of friends, spending several mornings with Lévi-Strauss discussing anthropology and with Jacques Lacan learning about psychoanalysis.

When *The Second Sex* appeared, there were those critics (as there always are those critics) who complained that she didn't say anything new. But there were many more who felt she had put her finger on something that other people, other women, were working out for themselves at the time, and moreover that, in doing her research, she had provided them with ammunition.[20]

Beauvoir's provocative idea that women represented 'the other' in society caught on and would much infuse the feminist movement in years to come. In fact, her idea of 'the other' would form a link with the predominantly French idea of postmodernism later in the century.

La Longue Durée: Civilisation, Capitalism, Colonialism

One of the academic activities at mid-century that was help-ing to reshape the very idea of 'culture' was the discipline of anthropology, where Claude Lévi-Strauss became influen-tial with two works published in 1955.

Born in Belgium in 1908, he grew up near Versailles and became a student at the University of Paris. He did fieldwork in Brazil where he was appointed in his twenties as professor of sociology at the University of São Paulo. Further fieldwork followed in Cuba, but he returned to France in 1939 for military service. In 1941 he arrived as a refugee in the New School for Social Research in New York, learning excellent English and a love of cowboy-style string ties, and after the war he became French cultural attaché to the United States.[1] He was appointed to the chair of social anthropology at the Collège de France in 1959, but by then he had begun his remarkable series of publications.

These fell into three kinds. There were his studies in kinship, examining the way familial relationships were understood among many different (but mainly indigenous American) tribes; there were his studies of mythologies, exploring what they reveal about the way people very different on the surface think about things; and third, there was a sort of autobiographical-philosophical travelogue, *Tristes Tropiques*, also published in 1955.[2]

Lévi-Strauss's theories were very complex and not helped by his own style, which was far from easy and on more than one occasion defeated his translators. Nevertheless, we may say that – his studies of kinship apart – Lévi-Strauss's work has two main elements. In his paper 'The Structural Study of Myth', published in the *Journal of American Folklore* in 1955, the year *Tristes Tropiques* appeared, and later developed in his four-volume *Mythologiques*, Lévi-Strauss examined hundreds of myths around the world. Though trained in anthropology, he came to this work, he said, with 'three mistresses' – geology, Marx and Freud. The Freudian element in his work is much more obvious than the Marxian, or the geological, but what he appears to have meant is that, like Marx and Freud, he was seeking to find the universal structures that underlie human experience.[3]

All mythologies, Lévi-Strauss said, share a universal, inbuilt logic. Any corpus of mythological tales, he observed, contains a recurrent harping on elementary themes – incest, fratricide, patricide, cannibalism. Myth was a kind of 'collective dream', an 'instrument of darkness', capable of being decoded. Over four volumes he examined 813 different stories with an extraordinary ingenuity that many, especially his Anglo-Saxon critics, have refused to accept.[4] He observes for instance that across the world, where figures from myth are born of the earth rather than from woman, they are given either very unusual names or some deformity – such as a club-foot – to signify the fact. At other times myths concern themselves with 'overrated' kin relationships (incest) or 'underrated' relationships (fratricide/patricide). Other myths concern themselves with the preparation of food (cooked/raw), whether there is sound or silence, whether people are dressed or undressed. It was Lévi-Strauss's claim, essentially, that if myth could be understood, it would explain how early man first came to decipher the world and would therefore represent the fundamental, unconscious structure of the mind. His approach, which came as a revelation for many people, also had one important secondary effect. He himself said explicitly that on the basis of his inquiries, there is really no difference between the 'primitive' mind and the 'developed' mind, that so-called 'savages' are just as sophisticated in their storytelling as we are ourselves. The thrust of Lévi-Strauss's work was to show instead how, at root, myths reveal the essential *similarity* of human nature and beliefs right across the globe.[5]

This was an immensely influential view in the second half of the twentieth century, not only helping to undermine the validity of evolved high culture, as advocated by T. S. Eliot, Lionel Trilling and others, but promoting the idea of 'local knowledge', the notion that cultural expression is valid even though it applies only to specific locations, whose reading of that expression may be much more complex and diverse – richer – than is evident to outsiders.

VIOLENCE AS CULTURE

The ideas of Sigmund Freud did not mean much to Frantz Fanon though he did train as a psychiatrist. Born in Martinique in 1925, after qualifying in psychiatry in Paris, Fanon was assigned to a hospital in Algeria during the rising against the French. The experience appalled him; he took the Algerians' side and wrote a number of books in which he became a spokesman for those suffering oppression. In *Black Skin, White Masks* (1952) and *A Dying Colonialism* (1959), Fanon proved himself an articulate critic of the last days of imperialism, and his activities for the FLN (National Liberation Front), including an address to the First Congress of Negro Writers in 1956, drew the attention of the French police. Later that year he was forced to leave Algeria for Tunisia, where he continued to be one of the editors of *El Moudjahid*, an anti-colonial magazine. His most poignant book was *The Wretched of the Earth* (1961), conceived at the time Fanon was diagnosed as suffering from leukaemia.

Fanon was a strongly polemical writer rather than a gifted phrasemaker. His works are designed to worry whites and convince his fellow blacks that the long battle – against racism and colonialism – can be won. Where *The Wretched of the Earth* was different was in Fanon's use of his experiences as a psychiatrist. He was intent on showing fellow blacks that the alienation they felt as a result of colonialism *was* a result of colonialism, and not some natural structural inferiority inherent in the black race. He reported a number of psychiatric reactions he had seen in his clinic and which, he said, were directly related to the guerrilla war of independence then being waged inside the country. In one case an Algerian taxi-driver and member of the FLN had developed impotence after his wife had been beaten and raped by a French soldier during interrogation. In another, two young Algerians, aged thirteen and fourteen, had killed their European playmate. As the thirteen-year-old put it, 'We weren't a bit cross with him ... One day we decided to kill him, because the Europeans want to kill all the Arabs. We can't kill big people. But we could kill ones like him.'

Fanon had many stories of disturbances in young people, and especially among the victims of torture. He pointed out that torture victims could be divided into two – 'those who know something' and 'those who know nothing'. He said he never saw those who knew something as patients (they never got ill; they had in a sense 'earned' their torture), but among those who knew nothing, there were all sorts of symptoms, usually related to the types of torture – indiscriminate, mass attack with truncheons or cigarette burns; electricity; and the so-called 'truth serum'. Victims of electric shock, for example, would develop an electricity phobia and become unable to touch an electric switch.

Fanon's aim was to show that mental illness was an extreme but essentially rational response to an intolerable situation. At that stage, he said, African culture (like black American culture) was the long *struggle* to be free; the fight – violence itself – was the shared culture of the Algerians and took most of their creative energy.[6]

Fanon did not live to see peace restored to an autonomous Algeria. He had been too busy completing his book to seek treatment for his leukaemia, and although he was taken to Washington in late 1961, the disease was too far advanced. He died a few weeks after his book was published, at the age of thirty-six.

THE KING'S EVIL

That decade – the 1960s – saw the publication of three enormously influential books from the so-called *Annales* school of French historians, some of whom were referred to in the Introduction. These books were: *Centuries of Childhood*, by Philippe Ariès (1960), *The Peasants of Languedoc*, by Emmanuel Le Roy Ladurie (1966); and *The Structures of Everyday Life*, by Fernand Braudel (1967), the first volume of his massive three-part *Civilisation and Capitalism*. The

1960s were in fact the third great flowering of the *Annales* school – the first had been in the 1920s and the second in the 1940s.

Of the three authors, Fernand Braudel was by far the most senior. He was older and a close colleague of the two original founders of the *Annales* school, Lucien Febvre and Marc Bloch. These two men came together at the University of Strasbourg in the 1920s, where they founded a new academic journal, the *Annales d'histoire économique et sociale*. The *Annales* from the first sought to concentrate on the social and economic context of events rather than 'the deeds of great men', but what set it apart was the imagination that Febvre and Bloch brought to their writing, especially after they both returned to Paris in the mid-1930s.

Bloch (a Resistance hero in the Second World War) wrote two books for which he is remembered today, *The Royal Touch* and *Feudal Society*. *The Royal Touch* was concerned with the belief, prevalent in both England and France from the Middle Ages to the Enlightenment, that kings – by the mere act of touching – could cure scrofula, a skin disease known as 'the king's evil'. But Bloch's study ranged much further than this curious belief: it drew on contemporaneous ideas in sociology, psychology and anthropology in search of the *mentalité* of the period. In *Feudal Society*, published on the eve of the Second World War, he attempted to recreate the historical psychology of feudal times, something that was completely novel. For example, he explored the mediaeval sense of time, better described perhaps as a lack of interest in the exact measurement of time.[7]

In the same way, Febvre's *Rabelais* explored the *mentalité* of the sixteenth-century world. By an analysis of letters and other writings, the author was able to show, for example, that when Rabelais was denounced as an atheist, his critics didn't mean what we would mean today. In the early sixteenth century, 'atheist' had no precise meaning, simply because it was inconceivable for anyone to be an atheist as we would recognise the term. It was a general smear word.[8] Febvre also explored time, showing for example that someone like Rabelais would not have known the year in which he was born, and that time was experienced not in a precise way, as measured by clocks, but rather by 'the length of an Ave Maria' or 'the flight of the woodcocks'. This *felt* more like history than the train of events many historians wrote about.

It applied even more to Braudel. His *The Mediterranean*, which appeared in 1949, created a bigger stir. Conceived and written in extremely unusual circumstances, it had begun as a diplomatic history in the early 1930s. Then, in 1935–7 Braudel accepted an appointment – as did Lévi-Strauss – to teach at the University of São Paulo, and on the voyage back he met a third French academic, Febvre, 'who adopted him as *un enfant de la maison*'. But Braudel didn't get round to writing the book until he was a prisoner of war in a camp near Lübeck. He lacked notes, but he had a near-photographic memory, and he drafted *The Mediterranean* in longhand in exercise books, which he posted to Febvre.[9]

The Mediterranean is 1,200 pages long and divided into three very different sections. In the first part, Braudel treats his readers to 300 pages on the geography of the Mediterranean – the mountains and rivers, the weather, the islands and the seas, the coastlines and the routes that traders and travellers would have taken in the past. This leads to a discussion of the various cultures in different geographical circumstances – mountain peoples, coastal dwellers, islanders. Braudel's aim here is to show the importance of what he called *la longue durée* – that the history of anywhere is determined by where it is and how it is laid out.[10] The second part of the book he called 'Collective Destinies and General Trends', and here the focus of his attention is on states, economic systems, entire civilisations – less permanent than the physical geography, but still more durable than the lives and careers of individuals. His gaze now centres on change that occurs over generations or centuries, shifts that individuals are barely aware of. Exploring the rise of both the Spanish and Turkish empires, for example, he shows how their growth was related to the size and shape of the Mediterranean (long from west to east, narrow from north to south); he also shows why they gradually came to resemble each other – communications were long and arduous, the land and the available technology supported similar population densities.

And finally, there is the level of events and characters on the historical stage. While Braudel acknowledges that people differ in character, he thinks these differences account for less than traditional historians claim. Instead, he argues that an understanding of how people in the past viewed their world can help explain a lot of their behaviour.

Whereas Bloch's books, and Febvre's, had created a sensation among historians, *The Mediterranean* broke out of its academic fold and became known well beyond France. People found the new type of information it contained every bit as fascinating as the doings of monarchs and prime ministers. For his part, Febvre invited his *enfant de la maison* (now turned fifty) to join him in an even more massive collaborative venture. This was a complete history of Europe, stretching from 1400 to 1800, exploring how the mediaeval world became the modern world, and using the new techniques. Febvre said he himself would tackle 'thought and belief', and Braudel could write about material life. The project hadn't gone very far when Febvre died in 1956, but Braudel carried on, with the book eventually taking almost as long to complete as did his earlier work. The first volume of *Civilisation et capitalisme*, known in English as *The Structures of Everyday Life*, appeared in 1967; the last in 1979.[11]

Here again Braudel's conception was three-fold – production at the base, then distribution, and consumption at the top (Marx-like, rather than specifically Marxist). In the realm of production, for example, Braudel explored the relationship of wheat and maize and rice to the civilisations of the world. Rice, he found, 'brought high populations and [therefore] strict social discipline to the regions where they prospered' in Asia. On the other hand, maize, 'a crop that demands little effort', allowed the native Americans 'much free time to construct their huge pyramids for which these civilisations have become famous'. A crucial factor in Europe's success was its relatively small size, plus the efficiency of grain, and the climate. The fact that so much of life was indoors fostered the development of furniture, which brought about the development of tools. The poorer weather meant that fewer days could be worked, but mouths still had to be fed, making labour in Europe relatively expensive. This led to a greater need for labour-saving devices, which, on top of the development of tools, contributed to the scientific and industrial revolutions. There was a certain inevitability about the way civilisations developed, which made Europe the cradle of both capitalism and science.[12]

Since the Second World War, the *Annales* school has spawned a very successful series of investigations. In *The Peasants of Languedoc* and *Montaillou*, Emmanuel Le Roy Ladurie, widely regarded as Braudel's most brilliant pupil, sought to recreate the *mentalité* of mediaeval Europe. Montaillou, in the Ariège region of south-west France, was in an area that had been 'home' to a number of nonconformists during the Cathar heresy of the fourteenth century. These heretics were captured and interrogated by the local bishop, and a written record has survived. This register was used by Ladurie, who interpreted it in the light of more recent advances in anthropology, sociology and psychology. Among the names on the register of interrogations, twenty-five came from one village, Montaillou, and Ladurie brought these individuals back to life.[13]

The first part of the book deals with the material aspects of village life – the structure of the houses, the layout of the streets, where the church was. This is done with wit and imagination – Ladurie shows, for instance, that the stones were so uneven that there were always holes in the walls so that families could listen in to their neighbours: privacy was unknown in Montaillou. But it is in the second part of the book, 'An Archaeology of Montaillou: From Body Language to Myth', that the real excitement lies. Here we are introduced, for example, to Pierre Maury, a gentle shepherd, but also politically conscious, and to Pierre Clergue, the obnoxious priest, too big for his boots and the seducer of Béatrice des Planissoles, all too eager to grow up.

The *Annales* school has proved very influential. Its attraction for many people lies in the imaginative use of new kinds of evidence, science added to a humanity that provides a technique to bridge the gap across the centuries, in such a way that we can really understand what happened in the past, how people thought. The very idea of recreating *mentalités*, the psychology of bygone ages, is ambitious, but for many people the closest thing to time travel we have ever had.[14]

'French Theory' and the Late Focus on Freud in France

The French Connection, William Friedkin's 1971 film about the Mafia and drug-running in America, wasn't really about France (some of the villains are French-speaking Canadians), but the film's title did catch on as a description of something that was notable in psychology, linguistics, and epistemology just as much as in historiography, anthropology and philosophy. This was a marked divergence between French and Anglo-Saxon thought that proved fruitful and controversial in equal measure.

In the United States, Britain and the rest of the English-speaking world, the Darwinian metanarrative was in the ascendant. But in France – in particular from the 1950s through to the 1990s – there was a resurgence of the other two great nineteenth-century metanarratives: Freudianism and Marxism. It was not always easy to distinguish between these theories for several authors embraced both, and some wrote in such a difficult and paradoxical style that their message was often obscure.

Jacques Lacan was a psychoanalyst in the Freudian tradition, who developed in highly idiosyncratic ways. Born in Paris in 1901, in the 1930s Lacan attended Alexandre Kojève's seminars on Hegel and Heidegger, along with Raymond Aron, Jean-Paul Sartre, André Breton, Maurice Merleau-Ponty and Raymond Queneau. Psychoanalysis was not taken up as quickly in France as in the US, and so it wasn't until Lacan began giving his public seminars in

1953 – which lasted for twenty-six years – that psychoanalysis in France was taken seriously.[1] His seminars were intellectually fashionable, with 800 people crammed into a room designed for 650, and many prominent intellectuals and writers in the audience. Although the Marxist philosopher Louis Althusser thought enough of Lacan to invite him in 1963 to transfer his seminar to the École normale supérieure (ENS), Lacan was forced to resign from the Société psychoanalytique de Paris and was expelled from the International Psychoanalytic Association because of his 'eclectic' methods. After May 1968, the Department of Psychoanalysis at Vincennes (part of Paris University) was reorganised as Le Champ freudien with Lacan as scientific director. Here was the mix of Freudianism and Marxism in action.

Lacan's first book, *Écrits* ('Writings'), published in 1966, contained major revisions of Freudianism, including the idea that there is no such thing as the ego. But the aspect of Lacan's theory that was to provoke widespread controversy was his attention to language, in which he was influenced by Wittgenstein and R. D. Laing, a British psychoanalyst. Like Laing, Lacan believed that going mad was a rational response to an intolerable situation. Like Wittgenstein, he believed that words are imprecise, meaning both more and less than they appear to mean to either the speaker or the hearer, and that it was the job of the psychoanalyst to understand this question of meaning, as revealed through language, in the light of the unconscious. Lacan did not offer a cure, as such; for him psychoanalysis was a technique for listening to, and questioning, 'desire'. In essence, the language revealed in psychoanalytic sessions was the language of the unconscious uncovering, 'in tortured form', desire. The unconscious, says Lacan, is not a private region inside us. It is instead the underlying and unknown pattern of our relations with one another.[2]

Influenced by surrealism, and by the linguistic theories of Ferdinand de Saussure, Lacan became fascinated by the devices of language. For him there were 'four modes of discourse' – those of the master, the university, the hysteric and the psychoanalyst, though they are rarely seen in pure form, the categories existing only for the purpose of analysis. A final important concept of Lacan is that there is no such thing as the whole truth, and it is futile waiting until that point has been reached. This is where language helps in the achievement of meaning; language brings home to the patient the true nature – the true meaning – of his situation. This is one reason, say Lacan's followers, why his own writing style is so dense and, as we would normally describe it, obscure. The reader has to 'recover' his own meaning from the words.[3]

This is of course an oversimplification of Lacan's theories. Towards the end of his life, he even introduced mathematical symbols into his work, though this does not seem to have made his ideas much clearer for most people, and certainly not for his considerable number of critics, who believe Lacan to have been eccentric, confused and very wrong.

Not least among the criticisms is that, despite a long career in Paris, in which he made repeated attempts to synthesise Freud with Hegel, Spinoza, Heidegger and the existentialism of Sartre, he nevertheless ignored the most elementary developments in biology and medicine. Lacan's enduring legacy, if there is one, is to have been one of the founding fathers of 'deconstruction', the idea that there is no intrinsic meaning in language, that the speaker means more and less than he or she knows, and that the listener must play his or her part. This is why his ideas lived on for a time not just in psychology but in philosophy, linguistics, literary criticism, and even in film and politics.

A Noisy Beehive

Among psychiatrists, none was so political and influential as Michel Foucault. Born in Poitiers, in October 1926, Paul-Michel Foucault trained at the ENS, where he came under the friendship, protection and patronage of Louis Althusser, a slender man with 'a fragile, almost melancholy beauty' (see below, this chapter). Far from well, often in analysis and even electroshock treatment, Althusser had a huge reputation as a grand theorist.

Foucault failed his early exams – to general consternation – but after he developed an interest in psychiatry, especially in the early years of the profession and its growth, his career blossomed. The success of his books brought him into touch with very many of the luminaries of French intellectual culture: Claude Lévi-Strauss,

Roland Barthes, Fernand Braudel, Alain Robbe-Grillet, Jacques Derrida and Emmanuel Le Roy Ladurie. Following the events of 1968, Foucault was elected to the chair of philosophy at the new University of Vincennes. This university, officially known as the Vincennes Experimental University Centre, 'was the offspring of May 1968 and Edgar Faure', the French minister for education. 'It was resolutely interdisciplinary, introduced novel courses on cinema, semiotics and psychoanalysis, and was the first French university to open its doors to candidates who did not have the *baccalauréat*.' It therefore succeeded in attracting (for a time) many people outside the normal university recruitment pool. 'The atmosphere was like a noisy beehive.'

This aspect of Foucault's career, plus his well-publicised use of drugs, his involvement with the anti-Vietnam protests, his part in the campaign for prison reform, and his role in the gay liberation movement, show him as a typical central figure in what was being called the 'counter-culture'. Yet at the same time, in April 1970, Foucault was elected to the Collège de France, to a chair in the history of systems of thought, specially created around him.[4]

Foucault shared with Lacan (and R. D. Laing in Britain) the belief that mental illness is a social construct – it is what psychiatrists, psychologists and doctors say it is, rather than an entity in itself. In particular, he argued that modern societies control and discipline their populations by delegating to the practitioners of the human sciences the authority to make these decisions. These sciences of man, he said, 'have subverted the classical order of political rule based on sovereignty and rights and replaced them with a new regime of power exercised through the stipulation of norms for human behaviour'. As Mark Philp has put it, we now know, or think we know, what 'the normal child' is, what 'a stable mind' is, a 'good citizen' or 'a perfect wife'. In describing normality, these sciences and their practitioners define deviation. For Foucault, this idea 'of man as a universal category, containing within it a "law of being", is ... an invention of the Enlightenment' and both mistaken and unstable. His aim was to argue that there is no 'single, cohesive human condition'. His most important works examine the history of institutions: prisons, mental hospitals, clinics.[5]

DISEASE, DISTURBANCE, DEVIATION, DISCIPLINES, DECONSTRUCTION

But Foucault was not just writing a history of psychiatry, penology, economics, biology or philology, as the case may be. He was seeking to show how the way knowledge is organised reflects the *power structures* within a society and how the definition of the normal man, or mind, or body, is as much a political construct as one that reflects 'the truth'. 'We are subject to the production of truth through power,' Foucault wrote. It is the human sciences, he says, that have given us the conception of a society as an organism 'which legitimately regulates its population and seeks out signs of disease, disturbance and deviation so that they can be treated and returned to normal functioning under the watchful eye of one or other policing systems', revealingly known as 'disciplines'. Foucault calls his books 'archaeologies' because, as Lacan saw meaning as a 'recovering activity', Foucault saw his work too as an 'excavation'.[6]

There was something of the *homme révolté* about Foucault; he believed that man could exist only if he showed a 'recalcitrance' towards the normative pressures of the human sciences (as Sartre had said before him), and that there is no coherent or constant human 'condition' or 'nature', no rational course to history, no 'gradual triumph of human rationality over nature'. There is struggle but it is 'patternless'.[7]

Foucault's last important book was an investigation of the history of sexuality, in which he argued that but for rape and sex with children, there should be no restraint on behaviour. This was entirely in line with the rest of his oeuvre, but for him it had the unfortunate consequence that the development of gay bars and bathhouses, of which he positively approved (he adored California and went there a lot), was probably responsible for the fact that he died, in June 1984, of an AIDS-related illness, aged fifty-seven.

After the success of structuralism, it was no doubt inevitable that there should be a backlash. Jacques Derrida, the man who mounted that attack, was Algerian and Jewish. In 1962, at independence, the Jews in Algeria left *en masse*: France suddenly had the largest Jewish population on the continent, west of Russia.

Derrida began with a specific attack on a specific body of work. In France, by the 1960s, Claude Lévi-Strauss was not merely an anthropologist – he had the status of a philosopher, a guru, someone whose structuralist views extended well beyond anthropology to embrace psychology, philosophy, history, literary criticism and even architecture. We also have Lévi-Strauss to thank for the new term 'human sciences', *sciences* of the human, which he claimed had left behind the 'metaphysical preoccupations of traditional philosophy' and were offering a more reliable perspective on the human condition. As a result, the traditional role of philosophy as 'the privileged point of synthesis of human knowledge' seemed increasingly vitiated. Being an anthropologist, who had worked in Brazil, he also attacked the ethnocentric nature of much European thought, saying it was too culture-bound to be truly universal.

Derrida took Lévi-Strauss to task – for being imprisoned within his own viewpoint in a much more fundamental way. In *Tristes Tropiques*, Lévi-Strauss's autobiographical account of how and why he chose anthropology and his early fieldwork in South America, he had explored the link between writing and secret knowledge in primitive tribes like the Nambikwara. This led Lévi-Strauss to the generalisation that 'for thousands of years', writing had been the privilege of a powerful elite, associated with caste and class differentiation, that 'its primary function' was to 'enslave and subordinate'. Between the invention of writing and the advent of science, Lévi-Strauss said, there was 'no accretion of knowledge'.

Derrida advanced a related but even more fundamental point. Like Lacan and Foucault especially, he was struck by the 'inexactitudes and imprecisions and contradictions of words', and he thought these shortcomings philosophically important. Going further into Lévi-Strauss's text, he highlighted inconsistencies in the arguments. The Nambikwara, Derrida says, have all sorts of 'decorations' that, in a less ethnocentric person, might be called 'writing'. These include calabashes, genealogical trees, sketches in the soil and so on, all of which undoubtedly have *meaning*. Lévi-Strauss's writing can never catch these meanings, says Derrida. For him, as with Lacan and Foucault, language is the most important mental construct there is, something that (perhaps) sets humankind apart from other organisms, the basic tool of thought and therefore essential – presumably – to reason (though also to corruption). But, once we doubt language, Derrida says, once we 'doubt that it accurately represents reality, once we are conscious that all individuals are ethnocentric, inconsistent, incoherent to a point, oversimplifiers ... then we have a new concept of man'. Consciousness is no longer what it appears to be, nor reason, nor meaning, nor – even – intentionality. Derrida questions whether any single utterance by an individual can have one meaning, even for that person.[8] Words mean both more and less than they appear to, either in the person producing them or someone hearing or reading them.

This gap, or 'adjournment', in meaning he labelled the *différance* and it led on to the process Derrida called 'deconstruction', which for many years proved inordinately popular, notorious even. As Christopher Johnson says, in his commentary on Derrida's ideas, deconstruction was an important ingredient in the 'postmodern' argument or sensibility, enabling as many readings of a text as there are readers. He meant to say (in itself dangerous) not only that people's utterances have unconscious elements, but also that the words themselves have a history that is greater than any one person's experience of those words, and so anything anyone says is almost bound to mean more than that person means. This too is no more than extended common sense. Where Derrida grows controversial, or non-commonsensical, is when he argues that the nature of language robs even the speaker of any *authority* over the meaning of what he or she says or writes. Instead, 'meaning resides in the structure of language itself: we think only in signs, and signs have only an arbitrary relationship to what they signify'. For Derrida, this undermines the very notion of philosophy as we (think we) understand it. For him there can be no progress in human affairs, no sense in which there is any accumulation in knowledge, 'where what we know today is "better", more complete, than what was known yesterday'. It is simply that old vocabularies are seen as dead, but 'that too is a meaning that could change'. On this account even *philosophy* is a hardly useful word.

For Derrida, the chief aspect of the human condition is its 'undecided' quality, where we keep giving meanings to our experience, but we can never be sure that those meanings are the 'true' ones, and in any case 'truth' is an unhelpful concept, which itself keeps changing. There is no progress, there is no one truth that, 'if we read enough, or live life enough, we can finally grasp'.[9]

IDEOLOGICAL SMUGNESS

Like Derrida, Louis Althusser was born in Algeria. Like Derrida, says Susan James, he was more Marxist than Marx, believing that not even the great revolutionary was 'altogether aware of the significance of his own work'. This led Althusser to question the view that the world of ideology and the empirical world are related. For example, 'the empirical data about the horrors of the gulag do not necessarily lead one to turn against Stalin or the USSR'. For Althusser – thinking along the same lines as Derrida – empirical data do not carry with them any one meaning, therefore one can (and Althusser did) remain loyal to, say, Stalin, and the ideology of communism despite disparate events that happened inside the territory under Stalin's control. Althusser also took the view that history is overdetermined: so many factors contribute to any one event or phenomenon – be they economic, social, cultural or political – that it is impossible to specify causes. 'There is, in other words, no such thing as a capability of determining the cause of a historical event. Therefore, one can decide for oneself what is at work in history, which decision then constitutes one's ideology ... The theory of history is something the individual works out for himself; necessarily so, because it does not admit of empirical and rational demonstration.'[10]

More often than not, societies – and especially capitalist societies – have what Althusser calls ideological state apparatuses: the family, the media, schools and churches, for example, which propagate and receive ideas, so much so that we are not really self-conscious agents: 'We acquired our identity as a result of these apparatuses.' In Marxist terms, the key to Althusser is the relative autonomy of the superstructure, and he replaced the false consciousness of class, which Marx had made so much of, with 'the false consciousness of ideology and individual identity, the aim being to shake people out of their ideological smugness'.[11] Unfortunately, his published ideas stopped in 1980 after he murdered his wife and was unfit to stand trial.

A Postmodern Marxism

With their scepticism about language, especially as it relates to knowledge and its links with power in the search for meaning, structuralism and deconstruction amount to a criticism of both capitalist/materialist society *and* the forms of knowledge produced by the natural sciences. What the French thinkers produced was essentially a postmodern form of Marxism. It is not so much Marx's economic determinism or class-based motivations that are retained as his idea of 'false consciousness', expressed through the idea that knowledge, and reason, must always be forged or mediated by the power relations of any society – that knowledge, hermeneutics and understanding always serve a purpose. Just as Kant said there is no pure reason, so, we are told from France, there is no pure knowledge, and understanding this is emancipatory.

While it would not be true to say that these writers are anti-scientific (Foucault in particular was too well informed to be so crude), there is among them a feeling that science is by no means the only form of knowledge worth having, that it is seriously inadequate to explain much, if not most, of what we know. These authors do not exactly ignore evolution, but they show little awareness of how their theories fit – or do not fit – into the proliferation of genetic and ethological studies. It is also noticeable that almost all of them accept and enlist as support evidence from psychoanalysis. There is, for Anglophone readers, something rather unreal about this late French focus on Freud. There is also a feeling that Foucault, Lacan and Derrida have done little more than elevate small-scale observations – the undoubted misuses of criminals or the insane in the past, or in Lacan's case vagaries in the use of language – into entire edifices of philosophies. Ultimately, the answer here must lie in how convincing others find their arguments.

At the same time, the ways in which they have subverted the idea that there is a general canon, or one way of looking at humankind, and telling our story, has undoubtedly had an effect. If nothing else, they have introduced a scepticism that has proved useful. In 1969, in a special issue of *Yale French Studies*, structuralism crossed the Atlantic. Postmodernist thought had a big influence on philosophy in America.

THE DEATH OF THE AUTHOR

Roland Barthes is generally considered a poststructuralist critic. Born in 1915 in Cherbourg, the son of a naval lieutenant, he grew up with a lung illness that made his childhood painful and solitary. This made him unfit for service in the Second World War, during which he began his career as a literature teacher. A homosexual, Barthes suffered the early death of a lover (from TB), and the amount of illness in his life even led him to begin work on a medical degree. During his time in the sanatorium, when he did a lot of reading, he also became interested in Marxism and for a time was on the edge of Sartre's milieu. After the war he took up appointments in Bucharest in Romania (then of course a Marxist country) and Alexandria in Egypt. He returned to a job in the cultural affairs section of the French Foreign Office.

The enforced solitude, and the travel to very different countries, meant that Barthes added to his interest in literature a fascination with language, which was to make his name. Beginning in 1953, he embarked on a series of short books, essays mainly, that grew in influence until, by the 1970s, it was the prevailing orthodoxy in literary studies.

Barthes's argument was that there was more to modern culture than met the eye, that modern men and women are surrounded by all manner of signs and symbols that tell them as much about the modern world as traditional writing forms. In *Mythologies*, published in 1957, but not translated into English until 1972, Barthes focused his gaze on specific aspects of the contemporary world, and it was his choice of subject, as much as the content of his short essays, that attracted attention.

He was in essence pointing to certain aspects of contemporary culture and saying that we should not just let these phenomena pass us by without inspection or reflection. He had one essay on margarine, another on steak and chips. He was after the 'capillary meanings' of these phenomena. This is how he began his essay 'Plastic': 'Despite having names of Greek shepherds (Polystyrene, Polyvinyl, Polyethylene), plastic, the products of which have just been gathered in an exhibition, is in essence the stuff of alchemy ... as its everyday name indicates, it is ubiquity made visible ... it is less a thing than a trace of a movement ... But the price to be paid for this success is that plastic, sublimated as movement, hardly exists as a substance ... What best reveals it for what it is, is the sound it gives, at once hollow and flat; its noise is its undoing, as are its colours, for it seems capable of retaining only the most chemical-looking ones. Of yellow, red and green, it keeps only the aggressive quality.'[12]

Barthes's Marxism gave him, like Sartre, a hatred of the bourgeoisie, and his very success in the analysis of the signs and symbols of everyday modern life (semiology, as it came to be called) turned him against the scientific stance of the structuralists. Fortified by Lacan's ideas about the unconscious, Barthes came down firmly on the side of humanistic interpretation, of literature, film, music. His most celebrated essay was 'The Death of the Author', published in 1968. This echoed the so-called New Criticism, in the 1940s in America in particular, where the dominant idea was 'the intentional fallacy'. As refined by Barthes, this view holds that the intentions of the author of a text do not matter in interpreting that text. We all read a new piece of work having read a whole range of works earlier on, which have given words particular meanings that differ subtly from one person to another. An author, therefore, simply cannot predict what meaning his work will have for others.[13] In *The Pleasure of the Text* (1973), Barthes wrote: 'On the stage of the text, no footlights: there is not, behind the text, someone active (the writer) and out front someone passive (the reader); there is not a subject and an object ... The pleasure of the text is that moment when my body pursues its own ideas.' Barthes was aware that all writing, all creation, is bound by the cultural context of its production, and he wanted to help people break out of those constraints, so that reading, far from being a passive act, could be more active and, in the end, more enjoyable.

He was given a rather bad press in the Anglo-Saxon countries.* He was such a vivid writer, with a gift for phrasemaking and acute observation, that he cannot be dismissed so easily.

---

* Barthes's views contain one contradiction. If an author's intentions mean little, how can Barthes's own views mean anything?

SUBVERTING RATIONALISM, FRENCH THEORY, *TEL QUEL* AND 'THE EXCEPTIONAL TRUTH OF LITERATURE'

These various forms of activity came together, in the sociable French way, in the pages of a journal, *Tel Quel*, founded in 1964 by Philippe Sollers and published by Seuil, one of the leading Left Bank publishing houses. Founded in the 1930s, Seuil had published Mao Zedong's *Little Red Book* and works by Lacan, Barthes and Fanon, and specialised in the social sciences.[14] *Tel Quel* (which translates as 'as is', 'as such', 'verbatim') embodied a long-standing French tradition – that literature was and is a uniquely privileged activity over and above anything else in life – on top of which the journal's editorial policies very much reflected the Marxist, including Maoist, idea of permanent revolution, along with psychoanalytic and even surrealist achievements.

Born in 1936 in Talence, near Bordeaux, Sollers, originally Philippe Joyeaux, had a rather wild, liberal mother but he grew up also with two dominant sisters who may have contributed more to his psychology – a precocious sexuality and the embrace of femininity. In 1968 he married Julia Kristeva, a Bulgarian-born French theorist, three years after she had arrived in Paris to attend seminars by Barthes. She became a psychoanalyst with a keen interest in language.

'French theory' is in fact an English-language phrase used most widely in the United States after these ideas caught on there in university circles in the 1970s. But the concept is nonetheless useful more generally in that it does consolidate a definite phase of intellectual life in France (as considered earlier in this chapter) in which specific modes of thought hung together conceptually. And although the collective energies of these thinkers eventually dissipated (after much robust criticism from Anglophone writers), for a while this was a characteristic French accomplishment – *Tel Quel* lasted more than twenty years, from 1960 to 1983. In this community of theorists, *Tel Quel* occupied a quite specific place, 'intersecting perspectives from numerous disciplines', and contributing to a 'theoretical euphoria' (theory 'exploded' in 1967, following the publications of Derrida and Foucault). During the period of its publication, the journal's twin aims were the affirmation of literature 'as a value higher than the philosophical, sociological or theoretical', emphasising its 'exceptional and radical status' at the end of the twentieth century, together with the aim of subverting rationalism.[15]

The journal variously investigated the nature of creativity, reporting on the dissolution of the traditional novel format, then coming under attack from the *nouveau roman*, which explored the absence of plot and character, utilised alternative viewpoints, so that it was not always clear which character was speaking/thinking, and played with narrative as a way to escape what were felt to be the traditional confines of the genre. In this sense, the journal reflected the theories of Derrida and others in regard to the ambiguities of meaning, authorial intentions and power.

Tel Quel was interested in the extent to which language is 'exterior to' or 'independent of' the mind. It explored the *experience* of writing in the belief that language has its own rules and intentions that are beyond human reason. The journal's (postmodern) view of human nature was that it is *not* cohesive, but marked by contradiction, chance, breaks, inconclusive activity; it questions whether roots determine character or are overcome by it, whether perversity is as much a feature of life as reason.

What held it together for so long were four basic ideas, each of which is capable of endless theorising. The first was Marxism, including Maoism (Sollers and Kristeva visited China in 1974 and returned impressed), the second was psychoanalysis (its theories, as we have seen, in particular proliferated in France in the 1960s) and its tempting notion of the unconscious, which called into question our ideas about intention and motive. The third idea was surrealism and here, to argue by metaphor, French theory was entranced by some of the achievements of the surrealists in the way that they played around with, and called into question, reality – one thinks, for example, of Dalí's melting watches, Miró's biological stars, de Chirico's menacing architectures. Sometimes playful, sometimes not playful at all, what did such conceits say about reality, and could literature find and attempt equivalent adventures? Fourthly, *Tel Quel* was above all impressed and influenced by philosopher/anthropologist/art historian Georges Bataille's idea that literature was 'all or nothing', and could not be judged by any other criteria.

Another factor was geography. The main intellectual publishers of the time – Seuil, Gallimard, Minuit – were all located in the same small area of the Left Bank, in three almost contiguous streets. As before with cafés, this world was geographically minuscule. Were these events and theories as big as they seemed, or a distended function of a tiny intellectual echo chamber? Did this give them an inbred character, and in turn did that account for the fact that a major problem with French theory was its very intelligibility and (in)comprehensibility? This sounds like it ought to have been a peripheral issue, but it very definitely was not. Even a sympathetic account of *Tel Quel* and 'the time of theory', by, for example, Patrick Ffrench, a London professor of French, refers to the journal's articles as 'fairly difficult to understand', 'complex and often impenetrable', as having an 'almost oppressive complexity', and recommending that what was needed when reading such articles was 'a kind of detective work to find out what is happening'.

Tel Quel was dissolved in 1983, following editorial disagreements among its board members and because Seuil turned down Sollers's new novel, though he found a new home at Gallimard and started a new title, *L'Infini*, which continues to assert 'the exceptional truth of literature'.[16]

But *Tel Quel* (though it only ever sold about 8,000 copies) was a paradigm example of French exceptionalism – lauded by the French, scorned by many Anglo-Saxon academics and writers who thought that its late-arriving obsession with psychoanalysis was ludicrously out of date and out of kilter with the great ideas – of evolution, genetics, ethology – then dominating scholarship in the North Atlantic, and that French theory's conceptual and cerebral *hauteur*, combined with its considerable stylistic imperfections and myriad obfuscations, made it a perfect example of an emperor with no clothes.

WHAT IS CAPABLE OF PROOF?

Although science was offering material advance and intellectual excitement for those who wanted it, by 1979, as in the case of *Tel Quel*, there were also many countervailing voices. By the end of the 1970s, the critique of science, the scientific method, and science as a system of knowledge had become a central plank in postmodern thinking. *The Postmodern Condition*, by Jean-François Lyotard, was the first in a raft of books that began to question the very status of science. It is important to give the subtitle of Lyotard's book, 'A Report on Knowledge', for he was a French academic at the Institut polytechnique de philosophie of the Université de Paris VIII (at Vincennes), who was commissioned by the Conseil des universités of Quebec to prepare an investigation.[17]

Lyotard had begun adult life in postwar Paris as a left-wing political journalist. Later, while completing his academic qualifications in philosophy, he had developed an interest in psychoanalysis, trying to marry Freud and Marx, as so many colleagues were doing. His early writing he had grouped into 'the Libidinal', 'the Pagan' and 'the Intractable'. The first category clearly carried psychoanalytic overtones, but beyond that the use of 'libidinal' was meant to imply that, as he viewed the world, motivating sources were personal, individual and even unconscious, rather than overtly political or deriving from some particular metanarrative. Similarly, in using the term 'pagan', Lyotard intended to imply not so much false gods as alternative gods, and many different varieties, that one's interests in life could be satisfying and rewarding even when they had nothing to do with the official or most popular 'truths'. By 'intractable' he meant that some areas of experience are simply too complex ever to be understood.

In *The Postmodern Condition*, however, Lyotard's specific target was science as a form of knowledge. He wanted to know in what important ways scientific knowledge differs from other forms of knowledge, and what effects the success of scientific knowledge is having on us, as individuals and as a society. 'Simplifying to the extreme,' he begins, 'I define *postmodern* as incredulity toward metanarratives.' He goes on to compare different kinds of knowledge – for example, that contained in fairy tales, that produced by the law and that produced by science. For many scientists, as Lyotard concedes, scientific knowledge is the only form of knowledge there is, but if so, how then do we understand fairy stories and laws? The most important form of knowledge that isn't scientific – in the sense that most scientists would accept the term – is, he says, knowledge about the self. The self, Lyotard says, has a history, is in part at least a narrative, and like no other. It is, therefore, unavailable to science.[18]

In a historical excursion, Lyotard explains how, in his view, the traditional scientific approach originated in the University of Berlin in the nineteenth century; he argues that science has essentially been a child of universities ever since, and therefore has usually been paid for by governments. This is important to Lyotard as the central fact in the sociology of (scientific) knowledge, 'the tyranny of the experts'. This is why a certain kind of knowledge (such as 'The earth revolves around the sun') came to have a higher status than others (such as 'The minimum wage should be set at x dollars'). After 150 years of state-run science, science and power, we find it much easier to prove the former than the latter. Is that because of the science we have pursued, or because the latter statement is intractable, incapable of proof? If there are certain categories of problem, or experience, or simple ways of talking that are intractable *in principle*, where does that leave science? Where does that leave the universities and the optimism (in those who possess it) that, given time, science can solve all our problems?

Lyotard argued that other forms of knowledge have their place, that science can never hope to provide anything like a complete answer to the philosophical problems that face us (or we think face us). Science derives its power, its legitimacy, from technological successes, and rightly so. But there are many areas of life that will always remain intractable to science in principle.[19] Of these the most important is the self.

The End of the 'Theatre of the Exceptional'

On Saturday 19 April 1980, Jean-Paul Sartre was buried in Montparnasse cemetery in Paris. He had died four days before of a pulmonary oedema, aged seventy-four. His funeral was not quite the event that Victor Hugo's had been almost a century before, but it was impressive enough – between 15,000 and 20,000 turned out to watch the cortège, which passed La Coupole, the café where he and so many fellow intellectuals had gathered, and his home at 29 boulevard Edgar Quinet. Under a leaden sky, interspersed in the crowd were Michel Foucault, Yves Montand, Simone Signoret, Claude Mauriac, André Glucksmann and Françoise Sagan. Simone de Beauvoir, looking frail, was in a car behind the coffin, together with Arlette El Kaïm, Sartre's adopted daughter. As the Agence France Presse reported, 'It is the last time in France that such a crowd gathers around the body of an intellectual.'

In the months and years ahead, death would be a visitor to virtually all the great postwar names of French intellectuals: Barthes went also in 1980, Lacan in 1981, Aron in 1983, Foucault a year later and Braudel a year after that, in 1985.

This series of close-run deaths did mark a significant change in French culture but, with the benefit of hindsight, and despite the fact that French literature, in the days of Sartre, Camus and Beauvoir, probably enjoyed an international reputation unequalled in the post-Second World War world, the most important demise was not

Sartre's but that of Raymond Aron (interred in the same cemetery but with a much smaller crowd in attendance), and the change embodied a transfer in intellectual climate from one mainly led by Marxist philosophers to a new galaxy formed predominantly of liberal historians – François Furet, Pierre Rosanvallon, Pierre Nora, Daniel Lindenberg and Pascale Casanova, the last formally a literary critic but equally a literary historian.

THE RECALCITRANCE OF REALITY

Born in Paris in 1905, the son of a secular Jewish lawyer, Raymond Aron studied at the École normale supérieure, where he was influenced by Bergson and where one of his early friends was Sartre, though they became intellectual rivals almost from the start (Michel Winock describes them as like two sides of the same coin). Always of an international bent, Aron studied for several years in Germany in the 1930s, where he acquired a wide knowledge of German intellectual history and some strongly held views about national socialism. He was a socialist, and all his life he retained the humanitarian, secular, democratic and progressive views of social democracy. He also retained an interest in Marxism, but he became its most severe critic as well as of the communist order of society.[1] He was above all politically *practical*, understanding that ideals can be approached but never fully realised.

Seeing the weakness in French life in the 1930s, and then the collapse in 1940, Aron's agenda for the rest of his career was clear – the rehabilitation of French society and the renewal of its self-respect. In the war he made his way to London, where he became the political commentator of a journal de Gaulle wanted published to uphold the very idea of France. When Aron returned to Paris in 1944 he became a publicist, first with *Combat*, then *Le Figaro*. Later, he would work in the Ministry of Culture, with André Malraux.

Aron had a distinguished academic career – professor of sociology at the Sorbonne, later director of studies at the École pratique des hautes études and finally professor of European civilisation at the Collège de France until his retirement in 1978. He was a committed heir of the Enlightenment and at his death, in the words of Edward Shils, 'he was the most prominent and esteemed writer in the world on modern society and contemporary international politics ... accepted as a towering figure in intellectual circles in France, Great Britain, Germany, Italy, Israel, the United States and Latin America'.[2] Aron was equally at home in Britain, Germany and the United States, and a foreign member of all their respective academies.

He was elected to the Académie française in 1974 but in a sense this is misleading: he was nonetheless isolated in the French intellectual world. Most of his erstwhile friends, after the Second World War, were communists and often fellow travellers of the Soviet Union. *Le Monde*, 'when it was not hostile, kept him at a distance'.[3]

Yet he had a prolific career, writing thousands of articles and more than forty books. More than one of them shocked the French, none more so than the best known, enduring and influential, which made him even more isolated. In *Opium of the Intellectuals* ('a leading document of the Cold War'), he expanded on a remark of Simone Weil's, that Marxism had 'bewitched' French intellectuals (and not only *French* intellectuals) and had become the opiate of the people, a form of quasi-religion which stymied critical thinking. Aron, for his part, regarded Marxism as a retrograde step in the wake of the Enlightenment in that it denied people the right of freedom, the right of expression, of controversy and criticism – and even the vote. He did not see the proletariat as a collective saviour, rather he felt that intellectuals placed too much faith in reason and that the ultimate and unrealistic aim of Marxism was the abolition of politics. For him, however, he knew that 'the last word would never be said', owing to 'the recalcitrance of reality'. This, to many Marxists in postwar Paris, was anathema. Undaunted, he dismissed the politics of perfection as a self-indulgence, not practically minded, and this set him against the great majority of his colleagues, friends and acquaintances. He agreed with Orwell that 'there are some ideas so absurd that only intellectuals could believe them', and set himself firmly against what he termed 'the higher gullibility'.

Gradually, however, events turned his way – though it took time: Khrushchev's 'anti-Stalin' speech in February 1956; the Soviet occupation of Hungary in November that same year; the Prague Spring of 1968; the publication of *The Gulag Archipelago* in 1973, which caused as big a sensation as anywhere in France, which did not have as strong a tradition of Sovietology as other countries. Throughout, Aron maintained that reason allied to new knowledge were the proper guides of choice and the best routes to patriotism.[4] But he repeatedly asserted that he had no confidence that the 'international working class' – the shibboleth of the Marxists – could be counted on to prevent wars, and no confidence at all that public ownership of the instruments of production would improve the lot of men and women and increase freedom. As a result, says Shils, he was treated by most French intellectuals 'almost as a leper was treated in antiquity'.[5]

THE COHERENCE OF GRANDEUR

Aron was partly critical and partly supportive of de Gaulle's politics of grandeur. Unlike the general, Aron had an outstanding ability to put himself in other people's shoes. But he understood that grandeur makes possible national coherence and flourishing, and showed 'a willingness to be a player'.[6] And he had his own conception of greatness, writing: 'Always of the second rank when compared with the colossus [of the United States and the Soviet Union], France will recover a radiance and an influence of the first rank on the condition that, by its interior stability and its prosperity, it creates a political and a spiritual centre around which will gather the smaller nations.' He was not opposed to colonies in principle – he thought they would help France maintain its rank and position in the world. French grandeur, he concluded, would be a function of a double success: modernisation of the economy and continuity of the culture.[7] One finds meaning, he liked to say, only in what one makes of oneself. In this he was closer to Sartre than de Gaulle.

Many postwar intellectuals, Aron argued, 'fled to an illusory paradise buried in the future'. This led them in his view into two errors. They turned their backs on science (in particular biology) in favour of polemics, and on America, it being part of his achievement, later, to introduce Anglo-Saxon thought to France.*

---

* Although, in the wake of the Second World War, the *grandes écoles* specialised in world-class mathematics and statistics, beyond that, and especially outside Paris, science floundered in France.

From the moment the French position ceased to have universal significance, he noted that many fellow Parisian intellectuals sought out Russia or America, 'in hopes of attaining universality'. For him modern life was different from the past because no grandiose task was available, revolution and conquest being no longer on the cards. As he liked to say, 'history requires an inaccessible paradise to be possible' – this was the appeal of Marxism.[8] But for him, contrariwise, 'freedom equals work to enlarge the margin of our autonomy'. Which also involved – and this was crucial – the inward recognition of limits.

That events were moving his way was shown by the fact that, when he died in 1983, his memoirs became a bestseller. Because of his fervent internationalism, Aron had plentiful access to Anglo-Saxon literature, and this informed his liberalism and added to his popularisation of Condorcet, Constant, Montesquieu and above all Tocqueville. This change had begun in earnest in 1978 with the publication of the journal *Commentaire*, when, as Iain Stewart has pointed out, 'something akin to an ideological revolution' took place in France and when, as Perry Anderson has also pointedly observed, 'in the space of a few years Paris had made the transition from a beacon of revolutionary politics to the capital of European intellectual reaction'.[9]

In *Commentaire*, and then later, another journal, *Contrepoint*, a liberal revival – partly a response to the events of 1968, but largely due to Aron's ideas and writings – began to be heard more and more, and his reputation was transformed.[10] This is partly because he enabled the 'rediscovery' of a *French* tradition of liberalism, in particular a respect for legality and a spirit of compromise quite at variance with militant Marxism, with its 'insatiable egalitarianism', that had been the taste of Sartre and the fellow members of his *'famille'*. It was obvious to Aron, if not to those opposed to him, that the *trente glorieuses*, the thirty prosperous years from 1945 to 1975, had been accomplished by a 'politics of productivity' in which the interests of workers and employers were aligned rather than the old habit of incessant conflict.

Aron presented himself as a descendant of Condorcet (as an early scientist-mathematician), and the liberals Montesquieu, Constant and Tocqueville, in firm opposition to totalitarian Marxist tradition. He dismissed the events of 1968 as a 'psychodrama' ('a crusade without a cross, a fight without an object'), rather than a systemic revolutionary event. In fact, Aron was more worried by the loss of respect for the law that the events had demonstrated. In particular the demonstrators had shown a marked unwillingness to compromise, which he had always felt was the *sine qua non* of politics.

And it was this which appealed to some of the younger (former) demonstrators who proceeded to gather around Aron. *Contrepoint*, founded in May 1970 – the second anniversary of the *événements* – was a deliberate move, which carried a Tocqueville quote on each successive masthead. The journal was especially critical of those intellectuals – Michel Foucault, Jacques Lacan, Gilles Deleuze, Félix Guattari – whose nihilist libertarianism, Aron felt, had helped bring May 1968 into being.[11]

Reinterpreting the Revolution: France's Liberal Revival

The people who gathered around Aron were predominantly historians, who would combine academic careers alongside political involvement, even if that involvement was only as members of editorial boards: Jean-Claude Casanova, Marc Fumaroli, François Furet, Pierre Manent, Pierre Nora, Pierre Rosanvallon. At the same time this group was scornful of what were described as the 'telegenic' and 'lightweight' New Philosophers, such as Bernard-Henri Lévy ('grotesque', 'a crass booby') and André Glucksmann, former radicals who had undergone anti-totalitarian conversions; they were dismissed as opportunists.[12]

Commentaire and, to a lesser extent, *Contrepoint*, attracted interest from politicians such as Valéry Giscard d'Estaing and Raymond Barre, and Aron served as an informal advisor in the election campaigns of 1978 and 1981. Aron's French biographer would later work for Nicolas Sarkozy, all of which confirms the intellectual climate he had helped to stimulate. Aron was also the doctoral supervisor for Claude Lefort, who started the anti-Stalinist journal *Socialisme ou barbarie*, while Pierre Manent was Aron's assistant at the Collège de France and a director of *Commentaire*. Aron introduced Manent to the work of Leo Strauss, the German-American godfather of neoconservatism, Manent coming to share Aron's view that totalitarianism 'existed as a permanent possibility within democracy', stemming from, again, its 'insatiable egalitarianism'.[13] Manent and Lefort also shared Aron's view that figures such as Lacan and Foucault had created a 'crisis of professional authority' in France in trying to promote a 'radical civil society'. Aron thought it ludicrous that people should follow Foucault and others in seeing classrooms, hospital wards and offices as thinly disguised concentration camps, especially as, after Solzhenitsyn, they had to confront the real thing.[14]

In 1977, six years before Aron died, the first of his intellectual heirs emerged when François Furet established a seminar at the École des hautes études en sciences sociales (EHESS), which also explored political philosophy with an emphasis on the French liberal tradition. This seminar was an important forerunner of the Institut Raymond Aron, founded in 1985 at the EHESS, which played a central role in France's liberal revival, not least the reinterpretation of the French Revolution that Furet and Rosanvallon would produce later, and in their joint work on the end of French exceptionalism (see below, this chapter).

These events did not go entirely uncontested, of course. In 1983, for example, Gilles Lipovetsky, then a Marxist professor at Grenoble University, argued that France was entering an 'age of emptiness', but in the same year François Mitterrand's socialist government 'forgot' to mark the centenary of Marx's death. It was a further sign that the left in France was losing its symbolic power.[15]

THE TERMINAL PHASE OF FRANCE'S REVOLUTIONARY CULTURE

The changing intellectual-political landscape in France in the 1980s was sharpened by the approach of the bicentenary of the Revolution in 1989. This was when François Furet, the first of a small number of what one observer called 'impresario-academics' – whose lives ranged well beyond research, to include organising think tanks, commissioning and editing rafts of books for publishing houses and similar activities – would really make his mark.[16]

Furet had already raised some of the issues that were to make him famous – notorious – in two books, one published as early as 1965, the other his 1978 work, *Penser la Révolution française*, which, as Patrice Higgonet, the French-born Harvard historian, says, 'renewed the field [of Revolution studies] completely'. Nineteen eighty-nine, Higgonet confirms, was Furet's greatest moment, and a turning point for his reputation. 'Since that time, his understanding of Revolutionary history had held sway' and, says Higgonet, Furet's name should henceforth be linked with those of Michelet and Tocqueville.[17]

Born into a wealthy Parisian banking family in 1927, Furet joined the French Communist Party in 1949. He left in 1956, in protest at the Soviet invasion of Hungary. Graduating from the Sorbonne, he later abandoned a doctorate in history to become a journalist.

In 1965, with his then brother-in-law Denis Richet, he published *La Révolution française*, his first challenge to the understanding of the Revolution as driven by classical Marxist arguments – that is, as a result of class conflict and the economic conditions of the time. In this first account, one might even say that Furet found that the Revolution was 'insignificant'. As he remarked: 'Nothing more resembled French society under Louis XVI than the same society under Louis Philippe.' Most political thinkers before 1789 were reformist-minded, not revolutionaries.[18]

To get his message across, Furet knew he had to repeatedly challenge the idea that economic structure and class relations governed events and, moreover, held out the promise that revolutionary ideals could still triumph in present-day France. Instead, in the first instance, he portrayed the period from 1789 to the Terror as one of 'enlightened moderation', in which liberty and equality were prioritised and the excesses of church power efficiently dismantled. For Furet, this period of the Revolution was essentially no more than a liberal reform movement, while the period after 1793 was an aberration, veering away from enlightened moderation. He replied to criticism by identifying among his opponents a 'revolutionary catechism', in which he accused Marxist historians of being less concerned with historical accuracy than with defending socialist ideals.

Furet modified his view somewhat in *Penser la Révolution*

française, a polemical masterpiece nonetheless. He now conceded that the Terror was of a piece with what had gone before but that direct democracy, the 'bottomless pit of egalitarianism' and Rousseau's idea of the 'general will' had carried between them the seeds of demagoguery, though again and importantly class conflict was sidelined as he reoriented studies of the Revolution away from social history towards cultural and intellectual history. Like Tocqueville before him, Furet saw the Revolution as more a battle of ideas, with the likes of Sieyès imagining new political possibilities, but these advances were driven by sheer thought rather than anything else – this was a philosophical revolution, not an economic one.

Emphasising individual factors even further above economic structuralism, he later developed his ideas of the 'passions'. 'Fear', he now argued, was the overwhelming passion of the right and 'resentment' the defining passion of the left. 'Envy' and 'jealousy' were among the democratic passions, the result of a fundamental contradiction at the heart of democracy 'between the principle of equality and the realities of personal enrichment'. This contradiction was, Furet felt, both 'irreconcilable and intolerable'.

He argued that the primary passion was the 'egalitarian passion', but below it were a number of 'subsidiary' passions, including a 'revolutionary passion' and a specifically French passion 'for permanent revolution', incorporating 'hatred of the bourgeoisie', an 'anti-aristocratic passion' and 'money'.[19] He felt that the collapse of Marxism owed more to a passion for well-being (which communism had signally failed to provide) than a passion for liberty.

The central point of Furet's argument was that the egalitarian passion – the most fundamental – also embodied a paradox in that the desire for equality is a bottomless pit. 'Democracy produces inequality that cannot be fully eliminated without putting basic liberties at risk.' And although it can be said that it was the passion for equality that led to the Terror in the French Revolution, Furet also maintained that the fact that 'equality is unattainable gives democracy its inexhaustible strength ... Equality is the archetypal example of a passion since it is always beyond reach.' Democratic society can never be democratic enough.

Despite this predicament, Furet was aware of – and helped bring about, as he saw it – 'the terminal phase of France's revolutionary culture'.[20] He felt that the French Revolution itself had created the revolutionary passion, now coming to an end. Revolutionary passion had 'demanded' that 'every action be political' and to some extent this had shaped France and fuelled its enthusiasm for Marxism – which says much the same thing. And since bourgeois society is based on a spirit of competition, 'its values seemed to be directly opposed to the values of egalitarianism'.[21] Furet thus grasped that modern individuals are torn between fraternity, the horizon of humanity, and envy, which mix constitutes our modern psychology.* He described various stages by which the revolutionary passion had declined and, in a famous phrase, had 'come into port'.

A Future without a Horizon

More than that, though, between François Mitterrand's victory in the 1988 presidential election and the 200th anniversary of the Revolution in summer 1989, Furet – together with Jacques Julliard, a teacher and former union leader, and Pierre Rosanvallon – published *La République du centre: la fin de l'exception française*. This much-debated book argued that the 'French exception' had come to an end, that the political divisions that had 'afflicted' France since 1789 had been so much eroded that the central characteristics that made France different – the *dirigiste* centralised state, France's sense of its universal mission as the depository of the values of Enlightenment rationalism, the republican model of citizenship and the repeated, sudden transfers of power – no longer applied.

Many scholars, as late as 2017, have queried whether Furet and his associates were premature in this analysis and, in any case, Furet's idea of French exceptionalism overlaps but is by no means identical with the French exceptionalism being explored in this book. But Furet was accused more than once of being 'obsessed' with French exceptionality.[22]

---

* Furet has been criticised for 'somewhat simplistically' regarding Britain as 'completely bourgeois'. Unlike the British, the French have never believed in the 'hidden hand' of Adam Smith and the resulting harmonisation of interests.

He was in no doubt as to why 'centrism' had taken hold in France. Most of all, as Aron had noted, the *trente glorieuses*, Furet felt, had given France 'the fastest collective embourgeoisement in its history', making society 'more individualistic and more uniform ... less aristocratic and less revolutionary'. France, he concluded, wanted neither socialism nor neoliberalism, 'the reign of the market'. And the turn to European integration, in the background, also made it even clearer how like other nations France was, accepting that capitalism and democracy could not be separated.

But Furet did not think that political passion would now die. He remained convinced that passion would always be fuelled by the possibilities – inherent in democracy – of new utopias. This was his concluding argument in *Le Passé d'une illusion*, another work which took France by storm, in 1995, in which he nailed communism as a mirage. This was not his most original idea but in great style he laid it against the backdrop of the Revolution and the book sold more than 100,000 copies. He wasn't entirely sanguine. He felt that the collapse of communism, which he now dismissed as an 'absurd' idea, had nonetheless left us with a future without a horizon, and this, he said, entailed a crisis of imagination. This crisis of imagination would be keenly felt all the more when set against the relatively recent arrival of so many Muslim migrants.

Furet, who lectured at the University of Chicago every autumn, where he was a member of the Committee on Social Thought, died in hospital in July 1997, where he was being treated for a head wound he suffered while playing tennis with the philosopher/politician Luc Ferry. It was only four months after he had been elected to the Académie française. He was seventy.

THE PATHOLOGIES OF DEMOCRACY

Furet was always clear about his debt to Aron and others. While he was director of the EHESS, he founded the Raymond Aron Institute and, together with Rosanvallon, jointly created the Fondation Saint-Simon (FSS) in 1982. Twenty-one years younger than Furet, Rosanvallon was nonetheless a close collaborator. The FSS was a think tank designed to spread Aron's liberal ideas and, according to

Pierre Nora, brought together the people with 'the means' (i.e., the money) and those with the ideas, in an attempt to influence government policy and public thinking in general. Named after the Comte de Saint-Simon, who had been so concerned about the social effects of industrialism (chapter 31), its aim was to encourage industrialists and businesspeople to involve themselves more fully with intellectual culture, and during the two decades it was active the foundation gathered together influential civil servants, business leaders, intellectuals, journalists and elected officials, meeting monthly for lunch followed by talks which were printed and circulated, and some of which led to new legislation.

The activities of the foundation overlapped with those of the influential journals *Commentaire* (the 'anchor') and *Contrepoint*, whose steering committee included the historians Pierre Manent and Marc Fumaroli and was 'unquestionably pro-American', disseminating the views of such American authors as Allan Bloom and Francis Fukuyama. In time, the FSS would be disbanded but by then a number of other clubs and associations of like-minded souls had been formed. Among these, Pierre Rosanvallon founded *La République des idées* in 2002, a collection of works published by Seuil, and organised large-scale forums, while Gallimard's senior history editor, Pierre Nora (another of Furet's brothers-in-law), and Marcel Gauchet launched *Le Débat*, a journal that became a springboard for Alain Finkielkraut, Alain Minc and Luc Ferry. It was almost as if the *'famille Sartre'* had been superseded by the *'fraternité Furet'*.*

After Furet, Rosanvallon proved to be one of the more productive of this group. He too would become an 'impresario-academic', helping to run the FSS and acting as editor for a series of historical books. Born in Blois in 1948, he came on stream at the time of the events of 1968. He began his career in the Confédération française démocratique du travail (CFDT), the leading French trade union after the Confédération générale du travail (CGT).[23] The attraction of the CFDT for him was the possibility of uniting intellectual and practical concerns, this practicality linking him, conceptually, to Aron and Furet.

The CFDT became known as the 'second left' because, following

---

* The press referred to it as the 'galaxy'.

the events of 1968, Rosanvallon and others adopted the anti-hier-archical political ideal of *autogestion* (self-management), based on the Yugoslav practice of worker-elected management in industry. Rosanvallon made himself one of the most important theorists of this libertarian and pluralist form of left-wing radicalism.[24] Published in 1976, his *L'Âge de l'autogestion* appeared at the time to represent a new foundational principle for organising society as a whole, 'one that would break with hierarchy and decentralise authority in all sec-tors of life'. Although *autogestion* did give birth to a number of social movements, in the end it went nowhere, but because of it Rosanvallon would always retain a sharp interest in the history and philosophy of democracy and – as he came to see it – its pathologies.

'NEW FRENCH THOUGHT': THE DECISIVE BREAK WITH MARXISM

In 1978, Rosanvallon joined the University of Paris-Dauphine where he took charge of the sociology section of the Work and Society Research Centre, founded by Jacques Delors, minister of finance under Mitterrand and later president of the European Commission.

The battles between the 'two cultures of the left' came to a head in the fight between Michel Rocard and Mitterrand in the contest for leadership of the Socialist Party (PS). Rosanvallon was in the Rocard camp, but Mitterrand won. It was in this atmosphere, however, that Rosanvallon and many others began to see totalitarianism as the chief threat in politics.

At this point Rosanvallon encountered Furet, then putting together an informal group of like-minded liberal souls at the EHESS. One of the unusual things about this group was that it was made up of two different generations. There was Furet's own generation, consisting of Claude Lefort, a student of Maurice Merleau-Ponty and editor of his posthumous writings, Cornelius Castoriadis, a Greek-French psychoanalyst and philosopher, and Krzysztof Pomian, a Polish phi-losopher and historian; and there was a younger group, made up of Marcel Gauchet, historian and sociologist and editor-in-chief of *Le Débat*, Bernard Manin, a political philosopher and historian from Marseilles, Pierre Manent, who, like Furet, taught for part of the year in the United States, and Rosanvallon himself. This seminar became the nucleus of what was referred to in the United States as 'New French Thought'.[25]

Rosanvallon had spent the middle years of the 1970s fully engaged in the polemical battles within the PS but by the time it came to power in 1981 he had quit and turned more fully to the role of analyst rather than actor.[26] This was when he published *Le Capitalisme utopique* (1979), his first work of historical scholarship, in which he conceded that, with the fundamental critiques of totalitarianism that had by then been launched, what was now required was the imagining of a horizon very different from what had been conceived until then, under predominantly Marxist eyes. In line with this, his later book, published in 1985, was *Le Moment Guizot*, a study of François Guizot (1787–1874), a literary figure and professor of history at the Sorbonne but also, later, a moderate liberal politician, and a passionate advocate of liberty and toleration and of the *juste milieu*, a middle path between absolutism and popular government. Guizot helped the creation of primary schools all over France, though he opposed the extension of the franchise, wanting it confined to propertied men only and famously advising anyone who wanted the vote to '*enrichissez-vous*'. The title of Rosanvallon's book therefore described 'the time of Guizot' and in doing so hinted – more than hinted – at what it had to teach the France of the late twentieth century. It was the success of this book that caused Rosanvallon to be invited to join the EHESS, where he later became director of studies and head of the research section of the Institut Raymond Aron.[27] In an article in Nora and Gauchet's *Le Débat*, Rosanvallon argued forcefully that the death of Sartre marked a definitive break with Marxism.

DEMOCRACY AND LIBERALISM AT LOGGERHEADS

In the 1980s Rosanvallon would work with Furet, and to an extent stand in his shadow, as the latter released his various books on the Revolution, though Rosanvallon did co-author *La République du centre*. Later, however, he would publish his own trilogy of broad-sweeping and imaginative books on the intellectual history of democracy, in particular exploring where 'democratic energy' came from, why citizens distrust authority, the role of work, what the psychology of past phases of democracy felt like, what people in the past saw as rational in their time, what they saw as moral obligation, and how the world is different now from the time of, say, Voltaire or Dreyfus.[28] The French Revolution, Rosanvallon concluded, like Furet, 'had poisoned the well' of French democracy, as shown in the repeated confrontations between the sovereignty of the people and representative government.[29]

Following Furet, Rosanvallon also believed robustly that democracy contained within it what he called 'pathogens' – the familiar inherent contradiction between liberty and egalitarianism. He was to argue that this explained France's exceptionalism, that the Revolution had inaugurated both a democratic and a liberal revolution in France, and that this tension had existed throughout the nineteenth century. Along the way he made some telling observations. For example, he felt that the right to vote in France had become more a symbol of social belonging than a mechanism for the construction of the general interest. And this, he felt, helped account for the continued importance of elites in France – democracy and liberalism 'remained at loggerheads' throughout the nineteenth century.[30]

In 1871, he went on, France joined Switzerland, Andorra and San Marino as the only republics in Europe. For Rosanvallon, the advent of the Third Republic – and its consolidation later in the 1870s – signalled the Revolution's 'coming into port', and the end of 'the theatre of the exceptional in France'.[31]

Rosanvallon maintained further, in a series of books published throughout the 1990s and into the 2000s, that French democracy was actually 'normalised' by a series of extra-parliamentary developments that took place in a 'silent revolution' that lasted from 1880 to 1920 but centred on the 1890s, and which, above all, he said, saw 'the acknowledgement that society has to be understood as a conglomeration of social categories to be represented as such rather than as incidents of a monistic unity'. Through these developments, France, Rosanvallon argued, became more 'English'. A key factor in this was the rise of the social sciences as a discipline 'attempting to understand society as a diverse set of exactly such "categories"'. The emergence of trade unions further underlined this development. And so the end of the French exception, which Furet and Rosanvallon had initially placed in the 1970s and 1980s, in *La République du centre*, was now considered to have occurred a full century earlier. Others have, perhaps, put it more clearly, in arguing that France was a cultural nation before it was a political nation.[32]

Despite his argument that French exceptionalism ended in the 'silent revolution', in his most recent books, since his election to the Collège de France in 2001, Rosanvallon has said he does not consider that France became fully 'mature' politically until the 1970s (underlining the point that culture in France came before politics), by which he means that only then was democracy finally established, as the French came to accept that no final definition of democracy is possible, because of the tensions that will always underpin its attractions, much as Furet had said. Democracy is, in effect, 'an active laboratory of the present'. This is, perhaps, his most apt observation.

Reviewers of Rosanvallon's books, such as Marcel Gauchet, have begged to differ and continue to argue that French exceptionalism still persists, that the collective power of the state has not gone away. Furet might have been obsessed by French exceptionalism, as his critics claimed, but there is no doubt that he shaped a generation of more or less like-minded fellow historians.

'THE REVOLUTION IS OVER': THE NEED FOR COMMEMORATIVE VIGILANCE

One of these is Furet's other one-time brother-in-law, Pierre Nora. Born in 1931 and elected to the Académie française in 2001, Nora is another of the many distinguished graduates of the Lycée Louis-le-Grand. In 2021 he published a very moving account of his early years as an educated Jew in France through the Second World War and in postwar Algeria, a story with certain parallels with the lives of Jews in Germany between the great wars.[33] For a time Nora taught at a lycée in Algeria, publishing an account of his experiences as *Les Français d'Algérie* in 1961. From 1965 to 1977 he held positions at the Institut d'études politiques de Paris and then joined Furet and Rosanvallon at the EHESS, where he became director of studies.

In his impresario role he also had an influential career in publishing.

From 1965 he was an editor at Gallimard, where he was responsible for publishing a wide-ranging selection of works (many titles considered earlier in this book) by Raymond Aron, Georges Dumézil, Claude Lefort, Michel Foucault, Emmanuel Le Roy Ladurie, Jacques Le Goff, Georges Duby, Michel de Certeau, Maurice Agulhon and François Furet, not to mention foreign authors such as Ernst Kantorowicz, Thomas Nipperdey and Karl Polanyi. In 1980 Nora also founded the journal *Le Débat* with the philosopher Marcel Gauchet, its editors over the years including Aron, Dumézil, Foucault, Ladurie, Furet and Le Goff. Nora was and is at the centre of a glittering network.

Traditionally, as we have seen, literature was always the queen of activities in French culture, with philosophy not far behind. Gradually, however, since the death of Sartre, letters in their classical clothing have – to an extent – lost their lustre, to be replaced by social analysis, though many of these have been, in the French way, 'virtuoso exercises of style', drawing on the rhetoric of artistic rather than academic forms. Attractive though all this was and is, there has been a price to pay for arguments 'freed from logic, propositions from evidence', for 'imaginative and discursive forms of writing'. *Le Débat*, on the other hand, turned more and more to evidence from the social sciences, culled from the universities. *Commentaire*, *Le Débat* and *Esprit* comprised the core axis of Cold War liberalism in France.

But arguably Nora's greatest achievement is his conception and bringing to fruition of a mammoth work of historical scholarship, *Lieux de mémoire*, seven volumes of 132 chapters in French, three volumes of forty-six chapters in the English translation, under the title *Realms of Memory*. This book is also a reflection of Furet's argument, that the Revolution is over, insofar as the underlying theme of *Lieux/Realms* is that 'the great divisions and conflicts that began with the revolution have now lost their power to convulse the French nation and topple governments'.[34]

'THE SPECTACULAR BEREAVEMENT OF LITERATURE': A NEW HISTORICAL TURNING POINT

The founding ideas of *Realms of Memory*, Nora says, are two-fold. First, that we live at a time when there is no spontaneous memory,

so we must deliberately create archives, acknowledge anniversa-
ries, organise celebrations, celebrate eulogies and notarise bills
because such activities no longer occur naturally – we must create
a 'commemorative vigilance', otherwise history will sweep away
our memories.

The second reason, is, as he puts it, 'the spectacular bereavement
of literature'.[35] By this he means that the era of great multi-volume
realist/naturalist novels, with meticulous attention to detail describing a particular epoch – Stendhal, Balzac, Flaubert, Zola, the early
Huysmans, Maupassant, Daudet – is long gone and their important
function needs replacing.

A change occurred, Nora says, with Bergson, Freud and Proust,
roughly contemporaries. For each of these seminal figures, memory –
looking back, time – was at the centre of their attention. This
transformation of memory, Nora says, 'implies a decisive shift from
the historical to the psychological, from the social to the individual' (as
we saw earlier, in the works of Céline, Malraux and Saint-Exupéry),
and above all from the content of a message to its cognitive, subjective
reception.[36] The very nature of memory, in other words, is now at the
centre of historical studies.

The volumes of *Lieux* were divided into three – *La République*,
La Nation and *Les Frances* (in the plural, note), the last containing, Nora maintained, the most typical and revealing lineaments of
'Frenchness'.[37] French historiography, he added, has been through
several phases: 'We go from a "royal memory" of the feudal age to a
"state memory" of the absolute monarchy to a "national memory"
of the immediate post-Revolutionary period, and from there to a
"citizen memory" of the republican schools and finally to the "patri-
monial memory" of our age.'[38] This approach, he argues, allows us to
explore radically new subjects, 'which no linear thematic or chrono-
logical history of France would have any reason to take into account'.
He insists that this approach, considering where French identity can
be said to have become symbolically focused, allows us to think
about the nation 'without nationalism and about France without any
universalistic *a priori*'.[39]

Noting also that there have been several discontinuities in French
historiography, brought about by transformative advances in

statistics, the social sciences and psychoanalysis, by the demise of the revolutionary idea, and most recently by the influx of immigrants 'not easily adaptable to the traditional norms of "Frenchness"', Nora is led to conclude that we are at a new historical turning point. This new kind of history, as he puts it, is 'a history less interested in causes than in effects; less interested in actions remembered or even commemorated than in the traces left by those actions and in the interactions of those commemorations; less interested in events themselves than in the construction of events over time, in the disappearance and reemergence of their significance; less interested in "what actually happened" than in its perpetual reuse and misuse, its influence on successive presents; less interested in traditions than in the way in which traditions are constituted and passed on ... a history that is interested in memory not as remembrance but as the overall structure of the past within the present'.[40]

And so these 132 chapters include some familiar topics – Versailles, Notre-Dame de Paris, Joan of Arc, Verdun, the Louvre, the tricolour – but also others much less so: the monarchical anointment ritual of Reims; the ways in which scholars and painters organised the 'landscape of France'; Parisian snobbery towards the provinces; the Tour de France; the forest; the generation; conversation; two ideas on which Nora says the nation was built – 'glory' and 'words'; figures such as Prosper Mérimée and Eugène Viollet-le-Duc, who did so much to preserve the buildings of France.[41] Taken together, Nora argues, the chapters form a return to France's collective heritage and focus 'on the country's shattered identities ... [its] deep consciousness of its threatened countryside, lost traditions, wrecked ways of life – its very "identity"'.[42] These sites, and their study by historians, he says, reproduce what literature once did and now in Nora's view no longer can accomplish. 'Memory has been promoted to the centre of history; thus do we mourn the loss of literature.'[43]

This dismissive claim for literature, which, as we have repeatedly seen, has been a central lineament of Frenchness for centuries (and we are not done yet), has been criticised as being either the outburst of a kind of French rhetoric that claims too much, goes too far, or is elsewhere slighted as 'just Frenchness at large' and as, quite simply, wrong.[44] Others have pointed out that film has taken the place of the novel as the main narrative form these days, so that someone like Jean Luc Godard is now the equivalent of Balzac or Zola.

Another criticism has been that although there may be an 'overabundance' of memory and commemoration in regard to the Second World War in France, there has been an equal overabundance of amnesia in regard to the compromises the French had to make in order to survive in those years and that it has been American, not French, scholarship that has rectified the situation, something reflected in the references to *Lieux de mémoire* if not in the text itself.[45] Overall, it was, said one critic, 'as if France was ceasing to be a history of what divides us to become a culture that unites us'.

Despite these caveats, the project was widely welcomed as an extraordinary exercise, 'indispensable', which moved the discussion of cultural history to a new level, and even comprised 'one of the great French intellectual achievements of the Mitterrand era'.[46]

The Literary Pre-eminence of Paris
in an Age of English

In his preface to the English edition of *Realms*, published in 1996, four years after the French edition, Pierre Nora spoke of an 'explosion' of memory studies, not just in France, but in America and the Far East. There was also a simultaneous explosion in studies about French identity. He did refer to Fernand Braudel's *Identity of France*, another multi-volume work that could not be properly completed because of Braudel's untimely death in 1985, but this scarcely did justice to the proliferation of works investigating this or that aspect of French identity that had been brought about partly by the ending of France's empire, the changes to political understanding that were the subject of the previous chapter, and of course the influx of large numbers of immigrants who, as Nora himself put it, were and are 'not easily adaptable to the traditional norms of Frenchness'. This latter phenomenon is treated more fully in chapter 52 but here we need to show that the concerns about French identity went far and wide and reached into many corners of French life.

There were studies about what it means to be Jewish in France today – that was perhaps not so surprising – how the culture of Brittany differed from the rest of France, what Franglais said about French identity – why were so many loan words needed? There were studies of the different understandings of the English Channel/*La Manche* between France and Britain, of France's more wide-ranging maritime identity, the place of sexuality in Frenchness, the understanding of – and attitudes towards – the aristocracy down the ages, Catholicism and Frenchness, the influence of wine and food on French self-consciousness, the difference between Belgian and Flanders Frenchness and metropolitan Frenchness, how French feminism differed from feminism elsewhere, how French concepts of secularism were changing (also considered in chapter 52), the special place in the French mind for culture, what – precisely – the Francophone world means for the French today, how the people of Alsace-Lorraine understand their Frenchness (or Germanness), and of course several works explored the extent to which Vichy 'was or was not' French.

Underlying many of these works was the idea that the life of what was once the 'French exception' was being squeezed out of the country by 'mediocre' forms of liberalism and the English language. No other nation, it was clear, has so conspicuously based its identity on culture.[1]

THE CATECHISM OF FRANCE

Arguably the most radical and contentious of these works was that by Suzanne Citron, a schoolteacher who died in 2018, aged ninety-five. Born in 1922 to a Jewish father who had been an earnest Dreyfusard, she herself had ended the Second World War in Drancy, lucky to survive, though at that stage she said she took pride in the fact that France had been the first country to totally emancipate the Jews.[2] This experience made her especially sensitive to the way the French behaved towards their colonies, especially Algeria, and her pride in France took a hit when she came to understand that the way the French treated the Algerians was much the same as the way the Nazis had treated the French, especially French Jews. In 1956, she said, 'I discovered torture', the special powers granted to the army that made it for her 'an Algerian Gestapo . . . life went on, but the Algerian question ended up invading each of our moments'.[3]

As she later recalled, this 'intimate upheaval' led her to write a series of books of which the best known was *Le Mythe national*. In it she had the novel idea to examine the history of France not as the nation's famous historians, like Michelet or Furet, understood it, but as it was taught in school textbooks. Published originally in 1987, her book was an irritant for many but went through several reincarnations, in 1989, 1991, 2008 and 2017, its argument being somewhat at variance with that of Pierre Nora and his collaborators. Citron's findings were that most children in the nineteenth century were taught about France 'as if it were a religion' incorporating a 'cult of the Revolution'. In schools there was, in effect, as she put it, 'a catechism of France' in books by such authors as Ernest Lavisse, another of those French figures nominated several times for the Nobel Prize, which signally failed to acknowledge that there was *no generally accepted principle of legitimacy throughout the nineteenth century*, and held that the monarchy by divine right had been replaced by a democratic republic which had been solidified by military victories, France fighting only 'just wars', and which had given the values of liberty to other nations. She found that there were two 'taboos' in the teaching of school history – the Terror aspect of the Revolution, and the horrors and setbacks of the First World War, which was instead presented as an unambiguous victory, a series of glorious campaigns.

Her overall argument was that French children were being given – to her way of thinking – an unreasonably rosy picture of French history, and her conclusions shocked many people, some of whom agreed with her and some of whom very much didn't. She also said that for many – journalists and politicians for instance – this essentially rosy view of France was retained into adult life, that it shaped their careers and the way they looked at the world, thinking France exceptional, and giving them a more positive image of themselves and their country than was, she dared to say, deserved.[4]

THE LITERARY EXCEPTIONALISM OF PARIS

Pascale Casanova's view of French exceptionalism was very different to Citron's. A former television journalist, she produced her masterpiece as a scholar at the Centre for Research in Arts and Languages in Paris. She died a few months after Citron, also in 2018, but aged only fifty-nine after suffering from an incurable disease for some years. Her book *The World Republic of Letters* was put by some on a par with Edward Said's *Orientalism*, its range of scholarship hailed as 'staggering'. It introduced a raft of new literary and historical scholarship and argued for the literary exceptionalism of France, Paris especially.

Casanova's aim, as one reviewer put it, was 'a radical remapping of global literary space – which means, first of all, the recognition that there *is* a global literary space'.[5] Among the examples she gives in support of her argument was that Sartre, despite his anti-Americanism, played a key role in 'consecrating' William Faulkner and John Dos Passos in France, that Faulkner was influential in places as disparate politically, historically and economically as South America and Algeria, that often avant-garde writers (rule-breakers) translate avant-garde writers into other languages, and that the achievements of Samuel Beckett and James Joyce lay in their production of their own literary languages also existing outside politics, economics or history.[6]

Her argument was that a 'world republic of letters' has gradually emerged, in which France, England and other 'major' European nations built up reserves of 'literary capital' over several centuries, due to cultivated aristocracies, the existence of salons, and a specialist press which together created a 'literary milieu' (see chapter 21), to the point where these 'core cultures' controlled the means of cultural legitimation for countries on the periphery – 'literary suburbs' as someone put it. In other words, literatures and authors all across the world – in Latin America, North America, Asia, Africa, eastern Europe – needed the imprimatur of the core, in particular Paris, to be legitimated. Casanova insists, for example, that Shakespeare, Scott, Byron and Poe were long read in French translations before they were more widely accepted, that many English-language novels (*Tropic of Cancer*, *Lolita*, *Naked Lunch*, *Ulysses*) were published in Paris first, that Paris has been the capital of literary exiles for the past two centuries (Ibsen, Joyce, Borges, García Márquez, Faulkner), and that a number of authors (Beckett, Kundera, Natalie Clifford Barney) moved from their native languages and began writing in French. She identified Paris as the 'Greenwich meridian' of literary modernity, partly because of its unique hospitality to the avant-garde that has ensured it has endured as 'the world literary centre'.[7]

Because of all this, she argued, literature has its own autonomous history. 'The world republic of letters is governed by its own rules, keeps time by its own historical clock, partitions the world according to its own map.'[8] She cherished – and argued for – the notion of literary values 'that transcend political and historical particulars', her ultimate goal being 'a new literary universality'.

The emergence of an international literary sphere began, she says, with a 1549 essay by Joachim du Bellay, poet and critic and founder of the group of French Renaissance poets known as the Pléiade, of whom the best known today is probably Pierre de Ronsard. Du Bellay's essay 'The Defence and Illustration of the French Language' was, as Casanova phrases it, a declaration of 'war against Latin', and in this she echoes the argument of Marc Fumaroli, in his book *When the World Spoke French*, in which he shows how French took over from Latin as the most favoured European language in which to write (briefly discussed in chapter 21). As a result of this, Casanova says, France built up its 'literary assets' through – among other innovations – the translation and imitation of classical models, linguistic standardisation and purification (partly through the Académie française), and the regimentation of poetic forms, also discussed in the early chapters of this book, so that, by the reign of Louis XIV, the age of Pascal, Molière and Racine, French had accomplished 'the unthinkable', displacing Latin as the language of literary classicism and philosophy.[9]

A second development encompassed the theories of Herder, who championed the depth and reach of folk culture as an exposition of a nation's 'soul' or 'genius', but the legitimation of which had to go through the centre of the literary world – in Paris. It is this creation of national literatures that led to the emergence of an international literary space. 'The capital of the world republic of letters, the place to which even other countries of the core must look for ultimate consecration and the global reputation it brings, is Paris.' It was Paris that made possible the creation of an avant-garde. Other nations began to compete with France, says Casanova, but France kept its advantage up, at least, to the 1960s if not longer. Even now, she says, New York may be a commercial centre of publishing but 'cannot be said to have become a centre of consecration'.[10]

Though the range of Casanova's scholarship was highly impressive, and built on the ideas that underpinned *Tel Quel* – in regard to the independence, autonomy and supremacy of literary values – she was criticised for minimising early Italian literature (Dante, Ariosto, Tasso, Machiavelli, Castiglione) and for being 'laughably' ignorant of English literature, baldly stating at one point in her text that Shakespeare did not become canonical until the turn of the twentieth century – some two centuries too late.[11]

People all over the world liked her idea of an autonomous literary space – outside politics and economics – and accepted that many writers had sought exile in Paris, had published their books there, and that some had even taken to writing in French. But they baulked somewhat at her insistence on the centrality of Paris, that it constitutes *the* centre of world literary space, especially with the recent advance of English as a global language, centred increasingly on London and New York, and her flat assertion that 'universality is best determined by Parisian taste'.[12]

The well-known Marxist critic Perry Anderson welcomed Casanova's work as 'pathbreaking', as 'an outstanding example of an imaginative synthesis', and linked it to other ways in which Paris still stands out. 'On any day, about five times as many foreign films, past or present, are screened in Paris as in any other city on Earth. Much of what is now termed "world cinema" – Iranian, Taiwanese, Senegalese – owes its visibility to French consecration and funding. Had directors like Kiarostami, Hou Xiao Xien or Sembène depended on reception in the Anglo-American world, few outside their native lands would ever have glimpsed them.' Anderson found it not meaningless to speak of French decline since the mid-1970s but argued that focusing on economic and social performance was too narrow and were France to become 'just another denizen of the cage of Atlantic conformities, a great hole would be left in the world'.[13]

In the run-up to the 2017 presidential elections, the centre-right candidate, François Fillon, formerly prime minister under the presidency of Nicolas Sarkozy, called for 'a history made up of men and women, symbols, places, monuments, events that find their meaning and sense in the progressive construction of the unique civilisation of France', an echo – but a nationalistic echo – of what Pierre Nora's *Lieux/Realms* had been about, a history to make Frenchmen and women proud. In March that year, however, right in the middle of the election campaign – contested between Fillon, Emmanuel Macron with his new En marche! party, and Marine Le Pen of the Front national – Laurence de Cock, a professor of history and geography, an erstwhile colleague of Suzanne Citron and a frequent guest on political television programmes, made a show during a TV debate on the history of France of presenting Fillon with a copy of *Le Mythe national*, which had just been reissued for the eighteenth time, and had a very different message. He had no choice but to accept the book on camera. Unfortunately, Fillon was charged with embezzlement crimes a few days later and this, not surprisingly, affected his campaign (he came third). And so we cannot say whether, had he been elected, he would have implemented the changes to the French educational system that are implicit in Suzanne Citron's work. But the episode – and the fact that this was the *eighteenth* edition of her book – shows that her criticism of a self-satisfied French exceptionalism still resonates.

'An Immense Vanity for France': De Gaulle, the French and the Anglo-Saxons

The concept of the 'other' is – as we have repeatedly seen – a central plank of French postmodernism. Postmodern philosophy was arguably the main achievement of French thought in the last half of the twentieth century and helped produce the modern mindset. It stemmed partly from the French left's acknowledgment in the wake of the Second World War of Négritude, a movement that began before the war, among a group of African and Caribbean black intellectuals in Paris, as a revolt against French colonialism (chapter 44), and which led to a recognition of the *tiers monde*, or 'Third World', which, after the fighting, had a more urgent political and philosophical significance for the French. But the concept of the 'other' embodied a profound irony.

Historically, the 'other' that has most concerned the French is Great Britain, as often as not referred to by them as 'England'. This may be brought into focus by an extraordinary publication that was released in Britain in 2006. It was a massive, 706-page history of the 'love–hate' relationship between Britain and France, titled *That Sweet Enemy*. Very readable, immensely detailed and beautifully organised, it enjoyed a well-deserved success but that is not what made it extraordinary. What was extraordinary about the book was that it was written by a very distinguished husband-and-wife couple, the Englishman Robert Tombs, professor emeritus of French history at the University of Cambridge, and his French wife,

Isabelle, née Bussy, who was then in charge of French training at the British Foreign & Commonwealth Office. As a result of having two authors – one British and the other French – the text showed some areas of piquant disagreement.[1]

But what concerns us here, given our theme of France as a culture of defeat, with a longing for grandeur, is the Tombses' compendious catalogue of French arrogance, directed at Britain, combined with their grievances – as was mentioned in the Introduction, French Anglophobia far exceeds British Francophobia. Here is a sample, by no means exhaustive, and I haven't even bothered to count the number of times over the centuries that the French have compared Britain to Carthage, characterising it as a nation of greedy shopkeepers interested only in material prosperity, while Paris is invariably compared to Rome, a noble city of artistic and philosophical grandeur:

Louis XIV once asked his ambassador whether England had any writers or men of learning.

Montesquieu found the English to be freer than other nations, but 'money is more important than honour or virtue and the people are coarse, insociable and, worst of all, corrupt'.

'What a nasty people [the English are], as ferocious as they appear to be philosophical.' – Marquis d'Argenson.

'The English language was probably now in decline.' – Voltaire.

'It seems to me impossible to be French without wishing ill to England, but this sentiment, so just and so reciprocal, increases every day that one is obliged to live among the English.' – Duc du Châtelet, ambassador to London, 1769.

'The "Great" will be soon gone from Britain ... in a few years she will fall to the second or third rank of European powers without hope of ever rising again.' – French Foreign Ministry report, 1777.

'The English ... can forge iron, harness steam, twist matter in every way, invent frighteningly powerful machines ... but real art will always escape them ... despite their stupendous material advances, they are only polished barbarians.' – Théophile Gautier.

'If France overcomes, the world will be governed by twenty-four letters of the alphabet; if England prevails, it will be tyrannised by the ten figures of arithmetic. Thinking or counting; those are the alternative futures.' – Victor Hugo.

'When England wishes to converse with me, it will learn to speak French.' – Victor Hugo.

'The English, who had not been conquered by an invader for nearly one thousand years, knew in their bones that their defeat would mean a kind of death for England, that its effect would not be temporary. The French, on the other hand, knew in their heads . . . the memory of national defeats together with the memory of their national recoveries.' – John Lukacs.

'Frenchmen are the gastronomes of love; Englishmen merely do it.' – Pierre Daninos.

'The Anglo-Saxons are not interested in women as women . . . It is a problem of upbringing and I consider it a sort of disease.' – Édith Cresson, France's first female prime minister.

In the 1990s, for the first time ever, there were more French in Britain than British in France. London suddenly became the world's eighth-largest French-speaking city.[2]

Even among educated French, this attitude persists, as Prime Minister Cresson's remarks show. In their recent book *Napoléon, le monde et les Anglais: Guerre des mots et des images*, published in 2004, Jean-Paul Bertaud, Alan Forrest and Annie Jourdan write: 'In England the throne was surrounded by merchants and bankers . . . England spoke the language of account books, France that of the warrior thirsty for honour and supremacy.'[3]

Which brings us to Charles de Gaulle. His career was dominated by one thing above all else – his desire to see France back at the forefront of nations after its massive humiliation in 1940, which set of events helped to create him, in the sense that de Gaulle found himself at the right place at the right time.

De Gaulle's Anglophobia is all the more noteworthy because he was a well-educated military man, with a range of intellectual friends, at least in the wake of the First World War where, as we have seen, he had been captured and undergone years of humiliation (chapter 41). In 1925, however, Philippe Pétain had decided to bring de Gaulle into his ambit. One reason, Julian Jackson says in his brilliant biography, is because de Gaulle was a stylish writer. Pétain had his eye on the Académie française and was planning a grand history of the French army, and since he himself had few literary gifts, de Gaulle was the perfect ghostwriter.[4] It was while de Gaulle was working for Pétain that he began frequenting the circle and salon of Colonel Émile Mayer. Mayer held a salon every Sunday morning in his Paris apartment, his guests comprising an 'eclectic' mix of mainly left-wing republican journalists, writers, publishers and politicians. Here too de Gaulle learned how to be with people with whom he disagreed without (too much) rancour, and it was certainly a much more liberal atmosphere than in the Pétain entourage. Jean Auburtin, himself a journalist and lawyer, was there, and this is how he described those mornings: 'It was not quite a political circle, nor a literary one ... [Mayer] gathered every Sunday, in an oval salon thick with cigarette smoke, a faithful group where students ... rubbed shoulders with French and foreign personalities, and with ministers ... in an atmosphere of fraternal animation.' The Mayer salon, says Jackson, 'opened new intellectual horizons, introduced de Gaulle to a world outside the army and extended his range of contacts to include journalists and intellectuals'.[5]

He was, from the start, authoritarian, Jackson says, insisting on all signs of respect due to his rank, stipulating that his officers kept the regulation six paces away, receiving reports without a response, and disconcerting subordinates with ironic put-downs. Others observed that he could not express affection or gratitude and was 'incapable of apologising'.[6]

A suspicion of Britain was never far under the surface among Frenchmen and women of de Gaulle's generation. This was not helped by his time in London, at the beginning of the Second World War, when every day provided a reminder of his (and France's) humiliatingly total dependence. All telegrams had to go via the British, he could only travel on British planes, he had to ask British permission to leave, his speeches had to be submitted in advance for clearance by the BBC.[7] He only ever sent Churchill one telegram in English.

Early in the war, in 1941, during the troubles in Syria and Lebanon, when Free French forces had fought Vichy French, de Gaulle had been in and out of the area. He was often in a violent mood, to such an extent that the British representatives there, Oliver Lyttelton, minister of state for the Middle East, and General Louis Spears, Churchill's liaison officer with the French government, both began to doubt de Gaulle's mental balance, referring to him as 'slightly cracked', and noting that he had lost control of himself to the extent that they even considered putting him in prison. 'I don't think I shall ever get on with *les Anglais*,' he told Spears at one point. 'You think I am interested in England winning the war? I am not. I am only interested in France's victory.' When Spears commented that these were the same, de Gaulle retorted: 'Not at all.' In the same vein, he added later: 'Our force and our grandeur reside only in our intransigence regarding the interests of France.' Mary Borden, Spears's wife, saw the situation clearly: 'He felt the dishonour of his country as few men can feel anything, as Christ according to the Christian faith took on himself the sins of the world.'[8]

Harold Macmillan had to deal with de Gaulle on many occasions and summed him up thus: 'The arrogance that makes him from time to time almost impossible to deal with is the reverse side of an extreme sensibility. I have never known any man so ungracious and so sentimental ... He belongs to the race of unhappy and tortured souls to whom life will never be a pleasure but an arid desert.' Later, after the war, Macmillan and de Gaulle alike had no wish to see a revived Germany but to the British prime minister the French president was only ever half welcome: 'We agree; but his pride, his inherited hatred of England ... his bitter memories of the last war; above all his immense vanity for France ... Sometimes when I am with him, I feel I have overcome it. But he goes back to his disgust and his dislike, like a dog to his vomit.'[9]

For de Gaulle, the smallest slight could spark any number of resentments that he felt he had accumulated during the war. He even said, only half in jest, that the British had found a place for him to operate from in Carlton Gardens 'because it's a dead end with the only way out through Waterloo Place'. Appalled by de Gaulle's refusal to allow Britain to join the European Economic Community in 1963 and 1967, Paul Reynaud, a wartime collaborator of de Gaulle and a minister, wrote him a long letter protesting against his treatment of an ally who had stood by France in its hour of need. When

Reynaud received a reply, the envelope contained nothing at all but on the back in de Gaulle's hand was written: 'If absent, forward to Agincourt (Somme) or Waterloo (Belgium).' Revenge for 'unforgiven defeats', says Jack Hayward, was a deep-seated sentiment that de Gaulle shared with 'most' of his countrymen.[10]

But de Gaulle had few illusions about the decline of France's material power, Jackson concludes. He exhorted France to believe in herself as a grand nation – but grandeur 'was an attitude rather than a concrete goal'.[11]

De Gaulle's philosophy – and we can call it that – was quite clear, and made in several public speeches: 'The conflict between nations was the eternal law of history ... One needs adversaries to exist ... To be great is to sustain a great quarrel ... Nations were the repositories of historical legitimacy ... The precondition of a nation state was its ability to wage war ... French power and grandeur ... are directed to the well-being and fraternity of mankind ... While other countries, when they develop their interests, try to subject others to their interests, France, when she succeeds in developing her interests, does so in the interest of all ... Everyone feels it obscurely in the world: France is the light of the world, her genius is to light up the universe ... France cannot be France without grandeur ...'[12] All the more remarkable for a man who, when president, still read two or three books a week, usually history, novels or poetry.

In the last half of the twentieth century, however, and despite de Gaulle's all-consuming Anglophobia, the 'other' that was most troublesome for the French was not Africa or the Caribbean, nor even communist Russia or China, but America. The historian who has studied this phenomenon most closely is Richard Kuisel, referred to briefly in the Introduction, a professor emeritus at Georgetown University. Kuisel detects that a certain snobbishness reigns still in France, in respect of American culture. Though it is nowhere near as strident as in the days of Sartre, a more trenchant anti-Americanism resurfaced at the very end of the century. Professor Kuisel even identifies a condition, 'anti-américaine primaire', a stance which 'conveys a confrontational intent'. As several French historians have pointed out, the modern French identity is, as in the past, defined – at least in part – by opposition to another country/civilisation, a point underlined here, too.

French criticism of America has been made largely on two grounds – the political and the cultural. There is nothing particularly exceptional in one country's political aims being different from another's, and instead it is the cultural exceptionalism that is of interest here. This was for the most part a preoccupation of the French elite and Kuisel identifies a raft among that elite whose actions and views in particular epitomised the various dimensions of the antagonism.

Although the French dislike of America received a boost in the postwar world, this attitude did not come out of nowhere. As far back as the middle of the nineteenth century, Philippe Buchez, journalist, historian, briefly a politician, had described America as 'socially organised egotism'. Already in the 1930s, there was no shortage of brickbats aimed across the North Atlantic. Here is Marguerite Yerta-Méléra, an authority on Rimbaud and author of a sensitive wartime memoir of the six women in her family left at home while the men were away at the front; writing in 1931, she said: 'There is no American civilisation ... there is still no American civilisation ... The only civilisation in America is the old civilisation of Europe which is still the theoretical basis of institutions and customs. But for the rest ... the box-like skyscrapers, the vile speakeasies, the oversized cities spoiled by racketeering, the government of gangsters ... Civilisation?'[13]

Kuisel also finds that through the interwar period French writers dismissed America as a wasteland of mass culture and dull standardisation. The post-1945 stereotype was essentially that established in the 1930s – Americans were adolescents, materialists, conformists and puritans. In 1951, Louis Aragon described America as 'a civilisation of bathtubs and frigidaires'.[14]

A repeated French criticism of America was that its standardised production methods encouraged conformity, that material prosperity was the only aim of life there. Sartre's *Les Temps modernes* and *Le Monde*, 'the anti-American voice of St-Germain-des-Prés', according to Kuisel, both turned out to be regular critics, claiming for example that the US was 'afraid of its own emptiness'.[15]

L'Amérique est-elle trop riche? (1960), by Claude Alphandéry, a noted *résistant*, identified an American psychological and philosophical malaise, namely that consumerism generated an endless escalation of desires that could not be satisfied, a form of alienation in which wealth, which 'ought to bring more freedom', actually 'rebounds against them' and traps them. The 'can-do' approach of America was contrasted critically with the much more enjoyable French habit of *flânerie*.

THE PATHOLOGY OF ABUNDANCE

Anti-Americanism was especially prevalent in France in the 1960s, owing at least in part to the foreign policies of Charles de Gaulle. De Gaulle was anti-American in two basic ways. First, he challenged – but failed to contain – American hegemony in geo-politics. Second, he simply harboured an antipathy to what he thought American society *was*. Among other things, de Gaulle's attitude sanctioned the student revolt against America's war in Vietnam, seen as neo-imperialism. This coincided with a raft of books and articles by intellectuals – Jean Baudrillard, Bertrand de Jouvenel, Alain Touraine, Henri Lefebvre – drawing attention to the 'pathology of abundance', which placed relations with objects above social interaction and saw personal gratification as the be-all and end-all of life, with the elevation of 'prefabricated desires over real needs'.[16]

In Alain Bosquet's *Les Américains sont-ils adultes?* (1969) – an insulting title if ever there was one – the author created an imaginary couple living in Chicago. The couple define themselves by what they own – which is more or less the same as what everyone else owns – and their life has no ups and downs, everything is bland, there are no passions and even God is 'affable and boring'. 'They strove to please everyone and avoided introspective or philosophical conversation.' There was no need for this latter because America, for this couple, was ideal, they were living their dream. It was this, Bosquet felt, that made them less than adult.

One of the biggest splashes was made in 1967, when Jean-Jacques Servan-Schreiber published *Le Défi américain* ('The American Challenge'). Servan-Schreiber, then forty-three, was a right-of-centre politician and journalist who founded *L'Express* newspaper. His book sold 400,000 copies that year with an argument that was simple but powerful. 'Next to the United States and the Soviet Union, the emerging economic power was not Europe – it was American business in Europe.'[17] American managers were better than their European counterparts at making the most of what Europe had to offer. Servan-Schreiber had identified an unconscious nerve that stretched across the continent but was especially near the surface in France, which was largely alone in trying to control American input.

This nerve, combined with the vivid reactions to the Algerian War and the events of May 1968, provoked several knock-on effects of which the most remarkable was the ethno-nationalist think tank the Groupement de recherche et d'études sur la civilisation européenne (GRECE, French for 'Greece'), part of what was known then as the New Right. GRECE sponsored conferences and opened a publishing house and a number of magazines, all of which shared its aim of combating the 'Judeo-Christian cosmopolitanism' of the Enlightenment, but it also became the only political outfit of any kind anywhere to make America its principal enemy.

Its main spokesman was Alain de Benoist, a journalist who wrote under several names, who embraced the Third World and 'the right to be different', was opposed to representative democracy, and saw Americanisation as the principal threat to the spoliation of French culture. The flat, universal civilisation that America was trying to impose on Europe, Benoist insisted, had little to do with European culture; instead Europe should embrace Third World peoples as their natural allies. Americans were bible-toting preachers, immersed in a 'gadget culture' and – worst of all – they were obese. They preached morality to the rest of the world, after exterminating the Indian; they pretended to be worldly while being intensely parochial – Benoist going so far as to say that 90 per cent of Americans had never read a book. In 1986 GRECE hosted a conference on 'The Challenge of Disneyland' in which Benoist called for the 'extermination' of Mickey Mouse and 'a cultural war against the United States'.[18]

The Impossible Dialogue

Less extreme, and closer to political power and the intellectual mainstream, was a raft of elite intellectuals: Jack Lang, Pierre Nora,

Jean-Marie Domenach and Régis Debray. Their views – between them – neatly encapsulate the French mindset vis-à-vis the United States and French culture.

Jack Lang was minister of culture for two periods, from 1981 to 1986 and again from 1988 to 1993. Part of his policy also was to champion the *tiers monde*, or Third World, which in his case had two broad elements. One was to reinforce the cultural strength of Francophone Africa and the other was to support left-wing – even Marxist – regimes in America's backyard, for example, Cuba and Nicaragua. Partly, this policy of *tiers-mondisme* was in effect a way to snipe at America as a culture that Lang saw as in many ways the very opposite of what France stood for.[19]

Lang was a telegenic figure, handsome, with a winning smile, who made the most of contemporary fashions, including a stylish pink jacket, and hosted equally stylish lunches with fashionable intellectual guests such as Roland Barthes. He was articulate and up-front in his dislike of American culture, particularly their movies. Lang would later take his crusade to Brussels and persuade the European Commission to investigate the growing 'power' of American films. In April 1988 the Television without Frontiers movement ensured that a law was passed which required broadcasters to show overall output that was at least 50 per cent French-made.[20]

Lang was bold and crude. Under the surface, however, other figures offered a more nuanced version of the Franco-American cultural divisions.

In the 1980s, Pierre Nora was in the middle of editing *Les Lieux de mémoire*, outlined in chapter 49. Nora was also history editor for the Gallimard publishing house, where he commissioned translations of important works in American social science and history. Nonetheless, Kuisel detects 'a certain hauteur' in his assessment of American culture.

Nora accepted the notion of American exceptionalism 'or, at least, the American construction of its uniqueness'. He thought, in fact, that there was an 'impossible dialogue' between Americans and French because it was part of the American ideology to escape 'the weight of the past'; they could never accept the European sense of history 'with its ruptures, ideologies and conflicts' and were always

seeking a 'narrative of consensus and progress'. The Americans suspected their French historian colleagues of lacking objectivity 'by
straying into Marxism' (for example), whereas the French saw the
Americans as 'docile', given to ratifying the status quo.[21]

American intellectuals sought refuge from reality in empiricism,
parochialism 'or an illusion of a happy past and a happier future' and
could not master the intricacies of France's cultural life. America,
Nora added, has never occupied the central position in the mental
geography of France that England did in the eighteenth century,
Germany in the nineteenth, and Soviet Russia and the Third World
in the twentieth.

Nora thought that France had been 'wrenched into modernity by
a revolution', whereas consensus was the basis of the American identity, albeit with so many minorities, and he concluded in a strikingly
original way: 'Our national rapport with the United States is not
knowledge but fascination.'[22]

Régis Debray, a confidant of President Mitterrand and, of
course, well known as a companion of Che Guevara, saw knee-jerk
anti-Americanism as a pathology, itself a form of hysteria. America
was not only Las Vegas but also Harvard. If he had to go into exile,
he said, he would choose either Italy or the United States – how
can you be anti-American 'when America makes us all dream'? At
the same time, he didn't think that what he saw as a widening gap
between the American dream and the reality could be ignored – the
shabby cities, high infant mortality rates, disastrous pollution, low
political participation and 'ubiquitous religious practice'. He thought
television had replaced intellectuals, the TV anchor had usurped the
poet. And he said he did not wish to be condemned as anti-American simply because he still believed in a civilisation 'where one reads
books, respects Sundays and the circumflex accent ... where people
are more than the sum of opinion polls'.[23]

America Becomes 'Unbearable'

'At the very *fin de siècle*,' says Kuisel, 'the French were more suspicious
of Americans than at any time since the tense days of the Cold War.'
He puts this down to the fact that both countries shared a narcissism,

that each nation was convinced it had a special global mission. 'For Americans it was the spread of democracy and free enterprise; for the French it was the *mission civilisatrice*. Such presumptions were bound to clash.' But what intensified this was the French sense of cultural superiority, the conviction that France was the *guardian* of high culture and America the *pedlar* of mass culture. When America's triumphalism was added to this mix ... 'America became unbearable.'[24]

Even now, these attitudes still linger, as shown by the comments of Eric Zemmour, a TV pundit and an early wild-card contender in the spring 2022 Presidential election in France. To the delight of his supporters, on the campaign trail in Normandy, in October 2021, he described the English as 'our greatest enemies for a thousand years', adding that the D-Day landings, about which de Gaulle 'had not even been consulted, was an enterprise of liberation but also one of Occupation and colonization by America'. Zemmour told his audience that France had not only to combat Islam but free itself from 'maleficent influences' that includes Washington, Brussels and Britain. 'It is the British who stopped us dominating Europe.'[25]

Such anti-Americanism did not replace French anti-British feeling, it was merely grafted on, forming part of a general anti-Anglo-Saxon mindset that never entirely went away. In the memoirs of Madeleine Albright, President Clinton's secretary of state, published in 2003, she says she tussled at one international conference with Hubert Védrine, then the (Socialist) French foreign minister. At the conference, France had refused to sign an American-sponsored manifesto designed to advance world-wide democracy, the only country to do so. Albright chided Védrine for letting down the side, reminding him that France had sent the Marquis de Lafayette to assist America's struggle for freedom. Védrine's sardonic reply was: 'Ah, but you see, *chère* Madeleine, Lafayette did not go to help the Americans, he went to defeat the British.'[26]

France's Other 'Other'

On Wednesday 12 September 2001, the day after two American Airlines passenger jets slammed into the World Trade Center in lower Manhattan, destroying the twin 110-storey skyscrapers and causing 2,977 fatalities, *Le Monde*, in Paris, published on its front page the headline 'NOUS SOMMES TOUS AMÉRICAINS'. This was a fine piece of stirring sympathetic rhetoric from a source that had not always been quite so enamoured of the United States. It was written by Jean-Marie Colombani, the paper's director since 1994, and eight months later he would publish a short, pithy book, *All Americans? The World after 11 September 2001*. In this title, he reflected on the aftermath, including the fact that, in the wake of the editorial, he received several letters from French readers insisting they were *not* American. 'Why didn't you write we are all Palestinians, or Afghans?' one complained. Colombani told an interviewer when his book was released that a 'necessary compassion' was required at that time, but he also confessed that even then he thought 'solidarity' between the US and Europe was breaking down, that the danger being faced was of a 'unilateralist' America, an isolationist nation in which President George W. Bush 'should stop seeing, and advertising [himself], as headmaster of the school ... presiding over the class'.[1]

But America today is not quite the threatening 'other' it was at the turn of the twenty-first century, simply because other 'others' have taken over as more worrisome to French civilisation and its sense of identity. None has been, or is, more threatening than the presence of millions of Muslims in metropolitan France. The exact number – though undoubtedly large – is a matter of some dispute, since various research bodies and government departments have come up with widely different answers. One reason for this is that it is against the law in France for government surveys to ask the ethnicity of respondents, though recently there have been calls for that to change.

The most popular figures would appear to be between 5 and 6 million, with a range from 4 million to 8 million, or some 8 per cent of the population, of which a third describe themselves as fully observant and half go regularly to the mosque for the Friday service. Between 70,000 and 110,000 are converts.

France has a far greater Muslim population than other European countries. During a demonstration held in Stockholm on 23 October 2020, called to mark the grim beheading of Samuel Paty, a teacher in France who had shown his class images of the Prophet, and in which there was an attempt to burn a copy of the Qur'an, the French ambassador described his country as 'a Muslim country'. 'Islam is the second largest religion in France,' said Étienne Gonneville.

The Paty beheading was the latest in a line of grisly Islamic terrorist episodes that have afflicted France more than anywhere else. The main reason for this – which sets the country apart, to an extent – is its troubled relationship with Algeria, which has involved levels of organised violence rarely seen elsewhere and a virulent Islamophobia also not seen elsewhere to the same extent.

In the wake of the Second World War, since Algerian ports were so close to Marseilles, migrants tended to rotate constantly between factories in France and their home village. At the time it was assumed that all Muslims would, eventually, go home and they were not seen as a threat. However, the separate status of Algerians in their own country was always going to be a source of friction. Not long after 1945, Algerians in Paris became the target of the BAV, the Brigade des aggressions et violence, who conducted large-scale 'sweeps' of the 'counter-society' that had formed among supporters of Algeria's National Liberation Front (FLN), and which accelerated as the Algerian War developed (1954–62). These aggressions were followed by those of the *harkis*, units which employed psychological warfare techniques and torture against the FLN, especially when it opened a 'second front' in France. All this was further aggravated by the presence of *pieds noirs*, white French settlers from Algeria, many Jewish, who were resettled in mainland France and were now living among the Muslim migrants they regarded as the cause of their displacement.

Relations were not improved by political figures such as Pierre Mauroy, prime minister in the early 1980s, and Gaston Defferre, minister of the interior at the same time and mayor of Marseilles, who were loud in their denunciations that Muslims were refusing to integrate and were a fundamental danger to the melting-pot ideology of republican France.

According to some historians 1980–84 was a 'racist turning point' in France. One catalyst occurred in December 1980, when the mayor of the Parisian 'red-belt' commune ordered a bulldozer attack on a hostel in Vitry to prevent its occupation by immigrant workers. Like the extreme right at the time (the Front national was just beginning) the communists sensed a grass-roots racism. The statistics of the time show the extent and pace of change: between 1975 and 1986, the number of mosques in France increased from 68 to 912. And in the political rhetoric of the time there was a shift from biological racism to cultural racism. In 1989 there was another bulldozing when the mayor of Charvieu-Chavagneux, near Lyons, ordered a Muslim prayer room to be razed, 'fearing an invasion of Islamic fundamentalists'. By 1989, says Neil Macmaster, Islamophobia in France 'had come of age'.[2]

For two decades, in the 1980s and 1990s, France was to become a territory for the extension of violent conflicts originating in the Arab world. Mohamed-Ali Adraoui, a French academic at the London School of Economics, says that the presence of radical Islam should be considered a fallout from French policy towards the Middle East and north Africa – metropolitan France was then a scene of anti-colonial struggle – not an antagonism based on religious views. However, the Islamist dimension started to be seen in the 1980s, in the wake of the Iranian Revolution. In February 1985 France experienced the first bomb attack in front of a Marks & Spencer shop in Paris and suffered twenty more in the following months, with September 1986 being the bloodiest period. In the 1990s France became directly targeted as a major enemy of Islam and the only country to which the Algerian Civil War was exported. Adraoui says: 'Islamist leaders reproached the French authorities for helping the Algerian government to stop them winning elections. Second, society was dumbstruck to discover that some of the radical activists in the civil war were French-born citizens with Algerian backgrounds. This phenomenon is still today at the root of a massive fear of a large part of the French population ... Ideologically, for the first time Islamists targeting France came from Salafi groups [see below] promoting a fundamentalist rhetoric clearly influenced by groups taking part in the war in Afghanistan against the Soviet Union.'

In 1994, after the Algerian army cancelled elections, the radical Armed Islamic Group mounted nine bomb attacks in France extending into 1995, targeting aeroplanes, shops, schools and mosques. Since 9/11, France has seen more Islamic terrorist outrages than America, which has contributed to what some have called a French identity crisis. In September 2005, the Groupe Salafi pour la prédication et le combat, the Salafi Group for Preaching and Combat, issued a communiqué in which France was threatened as 'Enemy Number One'.

There have been four particularly marked post-9/11 episodes. The first was the shooting in Toulouse in March 2012, when seven were killed and five injured – with the attacker being shot dead a week later. In the second, in January 2015, at the offices of the satirical magazine *Charlie Hebdo*, twelve employees of the publication were killed and eleven injured. A friend of the two brothers who fomented the assault also attacked the Hypercacher supermarket nearby, where a further four were murdered. Both brothers were killed by police.[*] In November 2015, in the worst episode, 130 were killed in the Bataclan theatre in Paris, and 413 injured. The seven terrorists were shot dead by police.[†] The fourth was the occasion when on Bastille

---

[*] Fourteen accomplices were found guilty by a Paris court shortly before Christmas 2020, three of whom were tried in absentia.

[†] In early September 2021, 20 men went on trial as accomplices in this attack, including Sala Abdeslam, believed to be part of the main group. The court was attended by 3330 lawyers, 1,800 plaintiffs and guarded by 1,000 police. The trial was expected to last 8-9 months.

Day 2016, 14 July, in Nice, 86 were killed and 458 injured when a terrorist drove a truck down the promenade des Anglais.

France is, of course, by no means the only Western or western European country to have been faced with Islamic terrorism. But in some ways it *is* exceptional in this regard. In addition to having a larger Muslim population, its controversial colonial past, particularly its troubled relationship with Algeria, is more recent and therefore more raw. President Macron admitted only as late as September 2018 that torture had been official French policy during those turbulent times, an admission that served to keep the wound – the searing legacy of colonialism – open in France more than elsewhere..

Not to be overlooked either is a perhaps deeper point where France is concerned, in that both French culture and Islamic culture have universal aspirations. The French *mission civilisatrice* has been mentioned throughout this book, but the desire of some Muslims to make Islam a universal culture, while not true of all the faithful, is widespread enough – especially among radicals – to bring the possibility of a clash more fully into focus. For all these reasons France sees itself as more under threat from Islamic culture than do its near neighbours.

It could be argued that France is betraying its new-found liberal principles in demanding that Muslims conform to Western ideas of religious tolerance and the (confined) place of religion in wider cultural practices. But, put alongside its tense relationship with the Anglosphere, and its repeated history of military defeat, any serious threat to French culture, its way of life, must be keenly felt. Paraphrasing Pierre Nora, it could also be said that culture is what France has left. When a country places so much reliance on culture as its defining attribute, mass migration of the 'other' must be especially threatening.

CULTURAL RESISTANCE AND A 'COUNTER-SOCIETY'

A final factor may prove to be the most intractable in the long run. This is the development of a Salafist minority in France that is much larger than anywhere else. Salafism is a branch of Sunni Islam whose modern-day followers claim to emulate 'the pious predecessors' (*al-salaf al-ṣāliḥ*, often equated with the first three generations of

Muslims) as closely and in as many spheres of life as possible. These first three generations are regarded as the finest Muslims the world has ever seen or will ever see.

Salafism grew in the twentieth century for three reasons, notably through one particular form, known as Wahhabism, grounded in Saudi Arabia. The first factor was the rise of the oil industry in Saudi and the rest of the Gulf, causing many Muslims to migrate there, to find jobs. Apart from jobs, they also found Wahhabi ideas. Second, in response to socialist developments in Egypt and Iran, Saudi Arabia began actively spreading Wahhabism as a conservative counter-narrative, backed up by oil money. Third, the abject defeat of several Arab states in the June 1967 war with Israel which, by extension, also delegitimised Arab socialism, led to a search for an alternative narrative. This proved fertile ground for Wahhabism, so that Salafism was spread not just across the Muslim world but beyond.

Theologically, Salafis exhibit a strong tendency to rely on what believers consider 'inerrant revelation' (*waḥy*) as expressed in the writings of the Qur'an, and reject what they see as the 'excessive spiritualism' associated with Sufism and the 'deviant' doctrines of the mediaeval rationalist Mu'tazila movement. In practice, Salafism comes in what we might call three 'temperatures'. At the coolest are the 'Quietist Salafis', who form the majority. They are politically quietist in that they stay away from political activism, such as running for parliament, attending demonstrations, signing petitions, engaging in political debate or founding political parties. Instead, they focus on 'cleansing' their Islamic tradition. They do not believe that an Islamic nation will arise before society is ready for it.

Unlike apolitical Quietists, Political Salafis – the second group – do engage in politics and sometimes even run for office. Under the leadership of Salmān al-'Awda (b. 1955) and Safar al-Ḥawālī (b. 1950), the trend became sharper after the Saudis invited 500,000 American troops on to their soil in 1990, nervous about Iraq and Iran's intentions. But the activities of Political Salafis have been mainly confined to the Middle East.

The 'hottest' Salafis are the Jihadi-Salafis, who support or wage jihad. This revolutionary type of jihad – which targets not just non-Muslims but also Muslim regimes judged to be apostates – is

rooted ideologically in the writings of Muslim Brotherhood thinkers such as the Egyptian Sayyid Qutb (1906–66). It is this group
that gave rise to al-Qaeda in Afghanistan and elsewhere, to Osama
bin Laden (1957–2011) and other forms of so-called 'global jihad',
espoused by a host of Islamic scholars around the world from 9/11
onwards, culminating in the Islamic State (Daesh in France), whose
openly declared aim is the establishment of a caliphate.

Not unnaturally, Jihadi-Salafis attract all the headlines. But terrorism doesn't bring down regimes or pose a permanent threat to
entire societies, unsettling as it is at times. Quietist Salafis, however,
are much thicker on the ground and for that reason are more of an
ever-present reminder of alternatives to the traditional French way of
life. To an extent, they provide a 'deep background' to the Jihadis.

Mohamed-Ali Adraoui, of the LSE in London, and Leyla Arslan,
at the Collège de France in Paris, have each examined Quietist Salafi
culture in France, a population which is not especially large but is
growing quite fast, numbering between 20,000 and 30,000 people
in late 2019, up from 12,000 in 2010 and just 100 in 2005. At one
level Salafis are urged to remove themselves to countries where Islam
is the majority faith but, being practical, acknowledging that people
need to work to live, and that many Middle Eastern countries are
less prosperous than France, the principles of Salafism allow for 'an
internal process of migration/isolation from French society'. Adraoui
conducted more than 100 in-depth interviews of Salafis for a paper
published in the academic press, and spent hours among them,
observing. His most important finding is that many Quietist Salafis
fashion a successful economic life of entrepreneurship *entirely among*
their own faith community.

Adraoui found that this form of faith particularly appealed to
young Muslims disappointed with their families' religious social-
isation, that the Salafist faith 'legitimised the disavowal of French
society in favour of a desire to build a counter-society based on its
own norms ... their way of life is principally designed to allow a fundamentalist counter-society to rise and oppose the un-Islamic society
without entirely breaking away from it'. They feel especially targeted
by the 2004 law banning religious signs from public schools and the
2010 law prohibiting the full veil.

Adraoui keenly observes that there are some parallels between Salafists and Max Weber's Protestants of the eighteenth and nineteenth centuries in that, in their own eyes, economic success is a reward granted by God for their puritanical observance. He concludes: 'This allows Salafist economic ethics to become a means of opposition to a society whose principles and norms are understood as vile, pushing these communities to convey their repudiation of French society ... thus leading to an antagonistic relationship.'[3]

What French Salafis value the most is an 'intense faith combined with being a shopkeeper/trader whose wealth is morally good as long as piety directs material success in a moral direction, including generosity toward those in need and lack of vanity in one's spending'. Believers advocate 'getting by' rather than relying on state benefits and many even think that voting is contrary to faith. Being one's own boss provides a feeling of being chosen by God, as with Weber's Protestants in the nineteenth century.

Perhaps the most notable aspect of the Quietist Salafists is that they promote primarily religious values within the economic sphere 'without any desire to use it for political revolution'. Theirs is an ideology of 'cultural resistance' rather than politics for institutional power.

A FASCINATION WITH DEATH

Clearly, even Quietist Salafism, were it to grow substantially in numbers, would pose a major headache for French society, French identity and France's famed sociability. The Salafis' point-blank refusal to have anything to do with mainstream French society goes against the whole idea of France that we have been considering.

A common saying in the past decades has been 'Not all Salafis are Jihadis but all Jihadis are Salafis'. In line with this, Adraoui and his colleagues say that, among the 20,000–30,000 French Salafis, there are roughly 100 Jihadis.

Not so, says Olivier Roy, a French Protestant historian and sociologist, who was born in La Rochelle and attended the Lycée Louis-le-Grand, taking his degree at the École normale supérieure – the classic French educational background – and is now chair of Mediterranean studies at the European University Institute in Fiesole,

Italy. Since an early six-week hitch-hiking trip to Afghanistan as a student, which fuelled his interest in the Middle East, he has made several inquiries into Islamic-inspired terrorism and he has decided views – backed by evidence – on who the terrorists are. And they are not, he says, Salafis, not in any accepted use of the word, though they invariably come from that background. Indeed, by some ways of reckoning, they are hardly Muslim.

Roy starts from the point of view that it is not only the French who feel that their identity is under threat – the same goes for Muslims. Because of economic pressures, an Algerian, for example, will live in France simply because it is, just now, better to live in France than in Algeria. Someone will live in the West, even *prefer* to live in the West, but they don't want to become Western. Their ethnic and moral values are not supported by the social environment. Further, the puritanical zeal that fires Salafis derives, he says, from an emphasis on virtue and, as he puts it, the French in particular know that the search for virtue leads only to terror, in particular 'the Terror'. 'We know', he says, 'since the French Revolution that once virtue is in charge, it leads to terror, for a simple reason: nobody is virtuous enough.'[4]

Roy can see the attraction of Salafism. 'By joining a neo-fundamentalist movement, which tells them, "Don't care about society, any kind of society; don't care about culture; don't care about politics; just try to be a good Muslim and to recreate the true Muslim community", they feel at home. They would say this is an identity for me.'[5] Thus the Salafis are 'at home' in France, but not in any way that traditional French would recognise.

But, says Roy, when you study the actual jihadis, whatever they *say* about their lives, their motives and their ideas, their Islam is a cross between the banal and the imaginary. His first point about them is that their systematic choice of death is a relatively recent development. 'The perpetrators of terrorist attacks in France in the 1970s and 1980s, whether or not they had any connection with the Middle East, carefully planned their escape. Muslim tradition, while it recognises the merits of the martyr who dies in combat, does not prize those who strike out in pursuit of their own deaths, because doing so interferes with God's will.' But over the past twenty-five years, from Khaled Kelkal, the leader of a plot to bomb Paris trains in 1995, nearly every terrorist in France has blown themselves up or got killed by the police, a situation perhaps best summed up by Mohammed Merah, who killed a rabbi and three children at a Jewish school in Toulouse in 2012. He quoted a variant of the notorious statement attributed to Osama bin Laden, which subsequently became almost routine: 'We love death as you love life.' The same fascination with death is found among many jihadis, suicide attacks being seen as the ultimate goal of their engagement. Yet, says Roy, suicide terrorism cannot be effective from a military standpoint: 'The fact that hardened militants are used only once is not rational.'[6]

His central point is that we are not seeing the radicalisation of Islam but the Islamisation of radicalism. And this is underlined by his analysis of jihadis themselves. 'Those who perpetrate attacks in Europe are not inhabitants of the Gaza Strip, Libya or Afghanistan. They are not necessarily the poorest, the most humiliated or the least integrated. The fact that 25 per cent of jihadis are converts shows that the link between radicals and "their people" is ... a largely imaginary construct. Revolutionaries almost never come from the suffering classes ... It was not Palestinians who shot up the Bataclan.'[7]

Just as Adraoui studied a hundred Salafis in detail, so Roy has studied a hundred jihadis. He concluded that there is no standard profile 'but there are recurrent characteristics' which have hardly changed since the beginning of the twenty-first century. These common features include the following: they are second generation; they are fairly well integrated at first, chasing women, enjoying nightclubs and consuming alcohol; but they succumb to a period of petty crime and end up in prison, where they are radicalised. The Abdeslam brothers, who carried out the Bataclan attack, had run a bar in Brussels and went out to nightclubs in the months preceding the attack. The fact that they were brothers was also significant – the group membership of jihadi terrorist cells often includes brothers (the number of sets of siblings found is remarkable), childhood friends and acquaintances from prison, sometimes from a training camp. The radicals are also often orphans or come from dysfunctional families. 'They are not necessarily rebelling against their parents personally, but against what they represent: humiliation, concessions made to society, and what they view as their religious ignorance.' They enjoy streetwear – baseball caps, hoods, 'not even the Islamic variety'. Their musical tastes are of their time – for example, rap. 'The language spoken by radicals is always that of their country of residence.' In France they often switch to a Salafised version of *banlieue* speech.[8]

Prison is often the defining event, putting them 'far outside' any institutionalised religion, introducing them to a simplified Salafism, the search for dignity, the formation of a tight-knit group and the reinterpretation of crime as legitimate political protest. This can occur quickly, Roy says, because they have never lived in a particularly religious environment. 'Their relationship to the local mosque was ambivalent; either they attended episodically, or they were expelled for having shown disrespect for the local imam.' None of them had worked for a Muslim charity, none were members of a Palestinian solidarity movement. Above all, they had practically no religious education and the embrace of religion does not necessarily correspond to immersion in religious practice. Jihadis do not descend into violence after poring over sacred texts. 'The paucity of religious knowledge among jihadis is glaring.'[9]

On top of all this, jihadis 'never refer to the colonial period ... they do not align themselves with the struggles of their fathers ... they read texts circulating on the Internet in French or English but not works in Arabic.' And, perhaps most controversially, 'living in an Islamic society does not interest jihadis'.[10]

In yet another controversial – but perhaps astute – observation, Roy compares jihadis with the American school shooter, who is usually heavily armed and kills as many as he can before either shooting himself or letting himself be shot by police.

Roy thinks that what the jihadis want is unobtainable, a 'grandiose imaginary system'. In truth they are a certain psychological type who want to use their faith as a badge of convenience. But that does appear to mean that so long as even Quietist Salafis exist in any numbers, they will continue to serve as the context for badges of convenience.[11]

SOMETHING CALLED FRANCE

But Roy does fear that France has a problem with religion, which stems ultimately from its 1904 law about *laïcité*. This law was intended to be neutral as regards religion – people could be religious in their private lives, but not carry it into the public sphere. Roy believes that in the post-Second World War world, however, France's secular rhetoric has become increasingly intolerant, that there is a 'secular prejudice' in France, which has to an extent sacrificed the view that although the *state* is neutral so far as religion is concerned, that doesn't apply to *individuals*.

As he has pointed out, when he was a student there were nuns in his class, dressed as nuns, and no one objected. Now *laïcité* is anti-religious. The right and far right in France are intent on affirming the country's Christian identity, while the left is anti-religion *tout court*, going far beyond Islamophobia to all forms of worship. This moral cleavage, Roy says, first emerged in the 1960s – in respect of sexual freedom, gay marriage, IVF and so on – when *laïcité* turned from the principle of neutrality into an 'ideology affirming values', namely that one must accept homosexuality, feminism etc., a demand that the state take into account Christian values and therefore take sides. 'Today there is a *laïc* intolerance ... We are no longer in a democracy when we impose a normative system on people.'

The term 'identity', Roy says, is new. 'If you look at texts forty, fifty, one hundred years ago, no one spoke of French identity. Some people spoke of French culture, the French Republic, of many things, but not identity, the idea that a culture could be reduced to an identity ... [but] no one questioned the existence of something called "France". Today there is a serious crisis of political identification. We have two profound changes of French society that happened at the same time. The first is immigration, and the second is the European project.' Decisions are taken in Brussels, he says, that do not resonate with the French, and immigration has brought not just a different religion but a different culture to France. Between them these have caused a crisis of identity, not helped by the existence of a counter-society. 'It is not understood in French society how someone can be religiously radical while being politically moderate.' Which of course Quietist Salafis are. 'A Muslim who prays five times a day is considered a potential radical.'

NINETY-THREE: A FRACTURE IN FRENCH SOCIETY

Ariane Bonzon, a journalist, agrees with Mohamed Ali Adraoui about the Salafis' enjoyment of modern fashions and that the Quietists will take off the veil, for example, if the law requires it. Pierre Merle, a sociologist, agrees with Roy that in France recently there has been a change in the concept of *laïcité* from 'the *laïcité* of liberation to the *laïcité* of exclusion'. Secularism, he points out, was a value renewed in the 1958 constitution, when de Gaulle brought in the Fifth Republic: the laws of the land should apply equally to all, irrespective or race or religion. But as time has gone by, instead of any pupil in school being allowed to wear signs of their religious affiliation, no one now is allowed to show any such signs. Jean-Pierre Filiu, a French Arabist at SciencesPo (the Paris Institute of Political Studies) and an advisor to François Hollande when he was president, has also pointed out that French *laïc* law prevents the state from funding churches or mosques, which has had the effect that many mosques in France have been built with Algerian or Moroccan money, further compromising the identity of French Muslims.

At the same time, Roy has come under a fulsome attack by another academic, Gilles Kepel, a historian and linguist also at SciencesPo, and a sometime colleague of Adraoui. The son of an immigrant playwright, who translated Václav Havel's plays into French, and married to a woman whose family are from north Africa, Kepel was part of the government commission that recommended the introduction of the 2004 law banning headscarves and other religious clothing in schools, as a result of which he was one of several individuals placed on a death list.

Kepel accuses Roy of naïvety, of not understanding the true situation, partly because he doesn't speak Arabic and so can't consult the necessary documents and writings of the extremists. Kepel dismisses the idea that there is rampant Islamophobia in France – the country, he says, has a proud record of immigration and its *laïc* law has encouraged many immigrants to settle in France because they can practise their faith there in much more agreeable surroundings than their countries of origin.

He sees the root of the problem in the *banlieues*, the rough areas of urban localities – in Paris, Lyons, Lille, Marseilles – where he sees Salafism as *the* gateway to jihadist violence. In 2012 he published a two-volume examination of the *banlieues*, to the second part of which he gave the title *Ninety-Three*. This has a double resonance in France. That number is the government designation for the Seine-Saint-Denis *département*, which has some of the worst-affected *banlieues* in France, but it is also an allusion to Victor Hugo's novel of the same title, about the Terror of 1793, 'the heyday of the guillotine'.

The *banlieues*, Kepel insists, are a source of both 'isolation and camouflage', which he implies Roy misses, not having the language. Though Kepel speaks Arabic, in the *banlieues* they speak a variety of Arabic and local patois, so it is not entirely clear what advantage he has. But for Kepel there is a *fracture* in French society, in which 'a distressingly large number of Muslims are in open revolt against French cultural and political norms'. In September 2016 a survey by the Montaigne Institute found that 28 per cent of Muslims had adopted values 'clearly opposed to the values of the Republic', a mix of 'authoritarian' and 'secessionist' views, including support for polygamy and the *niqab*, or full-face veil, and were opposed to the French laws enforcing secularism in public. Their hatred of the police is intense, he says.

He too sees the prisons as a problem. He says there are more than 400 Islamic terrorists in French prisons and around 1,200 identified as 'radicalised', plus 700 French citizens with Islamic State in Iraq and Syria (others put the number as high as 1,700). Farhad Khosrokhavar, a sociologist who works in French prisons, agrees with Kepel that such individuals have become much better at disguising their beliefs, making it impossible to get honest testimony out of these inmates.[12]

The basic problem seems to be that Salafism, even Quietist Salafism, is a religion without a home, which is another point Roy has made. As such, it is all too susceptible to influence from outside, from the Middle East in particular.

A FRENCH ISLAM

In February 2018, the same year that he confessed that torture had been official French policy in the Algerian War of Independence,

President Emmanuel Macron announced that he was looking at plans for reorganising Islam in France, one that conformed to the nation's values. He was building on an initiative of his predecessor, François Hollande, who in 2015 had developed a plan for French imams to give instruction at a training institute in Rabat, Morocco. Many saw this as a patronising attempt to manage and 'domesticate' the faith 'to the point of invisibility'. 'The Muslim community is tired and disappointed with a series of ridiculous and humiliating offers,' said M'hammed Henniche, the president of the Union of Muslim Associations of Seine-Saint-Denis. As Roy says, such an attempt may even be illegal under the French constitution, and in any case, the effort is not a religious initiative so much as one designed to increase national security.[13] In that same month, February 2018, a poll showed that 43 per cent of the French public considered Islam 'incompatible with the values of the republic'. A poll published in October 2021 showed that 67 per cent of French people worry that Muslims are taking over the country, with far-right wing politicians talking of *le grand remplacement*, 'people of foreign origin who are driving out, little by little, what in demography we call natives' and 'the implant on our soil of a civilization with which we share nothing'.[14]

Hakim El Karoui, a fellow at the Institut Montaigne, welcomes Macron's attempts to distance French Islam from the Arab world but does not think a French Islam can be imposed on the country's Muslims – better simply to 'enable [its] emergence'. 'I am proposing that we shift responsibility to French Muslims who have no interest other than that of France.'[15]

Do the Quietist Salafis hold a prime position in such a plan? On the one hand, they like the material aspects of Western society, but at the same time reject more association than is strictly necessary. The Quietist Salafi counter-society seems to be both an opportunity and a problem at the same time.

'Je Suis Notre-Dame'

On Wednesday 7 January 2015, just after eleven o'clock in the morning, two hooded men, weighted down with Zastava M70 AB2 rifles, Tokarev TT pistols and Škorpion vz. 61 submachine guns, forced their way into 6 rue Nicolas Appert in the eleventh arrondissement of Paris, not too far from the Bastille. 'Is this *Charlie Hebdo*?' they demanded. Realising from the expressions of the people they met there that they had made a mistake, they fired off one round through a glass door to show that their weapons were real, and quickly found their way along the street to number 10.

In a way the mistake made by the gunmen was understandable. The satirical magazine *Charlie Hebdo* was no stranger to controversy or violence. It had been publishing cheeky – and more than cheeky – cartoons of the Prophet Muhammad since 2011, including one in 2012 showing him naked, which had proved so contentious that the French government was forced to temporarily close embassies and lycées in more than twenty countries, because of the threat of reprisals. The weekly's offices had been firebombed, its website hacked, it had been unsuccessfully sued for contravening hate-speech laws, and cartoonist and editorial director Stéphane Charbonnier ('Charb') had been placed on a 'most wanted' list by al-Qaeda in 2013. As a result, and not before time, the magazine had moved into anonymous, unmarked offices.

The two men reached the *Charlie Hebdo* building about 11.30 that morning. Just arriving at the building, ahead of an editorial meeting, was one of the magazine's cartoonists, Corinne 'Coco' Rey, accompanied by her young daughter. At gunpoint the men forced Corinne to enter the passcode so they could gain access through the electronic door. Once inside they immediately opened fire, spraying the lobby with bullets and instantaneously killing a maintenance worker seated at a reception desk.

Upstairs on the second floor, where fifteen journalists were holding the first editorial meeting of the year, the noises from the lobby could be heard but, despite the magazine's history, they were mistaken for fireworks. 'The atmosphere was joyous,' said one of those present, Laurent Léger.

Not for long. The gunmen soon found the editorial room, burst in and immediately began shooting. Ten cartoonists or journalists would be killed that day, plus the maintenance man and a security officer. Four would be injured and four would survive, mainly by hiding under the tables.

The gunmen made off but were quickly identified by police as the Kouachi brothers, Chérif and Saïd, both of whom had prison records and had been involved in terrorist Islam-related offences earlier. Both had received military training in Yemen and were known to have mixed with other jihadis. They were spotted the day after the attacks in Aisne, north-east of Paris, and eventually holed up the following day in the offices of a signage production company. There, a terrified but ingeniously brave employee hid in a cardboard box, where she was never discovered and cunningly sent the police text messages for several hours describing exactly where in the building the brothers were.

The siege lasted for eight to nine hours and was so close to Charles de Gaulle airport that two runways were closed. An anti-terrorist team was landed by helicopter on the roof of the building but before the brothers could be reached, alerted by the noise, they ran outside and exchanged fire with the gendarmes. Both were killed.

During the stand-off near the airport, another jihadi, Amedy Coulibaly, who had met the brothers in prison, took more hostages at a kosher supermarket at Porte de Vincennes in eastern Paris, relaying to the police that he would kill hostages if the brothers were harmed. He killed four victims who were Jewish while leaving the others alive. He was shot and killed within minutes of the brothers.

The surviving staff of the magazine continued determinedly with production of the next issue, which – famously – had a print-run of nearly 8 million copies, as compared with its normal 60,000 copies, though most weeks it sold barely half of that.

Four days after the shooting, 2 million people, with several dozen world leaders in attendance, gathered in Paris for a rally of national unity. That was when the phrase *'Je suis Charlie'* became common currency. In wider France, more than fifty anti-Muslim incidents were reported in the week after the attack, including twenty-one shootings, with grenades being thrown at mosques. On the first anniversary of the attacks a Tunisian Muslim charged at police officers with a meat-cleaver and was shot and killed. Fourteen accomplices were found guilty in a Paris court at Christmas 2020.

The *Charlie* episode and the attack at the Bataclan café/concert theatre, in the same arrondissement, in November of the same year, when three gunmen of Algerian descent, all wearing suicide vests, killed 130 and injured more than 400 during a rock concert, before killing themselves or being killed by police, made it a bleak year for France. After the outrages a new state-of-emergency law was introduced, based on *suspicion* of people rather than firm evidence of guilt. Within the space of two years, the authorities reported that they had managed to thwart 32 terror attacks, search 4,457 apartments, put 439 people under house arrest and shut down 17 mosques. Nonetheless, many lawyers felt that being able to act merely on suspicion, rather than firm evidence, was a step backwards for a liberal democracy.

'THERE IS NO PURITY TO FRANCE'

The longer-term effects of this law remain to be seen, but a group of historians, responding to what they saw as the 'urgency' of the post-*Charlie* situation, produced as quickly as they could a striking new history of France, a history that, perhaps, could only be written in France about France, and only there could take the shape that it did.

The parallels – some parallels – with Nora's *Lieux de mémoire* are striking: a team of 132 historians, corralled together by an academic-impresario from the Collège de France. In double-quick time, the team produced a massive work of 900 pages that, despite its bulk, became an instant bestseller in 2017, selling out the initial print-run on the day it was published, and it has since been released in several formats, including pocket paperbacks and glossy coffee-table versions. Despite superficial parallels with *Lieux*, the substance of this latest history is very different.

For a start, the central editor/conceptualist of *France in the World*, Patrick Boucheron, is a mediaevalist, a specialist of a time that was – significantly – far less nationalistic than now. He saw the work as *part* of history, not just as *about* history. And the origin of the work lay not just in the horrific events of *Charlie Hebdo* and the Bataclan, but in the calls by politicians – such as Fillon and Macron in the 2017 election campaign – for a return to 'traditional values' and for the French to take pride in 'dreams of grandeur' and the established 'identity/unity/uniqueness' of France. It was also a determined intent by historians to reclaim French history from politicians, journalists, television reporters and other non-professionals who had, they felt, usurped the proper role of academic research to tell France's story as it was rather than how people wanted it to be. In this they reflected the work and ideas of the Comité de vigilance face aux usages publics de l'histoire (Committee of Vigilance on the Public Use of History), a professional association which also argued that it fell to historians, not legislators, to adjudicate on historical truth. The book also showed some sympathy with the wider aims of the *gilets jaunes* demonstrators, who were just then claiming that *la France profonde* was being forgotten.

The 132 authors were each asked to explore the significance of a single year and to confine their remarks to six printed pages, making for a great variety but also meaning that although the book is a linear, episodic chronology, it never amounts to a narrative, and means also that events and people with very different historical weight or significance are given equal treatment. This makes for some oddities, which some commentators found fruitful and provocative in the best sense and others very much did not.

The underlying aim of *France in the World* – the first sentence of which, in the introduction to the English version, is: 'This is an urgent book' – was to show that France 'is not a physical entity so much as a psychological creation of the modern mind', and cannot be properly understood without its wider context, and without challenging the traditional idea of 'a France alone and above all others'.[1] To this end, the book tells the story of a France that begins not with Vercingetorix, in the first century BC, or with Charlemagne, in the eighth century AD, but with the cave paintings at Lascaux and elsewhere 36,000 years ago, the point being that when France began there was no such thing as France. Continuing in this vein, the book's exploration of, for example, Descartes and Voltaire is both idiosyncratic and original, describing less their thought than the fact that both endured French intolerance that forced these great minds into exile. The year 1973 is selected because it was the year that Salvador Allende, the first elected Marxist president, in Chile, was assassinated, the point here being that Allende was a seminal figure for many French Marxists.[2] The six-page limit means that the interment of an unknown Celtic woman in the Vix Grave (a burial ground in northern Burgundy) is given the same space as the Holocaust, or the 1848 revolution.

Not that everything you would expect to be given its six pages *is* given its six pages. There is nothing in the book on Verdun, nothing on the fall of France in May 1940, although there is an article on how Brazzaville, in what was then French Congo, became the capital of Free France between 1940 and 1942. There is nothing on de Gaulle's appeal from London on 18 June 1940, nothing on Lévi-Strauss, Lacan or Aron, but there are chapters on the opening of the Negresco hotel in Nice in 1913 and on Coco Chanel, both lauding French fashion. There is nothing on wine and food. We have Napoleon's coronation but not his death, we have the revolution of 1848 but not that of 1830. There is no Franco-Prussian War.

The overall aim of the book, despite Boucheron's admission that it 'lacks coherence', is to upend assumptions, to encourage reassessment, to explore discontinuities and disruptions in chronology so as to cast into doubt the national and nationalistic narrative, to overcome what the authors see as a constricting narrow-mindedness, when France in the past has so often benefitted from immigrants.[3] There is no such thing, the book argues, as a racial, religious or intellectual purity to France.

The book – though written by well-qualified (if largely unknown) historians, mainly from Paris, and predominantly but not entirely male – was roundly criticised by more mainstream figures, who claimed that many of the 'decentred' episodes and personages in its chapters 'have no real historical significance', that the book is no more than 'a quasi-flippant pirouette through history'. Alain Finkielkraut damned the authors as 'gravediggers of the great French heritage'. Pierre Nora declared himself worried by Boucheron's 'alternative dates' in French history, comparing them to the 'alternative facts' then being made so much of by the Trump administration in Washington, and insisting that 'verifiable truth is the historian's aim'.[4] On the other hand, Robert Darnton, the great American historian of eighteenth-century France, said the book was 'a breath of fresh air'.

Boucheron was robust in his defence of the 'joyous polyphony' and experimentalism of the book and of what is and isn't in it, defending its scholarship, anxious that historians do not retreat from the public square, and equally anxious 'to denationalise history', arguing that his nation is a country that has made 'an extravagant claim to speak in the name of the universal, as if France could encompass the world'. In other words, France should not regard itself as exceptional. In response to the criticism that French literature, music and art are mostly missing from his book, he responded: 'Why should France be more defined by its literature than by its landscapes?'

Yet thoughtful critics have wondered: why – without its books, culture, wine and food – should the world take a special interest in France? They have also pointed out that the limit of each chapter to six pages constricts space for sustained analysis and theory, so that more thoughtful readers will find the book overall thin fare, in which too little of what a nation shares is considered. And there is precious little in *France in the World* on the inequalities that have dogged France's past no less than in other countries.[5]

Whatever criticisms have been levelled at the book, *France in the World* sold more than 100,000 copies in France, making it no surprise when plans were made to release an English-language version. And there, Boucheron's aim to make the book part of history as well as about history was again reinforced. Having been sparked by the events at *Charlie Hebdo* and the Bataclan, the book's American publication was bracketed with another world-worrying event.

THE 'INNER SHIVER'

On the morning of Monday, 15 April 2019, Boucheron and Stéphane Gerson, of New York University, the book's English-language editor, were preparing to launch *France in the World* at the Cultural Services Department of the French embassy at 972 Fifth Avenue in Manhattan. Before they could complete their preparations, however, distressing word came through that morning that the cathedral of Notre-Dame in Paris was on fire. Crimson flames were already engulfing its slender, iconic tower. The American launch of the title was immediately overtaken and put into the shade by this dark and dramatic turn of events.

The first fire alarm had gone off at 6.18 p.m. in Paris, 12.18 p.m. in New York, though it would be another half an hour before the fire brigade became involved, before word began to spread and shocked crowds started to gather on the Île de la Cité, which slices the River Seine in two and where Notre-Dame is located.

In Paris the springtime weather was wonderful – bright blue skies with the chestnut and cherry trees in full blossom. Notre-Dame's bells were about to ring for vespers. Inside the cathedral, Canon Jean-Pierre Caveau, aided by soprano Emmanuelle Campana and organist Johann Vexo, led the service.[6] President Macron was scheduled to give a big speech on television at 8.00 that night in which it was hoped he would signal an end to the weeks of unrest brought about by the *gilets jaunes'* radical *'manifestations'*. (For twenty-two consecutive Saturdays, protests had been held throughout France, not just in Paris, resulting in havoc and no shortage of material damage, and though some of the protestors had sabotaged their cause by aggressively criminal behaviour, people expected Macron to rise to the challenge.) It was even rumoured that some 'big' policy announcements would be made, such as the abolition of the fuel tax, which the *gilets jaunes* had been campaigning for, and even the dismantling of the École nationale d'administration, the elitist school that trained France's senior civil servants.

It was soon clear that the president's speech would have to be cancelled. So vast is the building of Notre-Dame that by the time the fire was discovered – by a security guard who, in response to an alarm, had climbed 300 narrow steps to the cathedral attic – red and yellow flames and plumes of acrid, black smoke had already begun to engulf a frightening number of the 1,300 oak beams that comprised the roof. Most dated from the thirteenth century and had dried out long ago, making them excellent timber for burning.

The fire brigade arrived, led by its commander-in-chief, Jean-Claude Gallet, a three-star general and a veteran of Afghanistan. The Paris fire brigade was established by Napoleon in 1811 and to this day its members are subjected to a number of demanding physical exercises, the most celebrated of which is the 'plank', which must be performed twice a day, fully dressed in uniform, including helmet. In the plank, the firefighters must pull themselves up almost eight feet, using only their arms. This is a safety routine to ensure that they can escape if floors below them have collapsed. At fifty-four, Gallet could still do this.

The general registered at once the sound of timber cracking in the evening air. At 7.57 p.m., just before 2.00 p.m. in Manhattan, the 750-ton iconic spire of the cathedral – made of heavy oak and lead – crashed down, fracturing the stone vault of the nave. The blast caused by the collapse forced open all the cathedral doors at once.[7]

Now the thought was to save Notre-Dame's treasury of several thousand religious relics. The firefighters approached the reliquaries deep in the cathedral, forcing locks or breaking glass when they had to, while a chain of human volunteers formed to pass the relics to safety. These included the white linen tunic of St Louis, said to have been worn by King Louis IX, known as St Louis since his canonisation in 1297, when he brought Jesus' crown of thorns to Paris from Byzantium in 1239, having paid a fortune for it. At 8.42 p.m., after a delay brought about by not knowing the access code, the red leather casket containing the crown of thorns itself was rescued by Marie-Hélène Didier – who had rushed back from Versailles, where she had been attending a ceremony – together with a nail from the holy cross and a piece of the cross itself. A hail of embers and molten metal rained down around her. She would safely reach the haven of the Louvre, driven in a truck, with the precious objects on her lap.

The police had commissioned drones to hover in the sky above the cathedral, for a better inspection of the damage, their view being shown on a huge screen that almost everyone could see. The screen showed 'terrifying images of a giant burning crimson cross, covering the nave and transepts like a kind of sorcerers' Sabbath, strik[ing] everyone to the core'.[8]

The situation was so grave that the GRIMP were brought in. GRIMP stands for Groupe de reconnaissance et d'intervention en milieu périlleux, an elite, highly trained, extremely tough unit, specially designed for intervention in dangerous assignments. A squad of fifty men was sent up the spiral staircase of the north tower, placing grapplers and tethers and ropes as they went, in case an emergency evacuation was needed and the men had to abseil down. They took hoses with them, 133 feet long, up into a tower that by now was an inferno, with flames 31 feet high. The floor separating the two sets of bells was already on fire.

As the GRIMP team doused the bells and the surrounding woodwork with water an amazing sound greeted them. The bells – some in situ since 1686 – started what Agnès Poirier, in her vivid account of the fire, described as a 'lament'. In the heat and steam the bells were gently vibrating: 'Notre-Dame is weeping.'[9]

At 9.35 General Gallet stepped in front of the television cameras to say that, as of that moment, he didn't know whether the north tower, with its bells, could be saved. At this, Archbishop Aupetit of Paris intervened on Twitter, in what was surely one of Twitter's finest moments: 'To all the priests of Paris; the firemen are currently still fighting to save the towers of Notre-Dame ... Let us pray. Ring your bells and spread the word.'

The bells started chiming all over Paris; and the rest of the country joined in.

Gallet asked for laser rangefinders to be placed where they could monitor the integrity of the masonry. He was told that the north gable had swayed half an inch. A building is normally said to be on the verge of collapse if it has moved just a tenth of an inch.[10]

At 11.00 p.m. – 5.00 p.m. in Manhattan – Gallet at last was reassured enough to tell President Macron – who had been present for some time near the scene with his wife, Brigitte – that the fire in the north tower had been brought under control. Half an hour later, Macron, flanked by his prime minister, Édouard Philippe, by Anne

Hidalgo, mayor of Paris, and by the Archbishop of Paris, addressed the nation, to praise the work of the fire brigade and the GRIMP, to say that he shared the 'inner shiver' of all who had witnessed the evening's disaster, and to reassure everyone watching, or listening, that it was France's destiny to rebuild the cathedral and to make her 'even more beautiful ... Notre-Dame is our history, our literature, our collective imagination, the place where we have lived all our great moments, our wars and our liberations. It is the epicentre of our life, the kilometre zero of France ... we will rebuild Notre-Dame ... because this is our profound destiny.'[11]

PARIS ON ITS KNEES

The battle for the rebuilding of Notre-Dame had its share of magnanimity and farce. Some of the richest people of France – François Pinault, Bernard Arnault, the Bettencourt family – and some of the major companies, such as Total, offered hundreds of millions of euros, literally overnight, at least in theory, and though this was welcomed it was also denounced by those aggrieved that such sums should be so readily available to be spent on a building when so many fellow French *people* were going hungry. A cascade of smaller donations came in from all over the world, not least from the municipality of Szeged in Hungary, which sent 10,000 euros because it had not forgotten how, in 1897, when it suffered a devastating flood, Paris had sent funds to help its rebuilding. The 80 million euros raised by small donors proved more than useful, in fact, as it could be used straight away, whereas the big donations had to go through arcane bureaucratic delays.

After this cascade of magnanimity, when it was announced that there was to be an international competition for the design of the new spire, this was when farce kicked in. There was one scheme suggested for a giant greenhouse in place of the spire, another for a forest where 'endangered animal species could find refuge', and a third (from Norway) for a cross-shaped swimming pool filled with rainwater.

A Notre-Dame Emergency Act was passed after three months, with Jean-Louis Georgelin, a five-star general and the army's former chief-of-staff, placed in charge of the 'building site of the century' as the French termed it, with a small office in the Élysée Palace.[12] But one fact escaped many people. Since the 1905 act separating church and state, the clergy has occupied the churches of France but has not been responsible for them. This seems like a significant anomaly. Notre-Dame attracts 14 million visitors a year, who enter free of charge. Had the church chosen – or been allowed – to charge a nominal sum, it could have generated funds that might have avoided the fire in the first place, which was seemingly caused by either a short circuit or a cigarette butt not being properly extinguished by workmen. (Doubts remain because even by the time investigators had finished their inquiry into the causes of the fire, they had not been given full access to the cathedral, not all of the areas yet being judged totally safe.)

Let Agnès Poirier end the story for us. While the fire was raging, that spring night in April 2019, when no one could be sure what the final outcome might be, all along the quai Saint-Michel, which borders the River Seine opposite the Île de la Cité, 'young and not-so-young Parisians have fallen to their knees. When was Paris last the setting for such stupefying scenes? Some are silently praying, while others are quietly singing Ave Marias. Those images, relayed on TV screens, stun this staunchly secular country, this viscerally sceptical people, and touch them to the core. Awestruck, France realises how profoundly Christian its history is, even if it is buried under a century or more of secularism.'[13]

The image of young and old kneeling side by side by the Seine to pray and sing Ave Marias on a spring evening is deeply affecting. And yes, perhaps very French. But is the fundamental paradox of a Christian heritage, in today's secular world – though brought into stark relief by the fire at Notre-Dame – really so exceptional? This paradox is surely something that France shares with many of its neighbours, who have perhaps not been given the opportunity, awful though it was, to show their feelings in quite the same way. In ending with this powerful image, we are reminded once again how France is – and is not – exceptional.

'The Uncanny Power of Literature': How and Why the French Became French

In November 2018, Emmanuel Macron attended a G-20 summit in Buenos Aires, while the *gilets jaunes* protests back home were erupting. During the proceedings, he broke away from the diplomatic gathering to meet with a group of Argentinian writers at a popular bookshop, El Ateneo, in the host nation's capital. There, the discussion that day ranged over the 'infinite and inexhaustible' sources of imagination in Latin American literature, and Macron made a promise that he would help publish the personal diary of the Argentine author Jorge Luis Borges (1899–1986) in France. Afterwards he returned to the 'grind' of the G-20 summit, calling his spell of truancy 'an enchanted break' from the drudgery of his day job. And, as he bade the writers farewell, he made another promise: 'Once I will be done with all that [he meant his day job], I will come back to the truth.'[1]

One cannot imagine Angela Merkel, the German chancellor, or Theresa May, the British prime minister at the time, still less Donald Trump, all of whom were at the summit, making that sort of excursion, or those sorts of promises. We have to assume – in this media-cynical world – that Macron, who has made it known that he keeps a copy of Stendhal's *Le Rouge et le noir* with him at all times, did what he did because he really enjoyed his outing, and not because it offered a convenient opportunity for an educated high-profile Frenchman to live up to the stereotype of the French as more civilised than the rest of us. It did his prospect of re-election in 2022 no harm.

Michel Houellebecq's 2015 novel, *Submission*, is ostensibly about the French general election of 2022, when he imagines not Macron but a Muslim government being voted into office. However, the book is also as much about the idea that literature 'is *the major art form* of a Western civilisation now ending before our very eyes'. 'Like literature,' Houellebecq writes in *Submission*, 'music can overwhelm you with sudden emotion, can move you to absolute sorrow or ecstasy; like literature, painting has the power to astonish, and to make you see the world through fresh eyes. But only literature can put you in touch with another human spirit, as a whole, with all its weaknesses and grandeurs, its limitations, its pettinesses, its obsessions, its beliefs; with whatever it finds moving, interesting, exciting or repugnant. Only literature can give you access to a spirit from beyond the grave ... to love a book is, above all, to love its author: we want to meet him again, we want to spend our days with him.' Elsewhere, in mentioning the work of Zola, Huysmans, Maupassant, Barbey and Bloy, he refers to 'the uncanny power of literature'.[2]

Houellebecq is not easily assimilable. A misanthrope in general, he has admitted to being 'probably' Islamophobic, based on his view that Islam is the 'dumbest' religion ('*la religion la plus conne*') and the 'most dangerous', but he claims he is not against Muslims. In 2002 he faced trial on charges of inciting racial hatred in a press interview but was acquitted in court.

Generally regarded as the *enfant terrible* of modern French fiction-writers, the character Houellebecq gives himself, as the protagonist and author of *Submission*, who makes the claim for the uncanny power of literature, is an academic, an authority on J. K. Huysmans, whose *À rebours* was covered in chapters 32 and 37, a book which Houellebecq describes as 'unrivalled even today in all of literature'. *Submission* is itself a form of *À rebours*, which is not easy to translate, but which we saw in chapter 32 means in English something like 'against the grain', or 'against nature', in the sense of rubbing a cat's fur the wrong way, or to run counter to the general trend, or to surprise an enemy from behind. In *Submission*, France certainly goes against the general trend of the country's history – under

Houellebecq's guidance it turns its back on the cultural achievements that have made the country what it is, and surrenders all too willingly to alien forces. Houellebecq's protagonist/character describes himself as a 'Huysmanist', not quite a humanist, and means that he too turns against the familiar strengths and traditions of French culture and converts to Islam and writes *against*.[3]

This way out is not so special because much of French literature has been writing against. But it does lead us neatly into our concluding remarks about the real nature of French exceptionalism, and returns us to the questions and predicaments we began with in the Introduction, but which we have been rubbing up against throughout the book.

In the most recent decades, many historians – French and non-French – have tended to conclude that 'French exceptionalism' is no longer all that useful as a heuristic device. It has been argued more or less energetically that the country is not more Jacobin or *dirigiste* than anyone else, is not more politically polarised or confrontational than other nations, is not more revolutionary, that the tradition of revolution no longer has a dynamic of its own, if it ever did, that the crucial role played by ordinary people in France's history no longer separates it out, that it no longer presents itself as a model for the rest of the world, that it no longer gives a primacy to politics any more than anyone else, that it no longer claims for itself a mission to civilise the world, or that its struggles point the way for humanity as a whole.[4] Intellectuals and intellectuality, they say, may have been a French characteristic after the Dreyfus affair and the Resistance in the Second World War but those circumstances have long since been over. France, they insist, despite the fact that there are 2,000 book prizes awarded there each year, no longer claims to be the home of a *pensée unique*, and its own claim, that the country *is* exceptional, can now be dismissed as merely a patriotic form of arrogance. Exceptionality, they conclude, is no longer an established feature of French identity. Not all historians or other commentators share this view, but it comes close to being the orthodoxy.

Yet it remains the case that it was Macron, and no one else, who played truant from the G-20 summit. It will be now argued that this episode was not a maverick one-off and that there is still something to French exceptionalism and that it runs through the preceding chapters with a definitive consistency.

A CHARACTERISTICALLY AND UNIQUELY FRENCH FIGURE

Houellebecq's perspective about the uncanny power of literature is itself particularly French and echoes many episodes in this narrative. The very conception of the Académie française was to support the primacy and purity of the French language. Throughout the book, conversation has been held as the defining characteristic of the salons. We saw in chapter 21 that the 'literification' of French culture took place on the eve of the Revolution. Napoleon told Mme de Staël's son that he well recognised that literature could be politicised as easily as any other activity. In the nineteenth century, the salons and the Goncourt brothers did all they could to prevent literature from being degraded by the influence of the market. In the First World War, science was subordinated to literature in schools. In the Second World War, Otto Abetz, the Nazis' ambassador to Paris, argued that France's three powers were 'banking, the Communist Party and the *Nouvelle Revue française*'.[5] Marc Fumaroli argues that only the French language can truly convey happiness and intelligence on earth. Pascale Casanova argued for a world civilisation of literature and literary values, headquartered in Paris. Pierre Nora contends that 'words' are one of the defining characteristics of French history and feels that the 'spectacular bereavement of literature' has brought about a new historical turning point. Writers as varied as Jean Guéhenno, Jean-Paul Sartre and even General de Gaulle subscribed to the view that, as Pierre Drieu La Rochelle phrased it, 'writers [in France] have duties and rights above those of others'. Between them, these writers and other observers/authorities have identified a *literary culture* that is the very embodiment of Frenchness – and which, as we shall now see, explains so much else.

One academic who has explored this at length is Priscilla Parkhurst Ferguson, emerita professor at Columbia University in New York, who parallels Houellebecq's argument, adding that she thinks the uncanny power of literature in particular helps explain a great deal about the French way of life, French culture, and why it is exceptional. Ferguson's explicit argument, following these others, is that French writers 'have constructed a certain notion of France', one that transcends politics and national developments, and that 'the crucial identification of Frenchness with the French language confirms literature as the privileged source of a certain national consciousness'.[6] There is in France, she says, the institution of 'public writer' that is a characteristically and indeed uniquely French figure. 'Only France has a literary culture that elects the writer as spokesman and invests literature with such powers.'[7]

As a sociologist as well as a scholar of French, Professor Ferguson (who is perhaps better known by her earlier name of Priscilla Parkhurst Clark) is alive to the fact that writers in France drew and draw their prestige from their association with upper-class milieux and government help. She observes, for example, that French banknotes give pride of place to literary figures, that street prostitutes paid off the police with '*des Pascal*' – street slang for the 500-franc note (when francs existed) that bore Blaise Pascal's mournful image. She notes an advertisement for Johnnie Walker Red Label whisky that plays on Stendhal's novel *Le Rouge et le Noir,* President Macron's favourite, the advert leaving off the words 'Le Rouge' and replacing them with '*Sans Rouge rien ne vas plus*': 'Without the red, nothing works'. She notes that Victor Hugo's name is all over the streets and squares of Paris.

Ferguson points to how the Académie française exemplifies a characteristic mingling of writers and the upper classes 'in and around a central cultural institution'. Academicians are *still* recruited from all the traditional sectors of the upper classes – the aristocracy, the clergy, the military – 'to which have been added the new aristocracies of academics, savants, and politicians'. The long-term norms of the lycées have always met and fostered the *expectations* of French literary culture. Even for students who specialised in mathematics and philosophy, literary studies were compulsory. Traditionally, French was taught through translation from Latin, which, along with the general culture in which it was immersed, united the upper classes even as it distinguished them from everyone else. This created a public for literature that extended – importantly and uniquely – *beyond readers* to include a much larger population that might only be 'touched' by these institutions. Ferguson notes how President Valéry Giscard d'Estaing confessed he would have preferred a career in literature to politics had he been sure of emulating Flaubert or Maupassant.[8] President Mitterrand wrote one of his twelve books while he was in office. Even de Gaulle wanted to be known for his writing style and only a French president, in declining Jean-Paul Sartre's request to hold a war crimes tribunal in France, would address his reply, without irony, as de Gaulle did, '*Cher Maître*'.[9] Macron is conforming to a tradition among French leaders.

An impressive line of writers has been directly involved in politics. Public writers 'conflate' their social and literary commitments, and in doing so acquire a symbolic power that makes them both insider and outsider. 'No British or German or American academy matches the prestige of the Académie française; patronage of letters never became in other countries what it has been in France.'[10]

In the early years, poetry and drama had the edge over the novel and what we now call non-fiction. This was more suited to aristocratic tastes, being shorter and more evanescent, and so fitted snugly into a salon environment. Patronage mattered because authors were paid badly, if at all – Descartes, for example, received 200 copies of *Discours de la méthode* as sole payment for his great effort. Books in the *ancien régime* rarely sold more than 2,000 copies. Kings knew this and made it clear that culture very much concerned the state, paying many pensions, as listed in earlier chapters.

The status of the writer in France was privileged from the beginning. Alone among the arts, literature permitted access to the salons because literary works were never considered incompatible with nobility, unlike painting, and writers needed no training beyond a general education. The salons enabled talented writers from outside the aristocracy to associate themselves with their social 'betters' and allowed those 'betters' to associate themselves with new ideas. Added to which, there was no shortage of aristocratic writers (as Mathieu Marraud's statistical survey made clear in chapter 21). The symbol of these ties, as Émile Gassier pointed out, was the Académie française itself.[11] It marked social as well as intellectual distinction.

More than this, writers lacked a specific 'literary consciousness' because they were not a distinct occupational group. Writing was a form suited for consumption in Paris salons or at the court (and at Sceaux). Not all genres were suited to salon presentation, but a number were: poetry was read aloud; plays were premiered in private readings before wider public performance; maxims and portraits, often composed on the spur of the moment (or it was pretended that they were), enjoyed the limelight for several years. There was a harmonious ideal, particularly French – namely, the integration of literary and elite social activities.[12] In this environment, writing was not only an intellectual/artistic activity, it was a social activity too.

As cultural authority was gradually removed from Versailles to the salons of Paris, the Republic of Letters became a force to be reckoned with, as underlined by the extension of censorship and the imprisonment of writers. In the late eighteenth century, the *philosophes* in the salons led the growth of public opinion, and as Napoleon also quickly grasped, politics entered all discussions, whatever the notional subject (chapter 27). As Mathieu Marraud put it: 'More and more the act of writing became a means of contestation.' Ferguson is more specific: 'Politics enters French literature with éclat, never to leave it.'[13] Added to which, the *philosophes* brought in not just a political sensibility, but a social commitment and a critical mode – this too arrived to stay. *Social class*, *politics* and the *critical spirit* characterise French literature and give it its distinctive edge. Only in France could critics such as Charles-Augustin Sainte-Beuve and Jules Lemaître occupy such an exalted position.

Writing in France was also influenced by the increased centralisation of French society under the Revolution and Napoleon. Paris became the overwhelming cultural centre, and the close proximity of so many notable personages made conflicts more personal – and therefore more confrontational – than elsewhere. Such was the effect of the concentration of talent in such a small space that James Fenimore Cooper (1789–1851) remarked that 'great men were so common that one did not even bother to turn around in the street to take a look'.[14]

In the nineteenth century France had a hybrid system that also aided the emergence of a distinctive literary culture. Patronage in the salons continued alongside the market and, most characteristically, *in opposition* to it, helping to shape an adversarial literary culture. One of the things that follows from this is that what we might call high-brow non-commercial taste flourished in France more than elsewhere. This in turn provoked the development of literary cenacles, more militant groups often wedded to one approach above others and closed to outsiders, and further adding to the adversary mindset.

The salons in the nineteenth century sustained their influence partly by maintaining an association with *le monde*, and likewise jealously cementing an association with the Académie française. The prestige of the academy and its symbolic connection with the past – dating back to the seventeenth century – its identification with the great classics of that time, its sheer *durability* (notwithstanding its closure and reopening in the Revolutionary and Napoleonic years, which only made it a 'national treasure' alongside Versailles, Notre-Dame and the Louvre), meant that it acquired an authority unmatched in a country where political regimes changed with such frequency. It is *this* which ensured the unrivalled prestige of the Académie française and the salons and helps explain why they mattered and endured.

This is brought into relief by the Académie des sciences, which had been founded in 1666 and therefore might be seen as nearly as venerable as the Académie française. But no. At the end of the eighteenth century the Abbé Maury summed up prejudices that would be shared widely. 'The Académie française alone was esteemed in France and gave real status. No one thought much of the Académie des sciences ... D'Alembert was ashamed of being a member ... At the Académie française we looked on the members of the Académie des sciences as our valets.'[15]

Not until 1862 did the Académie française elect a novelist *as* a novelist. Others who had written novels, such as Victor Hugo, had been elected but for work in the more established realms of poetry and drama – it had taken 200 years for the Académie to recognise the novel as a legitimate genre worthy of consideration. No naturalist was ever elected, one reason being that the Académie operated like a salon: it did not bestow elevated status but *required* it. The political conservatism of the Académie reflected the conservatism of *le monde*.

As the nineteenth century wore on, of course, the salons were forced to recognise that there were other literary institutions out in the world, even as they continued to oppose these new developments. But this meant that the various strands of literary life had a self-assured self-consciousness in France that rarely existed elsewhere. The best salons remained intellectually open, receptive to any subject that was felt to reflect *l'esprit français*, whereas the cenacles were invariably closed to ideological outsiders.

Ferguson argues that the Académie Goncourt – established in 1902 – formalised the cenacle much as the Académie française gave the *esprit de salon* an organisational base. But the Académie Goncourt was also created to counter the market, whose effects on taste and education the two brothers deplored. They made it clear that 'to have the honour of belonging to this Society [the jury who selected the prize-winners] it will be necessary to be a man of letters. Nothing but a man of letters, we will accept neither great lords nor politicians.' Very soon the Académie Goncourt was spoken of as 'an academy that would revenge and console the unfortunates who never made it into the Académie française'. Despite its success (winning the Prix Goncourt even today means a book will sell 200,000 copies), the Académie Goncourt underscored the greater prestige of the Académie française.

Unlike cenacles, which in some senses were 'professional dinners', salons mixed writers and the upper classes more generally, and were gatherings of friends and sympathisers rather than masters and disciples. That was their strength, the idea of the salon being also to test ideas and to receive criticism in a helpful environment. Even when more writers from the lower classes began to shine, the bourgeois and upper classes still held sway as the nineteenth century progressed. Gautier took care to point out that his fellow 'bohemians' were 'all from good families' and so the upper-class character of French literary life was never fully sacrificed.[16]

The exceptional fact was that traditional institutions like the salons and the Académie française allowed writers to conceive of their works as *other* than commercial properties. Balzac was just one who refused to think of himself in this – as he saw it – one-dimensional way. He went after market success, but he also played the salons and tried to evoke the interest of the academy.

A GENERAL – AND CRITICAL – INTELLECTUAL CULTURE

French literature, as Anatole France and Priscilla Parkhurst Ferguson both point out, can boast no Dante, Shakespeare, Cervantes or Goethe, 'no "universal genius" who', as Ferguson phrases it, 'both subsumes and stands apart from the entire tradition'. But, according to Edith Wharton, 'French culture is the most homogenous and uninterrupted culture the world has known.'[17] Building on this, Ferguson argues – as Guéhenno did before her – that it is the literary *tradition* of France, rather than any individual writer, which embodies the 'incomparable personality' of the nation. The French language – with its alleged clarity – is seen in France as a value in itself, as perfect in ways that other languages are not, reflecting most of all the spirit of Descartes, an *esprit de géométrie*, meaning a sense of order, system, logic, a respect for rules, based on Jean Chapelain's expressed idea in the seventeenth century (chapter 1) that 'pleasure is the product of order and verisimilitude'.

No one insists on the pre-eminence of the French language more than Marc Fumaroli. It was, he insists, the exigencies of style that constituted its universal prestige, 'whereas the English that prevails today the world over is a vernacular and technological language dispensing with style altogether ... Demanding of its speakers no commitment either in the manner or the matter of their utterance, that constitutes the essence of its power of attraction. The soft "transparency" of this global English is the contrary of the precise and lively claret required by the French of the Enlightenment, even when it was spoken by Robespierre, whose bearing was impeccable, whose hair was always freshly powdered, whose diction and manners were those of a courtier.'

What we have lost, Fumaroli says, is what the French language of the past excelled in, 'notably the intimate genres, the letter, the diary, the poetry of occasion, memoirs, and that oral literary genre that is conversation between friends ... It was altogether different from communicating. It was entering into company.'

If we wish to participate in the 'banquet of minds of which France was long the expert hostess', he says, 'then we must shake off the "leaden cloaks" of our modern forms of mass communication ...

Anyone who discovers that he wants before dying to participate in a civilised conversation, the image on this earth of *nostra conversatio quæ est in cœlis*, does so in French.'[18]

Like Fumaroli, Ferguson argues that the French have an 'intellectualised view of literature', one that places a premium on what they call the *esprit critique*, the practice of criticism itself, the idea and belief that all writers must also be critics. 'The association between French "genius" and criticism', she tells us, 'amounted to an elective affinity; for many the critical spirit *was* the French spirit.' (As we saw in chapter 46, Sartre was just one who argued that critics led 'fuller' lives.) She draws support from Ernest Renan, who regarded the Académie française as 'a guardian of useful prejudices', its role being to resist rather than create, and to 'resist in the name of a certain intellectual conception of literature and of culture'. And as Renan went on to say: 'The French genius is certainly the most complete, the most balanced and the most able to create a form of general, intellectual culture.' Matthew Arnold likewise singled out the Académie française as the 'intellectual conscience' of France and at the same time identified the French genius as a 'critical spirit that produced an essentially critical literature'.[19]

In the *ancien régime* the sophisticated public did not compartmentalise its reading. Descartes was read alongside Molière, Buffon and Beaumarchais, on the premise that anything that was properly presented could be understood by the educated public, reinforcing the *philosophes*' bias against specialised discourse, the French maintaining a predilection for literary forms that replicated salon conversational exchanges. Even today, Ferguson says (the paperback of her book was published in 1991), French literary culture easily incorporates specialised disciplines into a more general intellectual exchange, via the process of *haute vulgarisation*. One result is that French literary culture brings together the narrow world of science or scholarship with the broader world 'of beyond'.[20]

WRITERS AS THE 'LEADERS OF HUMANITY'

As so many have said before her, Ferguson concludes that conversation in France goes beyond mere talk or *bavardage*. She goes so far as to say that French conversation prizes brilliance of performance over profundity of thought. The French speaker knows he or she is surrounded by jealous rivals. Mme de Staël spoke of the 'aggressive sociability' of literary France, while Hippolyte Taine characterised literary life in his era as a 'daily duel'.

In France an elite public always played an important role in literary life, and as a result this educated public made literature more than literary because in France, as Ferguson puts it, 'literature and society seem to go together', making French literature a privileged social activity. Matthew Arnold, again, recognised this: 'The great place of France in the world is due to her eminent gift for the social life and development, and this gift French literature has accompanied, fashioned, perfected, and continues to reflect. This gives a special interest to French literature, and an interest independent of the excellence of individual French writers, high as that often is.'[21]

It was the Enlightenment which made literature the most general medium through which knowledge could be diffused. Literature took in whole territories of science and subsumed erudition of all sorts. 'With his knowledge of literature – French, classical, Italian, and English – and of philosophy, history, theology, mathematics, and science, Voltaire felt compelled and fully authorised to speak on every front.' For writers like Voltaire and, later, Balzac, their sheer range of knowledge encouraged them to consider themselves leaders of humanity who were equal, even superior, to statesmen.[22]

One of the important features of literature, especially visible in France – and perhaps not enough is made of this – is that the novel's holistic view of life was a direct challenge to the fragmentation inherent in specialised knowledge. Literature has a unique capacity to integrate every other intellectual pursuit, making the writer the quintessential intellectual by virtue of an occupation that is able to confront the clash between the particular and the universal. In an age of ever greater specialisation – fragmentation – literature at its best remains a *general* medium, drawing part of its strength from its ability to situate and synthesise the more general relevance of specialist knowledge.[23]

Ferguson ends her *tour d'horizon* (and *tour de force*) by noting the relatively curious fact that, in France until recently, and in contradistinction to Germany, the UK and the USA, the university 'stood apart' from general intellectual life. It was the locus of special- ised intellectual activity but, as this book has shown, it was hardly ever central (chapter 41, for example).[24] Nevertheless, since the death of Sartre, novelists and poets have given way to historians and phi- losophers, so this could be another area where French exceptionalism is dying. And yet, literary prizes still flourish (more than 2,000), and the Académie française is still 'the guardian of useful prejudices'. Film directors, women and people of colour have been admit- ted among the Immortals, and in 1975 the television programme *Apostrophes*, a remarkably successful book-review show, adapted the salon idea to the mass media age. The host's explanation of the success of the programme – quite different from anything anywhere else in the world – was that 'the French like to talk a lot'. The French, he said, typically 'savour the sociability, the contentiousness, the love of conversation, the mixture of literature with politics, with science and scholarship . . . the spectacle of French literary culture on parade'.

Serious literature, Ferguson concludes, is like *haute cuisine* (another of her interests) in that it is carried out by and for elites, and both practices still matter in France – in this sense a national culture does exist there that differs from elsewhere. Above all, and arguably most important, up against the endlessly complex and multi-faceted nature of modern [scientific] society, 'French literary culture provides a means to combat the anomie that fragmentation so often betokens'.[25]

This analysis helps to explain why French culture is what it is, and why and how it differs from other cultures. To an important extent it really does stem from the initial decision by the Marquise de Rambouillet to break away from the court in the early seventeenth century and set up her own salon – a rival 'court', a rival (but not at that stage a competitor) to the king's – that extended the act of *patronage*, which was to have such far-reaching consequences, albeit consequences neither she nor her immediate entourage could foresee.

Catherine de Vivonne was no 'intellectual' as we understand the term today. She was as interested in practical jokes as she was in books or philosophy (not that there is anything necessarily wrong with that). But her salon – small in comparison with the court – offered an intimate alternative form of sociability that, as we saw in the case of Simon Arnauld, was intoxicating. And, in an age before radio, before cinema, before television – but not before theatre – books, the written word and the spoken word were irresistible entertainment. Sociability in a salon offered a relatively intimate and safe space for gossip, chatter, banter, flirting, showing off, but also learning new things – all well away from the formal rigorous etiquette of the court. No one in the early salons appears to have expected too much from them but there seems little doubt that, as for Simon Arnauld, they quickly caught on as an appealing alternative way of life.

It was, it goes without saying, an age when the aristocracy were far better educated than the other classes in society, except for the clergy, and possibly the military. It was therefore natural for the salons, which offered by definition a different way of life to the court, to align themselves with the creative and innovative elements of society, which were anxious for recognition so that, as the salons caught on and grew in number and stature, salon society acquired its distinctive cachet, as a mix of aristocratic finery and fashion, and creative, artistic and intellectual brilliance.

What then happened was fortuitous. The Fronde played its part, in epitomising and solidifying the break between the Crown and the aristocracy, and by eventually driving the king to Versailles and, to an extent, freeing Paris to play host to the salons. In chapters 8 and 9 we saw that most aspects of what we might call the characteristic 'French style' – *haute cuisine, haute coiffure, haute couture*, fine wines, fine furniture – came on stream more or less together in the latter few decades of the seventeenth century, just when the salons were finding their feet, and sophisticated entertainment was in the process of formation. Not only that: this was the great era of French classicism. It was in the century 1618–1715 that modern France found its feet, when intellectual, artistic, fashionable France coalesced into a recognisable culture. It was a mix of the aristocratic and the creative elements that occurred nowhere else to the same extent, and was encouraged, enabled and facilitated by the phenomenon of the salons.

The two most important characteristics of the salons were that the great majority of them were organised by women, and – second – that they mixed the aristocracy with individuals of creative genius.

This is an important reason why, to return to the discussion in the Introduction, intellect is held in higher regard in France than elsewhere – it has for centuries been associated with the social elite. This is where the French love of grandeur comes from – intellect was associated with the grandest elite of what was, in the seventeenth and early eighteenth centuries, the grandest nation. It is why in French culture we have the prominent concept of *hauteur* – *haute cuisine*, *haute coiffure*, *haute couture*: the presence of the aristocracy in the fashionable salons of Paris brought with it the very idea of high excellence. This is where the French intellectual self-assurance comes from, being always associated with the aristocratic elite; this is where the taste for collective redemption comes from, awkward ethical and philosophical matters being sorted out in agreeable, private surroundings. This is why the philosophical spirit is valued in France more than elsewhere – the salons allowed its free expression, again in agreeable private surroundings. This is why intellectuals have mattered more in France than elsewhere – it is the salons that sparked the critical spirit in France, the love of abstract argument, the combative spirit in artistic and intellectual affairs, unburdened by the need to work. This intellectual self-assurance helped create the idea that the France of the salons was a beacon to others, that it was a form of civilisation that ought to be spread to the rest of the world. It is due to the salons that conversation, wit and refined language are such a characteristic of the traditional French way of life. The salons also fostered and embellished the practice of gallantry. Many of the *salonnières* were no longer young and seductive when they opened their salons but even so relations between the sexes had to be negotiated, and the sexual make-up of salons was important to their success and longevity.

It is worth repeating here the words of the British historian J. H. Plumb: 'Too much attention, it seems to me, is paid to the monopoly of ideas amongst the intellectual giants, too little to their social acceptance.' This too is what has set the French apart – the social acceptance of intellectual matters. The intellectual approach – intellectuality itself – has been far wider among the (social) elite in France than in other countries, and much of that was brought about by life in the salons.

*

Perhaps not enough has been made in these pages of the overlap in the membership of the salons. As we have had cause to remark, there were far more salons than have been covered here. What follows from this is that, although in any one salon a sympathetic environment was the aim, there was, as we have also noted, competition *between* salons, competition for members and what they could offer. This made for progress – in fashions, in ideas, in cuisine, in interior decoration. Salons provided continuity but also measured advances.

Broadly speaking, salons went through at least three major changes throughout their history. Between the middle of the seventeenth century and the Revolution, and the advent of the Enlightenment, philosophy and science were added to the main interests of the first salons – history, poetry, theatricals, maxims, pen portraits of individuals, some discussion of the sexes and their relative relationships (love), and the very early novels. From the Revolution through the early decades of the nineteenth century, salons became both more politically conscious and more politically divided. In the later decades of the nineteenth century, up to the First World War, as the political divisions in France became ever sharper, the salons – to an extent – played a role in preventing these divisions becoming even worse.

Nor should we overlook the fact that, in being the location of elite sociability, French intellectual and artistic life was, if not immune, then shielded from the modernising effects of the marketplace. This is another reason why France has always been a more 'high-brow' nation than others, why intellect has always played more of a role there than anywhere else: salons preserved – again to an extent – high-brow taste.

It is also largely thanks to the salons that literature became the wider, more 'general' subject that Priscilla Parkhurst Ferguson identifies it as in France – the belief that anyone who was educated could understand anything important from literature to philosophy to science was part and parcel of salon culture. It is why *haute cuisine*, *haute couture*, *haute coiffure*, interior decoration, all the pleasures of the table, go together in France and at a 'high' level. Perhaps we need a phrase along the lines of '*haute écriture*'. Marc Fumaroli certainly speaks of what he calls '*haute vulgarisation*'.[26] *Hauteur*, grandeur, is a final lineament of Frenchness.

THE SOFT POWER OF THE SALONS

Alongside these changes, three other long-term effects of salon life are worth highlighting. Throughout the period covered in this book, music has featured strongly in salon life. The salon contribution to French musical life can hardly be overstated – the relationship of the Paris Conservatoire to the salons was not unlike that between the Académie française and the salons: they were a convenient and efficient way for fledgling composers and instrumentalists, often newly graduated, to become more widely known.

Second, we can return to the fact that French history has been marked by a series of humiliating defeats, but also by remarkable recoveries. The salons were partly – not wholly, but partly – responsible for these recoveries, what de Gaulle called France's genius for renewal, in that, at times of crisis, they provided venues where people could congregate, where rivals could meet on territory that may not have been totally neutral but was more neutral than elsewhere, and those rivals could at least attempt to sort out a way forward, because the salons were, in effect, rehearsal rooms for new, innovative ideas, where would-be leaders could try out their thoughts in relative safety and privacy, and receive encouragement and, where necessary, correction. Salons were places where the wounds of defeat could be licked away from the public eye and where new thoughts about the different ways ahead – not necessarily political or military – could be aired. Where adjustment could be conceived and debated.

Moreover, the close association between the salons and the Académie française, most notably its sheer longevity at the pinnacle of prestige, kept the salons near the centre of all forms of soft power – political, intellectual, artistic, social. It was one of the reasons why the universities in France did not have the 'presence' in French affairs that they have had in other comparable countries. Neither Zola nor Gide, to give just two examples, ever held a university position. *Le monde* was always more worldly than the university campus. This was the difference between the Left Bank and the Sorbonne.

Then there is the fact that the French have a more or less holistic view of the arts and sciences, whereas in the Anglo-Saxon nations (the United Kingdom, Germany, the United States), a 'two cultures' mentality still persists, even today.

Finally, the narrative outlined here should surely put to bed the perennial carping by some historians that the business of the salons was 'trivial' and superficial, hardly worth taking seriously, and that the female *salonnières* were at root responsible for this. It is true that, besides conversation, salons offered opportunities for gambling, dancing, singing, drinking and eating, flirting and showing off. Women were usually in the minority but there was often a sexual frisson in the atmosphere, which no doubt added to the allure of salon life. At the same time, salons were in many cases arenas of sexual toleration, at times even refuges for homosexuals, and although this may not have been spoken about openly, it was widely known and accepted and in part responsible for the reputation Paris gained for being not just a city of sexual opportunity but of sexual tolerance. Voltaire would appear to have been right when he said the French were a more sociable people than others, better at it and better for it.

Above all, each of the *salonnières* considered here was formidable in her own right and, although females in France did not get the vote until 1945, each fashioned an interesting and satisfying life for herself that pushed forward the intellectual or artistic or political life of France. Each led a life based on more than motherhood.

Paris in the late nineteenth century was described as 'The Capital of Power and Desire' and that is true enough. Desire runs through these pages, through the great chain of salons, more obvious at some times than at others, but never far away. And this too helps show how female-led salons marked the French way of life: intellect, conviviality, the sensual and social pleasures of art and the table, political power, gallantry and sexual adventure, all go together in a full life – what else *is* a full life?

In 2021 Michel Onfray, a prolific philosopher and robust critic of Freud, based in Caen, released *L'Art d'être français*, 'The Art of Being French'. In his view that art depends on six building blocks: the epicurean but truculent appetite of Rabelais, the 'clear, simple and droll laicity' of Montaigne, and the deft essay style, the critical methodicalness of Descartes, the practical irony of Voltaire, the 'incandescent' charm of intelligent conversation sparked by

Marivaux's plays ('manifest in the salons' with women 'taking a major role') and the volcanic talents of Victor Hugo, combining politics, theatre, poetry and novels (the French word 'romancier' has a better ring to it) into one almighty 'republican earthquake.' And he can't resist adding: 'Hugo writes against English capitalism', which Onfray sees as, combined with republicanism, eventually leading to the *créolisation* of the world, a 'sublime catastrophe' against which the French, he insists, are exceptionally placed to take a stand.[27]

This may be attributing too much to salons. But we began this narrative with the striking story of Simon Arnauld arriving back in Paris in 1665 after a year in the provinces, and rushing to Mme du Plessis-Guénégaud's salon without even changing out of his dirty travelling clothes, so excited was he to be back from exile and again in the swim. We can end our story in 1859, *two whole centuries later*, when Théophile Gautier returned to Paris from a long trip to Russia. That evening he too turned up at Apollonie Sabatier's salon in the rue Frochot, again without even changing out of his travelling clothes, 'startling and delighting the other guests by his sudden appearance in a fur hat and voluminous overcoat'. Could anything better illustrate the intoxicating nature of the French salons or underline the part they played in originating and helping to shape the exceptional nature of the French way of life and the French mind?

ACKNOWLEDGEMENTS

In the Introduction I explained the immediate influences that sparked the idea for this book. But there was also a deeper context. From 1984 until 2018, I lived for part of each year in a lovely village in the pre-Alps in the south of France, a few kilometres outside Grasse. Quite by chance, the village was also the holiday home of Jean Lartéguy, a soldier and well-known writer, who had escaped France in 1942 and, after spending time in a Spanish jail, joined the Free French forces and fought in Italy and the Vosges, winning two Croix de guerre and the Légion d'honneur. After the war, Jean worked as a war correspondent for *Paris-Match*, covering hostilities in Korea (where he was wounded), Israel, Vietnam, Latin America (where he met Che Guevara) and Algeria. By the time I met him in Saint-Cézaire-sur-Siagne, and we became friends, he was best known for his two novels about Algeria, *The Centurions* and *The Praetorians*.

But Jean, and his wife Thérèse Lauriol, in this small mountain village, as beautiful as an opera set, had their own salon, as only the French know how. In their splendid house, with its magnificent oak dominating the patio, and overlooking the dramatic gorge of the Siagne and beyond, deep into the *département* of Var, they imported some of the greatest writers, journalists, politicians, civil servants, theatre people, academics and television commentators that France had to offer. It was like the Mediterranean branch of the Left Bank. These gatherings were glittering, but they were private affairs, so I won't identify the people (though one or two are included in the alphabetical list below), but it was the discussions around the

Lartéguy table that really drew me into the French mindset, and I began to appreciate how it differed – and still differed, then – from its Anglo-Saxon equivalent. Jean died in 2011 when he was considering a critical look at Vichy France. I'm not sure he ever started that book, but he certainly started something in me, *The French Mind* being the eventual result. My first thank-yous are to his memory and to Thérèse.

Thérèse is in fact herself an accomplished translator, as well as an author, and the translators of the many books referenced here are my second set of thank-yous. Translation is such an underappreciated art but how many authors could shine without it? Arthur Goldhammer is probably the doyen of translators, and the best-known, four times winner of the French–American translation prize, but I include all the others mentioned in these references in this encomium.

That raises another way in which the French are exceptional. London, where I live, is home to one of the greatest libraries in the world, if not the greatest. The London Library is not the largest library in the world, nor the oldest, but it has been in existence since 1841, established on the initiative of Thomas Carlyle, when he couldn't find a seat in the British Library. Since then, it has been collecting books in English, French, Italian, German, Spanish and Russian, to the point where it now houses more than a million volumes. But what makes it special is that almost all of that million *are on open access*. You can browse the shelves to your heart's content. How many other libraries offer such an intellectual adventure?

With its collecting history, the catalogue of the library is of particular interest in these acknowledgements. Here are the number of titles the library holds on various countries:

France	39,027
Germany	23,891
Italy	19,329
Russia	12,961
Spain	8,106
USA	7,467
China	6,524

As this shows, France leads the way comfortably. Many of these titles are in the English language, and this shows another way in which the French are exceptional: on this count there would appear to be more books about France than about any other country. A subset of these titles, especially since the Second World War, are by Americans, and this explains why it may seem to some readers that a surprising number of the references which follow are in English. Some, of course, are translations of original French titles, but there is a strong representation of original, English-language research-based books by Americans, the fascination of France and the French way of life being as strong among them as among anyone, possibly for the reasons outlined in the Introduction. In particular, I would like to thank Faith Beasley at Dartmouth College, Carolyn Lougee Chappell at Stanford, Priscilla Parkhurst Ferguson at Columbia, Elizabeth Goldsmith at Boston, Dena Goodman at Michigan, Daniel Gordon at Massachusetts, Martha Hanna at Colorado, Erica Harth at Brandeis, Steven Kale at Washington State, Joan Landes at Penn State, Sarah Maza at Northwestern, Jolanta Pekacz at Dalhousie and Lisa Tiersten at Barnard College.

The Covid-19 pandemic put paid to a number of planned visits to France and its libraries, and interviews were conducted by phone and email rather than face to face. But that only means I am more than grateful for the understanding and cooperation of Iralia Albani, Jaquine Arnold, Anne d'Asch, Pierre Assouline, John Bachofen, Diane de Beauvau, Gilles Berthoud, Roger Berthoud, Aurelie Bonal, Derek Bormann, Sophie Charbonnel, Dale Coudert, didi Danglejan, Catherine Deen, Laurence Droz-Georget, Roger Duchêne (for his many excellent books), Jane Foster, Louise Frank, Juliana Galvis, Bernard de Ganay, Philippe Garner, Didier Garnier, Jean de Gruchy, Vincent Guy, Noémi Hepp, Ruth Iskin, Richard Kuisel, Howard Leach (US ambassador to France, 2001–5), Gerard Leroux, Ann Manuel, Anne Martin-Fugier, François Mitterrand (for showing me the antiquarian bookshops of the Left Bank), Guislaine Vincent Morland, Ben Murphy, Hélène Nozières, Monique Ogilvie, Isabelle and Douglas Ortmans, Luc Petre, Darian Pictet, Marei Pittner, Michael Pochna, Agnès Poirier, Anna Pojer, Jean-Charles de Ravenal, Jean-François Revel, Jean Ribault, Martine and Edouard de Royère, Gonzague Saint Bris, Assallah Tahir, Antony Terry, Mark Tompkins, Christian Tual, Dominique Tutoni, Robert Vallois,

Marco Vianello-Chiodo, Hugo Vickers, Isabel and Jimmy de Viel-Castel, Ann de Vigier and Jonathan Wadman.

Materials used from earlier books are indicated in the notes. Such errors, solecisms and omissions as remain are the author's responsibility alone.

London, 2021

NOTES

Introduction: The Fascination with France, the French and the French Way of Life

1. Elaine Sciolino, *La Seduction: How the French Play the Game of Life*, New York: Times Books, 2011. Pierre-Louis Colin, *Guide des jolies femmes de Paris*, Paris: Robert Laffont, 2008.
2. Jean-Benoît Nadeau and Julie Barlow, *Sixty Million Frenchmen Can't Be Wrong (Why We Love France but Not the French)*, Napierville, IL: Sourcebooks, 2004.
3. Sudhir Hazareesingh, *How the French Think: An Affectionate Portrait of an Intellectual People*, London: Penguin, 2016.
4. Jean Baudrillard, *Amérique*, Paris: Livre de Poche, 1988.
5. François Furet, Jacques Julliard and Pierre Rosanvallon, *La République du centre: la fin de l'exception française*, Paris: Calmann-Lévy, 1988.
6. Richard Kuisel, *Seducing the French: The Dilemma of Americanization*, Berkeley: University of California Press, 1993; *The French Way: How France Embraced and Rejected American Values and Power*, Princeton, NJ: Princeton University Press, 2011.
7. Robert Tombs and Isabelle Tombs, *That Sweet Enemy: The French and the British from the Sun King to the Present*, London: William Heinemann, 2006.
8. Robert Gildea, *Children of the Revolution: The French 1799–1914*, Cambridge, MA: Harvard University Press, 2008.
9. A very useful introduction to contemporary French historians in English is to be found in: Philip Daileader and Philip Whalen (eds), *French Historians 1900–2000: New Historical Writing in Twentieth-Century France*, Chichester: Wiley-Blackwell, 2010, with essays on forty individuals. But see also Raoul Max Luca da Costa, 'Michel de Certeau: entre a história e a psicanálise', *História da Historiografica*, 5 (10), 2012, which shows his approach and range; Maurice Agulhon, *La République au village: les populations du Var de la Révolution à la Seconde République*, Paris: Plon, 1970; Hazareesingh, *How the French Think*, p. 290.
10. Wolfgang Schivelbusch, *The Culture of Defeat: On National Trauma, Mourning and Recovery*, tr. Jeffrey Chase, London: Granta, 2003.
11. Ibid., p. 2.
12. Ibid., p. 4.
13. Tombs and Tombs, *That Sweet Enemy*, for example, p. 293.
14. Ceri Crossley, *French Historians and Romanticism: Thierry, Guizot, the Saint-Simonians, Quinet, Michelet*, London: Routledge, 1993.
15. Schivelbusch, *The Culture of Defeat*, p. 20.

16. Tombs and Tombs, *That Sweet Enemy*, p. 292.
17. Schivelbusch, *The Culture of Defeat*, pp. 135ff.
18. Ibid. Linda Colley, *Britons: Forging the Nation 1707–1837*, London : Pimlico, 1994, pp. 149, 192, 212 and 352.
19. Schivelbusch, *The Culture of Defeat*, pp. 163ff.
20. Ibid., p. 126.
21. Ibid.
22. Ibid., p. 65, and see pp. 16–17.
23. Jean-Marc Largeaud, *Napoléon et Waterloo: la défaite glorieuse de 1815 à nos jours*, Paris: Boutique de l'histoire, 2006.
24. Published as *A Sentimental Journey through France and Italy*, by 'Mr Yorick', London: T. Becket and P. A. De Hondt, 1768.
25. Quoted in Daniel Gordon, *Citizens without Sovereignty: Equality and Sociability in French Thought 1670–1789*, Princeton, NJ: Princeton University Press, 1994, pp. 72–3.
26. Ibid., p. 74.
27. Ibid.
28. Voltaire, 'Epître dédicatoire à M. Falkner', in *Zaïre*, Paris: E. Leroux, [1732] 1889. p. 22.
29. Schivelbusch, *The Culture of Defeat*, p. 4.
30. Benedetta Craveri, *The Age of Conversation*, tr. Theresa Waugh, New York: New York Review Books, 2005, pp. ix–xv.
31. Ibid., p. 7.
32. Gordon, *Citizens without Sovereignty*, p. 3.
33. Craveri, *The Age of Conversation*, p. 8.
34. Jolanta T. Pekacz, 'The Salonnières and the Philosophes in Old Régime France: The Authority of Aesthetic Judgment', *Journal of the History of Ideas*, 60 (2), 1999, p. 227.
35. Steven Kale, *French Salons: High Society and Political Sociability from the Old Regime to the Revolution of 1848*, Baltimore: Johns Hopkins University Press, 2004, p. 2.
36. Ibid., p. 3.
37. Ibid.
38. Ibid.
39. Ibid., p. 4.
40. Ibid., p. 6.
41. Anne Martin-Fugier, *Les Salons de la IIIe République: arts, littérature, politique*, Paris: Perrin, 2003, pp. 88–91; Marc Fumaroli, *La République des lettres*, Paris: Gallimard, 2015, pp. 171ff.
42. Kale, *French Salons*, pp. 102–3.
43. Dena Goodman, *The Republic of Letters: A Cultural History of the French Enlightenment*, Ithaca, NY: Cornell University Press, 1994, pp. 99, 104, 141–5.
44. Faith Beasley, *Salons, History, and the Creation of 17th-Century France*, Aldershot: Ashgate, 2006, p. 21. A recent French book to address some of these issues, albeit in a narrow time frame, is: *Éliane Viennot. L'Âge d'Or de L'Ordre Masculin: La France, Les femmes et le Pouvoir: 1804-1860*, Paris: CNRS Éditions, 2020, especially chapter 1, 'La Contagion de l'exception française' and chapter 5: 'Légitimer la sujétion des femmes.'
45. Ibid., pp. 27–8.
46. Antoine Lilti, *The World of the Salons: Sociability and Worldliness in Eighteenth-Century Paris*, tr. Lydia G. Cochrane, Oxford: Oxford University Press, 2015; the original French version, *Le Monde des salons: sociabilité et mondanité à Paris au XVIIIe siècle*, Paris: Fayard, 2005, is somewhat longer.
47. Lilti, *The World of the Salons*; see in particular chapters 2 and 3.

48. Beasley, *Salons, History, and the Creation of 17th-Century France*, p. 101. See also: Joan DeJean, *Tender Geographies: Women and the Origins of the Novel in France*, New York: Columbia University Press, 1991, p. 194.

49. Linda Timmermans, *L'Accès des femmes à la culture sous l'Ancien régime*, Paris: Champion Classiques, 2005, especially pp. 95–133; Charles Perrault, *Œuvres posthumes de M. Perrault, de l'Académie francoise avec l'apologie des femmes*, Cologne: Pierre Marteau, 1729; see also Beasley, *Salons, History, and the Creation of 17th-Century France*, pp. 40, 43.

50. Beasley, *Salons, History, and the Creation of 17th-Century France*, p. 70.

51. Ibid., pp. 100–1.

52. Ibid., p. 114.

53. Ibid.

54. Ibid.

55. Ibid., p. 176.

56. Ibid., p. 272.

57. Ibid., pp. 222, 224.

58. Ibid., p. 243.

59. Ibid., p. 210.

60. Ibid., p. 317.

61. Lilti, *The World of the Salons*, especially the Introduction, pp. 1–11.

62. Arno J. Mayer, *La Persistance de l'ancien régime: l'Europe de 1848 à la Grande guerre*, tr. Jonathan Mandelbaum, Paris: Aubier/Flammarion, 2010, pp. 23ff.

63. Ibid., p. 109.

64. Martin-Fugier, *Les Salons de la IIIe République*, p. 7.

65. David A. Bell, *The Cult of the Nation in France: Inventing Nationalism 1680–1800*, Cambridge, MA: Harvard University Press, 2001, pp. 149–52.

66. Ibid., p. 149

Prologue: The Intoxication of Simon Arnauld

1. Benedetta Craveri, *The Age of Conversation*, tr. Theresa Waugh, New York: New York Review Books, 2005, p. 188.

Chapter 1: Catherine de Vivonne, the Blue Room and the Académie française

1. Benedetta Craveri, *The Age of Conversation*, tr. Theresa Waugh, New York: New York Review Books, 2005, p. 4. For the palace itself, see Susan B. Taylor, 'Rambouillet, Château of', *Grove Art Online*, Oxford University Press, 2003.

2. Craveri, *Op. cit.*, p. 4. I have also used Nicole Aronson, *Madame de Rambouillet, ou La Magicienne de la Chambre bleue*, Paris: Fayard, 1988.

3. Craveri, *The Age of Conversation*, p. 28.

4. Ibid., p. 29.

5. Ibid. But see also Aronson, *Madame de Rambouillet*.

6. Craveri, *Op. cit.*, pp. 138–74.

7. W. l. Wiley, *The Formal French*, Cambridge, MA: Harvard University Press, 1967, p. 88.

8. Wiley, Op. cit., p. 90.

9. Nicolas Boileau-Despréaux, *Satires: texte établi et présenté par Charles H. Boudhors*, Paris: Société des belles lettres, 1934; W. L. Wiley, *The Formal French*, Cambridge, MA: Harvard University Press, 1967, p. 88.

10. This is especially clear in Charles Mauron, *L'Inconscient dans l'œuvre et la vie de Racine*, Gap: Ophrys, 1957.

11. Craveri, *The Age of Conversation*, p. 458.

12. Fitzsimmons, *The Place of Words*, p. 4.
13. Ibid., p. 5.
14. Craveri, *The Age of Conversation*, pp. 34, 140; Joan DeJean, *Tender Geographies: Women and the Origins of the Novel in France*, New York: Columbia University Press, 1991, p. 68.
15. Alain Niderst, *Pierre Corneille*, Paris: Fayard, 2006.
16. Craveri, *The Age of Conversation*, pp. 51–7.
17. Charles Clerc, *Un Matamore des lettres: la vie tragi-comique de Georges de Scudéry*, Paris: Spes, 1929.
18. Picard, *Les Salons littéraires et la société française*, p. 94.
19. Ibid., p. 35.
20. Ibid., p. 40. Note also that Craveri used the phrase for the title of her book.
21. Robert A. Schneider, *Dignified Retreat: Writers and Intellectuals in the Age of Richelieu*, Oxford: Oxford University Press, 2019, p. 113. Erica Harth, in *Cartesian Women: Versions and Subversions of Rational Discourse in the Old Regime*, Ithaca, NY: Cornell University Press, 1992, p. 23, says it was in the seventeenth century that bourgeois and nobles first began 'to rub shoulders'.
22. Craveri, *The Age of Conversation*, p. 42.

Chapter 2: A Woman's War: Élisabeth du Plessis-Guénégaud and Blaise Pascal

1. Benedetta Craveri, *The Age of Conversation*, tr. Theresa Waugh, New York: New York Review Books, 2005, p. 22.
2. Ibid., pp. 78–9.
3. Jeanine Delpech, *L'Âme de la Fronde*, Paris: Fayard, 1957, p. 88. See also Craveri, *The Age of Conversation*, p. 81; Joan DeJean, *Tender Geographies: Women and the Origins of the Novel in France*, New York: Columbia University Press, 1991, p. 38; Linda Timmermans, *L'Accès des femmes à la culture sous l'Ancien régime*, Paris: Champion Classiques, 2005, p. 107.
4. Craveri, *The Age of Conversation*, p. 79.
5. Delpech, *L'Âme de la Fronde*, p. 174. Michael Pernot, *La Fronde: 1648-1653*, Paris: Éditions Tallandier, 2019, pp. 168ff.
6. Craveri, *The Age of Conversation*, p. 86. Michel Pernot, *La Fronde: 1648-1653*, Paris: Éditions Tallandier, 2019, p. 168ff.
7. Ibid., p. 88.
8. Ibid., p. 90.
9. For Boileau's preferred literary form, see Nicolas Boileau-Despréaux, *Satires: text établi et présenté par Charles H. Boudhors*, Paris: Société des belles lettres, 1934; W. L. Wiley, *The Formal French*, Cambridge, MA: Harvard University Press, 1967, p. 88.
10. This is again clear in Charles Mauron, *L'Inconscient dans l'œuvre et la vie de Racine*, Gap: Ophrys, 1957; see also Craveri, *The Age of Conversation*, p. 94.
11. David Simpson, 'Blaise Pascal (1623–1662)', *Internet Encyclopedia of Philosophy*, https://iep.utm.edu/pascal-b (accessed 15 July 2021).
12. On the medical aspect of Pascal, see Marc Zanello *et al.*, 'The Mysteries of Blaise Pascal's Sutures', *Child's Nervous System*, 31 (4), 2015, pp. 503–6; Simpson, 'Blaise Pascal'.
13. Simpson, 'Blaise Pascal'.
14. Brought out in Mary Ann Caws, *Blaise Pascal: Miracles and Reason*, London: Reaktion, 2017.
15. H. F. Stewart, *The Heart of Pascal*, Cambridge: Cambridge University Press, 1945.
16. For Pascal's style, see Jacques Attali, *Blaise Pascal, ou Le Génie français*, Paris: Fayard, 2000.
17. Simpson, 'Blaise Pascal'.

18. John J. Conley SJ, *The Other Pascals: The Philosophy of Jacqueline Pascal, Gilberte Pascale Périer, and Marguerite Périer*, Notre Dame: Indiana University Press, 2019.

Chapter 3: Marie de Sévigné, Molière and the Gradations of Love

1. Of the many biographies, I have used Roger Duchêne, *Naissances d'un écrivain: Madame de Sévigné*, Paris: Fayard, 1996; Roger Duchêne, *Madame de Sévigné, ou La Chance d'être femme*, Paris: Fayard, 1982; and Madeleine Sainte-René Taillandier, *Madame de Sévigné et sa fille*, Paris: Grasset, 1938.

2. Benedetta Craveri, *The Age of Conversation*, tr. Theresa Waugh, New York: New York Review Books, 2005, pp. 138–74.

3. Ibid.

4. Ibid., especially p. 166.

5. Antoine Baudeau de Somaize, *Le Dictionnaire des Précieuses*, Paris: Jannet, 1856. With a section on 'the key to the language of the *ruelles*'.

6. Craveri, *The Age of Conversation*, p. 166.

7. Ibid., pp. 175–204.

8. *Lettres choisies de Madame de Sévigné*, with a preface by Charles Boreux, London: Dent, 1906, pp. 94ff; Harriet Ray Allentuch, *Madame de Sévigné: A Portrait in Letters*, Baltimore: Johns Hopkins University Press, 1963. See also Duchêne, *Naissances d'un écrivain*.

9. Craveri, *The Age of Conversation*, p. 166.

10. Duchêne, *Madame de Sévigné*.

11. Madame de Sévigné, *Sevigniana, ou Recueil de pensées ingénieuses, d'anecdotes littéraires, historiques et morales*, Paris: Durand père et fils, 1788.

12. Roger Duchêne, 'Bussy épistolier', in Daniel-Henri Vincent and the Société des amis de Bussy-Rabutin, eds, *Rabutinages* (special edition, 1988).

Chapter 4: Marie-Madeleine de Lafayette, La Rochefoucauld and La Fontaine: Three Literary Revolutions

1. Benedetta Craveri, *The Age of Conversation*, tr. Theresa Waugh, New York: New York Review Books, 2005, p. 196.

2. Roger Duchêne, *Madame de La Fayette: la romancière aux cent bras*, Paris: Fayard, 1988. Also useful: Émile Magne, *Madame de Lafayette en ménage*, Paris: Émile-Paul frères, 1926.

3. The original work is Anne Dacier, *Des causes de la corruption du goust*, Paris: Rigaud, 1714.

4. Linda Timmermans, *L'Accès des femmes à la culture sous l'Ancien régime*, Paris: Champion Classiques, 2005, p. 107.

5. Joan DeJean, *Tender Geographies: Women and the Origins of the Novel in France*, New York: Columbia University Press, 1991, pp. 68, 103.

6. Timmermans, *L'Accès des femmes à la culture sous l'Ancien régime*, pp. 112ff.

7. François, Duc de La Rochefoucauld, *Reflections, or Sentences and Moral Maxims*, tr. J. W. Willis Bund and J. Hain Friswell, London: Sampson Low, Son & Marston, 1871, available at Project Gutenberg, Ebook 9105, p. 6 (of 74), 2013.

8. Ibid.

9. Jean Lafond (ed.), *Moralistes du XVIIe siècle*, Paris: Robert Laffont, 1992, pt 3.

10. La Rochefoucauld, *Reflections*, 8/74.

11. François de La Rochefoucauld, *Réflexions, sentences et maximes morales de La Rochefoucauld*, new ed., Paris: Jannet, 1853. A convenient and witty introduction may be found in Larry F. Norman, review of François Jaouën, 'De l'art de plaire en petits morceaux: Pascal, La Rochefoucauld, La Bruyère', *Modern Philology*, 96

(3), 1999, pp. 387–90.
12. La Rochefoucauld, *Op. cit.*
13. Ibid.
14. Lafond, *Moralistes du XVIIe siècle*, pp. 1161–6, 1238–40.
15. Jean-Pierre Collinet, *Le Monde littéraire de La Fontaine*, Paris: Presses Universitaires de France, 1970. See also Marc Fumaroli, *Le Poète et le roi: Jean de la Fontaine et son siècle*, Paris: Fallois, 1997.
16. For La Fontaine in context, see: Saint-Marc Girardin, *La Fontaine et les fabulistes*, Paris: Michel Lévy, 1867.
17. Racine (Louis), *Bulletin de la Société de l'histoire de France*, 1859, p. 27.

Chapter 5: Magdeleine de Sablé and the *Journal des Savants*, Madeleine de Scudéry and the Tender Game of Love

1. Benedetta Craveri, *The Age of Conversation*, tr. Theresa Waugh, New York: New York Review Books, 2005, p. 168.
2. Ibid., p. 117.
3. W. L. Wiley, *The Formal French*, Cambridge, MA: Harvard University Press, 1967, p. 151.
4. For the state of women in seventeenth-century France, see: Linda Timmermans, *L'Accès des femmes à la culture sous l'Ancien régime*, Paris: Champion Classiques, 2005, passim but especially pt 1, chs 1–6 and pt 2, ch. 6. For widowhood in the seventeenth century, see Joan DeJean, *Tender Geographies: Women and the Origins of the Novel in France*, New York: Columbia University Press, 1991, p. 123. And for women being mocked for both their learning and their ignorance, see Erica Harth, *Cartesian Women: Versions and Subversions of Rational Discourse in the Old Regime*, Ithaca, NY: Cornell University Press, 1992, p. 38. See also Craveri, *The Age of Conversation*, p. 119.
5. Timmermans, *Op cit., passim.*
6. Nicola Ivanoff, *La Marquise de Sablé et son salon*, Paris: Presses modernes, 1927.
7. Ibid., p. 211.
8. The salons in the late seventeenth century were beset by Cartesianism. See Harth, *Cartesian Women*, pp. 61, 64.
9. Ivanoff, *Op. cit*, p. 212.
10. Useful here is Gordon Pocock, *Boileau and the Nature of Neo-classicism*, Cambridge: Cambridge University Press, 1980. Wiley, *The Formal French*, pp. 158–9.
11. Roger Picard, *Les Salons littéraires et la société française 1610–1789*, New York: Brentano's, 1943, p. 112. See also Marc Soriano, *Le Dossier Perrault*, Paris: Hachette, 1972.
12. Georges Mongrédien, *Madeleine de Scudéry et son salon*, Paris: Tallandier, 1946. DeJean, *Tender Geographies*, p. 127.
13. Picard, *Les Salons littéraires et la société française*, p. 77 for the whereabouts of the Scudéry salon.
14. Ibid., pp. 74, 75; DeJean, *Tender Geographies*, p. 64.
15. The other great debate in Mme de Sablière's salon was whether animals had souls. See: Jean de la Fontaine, *Discours à Mme de la Sablière (sur l'âme des animaux)*, Geneva, Droz, 1950.
16. Harth, *Cartesian Women*, p. 56.
17. Ibid., p. 93. Mme de Scudéry felt the salons lent a new dignity to female friendships.
18. A. Steiner, 'Les Idées esthétiques de Mlle de Scudéry', *Romantic Review*, Vol. 16, 1925, p. 174.
19. DeJean, *Tender Geographies*, p. 183. See also Constant Venesoen, *Etudes sur la*

littérature féminine au XVIIe siècle: Mademoiselle de Gourney, Mademoiselle de Scudéry, Madame de Villedieu, Madame de Lafayette, Birmingham, AL: Summa, 1990.

20. Picard, *Les Salons littéraires et la société française*, pp. 98–9.

Chapter 6: The Philosophical Eroticism of Ninon de Lenclos

1. Roger Duchêne, *Ninon de Lenclos: la courtisane du Grand Siècle*, Paris: Fayard, 1984, pp. 22ff; see also Émile Colombey, *Ninon de Lenclos et sa cour*, Paris: Adolphe Delahays, 1854, for colour.
2. Katia Béguin, *Les Princes de Condé: rebelles, courtisans et mécènes dans la France du Grand Siècle*, Seyssel: Champ Vallon, 1999.
3. Duchêne, *Ninon de Lenclos*.
4. Edgar H. Cohen, *Mademoiselle Libertine: A Portrait of Ninon de Lenclos*, London: Cassell, 1971; F. U. Wrangel, *Première visite de Christine de Suède à la cour de France, 1656*, Paris: Firmin-Didot, 1930.
5. For Philippe d'Orléans, Boileau and others in her salon, see Roger Picard, *Les Salons littéraires et la société française 1610–1789*, New York: Brentano's, 1943, p. 138.
6. Bernard le Bovier de Fontenelle, *Conversations on the Plurality of Worlds*, tr. H. A. Hargreaves, Berkeley, CA: University of California Press, 1990.
7. Alain Niderst, *Fontenelle à la recherche de lui-même 1657–1702*, Paris: A.-G. Nizet, 1972. See also Cousin d'Avallon, *Fontenelliana, ou Recueil des bons mots, réponses ingénieuses, pensées fines et délicates de Fontenelle*, Paris: Marchand, 1801. For his relation to Corneille, see Picard, *Les Salons littéraires et la société française*, p. 194, and for his writing as especially accessible to women, see ibid., p. 195.
8. Cousin d'Avallon, *Fontenelliana*.
9. For a fairly recent, and accessible, work on this topic see Lucy Norton (ed. & tr.), *Saint-Simon at Versailles*, new ed., London: Hamish Hamilton, 1980; but also Jean de La Varende, *M. le duc de Saint-Simon et sa comédie humaine*, Paris: Hachette, 1955.
10. Niderst, *Fontenelle à la recherche de lui-même*.
11. Emmanuel Le Roy Ladurie and Jean-François Fitou, *Saint-Simon and the Court of Louis XIV*, tr. Arthur Goldhammer, Chicago: Chicago University Press, 2001.
12. La Varende, *M. le duc de Saint-Simon et sa comédie humaine*, pp. 14, 89.
13. Lenclos's relationship with Voltaire (since he was a child) is discussed in: Philippe Erlanger, *Ninon de Lenclos et ses amis*, Paris: Perrin, 1985.
14. Léon Petit, *La Fontaine de Saint-Évremond, ou La Tentation de l'Angleterre*, Toulouse: Privat, 1953.
15. Duchêne, *Ninon de Lenclos*. See also Colombey, *Ninon de Lenclos et sa cour*.
16. Émile Colombey, *Correspondance authentique de Ninon de Lenclos*, Paris: E. Dentu, 1886.
17. Ibid.
18. Ibid.

Chapter 7: The Formal French: Colbert and the Academies

1. Cornelia Otis Skinner, *Elegant Wits and Grand Horizontals: Paris, La Belle Epoque*. London: Michael Joseph, 1963, p. 208; Anne Martin-Fugier, *Les Salons de la IIIe République: arts, littérature, politique*, Paris: Perrin, 2003, pp. 233–4.
2. Anthony Blunt, *Art and Architecture in France 1500–1700*, London: Penguin, 1953, p. 345.
3. Michel Vergé-Franceschi, *Colbert: la politique du bon sens*, Paris: Payot &

Rivages, 2005, p. 115.

4. Daniel Dessert, *Colbert, ou Le Mythe de l'absolutisme*, Paris: Fayard, 2019. For the Tuileries decoration see Charles Woolsey Cole, *Colbert and a Century of French Mercantilism*, New York: Columbia University Press, 1939, vol. 2, p. 302.

5. Cole, *Colbert and a Century of French Mercantilism*, vol. 2, p. 89.

6. Gill Perry and Colin Cunningham (eds), *Academies, Museums and Canons of Art*, New Haven, CT: Yale University Press, 1999, p. 91.

7. Ibid., pp. 92, 101.

8. Blunt, *Art and Architecture in France*, p. 92.

9. Ibid., p. 346.

10. Perry and Cunningham, *Academies, Museums and Canons of Art*, p. 98.

11. Ibid., p. 93.

12. Vergé-Franceschi, *Colbert*, pp. 199–203.

13. For Séguier, see Cole, *Colbert and a Century of French Mercantilism*, vol. 1, pp. 315–16.

14. Vergé-Franceschi, *Colbert*, p. 316 reflects on Colbert's effect on the artistic 'tone' of Paris. The Rome academy was discontinued in 1968.

15. Alice Stroup, *A Company of Scientists: Botany, Patronage, and Community at the Seventeenth-Century Parisian Royal Academy of Sciences*, Berkeley: California University Press, 1990, p. 123.

16. Ibid., p. 139.

17. Ibid., p. 186.

18. Ibid., p. 187.

19. Maria Rose Antognazza, *Leibniz: An Intellectual Biography*, Cambridge: Cambridge University Press, 2009, p. 138.

20. Cole, *Colbert and a Century of French Mercantilism*, vol. 2, p. 141.

21. Stroup, *A Company of Scientists*, p. 7.

22. Ibid., p. 13.

23. Lisa Jardine, *Ingenious Pursuits: Building the Scientific Revolution*, London: Little, Brown, 1999. p. 55.

24. Ibid., p. 249.

25. Ibid., p. 251.

26. Stroup, *A Company of Scientists*, pp. 132–6.

27. Antognazza, *Op. cit.*, p. 162, 167. For the architecture academy, see Christopher Drew Armstrong, 'The Académie Royale d'Architecture (1671–1793)', in Harry Francis Mallgrave (ed.), *Companions to the History of Architecture*, New York: John Wiley & Sons, 2017, vol. 2. For the music academy, see Lucy Robinson, review of *Musique française classique*, *Early Music*, 45 (2), 2017, pp. 337–40.

28. Vergé-Franceschi, *Colbert*, pp. 314ff discusses the effect of Colbert's 'embellishment' of the arts in Paris.

29. Maurice Pellisson, *Les comédies-ballets de Molière: originalité du genre, la poésie, la fantaisie, la satire sociale dans les comédies-ballets*, Paris: Hachette, 1914.

30. Vergé-Franceschi, *Colbert*, pp. 326ff discusses Colbert's initiatives in foreign trade.

Chapter 8: *Haute Cuisine, Haute Couture, Haute Coiffure*: The French Taste for Grandeur

1. The fullest early account of the mirror affair, in English, is given in Charles Woolsey Cole, *Colbert and a Century of French Mercantilism*, New York: Columbia University Press, 1939, vol. 2, pp. 304–15. But see also Joan DeJean, *The Essence of Style: How the French Invented High Fashion, Fine Food, Chic Cafés, Style, Sophistication, and Glamour*, New York: Free Press, 2005, p. 179; Jeanine Delpech, *L'Âme de la Fronde*, Paris: Fayard, 1957; Arlette Lebigre, *La Duchesse*

de Longueville, Paris: Perrin, 2004.

2. DeJean, *The Essence of Style*, p. 180.
3. Cole, *Colbert and a Century of French Mercantilism*, vol. 2, p. 304.
4. Ibid., vol. 2, pp. 314–15.
5. Ibid., vol. 2, p. 306. Colbert's many activities have been brought together in Jacob S. Soll, *The Information Master: Jean-Baptiste Colbert's Secret State Intelligence System*, Ann Arbor: University of Michigan Press, 2009.
6. DeJean, *The Essence of Style*, p. 193.
7. Cole, *Colbert and a Century of French Mercantilism*, vol. 2, pp. 315–18.
8. There are many books on this subject, several in English. Among those I have used are: Susan Pinkard, *A Revolution in Taste: The Rise of French Cuisine 1650–1800*, Cambridge: Cambridge University Press, 2009; Priscilla Parkhurst Ferguson, *Accounting for Taste: The Triumph of French Cuisine*, Chicago: University of Chicago Press, 2004; Amy B. Trubek, *Haute Cuisine: How the French Invented the Culinary Profession*, Philadelphia: University of Pennsylvania Press, 2000.
9. Leon G. Fine, 'The Transformative Influence of La Varenne's *Le Cuisiner François* (1651) on French Culinary Practice', *Frontiers in Nutrition*, 7, 2020.
10. Ibid., p. 42.
11. DeJean, *The Essence of Style*, p. 114. DeJean's book does not have footnotes so it is not easy to be exact about her sources. For this reference she quotes Sabine Coron *et al.* (eds), *Livres en bouche: Cinq siècles d'art culinaire français*, Paris: Hermann, 2001; Jean-Louis Flandrin and Massimo Montani (eds), *Histoire de l'alimentation*, Paris: Fayard, 1996; and other titles.
12. DeJean, *The Essence of Style*, p. 115.
13. Papin was protected by Colbert: see Michel Vergé-Franceschi, *Colbert: la politique du bon sens*, Paris: Payot & Rivages, 2005, p. 323; Charles Cabanes, *Denys Papin, inventeur et philosophe cosmopolite 1647–1714*, Paris: Société française d'éditions littéraires et techniques, 1935.
14. DeJean, *The Essence of Style*, p. 122 (see note 11).
15. Ibid., p. 126 (see note 11).
16. Cole, *Colbert and a Century of French Mercantilism*, vol. 1, ch. 8 explores France's East India Company. For Colbert's influence on the soap business, leather, silk-dyeing, gold and silver, see Cole, *Colbert and a Century of French Mercantilism*, vol. 2, especially chapters 6 and 12 on Lace, Tapestry and Mirrors and the Regulation of Industry. See also Simon Barbe, *Le Parfumeur français*, Lyon: Thomas Amaulry, 1693; Simon Barbe, *Le Parfumeur royal*, Paris: Simon Augustin Brunet, 1699.
17. See Cole, *Colbert and a Century of French Mercantilism*, vol. 2, Appendix 3 for a fascinating list of French towns and the industries associated with them, just as Grasse became associated with perfume. Jim Chevallier, *A History of the food of Paris: From Roast Mammoth to Steak Frites*, Lanham, MD: Rowan & Littlefield, 2018, p. 22.
18. For the soap business, see Cole, *Colbert and a Century of French Mercantilism*, vol. 2, pp. 349–55; DeJean, *The Essence of Style*, p. 259 (see note 16).
19. G. d'Eze and A. Marcel, *Histoire de la coiffure des femmes en France*, Paris: Paul Ollendorff, 1886, p. 139; Valerie Cumming, *Gloves*, London: Batsford, 1982; Octave Uzanne, *The Sunshade, the Glove, the Muff*, London: J. C. Nimmo & Bain, 1884; B. Eldred Ellis, *Gloves and the Glove Trade*, London: Pitman, 1921; John Grand-Carteret, *Les Élégances de la toilette*, Paris: Albin Michel, 1911; DeJean, *The Essence of Style*, p. 93.
20. DeJean, *The Essence of Style*, p. 22. She quotes Catherine Lebas and Annie Jacques (eds), *La Coiffure en France du Moyen Âge à nos jours*, Paris: Delmas International, 1979.
21. DeJean, *The Essence of Style*, p. 22 (see also note 20).

22. For the wide range of Mme de Sévigné's letters, see Vergé-Franceschi, *Colbert*, pp. 198–206. And for her obsession with fashion, see Cole, *Colbert and a Century of French Mercantilism*, vol. 2, p. 253.

23. Pierre Mélèse, *Donneau de Visé, fondateur du 'Mercure Galant'*, Paris: E. Droz, 1936; Barbara Selmeci Castioni, 'Donneau de Visé, amateur des étampes et visionnaire. Le Mercure galant en 1686', *Dossiers du Grihl*, 2017 (2).

24. DeJean, *The Essence of Style*, p. 49. She quotes Henry d'Allemagne, *Les Accessoires du costume et du mobilier depuis le XIIe siècle jusqu'au milieu du XIXe siècle*, 3 vols, Paris: Schemit, 1928.

25. DeJean, *The Essence of Style*, p. 59 (see note 24).

26. Ibid., p. 93. These fashion issues are explored in Virgil Josz, *Fragonard: mœurs du XVIIIe siècle*, Paris: Société du Mercure de France, 1901.

27. DeJean, *The Essence of Style*, p. 153. She quotes René Gandilhon, *Naissance du champagne: Dom Pierre Pérignon*, Paris: Hachette, 1968.

28. DeJean, *The Essence of Style*, p. 154ff (see note 27).

29. André L. Simon, *The History of Champagne*, London: Ebury Press, 1962; Kolleen M. Guy, *When Champagne Became French: Wine and the Making of a National Identity*, Baltimore: Johns Hopkins University Press, 2003; DeJean, *The Essence of Style*, pp. 209–12; René Gandilhon, *Naissance du champagne*.

30. DeJean, *The Essence of Style*, p. 154 (see note 27).

31. Jean Moura and Paul Louvet, *Le Café Procope*, Paris: Perrin, 1930; and see the review in *Annales historiques de la Révolution française*, 7, 1930, p. 291. For the Marseilles trade: Paul Masson, *Marseille et la colonisation française*, Marseilles: Barlatier, 1906, Appendix 12: 'Marseille Port Colonial'.

32. E. C. Spary, *Eating the Enlightenment: Food and the Sciences in Paris 1670–1760*, Chicago: University of Chicago Press, 2012, pp. 135–42.

33. Ibid.

34. Marie-France Boyer, *The French Café*, tr. Jacqueline Taylor, London: Thames & Hudson, 1994.

35. Sévigné quoted in DeJean, *The Essence of Style*, p. 209.

Chapter 9: Salons as 'Schools of Civilisation': Intellect in Fashion, Intellect *as* Fashion

1. Steven Kale, *French Salons: High Society and Political Sociability from the Old Regime to the Revolution of 1848*, Baltimore: Johns Hopkins University Press, 2004, p. 2.

2. Ibid., p. 3.

3. Ibid., p. 10.

4. Roger Picard, *Les Salons littéraires et la société française 1610–1789*, New York: Brentano's, 1943, p. 150.

5. Kale, *French Salons*, p. 53.

6. Ibid., p. 65.

7. Ibid., p. 111.

8. Ibid., p. 118. Mme de Sévigné made wide use of fashion prints. See Elizabeth Davis, '*Habit de qualité*: Seventeenth-Century French Fashion Prints as Sources for Dress History', *Dress*, 40 (2), 2014, pp. 117–43.

9. Daniel Roche, *La Culture des apparences: une histoire du vêtement (XVIIe–XVIIIe siècles)*, Paris: Fayard, 1989, ch. 5. I have also used the English-language version: *The Culture of Clothing: Dress and Fashion in the Ancien Regime*, tr. Jean Birrell, Cambridge: Cambridge University Press, 1994.

10. Roche (English-language version), *op. cit.*, pp. 259, 282.

11. Ibid., p. 307.

12. Ibid., p. 436.

13. Ibid., pp. 451–2. See for example M de Garsault, 'L'Art du perruquier', *Journal des savants*, 31 (6), 1768, p. 404.
14. Roche (English-language version), *op. cit.*, p. 457.
15. Ibid., p. 460. See also: Helen Clergue, *The Salon: A Study of French Society and Personalities in the Eighteenth Century*, New York and London: G. P. Putnam, 1907, p. 180.
16. Lucy Moore, *Liberty: The Lives and Times of Six Women in Revolutionary France*, London: HarperPress, 2006, pp. 7, 365.
17. Piero Camporesi, *Exotic Brew: The Art of Living in the Age of Enlightenment*, tr. Christopher Woodall, Cambridge: Polity Press, 1994, p. 8. See also: Picard, *Les Salons littéraires et la société française*, p. 143.
18. Camporesi, *Exotic Brew*, pp. 30–1.
19. Ibid., p. 99.
20. Roche (English-language version), *op. cit.*, pp. 464–6.
21. Ibid., p. 475.
22. Ibid., p. 472.
23. Du Bled's many books include: *La société française du XVIe siècle au XXe siècle*, 9 vols, Paris: Perrin, 1900–13. See also Kale, *French Salons*, p. 213.
24. Dena Goodman, *The Republic of Letters: A Cultural History of the French Enlightenment*, Ithaca, NY: Cornell University Press, 1994, p. 4.

Chapter 10: The Orléans Alternative

1. Orest A. Ranum, *The Fronde: A French Revolution 1648–1652*, New York: W. W. Norton, 1993.
2. I have used Philippe Amiguet, *Une Princesse à l'école du Cid: la Grande Mademoiselle et son siècle, d'après ses Mémoires*, Paris: A. Michel, 1957. A more recent title in English is Vincent J. Pitts, *La Grande Mademoiselle at the Court of France 1627–1693*, Baltimore and London: Johns Hopkins University Press, 2000.
3. Ruth Norrington, *My Dearest Minette: The Letters between Charles II and His Sister Henrietta, Duchesse d'Orléans*, London: Peter Owen, 1996.
4. Nancy Nichols Barker, *Brother to the Sun King: Philippe, Duke of Orléans*, Baltimore: Johns Hopkins University Press, 1989, especially ch. 3; Nancy N. Barker, 'Philippe d'Orléans, *frère unique du roi*: Founder of the Family Fortune', *French Historical Studies*, 13 (2), 1983, pp. 145–171.
5. Barker, *Brother to the Sun King*, pp. 167–8.
6. Ibid., pp. 88–9.
7. Peter Watson, *Wisdom and Strength: the Biography of a Renaissance Masterpiece*, London: Hutchinson, 1989, pp. 184ff.
8. Ibid., pp. 189ff.
9. Ibid., pp. 195ff.
10. Ibid., p. 191.
11. Ibid., p. 189.
12. Benedetta Craveri, *The Age of Conversation*, tr. Theresa Waugh, New York: New York Review Books, 2005, p. 255.
13. Ibid., p. 256.

Chapter 11: 'Esteem Is the Soul of Society'

1. Roger Marchal, *Madame de Lambert et son milieu*, Oxford: Voltaire Foundation at the Taylor Institution, 1991.
2. Ibid., pp. 200–1.
3. Ibid., p. 219.
4. The changing intellectual climate of the salons as reflected by Mme de Lambert's

salon is discussed in Dena Goodman, *The Republic of Letters: A Cultural History of the French Enlightenment*, Ithaca, NY: Cornell University Press, 1994, pp. 24, 145; Joan DeJean, *Tender Geographies: Women and the Origins of the Novel in France*, New York: Columbia University Press, 1991, pp. 21, 77, 103, 106, 109; Erica Harth, *Cartesian Women: Versions and Subversions of Rational Discourse in the Old Regime*, Ithaca, NY: Cornell University Press, 1992, pp. 5, 21, 38, 46, 56, 64, 130, 140. Montesquieu's *Persian Letters* are available in English translation via Open Access Books (JSTOR), a digital library of academic journals and historically important books.

5. I have used Jules Lemaître, *Fénelon*, Paris: A. Fayard, 1910; and Sabine Melchior-Bonnet, *Fénelon*, Paris: Perrin, 2008.

6. Lemaître, *Op. cit.* 'Cinquième conference', pp. 127ff. (Chapters are presented as 'Conferences'.)

7. Marchal, *Madame de Lambert et son milieu*, p. 265.

8. Ibid., p. 266.

9. Ibid., p. 268.

10. See Marie de Vichy Chamrond, Marquise du Deffand, *The Unpublished Correspondence of Madame du Deffand*, tr. Mrs Meeke, London: A. K. Newman, 1810; Marchal, *Madame de Lambert et son milieu*, p. 269.

11. Roger Picard, *Les Salons littéraires et la société française 1610–1789*, New York: Brentano's, 1943, p. 186.

12. Peter Watson, *Wisdom and Strength: The Biography of a Renaissance Masterpiece*, London: Hutchinson, 1990, pp. 190–1.

13. See Duc de Castries, *La Scandaleuse Madame de Tencin 1682–1749*, Paris: Perrin, 1987; more accessible for English readers is Julia Kavanagh, *French Women of Letters: Biographical Sketches*, London: Hurst & Blackett, 1862.

14. Jean Louis Aujol, *Le Cardinal Dubois: ministre de la paix*, Paris: Bateau Ivre, 1948.

15. Benedetta Craveri, *Madame du Deffand and Her World*, tr. Teresa Waugh, Boston: David Godine, 1994; Louis de Rouvroy, Duc de Saint-Simon, *Memoirs of the Duc de Saint-Simon on the Times of Louis XIV and the Regency*, tr. Katharine Prescott Wormeley, Boston: J. B. Millet, [1899] 1909.

16. See, for instance, Joseph Bertrand, *D'Alembert*, Paris: Hachette, 1889.

17. Craveri, *Madame du Deffand and Her World*, p. 285.

18. Ibid.

19. Picard, *Les Salons littéraires et la société française*, p. 188; Ellen McNiven Hine, *Jean-Jacques Dortous de Mairan and the Geneva Connection: Scientific Networking in the Eighteenth Century*, Oxford: Voltaire Foundation, 1996.

20. Adolphe Lods, *Jean Astruc et la critique biblique au XVIIIe siècle*, Strasbourg: Librairie Istra, 1924.

21. Eamonn O' Doherty, 'The "Conjectures" of Jean Astruc 1753', *Catholic Biblical Quarterly*, 15 (3), 1953, pp. 300–4; see also Lods, *Jean Astruc et la critique biblique au XVIIIe siècle*, pp. 56–61.

22. For its reception, see Lods, *Jean Astruc et la critique biblique au XVIIIe siècle*, chapter 4, pp. 62ff.

23. Craveri, *Madame du Deffand and Her World*, p. 293.

24. Castries, *La Scandaleuse Madame de Tencin*, pp. 193ff.

25. Charles de Secondat, Baron de Montesquieu, *The Spirit of the Laws*, tr. Anne M. Cohler *et al.*, Cambridge: Cambridge University Press, 1989; also very useful is Ana J. Samuel, 'The Design of Montesquieu's *The Spirit of the Laws*: The Triumph of Freedom over Determinism', *American Political Science Review*, 103 (2), 2009, pp. 305–21.

Chapter 12: Sceaux: 'The Best of all Possible Worlds'

1. Roger Chartier, *The Cultural Origins of the French Revolution*, tr. Lydia G. Cochrane, Durham, NC: Duke University Press, 1991, p. 6 (original French edition: *Les Origines culturelles de la Révolution française*, Paris: Seuil, 1990).
2. Jürgen Habermas, *The Structural Transformation of the Public Sphere: An Inquiry into a Category of Bourgeois Society*, tr. Thomas Berger and Frederick Lawrence, Cambridge, MA: MIT Press, 1989, p. 155.
3. Chartier, *The Cultural Origins of the French Revolution*, pp. 154–7.
4. Benedetta Craveri, *Madame du Deffand and Her World*, tr. Teresa Waugh, Boston: David R. Godine, 1994, p. 3.
5. Ibid., p. 4. Her intellectual side is also explored in Claude Ferval, *Madame du Deffand: l'esprit et l'amour au XVIIIe siècle*, Paris: Arthème Fayard, 1933.
6. Craveri, *Madame du Deffand and Her World*, p. 8.
7. Ibid., p. 9.
8. Lucien Perey, *Le Président Hénault et Madame du Deffand: la cour du régent, la cour du Louis XV et de Marie Leczinska*, Paris: Calmann-Lévy, 1893. See also Craveri, *Madame du Deffand and Her World*, pp. 17–19.
9. Craveri, *Op. cit.*, p. 34. See also General de Piépape, *A Princess of Strategy: The Life of Anne Louise Bénédicte de Bourbon-Condé, Duchesse du Maine*, tr. J. Lewis May, London: Bodley Head, 1911, pp. vii, 8 and especially 89ff.
10. Piépape, *A Princess of Strategy*, p. 49.
11. Craveri, *Madame du Deffand and Her World*, p. 38.
12. Ibid., p. 56.
13. Ibid., pp. 60–1.
14. For the duchesse and Mme du Châtelet, see Marc Fumaroli, *La République des lettres*, Paris: Gallimard, 2015, p. 234; Craveri, *Madame du Deffand and Her World*, p. 63.
15. There are well over a thousand books in print on Voltaire, covering every imaginable aspect of his life. One that is especially interesting is Theodore Bestermann (ed.), *Voltaire's Household Accounts*, Geneva: Institut et Musée Voltaire, 1968; see also Piépape, *A Princess of Strategy*, p. 290.
16. Piépape, *Op. cit.*, p. 332.
17. For Émilie in a different context beyond Voltaire, see Robyn Arianrhod, *Seduced by Logic: Émilie du Châtelet, Mary Somerville, and the Newtonian Revolution*, New York: Oxford University Press, 2012. See also Craveri, *Madame du Deffand and Her World*, p. 214; Piépape, *A Princess of Strategy*, p. 282 for Mme du Deffand and Émilie.
18. Piépape, *A Princess of Strategy*, pp. 359ff.
19. For the context of d'Alembert's mathematics, see Edric Cane and Thomas L. Hankins, 'Jean d'Alembert between Descartes and Newton', *Isis*, 67 (2), 1976, pp. 274–8; for mathematics in France in Euler's time, see Ronald S. Calinger, *Leonhard Euler: Mathematical Genius in the Enlightenment*, Princeton, NJ: Princeton University Press, 2015, pp. 165ff.
20. Étienne Bonnot de Condillac, *Essay on the Origin of Human Knowledge*, tr. Hans Arsleff, Cambridge: Cambridge University Press, 2001, in particular part 2, pp. 113ff.
21. For context and perspective, I have used Émile Callot, *Six philosophes français du XVIIIe siècle: la vie, l'œuvre et la doctrine de Diderot, Fontenelle, Maupertuis, La Mettrie, d'Holbach, Rivarol*, Annecy: Gardet, 1963. See also Mary Terrall, 'Representing the Earth's Shape: The Polemics Surrounding Maupertuis's Expedition to Lapland', *Isis*, 83 (2), 1992, pp. 218–37.
22. Thomas L. Hankins, *Science and the Enlightenment*, Cambridge: Cambridge University Press, 1985, p. 28.

23. For an unusual but accessible take on these events, see François Moureau, *Le Roman vrai de l'Encyclopédie*, Paris: Gallimard, 1990; for a more prosaic but clear account of the birth of the *Encyclopédie*, in English, see P. N. Furbank, *Diderot: A Critical Biography*, London: Secker & Warburg, 1992, ch. 4, especially pp. 85ff.

Chapter 13: She Who Made Voltaire Tremble

1. Benedetta Craveri, *Madame du Deffand and Her World*, tr. Teresa Waugh, Boston: David R. Godine, 1994, p. 71.
2. Ibid., p. 130.
3. Camilla Jebb, *A Star of the Salons: Julie de Lespinasse*, London: Methuen, 1908, p. 6.
4. Craveri, *Madame du Deffand and Her World*, p. 150.
5. See Warren Hunting Smith (ed.), *Letters to and from Mme du Deffand and Julie de Lespinasse*, New Haven, CT: Yale University Press, 1938.
6. Craveri, *Madame du Deffand and Her World*, pp. 179–80.
7. Ibid., p. 187.
8. For context, see Abel-François Villemain, 'L'Académie française: introduction à une histoire de l'Académie française depuis d'Alembert', *Revue des deux mondes*, September 1852, pp. 1033–52; Craveri, *Madame du Deffand and Her World*, pp. 145–7.
9. Craveri, *Madame du Deffand and Her World*, p. 58.
10. Roger Picard, *Les Salons littéraires et la société française 1610–1789*, New York: Brentano's, 1943, p. 251. See also Louis Tenenbaum, 'Madame du Deffand's Correspondence with Voltaire', *French Review*, 27 (3), 1954, pp. 193–200.
11. Picard, *Les Salons littéraires et la société française*, p. 160.
12. Jebb, *A Star of the Salons*, p. 170.
13. Ibid., has a full account, pp. 181–5.
14. See Anna de Koven, *Horace Walpole and Madame du Deffand: An Eighteenth-Century Friendship*, New York and London: D. Appleton, 1929; Craveri, *Madame du Deffand and Her World*, pp. 261–4.
15. Craveri, *Madame du Deffand and Her World*, pp. 362–3.
16. Charles-Augustin Sainte-Beuve, *Quelques portraits féminins extraits des œuvres de C.-A. Sainte-Beuve*, Paris: J. Tallandier, 1927, ch. 6; Tenenbaum, 'Madame du Deffand's Correspondence with Voltaire'; Craveri, *Madame du Deffand and Her World*, p. 198.
17. Craveri, *Op cit.*, p. 219.
18. Ibid.
19. Noted in Albert de Broglie, *Voltaire avant and pendant la guerre de sept ans*, Paris: Calmann-Lévy, 1898.
20. Ibid., p. 213.
21. Voltaire, *Dictionnaire philosophique*, tr. Theodore Besterman, Oxford: Voltaire Foundation, 1971, p. 10.
22. Ibid., p. 16.
23. The complete correspondence between Madame du Deffand and the Duchesse de Choiseul was published in Paris in 1866 by Michel Lévy frères, but a useful introduction is available in Charles de Mazade, 'La Duchesse de Choiseul et Mme du Deffand', *Revue des deux mondes*, December 1859, pp. 677–97.
24. Robert Tombs and Isabelle Tombs, *That Sweet Enemy: The French and the British from the Sun King to the Present*, London: William Heinemann, 2006, p. 155.
25. Ibid., p. 157.
26. Ibid., p. 158.

Chapter 14: 'All the Loose Knowledge of the World'

1. Benedetta Craveri, *Madame du Deffand and Her World*, tr. Teresa Waugh, Boston: David R. Godine, 1994, p. 298. See also Maurice Hamon, *Madame Geoffrin: Femme d'influence, femme d'affaires aux temps des Lumières*, Paris: Fayard, 2010.
2. Hamon, *Madame Geoffrin*, pp. 135ff.
3. Roger Picard, *Les Salons littéraires et la société française 1610–1789*, New York: Brentano's, 1943, p. 199; Craveri, *Madame du Deffand and Her World*, p. 299.
4. C.-A. Sainte-Beuve, *Monday Chats*, tr. William Matthews, Chicago: S. C. Griggs, 1878. Equally accessible is Sainte-Beuve, *Portraits de femmes*, Paris: Garnier frères, 1881, with assessments of Mesdames Sévigné, Roland, Lafayette and de Staël. See also: Picard, *Les Salons littéraires et la société française*, p. 219.
5. Craveri, *Madame du Deffand and Her World*, p. 300.
6. Ibid., p. 22.
7. Hamon, *Madame Geoffrin*, ch. 8.
8. An explanation is given in J. H. Müntz, *Encaustic: or, Count Caylus's Method of Painting in the Manner of the Ancients*, London: printed for the author, 1760.
9. Hamon, *Madame Geoffrin*, p. 63.
10. Hamon, *Madame Geoffrin*, p. 72; Craveri, *Madame du Deffand and Her World*, p. 75.
11. Janet Aldis, *Madame Geoffrin: Her Salon and Her Times 1750–1777*, London: Methuen, 1905, p. 87.
12. Ibid., p. 89.
13. Ibid., p. 91. Hamon, *Madame Geoffrin*, pp. 251–2.
14. For the full background see Daniel Delafarge, *La vie et l'œuvre de Palissot 1730–1814*, Paris: Hachette, 1912. For Saint-Lambert see Picard, *Les Salons littéraires et la société française*, p. 314.
15. Aldis, *Madame Geoffrin*, p. 142.
16. For Buffon's ideas in context, and his relationship with Diderot, see Devin Vartija, 'Revisiting Enlightenment Racial Classification: Time and the Question of Human Diversity', *Intellectual History Review*, published online 6 August 2020, DOI: 10.1080/17496977.2020.1794161; see also John Lough, *The Encyclopédie*, London: Longman, 1971, p. 196.
17. Lough, *The Encyclopédie*, p. 242.
18. Ibid., p. 271. For a relatively recent look at the *Encyclopédie* in the world of knowledge, and at the specific contribution of Diderot and d'Alembert, see Benoît Melançon, *Le savoir des livres*, Montreal: Presses de l'Université de Montréal, 2005.
19. Lough, *The Encyclopédie*, p. 397.
20. Aldis, *Madame Geoffrin*, p. 292.
21. Ibid., p. 108.
22. Ibid., p. 111.
23. For Marmontel as parasite see Picard, *Les Salons littéraires et la société française*, p. 344; also Lough, *The Encyclopédie*, p. 186.
24. Pierre de Ségur, *Le Royaume de la rue Saint-Honoré: Madame Geoffrin et sa fille*, Paris: Calmann-Lévy, 1898; Aldis, *Madame Geoffrin*, p. 289.
25. Picard, *Les Salons littéraires et la société française*, p. 230.
26. All the self-conscious strange details are in Constantin Photiadès, *La Reine des Lanturelus: Marie-Thérèse Geoffrin, Marquise de La Ferté-Imbault 1715–1791*, Paris: Plon, 1928.
27. For her satire on the *philosophes*, see Photiadès, *La Reine des Lanturelus*, pp. 117ff.
28. Craveri, *Madame du Deffand and Her World*, p. 307.

Chapter 15: The Multiple Ménages of Julie de Lespinasse

1. I enjoyed André Beaunier, *La Vie amoureuse de Julie de Lespinasse*, Paris: Ernest Flammarion, 1925; also Marilyn Yalom, *How the French Invented Love: Nine Hundred Years of Passion and Romance*, New York: HarperPerennial, 2013, p. 143.
2. Yalom, *How the French Invented Love*, p. 144.
3. Uniting the Académie and the *Encyclopédie*: Roger Picard, *Les Salons littéraires et la société française 1610–1789*, New York: Brentano's, 1943, p. 263. On Turgot: of the many biographies, the most classic is Léon Say, *Turgot*, Paris: Hachette, 1887; but for a more modern view, reflecting the outline in this book, see Malcolm Hill, *Statesman of the Enlightenment: The Life of Anne-Robert Turgot*, London: Othila Press, 1999.
4. Douglas Dakin, *Turgot and the Ancien Régime in France*, London: Methuen, 1939, pp. 16ff.
5. Benedetta Craveri, *Madame du Deffand and Her World*, tr. Teresa Waugh, Boston: David R. Godine, 1994, p. 343.
6. For a clear and concise discussion of Turgot's policies, see Camilla Jebb, *A Star of the Salons: Julie de Lespinasse*, London: Methuen, 1908, pp. 287–91. See also Marquis of Condorcet, *The Life of M. Turgot*, London: J. Johnson, 1787, chs 5 & 7 on the censures Turgot faced.
7. Jebb, *Op. cit.*, pp. 296–300.
8. Roger Pearson, *Unacknowledged Legislators: The Poet as Lawgiver in Post-Revolutionary France*, Oxford: Oxford University Press, 2016, p. 55.
9. Helen Clergue, *The Salon: A Study of French Society and Personalities in the Eighteenth Century*, New York and London: G. P. Putnam, 1907, p. 142.
10. Marquis de Condorcet, *Outlines of a Historical View of the Progress of the Human Mind*, London: J. Johnson, 1795, especially the section on the Ninth Epoch, 'Descartes to Republic'.
11. Picard, *Les Salons littéraires et la société française*, p. 266; Jebb, *A Star of the Salons*, p. 269.
12. All of Julie's letters can be found in Comte de Armand, *Correspondance entre Mademoiselle de Lespinasse et le Comte de Guibert*, Paris: Calmann-Lévy, 1906; the Comte de Armand was a nineteenth-century descendant of Guibert. See also Jebb, *A Star of the Salons*, pp. 258–9.
13. Robert Morrissey, *The Economy of Glory: From Ancien Régime France to the Fall of Napoleon*, Chicago and London: University of Chicago Press, 2014, p. 74.
14. Ibid., p. 78.
15. Jebb, *A Star of the Salons*, p. 264.
16. Ibid., p. 315.
17. Ibid., p. 330.
18. These events have been described well in several sources, for example Beaunier, *La Vie amoureuse de Julie de Lespinasse*; Jebb, *A Star of the Salons*, pp. 336–7; Yalom, *How the French Invented Love*, p. 155; Craveri, *Madame du Deffand and Her World*, p. 376.
19. Yalom, *How the French Invented Love*, p. 155; Craveri, *Madame du Deffand and Her World*, p. 376.

Chapter 16: An Elevated Level of Living: France as the New Greece

1. Charissa Bremer-David (ed.), *Paris: Life & Luxury in the Eighteenth Century*, Los Angeles: Getty, 2011, p. 16.
2. Joan DeJean, *The Age of Comfort: When Paris Discovered Casual and the Modern Home Began*, New York: Bloomsbury, 2009, p. 223.
3. Ibid., p. 233.

4. Ibid., p. 234.
5. Arthur Young, *Arthur Young's Travels in France During the Years 1787, 1788, 1789*, London: G. Bell, 1892.
6. DeJean, *Op. cit.*, p. 233.
7. Pierre Legrand d'Aussy, *Histoire de la vie privée des Français, depuis l'origine de la nation jusqu'à nos jours*, Paris: P.-D. Frères, 1782.
8. Bremer-David, *Paris*, p. 147.
9. DeJean, *The Age of Comfort*, p. 184.
10. Ibid., p. 63. See also Dena Goodman and Kathryn Norberg (eds), *Furnishing the Eighteenth Century: What Furniture Can Tell Us about the European and American Past*, New York: Routledge, 2007, p. 16.
11. Goodman and Norberg, *Furnishing the Eighteenth Century*, p. 16.
12. DeJean, *The Age of Comfort*, p. 20.
13. Dena Goodman, *The Republic of Letters: A Cultural History of the French Enlightenment*, Ithaca, NY: Cornell University Press, 1994, p. 140.
14. DeJean, *The Age of Comfort*, p. 111.
15. Goodman and Norberg, *Furnishing the Eighteenth Century*, p. 232.
16. DeJean, *The Age of Comfort*, p. 61. For wider context see Stéphanie Genand, *Le Libertinage et l'histoire: politique de la séduction à la fin de l'ancien régime*, Oxford: Voltaire Foundation, 2005.
17. Goodman and Norberg, *Furnishing the Eighteenth Century*, p. 234.

Chapter 17: The Fixation with Fashion

1. Kimberly Chrisman-Campbell, *Fashion Victims: Dress at the Court of Louis XVI and Marie-Antoinette*, New Haven, CT: Yale University Press, 2015, p. 53.
2. Ibid., p. 54.
3. Ibid.
4. Cousin d'Avallon, *Genlisiana, ou Recueil d'anecdotes, bons mots, plaisanteries, pensées et maximes, de Mme la Comtesse de Genlis*, Paris: Librairie politique, 1820. See also Jean Harmand, *A Keeper of Royal Secrets: Being the Private and Political Life of Madame de Genlis*, London: Eveleigh Nash, 1913.
5. Chrisman-Campbell, *Fashion Victims*, p. 55.
6. Ibid., p. 59.
7. Ibid., p. 64.
8. Tobias Smollett, *Travels through France and Italy*, ed. Frank Felsenstein, Oxford: Oxford University Press, 1979.
9. Chrisman-Campbell, *Fashion Victims*, p. 71.
10. Jennifer M. Jones, *Sexing la Mode: Gender, Fashion and Commercial Culture in Old Regime France*, Oxford: Berg, 2004, p. xvii.
11. Ibid., p. 1.
12. Daniel Roche, *La Culture des apparences: une histoire du vêtement (XVIIe–XVIIIe siècles)*, Paris: Fayard, 1989.
13. Jones, *Sexing la Mode*, p. 13.
14. Ibid., p. 17.
15. Ibid., p. 22.
16. Elizabeth Davis, '*Habit de qualité*: Seventeenth-Century French Fashion Prints as Sources for Dress History', *Dress*, 40 (2), 2014, pp. 117–43. Based on 'Conversations about Fashion' by Donneau de Visé, these prints give a good idea of his taste and how tastes change.
17. Jones, *Sexing la Mode*, p. 75.
18. Ibid., p. 74.
19. Roche, *La Culture des apparences*, p. 75.
20. Ibid.

21. Jones, *Sexing la Mode*, p. 83.
22. Roche, *La Culture des apparences*, p. 86.
23. Jones, *Sexing la Mode*, p. 90.
24. Ibid., p. 95.
25. Michell Sapori, *Rose Bertin: couturière de Marie-Antoinette*, Paris: Perrin, 2010.
26. Jones, *Sexing la Mode*, p. 114.
27. Ibid., p. 116.
28. Virey's views are analysed, in context, in Robert J. Richards, 'The Emergence of Evolutionary Biology of Behaviour in the Early Nineteenth Century,' *British Journal for the History of Science*, 15 (3), 1982, pp. 241–80.
29. *Almanach historique et raisonné des architectes, peintres, sculpteurs, graveurs, et cizeleurs*, Paris, 1777, p. 125.
30. Cynthia J. Koepp, 'The Alphabetical Order: Work in Diderot's *Encyclopédie*', in Stephen Laurence Kaplan and Cynthia J. Koepp (eds), *Work in France: Representations, Meaning, Organization and Practice*, Ithaca, NY: Cornell University Press, 1986, pp. 229ff.
31. In particular, see Mary K. Gayne, 'Illicit Wigmaking in Eighteenth-Century Paris', *Eighteenth-Century Studies*, 38 (1), 2004, pp. 119–37.
32. Jones, *Sexing la Mode*, p. 125.
33. Ibid., p. 128.
34. Lesley Ellis Miller, 'Representing Silk Design: Nicolas Joubert d'Hiberderie and *Le Dessinateur pour les étoffes d'or, d'argent et de soie* (Paris, 1765)', *Journal of Design History*, 17 (1), 2004, pp. 29–53. This article also discusses Joubert's links with Diderot and the *Encyclopédie*.
35. For example *Journal des dames*, December 1774, p. 192.
36. Nina Rattner Gelbart, *Feminine and Opposition Journalism in Old Regime France: Le Journal des dames*, Berkeley: University of California Press, 1987; Jones, *Sexing la Mode*, p. 138.
37. Jones, *Op. cit*, p. 146.
38. Craig Koslofsky, 'Parisian Cafés in European Perspective: Contexts of Consumption 1660–1730', *French History*, 31 (1), 2017, pp. 39–62, looks at the views of English and German travellers in France, Nemeitz included.
39. Jones, *Sexing la Mode*, p. 154.
40. Ibid., p. 160; Louis-Sébastien Mercier, *The Waiting City, Paris 1782–1788*, tr. Helen Simpson, London: G. G. Harrap, 1933. A useful introduction.
41. John Lough, *The Encyclopédie*, London: Longman, 1971, p. 183. For an original account see François Moureau, *Le Roman vrai de l'Encyclopédie*, Paris: Gallimard, 1990.
42. M. Lambert, *L'Avant-Coureur*, 1760.
43. Jones, *Sexing la Mode*, p. 195.
44. Ibid., p. 199.
45. Sarah Maza, *The Myth of the French Bourgeoisie: An Essay on the Social Imaginary 1750–1850*, Cambridge, MA: Harvard University Press, 2003; Christine Le Bozec, *Les Femmes et la Révolution 1770–1830*, Paris: Passés composés, 2019, passim. See also Jennifer M. Jones, 'Repackaging Rousseau: Femininity and Fashion in Old Regime France', *French Historical Studies*, 18 (4), 1994, pp. 939–67.
46. Jones, *Sexing la Mode*, p. 214.

Chapter 18: The Philosophy of Food, the Cult of Coffee and the Rise of the Restaurant

1. Sean Takats, *The Expert Cook in Enlightenment France*, Baltimore: Johns Hopkins University Press, 2011, p. 1.

2. Ibid., p. 2.
3. Ibid., p. 7.
4. Ibid., p. 104.
5. Ibid., p. 99.
6. Jean Flahaut, 'Les Pluvinet, pharmaciens et épiciers sous la Révolution et l'Empire', *Revue d'histoire de la pharmacie*, 338, 2003, pp. 265–80, looks at the chemists' dealings with grocers.
7. Stephen Mennell, *All Manners of Food: Eating and Taste in England and France from the Middle Ages to the Present*, Oxford: Basil Blackwell, 1986, p. 34.
8. E. C. Spary, *Eating the Enlightenment: Food and the Sciences in Paris*, Chicago: University of Chicago Press, 2012, p. 45.
9. Ibid., p. 38.
10. Ibid., p. 49.
11. Ibid., p. 39.
12. John Rivers, *Greuze and His Models*, London: Hutchinson, 1912.
13. Spary, *Eating the Enlightenment*, p. 41.
14. Mennell, *All Manners of Food*, p. 196.
15. Ibid., p. 197.
16. Ibid.
17. Ibid.
18. Spary, *Eating the Enlightenment*, p. 208.
19. Ibid., p. 210.
20. For Tronchin, see Henry Tronchin, *Un médecin du XVIIIe siècle: Théodore Tronchin 1709–1781*, Paris: Plon-Nourrit, 1906.
21. Spary, *Eating the Enlightenment*, p. 216.
22. The very idea of connoisseurship was a French concept, matured by P. J. Mariette. See Kristel Smentek, *Mariette and the Science of the Connoisseur in Eighteenth-Century Europe*, Farnham: Ashgate, 2014.
23. Spary, *Eating the Enlightenment*, p. 160.
24. Ibid., p. 161.
25. Ibid., p. 50.
26. The growth of cookbooks is explored and explained in Maryse Colson, 'La Naissance du livre de cuisine: étude discursive des ouvrages culinaires d'Ancien Régime (1651–1799)', doctoral thesis, University of Liège, 2014. Open access online.
27. Spary, *Eating the Enlightenment*, p. 273.
28. Ibid., p. 254. Spary has a whole page on dieting in salons.
29. Ibid., pp. 258–62; Sonja Boon, *Telling the Flesh: Life Writing, Citizenship, and the Body in Letters to Samuel Auguste Tissot*, Montreal: McGill-Queen's University Press, 2015.
30. Spary, *Eating the Enlightenment*, p. 91.
31. Ibid., p. 80.
32. See also Rose-Marie Herder-Mousseaux *et al.*, *Thé, café ou chocolat? Les boissons exotiques à Paris au XVIIIe siècle*, Paris: Paris musées, 2015.
33. Spary, *Eating the Enlightenment*, p. 98.
34. Ibid., pp. 109–11.
35. Ibid., p. 113.
36. Craig Koslofsky, 'Parisian Cafés in European Perspective: Contexts of Consumption 1660–1730', *French History*, 31 (1), 2017, pp. 39–62.
37. Spary, *Eating the Enlightenment*, p. 115.
38. For another view of café society see: Maria Teodora Comsa *et al.*, 'The French Enlightenment Network', *Journal of Modern History*, 88 (3), 2016, pp. 495–534.
39. Spary, *Eating the Enlightenment*, p. 117.
40. Ibid., p. 125.

41. Ibid., p. 138; Melissa Percival, 'Taste and Trade: The Drinking Portraits of Alexis Grimou (1678–1733)', *Art Bulletin*, 101 (1), 2019, pp. 6–25. Grimou, the 'French Rembrandt', depicted 'refined sociability' in the cafés of Paris.

42. Spary, *Eating the Enlightenment*, p. 144.

43. Politics and literature move together: see Roger Picard, *Les Salons littéraires et la société française 1610–1789*, New York: Brentano's, 1943, p. 302. But science could also be 'polite': see Cheryce Kramer et al., *Literature and Science 1660–1834, Vol. 1: Science as Polite Culture*, London: Pickering & Chatto, 2003.

44. Spary, *Eating the Enlightenment*, p. 148.

45. Ibid., p. 159.

46. Ibid., p. 161.

47. Rebecca L. Spang, *The Invention of the Restaurant: Paris and Modern Gastronomic Culture*, Cambridge, MA: Harvard University Press, 2000, p. 2.

48. Ibid., p. 2.

49. Ibid.

50. Ibid., p. 22. Another account of Roze de Chantoiseau is given in Whitney Walton, review of Spang, *The Invention of the Restaurant*, *Business History Review*, 75 (2), 2007, pp. 361–3.

51. Spang, *The Invention of the Restaurant*, p. 40.

52. Ibid., p. 134.

53. Ian Kelly, *Cooking for Kings: The Life of Antonin Câreme, the First Celebrity Chef*, London: Short, 2003, gives details of his recipes as well as of his life. See also A. Beauvilliers, *L'Art du cuisinier*, Paris: Pilet, 1814.

54. Spang, *The Invention of the Restaurant*, p. 266.

55. Joanna Hawke, 'Durbin, John Price (1800–1876)', *American National Biography Online*, 2000.

56. Spang, *The Invention of the Restaurant*, p. 25.

57. Ibid., p. 28.

Chapter 19: The Serious Game of Love

1. Michel Feher, *The Libertine Reader, Eroticism and Enlightenment in Eighteenth-Century France*, New York: Zone, 1997. p. 12.

2. Ibid., p. 13; Roger Picard, *Les Salons littéraires et la société française 1610–1789*, New York: Brentano's, 1943, pp. 118–19.

3. Feher, *The Libertine Reader*, p. 14.

4. Ibid., pp. 6–7.

5. For the new culture of letter-writing, see Dena Goodman, *Becoming a Woman in the Age of Letters*, Ithaca, NY: Cornell University Press, 2009, chs 3, 6, 8, 9.

6. Feher, *The Libertine Reader*, p. 11.

7. Gonzague Saint Bris, *Déshabillons l'histoire de France*, Paris: XO, 2017, especially chs 8 and 9.

8. Feher, *The Libertine Reader*, p. 25.

9. Ibid., p. 29. Here are some examples, illustrating the points made in the main text:
   • There were regular depictions of nudes, often given a classical bent, as in statuary, to distance the art from the more obviously pornographic.
   • There were a number of drawings and paintings showing female bodies (rarely if ever males) from behind, as often as not sprawled across untidy bedsheets and silks. It is as if the artists could not risk too much full-frontal nudity but, at the same time, realised that an artfully – and languidly – posed nude rear or buttock can be extremely erotic. (Boucher, *Study of Reclining Nude, Seen from the Back*, n.d.; Boucher, *Woman Stretched Out on a Bed, Back View*, 1719–26; Fragonard, *The Desired Moment*, 1755–60.)
   • A number of figures – usually women – are shown sleeping, mostly in bed, or

on the bed, and from the pose, and the thoroughness of the sleep, we are invited
to assume that this is the sleep of sexual exhaustion. (Fragonard, *Match to the
Powderkeg*, before 1778; Boucher, *Nude Woman on a Bed*, eighteenth century;
Watteau, *Young Woman Sleeping*, mid-eighteenth century.)

- Many paintings confirm that it was the fashion of the time for women – even
serving girls and maids – to wear bodices in which their breasts are forced
upwards, so that the upper part of the bulging bosom and cleavage draws the
eye. (Boucher, *The Charms of the Country Life*, 1737; Wille, *The Seduction*,
late eighteenth century; Boilly, *The Couple with an Escaped Bird*, end of
eighteenth century; Boilly, *The Visit Returned*, c.1789.)

- Lest we be minded to think that this is as far as artists could go, there is no
shortage of paintings in which a stylishly dressed woman – and not always
a young woman either – is depicted so that her décolleté shows not just her
bulging upper bosom but both nipples as well. (Greuze, *Head of a Young
Woman*, 1780; Boilly, *The Indiscreet*, 1795–1800; Duplessis, *Portrait of Marie
Thérèse Louise de Savoie-Carignan, Princesse de Lamballe*, n.d.; Greuze, *The
Broken Urns*, 1772; Boudouin, *Night*, 1767.)

- Women at their toilette, or in their boudoir, was another popular scene in
which female figures are shown in various states of undress, mostly tame by our
standards, but presumably eroticising at the time. (Pater, *The Boudoir*, 1733;
Boucher, *The Toilette*, 1742; Boucher, *Young Woman Attaching her Garter*,
eighteenth century; Fragonard, *The Useless Resistance*, 1770.)

- By the same token, depictions of women showing their ankles, or lower legs,
were also popular, not erotic to us but in the eighteenth century such exposure
was seen as sexually enticing.

- There were innumerable scenes of couples on couches, sofas, daybeds and
beds – in the music room, in the kitchen and sometimes out of doors – more
or less closely disporting, touching, undressing, stroking, occasionally kissing.
(Fragonard, *The Blouse Removed*, c.1770; Subleyras, *The Amorous Couple*,
c.1735; French school, *The Amorous Courtesan*, eighteenth century; Troy, *The
Declaration of Love*, 1724; Fragonard, *The Progress of Love, Love Letters*,
1771–2; Boucher, *The Pretty Kitchen Maid*, before 1735; Boudouin, *The
Indiscreet Husband*, 1767; Boucher, *Hercules and Omphale*, 1735, showing
Hercules grasping Omphale's bosom, none too gently; Lancret, *The Amorous
Couple*, first half of eighteenth century, showing fairly rough sex on a bed;
formerly attributed to Boucher, *Amorous Couple*, n.d., showing full-frontal
nudity and the man kissing the woman's breast.)

10. Feher, *The Libertine Reader*, p. 10.
11. For an English version, see Claude Prosper Jolyot de Crébillon, *The Wayward
Head and Heart*, tr. Barbara Bray, Oxford: Oxford University Press, 1963.
12. Originally published in English as *The Indiscreet Toys*, in 1749, without a
publisher's or author's name, the latest translation is *From Their Lips to His Ear*,
Lakeport, CA: Black Scat, 2020.
13. The classic English translation is *Dangerous Acquaintances (Les Liaisons
Dangereuses)*, tr. Richard Aldington, London: Routledge, 1924.
14. Feher, *The Libertine Reader*, pp. 912ff.

Chapter 20: The Discovery of the Bourgeois:
Unpoetic, Unheroic, Unerotic

1. Helen Clergue, *The Salon: A Study of French Society and Personalities in the
Eighteenth Century*, New York and London: G. P. Putnam, 1907, p. 123.
2. Ibid., p. 138. There are many editions of the *Confessions*, in both French and
English. One of the more recent editions is Isabelle Chanteloube and Maria Susana

Seguin (eds), *Un discours sur les origines de J.-J. Rousseau: 'Les Confessions',
livres I à VI*: Paris: CNED Presses Universitaires de France, 2012.

3. Clergue, *The Salon*, p. 20.
4. Cousin d'Avallon, *Grimmiana, ou Recueil des anecdotes, bons mots,
plaisanteries de Grimm*, Paris: J. M. Davi et Locard, 1813.
5. Roger Picard, *Les Salons littéraires et la société française 1610–1789*, New York:
Brentano's, 1943, p. 323; Clergue, *The Salon*, p. 142.
6. Clergue, *The Salon*, p. 150.
7. Ibid., p. 142. See also: Daniel Roche, *Les Républicains des lettres: Gens de
Culture et Lumières aux XVIII siècle*, Paris: Fayard, 1988, which, inter alia,
looks at the political engagement of the d'Holbach coterie and the library of
Jean-Jacques Dortous de Mairan. See also: Daniel Roche, *Les Républicains des
Lettres: Gens de Culture et Lumières aux XVIII siècle*, Paris: Fayard, 1988,
which, inter alia, looks at the political engagement of the d'Holbach coterie and
the library of Jean-Jacques Dortous de Mairan.
8. Mark S. Cladis, 'Redeeming Love: Rousseau and Eighteenth-Century Moral
Philosophy', *Journal of Religious Ethics*, 28 (2), 2000, pp. 221–51.
9. Michael O'Dea (ed.), *Rousseau et les philosophes*, Oxford: Voltaire Foundation,
2010, p. 239.
10. This section is based on David Edmonds and John Eidinow, *Rousseau's Dog:
Two Great Thinkers at War in the Age of Enlightenment*, London: Faber &
Faber, 2006.
11. Ibid.
12. Ibid.
13. Allan Bloom, *Giants and Dwarfs: Essays 1960–1990*, London and New York:
Simon & Schuster, 1991, p. 210.
14. Clergue, *The Salon*, p. 156.
15. Ibid., p. 167.
16. Henry Tronchin, *Un Médecin du XVIIIe siècle: Théodore Tronchin, 1709–1781*,
Paris: Plon-Nourrit, 1906. This book won a prize from the Académie française.
17. Clergue, *The Salon*, p. 177.
18. Ibid., p. 185.
19. Francis Steegmuller, *A Woman, a Man and Two Kingdoms: The Story of
Madame d'Épinay and the Abbé Galiani*, London: Secker & Warburg, 1992, p.
65.
20. Ibid., p. 72; *Diderot's Letters to Sophie Volland: A Selection*, tr. Peter France,
Oxford: Oxford University Press, 1972. See also: Picard, *Les Salons littéraires et
la société française*, p. 326.
21. Steegmuller, *A Woman, a Man and Two Kingdoms*, p. 123.
22. Ibid., p. 190.
23. Ibid., p. 188.

Chapter 21: 'Literification'

1. Marc Fumaroli, *When the World Spoke French*, tr. Richard Howard, New York:
New York Review Books, 2011, pp. xviii, xxi, xxii; French edition: *Quand
l'Europe parlait français*, Paris: Fallois, 2001. See also Marc Fumaroli, *La
Grandeur et la grâce*, Paris: Robert Laffont, 2014.
2. Fumaroli, *When the World Spoke French*, pp, xxiii, xxvii.
3. Dena Goodman, *The Republic of Letters: A Cultural History of the French
Enlightenment*, Ithaca, NY: Cornell University Press, 1994, p. 53.
4. Mathieu Marraud, *La Noblesse de Paris aux XVIIIe siècle*, Paris: Seuil, 2000,
pp. 401, 411.
5. Ibid., p. 431.

6. Ibid., p. 448.
7. Ibid., pp. 451–4, 461–2. See also: Daniel Roche, *Les Républicains des Lettres: Gens de Culture et Lumières aux XVIII siècle*, Paris: Fayard, 1988, which, inter alia, looks at the political engagement of the d'Holbach coterie and the library of Jean-Jacques Dortous de Mairan.
8. Ibid., p. 457.
9. Ibid., pp. 464–6.
10. Ibid., p. 469.
11. Ibid., p. 475. *Savoir vivre* also becomes a philosophy, says Fumaroli, in *La République des lettres*, Paris: Gallimard, 2015, p. 231.
12. Marraud, *La Noblesse de Paris aux XVIIIe siècle*, p. 545.

Chapter 22: Debt, Madame Deficit and an Undimmed Versailles

1. J. Christopher Herold, *Mistress to an Age: A Life of Madame de Staël*, London: Hamish Hamilton, 1959, p. 7.
2. Ibid., p. 8.
3. Ibid., p. 12.
4. Karen O'Brien and Brian Young (eds), *The Cambridge Companion to Edward Gibbon*, Cambridge: Cambridge University Press, 2018, has a chapter on Gibbon and Catholicism.
5. Herold, *Mistress to an Age*, p. 23.
6. For the Necker salon as 'sanctuary' see Roger Picard, *Les Salons littéraires et la société française 1610–1789*, New York: Brentano's, 1943, p. 339.
7. Vicomte d'Haussonville, *The Salon of Madame Necker*, tr. Henry M. Trollope, London: Chapman & Hall, 1882, vol. 1, p. 111.
8. Ibid., vol. 1, p. 119.
9. Ibid., vol. 1, p. 168.
10. Ibid., vol. 2, p. 4.
11. Herold, *Mistress to an Age*, p. 30.
12. Ibid., p. 39.
13. Malcolm Hill, *Statesman of the Enlightenment: The Life of Anne-Robert Turgot*, London: Othila Press, 1999, p. 14.
14. Ibid., p. 177.
15. Ibid., p. 183.
16. Ibid., p. 187.
17. Herold, *Mistress to an Age*, p. 40.
18. Francis Steegmuller, *A Woman, a Man and Two Kingdoms: The Story of Madame d'Épinay and the Abbé Galiani*, London: Secker & Warburg, 1992, p. 214.
19. Herold, *Mistress to an Age*, p. 28.
20. Ibid.
21. Ibid., p. 205.
22. But see Sonja Boon, 'Performing the Woman of Sensibility: Suzanne Churchod Necker and the Hospice de Charité', *Journal for Eighteenth-Century Studies*, 32 (2), 2009, pp. 235–54.
23. Herold, *Mistress to an Age*, p. 206.
24. Ibid., p. 207.
25. Ibid., p. 25.
26. For a wry look at Necker's finances, see Ghislain de Diesbach, *Necker, ou La Faillite de vertu*, Paris: Perrin, 1978.
27. Keith Michael Baker, *Inventing the French Revolution: Essays on French Political Culture in the Eighteenth Century*, Cambridge: Cambridge University Press, 1990, pp. 190–7; Herold, *Mistress to an Age*, p. 131.
28. Baker, *Op. cit.*, p. 210.

29. Ibid, pp. 190–7.
30. Herold, *Mistress to an Age*, p. 42.
31. Haussonville, *The Salon of Madame Necker*, vol. 2, p. 115.

Chapter 23: The Maître d'Hôtel de la Philosophie

1. Alan Charles Kors, *D'Holbach's Coterie: An Enlightenment in Paris*, Princeton, NJ: Princeton University Press, 1976, p. 10. But see also W. H. Wickwar, *Baron d'Holbach: A Prelude to the French Revolution*, London: George Allen & Unwin, 1935.
2. Roger Picard, *Les Salons littéraires et la société française 1610–1789*, New York: Brentano's, 1943, p. 305; Kors, *D'Holbach's Coterie*, p. 5.
3. Picard, *Les Salons littéraires et la société française*, p. 306; Kors, *D'Holbach's Coterie*, p. 12.
4. Baron d'Holbach, *Système de la nature, ou Des lois du monde physique et du monde moral*, new ed., Paris: Étienne Ledoux, 1821; Picard, *Les Salons littéraires et la société française*, p. 305.
5. Kors, *D'Holbach's Coterie*, p. 45.
6. Ibid., p. 77.
7. Ibid., p. 134.
8. Ibid.
9. Ann Thomson, review of Charles-Georges Le Roy, *Lettres sur les animaux*, ed. E. Anderson, Langres: Soc. Diderot, *Recherches sur Diderot et sur l'Encyclopédie*, 20, 1996, pp. 166–7.
10. Kors, *D'Holbach's Coterie*, p. 136.
11. Ibid., p. 137.
12. Jacques-André Naigeon and Jean-Baptiste de Mirabaud, *Opinions des anciens sur les juifs*, London, 1769.
13. Kors, *D'Holbach's Coterie*, p. 141.
14. Picard, *Les Salons littéraires et la société française*, pp. 311–12.
15. Paul Sadrin, *Nicolas-Antoine Boulanger (1722–1759), ou Avant nous le déluge*, Oxford: Voltaire Foundation, 1986.
16. Kors, *D'Holbach's Coterie*, p. 39.
17. Ibid., p. 93.
18. Ibid.
19. Daniel Gordon, '"Public Opinion" and the Civilizing Process in France: The Example of Morellet', *Eighteenth-Century Studies*, 22 (3), 1989, pp. 302–28.
20. Kors, *D'Holbach's Coterie*, p. 97.
21. Ibid., p. 121.
22. Jean-Francois Marmontel, *Bélisaire*, new ed., Paris: Merlin, 1770. See also John Renwick, *Marmontel, Voltaire and the Bélisaire Affair*, Banbury, Voltaire Foundation, 1974; Jacques Wagner (ed.), *Jean-François Marmontel: un intellectual exemplaire aux siècle des Lumières*, Tulle: Mille sources, 2003.
23. Kors, *D'Holbach's Coterie*, p. 79.
24. Ibid., p. 124.
25. Ibid., p. 125.
26. Jean-François Marmontel, '"Minds are Not Enlightened by the Flames of an Executioner's Pyre", from *Belisarius*, 1767', in Caroline Warman (ed.), *Tolerance: The Beacon of the Enlightenment*, Cambridge: Open Book Publishers, 2016.
27. Translated into English as *An Essay on Public Happiness*, New York: Augustus M. Kelley, 1969.

Chapter 24: Félicité de Genlis and *Égalité* in the Palais-Royal

1. Jean Harmand, *Madame de Genlis: sa vie intime et politique 1746–1830*, Paris: Perrin, 1912, p. 43.
2. Ibid., p. 17.
3. Ibid., p. 26.
4. Ibid., p. 51.
5. The original ten volumes are available in a convenient two volumes: Stéphanie Félicité, Comtesse de Genlis, *Mémoires de Madame de Genlis*, Paris: Firmin-Didot, 1928.
6. Roger Picard, *Les Salons littéraires et la société française 1610–1789*, New York: Brentano's, 1943, p. 300.
7. Harmand, *op. cit.*, pp. 93–4.
8. Olivier Deshayes, *Le Destin exceptionnel de Mme de Genlis (1746–1830): une éducatrice et femme de lettres en marge du pouvoir*, Paris: Harmattan, 2014.
9. Edward Rigby, *Dr Rigby's Letters from France &c. in 1789*, ed. Lady Eastlake, London: Longmans, Green, 1880.
10. Julien Puget, 'From Public Garden to Public City: The Controversy over the Housing Project at the Palais-Royal in 1781', *French History*, 31 (2), 2017, pp. 174–93.
11. André Castelot, *Le Prince rouge, Philippe-Égalité*, Paris: Livre contemporain, 1961.
12. Puget, 'From Public Garden to Public City'.
13. Ibid.
14. Clyde Plumauzille, 'Le "marché aux putains": économies sexuelles et dynamiques spatiales du Palais-Royal dans le Paris révolutionnaire,' *Genre, sexualité et société*, 10, 2013, https://doi.org/10.4000/gss.2943 (accessed 26 July 2021).
15. Darrin M. McMahon, 'The Birthplace of the Revolution: Public Space and Political Community in the Palais-Royal of Louis-Philippe-Joseph d'Orléans 1781–1789', *French History*, 10 (1), 1996, p. 1; George Armstrong Kelly, 'The Machine of the Duc d'Orléans and the New Politics', *Journal of Modern History*, 51 (4), 1979, pp. 667–84.
16. Kelly, 'The Machine of the Duc d'Orléans and the New Politics', p. 672. For his life as a general, see: Jean-Paul Bertaud, *Choderlos de Laclos: l'auteur des Liaisons dangereuses*, Paris: Fayard, 2003, pp. 472ff.
17. Kelly, 'The Machine of the Duc d'Orléans and the New Politics', p. 673. The most vivid account, though dated, is Camille Desmoulins, *Histoire des Brissotins, ou Fragment de l'histoire secrète de la révolution et des six premier mois de la république*, Paris: Imprimerie patriotique et républicaine, 1793.
18. Kelly, 'The Machine of the Duc d'Orléans and the New Politics', p. 678; Harmand, *op. cit.*, pp. 48–50. See also François Furet, *Interpreting the French Revolution*, tr. Elborg Forster, Cambridge: Cambridge University Press, 1981 (original French edition: *Penser la Révolution française*, Paris: Gallimard, 1978); Konrad Engelbert Oelsner, *An Account of the Life of Sieyes, Member of the first National Assembly, and of the Convention*, London: J. Johnson, 1795.
19. Kelly, 'The Machine of the Duc d'Orléans and the New Politics', pp. 674 ('receiving line'), 679ff; Madame de Genlis, *Adèle et Théodore, ou Lettres sur l'éducation*, Paris, 1782. See also Harmand, *Madame de Genlis*, p. 131.
20. Harmand, *op. cit.*, p. 164.
21. Simon Schama, *Citizens: A Chronicle of the French Revolution*, London: Viking, 1989, p. 370.
22. Nicolas Restif de La Bretonne, *Le Palais-Royal*, Paris: Louis Michaud, 1980.
23. André Castelot, *Philippe Égalité: le régicide*, Paris: Picollec, 1991, p. 302.
24. Ibid.

25. Ibid.
26. The latest study I have been able to find is Jacques Janssens, *Camille Desmoulins: le premier républicain de France*, Paris: Perrin, 1973.
27. Kelly, 'The Machine of the Duc d'Orléans and the New Politics', p. 683.
28. Deshayes, *Le Destin exceptionnel de Madame de Genlis*.
29. Peter Watson, *Wisdom and Strength: The Biography of a Renaissance Masterpiece*, London: Hutchinson, 1990, pp. 233–8.
30. Castelot, *Philippe Égalité*, p. 302..

Chapter 25: 'The Most Eloquent Love–Hate Affair in History'

1. J. Christopher Herold, *Mistress to an Age: A Life of Madame de Staël*, London: Hamish Hamilton, 1959, p. 52. In addition, among the scores of books on Mme de Staël, the most recent include Biancamaria Fontana, *Germaine de Staël: A Political Portrait*, Princeton, NJ: Princeton University Press, 2016; Renee Winegarten, *Germaine de Staël and Benjamin Constant: A Dual Biography*, New Haven, CT, and London: Yale University Press, 2008; Jean-Denis Bredin, *Une Singulière Famille: Jacques Necker, Suzanne Necker et Germaine de Staël*, Paris: Fayard, 1999. I have also used Ghislain de Diesbach, *Madame de Staël*, Paris: Perrin, 2008.
2. Herold, *op. cit.*, pp. 67–9.
3. Christine Le Bozec, *Les Femmes et la Révolution 1770–1830*, Paris: Passés Composés, 2019, p. 156.
4. Harmand, *op. cit.*, p. 91.
5. Casimir Carrère, *Talleyrand amoureux*, Paris: France-Empire, 1975; Duff Cooper, *Talleyrand*, New York: Harper & Bros, 1932. Though dated this is a book by a diplomat about a diplomat.
6. Harmand, *Madame de Genlis*, *Op. cit.*, p. 93.
7. Georges Solovieff (ed.), *Madame de Staël: lettres à Narbonne*, Paris: Gallimard, 1960.
8. Harmand, *op. cit.*, p. 100.
9. Ibid., p. 105.
10. Ibid., p. 106. For Rivarol's wider role, see G. W. Harris, *Antoine Rivarol: Journalist of the French Revolution*, Oxford: Blackwell, 1940.
11. Harmand, *op. cit.*, p. 112.
12. In English: G. Lenôtre, *The September Massacres*, London: Hutchinson, 1929.
13. Harmand, p. 121.
14. Ibid., p. 135.
15. Ibid., p. 139.
16. Among the more recent works see Paul Delbouille, *Benjamin Constant (1767–1830): les égarements du cœur et les chemins de la pensée*, Geneva: Slatkine, 2015; see also: Benjamin Constant, *Journal intime de Benjamin Constant et lettres à sa famille et ses amis*, Paris: Paul Ollendorff, 1895.
17. Harmand, *op. cit.*, p. 356.
18. Ibid., p. 154.
19. Ibid., p. 157.
20. Jean-Paul Garnier, *Barras, le roi du Directoire*, Paris: Perrin, 1970.
21. Harmand, *op. cit.*, p. 163.
22. Ibid., p. 168.
23. Ibid., p. 176; Kari E. Lokke, 'Women and Fame: Germaine de Staël and Regency Women Writers', *Keats–Shelley Journal*, 55, 2006, pp. 73–9.
24. Harmand, *Madame de Genlis*, *Op. cit.*, pp. 179–80.
25. Jean de Pange, 'Un amour de Madame de Staël: lettres au Chevalier de Pange', *Revue des deux mondes*, 23 (4), 1924, pp. 827–64.
26. Harmand, *Madame de Genlis*, *Op. cit.*, p. 193.
27. Ibid., p. 205.

28. Karyna Szmurlo (ed.), *Germaine de Staël: Forging a Politics of Mediation*, Oxford: Voltaire Foundation, 2011.
29. Harmand, *op. cit.*, p. 212.
30. Ibid., p. 218.
31. For the 'double games' of Constant, see Diesbach, *Madame de Staël*, pp. 516ff.
32. Harmand, *op. cit.*, p. 229.
33. Madame de Staël-Holstein, *Delphine: A Novel*, London: G. & J. Robinson, 1803; see also Angelica Goodden, *Madame de Staël: 'Delphine' and 'Corinne'*, London: Grant & Cutler, 2000.
34. Harmand, *op. cit*, p. 233.
35. Ibid., p. 236.
36. See Delbouille, *Benjamin Constant*, pp. 307ff for his unhappiness with Germaine.
37. Harmand, *op. cit.*, p. 247.
38. Ibid., p. 259.
39. A recent English-language edition of Germaine's book on Germany was published in 2015 by Palala Press on the internet.
40. Harmand, *op. cit.*, p. 281.
41. Ibid., p. 310.
42. Ibid., p. 311.
43. Goodden, *'Delphine' and 'Corinne'*.
44. Harmand, *op. cit.*, p. 344.
45. Ibid., p. 357.
46. Ibid., p. 390. Yota Batsaki picks up on this in 'Exile as the Inaudible Accent in Germaine de Staël's *Corinne, ou L'Italie*', *Comparative Literature*, 61 (1), 2009, pp. 26–42.
47. Harmand, *op. cit.*, p. 393.
48. Paul Gautier, *Madame de Staël et Napoléon*, Paris: Plon-Nourrit, 1903.
49. Harmand, *op. cit.*, p. 405.
50. Ibid., p. 406.
51. Ibid., p. 502.
52. Ibid., pp. 437–44; Gautier, *Madame de Staël et Napoléon*.
53. Harmand, *op. cit.*, p. 538.
54. Stephen Holmes, *Benjamin Constant and the Making of Modern Liberalism*, New Haven, CT: Yale University Press, 1984.
55. Harmand, p. 448.
56. Benjamin Constant, *'Adolphe' and 'The Red Note-Book'*, tr. Carl Wildman and Norman Cameron, London: Hamish Hamilton, 1969.
57. Ibid., p. 465.

Chapter 26: Napoleon Spurned

1. As with Germaine de Staël, there is no shortage of books and articles on Juliette Récamier. One of the more recent is Catherine Decours, *Juliette Récamier: l'art de la séduction*, Paris: Perrin, 2013. Also useful for colour is Maurice Levaillant, *Une amitié amoureuse: Madame de Staël et Madame Récamier*, Paris: Hachette, 1956, available in English as *The Passionate Exiles: Madame de Staël and Madame Récamier*, tr. Malcolm Barnes, New York: Farrar, Straus & Cudahy, 1958. See also Joseph Turquan, *Madame Récamier*, Paris: Jules Tallandier, 1928; and Lucy Moore, *Liberty: The Lives and Times of Six Women in Revolutionary France*, London: HarperPress, 2006, p. 182.
2. Turquan, *Madame Récamier*, p. 32.
3. Ibid., p. 40.
4. Ibid., p. 35.
5. Moore, *Liberty*, p. 184.

6. Turquan, *Madame Récamier*, p. 42.
7. J. Christopher Herold, *Mistress to an Age: A Life of Madame de Staël*, London: Hamish Hamilton, 1959, p. 358.
8. Turquan, *Madame Récamier*, p. 45.
9. Ibid., p. 47.
10. Quoted in Herold, *Mistress to an Age*, p. 351.
11. Moore, *Liberty*, pp. 71–2.
12. Ibid., p. 59.
13. Herold, *Mistress to an Age*, p. 364.
14. Moore, *Liberty*, p. 76.
15. Herold, *Mistress to an Age*, p. 365.
16. Moore, *Liberty*, p. 77.
17. Herold, *Mistress to an Age*, p. 366.
18. Turquan, *Madame Récamier*, p. 87.
19. A good account of the whole business is in Decours, *Juliette Récamier*, ch. 7.
20. Herold, *Mistress to an Age*, p. 369.
21. Turquan, *Madame Récamier*, p. 59.
22. Ibid., p. 122.
23. Herold, *Mistress to an Age*, p. 381.
24. Ibid., p. 382.
25. A helpful introduction to Chateaubriand in English may be found in *The Memoirs of Chateaubriand*, ed. and tr. Robert Baldick, New York: Knopf, 1961. See also Chateaubriand, *Lettres à Madame Récamier*, ed. Maurice Levaillant and E. Beau de Lomenie, Paris: Flammarion, 1951; Moore, *Liberty*, p. 65.
26. Decours, *Juliette Récamier*, ch. 20 is headed 'Passion according to Juliette'.
27. Moore, *Liberty*, p. 196.
28. Ibid., p. 226; Chateaubriand, *Lettres à Madame de Récamier*. Levaillant, *Une amitié amoureuse* offers a crisp double portrait and an amusing account of the rivalries at the time between beautiful women.
29. Moore, *Liberty*, p. 228.
30. Ibid., p. 64.
31. Ibid., p. 63. For a critique, see Raymond Lebègue, 'Le Problème du voyage de Chateaubriand en Amérique', *Journal des savants*, 1965 (1), p. 456.
32. Moore, *Liberty*, p. 63.
33. Chateaubriand, *Mémoires d'outre-tombe*, 2 vols, Paris: Gallimard, 1948, but there are numerous editions, including, most recently in English, *Memoirs from Beyond the Grave 1768–1800*, tr. Alex Andriesse, New York: New York Review Books, 2018. See also Moore, *Liberty*, pp. 66–7.
34. Peter Watson, *Ideas: A History from Fire to Freud*, London: Weidenfeld & Nicolson, 2005, p. 292.
35. Tocqueville and Beaumont both wrote books on the USA.
36. André Jardin, *Tocqueville*, tr. Lydia Davis and Robert Hemenway, London: Peter Halban, 1988, p. 149.
37. Ibid.
38. Ibid., p. 117. See also James T. Schleifer, *The Making of Tocqueville's 'Democracy in America'*, Chapel Hill: University of North Carolina Press, 1980, esp. pp. 62ff, 191ff, 263ff.
39. Jardin, *Tocqueville*, p. 126.
40. Ibid., p. 158. See also Sudhir Hazareesingh, *How the French Think: An Affectionate Portrait of an Intellectual People*, London: Penguin, 2016, p. 106.
41. Jardin, *Tocqueville*, p. 114. An alternative view is that Tocqueville thought equality the most important factor in America, but that the revolution had been of little importance in producing that spirit. He also said that the two great powers of the future would be America and Russia.

42. Alexis de Tocqueville, *Œuvres complètes*, ed. J. P. Mayer, Paris: Gallimard, 1951–2002, vol. 1, p. 236.
43. Jardin, *Tocqueville*, p. 162. See also: Decours, *Juliette Récamier*, p. 557.

Chapter 27: 'The Return of Conversation'

1. Robert Tombs and Isabelle Tombs, *That Sweet Enemy: The French and the British from the Sun King to the Present*, London: William Heinemann, 2006, p. 293.
2. Ibid., p. 289.
3. Ibid., p. 290.
4. Jean-Marc Largeaud, *Napoléon et Waterloo: La défaite glorieuse de 1815 à nos jours*, Paris: Boutique d'histoire, 2006.
5. Tombs and Tombs, *That Sweet Enemy*, p. 290.
6. Steven Kale, *French Salons: High Society and Political Sociability from the Old Regime to the Revolution of 1848*, Baltimore: Johns Hopkins University Press, 2004, p. 105.
7. Ibid., p. 106.
8. Philip Mansel, *Paris between Empires 1814–1852*, London: John Murray, 2001, p. 130.
9. Ibid., p. 131.
10. Ibid., p. 132.
11. Kale, *French Salons*, p. 107.
12. Ibid.
13. Ibid., p. 109; Roxana M. Verona, 'Madame Récamier: entre portrait et causerie', *Romantisme*, 109, 2000, pp. 99–106.
14. Kale, *French Salons*, p. 107.
15. Ibid., p. 111.
16. Albertine de Staël-Holstein, Duchesse de Broglie, *Lettres de la Duchesse de Broglie 1814–1838*, Paris: Calmann-Lévy, 1896.
17. Kale, *French Salons*, p. 126.
18. Mansel, *Paris between Empires*, p. 122. See also Daniel Stern, *Esquisses morales: pensées, réflexions et maximes*, 2nd ed., Paris: J. Techener, 1856.
19. Mansel, *Paris between Empires*, p. 134.
20. Kale, *French Salons*, p. 130.
21. Xavier Salmon, *François Gérard, 1770–1837, portraitiste: peintre des rois, roi des peintres*, Paris: Réunion des musées nationaux – Grand Palais, 2014; Mansel. *Paris between Empires*, p. 135.
22. Mansel, *Paris between Empires*, p. 139.
23. W. A., *Mémoires de Mme Boigne 1-111*, Paris: E. Leroux, 1907. Kale, *French Salons*, p. 133.
24. Madame M*** (Mary Clark Mohl), *Madame Récamier: With a Sketch of the History of Society in France*, London: Chapman & Hall, 1862. Mansel, *Paris between Empires*, p. 143.
25. Mansel, *Paris between Empires*, p. 161.

Chapter 28: Delphine de Girardin and her 'Collection of Superiorities'

1. Léon Séché, *Delphine Gay, Mme de Girardin*, Paris: Mercure de France, 1910.
2. Anne Martin-Fugier, *La Vie élégante, ou La Formation du Tout-Paris 1815–1848*, Paris: Perrin, 1990, p. 366.
3. Ibid., p. 367.
4. William Weaver, *The Golden Century of Italian Opera from Rossini to Puccini*, London: Thames & Hudson, 1980.
5. Martin-Fugier, *La Vie élégante, Op. cit.*, p. 358.

6. Ibid., pp. 366–7.
7. Ibid., p. 358.
8. Théophile Gautier, *Portraits et souvenirs littéraires*, Paris: Michel Lévy frères, 1875.
9. Martin-Fugier, *La Vie élégante*, pp. 364–9.
10. Ibid., p. 370.
11. Ibid., p. 372.
12. Ibid., p. 375.
13. Marianne de Lamartine was quite something. See William Fortescue, 'The Role of Women and Charity in the French Revolution of 1848: The Case of Marianne de Lamartine', *French History*, 11 (1), 1997, pp. 54–78.
14. Martin-Fugier, *La Vie élégante*, pp. 377ff.
15. F. W. J. Hemmings, *Culture and Society in France 1789–1848*, Leicester: Leicester University Press, 1987, p. 168.
16. For Stendhal and the romantics, see ibid., pp. 163–6.
17. Ibid., p. 168.
18. Ibid., pp. 260ff. See also Martin-Fugier, *La Vie élégante*, pp. 333–4.
19. Hemmings, *Culture and Society in France 1789–1848*, p. 141.
20. Ibid.
21. Ibid., pp. 262–3.
22. J. Tripier Le Franc, *Histoire de la vie et de la mort du Baron Gros, le grand peintre*, Paris: Jules Martin etc., 1880.
23. Hemmings, *Culture and Society in France 1789–1848*, p. 263.
24. Of the many biographies, see George Sand, *Histoire de ma vie*, 4 vols, Paris: C. Lévy, 1898–9; Roger Pierrot *et al.*, *George Sand: visages du romantisme*, Paris: Bibliothèque nationale de France, 1977; Martine Reid, *George Sand*, tr. Gretchen van Slyke, University Park: Pennsylvania State University Press, 2018.
25. An English-language translation of *Consuelo* was published in 1908 by Walter Scott in London.
26. F. W. J. Hemmings, *Culture and Society in France 1848–1898: Dissidents and Philistines*, New York: Charles Scribner's Sons, 1971, pp. 30–1.
27. For context, see: H. Sutherland Edwards, *Famous First Representations*, London: Chapman & Hall, 1886, which compared the first night of *Hernani* with some others that were equally notorious, such as Molière's *Le Tartuffe* and Wagner's reworked *Tannhäuser* at the Paris Opera in 1861.
28. See J. C. Ireson, *Victor Hugo: A Companion to His Poetry*, Oxford: Clarendon Press, 1997.
29. See Catherine Hewitt, 'Théophile Gautier, Orator to the Artists: Art Journalism of the Second Republic, *French Studies*, 64 (2), 2010, pp. 213–14.
30. See, for a general discussion, Sylvie Guillaume, *Le Centrisme en France aux XIXe et XXe siècles: un échec?*, Pessac: Maison des sciences de l'homme d'Aquitaine, 2005.
31. Martin-Fugier, *La Vie élégante*, pp. 375–82.
32. Alexandre Dumas, *Souvenirs d'Antony*, Paris: Michel Lévy frères, 1862.
33. Hemmings, *Culture and Society in France 1789–1848*, p. 288.
34. One of the most recent studies is Marie-Christine Natta, *Eugène Delacroix*, Paris: Tallandier, 2010, but, for contemporary context, see also Charles Baudelaire, *Eugène Delacroix*, Paris: G. Crès, 1927.
35. Hemmings, *Culture and Society in France 1789–1848*, pp. 181–90.
36. A helpful introduction can be found in Ceri Crossley, *French Historians and Romanticism: Thierry, Guizot, the Saint-Simonians, Quinet, Michelet*, London: Routledge, 1993, but see also Roland Barthes, *Michelet*, tr. Richard Howard, Oxford: Blackwell, 1987; and, more recently, Paul Viallaneix, *Michelet: les travaux et les jours 1798–1874*, Paris: Gallimard, 1998.

37. Martin-Fugier, *La Vie élégante*, pp. 376ff.
38. Ibid., p. 381.

Chapter 29: 'A Life Based on More than Motherhood'

1. E. Preston Dargan and Bernard Weinberg (eds), *The Evolution of Balzac's Comedie humaine*, Chicago: University of Chicago Press, 1942, especially the chapter by B. I. Dedinsky, 'Development of the Scheme of the Comédie Humaine: Distribution of the sources.'
2. Richard Bolster, *Marie d'Agoult: The Rebel Countess*, New Haven, CT, and London: Yale University Press, 2000, p. 2.
3. Ibid., p. 43.
4. Ibid., p. 60.
5. Ibid., pp. 91–8; reflected in Daniel Stern, *Lettres républicaines du Second Empire*, ed. Jacques Vier, Paris: Cèdre, 1951.
6. Bolster, *Marie d'Agoult*, p. 110.
7. For an introduction to Eugène Scribe, see Neil Cole Arvin, *Eugène Scribe and the French Theatre 1815–1860*, Cambridge, MA: Harvard University Press, 1924.
8. Bolster, *Marie d'Agoult*, p. 115.
9. Ibid.
10. Ibid.
11. Wagner hated Meyerbeer because of his Jewishness, though he thought it 'impossible to surpass him'. Harold C. Schonberg, *The Lives of the Great Composers*, London: Davis-Poynter, 1971, p. 208; Bolster, *Marie d'Agoult*, pp. 201, 205.
12. Bolster, *Marie d'Agoult*, p. 122.
13. Quoted ibid., p. 125.
14. For appropriate detail, see Étienne Rey, *La Vie amoureuse de Berlioz*, Paris: Ernest Flammarion, 1929.
15. Bolster, *Marie d'Agoult*, p. 130.
16. Ibid., p. 122.
17. Ibid., p. 148.
18. For other background see Joachim Merlant, 'Le Manuscript de *Béatrix* de Balzac', *Revue d'histoire littéraire de la France*, 20 (3), 1913, pp. 602–36.
19. For a modern orientation to Sainte-Beuve, see Marcel Proust, *By Way of Sainte-Beuve*, tr. Sylvia Townsend-Warner, London: Hogarth Press, [1958] 1984.
20. For full context, see Christopher Prendergast, *The Classic: Sainte-Beuve and the Nineteenth-Century Culture Wars*, Oxford: Oxford University Press, 2007.
21. Bolster, *Marie d'Agoult*, p. 201.
22. Ibid., p. 176.
23. Joseph J. O'Malley, reviews of William J. Brazill, *The Young Hegelians* and David McLellan, *Marx before Marxism*, *Review of Politics*, 34 (2), 1972, pp. 244–9, discusses how art and politics were linked in their minds.
24. Bolster, *Marie d'Agoult*, pp. 203–4.
25. Ibid.
26. Ibid., p. 215.
27. Ibid., p. 226; Hope Christiansen, '"May I Have This Waltz?" Madame Bovary and Nélida,' *Dalhousie French Studies*, 55, 2001, pp. 31–9.
28. Franz Liszt, *Lettres à Cosima et à Daniela*, ed. Klára Hamburger, Liège: Pierre Mardaga Sprimont, 1996, shows how close Liszt was to his children, more so than d'Agoult.
29. Bolster, *Marie d'Agoult*, p. 248.
30. Ibid., p. 256.

Chapter 30: 'Notre-Dame des Arts'

1. I have used Joanna Richardson, *Princess Mathilde*, London: Weidenfeld & Nicolson, 1969; and Jean des Cars, *La Princesse Mathilde: l'amour, la gloire et les arts*, Paris: Librairie académique Perrin, 1988.
2. Richardson, *Princess Mathilde*, p. 51.
3. Ibid., p. 27.
4. Ibid., p. 34.
5. Ph. de Chennevières, 'Le Comte de Nieuwerkerke', *Gazette des beaux-arts*, 3 (7), 1892, p. 265.
6. Richardson, *Princess Mathilde*, pp. 46ff.
7. Ibid., p. 34.
8. Ibid., p. 62.
9. John Julius Norwich, *France: A History from Gaul to de Gaulle*, London: John Murray, 2018, pp. 279–80.
10. For Ponsard see Siegbert Himmelsbach, 'François Ponsard: poète du juste milieu', *Revue d'histoire littéraire de la France*, 81 (1), 1981, pp. 99–109; for Augier see Brander Matthews, *French Dramatists of the Nineteenth Century*, London: Remington, n.d. chapter 5.
11. Harold C. Schonberg, *The Lives of the Great Composers*, London: Davis-Poynter, 1971, p. 303. See also Roger Nichols (ed. & tr.), *Camille Saint-Saëns on Music and Musicians*, New York: Oxford University Press, 2008.
12. Schonberg, *The Lives of the Great Composers*, p. 303.
13. See Geoff Dyer, 'Succès de scandale', *The Guardian*, 9 December 2006.
14. André Billy, *The Goncourt Brothers*, tr. Margaret Shaw, London: André Deutsch, 1960.
15. Richardson, *Princess Mathilde*, p. 130.
16. F. W. J. Hemmings, *Culture and Society in France 1848–1898: Dissidents and Philistines*, New York: Charles Scribner's Sons, 1971, p. 114.
17. Ibid.
18. Ibid., p. 115.
19. Ibid., p. 117; Michael Tilby, 'Flaubert, Edmond de Goncourt, and Gavarni's "Immoral" *Débardeurs*', *French Studies Bulletin*, 39 (146), 2018, pp. 1–6.
20. James Wood, *How Fiction Works*, London: Jonathan Cape, 2008, p. 29.
21. Richardson, *Princess Mathilde*, p. 129.
22. Ibid., p. 162.
23. Ibid, p. 162, 167. Pierre Pinon, *Paris pour mémoire: le livre noir de destructions haussmanniennes*, Paris: Parigramme, 2012, gives a good account of what was destroyed.
24. Richardson. *Princess Mathilde*, p. 171.
25. Ibid., p. 210.

Chapter 31: *La Grande Française*

1. Winifred Stephens, *Madame Adam (Juliette Lamber): La Grande Française, from Louis Philippe until 1917*, London: Chapman & Hall, 1917, p. 3.
2. Ibid., p. 7.
3. Ibid., p. 17.
4. P.-J. Proudhon, *Système de contradictions économiques, ou La Philosophie de la misère*, Elibron Classics, 2 vols, [1850] 2005.
5. Stephens, *Madame Adam*, p. 23.
6. Ibid., p. 39.
7. Ibid., p. 43.
8. Ibid., p. 46. Among Karr's whimsical titles are *L'Art d'être malheureux*, Paris:

Calmann-Lévy, 1876; and *Voyage autour de mon jardin*, 2 vols, Brussels: Société Belge Librairie, 1844–5.

9. Peter Watson, *Ideas: A History from Fire to Freud*, London: Weidenfeld & Nicolson, 2005, pp. 881–2.
10. Stephens, *Madame Adam*, p. 47.
11. Ibid., p. 49.
12. Mark Everist, *Giacomo Meyerbeer and Music Drama in Nineteenth-Century Paris*, Aldershot: Ashgate, 2005.
13. Stephens, *Madame Adam*, p. 52.
14. Ibid.
15. Ibid., p. 56.
16. Ibid, p. 58. See also: Juliette Adam, *Le Roman de mon enfance et de ma jeunesse*, Paris: Alphonse Lemerre, 1902.
17. Juliette Adam, *Mes sentiments et nos idées avant 1870*, Paris: Alphonse Lemerre, 1905.
18. Stephens, *Madame Adam*, p. 61.
19. Ibid., p. 64; Karen Offen, 'A Nineteenth-Century French Feminist Rediscovered: Jenny P. d'Héricourt, 1809–1875', *Signs: Journal of Women in Culture and Society*, 13 (1), 1987, pp. 144–78.
20. Stephens, *Madame Adam*, p. 66.
21. Ibid.
22. Émile Littré, *Dictionnaire de la langue française*, Paris: Hachette, 4 vols, 1863–72; Sudhir Hazareesingh, *How the French Think: An Affectionate Portrait of an Intellectual People*, London: Penguin, 2016, p. 96.
23. Stephens, *Madame Adam*, p. 7.
24. Watson, *Ideas*, pp. 962–3. See also Hazareesingh, *How the French Think*, p. 231.
25. Stephens, *Madame Adam*, p. 97.
26. Ibid., p. 28.
27. Ibid., p. 102.
28. What Adam faced is brought out starkly in Jill Harsin, *Barricades: The War in the Streets of Revolutionary Paris 1830–1848*, New York: Palgrave, 2002.
29. J. P. T. Bury, *Gambetta and the Making of the Third Republic*, London: Longman, 1973.
30. Stephens, *Madame Adam*, p. 116.
31. Juliette Adam, *Mes illusions et nos souffrances pendant le siège de Paris*, Paris: Alphonse Lemerre, 1906.

Chapter 32: The *Flâneur*, the *Boulevardier* and the Dandy

1. Stanley Karnow, *Paris in the Fifties*, New York: Times Books, 1997, p. 5.
2. Edmund White, *The Flâneur: A Stroll through the Paradoxes of Paris*, London: Bloomsbury, 2001, p. 10; James Cannon, *The Paris Zone: A Cultural History 1840–1944*, Farnham: Ashgate, 2015, pp. 8, 13, 68, 74. See also Catherine Nesci, *Le Flâneur et les flâneuses: les femmes et la ville à l'époque romantique*, Grenoble: Ellug, 2007; and Aruna D'Souza and Tom McDonough (eds), *The Invisible Flâneuse? Gender, Public Space and Visual Culture in Nineteenth-Century Paris*, Manchester: Manchester University Press, 2006.
3. Walter Benjamin, *The Writer of Modern Life: Essays on Charles Baudelaire*, tr. Howard Eiland *et al.*, Cambridge, MA: Belknap Press, 2006, p. 8.
4. Keith Tester (ed.), *The Flâneur*, London: Routledge, 1994, p. 1.
5. Ibid., p. 2.
6. Ibid., p. 36.
7. Ibid., p. 40–1.
8. Benjamin, *The Writer of Modern Life*, p. 81.

9. Ibid., p. 85.
10. Ibid., p. 92.
11. Tester, *The Flâneur*, p. 7.
12. Benjamin, *The Writer of Modern Life*, p. 96.
13. Cornelia Otis Skinner, *Elegant Wits and Grand Horizontals – Paris, La Belle Époque*, London: Michael Joseph, 1963, p. 102.
14. Ibid., p. 114.
15. Ibid., p. 117.
16. Ibid., p. 122.
17. Vincent Cronin, *Paris on the Eve: 1900–1914*, London: Collins, 1989, p. 332.
18. Skinner, *Elegant Wits and Grand Horizontals*, p. 136.
19. Julian Barnes, *The Man in the Red Coat*, London: Vintage, 2019, p. 60; Louis Piaget Shanks, *Charles Baudelaire: Flesh and Spirit*, London: Noel Douglas, 1930, p. 36.
20. Nigel Rodgers, *The Dandy: Peacock or Enigma?* London: Bene Factum, 2012, pp. 9–10.
21. Skinner, *Elegant Wits and Grand Horizontals*, p. 78.
22. Ibid., p. 81.
23. Anne Martin-Fugier, *La Vie élégante, ou La Formation du Tout-Paris 1815–1848*, Paris: Perrin, 1990, p. 464.
24. Shanks, *Charles Baudelaire*, p. 90.
25. Martin-Fugier, *La Vie élégante*, p. 464.
26. Ibid., pp. 464–6.
27. Virginia Rounding, *Grandes Horizontales: The Lives and Legends of Marie Duplessis, Cora Pearl, La Païva and La Présidente*, London: Bloomsbury, 2003, p. 100.
28. Shanks, *Charles Baudelaire*, p. 38.
29. Ibid., p. 36.
30. Ibid., p. 41.
31. Skinner, *Elegant Wits and Grand Horizontals*, p. 121.
32. Shanks, *Charles Baudelaire*, p. 42.
33. Rodgers, *The Dandy*, p. 137.
34. Ibid., p. 139
35. Ibid., p. 145.
36. Skinner, *Elegant Wits and Grand Horizontals*, p. 47.
37. Ibid., p. 49.
38. Ibid., p. 51.
39. One typical title was *La Trépidation: scènes de mœurs mondaines*, Paris: Émile-Paul frères, 1922; see Edgar Munhall, *Whistler and Montesquiou: The Butterfly and the Bat*, Paris: Flammarion, 1995.
40. Barnes, *The Man in the Red Coat*, p. 18; Skinner, *Elegant Wits and Grand Horizontals*, p. 46.
41. Caroline Weber, *Proust's Duchess: How Three Celebrated Women Captured the Imagination of Fin-de-Siècle Paris*, New York: Alfred A. Knopf, 2018, p. 68.
42. Cannon, *The Paris Zone*, p. 60.
43. Weber, *Proust's Duchess*, p. 225.
44. Ibid.
45. Ibid.; Lawrence Danson, review of Tony Howard, *Women as Hamlet: Performance in Interpretation in Theatre, Film and Fiction*, *Shakespeare Quarterly*, 59 (1), 2008, pp. 109–11.
46. Weber, *Proust's Duchess*, p. 553.
47. Barnes, *The Man in the Red Coat*, p. 64.

Chapter 33: The Splendours and Spleen of No-Man's-Land

1. Rosemary Lloyd (ed.), *The Cambridge Companion to Baudelaire*, Cambridge: Cambridge University Press, 2005, p. 2.
2. Ibid., p. 3.
3. Ibid., p. 37.
4. Virginia Rounding, *Grandes Horizontales: The Lives and Legends of Marie Duplessis, Cora Pearl, La Païva and La Présidente*, London: Bloomsbury, 2003, p. 133.
5. Ibid., pp. 134ff.
6. Émile Reinaud, *Charles Jalabert: l'homme, l'artiste*, Paris: Hachette, 1902.
7. Ibid., p. 100.
8. James S. Patty, review of Thierry Savatier, *Une femme trop gaie: biographie d'un amour de Baudelaire*; *Nineteenth-Century French Studies*, 33 (1–2), 2004–5, p. 198.
9. Rounding, *Grandes Horizontales*, p. 106.
10. Ibid., p. 107.
11. Edith Melcher, *The Life and Times of Henri Monnier 1799–1877*, Cambridge, MA: Harvard University Press, 1950; J.-F. Schnerb, 'Henry Monnier et Joseph Prudhomme', *Gazette des beaux arts*, 3 (27), 1902, pp. 489–99.
12. Rounding, *Grandes Horizontales*, p. 114.
13. Ibid., p. 115.
14. Ibid., p. 117; Théophile Gautier, *Voyage en Russie*, Paris: Charpentier, 1867.
15. Rounding, *Grandes Horizontales*, p. 118.
16. Ibid.
17. Théophile Gautier, *La Nature chez elle et Ménagerie intime*, Paris: Charpentier, 1891. For more on his attitude to sex see Théophile Gautier, *Les Roués innocents*, Paris: Librairie nouvelle, 1853.
18. Rounding, *Grandes Horizontales*, p. 135.
19. Ibid., p. 146.
20. Ibid.; Thierry Savatier, *Une femme trop gaie: biographie d'un amour de Baudelaire*, Paris: CNRS, 2003; Armand Moss, *Baudelaire and Madame Sabatier*, Paris: A. G. Nizet, 1978. The latter also claims that a sexual relationship did not exist.
21. Ronjaunee Chatterjee, 'Baudelaire and Feminine Singularity', *French Studies*, 70 (1), 2016, pp. 17–32.

Chapter 34: *Fumisterie* and the Poetics of the Café

1. Virginia Rounding, *Grandes Horizontales: The Lives and Legends of Marie Duplessis, Cora Pearl, La Païva and La Présidente*, London: Bloomsbury, 2003, p. 156.
2. Matthew Gandy, 'The Paris Sewers and the Rationalization of Urban Space', *Transactions of the Institute of British Geographers*, 24 (1), 1999, pp. 23–44.
3. Rounding, *Grandes Horizontales*, p. 157.
4. Ibid., p. 158.
5. Ibid.
6. T. J. Clark, *The Painting of Modern Life: Paris in the Art of Manet and His Followers*, London: Thames & Hudson, 1985, p. 212.
7. Gérard-Georges Lemaire, *L'Europe des cafés*, Paris: Eric Koehler, 1991. See also Leona Rittner *et al.* (eds), *The Thinking Space: The Café as a Cultural Institution in Paris, Italy and Vienna*, Farnham: Ashgate, 2013.
8. Pierre Assouline, *Discovering Impressionism: The Life and Times of Paul Durand-Ruel*, tr. Willard Wood and Anthony Roberts, New York: Vendome Press, 2004, p. 117.

9. Ibid.
10. Ibid., p. 97.
11. Ibid., p. 53.
12. Rittner *et al.*, *The Thinking Space*, p. 13.
13. Ibid., p. 14.
14. Ibid., p. 15. Perhaps the most surprising reference here is Giordana Charuty, '"Cher Grand Professor Freud": une correspondance entre Yvette Guilbert et Sigmund Freud,' *L'Homme*, 215–16, 2015, pp. 81–102.
15. Rittner *et al.*, *The Thinking Space*, p. 36.
16. Steven Moore Whiting, *Satie the Bohemian: From Cabaret to Concert Hall*, Oxford: Oxford University Press, 1999, p. 69.
17. Ibid., p. 81.
18. Ibid., p. 98.
19. Ibid., p. 107.
20. Albert Dubeux, *La Curieuse Vie de Georges Courteline*, Paris: P. Horay, 1958.
21. Whiting, *Satie the Bohemian*, p. 129.
22. Ibid., p. 120.
23. Ibid., p. 122.
24. Eunice Lipton, 'Representing Sexuality in Women Artists's Biographies: The Cases of Suzanne Valadon and Victorine Meurent', *Journal of Sex Research*, 27 (1), 1990, pp. 81–94.
25. Whiting, *Satie the Bohemian*, p. 263.
26. Roger Shattuck, *The Banquet Years: The Arts in France 1885–1918*, London: Faber & Faber, 1959, p. 263.
27. Ibid., p. 179.
28. Ibid., p. 263.

Chapter 35: *Chic*: The Parisienne as a Work of Art

1. Ruth E. Iskin, *Modern Women and Parisian Consumer Culture in Impressionist Painting*, Cambridge: Cambridge University Press, 2007. p. 195.
2. Ibid.
3. Ibid.
4. Lisa Tiersten, *Marianne in the Market: Envisioning Consumer Society in Fin-de-Siècle France*, Berkeley: University of California Press, 2001, p. 3.
5. Iskin, *Modern Women and Parisian Consumer Culture in Impressionist Painting*, p. 184.
6. Ibid., p. 102. Scott Allan *et al.* (eds), *Manet and Modern Beauty: The Artist's Last Years*, Los Angeles: J. Paul Getty Museum, 2019, contains two chapters on Manet and the Parisienne.
7. Iskin, *Modern Women and Parisian Consumer Culture in Impressionist Painting*, p. 185.
8. Ibid., p. 190.
9. Though Léon Gozlan is largely forgotten now, his standing in his lifetime can be gauged from his inclusion in Annie Challice, *French Authors at Home*, London: L. Booth, 1844, alongside the likes of Balzac, Sand and Hugo.
10. Iskin, *Modern Women and Parisian Consumer Culture in Impressionist Painting*, p. 87.
11. Tiersten, *Marianne in the Market*, p. 190.
12. Ibid., p. 211.
13. Iskin, *Modern Women and Parisian Consumer Culture in Impressionist Painting*, p. 17.
14. Tiersten, *Marianne in the Market*, p. 191.
15. Ibid., p. 192.

16. For Paquin, see Charles Dawbarn, *Makers of New France*, London: Mills & Boon, 1915.
17. Tiersten, *Marianne in the Market*, p. 5.
18. Ibid., p. 6.
19. Ibid. See Judith G. Coffin, *The Politics of Women's Work: The Paris Garment Trades 1750–1915*, Princeton, NJ: Princeton University Press, 1996.
20. Tiersten, *Marianne in the Market*, p. 9.
21. Brian Wemp, 'Social Space, Technology and Consumer Culture at the Grands Magasins Dufayel', *Historical Reflections*, 37 (1), 2011, pp. 1–17, looks at a huge department store built on the fringes of Paris in the late nineteenth century and, unlike the stores considered by most writers, one that had a big impact on the cultural life of the working class rather than *mondaines*.
22. Tiersten, *Marianne in the Market*, p. 29.
23. Ibid., p. 47.
24. Ibid., p. 61. But see Sara Maza, *The Myth of the French Bourgeoisie: An Essay on the Social Imaginary 1750–1850*, Cambridge, MA: Harvard University Press, 2003. Despite the date limits, it is still relevant.
25. Tiersten, *Marianne in the Market*, p. 85.
26. But sent up in Richard O'Monroy, *Le Chic et le chèque*, Paris: Calmann-Lévy, 1893.
27. Tiersten, *Marianne in the Market*, p. 91.
28. Ibid., p. 105.
29. Ibid., p. 119.
30. Journals aimed explicitly at the Parisienne included *La Revue parisienne, Semaine parisienne, Comédie parisienne, La Patriote parisienne* and *La Parisienne*.
31. Tiersten, *Marianne in the Market*, p. 144.
32. Octave Uzanne, *La Femme et la mode: métamorphoses de la Parisienne de 1792 à 1892*, Paris: Ancienne maison Quantin, 1893.
33. Tiersten, *Marianne in the Market*, p. 178.
34. Ibid., p. 179.
35. Iskin, *Modern Women and Parisian Consumer Culture in Impressionist Painting*, p. 233.
36. *The Times*, 23 October, 2021.

Chapter 36: 'All Progress Depends on France Remaining Intact'

1. Roger Shattuck, *The Banquet Years: The Arts in France 1885–1918*, London: Faber & Faber, 1959, p. 5.
2. Ibid., p. 6.
3. Ibid., p. 7.
4. Ibid. More recent is Antoine Prost, *Les Français de la Belle Époque*, Paris: Gallimard, 2019, with maps showing where different activities took place.
5. Nancy J. Troy, *Couture Culture: A Study in Modern Art and Fashion*, Cambridge, MA: MIT Press, 2003. See also *Paul Poiret et Nicole Groult: maîtres de mode art-déco*, Paris: Paris Musées, 1986, a catalogue to accompany an exhibition in Tokyo and Paris.
6. Shattuck, *The Banquet Years*, p. 8.
7. Wolfgang Schivelbusch, *The Culture of Defeat: On National Trauma, Mourning and Recovery*, tr. Jeffrey Chase, London: Granta, 2003, p. 104.
8. Ibid., p. 105.
9. Ibid., p. 107.
10. Ibid., p. 108.
11. J. P. T. Bury, 'Gambetta and the Revolution of 4 September 1870', *Cambridge Historical Journal*, 4 (3), 1934, pp. 263–82. The title reflects the author's argument.

12. Schivelbusch, *The Culture of Defeat*, p. 113.
13. Ibid., p. 115.
14. Ibid.
15. Francine du Plessix Gray, *Rage and Fire: A Life of Louise Colet – Pioneer Feminist, Literary Star, Flaubert's Muse*, London: Hamish Hamilton, 1994.
16. Schivelbusch, *The Culture of Defeat*, p. 120.
17. Ibid., p. 122.
18. Victor Hugo, *L'Année terrible*, Paris: J. Hetzel, 1872.
19. Schivelbusch, *The Culture of Defeat*, p. 128.
20. Karine Varley, *Under the Shadow of Defeat: The War of 1870–71 in French Memory*, Basingstoke: Palgrave Macmillan, 2008, p. 152.
21. Ibid., pp. 165–6.
22. Ibid., p. 168.
23. Ibid., p. 173.
24. Bernard Taithe, *Defeated Flesh: Welfare, Warfare and the Making of Modern France*, Manchester: Manchester University Press, 1999, pp. 4–5.
25. Ibid., p. 12.
26. Schivelbusch, *The Culture of Defeat*, p. 129.

Chapter 37: 'Vegetations of the Sick Mind'

1. Daniel Pick, *Faces of Degeneration: A European Disorder c.1848–c.1918*, Cambridge: Cambridge University Press, 1989, p. 72.
2. Peter Watson, *Ideas: A History from Fire to Freud*, London: Weidenfeld & Nicolson, 2005, p. 914.
3. Peter Watson, *The Modern Mind: An Intellectual History of the Twentieth Century*, New York: HarperCollins, 2000, p. 483.
4. Jean-Marie Augustin, *George Vacher de Lapouge: juriste, raciologue et eugéniste 1854–1936*, Toulouse: Presses de l'Université Toulouse 1 Capitole, 2011.
5. Watson, *Ideas*, pp. 914–15.
6. Geneviève Fraisse, *Les femmes et leur histoire*, Paris: Éditions Gallimard, 2010, p. 448ff.
7. Pick, *Faces of Degeneration*, p. 74.
8. Ibid., p. 91.
9. Gustave Le Bon, *La Révolution française et la psychologie des révolutions*, Paris: Ernest Flammarion, 1912.
10. Pick, *Faces of Degeneration*, p. 91.
11. Ibid., p. 100.
12. Diana Holmes, *Rachilde: Decadence, Gender and the Woman Writer*, Oxford and New York, Berg, 2001, p. 37.
13. Ibid., p. 74.
14. Ibid., p. 75.
15. Joseph Acquisto, 'The Decadent Writer as Collector and Flâneur: On Intertextual Networks and Literary Spaces in Huysmans', *French Forum*, 32 (3), 2007, pp 65–80.
16. Pick, *Faces of Degeneration*, p. 12.
17. Ibid., p. 18.
18. Ibid., p. 25.
19. Ibid., p. 28. Rachilde's various thoughts about love are explored in Vicky Gauthier, 'Le Banquet de Rachilde', *Voix plurielles*, 14 (2), 2017, pp. 92–102.
20. For Catulle Mendès, see Liz Constable, 'Being under the Influence: Catulle Mendès and Les Morphinées, or Decadence of Degeneracy', *L'Esprit créateur*, 37 (4), 1997, pp. 67–81; for Felix Fénéon, see Isabelle Cahn (ed.), *Félix*

Fénéon: critique, collectionneur, anarchiste, Paris: Musée du quai Branly Jacques Chirac, 2019, a catalogue to accompany an exhibition in Paris and New York.

21. Pick, *Faces of Degeneration*, p. 41.
22. Ibid., p. 42.
23. Ibid., p. 51; see also Alfred Jarry, *Le surmâle*, Paris: Fasquelle, [1902] 1953, p. 12.
24. Holmes, *Rachilde*, p. 52.
25. Ibid., p. 53.
26. Ibid., p. 57.
27. Rachilde, *Dans le puits, ou La Vie inférieure 1915–1917*, Paris: Mercure de France, 1918.
28. G. Bruno, *Le Tour de la France par deux enfants: devoir et patrie*, Paris: Belin, 1877.
29. Édouard Drumont, *La France juive: essai d'histoire contemporaine*, Paris: Marpon & Flammarion, 1886; see also Grégoire Kauffmann, *Édouard Drumont*, Paris: Perrin, 2008.
30. Robert Gildea, *Children of the Revolution: The French 1799–1914*, Cambridge, MA: Harvard University Press, p. 275.
31. Typical Barrès views can be found in *Scènes et doctrines du nationalisme*, Paris: Félix Juven, 1902; and *Les Déracinés*, Paris: Eugène Fasquelle, 1897.

Chapter 38: 'The Old Brilliance Revives'

1. Caroline Weber, *Proust's Duchess: How Three Celebrated Women Captured the Imagination of Fin-de-Siècle Paris*, New York: Alfred A. Knopf, 2018, p. 5.
2. Ibid., p. 59.
3. Winifred Stephens, *Madame Adam (Juliette Lamber): La Grande Française, from Louis Philippe until 1917*, London: Chapman & Hall, 1917, p. 172.
4. Ibid., p. 181.
5. Ibid., pp. 197–8; see also Janine Alexandre-Debray, *La Païva 1819–1884: ses amants, ses maris*, Paris: Perrin, 1986.
6. Stephens, *Madame Adam*, p. 207.
7. Among his sitters are several individuals who appear elsewhere in this book, such as Édouard Manet, Natalie Clifford Barney and Georges Feydeau; his pupils included John Singer Sargent, Maximilien Luce and Paul Helleu.
8. Stephens, *Madame Adam*, p. 239.
9. Ibid., p. 219.
10. Ibid., p. 239.
11. Her attitude comes across clearly in *L'Heure vengeresse des crimes bismarckiens*: Paris: Nouvelle Librairie nationale, 1915.

Chapter 39: Proust's Prototypes

1. Cornelia Otis Skinner, *Elegant Wits and Grand Horizontals: Paris, La Belle Epoque*. London: Michael Joseph, 1963, p. 154.
2. Ibid., p. 152.
3. Anne Martin-Fugier, *Les Salons de la IIIe République: arts, littérature, politique*, Paris: Perrin, 2003, pp. 208ff.
4. Ibid., p. 209.
5. Skinner, *Elegant Wits and Grand Horizontals*, p. 155.
6. Julie Kavanagh, *The Girl Who Loved Camellias: The Life and Legend of Marie Duplessis*, New York: Alfred A. Knopf, 2013.
7. Virginia Rounding, *Grandes Horizontales: The Lives and Legends of Marie Duplessis, Cora Pearl, La Païva and La Présidente*, London: Bloomsbury, 2003, p. 43.

8. Skinner, *Elegant Wits and Grand Horizontals*, p. 159.

9. Ibid., p. 161.

10. See for instance Pierre Loti, *Siam*, tr. W. P. Baines, London and New York: Kegan Paul International, [1913] 2002; *Vers Ispahan*, Paris: Calmann-Lévy, 1904; *Un Pélerin d'Angkor*, Paris: Calmann-Lévy, 1912; *Lettres de Pierre Loti à Madame Juliette Adam 1880–1922*, Paris: Plon-Nourrit, 1924.

11. Jeanne Maurice Pouquet, *Le Salon de Madame Arman de Caillavet*, Paris: Librairie Hachette, 1926.

12. See in particular Anatole France, *Penguin Island*, tr. A. W. Evans, London: John Lane, the Bodley Head, 1919; Paul Gsell (ed.), *Anatole France and His Circle: Being His Table Talk*, tr. Frederic Lees, London: John Lane, the Bodley Head, 1922.

13. Skinner, *Elegant Wits and Grand Horizontals*, p. 197. Less is written about the Comtesse de Loynes than many other *salonnières* but see Arthur Meyer, *Ce que je peux dire, avec un portrait de Mme la Comtesse du Loynes*, Paris: Plon-Nourrit, 1912.

14. Skinner, *Elegant Wits and Grand Horizontals*, p. 201.

15. Ibid., p. 213.

16. Ibid. For Henry Becque, see Paul Blanchart, *Henry Becque: son œuvre – portrait et autographe*, Paris: Nouvelle revue critique, 1930.

17. Skinner, *Elegant Wits and Grand Horizontals*, p. 216.

18. Caroline Weber, *Proust's Duchess: How Three Celebrated Women Captured the Imagination of Fin-de-Siècle Paris*, New York: Alfred A. Knopf, 2018.

19. Ibid., p. 11.

20. An earlier view is given in Laure Hillerin, *La Comtesse Greffulhe: à l'ombre des Guermantes*, Paris: Flammarion, 2014.

21. Weber, *Proust's Duchess*, p. 25.

22. Ibid., p. 79.

23. Works by or on Madrazo are much rarer than those on Helleu. All I have been able to find is Federico de Madrazo y Kuntz, *Epistolario*, 2 vols, Madrid: Museo del Prado, 1994.

24. Weber, *Proust's Duchess*, p. 14.

25. Ibid., p. 176.

26. Ibid., p. 273; Guy de Maupassant, *Bel-Ami*, Paris: Louis Conard, [1885] 1910; see also Heidi Brevik-Sender, 'Fashion and Fractured Flânerie in Guy de Maupassant's *Bel Ami*', *Dix-Neuf*, 16 (2), 2012, pp. 224–42.

27. Among the many biographies, see Mina Kirstein Curtiss, *Bizet and His World*, London: Secker & Warburg, 1959.

28. Weber, *Proust's Duchess*, p. 122.

29. Ibid., pp. 429ff.

30. Ibid., pp. 436–40.

31. Maupassant's *Strong as Death* is now available online.

32. G. M. Fess, 'Personal Sources for Maupassant's *Contes*', *Modern Language Notes*, 59 (4), 1944, pp. 277–81. See note 31, immediately above.

33. Weber, *Proust's Duchess*, p. 15.

34. A recent biography is Ariane Charton, *Alain-Fournier*, Paris: Gallimard, 2014. But for more specific interpretation see Jean Loize, *Alain-Fournier: sa vie et le Grand Meaulnes*, Paris: Hachette, 1968.

35. Julien Benda, *Belphégor: essai sur l'esthétique de la présente société française*, Paris: Émile-Paul frères, 1919.

36. Anne Martin-Fugier, *Les Salons de la IIIe République: arts, littérature, politique*, Paris: Perrin, 2003, p. 321.

37. Ibid.

38. Lewis A. Coser, *Men of Ideas: A Sociologist's View*, New York: Free Press, 1965, pp. 11ff.

Chapter 40: The Crossroads of French Musical Life

1. Sylvia Kahan, *Music's Modern Muse: A Life of Winnaretta Singer, Princesse de Polignac*, Rochester, NY: University of Rochester Press, 2003.
2. Michael de Cossart, *The Food of Love: Princesse Edmond de Polignac (1865–1943) and Her Salon*, London: Hamish Hamilton, 1978, p. 2.
3. Ibid., p. 11.
4. Ibid., p. 9.
5. Ibid., p. 11.
6. Kahan, *Music's Modern Muse*, p. 17.
7. Ibid., pp. 19, 23.
8. Ibid., p. 15.
9. A useful introduction in English is Jean-Michel Nectoux (ed.), *Gabriel Fauré: His Life through His Letters*, tr. J. A. Underwood, London: Marion Boyars, 1984. But see also Vladimir Jankélévitch, *Gabriel Fauré: ses mélodies, son esthétique*, new ed., Paris: Plon, 1951.
10. Harold C. Schonberg, *The Lives of the Great Composers*, London: Davis-Poynter, 1971, pp. 364–6.
11. Kahan, *Music's Modern Muse*, p. 36.
12. Ibid., p. 37.
13. Ibid.
14. Bernard Gavoty, *Reynaldo Hahn: le musicien de la Belle époque*, Paris: Buchet-Chastel, 1976.
15. For the friendship with Proust, see Martin Robitaille, *Proust épistolier*, Montreal: Presses de l'Université de Montréal, 2003. This gives Proust's letters to his mother, to Robert de Montesquiou and Hahn.
16. Kahan, *Music's Modern Muse*, p. 40.
17. Roger Delage, *Emmanuel Chabrier*, Paris: Fayard, 1999.
18. Kahan, *Music's Modern Muse*, p. 53.
19. Auguste Dorchain, *Chant pour Léo Delibes*, Paris: Alphonse Lemerre, 1899.
20. Cossart, *The Food of Love*, p. 25.
21. Kahan, *Music's Modern Muse*, p. 53.
22. Ibid., p. 56.
23. Cossart, *The Food of Love*, p. 39.
24. Ibid., p. 41. But see also Sylvia Kahan, *In Search of New Scales, Prince Edmond de Polignac, Octatonic Explorer*, Rochester, NY: University of Rochester Press, 2009.
25. Kahan, *Music's Modern Muse*, p. 47.
26. Ibid., p. 49.
27. Cossart, *The Food of Love*, p. 51.
28. Kahan, *Music's Modern Muse, Op. cit.*, p. xx.
29. Ibid., p. 63. See also Stephan Zank, *Irony and Sound: The Music of Maurice Ravel*, Rochester, NY: University of Rochester Press, 2009.
30. Cossart, *The Food of Love*, p. 83.
31. Kahan, *Music's Modern Muse, Op. cit.*, p. 65.
32. Cossart, *The Food of Love*, p. 83.
33. Ibid., p. 84.
34. Kahan, *Music's Modern Muse, Op. cit.*, p. 134.
35. Ibid., p. 5.
36. Cossart, *The Food of Love*, p. 86.
37. Kahan, *Music's Modern Muse, Op. cit.*, p. 148.
38. Ibid.
39. Ibid., p. 105. There are numerous biographies and more than one autobiography. But see also Jean Cocteau and Anna de Noailles, *Correspondance*, ed. Claude Mignot-Ogliastri, Paris: Gallimard, 1989.

40. Kahan, *Music's Modern Muse, Op. cit.*, p. 154.
41. There is no shortage of biographies and other studies of Diaghilev's life and art, but a detailed look at the artefacts he used can be found in *Catalogue Principally of Diaghilev Ballet Material: Costumes, Costume Designs and Portraits*, London: Sotheby's, 1967.
42. Kahan, *Music's Modern Muse, Op. cit.*, p. 159.
43. Cossart, *The Food of Love*, p. 103.
44. Henri de Régnier, *Esquisses Vénitiennes*, rev. ed., Paris: Mercure de France, 1920.

Chapter 41: Miracle, Mutiny, Mourning, *Mondains*

1. Alistair Horne, *Friend or Foe: An Anglo-Saxon History of France*, London: Weidenfeld & Nicolson, 2004, p. 276.
2. Ibid., p. 277.
3. Ibid., p. 278.
4. Ibid., p. 279. Suggested reading on the Schlieffen plan: Benoît Lemay, 'Le Mythe de la bataille de la Marne ou de l'échec du "Plan Schlieffen" en septembre 1914 dans l'historiographie allemande', *Guerres mondiales et conflits contemporains*, 252, 2013, pp. 7–26.
5. There are well over fifty books on the Battle of the Marne. One of the more up to date is Holger H. Herwig, *The Marne, 1914: The Opening of World War I and the Battle That Changed the World*, New York: Random House, 2009.
6. Horne, *Friend or Foe*, p. 282.
7. Ibid., p. 287.
8. André Loez, 14-18: *Les refus de la guerre: Une histoire des mutins*, Paris: Éditions Gallimard, 2010, pp. 235, 240 and 550ff.
9. Ibid.; Henri Sellier *et al.*, *Paris pendant la guerre*, Paris: Presses Universitaires de France, 1926.
10. Julian Jackson, *A Certain Idea of France: The Life of Charles de Gaulle*, Allen Lane, 2018, p. 38.
11. Ibid., p. 40.
12. Ibid., p. 42.
13. Ibid., p. 43.
14. The classic title is Paul Gaultier, *Les Maîtres de la pensée française: Paul Hervieu, Émile Boutroux, Henri Bergson, Maurice Barrès*, Paris: Payot, 1921. But see also R. M. Ogden, reviews of *Émile Boutroux*, William James and A. Ménard, *Analyse et critique des principes de la psychologie de W. James*, *Philosophical Review*, 20 (6), 1911, p. 658.
15. Jackson, *A Certain Idea of France*, p. 43.
16. Ibid., p. 46.
17. Francis E. McMahon, *New York Times*, 14 November 1971.
18. Martha Hanna, *The Mobilization of Intellect: French Scholars and Writers during the Great War*, Cambridge, MA: Harvard University Press, 1996, pp. 28 and especially 170.
19. Ibid., p. 47.
20. Ibid., p. 65.
21. Ibid., p. 91.
22. Ibid., p. 22; see also Karin Stephen, *The Misuse of Mind: A Study of Bergson's Attack on Intellectualism*, London: Kegan Paul, Trench, Trubner, 1922, which comes with an introductory letter by Bergson himself.
23. Hanna, *The Mobilization of Intellect*, pp. 8, 99.
24. Ibid., p. 11.
25. This was also evident in the letters of the time. See Martha Hanna, 'A Republic

of Letters: The Epistolary Tradition in France during World War I', *American Historical Review*, 108 (5), 2003, pp. 1338–61.

26. Hanna, *The Mobilization of Intellect*, p. 147.
27. Ibid., p. 149.
28. Étienne Lamy, *Au service des idées et des lettres*, Paris: Bloud, 1909.
29. René Doumic, *La Défense de l'esprit français*, Paris: Bloud et Gay, 1916.
30. Hanna, *The Mobilization of Intellect*, p. 158.
31. Norman Demuth, *Vincent d'Indy 1851–1931: Champion of Classicism*, London: Rockliff, 1951.
32. Stephen, *The Misuse of Mind*.
33. Hanna, *The Mobilization of Intellect*, p. 200.
34. *Un demi-siècle de civilisation française (1870–1915)*, Paris: Hachette, 1916. Collaborators organised by Raphaël-Georges Lévy.
35. Hanna, *The Mobilization of Intellect*, p. 211.
36. Ibid., p. 229; François Duhourcau, *La Voix intérieure de Maurice Barrès*, Paris: Bernard Grasset, 1929.
37. J. Théodoridès, 'Maurice Caullery (1868–1958)', *Revue d'histoire des sciences et de leurs applications*, 12 (1), 1959, pp. 60–2.
38. Terry Nichols Clark, *Prophets and Patrons: The French University and the Emergence of the Social Sciences*, Cambridge, MA: Harvard University Press, 1973.
39. Ibid., pp. 14–15.
40. Ibid., p. 23.
41. Ibid., p. 51.
42. See also Antoine Albalat, *Trente ans de Quartier latin: nouveaux souvenirs de la vie littéraire*, Paris: Edgar Malfère, 1930; Jean-Émile Bayard, *The Latin Quarter: Past and Present*, tr. Percy Mitchell, London: T. Fisher Unwin, 1926.
43. Clark, *Prophets and Patrons*, p. 22.
44. Ibid., p. 51.
45. Ibid., p. 52; Andrea Weiss, *Paris Was a Woman: Portraits from the Left Bank*, London: Pandora, 1995.
46. Hanna, *The Mobilization of Intellect*, p. 241.

Chapter 42: A Revolution in Kissing: The Landscape of Sex in Paris

1. Alistair Horne, *Friend or Foe: An Anglo-Saxon History of France*, London: Weidenfeld & Nicolson, 2004, p. 290.
2. Ibid., p. 293.
3. Peter Watson, *The Modern Mind: An Intellectual History of the Twentieth Century*, New York: HarperCollins, 2000, p. 199.
4. See Harold March, *The Two Worlds of Marcel Proust*, Oxford: Oxford University Press, 1948, pp. 241–2, for a discussion of Freud and Proust.
5. Charles Glass, *Americans in Paris: Life and Death under Nazi Occupation*, New York: Penguin Press, 2010.
6. Ibid., pp. 25–6.
7. Ibid.
8. Harold C. Schonberg, *The Lives of the Great Composers*, London: Davis-Poynter, 1971, p. 426.
9. Steven Moore Whiting, *Satie the Bohemian: From Cabaret to Concert Hall*, Oxford: Oxford University Press, 1999, p. 71.
10. Ibid., p. 84; Jean Cocteau, *La Voix humaine: pièce en un acte*, Paris: Stock, [1930] 1952.
11. Alain Goulet, *Fiction et vie sociale dans l'œuvre d'André Gide*, Paris: Association des amis d'André Gide, 1986.

12. Hervé Paindaveine and Jane Block, 'Van Rysselberghe Family', *Grove Art Online*, Oxford University Press, 2003.
13. Vincent Cronin, *Paris on the Eve 1900–1914*, London: Collins, 1989, pp. 45–7.
14. Sylvia Kahan, *Music's Modern Muse: A Life of Winnaretta Singer, Princesse de Polignac*, Rochester, NY: University of Rochester Press, 2003, p. 226.
15. Ibid.
16. Laurence Benaïm, *Marie Laure de Noailles: la vicomtesse du bizarre*, Paris: Grasset, 2001, p. 113.
17. Kahan, *Music's Modern Muse*, p. 248.
18. Léonie Rosenstiel, *Nadia Boulanger: A Life in Music*, New York: W. W. Norton, 1982.
19. William Wiser, *The Crazy Years: Paris in the Twenties*, London: Thames & Hudson, 1983, p. 111.
20. Ibid.
21. Ibid., p. 112.
22. Cronin, *Paris on the Eve*, p. 12. The high-brow tone of Berthelot is maintained in Jean-Luc Barré, *Le Seigneur-Chat: Philippe Berthelot 1866–1934*, Paris: Plon, 1988. See also George Wickes, *The Amazon of Letters: The Life and Loves of Natalie Barney*, London: W. H. Allen, 1977; Karla Jay, *The Amazon and the Page: Natalie Clifford Barney and Renée Vivien*, Bloomington: University of Indiana Press, 1988.
23. Jean Chalon, *Liane de Pougy: courtisane, princesse et sainte*, Paris: Flammarion, 1994. See also Cornelia Otis Skinner, *Elegant Wits and Grand Horizontals: Paris, La Belle Epoque*, London: Michael Joseph, 1963, p. 219.
24. Liane de Pougy, *Idylle saphique: roman*, Paris: J. C. Lattès, [1901] 1979.
25. Wickes, *The Amazon of Letters*, pp. 116, 199.
26. Wiser, *The Crazy Years*, p. 121.
27. Isabelle Cahn, *Misia: reine de Paris*, Paris: Gallimard, 2012, a catalogue to accompany an exhibition at the Musée d'Orsay.
28. Dominique Laty, *Misia Sert et Coco Chanel: une amitié, deux tragédies*, Paris: Odile Jacob, 2009.
29. Henri Albert, *Willy*, Paris: E. Sansot, 1904.
30. Colette Willy, *La Vagabonde*, Paris: Paul Ollendorff, 1910.
31. But see Steven C. Hause, *Hubertine Auclert: The French Suffragette*, New Haven, CT: Yale University Press, 1987. Auclert (1848–1914) helped form the National Council of French Women.

Chapter 43: Shell Shock, Surrealism and the Seventh Art

1. André Breton, *Manifestes du surréalisme*, Paris: J.-J. Pauvert, 1962.
2. Deborah Menaker Rothschild, *Picasso's 'Parade': From Street to Stage – Ballet by Jean Cocteau; Score by Erik Satie; Choreography by Léonide Massine*, London: Sotheby's in association with the Drawing Center, New York, 1991, a catalogue to accompany an exhibition at the Drawing Center.
3. Michel Winock, *Le Siècle des intellectuels*, Paris: Seuil, 1997, p. 176; Béatrice Mousli, *Philippe Soupault*, Paris: Flammarion, 2010.
4. This book was translated into English by Simon Watson Taylor as *Paris Peasant*, London: Jonathan Cape, 1971.
5. Paul Éluard, *Letters to Gala*, tr. Jesse Browner, New York: Paragon House, 1989. See also Tim McGirk, *Wicked Lady: Salvador Dalí's Muse*, London: Hutchinson, 1989.
6. Patrick Waldberg, introduction, in *Max Ernst: peintures pour Paul Éluard*, Paris: Denoël, 1969, a catalogue to accompany an exhibition at the Galerie André François Petit.

7. Of the many biographies, not all of them flattering, see Meryle Secrest, *Salvador Dalí: The Surrealist Jester*, London: Weidenfeld & Nicolson, 1986.

8. Billy Klüver and Julie Martin, *Kiki's Paris: Artists and Lovers 1900–1930*, New York: Abrams, 1989; Phyllis Birnbaum, *Glory in a Line: The Life of Foujita, the Artist Caught between East and West*, London: Faber & Faber 2007, in which the author frequently admits to finding Foujita's female friends more interesting than the artist himself.

9. Aya Louisa McDonald, 'The Artist's Widow Syndrome East and West: The Case of Foujita Kimiyo', *Art Journal*, 76 (1), 2017, pp. 177–88.

10. Frank Davis, 'Nasty, Brutish and Short', *Country Life*, 4 May 1989, pp. 190–1, discusses the several paintings Modigliani made of Hébuterne.

11. Discussed in Mary Matthews Gedo, 'Picasso's Projective Paralysis', *Source Notes in the History of Art*, 15 (2), 1996, pp. 32–9.

12. Olivier Widmaier Picasso, *Picasso: The Real Family Story*, tr. Bernard Wooding *et al.*, Munich and New York: Prestel, 2004. Written by the artist's grandson, in relation to more sensational accounts by others in Picasso's family, it nonetheless gives a fullish account of his many women.

13. Georges Charensol and Roger Régent, *Un maître de cinéma: René Clair*, Paris: Table ronde, 1952.

14. R. C. Dale, 'A Clash of Intelligences: Sound versus Image in René Clair's *À nous la liberté*', *French Review*, 38 (5), 1965, pp. 637–44, argues that the advent of sound was more of a shock to the French cinema system than anywhere else.

15. Kevin Brownlow, *Napoleon: Abel Gance's Classic Film*, London: Jonathan Cape, 1983. Brownlow, a distinguished film historian, is best known for his work on the silent era.

16. Pascal Mérigeau, *Jean Renoir*, Paris: Flammarion, 2012. With a 28-page filmography.

17. Julien Benda, *La Trahison des clercs*, Paris: Bernard Grasset, 1927, pp. 6, 10.

18. Ibid., p. 42.

19. Ibid., p. 18.

20. In 1921 the *New York Times* revisited the ninety-three. Seventeen had died but a number of the survivors now said they regretted signing the document. Sixteen retained their original views.

21. Benda, *La Trahison des clercs*, p. 20.

22. Ibid., p. 60.

Chapter 44: Solitude, *Négritude* and Other Half-Way Houses

1. Vincent Cronin, *Paris: City of Light 1919–1939*, London: HarperCollins, 1994, pp. 243ff.

2. A brief narrative is given in ibid., pp. 249ff.

3. Tibor Fischer, 'Céline's journey to the cutting edge of literature', *The Guardian*, 15 June 2013.

4. English version: Louis-Ferdinand Céline, *Journey to the End of the Night*, tr. John Marks, London: Chatto & Windus, 1934. For Bardamu in the Zone, see also James Cannon, *The Paris Zone: A Cultural History 1840–1944*, Farnham: Ashgate, 2015, pp. 136ff.

5. Arthur Herman, *The Idea of Decline in Western History*, New York: Free Press, 1997, p. 333.

6. Ibid., p. 339.

7. The classic English-language translation is Alexandre Kojève, *Introduction to the Reading of Hegel*, tr. James H. Nichols Jr, New York: Basic, 1969.

8. Stefanos Geroulanos, *An Atheism That Is Not Humanist Emerges in French Thought*, Stanford, CA: Stanford University Press, 2010, p. 227.

9. For context, see Walter G. Langlois, *André Malraux: The Indochina Adventure*, London: Pall Mall Press, 1966.

10. Peter Watson, *The Age of Nothing: How We Have Sought to Live Since the Death of God*, London, Weidenfeld & Nicolson, 2014, p. 495

11. Emile Musil Church, 'In Search of Seven Sisters: A biography of the Nardal Sisters of Martinique', *Callaloo*, 36 (2), 2013, pp. 375–90.

12. Michel Fabre, 'René, Louis, and Léopold: Senghorian Négritude as a Black Humanism', tr. Randall Cherry and Jonathan P. Eburne, *Modern Fiction Studies*, 51 (4), 2005, p. 924.

13. Robert P. Smith Jr, 'Black like That: Paulette Nardal and the Negritude Salon', *CLA Journal*, 45 (1), 2001, pp. 53–68.

14. Fabre, 'René, Louis, and Léopold', p. 921.

15. Jane Nardal, 'Black Internationalism', tr. T. Denean Sharpley-Whiting and Georges Van Den Abbeele, in T. Denean Sharpley-Whiting, *Négritude Women*, Minneapolis: University of Minnesota Press, 2002, pp. 105–7.

16. Fabre, 'René, Louis, and Léopold', p. 926.

17. Antoine de Saint-Exupéry, *Pilote de guerre*, New York: Maison française, 1942; Antoine de Saint-Exupéry, *Vol de nuit*, Paris: Gallimard, 1931.

18. Geroulanos, *An Atheism That Is Not Humanist Emerges in French Thought*, p. 159.

19. Antoine de Saint-Exupéry, *Citadelle*, Paris: Gallimard, 1948.

20. Cronin, *Paris: City of Light*, p. 310.

21. Ibid.

22. In 1946 this remarkable woman was appointed to the United Nations as a delegate. In 1976 she was awarded the Légion d'honneur.

Chapter 45: The Collaboration of Culture and the Culture of Collaboration

1. Charles Glass, *Americans in Paris: Life and Death under Nazi Occupation*, New York: Penguin Press, 2010, p. 24. Among the latest books on collaboration are: Collection Pluriel/Anthony Rowley, *Les Collabos*, Paris: Sophie Publications, Arthème Fayard, 2011, with several sections on collaboration in other European countries; and Jacques Cantier, *Lire sour l'Occupation*, Paris: CNRS Éditions, 2019, which discusses the conflict between the natural sociability of readers and the difficulty of occupation.

2. Frederic Spotts, *The Shameful Peace: How French Artists and Intellectuals Survived the Occupation*, New Haven, CT, and London: Yale University Press, 2010, p. 2.

3. Ibid., p. 4. For the ambassador's largesse, see Anne Sebba, *Les Parisiennes: How the Women of Paris Lived, Loved and Died in the 1940s*, London: Weidenfeld & Nicolson, 2016, pp. 59–60.

4. Spotts, *The Shameful Peace*, p. 11.

5. Stéphanie Corcy, *La Vie culturelle sous l'Occupation,* Paris: Perrin 2005; Varian Fry, *Surrender on Demand*, Boulder, CO: Johnson, [1945] 1997.

6. Spotts, *The Shameful Peace*, p. 25.

7. Ibid., p. 42.

8. Robert Belot, *Lucien Rebatet: un itinéraire fasciste*, Paris: Seuil, 1994.

9. Spotts, *The Shameful Peace*, p. 56. See also Martin Mauthner, *Otto Abetz and His Paris Acolytes: French Writers Who Flirted with Fascism 1930–1945*, Brighton: Sussex Academic Press, 2016; Barbara Lambauer, *Otto Abetz et les Français, ou L'Envers de la Collaboration*, Paris: Fayard, 2001.

10. Spotts, *The Shameful Peace*, p. 57.

11. Susan Ronald, *A Dangerous Woman: American Beauty, Noted Philanthropist, Nazi Collaborator – The Life of Florence Gould*, New York: St Martin's Press, 2018.

12. Ibid., p. 234; Alan Riding, *And the Show Went On: Cultural Life in Nazi-Occupied*

Paris, London: Duckworth, 2011, p. 259. Anne Sebba says the Bousquet salon was partly financed by Count René de Chambrun, known as Bunny, a descendant of the Marquis de Lafayette. See Sebba, *Les Parisiennes*, p. 101.

13. Ronald, *A Dangerous Woman*, p. 235.
14. Ibid.
15. Ibid., p. 247.
16. Glass, *Americans in Paris*, p. 96.
17. Ronald, *A Dangerous Woman*, p. 233; Sebba, *Les Parisiennes*, p. 187.
18. Spotts, *The Shameful Peace*, p. 50.
19. Riding, *And the Show Went On*, p. 261.
20. Ibid., p. 265.
21. Ibid., p. 266.
22. The latest book on this always-controversial subject is Annie Lacroix-Riz, *Le Non-épuration en France: de 1943 aux années 1950*, Malakoff: Armand-Colin, 2019.
23. Ronald, *A Dangerous Woman*, p. 232.
24. Spotts, *The Shameful Peace*, p. 62.
25. Ibid., p. 65.
26. Myriam Chimènes, *La Vie musicale sous Vichy*, Paris: Editions Complexe, 2001; Riding, *And the Show Went On*, p. 227.
27. Ibid., p. 225.
28. Ibid., p. 230; Audrey Garcia and David Gullentops (eds), *Cocteau sous l'Occupation*, Paris: Non lieu, 2016.
29. Laurence Benaïm, *Marie Laure de Noailles: la vicomtesse du bizarre*, Paris: Grasset, 2001, pp. 319ff; Sebba, *Les Parisiennes*, pp. 102–3.
30. Spotts, *The Shameful Peace*, p. 241.
31. Glass, *Americans in Paris*, p. 234.
32. Simon Singh, *The Code Book: The Science of Secrecy from Ancient Egypt to Quantum Cryptography*, London: Fourth Estate, 1999, p. 140.
33. Christian Chaput, 'Autour de Lévy-Dhurmer, visionnaires et intimistes en 1900', *Esprit*, April 1973, p. 971.
34. This section is mainly taken from Christine Bard, *Les Filles de Marianne: histoire des féminismes 1914–1940*, Paris: Fayard, 1995. For her own books, see Edmée de La Rochefoucauld, *Anna de Noailles*, Paris: Éditions universitaires, 1956; and *Léon-Paul Fargue*, Paris: Éditions universitaires, 1959.

Chapter 46: Anti-Americanism and *la Famille Sartre*

1. Antony Beevor and Artemis Cooper, *Paris after the Liberation 1944–1949*, London: Hamish Hamilton, 1994, pp. 81, 200. For Sartre and Beauvoir's relationship, see for example Liliane Lazar's review of Claudine Monteil, 'Sartre, Jean-Paul, and Simone de Beauvoir. (Les amants de la liberté: L'aventure de Jean-Paul Sartre et Simone de Beauvoir dans le siècle', *The French Review*, volume 76 (4), pp. 822–3, 2003.
2. Hanne Jacobs, 'Husserl on Reason, Reflection and Attention', *Research in Phenomenology*, 46 (2), 2016, pp. 257–76.
3. Jean-Paul Sartre, *La Nausée*, Paris: Gallimard, 1938. And see Arthur Herman, *The Idea of Decline in Western History*, New York: Free Press, 1997, p. 339.
4. Jean-Paul Sartre, *L'Existentialisme est un humanisme*, Paris: Nagel, 1946.
5. Maurice Merleau-Ponty, *Humanism and Terror: An Essay on the Communist Problem*, tr. John O'Neill, Boston: Beacon Press, 1969, pp. xvi–xvii; Herman, *The Idea of Decline in Western History*, p. 346.
6. Annie Cohen-Solal, *Sartre: A Life*, London: Heinemann, 1987, p. 250; Howard Davies, *Sartre and 'Les Temps Modernes'*, Cambridge: Cambridge University Press, 1987. See also Herman, *The Idea of Decline in Western History*, p. 335.

7. Beevor and Cooper, *Paris after the Liberation*, p. 158. Aragon would later write *A History of the USSR: From Lenin to Khrushchev*, tr. Patrick O'Brian, London: Weidenfeld & Nicolson, 1964.

8. Beevor and Cooper, *Paris after the Liberation*, p. 382; Juliette Gréco, 'La petite musique du chagrin', *Nouvelle Revue des deux mondes*, May 1977, p. 358.

9. For Zhdanov's views, see his *On Literature, Music and Philosophy*, tr. Eleanor Fox *et al.*, London: Lawrence & Wishart, 1950, which includes his speech to the Conference of Soviet Philosophical Workers in 1947. Some idea of the emotions this episode can still raise may be seen from the fact that Annie Cohen-Solal's 1987 biography of Sartre, 500 pages, makes no reference to the matter, or to Kravchenko, or to other individuals who took part.

10. Athan Theoharis, 'A Creative and Aggressive FBI: The Victor Kravchenko Case', *Intelligence and National Security*, 20 (2), 2005, pp. 321–31.

11. For the link between Bourbaki and Messiaen, see Julian L. Hook, 'Rhythm in the Music of Messiaen: An Algebraic Study and an Application in the Turangalîla Symphony', *Music Theory Spectrum*, 20 (1), 1998, pp. 97–120. For Messiaen, see Arnold Whittall, *Music since the First World War*, Oxford: Oxford University Press, [1977] 1995, pp. 216–19.

12. Mildred Glimcher, *Jean Dubuffet: Towards an Alternative Reality*, New York: Pace, 1987. Published two years after the artist's death.

13. Olivier Todd, *Albert Camus: une vie*, Paris: Gallimard, 1996, pp. 296ff; Albert Camus, *L'Homme révolté*, Paris: Gallimard, 1951.

14. Albert Camus, *Carnets 1942–1951*, tr. Philip Thody, London: Hamish Hamilton 1966 *circa* p. 51 for his note-books, thoughts on Tarrou and the symbolic effects of the plague; Albert Camus, *La Peste*, Paris: Gallimard, 1947.

15. Kate Millett, *Sexual Politics*, London: Rupert Hart-Davis, 1971, p. 346; Jean-Paul Sartre, *Saint-Genet: Actor and Martyr*, tr. Bernard Frechtman, London: W. H. Allen, 1964.

16. Jean Genet, *Les Nègres: clownerie*, Décines: M. Barbezat, 1958. See also Gene A. Plunka, *The Rites of Passage of Jean Genet: The Art and Aesthetics of Risk-Taking*, Rutherford, NJ: Fairleigh Dickinson University Press, 1992.

17. The best biography of Beauvoir that I have read is Deirdre Bair, *Simone de Beauvoir: A Biography*, London: Jonathan Cape, 1990. See p. 383, chapter 40.

18. Claude Francis and Fernande Gontier, *Simone de Beauvoir*, tr. Lisa Nesselson, London: Sidgwick & Jackson, 1987, p. 207; Simone de Beauvoir, *Lettres à Nelson Algren: un amour transatlantique 1947–1964*, tr. Sylvie Le Bon de Beauvoir, Paris: Gallimard, 1997.

19. Bair, *Simone de Beauvoir*, pp. 432–3.

20. *The Second Sex* was translated into sixteen languages: see Francis and Gontier, *Simone de Beauvoir*, p. 254. See also Caroline Evans, 'On Rereading Simone de Beauvoir's *The Second Sex* after Thirty-Five Years', *Women's Studies Quarterly*, 41 (1/2), 2013, pp. 194–6.

Chapter 47: *La Longue Durée*: Civilisation, Capitalism, Colonialism

1. Claude Lévi-Strauss and Didier Eribon, *Conversations with Lévi-Strauss*, tr. Paula Wissing, Chicago: University of Chicago Press, 1991, p. 145. See also Claude Lévi-Strauss, *The Savage Mind*, London: Weidenfeld & Nicolson, 1966; *The Elementary Structures of Kinship*, rev. ed., London: Eyre & Spottiswoode, 1969. For a recent study of the man and his work, see Maurice Godelier, *Claude Lévi-Strauss: A Critical Study of His Thought*, tr. Nora Scott, London: Verso, 2018.

2. Claude Lévi-Strauss, *Tristes Tropiques*, tr. John and Doreen Weightman, New

York: Atheneum, 1973; Lévi-Strauss and Eribon, *Conversations with Lévi-Strauss*, p. 145.

3. For an introduction see Simon Clarke, *The Foundations of Structuralism: A Critique of Lévi-Strauss and the Structuralist Movement*, Brighton: Harvester, 1981. Lévi-Strauss and Eribon, *Conversations with Lévi-Strauss*, p. 106.

4. Edmund Leach, *Lévi-Strauss*, rev. ed., London: Fontana, 1974, especially pp. 60, 63, 82ff.

5. Ibid., pp. 60, 63. See also, for example, Claude Lévi-Strauss, *Mythologiques 3: L'Origine des manières de table*, Paris: Plon, 1968.

6. Frantz Fanon, *The Wretched of the Earth*, tr. Constance Farrington, London: McGibbon & Kee, 1965, p. 221; see also Leo Zeilig, *Frantz Fanon: The Militant Philosopher of the Third World Revolution*, London: I. B. Tauris, 2016.

7. Peter Burke, *The French Historical Revolution: The 'Annales' School 1929–1989*, Cambridge: Polity Press, 1990, pp. 27ff; Marc Bloch, *La Société féodale: les classes et le gouvernement des hommes*, Paris: Albin Michel, 1940; Marc Bloch, *The Royal Touch: Sacred Monarchy and Scrofula in England and France*, tr. J. E. Anderson, London: Routledge & Kegan Paul, 1973.

8. Burke, *The French Historical Revolution*, p. 29; Lucien Febvre, *Le Problème de l'incroyance au XVIe siècle: la religion de Rabelais*, Paris: A. Michel, 1942.

9. François Dosse, *New History in France: The Triumph of the Annales*, tr. Peter V. Conroy Jr, Urbana: University of Illinois Press, 1994, pp. 42ff; Fernand Braudel, *The Mediterranean and the Mediterranean World in the Age of Philip II*, tr. Siân Reynolds, 2 vols, London: Collins, 1972–3.

10. Also explained in his *Grammaire des civilisations*, Paris: Flammarion, 1993 (published posthumously). See also Burke, *The French Historical Revolution*, pp. 35–6.

11. Burke, *Op. cit.*, pp. 45ff; Fernand Braudel, *Civilisation matérielle et capitalisme: XVe–XVIIIe siècle*, Paris: Armand Colin, 1967.

12. Again, a shorter account is given in *Grammaire des civilisations*. Burke, *The French Historical Revolution*, pp. 48ff.

13. Emmanuel Le Roy Ladurie, *Montaillou, village Occitan de 1294 à 1324*, Paris: Gallimard, 1975; *The Peasants of Languedoc*, tr. John Day, Urbana, University of Illinois Press, 1964. See Dosse, *New History in France*, p. 157 for a critique of Ladurie. Burke, *The French Historical Revolution*, p. 81.

14. For another view of the *Annales* school, see André Burguière, *The Annales School: An Intellectual History*, tr. Jane Marie Todd, Ithaca, NY: Cornell University Press, 2009.

Chapter 48: 'French Theory' and the Late Focus on Freud in France

1. Sherry Turkle, *Psychoanalytic Politics: Freud's French Revolution*, New York: Basic, 1978; Jacques Lacan, *Formations of the Unconscious: The Seminar of Jacques Lacan, Book V*, ed. Jacques-Alain Miller, tr. Russell Grigg, Cambridge: Polity, 2017.

2. Philip Julien, *Jacques Lacan's Return to Freud: The Real, the Symbolic, and the Imaginary*, tr. Devra Beck Simiu, New York: New York University Press, 1994, pp. 178ff; Bice Benvenuto and Roger Kennedy, *The Work of Jacques Lacan: An Introduction*, London: Free Association, 1986, pp. 166–7; Jacques Lacan, *Desire and Its Interpretation: The Seminar of Jacques Lacan, Book VI*, ed. Jacques-Alain Miller, tr. Bruce Fink, Cambridge: Polity, 2019.

3. Jacques Lacan, *Le Séminaire de Jacques Lacan, livre XVI: D'un autre à l'autre 1968–69*, Paris: Seuil, 2006. Julien, *Jacques Lacan's Return to Freud*, pp. 178ff.

4. Recommended: Didier Eribon, *Michel Foucault 1926–1984*, Paris: Flammarion,

1989, pp. 201ff. See also David Macey, *The Lives of Michel Foucault*, London: Hutchinson, 1993, pp. 219–20.

5. For example Michel Foucault, *La Société punitive: cours au Collège de France 1972–73*, Paris: EHESS/Gallimard/Seuil, 2013. For an excellent summary, see also Mark Philp, 'Michel Foucault', in Quentin Skinner (ed.), *The Return of Grand Theory in the Human Sciences*, Cambridge: Cambridge University Press, [1985] 1990, pp. 67–8.

6. Eribon, *Michel Foucault*, pp. 269ff.

7. See Philp, 'Michel Foucault', pp. 74–6 for 'power relations', p. 78 for our 'patternless condition'. Also explored in Jean-François Bert and Jérôme Lamy (eds), *Michel Foucault: un heritage critique*, Paris: CNRS, 2014.

8. Geoffrey Bennington and Jacques Derrida, *Jacques Derrida*, tr. Geoffrey Bennington, Chicago: Chicago University Press, 1993, pp. 133–48; John Llewelyn, *Derrida on the Threshold of Sense*, Basingstoke: Macmillan, 1986.

9. Jacques Derrida, *The Beast and the Sovereign*, ed. Michel Lisse *et al.*, tr. Geoffrey Bennington, 2 vols, Chicago: University of Chicago Press, 2009–11. And see Jacques Derrida, *'Différance'*, in *Margins of Philosophy*, Brighton: Harvester Press, 1982, pp. 3–27.

10. Susan James, 'Louis Althusser', in Skinner, *The Return of Grand Theory in the Human Sciences*, p. 151; Louis Althusser, *The Future Lasts a Long Time and The Facts*, ed. Olivier Corpet and Yann Moulier Boutnag, tr. Richard Veasey, London: Chatto & Windus, 1993.

11. For a detailed discussion of ideology and its applications, see Louis Althusser, *Philosophy and Spontaneous Philosophy of the Scientists and Other Essays*, ed. Gregory Elliott, London: Verso, 1990, pp. 73ff. See also: Louis Althusser, *On the Reproduction of Capitalism: Ideology and Ideological State Apparatuses*, tr. G. M. Goshgarian, London: Verso, 2014.

12. Roland Barthes, *Mythologies*, tr. Annette Lavers, London: Jonathan Cape, 1972, p. 98; Roland Barthes, *Le Bruissement de la langue*, Paris: Seuil, 1984.

13. Roland Barthes, *The Pleasure of the Text*, New York: Hill & Wang, 1975, p. 16; Roland Barthes, *L'Aventure sémiologique*, Paris: Seuil, 1985.

14. Patrick Ffrench, *The Time of Theory: A History of 'Tel Quel' 1960–1983*, Oxford: Clarendon Press, 1995, p. 41.

15. Ibid., p. 42.

16. Ibid., p. 272.

17. Jean-François Lyotard, *The Postmodern Condition: A Report on Knowledge*, tr. Geoff Bennington and Brian Massumi, Manchester: Manchester University Press, 1984.

18. See Jean-François Lyotard, 'The Psychoanalytic Approach to Artistic and Literary Expression', in *Toward the Postmodern*, Atlantic Highlands, NJ: Humanities Press, 1993, pp. 2–11. Part 1 of this book is headed 'Libidinal', Part 2 'Pagan', and Part 3 'Intractable'. See also Jean-François Lyotard, *Instructions païennes*, Paris: Galilée, 1977.

19. Lyotard, *The Postmodern Condition*, p. 60; Jean-François Lyotard, *La Phénoménologie*, 8th ed., Paris: Presses universitaires de France, 1976.

Chapter 49: The End of the 'Theatre of the Exceptional'

1. Michel Winock, *Le Siècle des intellectuels*, Paris: Seuil 1997, pp. 606–8; Mark Lilla, 'The Strange Birth of Liberal France', *Wilson Quarterly*, Autumn 1994, pp. 106–20, at 113.

2. Edward Shils, 'Raymond Aron', *American Scholar*, Spring 1985, p. 163.

3. Ibid., p. 164.

4. Winock, *Le Siècle des intellectuels*, p. 609; Shils, 'Raymond Aron', p. 174.

5. Shils, 'Raymond Aron', p. 176.
6. Reed Davis, 'A Once and Future Greatness: Raymond Aron, Charles de Gaulle and the Politics of Grandeur', *International History Review*, 33 (1), 2011, pp. 27–41.
7. Ibid., p. 37.
8. Ibid., p. 39.
9. Iain Stewart, 'France's Anti-68 Liberal Revival', in Emile Chabal (ed.), *France since the 1970s: History, Memory and Politics in an Age of Uncertainty*, London: Bloomsbury, 2015, p. 199.
10. Ibid., p. 201.
11. Winock, *Le Siècle des intellectuels*, p. 566.
12. A typical title of Glucksmann's is *Cynisme et passion*, Paris: Grasset, 1981.
13. Stewart, Op. cit., p. 211.
14. Lilla, 'The Strange Birth of Liberal France', p. 115.
15. Stewart, *Op. cit.*, p. 83.
16. Perry Anderson, 'Dégringolade', *London Review of Books*, 2 September 2004.
17. Patrice Higgonet, 'On the Death of François Furet', *French Politics and Society*, 15 (3), 1997, pp. 65–7.
18. François Furet, 'The French Revolution Revisited', *Government and Opposition*, 24 (3), 1989, p. 276.
19. Daniel Steinmetz-Jenkins, 'The French Revolution is not over', *Prospect*, 10 March 2014, p. 85.
20. Ibid., p. 87.
21. Ibid., p. 90.
22. William Scott, 'François Furet and Democracy in France', *Historical Journal*, 34 (1), 1991, p. 150.
23. Andrew Jainchill and Samuel Moyn, 'French Democracy between Totalitarianism and Solidarity: Pierre Rosanvallon and Revisionist Historiography', *Journal of Modern History*, 76 (1), 2004, pp. 107–54.
24. Ibid., p. 112.
25. Ibid., p. 115.
26. Ibid., p. 117.
27. Ibid., p. 118. On this, see Nick Bromell, '"Where the Distinction between Action and Knowledge Vanishes": Pierre Rosanvallon's "Philosophical History of the Political"', *Political Theory*, 44 (4), 2016, pp. 578–85.
28. Javier Fernández Sebastián, 'Intellectual History and Democracy: An Interview with Pierre Rosanvallon', *Journal of the History of Ideas*, 68 (4), 2007, pp. 703–16.
29. Jainchill and Moyn, 'French Democracy between Totalitarianism and Solidarity', p. 139.
30. Ibid., pp. 130–3.
31. Ibid., p. 138.
32. Pierre Rosanvallon, 'Citoyenneté politique et citoyenneté sociale au XIXe siècle', *Mouvement social*, 171, 1995, pp. 9–30. Regarding culture coming before politics, see for example Joseph F. Byrnes, *Catholic and French for Ever: Religious and National Identity in Modern France*, University Park: Pennsylvania State University Press, 2005, pp. 222–3.
33. Pierre Nora, *Jeunesse*, Paris: Gallimard, 2021; Anderson, 'Dégringolade', p. 1.
34. Hue-Tam Ho Tai, 'Remembered Realms: Pierre Nora and French National Memory', *American Historical Review*, 106 (3), 2001, pp. 906–22, especially 909.
35. Pierre Nora, 'Between Memory and History: Les Lieux de Mémoire', *Representations*, 26, 1989, p. 24.
36. Ibid., p. 15.
37. Pierre Nora, 'Preface', in Pierre Nora (ed.), *Realms of Memory: Rethinking the*

French Past, vol. 1: Conflicts and Divisions, tr. Arthur Goldhammer, New York: Columbia University Press, 1996–8, vol. 1, p. xvii.

38. Ibid., p. xx.
39. Ibid., p. xxi.
40. Ibid., p. xxiv.
41. Nora, 'Between Memory and History', p. 12.
42. Nora, 'Preface', p. xxiii.
43. Jay Winter, review of Pierre Nora, *Realms of Memory: Rethinking the French Past*, H-Net Reviews, October 1997, p. 2.
44. Ibid., p. 3.
45. Tai, 'Remembered Realms', p. 919.
46. Ibid., p. 909.

Chapter 50: The Literary Pre-eminence of Paris in an Age of English

1. Perry Anderson, 'Union Sucrée', *London Review of Books*, 23 September 2004, p. 2.
2. Suzanne Citron put this into a wider context in: 'Le mythe national et l'accueil des étrangers', *Autres Temps*, 1993, vol. 38. pp. 110-117. See note 4 for her main work.
3. Ibid.
4. Suzanne Citron, *Le Mythe national: l'histoire de France en question*, Paris: Éditions ouvrières, 1987.
5. English edition: Pascale Casanova, *The World Republic of Letters*, tr. M. B. DeBevoise, Cambridge, MA: Harvard University Press, 2004. French edition: *La République mondiale des lettres*, Paris: Seuil, 1999. See also William Deresiewicz, 'The Literary World System', *The Nation*, 16 December 2004.
6. Casanova *The World Republic of Letters*, *Op. cit.*, p. 320. The English version is referenced below in notes 9, 10 and 12.
7. Ibid., pp, 23, 25, 95, for example.
8. Ibid., pp. 69–70. But see David Cottington, 'The Formation of the Avant-Garde in Paris and London, c.1880–1915', *Art History*, 35 (3), 2012, pp. 596–621.
9. Casanova, *Op. cit.*, pp. 47–56; Marc Fumaroli, *When the World Spoke French*, tr. Richard Howard, New York: New York Review Books, 2011, passim.
10. Casanova, *Op. cit.*, p. 168.
11. 'Bali Sabola', *Bryn Mawr Review of Contemporary Literature*, 6 (2), 2007.
12. Casanova, *Op. cit.*, p. 109, using the example of James Joyce.
13. Perry Anderson, 'Union Sucrée', p. 2.

Chapter 51: 'An Immense Vanity for France': De Gaulle, the French and the Anglo-Saxons

1. Robert and Isabelle Tombs, *That Sweet Enemy: The French and the British from the Sun King to the Present*, London: Heinemann, 2006.
2. Ibid., passim.
3. Jean-Paul Bertaud, Alan Forrest and Annie Jourdan, *Napoléon, le monde and les Anglais: Guerre des mots et des images*, Paris: Autrement, 2004.
4. Julian Jackson, *A Certain Idea of France: The Life of Charles de Gaulle*, Allen Lane, 2018, p. 59.
5. Ibid., p. 108.
6. Ibid., p. 222. On the other hand, see Daniel Mahoney, 'A "Man of Character": The Statesmanship of Charles de Gaulle', *Polity*, 27 (1), 1994, p. 155.
7. Jackson, *A Certain Idea of France*, p. 223.
8. Mary Borden, *Journey down a Blind Alley*, New York: Harper & Bros, 1946.
9. Jackson, *A Certain Idea of France*, p. 592.

10. Peter Mangold, *The Almost Impossible Ally: Harold Macmillan and Charles de Gaulle*, London: I. B. Tauris, 2006; Jack Hayward, *Fragmented France: Two Centuries of Disputed Identity*, Oxford: Oxford University Press, 2007, p. 23.

11. Jackson, *A Certain Idea of France*, p. 778.

12. Ibid. See also Hayward, *Fragmented France*, pp. 30–1.

13. Hayward, *Fragmented France*, pp. 19–20; Richard F. Kuisel, *Seducing the French: The dilemma of Americanization*, Berkeley: University of California Press, 1993, p. 11.

14. Kuisel, *Seducing the French*, p. 38.

15. Ibid., p. 108.

16. Annelien De Dijn, 'Bertrand de Jouvenel and the Revolt against the State in Post-War America', *Ethical Perspectives*, 17 (3), 2010, p. 386.

17. Kuisel, *Seducing the French*, p. 154.

18. Richard F. Kuisel, *The French Way: How France Embraced and Rejected American Values and Power*, Princeton, NJ: Princeton University Press, 2012, pp. 74–6.

19. Ibid., p. 45.

20. Ibid., pp. 47–8.

21. Ibid., pp. 89–90.

22. Pierre Nora and Michael Taylor, 'America and the French Intellectuals', *Dædalus*, 107 (1), 1978, pp. 325–37.

23. Kuisel, *The French Way, Op. cit.*, pp. 96–7.

24. Ibid., p. 354.

25. *The Times*, 27 October 2021.

26. Madeleine Albright, *Madam Secretary*, New York: Miramax, 2003, p. 447.

Chapter 52: France's Other 'Other'

1. Jean-Marie Colombani, *Tous Américains?: Le monde après le 11 septembre 2011*, Paris: Fayard, 2002.

2. The main thrust of the first part of this chapter is a consolidated synthesis of three publications by Mohamed-Ali Adraoui: 'French Salafists' Economic Ethics: Between Election and New Forms of Politicization', *Religions*, 10 (11), 2019, article no. 635; 'Radical Milieus and Salafist Movements in France: Ideologies, Practices, Relationships with Society and Political Visions', EUI MWP Working Paper 2014/13; and 'Salafism, Jihadism and Radicalisation: Between a Common Doctrinal Heritage and the Logics of Empowerment', in Serafettin Pektas and Johan Leman (eds), *Militant Jihadism: Today and Tomorrow*, Leuven: Leuven University Press, 2019. On French Islamophobia see Neil Macmaster, 'Islamophobia in France and the "Algerian Problem"', in Emran Qureshi and Michael A. Sells (eds), *The New Crusades: Constructing the Muslim Enemy*, New York: Columbia University Press, 2003, pp. 288–313. In 2021, in memory of the beheaded teacher, Samuel Paty, the Presses universitaires de Lyon published a memoir he had written in 1995, ironically (in some ways) a study of the symbolism of the colour black: *Le Noir: société et symbolique 1815-1995: Memoire de recherche d'un apprenti historien*.

3. Rahsaan Maxwell and Erik Bleich, 'What Makes Muslims Feel French?', *Social Forces*, 93 (1), 2014, pp. 155–79. See also Vincent Geisser, 'La "Question musulmane" en France au prisme des sciences sociales', *Cahiers d'études africaines*, 206/207, 2012, pp. 351–66; Gérard Noiriel, *Le Creuset français: histoire de l'immigration XIXe–XXe siècles*, Paris: Seuil, 1988.

4. Olivier Roy, 'The Disconnect between Religion and Culture', *IWMpost*, 115, 2015, pp. 17–18.

5. Ibid.

6. See for example Olivier Roy, 'Who are the new jihadis?' *The Guardian*, 13 April 2017.

7. Ibid.
8. Olivier Roy, *Jihad and Death: The Global Appeal of Islamic State*, tr. Cynthia Schoch, London: Hurst, 2017.
9. Olivier Roy, *La Sainte Ignorance: le temps de la religion sans culture*, Paris: Seuil, 2012.
10. Roy, *Jihad and Death*.
11. Ibid.
12. Gilles Kepel, *Quatre-vingt-treize*, Paris: Gallimard, 2014; *Le Fracture*: Paris: Gallimard, 2016. Kepel has published ten books on the subject of Islam in France, six in English. Adam Nossiter, '"That ignoramus": 2 French scholars of radical Islam turn bitter rivals', *New York Times*, 12 July 2016.
13. Oliver Roy, In Search of the Lost Orient, Op. cit.
14. *The Times*, 27 October 2021.
15. Hakim El Karoui, *A French Islam Is Possible*, Institut Montaigne, Paris, September 2016. See also 'L'Islam français d'Hakim El Karoui', *L'Express*, 10 September 2018.

Envoi: 'Je Suis Notre-Dame'

1. Original French edition: Patrick Boucheron *et al.* (eds), *Histoire Mondiale de la France*, Paris: Seuil, 2017; English edition: *France in the World: A New Global History*, tr. Teresa Lavender Fagan *et al.*, New York: Other Press, 2019. See also Mark Mazower, 'Gauls, *gilets jaunes* and the fight for French identity', *Financial Times*, 26 April 2019; Paul Burke, review, *NB*, 24 April 2019.
2. J. P. Daughton, review of Patrick Boucheron *et al.* (eds), *France in the World: A New Global History*, *American Historical Review*, 125 (3), 2020, pp. 948–51.
3. Ibid.
4. Benjamin Ivry, 'This controversial history book is causing a stir in France and beyond. Here's why', *Time*, 9 April 2019.
5. See for example Jack Hayward, *Fragmented France: Two Centuries of Disputed Identity*, Oxford: Oxford University Press, 2007, p. 178; Steven Englund, 'The Ghost of Nation Past,' *Journal of Modern History*, 64 (2), 1992, pp. 300–11; Robert Gildea, *The Past in Frenc History*, New Haven, CT: Yale University Press, 1996, pp. 10–12.
6. Agnès Poirier, *Notre-Dame: The Soul of France*, London: Oneworld, 2020, p. 4, on which this account is based.
7. Ibid., p. 11.
8. Ibid., p. 14.
9. Ibid., p. 17.
10. For another discussion, see Valérie Rochaix, 'Patrimoine universel vs patrimoine communautaire: les mécanismes discursifs de reconstruction sémantique du patrimoine culturel dans le traitement médiatique de l'incendie de Notre-Dame de Paris', *SHS Web of Conferences*, 78, 2020, article no. 01020.
11. Poirier, *Notre-Dame*, p. 21.
12. Ibid., p. 174.
13. Ibid., p. 18.

Conclusion: 'The Uncanny Power of Literature': How and Why the French Became French

1. William Drozdiak, *The Last President of Europe: Emmanuel Macron's Race to Revive France and Save the World*, New York: Public Affairs, 2020, p. 64.
2. Michel Houellebecq, *Submission*, tr. Lorin Stein, London: William Heinemann, 2015, pp. 6–7.

3. Ibid., p. 54.

4. Jack Andrew, *The French Exception: Still So Special?*, 2nd ed., London: Profile, 2001; Tony Chafer and Emmanuel Godin (eds), *End of the French Exception? Decline and Revival of the 'French Model'*, Basingstoke: Palgrave Macmillan, 2010; Emmanuel Godin and Tony Chafer (eds), *The French Exception*, New York and Oxford: Berghahn, 2005, especially chapters 3 and 14.

5. Alan Riding, *And the Show Went On: Cultural Life in Nazi-Occupied Paris*, London: Duckworth, 2011, p. 65.

6. Priscilla Parkhurst Clark, *Literary France: The Making of a Culture*, Berkeley: University of California Press, 1989, p. xvi.

7. Ibid., p. 4.

8. Ibid., pp. 24–9.

9. Ibid., p. 29.

10. On this point, see also René de la Croix, Duc de Castries, *La Vieille Dame du quai Conti: une histoire de l'Académie française*, Paris: Perrin, 1978.

11. Clark, *Literary France*, p. 46.

12. Emile Gassier, *Les Cinq Cents Immortels*, Paris: Henri Jouve, 1906, pp. 210–11.

13. Mathieu Marraud, *La Noblesse de Paris au XVIIIe siècle*, Paris: Seuil, 2000, p. 469; Clark, *Literary France*.

14. James Fenimore Cooper, *Recollections of Europe*, Paris: Baudry, 1837, p. 181.

15. Charles-Augustin Sainte-Beuve, 'L'Abbé Maury', in *Causeries du lundi*, Paris: Garnier, n.d. but probably 1851, vol. 4, p. 283.

16. Matthieu Marraud, *La Noblesse de Paris au XVIIIe siècle*, p. 464. For the Goncourts, see: Jacques Robichon, *Le Défi des Goncourt*, Paris: Denoël, 1975, p. 332. See also Philip Crant, review of Robichon, *Le Défi des Goncourt*, *French Review*, 50 (2), 1976, pp. 378–9.

17. Clark, *Literary France*, p. 97.

18. Marc Fumaroli, *When the World Spoke French*, tr. Richard Howard, New York: New York Review Books, 2011, p. xxviii; Marc Fumaroli, *La République des lettres*, Paris: Gallimard, 2015, p. xxx.

19. Ernest Renan, 'L'Académie française', in *Essais de morale et de critique*, 2nd ed., Paris: Michel Lévy, 1860, p. 345.

20. On French eloquence, see Ferdinand Gohin, *La Langue française*, Paris: Didier, 1913, a short book examining the purity and clarity of French and whether it lends itself to poetry; and Marc Fumaroli, *L'Âge de l'éloquence: rhétorique et 'res literaria', de la Renaissance au seuil de l'époque classique*, Geneva: Droz, 1980.

21. Frank J. W. Harding, *Matthew Arnold, the Critic and France*, Geneva: Droz, 1964, p. 135. Arnold's self-imposed mission, according to one reviewer, was to inform the British of their 'manifold' faults while at the same time drawing attention to 'their one great fault', of being intellectually and artistically inferior to the French.

22. Clark, *Literary France*, p. 143.

23. Ibid., pp. 170, 192.

24. Ibid., p. 197; see also Fumaroli, *La République des lettres*, p. 212.

25. Clark, *Literary France*, p. 208.

26. Fumaroli, *La République des lettres*, p. 195.

27. Michel Onfray, *L'Art d'être français*, Paris: Éditions Bouquins, 2021, especially pp. 26-37 and 383-392.

INDEX